UNDERSTANDING AND MANAGING EMOTIONAL AND BEHAVIOR DISORDERS IN THE CLASSROOM

GRAD L. FLICK

The ADD Clinic, Ocean Springs, Mississippi

PEARSON

Boston Columbus Indianapolis New York San Francisco Upper Saddle River
Amsterdam Cape Town Dubai London Madrid Milan Munich Paris Montreal Toronto
Delhi Mexico City Sao Paulo Sydney Hong Kong Seoul Singapore Taipei Tokyo

Vice President and Editor in Chief: Jeffery W. Johnston
Executive Editor: Ann Castel Davis
Editorial Assistant: Penny Burleson
Vice President, Director of Marketing: Quinn Perkson
Marketing Manager: Erica DeLuca
Senior Managing Editor: Pamela D. Bennett
Project Manager: Sheryl Glicker Langner
Senior Operations Supervisor: Matthew Ottenweller
Operations Specialist: Laura Messerly
Senior Art Director: Diane C. Lorenzo
Cover Designer: Diane Y. Ernsberger
Cover Art: Super Stock
Full-Service Project Management: Andrea Stefanowicz, GGS Higher Education Resources, a division of PreMedia Global, Inc.
Composition: GGS Higher Education Resources, a division of PreMedia Global, Inc.
Printer/Binder: Hamilton Printing
Cover Printer: Lehigh-Phoenix
Text Font: New Caledonia

Credits and acknowledgments borrowed from other sources and reproduced, with permission, in this textbook appear on appropriate page within text.

Every effort has been made to provide accurate and current Internet information in this book. However, the Internet and information posted on it are constantly changing, so it is inevitable that some of the Internet addresses listed in this textbook will change.

Library of Congress Cataloging-in-Publication Data
Flick, Grad L.
    Understanding and managing emotional and behaviorial disorders in the classroom/Grad L. Flick.
        p. cm.
    Includes bibliographical references and index.
    ISBN-13: 978-0-13-041713-8 (alk. paper)
    ISBN-10: 0-13-041713-0 (alk. paper)
    1. Problem children—Education.   2. Problem children—Behavior modification.   3. Children with social disabilities—Education.   4. Emotional problems of children.   5. Behavior disorders in children.
6. Classroom management.   I. Title.
LC4801.F53 2011
370.15′28—dc22
                                                                         2009052073

www.pearsonhighered.com

10 9 8 7 6 5 4 3 2 1
ISBN 10: 0-13-041713-0
ISBN 13: 978-0-13-041713-8

This book is dedicated to Billy Malette.

He has faced many challenges in his life

and continues to adapt to them successfully.

I look forward to seeing what he will achieve in the future.

I will always be proud of him.

Preface

This book is intended for use by pre-service teachers, general education teachers, and special education teachers. There are a number of unique features of this book.

Beginning each chapter, the teacher will find case histories of issues in classroom management. The case ends with the question, "What would you do?" This is intended to prompt the teacher in designing a behavioral intervention to address each student's behavior problem(s). Possible solutions are provided in Appendix A. It should be noted that the solution offered is not the only possible solution to the problem behavior. It is essential that the teacher be able to apply behavioral principles to each case; a cookbook approach is not supported. This means that there may be more than one behavioral solution to the problem(s) presented. A critical analysis and use of thinking skills are needed. Once basic behavioral procedures are learned, they can be applied regardless of the type of behavioral problem presented. The format of these case histories was obtained online from Tobin (2000); the content of case histories comes from the author's cases.

It is important for the teacher to know and to be able to identify types of symptomatic behavior. One should have some familiarity with various diagnostic entities involving the emotional and behavioral disorders, as well as be able to appreciate how the diagnosis was reached and what, if any, medications are prescribed. It is important to remember that interventions are developed for behaviors, not diagnoses. Clinicians and teachers must, therefore, focus on the individual child or student and his/her behavioral pattern. Teachers must remember to always address specific problematic behavior and not diagnoses.

Interventions are clearly not established within a vacuum. There are other factors that must be considered. These surely include the student's physical environment and school-wide positive orientations.

Teachers need to know the statistics that are associated with various disorders and the behavior disorders in particular. Likewise, it is important to be familiar with the general outcome of students with behavior disorders as well as how these outcome statistics can be changed.

Many behavioral interventions are reviewed. Teachers will not only become familiar with some of the general positive oriented behavioral techniques, but also will review how functional behavioral assessments are conducted and how the behavioral intervention plan is developed. Finally, teachers will learn how to integrate this information into the IEP.

Teachers need to know how families and siblings are affected by a student with a disability. They also need information about involving families and the community in working with students who have behavior disorders along with other students who are without disabilities.

All teachers must learn the vocabulary that is used to describe some of the behavioral disorders and the research on these disorders. While teachers do not need to acquire this information to the same degree as a Ph.D. psychologist, they will need to know appropriate terms so that they will be better able to communicate with other medical and psychological specialists. For many disorders, there are case examples and vignettes within the chapters that provide examples of the disorder or the defined program.

Some teachers may wish to explore some of the techniques in greater detail. To this end, a comprehensive resources section has been provided. Teachers who wish to use some of the blank forms discussed may find these (available for copying) in the appendices.

Teachers must note that the 16 chapters of this book have been divided into 5 sections or parts. Part I addresses the foundation of behavior disorders, Part II concerns the recognition of emotional and behavioral disorders, Part III provides information on identifying and assessing behavior disorders, Part IV discusses the management of behavior disorders, and Part V covers school-wide management and promising directions.

It is essential that teachers remember that some of the behavior disorders have developed over a period of time; therefore, they will be quite resistant to change. This fact provides the primary reason to address these problems with early intervention in the lower grades. After many episodes of reinforced inappropriate behavior, it becomes more difficult to change that behavior. Teachers should always keep this in mind during the development of any intervention.

Each chapter contains an overview of topics covered as well as discussion questions at the end of each chapter. These discussion questions are designed to help teachers integrate and review the information covered.

AUDIENCE

This text targets both pre-service teachers, as well as established teachers in regular and special education. It is appropriate for undergraduate and graduate courses in the training of pre-school, elementary, and middle school educators. It is also appropriate for educational administrators, behavior therapists in training, school counselors, social workers, and psychologists.

ACKNOWLEDGMENTS

I wish to thank all those who gave permission to use their materials in the body of this text and for the forms that are used in conducting functional behavioral assessments, behavioral intervention plans, and the IEP.

I would like to thank Lynn Mourey (Ocean Springs Special Education), who not only read the entire text, but gave valuable suggestions and comments.

I would like to extend my sincere thanks to my wife, Alma, who provided continual encouragement and maintained a quiet environment with our five dogs.

I would like to thank my typists, Angela Johnson and, especially, Katherine Hopkins, who had the difficult task of reading my handwriting for the first time. Many thanks also go to my office manager, Anna Griffith, who copied and mailed the manuscript to the typist and publisher.

I would like to thank the following people who reviewed the manuscript and provided constructive feedback for changes: Ellen Arwood, University of Portland; Lawrence Beard, Jacksonville State University; Marie Brand, State University of New York at New Paltz; Jim Burns, The College of St. Rose; Leslynn Gallo, Southwestern College; Craig Hart, Brigham Young University; Jean Kueker, Our Lady of the Lake University; Kim Madsen, Chadron State College; Maureen Norris, Bellarmine University; Karen Peterson, Washington State University— Vancouver; Dean Richey, Tennessee Tech University; and Sandra Wanner, University of Mary Harden-Baylor.

Lastly, I would like to thank my editors: first, Allyson Sharp, who helped with the initial organization of the text, and second, Ann Davis, who completed the organization. Thanks also to Penny Burleson, who spent much time with faxes, mail, and e-mail to complete the project. I really appreciate all of the help from the staff at Pearson Education for their advice and their assistance.

Brief Contents

Contents

PART V

Promising Directions for School-Wide Management   285

CHAPTER 14
Developing a School-Wide Behavioral Program   286

PART 1

Foundations of Behavior Disorders

What are the interventions that teachers may use to incorporate students with behavior disorders in the general classroom? What basic background information will provide a basis for the development of specific interventions that are needed to deal with behavior disorders? To begin with, it is important to know the incidence of various emotional and behavioral problems along with their frequency in each disability category. In order to be eligible for special education, each student will have an evaluation that focuses on those aspects of behavior that interfere with his or her academic success. The final objective of such evaluations will be to provide a comprehensive list of behavior problems and the interventions needed to change them. The labeling that is sometimes used to determine eligibility and classification is also a topic of focus. Clearly, there are many pros and cons for labeling, and we focus here on an alternate classification system. Since all students will be governed by the Individuals with Disabilities Education Act (IDEA), a summary of the revised 2004 legal issues regarding the handling of behavior disorders is noted.

We next provide an overview of the development of behavior problems and the origins of behavior disorders and discuss the risk and protective factors that may contribute to the manifestation of behavior disorders. In addition, we outline various models that may be used to further understand behavior disorders as well as other emotional disabilities. The major models of child development are also presented in order to acquaint readers with some of the ways of viewing behavior disorders with regard to their trajectory of development.

This section concludes with a focus on the educational outcome of students with emotional and behavior disorders. The factors for improving postschool outcomes through the use of positive techniques are discussed as are the services that are delivered in special education as well as the types of classrooms in which these services are provided.

CHAPTER 1

Behavior Disorders and Intervention in Today's Classrooms

Overview

- Incidence of emotional and behavior disorders
- Statistical trends in special education
- Disability categories
- Problems with disability classification
- Labeling
- DSM-IV diagnostic classification
- Problems with the DSM-IV approach
- An alternative classification system

Case History

Lena is a 9-year-old fourth-grade student who has been placed in a class for the emotionally disturbed. She has a full-scale score of 80 on the WISC-III. Her teacher notes that she shows poor task engagement and has a high rate of problem behaviors that include aggression, critical verbal statements to other students and her teachers, and destruction of property. She is often out of her seat, annoying others. *What would you do?*

Diagnosing a student's emotional or behavior disorder may be a difficult process. To begin, it may be difficult to determine whether something has gone wrong in the brain that may be linked to behavior. Likewise, it may be hard to identify some problem behavior in the child's early life that may be associated with parental actions. Actually, there may be a combination of factors: biological, environmental, and psychological. The one thing that is clear, however, is that children with emotional and behavioral disorders may have much difficulty becoming integrated with the mainstream educational environment (Kauffman, 2001; Muscott, 1997); they may even need placement in some exclusionary and more restrictive setting that provides greater behavioral and therapeutic support than can be offered in any general educational setting. However, the main emphasis here is that in providing academic and behavior interventions, along with positive behavior supports, many of these children who are now classified as having an emotional or behavior disorder can be taught in general education classes.

Clearly, there is no simple or standard way of measuring emotional and behavior functions. Some judgment will always be needed to make such assessments and to determine whether a behavior pattern is *abnormal* or *disruptive*.

• •

Disruptive behavior is problem behavior that interferes with the teacher's ability to educate other students or impairs the other students' engagement in a school activity.

• •

Halgin and Whitbourne (2006) have noted that *disruptive* behavior can be defined as "persistent negative behavior patterns that usually incite caretakers or peers to respond with anger, impatience, punishment or avoidance." Young children today need to learn more than the basic skills of reading, writing, and arithmetic in school; they must also acquire many social adaptive skills necessary to succeed in our complex world.

Some children enter the school setting well rounded and well prepared; others present educational as well as social and behavior challenges for teachers. These children who are different for various reasons (some perhaps from birth) are the subjects of this book.

Some of them must be taught learning skills and many must acquire social and behavior skills so that they can function now in the classroom and later in the world of work and in society in general.

INCIDENCE OF EMOTIONAL AND BEHAVIOR DISORDERS

Approximately 9 percent of all students receiving special education are classified as having an emotional or behavior disorder. About 80 percent of all students with emotional or behavior disorders are taught in general education classes. Taking into consideration the incidence of emotional and behavior disorders, all classroom teachers must learn to deal with more of these students than any other disability group except learning disabilities.

CULTURAL SIMILARITY

The incidence of emotional and behavior disorders may vary some across cultures but mainly with regard to what constitutes a "serious problem." For example, in the United States in 1999, school principals reported data on eighth graders having two main problems: classroom disturbances (69 percent) and intimidation or verbal abuse of other students (46 percent) as shown in Figure 1.1.

While 69 percent of U.S. eighth graders were in schools where principals reported these weekly classroom disturbances, only 11 percent were in schools whose principals reported these disturbances as a severe problem. This was also true in Canada, where 60 percent of principals reported weekly classroom disturbances but only 21 percent reported these classroom disturbances as a serious problem (see Figure 1.2).

While a higher proportion of eighth-grade students in Japan were in schools where principals reported that theft, vandalism, and cheating were serious problems, the incidence of these classroom behaviors was still quite low. This was also the case with physical injury to other students, along with intimidation and verbal abuse of teachers.

Compared to U.S. eighth graders, a higher percentage of Japanese students were in schools where the principals perceived problems to be serious. Twenty-five percent of Japanese eighth graders were in schools

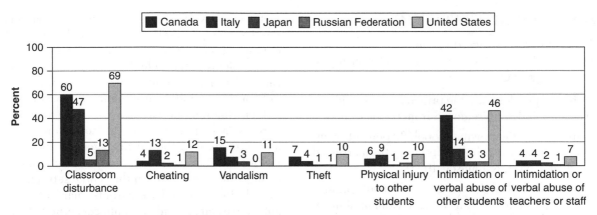

FIGURE 1.1   Percentage of eighth-grade students whose principals reported that behavior threatening a safe and orderly environment occurs at least weekly, by selected behavior and country.

Note: Response data for the United States are available only for 70–84 percent of students.

Source: International Association for the Evaluation of Educational Achievement, *TIMSS 1999 International Mathematics Report: Findings from IEA's Repeat of the Third International Mathematics and Science Study at the Eighth Grade, 2000*, Exhibits 7.7 and 7.8.

in which principals perceived that theft was a serious problem; 23 percent were in schools where vandalism was seen as a serious problem. The figures for the United States were 2 percent, 1 percent, and 1 percent, respectively. In addition, 22 percent of Japanese eighth graders were in schools where physical injury to other students was perceived as a serious problem, and 25 percent were in schools where intimidation or verbal abuse of other students was perceived as a serious problem, compared to the 3 percent and 16 percent, respectively, of U.S. students. Similarly, 23 percent of Japanese eighth graders were in schools where intimidation and verbal abuse of teachers was seen as a serious problem, compared to 3 percent of U.S. students.

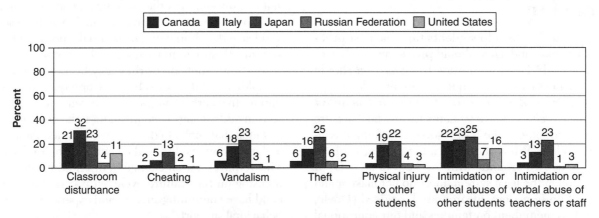

FIGURE 1.2   Percentage of eighth-grade students whose principals reported that behavior threatening a safe and orderly environment is a serious problem, by selected behavior and country.

Note: Response data for the United States are available for only 70–84 percent of students.

Source: International Association for the Evaluation of Educational Achievement, *TIMSS 1999 International Mathematics Report: Findings from IEA's Repeat of the Third International Mathematics and Science Study at the Eighth Grade, 2000*, Exhibits 7.7 and 7.8.

EDUCATIONAL STATISTICS

Some older statistics regarding school dropouts, untreated behavior problems, and their relationship to crime are staggering:

1. Behavior problems are the primary reason students with disabilities are removed from regular school.

2. Three years after leaving school, 20 percent of antisocial youth (or delinquents) have been arrested (Walker, Colvin, & Ramsey, 1995).

3. Students who had dropped out of school committed 82 percent of crimes (APA Commission on Youth Violence, 1994).

4. More than 50 percent of the crime in the United States is committed by 5 to 7 percent of youths between 10 and 20 years old (APA Commission on Youth Violence, 1994).

Walker and colleagues have noted that if antisocial behavior (i.e., behavior primarily involving aggression and crime toward others) is not changed by the end of third grade, it should be treated as a *chronic condition* much like diabetes. This means that such antisocial behavior may be a lifelong problem that cannot be cured but may be managed only with appropriate support and continuing intervention (Walker et al., 1995).

ADDRESSING BEHAVIOR PROBLEMS

Who is available to help students that manifest problems in school, and *when* should problematic behavior be addressed? The last question to ask is *what* should be done? Let's look at each question in more detail.

Who is available to help students that manifest problems in school? Once students leave school and are subjected to some of the "last resorts" of reform, it is already too late. While there are a few who are able to "turn their lives around" with the help of a GED, or even through the legal system, most do not make it and may end up homeless, incarcerated, or dead (Doyle, 2005). It is incumbent on families and our educational system to help such children adapt and succeed. Both parents and teachers may lack the basic knowledge or understanding about some of the challenging behaviors and their "diagnostic labels" as well as what they can do about these behaviors. Because there is a strong genetic factor in many of these conditions, some parents who may have had similar longstanding problems may be ill-equipped both cognitively and emotionally to cope with the problems of their children. In many cases, parents themselves may exhibit similar difficulties, which not only provides models of some inappropriate behavior to their children but may also contribute to one or both parents' lack of awareness that "something is wrong," and ultimately to the mismanagement of the child's problems. Consequently, most of the impetus for change must occur within the school setting. This approach does not exclude parents, many of whom are able to participate and are quite concerned about their child's behavior. Like teachers, they too may not understand the behavior or be aware of how to deal with it. Both parents and teachers will need information about disordered behavior and how to cope with it.

When should problematic behavior be addressed? This is perhaps the easier question to answer. All problematic and challenging behaviors should be addressed as early as possible. Such conditions are far less complex during early development and there are fewer associated and "learned conditions" to deal with. Early intervention is clearly the key. However, while intervening at the earliest possible time is necessary, it may not always work. Many of the conditions discussed here reflect the "lifelong" disorders of children who have inherited different nervous systems. It is possible that some neurodevelopmental changes may occur and result in a resolution of the challenging behaviors (in contrast to some seizure disorders, which may be resolved and leave the child with an essentially normal nervous system). However, in most cases the problems may remain throughout life or they may become even more complex and difficult to change. Consequently, it is important that early changes and interventions be the first step in addressing these problem behaviors. It is also essential that such children have continued monitoring and interventions during the course of their education. This requires a total change in orientation. Instead of focusing on the "failure cycle," it is essential that the child have continuing success and experience "positive behavioral support."

What should be done? This is not an easy question to answer. Clearly, there is a certain amount of basic information that needs to be imparted to the child. Perhaps the three Rs, but even here there is the question about what is the best way to teach this information that can be delivered to students with and without various disabilities. Beyond the basic information cluster, additional questions arise regarding which additional skills should be generally taught and which ones should be taught only in specific individual cases. Several basic skills are among those needed in school and beyond: social skills, problem-solving skills, conflict resolutions skills, coping skills, and stress management/relaxation skills. This clearly indicates that a skill development approach is needed. Although some medications may help with behavioral problems through modification of the child's neurophysiology (and neurotransmitters), there is no pill that will teach skills (Flick, 1996, 1998b, 2000). Such skill development must be planned with the establishment of clear goals and specific interventions geared toward teaching compensatory behaviors.

Much needs to be first accomplished in educational reform, specifically addressing how general education can be modified to teach children without disabilities the information they will need to successfully cope with the challenges they will face in the future. At the same time, educational reform must address those students *with disabilities* to teach them the basic information, within their capacity, that is needed to successfully deal with social and occupational challenges. In addition, such students must be taught skills that will assist them in dealing with interfering behaviors or in developing behaviors in areas where they are deficient. This involves modifying some inappropriate behavior—changing these behaviors or removing them completely.

Behavioral interventions will also be needed to teach many new behaviors. If teachers understand the characteristics of a disability, they will know how to approach that problem. For example, children who are "hyperactive" based on their physiology may have trouble sitting still for long periods and may need to get up and move around. This need to move around may not reflect a willful disobedience of "class rules"; it is a physiological and basic "survival" need for the child, much like the need to find food or water if lost in the forest. Hyperactivity as a reactive behavior may reflect the need to activate muscles due to increased tension associated with an assignment or task that is difficult or impossible for the child to complete. In such cases, getting out of his or her seat not only satisfies the "need to move" but may also result in being sent to the principal's office—a desirable consequence for the child (i.e., getting out of class and breaking the class rule), which

also reinforces a behavior that allows the child greater movement.

More importantly, the whole sequence is reinforced by the attention the child receives and the many interesting things that may occur while in the principal's office. Also, while many children with a learning disability can learn and have the capacity to learn as much as normal students, they may learn more slowly and process information differently, which may result in incomplete work or unfinished tasks. Some simple accommodations (or manipulations of environmental conditions) may effectively deal with some of these aforementioned problems. Effective modifications can be implemented and are based on either an understanding of the disability condition or a "functional analysis" of the child's behavior. Indeed, some solutions to these problem behaviors can be simple yet effective.

In addition to essential academic skills, it is important to note three basic areas that need to be the focus of behavioral interventions: (1) social skills, (2) impulse control skills, and (3) study skills. These skills need to be developed preferably from the preschool years and throughout elementary school, middle school, and high school. Because learning may occur slowly for some students, it is important that these skills be taught early and then reinforced throughout the school years. However, just like any other learned skills that are not frequently used, they may deteriorate and refresher sessions may be essential. In addition, schools must also maintain a positive behavioral orientation to encourage the use of appropriate motivational factors to support such a program. Schools must also offer ongoing parent training sessions to develop family awareness about behavioral or academic problems, and to promote the effective reinforcement of all appropriate learned skills whether academic, social-emotional, or behavioral in nature.

It is also essential that schools maintain continuing programs for teachers and administrators to increase awareness and information about the various disabilities, many of which appear in regular classes via inclusion. As Guskey (2002) points out, any successful professional development program for teachers should focus on three critical factors: (1) change is a slow, difficult, and gradual process for teachers and administrators; (2) teachers need to receive regular and frequent feedback on student learning outcomes (it is important to know what works); and (3) continued support and follow-up are necessary after initial training. A one-hour in-service training program may provide some ideas for the classroom and possibly result in some temporary changes, but it is most likely that teachers will return to their old habits with the result that few permanent changes will occur in dealing with children who show disordered behavior. Just as behavioral interventions with a child may need to be conducted on a regular basis to promote consistency, so must the education of teachers. In short, when student behavior needs to change, the behavior of teachers, parents, and administrators also needs to change. A complete and comprehensive reform of the educational system is clearly needed to achieve such a goal.

SPECIAL EDUCATION

Over time there have been significant changes—both positive and negative—in the definition of *special education*, in the methods of identifying children (ideally before they become students) with such behavior problems, and in the approaches to offering help for students, parents, and teachers.

••

Special education: Specially designed educational programs that meet the needs of eligible students. At

no cost to parents, this also includes classroom instruction and out-of-school instruction in residential settings and training centers. Special education also includes assistive technology, physical education, vocational education, or other changes in the curriculum that meet the individual's needs.

••

STATISTICAL TRENDS

The U.S. Department of Education has reported that the numbers and percentages of children that are being served for disabilities has been slowly increasing (see Table 1.1).

During the 1991–1992 school year, 11.6 percent of students were served in these programs, compared with 13.4 percent in 2001–2002. Some of the rise since 1991–1992 may be attributed to the increasing number of children identified as *learning disabled*, which rose from 5.3 to 6 percent of the enrollment in 2001–2002; another large increase occurred in the *other health impairments* category and this is probably due to the significant increase of those students identified with attention-deficit/hyperactivity disorder (ADHD).

TABLE 1.1 Changes in Number of Students Ages 6–21 Served Under IDEA by Disability Category, 1990–1991 and 1999–2000

	1990–1991	1999–2000	Difference	Change (%)
Specific learning disabilities	2,144,017	2,871,966	727,949	34.0
Speech or language impairments	987,778	1,089,964	102,186	10.3
Mental retardation	551,457	614,433	62,976	11.4
Emotional disturbance	390,764	470,111	79,347	20.3
Multiple disabilities	97,629	112,993	15,364	15.7
Hearing impairments	59,211	71,671	12,460	21.0
Orthopedic impairments	49,340	71,422	22,082	44.8
Other health impairments	56,349	254,110	197,761	351.0
Visual impairments	23,682	26,590	2,908	12.3
Autism	.	65,424	.	—[a]
Deafness-blindness	1,524	1,845	321	21.1
Traumatic brain injury	.	13,874	.	—[a]
Developmental delay	.	19,304	.	—[b]
All disabilities	4,361,751	5,683,707	1,321,956	30.3

[a]Reporting on autism and traumatic brain injury was first required in 1992–1993.
[b]Optional reporting on developmental delay for students ages 3 through 7 was first allowed in the 1997–1998 school year.
Source: U.S. Department of Education, Office of Special Education Programs, Data Analysis System (DANS), (1990–1991, 1999–2000).

DISABILITY CATEGORIES

There is no "official" special education classification system; category designations, concept definitions, and classification criteria may vary from one state to another. Thus a student may be classified as disabled in one state and not in another. The 13 disability categories as used and defined in this book are:

1. Autism
2. Deaf-blind
3. Deafness
4. Hearing impairment
5. Orthopedic impairment
6. Other health impairment
7. Serious emotional disturbance (e.g., psychotic disorders, schizophrenia)
8. Specific learning disability (e.g., reading or math disabilities)
9. Speech/language impairment
10. Traumatic brain injury
11. Mental retardation
12. Visual impairment (including blindness)
13. Multiple disabilities

The approximate percentages in each disability category (1999–2000) are shown in Figure 1.3.

Medical and Social System Models of Disabilities

A common system of classification via categorization involves a mix of two models of deviance: the *medical* and *social systems* models (Reschly, 1996). A comparison of these two models is found in Table 1.2.

The social systems model places little emphasis on underlying causes of the presenting disorder(s), and focuses rather on direct assessment and treatment of the symptoms. Such disorders are defined as deviations from explicit patterns or level of behavior in special context or social roles.

The medical model, on the other hand, places more emphasis on the etiology of the presenting problem(s), thus implying significance of identification, assessment, and treatment based on the causation (perceived and

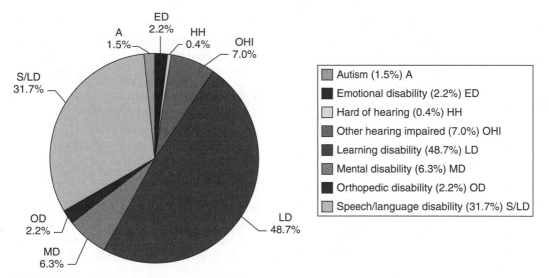

FIGURE 1.3   Percentages in each disability category.

Source: Information from www.ed.gov/teachers/how.tools/initiative/summerworkshop/lin.coln.county/edlite-slide003.html.

TABLE 1.2 Comparison of Medical and Social System Models of Disabilities

Characteristic	Medical Model	Social System Model
Definition of problem	Biological anomaly	Discrepancies between expected and observed behavior in a specific context
Focus on treatment	Focus on cause with purpose of curing or compensating for underlying problem	Eliminate symptoms through direct educational or behavioral interventions
Initial diagnosis	In preschool years by medical professionals	During school-age years by professionals in education or psychology
Incidence	Low (about 1% of school-age population)	High (about 9% of school-age population)
Prognosis	Lifelong disabilities	Disabilities may be recognized officially only during school years
Cultural context	Cross-cultural	Arguably, culturally specific
Comprehensiveness	Usually affects performance in most roles and in most contexts	May affect one or a few roles in a few or multiple contexts

Source: Information from Reschly (1996).

diagnosed). The medical model is used to denote disabilities with known biological bases (Reschly, 1996); a problematic result of this is that educational professionals seldom detect the biologically caused behavior and/or learning problems in school settings. The medical model does allude to underlying causes that can be biological, cognitive, or psychological; and it views the information about causes as essential to treatment. However, such a view is not supported by research on the outcome of psychological and educational interventions; treating symptoms is more effective (Bandura, 1986; Weisz et al., 1995).

The *dual approach*, using both the medical and the social system models, has serious consequences mostly for the specific learning disabled (SLD)—for example, a child with a specific reading disability, where there is confusion over the importance of underlying causes and symptoms in assessment, identification, and treatment. The major problem in applying the medical model to SLD and other mild disabilities is that the focus tends to be on underlying factors that basically have been irrelevant to successful treatment of symptoms.

Suggestions for reform of the current classification systems would be to continue the utilization of traditional diagnostic constructs for diagnosing biologically based disabilities such as deafness. Disabilities other than biologically based disorders might be more accurately diagnosed and designated using dimensions of behavior (rather than typologies). For instance, dichotomous decision rules imply that one child, with an IQ of 74 and therefore diagnosed as mentally retarded (MR), would be eligible for special education, but the child with an IQ of 75 would not be eligible. In all probability, both children would need special education services.

A functional classification system would have various applications to treatment depending on the level of severity of the disability and the student's age. In contrast, etiological formulations are not closely related to treatment. Even though students may be disabled in some way, they are nonetheless multidimensional with regard to their assets and limitations; the current classification system focuses mostly on intelligence level and achievement, often ignoring those vital areas of social skills and social competencies (Reschly, 1996; Maras & Kutnick, 1998). For example, some statistics may choose not to allow the use of the IQ discrepancy model. *Response to intervention (RTI)*—a three-tier process used to determine whether or not to proceed to an evaluation for eligibility—may instead be selected:

■ Level 1—The student assistance team (parents, teachers, and the student, if appropriate) complete a functional behavioral assessment and write a behavior plan for the classroom with the teacher as the implementor.

■ Level 2—The same team along with a behavior specialist conduct a more in-depth analysis using minimal pull-out of small groups.

■ Level 3—Behavior checklists and behavior rating scales are used. More intense intervention by the behavior specialist may occur outside the classroom on a daily and individual basis.

If these interventions fail to increase appropriate behavior and improve academic work, there will be a comprehensive evaluation (Mowrey, 2008).

Etiological events or characteristics are assessed less reliably than directly observable behavior. Over the past 30 years, there have been technological developments for directly measuring students' behavior in natural settings (Reschly, 1996; Daly & Murdoch, 2000; Peterson & Shinn, 2002; Shinn, Stoner, & Walker, 2002). Specifically, curriculum-based measures of behavior assessment provide reliable information directly related to treatment. Classification systems should facilitate the application of available knowledge in effective instructional interventions and/or psychological treatments; systems must focus on functional dimensions of behavior using curriculum-based or behavioral assessment procedures.

A developmental approach for the classification of child behavior disorders has been proposed by Achenbach (1999). He indicates that a comprehensive understanding of classification issues requires an in-depth analysis of the forms that psychopathology may assume across development. Some behavior problems may be similar across long periods of development, whereas others may undergo observable changes from one developmental period to another. Patterns of behavior problems and their intensity may thus vary systematically across situations and social interactions with parents, teachers, siblings, and peers. Consequently, taxonomic constructs that aggregate findings across situations, times, sources of data, and developmental periods are needed. Achenbach (1999) suggests new models that are both developmentally and contextually sensitive.

Changes are also needed to put more focus on effective interventions (Imlay, 2004) and the evaluation of outcomes. In the past, reports of educational outcomes have been defined primarily by the number of students served and the location of services. Using the now available knowledge base and current assessment technology will certainly further the goal of improving the outcomes for both educational and behavioral treatment interventions for disabled youths. Some of the factors that affect the outcome of special education students are summarized in the box below.

Factors Affecting Outcomes for Special Education Students

- Student academic and social success is affected more by the instructional models employed and the classroom environment than by placement in general or special education.
- Students with learning disabilities (LD) perform slightly better and think of themselves as more competent academically when placed in special education.
- Students with severe emotional disturbance (SED) are more likely to succeed in general education if they take part in vocational education and are integrated into the school, for example, through sports participation. However, students with SED who have a history of course failure may be more likely to drop out of school if placed in general education.
- Students with hearing impairments appear to gain some academic advantage but suffer some loss of self-concept when placed in general education. The strength of the child's auditory and oral skills is a critical determinant of success in general education. On average, hard-of-hearing students do not perform as well academically as normally hearing students in any setting, and the gap in performance increases with age.
- Students with educable mental retardation (EMR), usually defined as having an IQ between 70 and 50 combined with deficits in adaptive behavior, appear to be particularly sensitive to the classroom environment. A supportive teacher, instruction style, and classmates have a greater impact on outcomes for these students than for students without disabilities.
- Students with severe mental disabilities, usually with IQs below 50, typically have greater social integration as a primary goal. Programs providing supportive transitional services have been successful at avoiding placements in residential settings.
- Nondisabled students do not appear to be impacted by the inclusion in general education of students with learning disabilities, mild behavior disorders, or severe mental disabilities, as long as supportive services are provided. When the inclusion program brings a lower overall teacher–student ratio to the classroom, the nondisabled students are likely to benefit academically.
- Effective schools appear to be more likely to benefit nondisabled low achievers than to benefit special education students. Outcome data for students with disabilities in identified effective schools are inconclusive.

Source: Information from Holcutt (1996, pp. 77–102).

Focus on Emotional and Behavior Disorders

The types of disorders that are addressed in this book may be cross-referenced to the following four disability categories:

1. Autism
2. Other health impaired
3. Traumatic brain injury
4. Emotional and behavioral disorders (EBD)

Let's look at what's included in each category.

Autism   Autism is a developmental disability, generally evident before age three, that adversely affects a student's educational performance and significantly influences developmental rates and sequences, verbal and nonverbal communications, social interaction, and participation.

The autism category may also include students who have pervasive developmental disorder, Asperger's disorder, Rett's disorder, and childhood disintegrative disorder. It is also assumed that the student's educational performance is adversely affected and that the student meets the eligibility and placement requirements; autism may also coexist with other areas of disability.

Other Health Impaired   According to special education guidance, this category applies to students having limited strength, vitality, or awareness including a heightened attention to environmental stimuli that results in restricted alertness with respect to educational placement that (1) is due to chronic or acute health problems such as asthma, ADD or ADHD, diabetes, epilepsy or a heart condition, hemophilia, lead poisoning, leukemia, nephritis, rheumatic fever, and sickle-cell anemia; and (2) adversely affects a student's educational performance. In some cases, heightened awareness to an environmental stimulus results in difficulties starting, staying on, and completing tasks; making transitions between tasks; interacting with others; following directions; producing work consistently; and organizing multistep tasks.

Traumatic Brain Injury   Traumatic brain injury refers to an acquired injury to the brain caused by an external physical force, resulting in total or partial functional disability or psychosocial impairment, or both, that adversely affects the student's educational performance. The term applies to open or closed head injuries resulting in impairments that are immediate or delayed in one or more areas—for example, cognition, language, memory, attention, reasoning, abstract thinking, judgment, problem solving, sensory, perceptual, and motor abilities, psychosocial behavior, physical function speech and information processing. Such injuries may also intensify any preexisting problems in these areas. Resulting impairments may be temporary or permanent in nature. The term does not apply to brain injuries from birth trauma or those resulting from internal occurrences such as stroke, tumor, or aneurysm.

Emotional and Behavior Disorder   An emotional and behavior disorder (EBD) is characterized by the following: (1) an inability to build or maintain satisfactory interpersonal relationships with peers and/or teachers; for preschool children, this would include other care providers; (2) an inability to learn that cannot be adequately explained by intellectual sensory or health factors; (3) consistent chronic inappropriate types of behavior or feelings under normal conditions; (4) a pervasive mood of unhappiness or depression; (5) a tendency to develop physical symptoms, pains, or unreasonable fears associated with personal or school problems.

A student with EBD may exhibit one or more of the above characteristics for a sufficient duration, and their frequency and intensity will interfere significantly with educational performance to the degree that provision of special education services is necessary for preschool age children. Documented through an extended assessment period, these characteristics may appear within the preschool environment or in another setting. The student's difficulty is emotionally based and cannot be adequately explained by intellectual, cultural, sensory, or general health factors. The EBD category may include children who are schizophrenic but not socially maladjusted, unless it is determined that they are also emotionally disturbed [Federal Register, 42 (163) 42478].

CLASSIFICATION OF DISABILITY

Problems with Disability Classification

In 1975, Hobbs formed the Project on Classification of Exceptional Children to review how these children have been labeled and classified. This classic work is still relevant today. The section written by Goldstein and colleagues (1975) provides educators with a summary of arguments for and against the labeling of students. According to this study, there were only a few advantages to classification or labeling:

1. Some of the ways that students are labeled give more definitive *inclusion* and *exclusion* criteria, which reduces ambiguity of decision making and results in better communication among educators.

2. The labeling of the student documents physical symptoms, which may be important with regard to instruction of the child.

3. Labeling may assist the administrators in the delivery of services and also in providing a more convenient tool for funding various projects.

4. Labeling has helped to obtain public and governmental support for educational services.

Goldstein et al. (1975) and, more recently, Reschly (1996) have also noted a downside to labeling:

1. Labeling may often promote overgeneralizations about students with disabilities.

2. Categorization may seem to reify the label.

3. Labels de-emphasize student-environment interactions, focusing instead on factors within the child.

4. Labels remove the "burden of proof" for students learning from teachers.

5. Labeling fails to produce improved instructional planning for students.

6. Labeling often means that students may be "stuck" in special education with little hope of returning to a general educational placement.

The real question is whether some of these statements would apply to special education as we know it today. Let's now look at all of the advantages and disadvantages of labeling in special education.

Advantages of Labeling in Special Education

The advantages of labeling have generally not been supported, and the idea of clearly delineating students eligible for inclusion or exclusion has not held up. Yesseldyke, Algozzine, and Rickey (1982) show how difficult it is to make a differential diagnosis of a learning disability with students who are experiencing academic difficulty.

According to the National Academy of Sciences, minorities are often overrepresented in special education, and labels do not foster better instruction (Reschly, Tilly, & Grimes, 1999). These authors stated that it is the responsibility of the placement team that labels and places a child in a special program to demonstrate that any differential label used is related to a distinctive prescription for educational practices that lead to improved outcomes. In addition, students with labels such as mild mental impairment or learning disability had no impact on which students improved during the school year.

Using labels or categories to develop a delivery of services for special education students not only assisted in establishing the validity of these categories or labels but also helped schools secure funding for them. Others have argued that the proliferation of special education programs has fragmented services, which has not resulted in better learning environments for students. In addition, the National Association of State Boards of Education (NASBE) recommended in 1992 that "state boards with state departments of education should sever the link between funding, placement, and handicapping label. Funding requirements should not drive programming and placement decisions for students" (1992, p. 5).

The most effective argument for labels is their usefulness in communicating to the public about the special needs of students with disabilities. Labels or categories can provide a center point to obtaining governmental support for educational programs. A current example would be the focus on ADHD as a distinct category of disability.

Disadvantages of Labeling in Special Education

Clearly, there are many disadvantages of labeling. Goldstein and colleagues (1975) noted that while classification has been useful in other sciences, such procedures may not lead to improved instruction in special education. For most students, a label fails to indicate how they should be taught. Lovitt (1995) argued that disability labels have little relevance to instruction and likened the labeling approach to a grocer separating all foods by color.

While a label is designed to communicate information about a student's primary disability, it may assume an explanatory role rather than provide descriptive information. Such use may lead to a circuitous reasoning about the student's difficulty. For example, if a student has a reading disability, his difficulty reading may be explained by saying "he can't read because he has a reading disability." Yet, this difficulty was determined using tests that assess reading problems. This is tantamount to saying that he can't read because he can't read.

Labeling often emphasizes intrapersonal factors and de-emphasizes environmental factors. For example, Yesseldyke and Christenson (2002) have reasoned that problems in learning are not solely related to attributes of the child, and they may also be influenced by the environment, especially in the classroom. Howard, Krause, and Orlinsky (1986) suggest that "the greatest amount of attention should be directed toward variables that have the most impact on the interaction (of child and environment) and are easier to alter" (p. 325).

Lastly, Goldstein and colleagues (1975) point out that teachers may use the student's label to rationalize poor progress (Snell, 2002). They suggest moving away from labeling to help teachers focus on the student and classroom environmental issues.

The pros and cons of labeling are summarized in Figure 1.4.

DSM-IV DIAGNOSES IN CLASSIFICATION

The most familiar and widely used classification system for mental disorders today is the fourth edition of the *Diagnostic and Statistical Manual of Mental Disorders* (DSM-IV), published by the American Psychiatric Association. The following types of disorders fall into the special educational classification:

Autism

> Asperger's syndrome
> Pervasive developmental disorder
> Autism

Other Health Impaired

> Attention deficit hyperactivity disorder

Traumatic Brain Injury (TBI)

> Fragile X syndrome
> Fetal alcohol syndrome

Emotional and Behavioral Disorders

> Generalized anxiety disorder
> Separation anxiety disorder
> Obsessive-compulsive disorder
> Phobias
> Post-traumatic stress disorder
> Depression
> Bipolar disorder
> Schizophrenia
> Oppositional defiant disorder
> Conduct disorder
> Tourette's syndrome

Problems with DSM-IV Diagnostic Classifications

There are two primary problems in using the DSM-IV diagnostic classification scheme. First, there is lack of consistency in classification. Many disorders are grouped together in one category without a reasonable degree of association. Second, there is general lack of reliability of classification over time and across clinicians. This results in a dearth of guidelines for education and treatment. This means that distinctly different diagnostic groups may be taught using the same approach to instruction, and they may be treated using the same therapeutic techniques.

Although a variety of DSM-IV diagnostic categories will be discussed in later chapters, only those

Pros	Cons
1. Serves as focal point of advocacy groups supporting special education	1. Stigmatizes students
2. Provides a structure for passing legislation	2. Establishes categories that are unreliable
3. Becomes a basis for allocating monies for special education services	3. Develops a poor relationship between categories and treatment
	4. Focuses on outdated assumptions
	5. Represents disproportionate numbers of minorities

FIGURE 1.4 The pros and cons of labeling.

that fall into emotional or behavioral categories that involve difficult and problematic behavior in the classroom will be emphasized. The purpose of providing these descriptions is to familiarize teachers with those characteristics of the disorders that create the most difficult problems in the classroom. Ultimately, it will be shown that there is much overlap of symptoms and that specific behavior will be the focus of treatment in the classroom, not *diagnoses*, whether such diagnoses are related to the student's classifications or derived from DSM-IV criteria. Consequently, the focus of behavior change will be directed toward problematic behaviors that may be associated with certain DSM-IV diagnoses.

Labeling: A New Direction

Most arguments regarding the use of labels have been controversial. It should be clear now that labels and disability classifications are not the primary problem. The objective for special education is to identify those students who need special interventions without using labels or classifications. In fact, there is not much evidence to warrant the continued use of labels. Buehler (2004) has noted that every student has a right to be treated with dignity and as a "full person." As she points out, there is no issue with the idea that students are different, that they may vary intellectually, physically, and emotionally. What she proposes is a "paradigm shift" to specify which services are needed so that a student can function adequately in his or her environment. Thus, labels and classification schemes would not be essential.

Certainly, there needs to be some screening of which students need and which ones should get these services. However, labels and classification are not needed. What would be required are criteria for getting services and determining which ones will be available. Clearly, sensitive and neutral terminology is essential, and terms such as *idiot* and *retard* should be avoided.

It has been a well-documented fact that some parents seek to have their child labeled (in order to get services) while others avoid labels at all costs. Those who advocate full inclusion (Rothstein, 2000) wish to end labeling and to educate most students in the regular classroom while maintaining needed social supports and services. The Individuals with Disabilities Education Act (IDEA) is a law passed in 1997 and revised in 2004 that provides for a variety of educational placements in the least restrictive environment, whether this is in a general education class or in an outside agency such as a hospital. Clearly, some students will need to be educated apart from their general education classmates.

Perhaps the most important reason to remove and/or change the labeling process is the effect of the label on the student (Drew & Hardman, 2004). The most compelling reason for labeling to continue may be the issue that funds are tied to it. This may simply be changed to funds being allocated for specific interventions that are needed for individualized academic (and behavioral) success in school.

AN ALTERNATIVE CLASSIFICATION SYSTEM

The primary goal of special education is to improve the quality of interventions and the outcome for children with disabilities. Classification categories should be free of unpleasant connotations. It has been recommended that systems be organized around the supports and services needed by children with disabilities and especially with regard to dimensions of behavior (NASP, NASDE/OSEP, 1994; NASP, 1989).

Dimensional Versus Categorical Classification

••

Dimensional classification implies that mental disorders would lie on a continuum from normal to disturbed behavior. Parents or students who present abnormal behavior would be identified on specific dimensions of either intellectual or affective/behavioral capacity rather than being placed in a categorical box.

••

Categorical classification typically involves dichotomous typologies—retarded–not retarded, ADHD–not ADHD, etc. Such categories do not accurately reflect the diversity and continuous nature of many behaviors, many of which are best described on a continuum with varying degrees of expression. It is often obvious that students who are classified in the same category often have different educational needs. What is needed is a classification system that is based on broad dimensions with fine gradations that would allow for more accurate descriptions of students' behavior without the imposition of dichotomies. When the degree of disability can be measured but the response to treatment cannot be predicted, the optimal decision may be to offer multiple treatment options. This is often the best option because, in most cases, the student will present with more than one disability. If the focus is on the disability and the student's specific behavior—not the category—a comprehensive treatment program can be offered.

Etiological Versus Functional Classification

While current approaches may be based primarily on etiological classification, such formulations are generally not useful because they are not closely related to treatment. Functional classification typically involves greater emphasis on skill development and essential social competencies. Attempts at using functional classification criteria have been successful and offer great promise for improving services and how they are provided (Reschly, 1996).

SUMMARY

This chapter provides basic information about the incidence, labeling, and classification of behavior disorders.

DISCUSSION QUESTIONS

1. Are statistics of problem behaviors similar across other cultures? Explain.
2. When is the best time to intervene when a child presents problem behavior?
3. Compare and contrast the medical and social systems models of disability.

Multidimensional Versus Unidimensional Classification

Children with disabilities may exhibit a multidimensional array of complex strengths and weaknesses. When the current classification system is used, many children may be found to have a disability that encompasses differences on only one or two salient dimensions of behavior, such as intelligence and achievement. When there is a limited focus on only one or two such dimensions, there may be a corresponding restriction of programming for those dimensions, and relevant issues such as social skills may be ignored. It will thus be important to look at a student's total array of strengths and weaknesses so that a viable multidimensional program may be offered.

Providing Effective Intervention

Classification systems that focus on *functional dimensions* of behavior will facilitate the application of a knowledge base of effective interventions. In contrast, a classification system that focuses on *underlying and presumed etiology* that may have no relationship to treatment outcome may interfere with the provision of effective treatment. Much of the preceding material has been adapted from Reschly (1996).

An alternative to the current classification system is discussed.

4. Discuss the advantages and disadvantages of labeling.
5. Describe an alternative classification system that includes behavior disorders.

CHAPTER 2

Understanding Emotional and Behavior Disorders

Overview

- The origins of emotional and behavior disorders
- Risk and protective factors
- Theories of child development
- The biopsychosocial model
- Other models

Case History

Shawn is a 6-year-old first-grade student who has been classified as "other health impaired," specifically with attention deficit hyperactivity disorder (AHDH) and a seizure disorder that is not fully controlled. He functions in the average range of ability but has had some difficulty with both expressive and receptive language functions. Shawn's behavior problems include general noncompliance, kicking, hitting, biting, pinching, screaming, and grabbing things that do not belong to him. Because of his dangerous and disruptive behavior he is taken to a resource room when he is "out of control." However, it requires an aide and a teacher to get him to that location (where he is seen one-on-one), and his screaming and resistance disrupt the entire building. His rebellion leaves the resource room in shambles and his teachers are emotionally drained. These episodes have been occurring several times a day. *What would you do?*

An understanding of emotional and behavior disorders depends on a knowledge base that includes three key factors: (1) the possible origins of these disorders, focusing on both risk and protective factors that influence the development of deviant behavior; (2) an overview of the major theories that have helped to explain childhood disorders in the past; and (3) the use of the biopsychosocial model, a current model of psychopathology that includes a general overview of all factors that could affect the child. The present conceptualization of behavior orientation is reviewed as it relates to dealing with the primary emotional and behavior disorders.

DEVELOPMENT OF BEHAVIOR PROBLEMS

Maladaptive and dysfunctional behavior does not develop overnight. It develops over time, spilling into home and school environments, each affecting the other. Often there are multiple factors that lead to current problem behaviors in the classroom (Stokes, 2002).

The development of this pattern of disordered behavior begins in early childhood and continues to develop throughout life. It is important to realize that each child is different. While some behavior tendencies are inherited, all behavior can be better managed with behavior techniques. Note that problems can appear at any stage of the behavior development process, as shown in Figure 2.1. It is most important that risk and protective factors be considered early within the child's first five years of life.

Because all children inherit genes from their parents and grandparents, a good guide to some behavioral conditions may lie in genetic influence. There are also possible problems at conception and during the pregnancy that must be considered. Likewise, there are congenital factors at birth that have to be taken into account. Some of the early influences on the developing child at this stage involve family and community factors. When children enter school, they are influenced by the kind of teachers they have as well as the philosophy of the school regarding the management of behavior problems. If aggressive, disruptive behavior develops during the early school years, this may result in rejection by classmates along with increased aggression or other acting-out behaviors. Children who develop behavior problems such as aggressiveness may tend to associate with classmates who show similar behavior. Eventually, such aggressive behavior may lead to delinquent status.

Knowing the critical risk and protective factors and how they influence the probability of delinquency is essential for preventing such problems from escalating into chronic criminality. As indicated in Figure 2.1, early risk factors involve community, family, and the individual child. There are genetic factors along with the primary influences of family and community in which the child lives. It should be noted that no single risk factor leads a young child to delinquency. However, the overall risk for delinquency increases as the number of risk factors increases. Early on, the most important risks stem from individual factors that are genetic or perhaps congenital at birth. Family factors might reflect antisocial tendencies in the family, criminal behavior, substance abuse, or simply poor parenting. During school entry, the factors involving peer interactions influences the child's school; to a greater degree community factors may contribute to the overall risk. These factors continue to operate through the early school years. Children who are directly reinforced for aggressiveness or destructiveness and those who associate with deviant peers are most likely to model delinquent behavior and to be influenced by their actions. By preadolescence, there is an accumulation of deviant patterns of learned behavior as well as genetic or congenital factors that contribute to the overall risk status of these troubled students.

While many of these factors involve genetic and life experiences, they influence behavior in school and thus become a reality for the classroom teacher. Stokes, Mowery, Dean, and Hoffman (1997) identified some of the maladaptive behaviors of children: displaced aggression toward self or others; displaying depression or mood problems; and regression of cognitive, social, and emotional behavior. Aggression may be manifested as crying, screaming, hitting, cursing, and self-abuse. Depression may be seen as mood changes, sadness, pouting, and disorganized behavior. Regression may be seen as immaturity in cognitive or social-emotional behaviors; this means that the student acts like a child who is much younger.

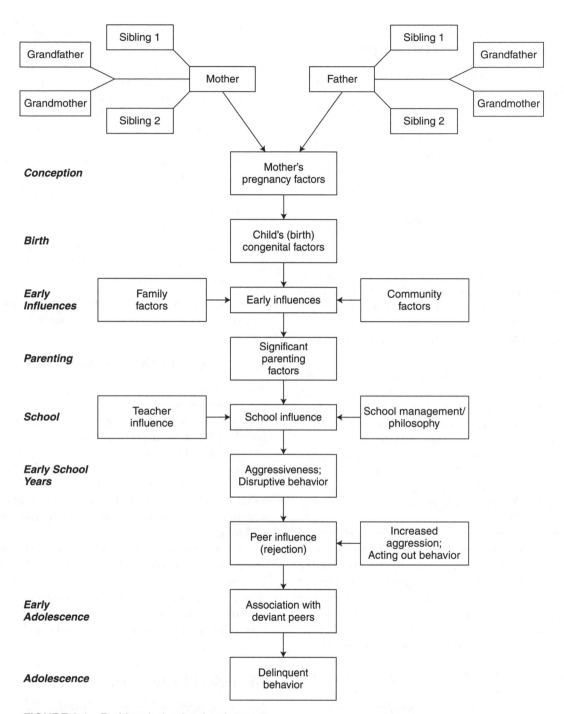

FIGURE 2.1   Problem behavior development.

ORIGINS OF EMOTIONAL AND BEHAVIOR DISORDERS

Psychopathology in children develops from the complex multiple interactions of biological, genetic, and psychological factors they experience in their environment, including family (parents and siblings), peers, school, and extended community factors. Consequently, it is important to understand the history and experiences of the child, including biological events that affect the development of the brain and nervous system. Some basic concepts underlying the development of psychopathology in children have been identified by various investigations (Pine, 2006; Cicchetti & Cohen, 2006; Jensen, 1998):

1. The continuity of development is emphasized, as early experiences form some part of the child's current behavior patterns. However, developmental discontinuities may reflect the emergence of new capabilities or incapabilities as developmental reorganization occurs.

2. Children have the tendency to adapt to a specific ecological place in order to get basic needs met. This process of adaptation may be difficult for those children who must adjust to highly disorganized or pathological environments, which may, in itself, result in some pathological behavior. Such behavioral adaptation may occur at several levels, including the level of the brain and nervous system—a process termed *neuroplasticity*.

••

Nuroplasticity, also known as *brain plasticity* or *cortical plasticity*: Changes in the organization of the brain and, in particular, those changes to the location of specific information-processing functions as a result of learning or experience. This is a developmental concept (e.g., the child's brain is more plastid than the adult's).

••

3. Age and time factors have an impact on the development of emotional and behavior disorders. For example, a behavior that might be acceptable at one age (a young child's temper tantrum) may be a significant problem at another age (the older child's temper outburst). Likewise, the stress of a risk factor may have little or no effect depending on the age at which it is experienced and whether the risk factor is greater alone or in combination with other risk factors.

4. Research has shown the importance of the child's environmental context, especially his or her caretaking experiences, Gross disruptions in the child's family environment may have both immediate and long-term effects on later social-emotional development as well as on physical health, long-term morbidity and mortality, later parenting practices, and the behavioral outcomes of their own children. It is also important to point out that a behavior seen as acceptable in one culture may be viewed as pathological in another culture.

5. In many cases, the difference between typical and abnormal behavior is one of degree and no sharp distinction can be made.

Table 2.1 provides an overview of the risk and protective factors across different age groups.

RISK FACTORS AND CAUSES

Both biological and psychosocial experiences influence but do not always cause the development of emotional and behavior disorders. Most children are influenced by adversity in their psychosocial environment; some are resistant to such adversity. However, some children who possess a genetically based biological vulnerability are more likely to be harmed by an adverse environment. Chronic or repeated exposure to an adverse environment is likely to induce psychopathology in all children.

Several risk factors negatively influence developmental psychopathology: (1) prenatal damage from alcohol, drugs, or smoking, (2) low birth weight, (3) inherited temperament problems, (4) external risk factors such as poverty, deprivation, abuse, and neglect, (5) unsatisfactory relationships, (6) parental psychopathology, and (7) exposure to trauma.

Biological Influences

Most emotional and behavior disorders develop from some combination of both genetic and environmental factors, the latter being biological or psychosocial (Pennington, 2004). In fact, there is accumulated research evidence that biological factors may have a marked influence on several disorders, including pervasive

TABLE 2.1 Overview of Risk and Protective Factors Across Domains for Different Ages

	Risk Factors		
Domain	**Early Onset (ages 6–11)**	**Late Onset (ages 12–14)**	**Protective Factors**[a]
Individual	• General offenses • Substance use • Being male • Aggression[b] • Psychological condition • Hyperactivity • Exposure to television violence • Medical, physical condition • Low IQ • Antisocial attitudes, beliefs • Dishonesty[b]	• General offenses • Psychological condition • Restlessness • Difficulty concentrating[b] • Risk taking • Aggression[b] • Being male • Physical violence • Antisocial attitudes, beliefs • Crimes against persons • Problem (antisocial) behavior • Low IQ • Substance use	• Intolerant attitude toward deviance • High IQ • Being female • Positive social orientation • Perceived sanctions for transgressions
Family	• Low socioeconomic status, poverty • Antisocial parents • Poor parent–child relations • Harsh, lax, or inconsistent discipline • Broken home • Separation from parents • Other conditions • Abusive parents • Neglect	• Poor parent-child relations • Harsh, lax, discipline; poor monitoring, supervision • Low parental involvement • Antisocial parents • Broken home • Low socioeconomic status, poverty • Abusive parents • Other conditions • Family conflict[b]	• Warm, supportive relationships with parents or other adults • Parents' positive evaluation of peers • Parental monitoring
School	• Poor attitude, performance	• Poor attitude, performance • Academic failure	• Commitment to school • Recognition for involvement in conventional activities
Peer group	• Weak social ties • Antisocial peers	• Weak social ties • Antisocial, delinquent peers • Gang membership	• Friends who engage in conventional behavior
Community		• Neighborhood crime, drugs • Neighborhood disorganization	

[a]Age of onset is not known.
[b]Males only.
Source: Information from www.surgeongeneral.gov/library/youthviolence/images/box_4-1.gif.

developmental disorder (Piven & O'Leary, 1997), autism (Piven & O'Leary, 1997), and early-onset schizophrenia (Jablensky & Kalaydieva, 2003). Biological factors may also be involved in the etiology of social phobia (Pine, 1997), obsessive-compulsive disorder (Leonard, Rapoport, & Swedo, 1997), and other disorders such as Tourette's syndrome (Lechman, Peterson, Pauls, & Cohen, 1997), and attention-deficit/hyperactivity

disorder (ADHD) (Acosta, Arcos-Burgos, & Muenke, 2004). Biological factors of a genetic nature may thus account for some mental disorders such as autism, bipolar disorder, schizophrenia, and ADHD according to the National Institute of Mental Health (1998).

There are two important points about the influence of biological factors. First, not all biological influences are based on genetics. For example, biological abnormalities of the central nervous system can be caused by injury, infection, poor nutrition (associated with poverty), or exposure to toxins (e.g., lead poisoning). Clearly, these are biological, not genetic, events.

Second, biological factors are not necessarily independent of environmental factors—they actually interact with them. For example, children with a biologically based behavior may unconsciously modify their environment. Consider the low birth weight infant who has sustained brain damage and become irritable; this child changes the behavior of caretakers by making it more difficult for them to provide good care. There are a number of biological risk factors that by affecting brain structure and function result in an increased probability of developing a mental disorder. These include intrauterine exposure to alcohol or cigarette smoke (Wakschlag et al., 2006; Mick et al., 2002); prenatal trauma (Whitaker et al., 1997); exposure to lead (Needleman et al., 1990); malnutrition during pregnancy, traumatic brain injury, some mental retardation, and some specific chromosomal syndromes. Some of these disorders and their accompanying behaviors will be explored in more detail in upcoming chapters.

Psychosocial and Environmental Influences

A pivotal study of environmental risks indicated that several factors can influence a child's mental health (Laucht et al., 2000). Dysfunction in the family setting, including parental discord, and psychopathology, overcrowding, and even large family size can predispose a child to develop a conduct disorder or antisocial personality, especially if the child does not have a loving relationship with at least one parent (Rutter, 1995). Poverty or low income can also increase a child's risk of developing a behavior disorder because of associated parental behavior problems or the increased risk of child abuse (Rutherford, Quinn, & Mathur, 2004; Peden et al., 2004). In a related sense, exposure to acts of violence may also predispose a child to develop a mental disorder (Jenkins & Bell, 1997).

Likewise, poor caregiving from depressed parents may affect a child (Elgar et al., 2003). The relationships between maternal problems and risk factors in children that predispose them to form insecure attachments as infants and toddlers may impact the development of mood and conduct problems. Some researchers have found that the nature and outcome of the attachment process are related to later depression, especially when the child is raised in an abusive relationship (Toth & Cicchetti, 1996), as well as to later conduct disorder (Sampson & Laub, 1993). Some authors (Van Ijzendoorn, Juffer, & Duvesteyn, 1995) have reviewed this relationship between attachment and the development of later mental disorders.

Kagan (1994, 1995) demonstrated that infants who were more prone to be active, agitated, and tearful at 4 months were less spontaneous and sociable; these children were more likely to show anxiety symptoms at 4 years of age (Kagan et al., 1998). Furthermore, long-term study of highly reactive behaviorally inhibited infants and toddlers found that they were excessively shy and avoidant during early childhood and that such behavior seemed to predispose them to later anxiety (Biederman et al., 1993). A more controversial theory is that some hard-to-manage, temperamental infants may actually be showing an early manifestation of a behavior problem and may later develop a conduct disorder (Olds et al., 1999).

Shaw and colleagues (2001) have noted that the relationship between a child's temperament and the parenting styles is complex (i.e., protective if the parenting style is good, or a risk factor if it is poor). A child who is difficult to manage may thus have a reduced chance of developing a behavior problem if the family rules are clear and reinforcement is consistent (Dishion & Patterson, 1996); conversely, the child who is reared in the context of inconsistent discipline and poor rule definition will be at greater risk for later behavior problems (Werner & Smith, 2001).

Family and Genetic Risk Factors

The relative contributions of biological and environmental influences are difficult to determine. For example, research has shown that from 20 to 50 percent of depressed children have a family history of depression (Williamson et al., 2004; Kovacs, Devlin et al., 1997). Both biological and environmental factors appear to interact and to result in increased risk (Weissman et al., 1997). Research has further shown that children of depressed parents are more than three times as likely as children of nondepressed parents to manifest a depressive disorder (Birmaher et al., 1996a, 1996b). However, it is clear that parental depression appears to result in increased risk for anxiety disorders, conduct disorders, and problems with alcohol (Pilowsky et al., 2006; Weissman et al., 2006;

Symptoms of Major Depression in Parents

Almost 20 percent of the parent population may have some form of depression—not just the blues. In order for a person to be diagnosed as depressed, at least five of the following symptoms must be present for a 2-week period, with one of those symptoms being (1) depressed mood, or (2) loss of interest or pleasure:

- Depressed mood
- Loss of interest or pleasure
- Significant weight loss (not dieting)
- Insomnia or hypersomnia
- Psychomotor agitation or retardation (slowing)
- Fatigue or loss of energy
- Feelings of worthlessness or excessive/inappropriate guilt
- Diminished ability to think or concentrate or indecisiveness
- Recurrent thoughts of death/suicidal ideation with/without a plan

Remember, a child may influence a parent's emotional state, but so too can a parent affect a child's emotional state.

Source: Adapted from Lyness, J.M. Patient information: Depression in Adults. In Up To Date, Rose, BD (Ed.) Up To Date, Waltham, M.A., 2008. Copyright 2008, Up To Date, Inc. For more information, visit www.uptodate.com.

Wickramaratne & Weissman, 1998). In addition, risk is increased if both parents have a depressive disorder or were depressed when they were young, or if a parent has had several episodes of depression (Merikangas et al., 1998; Wickramaratne & Weissman, 1998).

Parental Depression   Depressed parents may be withdrawn and lack energy and thus pay less attention to and provide inadequate supervision for their children. They may also be quite irritable and excessively critical, which frequently causes emotional upset, demoralization, and distance between themselves and their children (Crandell et al., 2003). In addition, a parent's emotional distress may cause anxiety in the child who is exposed to a pessimistic outlook, crying, or perhaps threats to commit suicide.

Depressed parents may also fail to model adequate and effective coping strategies during periods of stress, which may cause a sense of helplessness in their children as well (Garber & Hillsman, 1992). Parental depression may also be associated with marital difficulties, which may also adversely affect the child. A child's depression may in turn contribute to additional stress in the family as well as being a product of it. Impairment of concentration and thinking may then im-

pact the child's academic performance, further impair the child's self-esteem, and may make academic success improbable.

Stressful Life Events   The relationship between stressful life events and childhood mental disorders is well established but complicated (Jensen et al., 1999; Grant et al., 2002). For example, events such as the death of a parent, divorce, and depression when the child is young may sometimes lead to poor outcomes for the child later in life. However, the outcome may be different if the depression (stress) occurs later in the child's life (Birmaher et al., 1996a, 1996b; Garrison et al., 1997).

Child Abuse   Physical abuse toward children is a widespread problem that involves an estimated 3 million children in the United States (National Committee to Prevent Child Abuse, 1995). Such abuse may result in insecure attachment (Main & Solomon, 1990), mental disorders such as post-traumatic stress disorder, conduct disorder, ADHD (Cohen et al., 2002), depression (Lyon & Morgan-Judge, 2000) and impaired social functioning with peers (Salzinger et al., 2001). Emotional and psychological abuse occur more frequently than physical abuse, which is often associated with depression, conduct disorder, and delinquency (Lau & Weisz, 2003), and which can also impair both cognitive and social functions in children.

Peer and Sibling Influences The influence of a maladaptive peer's behavior can be potentially damaging to a child and can significantly increase the likelihood of delinquency, especially when the child comes from a family that is beset with many different forms of stress (Loeber & Farrington, 1998). The likelihood of a negative outcome such as delinquency can be reduced when youths are encouraged to interact under supervision with peers who show more appropriate behavior (Feldman, Caplinger, & Wodarski, 1983). Sibling rivalry can also contribute to a family's stress, especially when combined with other risk factors (Goldenthal, 2000), and it can cause a child to exhibit aggressive behavior toward others.

When parental attention is limited (as is seemingly the "norm" in our fast-paced society), sibling conflicts increase, which forces parents to pay attention. In these situations, parents may rarely focus on, or pay attention to, their child's *good behavior* yet will consistently direct attention to their inappropriate aggressive behavior, often in a very critical and negative way. Consequently, the aggressive behavior may be (inadvertently) rewarded and will more than likely be repeated.

RELATIONSHIPS AMONG RISK FACTORS AND PROTECTIVE FACTORS

Social and environmental risk factors may combine with physical risk factors such as low birth weight, neurological brain damage caused by complications at birth, fearlessness and stimulation-seeking behavior, learning impairments, underarousal in the autonomic nervous system (ANS), and insensitivity to physical pain and punishment (Raine, Brennan, & Mednick, 1997; Raine et al., 1998). Some of the risk factors are difficult to measure, as are their interactions and resulting effects on the development of emotional and behavioral disorders. Thus, the trend today is to avoid consideration of individual risk factors and instead to identify those measurable multiple risk factors while incorporating them into a single model that can be tested (Patterson, 1996).

Protective factors are those conditions that can improve resistance to risk factors and contribute to successful outcomes, adaptation, and resiliency in children. There are three main categories:

1. Personal characteristics within the child (e.g., high abilities, good social skills, diet, and positive temperament traits).
2. Relationship and parenting variables, especially having a warm, sympathetic adult who is consistent in discipline and provides a child with a safe and secure relationship.
3. A social environment or community that reinforces and supports positive efforts made by the child.

The relationship between risk factors and protective factors and the development of resiliency in children is complex. Rolland and Walsh (2005) have elaborated on possible protective mechanisms that can create resilience in children. Rutter (1995) describes a variety of ways in which involvement in risk conditions or negative effects of risk exposure can be reduced and thus serve to avoid the perpetuation of the risk effects. Situations that enhance the child's feelings of self-esteem, self-confidence, and the opportunities that are provided for them are also considered possible pathways to resilience.

COGNITIVE AND BEHAVIOR DEVELOPMENT: MAJOR THEORIES

Theories of developmental neuropsychology all stress different aspects of behavior development. Diamond (1990) has noted that the development of concrete and formal operations appears related to the late maturation of the frontal lobes; he ignores other areas of the brain that focus on sensory and motor control. The question about whether cognitive and/or brain development proceeds in steps or as a continuous and ongoing process continues to be debated (Foglianni et al., 2005; Paus, 2005; Toga et al., 2006). Recently, Evans (2006) established measurable and comparable MRI data on normal children ages 7 days to 18 years to serve as control data for future studies on childhood disorders.

A major conceptual development that relates to brain and cognitive development is that of growth spurts. Pond and colleagues (2000) found that there are periods of development when the brain is increasing its weight most rapidly. These growth spurts are related to the myelination of nerves, a process that begins at around 2 years of age and continues into the third and fourth years. Epstein and Epstein (1978) found that brain weight (relative to the weight of other organs) was related to mental growth. Epstein (1986) suggested that the peak growth for the brain's cortex occurs between ages 6 to 8, 10 to 12, and 14 to 16 years. However, if there is a period of slow development during one of these periods (i.e., 6 to 8, 10 to 12, and 14 to 16 years) Epstein and Epstein (1978) suggested that even additional stimulation during that period may have little or no effect on cognitive development; they also indicated that the "slow stage" may explain why some Head Start programs are aimed at preschool children. The concept of educational readiness and stage dependent periods of development (Piaget) imply a critical period hypothesis (Smart, 1991).

• •

Critical period: The time between the anatomical or functional emergence of a given bio-behavioral system and/or its maturation. The nervous system may be affected in this emergent but immature state (for better or worse) by outside stimuli, and this effect can be permanent should the system mature at that time (adapted from Cooke, 2006).

• •

The concept of a critical period has been well established in embryological terms; whether it has equal validity after birth has been debated. Some traces of the critical period hypothesis can be found in Freud's notion of the origin of human neuroses in early infancy as well as in his belief that early infancy is an especially sensitive period of development. Three major aspects of postnatal development can be identified: (1) the effects of early experience, (2) the establishment of basic social relationships (especially attachment), and (3) learning.

Early Experiences

Early experiences cannot only extensively modify genetically based characteristics, but also provide for one of the principal sources of individual differences in behavior. Sensory deprivation studies (Ornoy, 2003) have shown that there are critical periods during which suitable experiences must occur; for example, if the visual system is to develop and function normally, the developing brain must be sensitive to environmental deprivation.

Social Relationships

Some classic reports (Spitz, 1945; Bowlby, 1951) suggest a definite correlation between maternal deprivation in the first few years of life and later maladaptive behavior. These researchers hypothesized a critical period from birth into the preschool years for the development of social bonds. Some reviews of these studies (Pinneau, 1955; and Kagan, Kearsley, & Zelazo, 1978) suggest that early infancy may be sensitive rather than critical to the development of social relationships. The concept of attachment behavior also includes a sensitive period estimated to be between 6 and 9 months for the infant and mother to establish social relations (Steele, 2004).

• •

Attachment: A powerful emotional tie or bond between two people, regardless of age but typically referring to the relationship between children and caregivers (usually the mother). Attachment keeps infants close to their mothers, which is important for getting food and comfort and staying away from danger. (Based on information obtained from www.alleydog.com/glossary/definition.cfm?term=attachment.

• •

Learning

There are critical periods for learning as well. This was first observed by McGraw (1946) when he described varying periods to learn different motor activities that depended on degree of opportunity and stimulation. Michel (2001) later expanded on this concept.

Plasticity is a related concept that refers to the capacity of the central nervous system to adapt or change after environmental stimulation. Head injury in children may disrupt the developmental sequence—slowing the rate of subsequent development and possibly leading to deviant patterns of development. For example, Koeb, Gibb, and Gorny (2000) indicated that frontal lobe injury in the first year of life almost invariably leads to lowered IQ and poor performance on frontal lobe executive function tasks (inhibition, planning, flexibility, and self-monitoring). The same injury at an older age may not have the same effect. Koeb concluded that at least for this part of the brain, the earliest injury produced the worst behavioral outcome. Recent studies provide limited evidence for greater neuronal plasticity (i.e., growth) after early lesions (such as head injury) in children (Koeb, 2000).

Clearly, many factors must be taken into account when presented with a child who has behavior problems. Each child carries a biological and psychological developmental history within the context of his or her genetics, family, culture, and environment.

EDUCATION OF THE BEHAVIORALLY DISORDERED

During the 1950s, all special services for students with behavior problems were provided in segregated settings, with one grouping set aside for the "socially maladjusted" (Wood, 1990). Services were provided in hospitals and other residential settings. Many of these students were discouraged from attending school because of their behavior, and those who did come were punished or expelled. Teachers who worked with such students were lonely and isolated, with little sense of being part of a professional group.

By the mid-1950s, the situation began to change. With an emphasis on milieu therapy and the environment in treatment, there was greater recognition of the importance of these special teachers. The behavior modification era developed and began to claim an important part of treatment in schools. About the same time, there was a growth of special education programs recognizing the emotionally disturbed and "socially maladjusted" as categories of special need. Teachers moved rapidly to establish their professional competence in applying learning-based interventions in school settings.

There was a rapid growth of programs in the 1960s. The newly established Bureau of Education for the Handicapped provided financial support, teacher training, and program development. Clearly, special education was still in its infancy in dealing with problem behavior (Kauffman, Bantz, & McCullough, 2002). Before the end of the 1960s, there were several new books blending psychodynamic and behavioral principles with direct application to school settings. There was also the establishment of the Council for Exceptional Children (CEC established in 1922) and the Council for Children with Behavioral Disorders (CCBD established in 1962).

From 1970 on, educators of students with behavior disorders grew in numbers and in their professional accomplishments. Legal due processes (especially rights for students with disabilities to a Free Appropriate Public Education [FAPE] in the Least Restricted Environment [LRE]) have caused concern about the definition of the "problem." Special educators were forced to recognize that there are other ways to look at behavior disorders than those provided by psychology, which put prime emphasis on the "deviant individual" as the focus of the problem. Many challenged the current conceptualization, noting the role played by social systems. Still others pointed out that what is or is not to be considered as deviant behavior is culturally based, varying across cultures. Ecologists stressed the importance of setting as a determinant of disruptive behavior.

Special education, once dependent on the professional literature of related fields, began to develop a strong and vital literature of its own, including *Behavior Disorders*, a professional quarterly journal published by the Council for Children with Behavioral Disorders, as well as several excellent textbooks and teacher manuals.

However, in the course of this growth there has been a continuous struggle with some fundamental problems, such as the labeling/eligibility issue. In 1981, the National Society for Autistic Children had autism removed from the category of serious emotional disturbances. One serious consequence has been to fractionate the federal and state funds available for training and programs in the area of the "seriously emotionally disturbed." Also, while there have been many texts, the number of researched and effective interventions has not grown since the late 1960s. Some procedures have been evaluated singly (and in combination) to provide many documented intervention strategies (O'Conner et al., 2005; Corrigan et al., 2001).

Although there has been a blending of cognitive and behavioral procedures by earlier educators, the job of the teacher of behaviorally disordered students remains extremely difficult. While there have been many changes in the field of behavior disorders over the past 30 years, these changes have generally not been incorporated into the field of special education. Since many students with disabilities have been included in general education, teachers are now needing information on these behavioral interventions. Most recently, the emphasis has been on disseminating information to both special and general educators.

THEORIES OF CHILD DEVELOPMENT

There are many theories of child development and various models on which to base a developmental perspective and to understand emotional and behavior disorders. Crain (2000) has reviewed the concepts of several theorists, including Bandura's social learning theory, Freud's psychoanalytic theory, and Erickson's theory. Specific attention is given here to the developmental and the behavioral perspectives.

Historically, two models have been used to account for changes that occur in children throughout their development: (1) the *organismic model*, and (2) the *mechanistic model*. The organismic model, associated with Erickson (1968), Freud (1949), and Piaget (1951), alleges that the child's basic structures and functions change across age. This would be identified as Freud's *psychosexual stages*, Erickson's *stages of identity development*, and Piaget's *stages of cognitive development*. Description of these stages reflect emerging yet qualitatively different ways of interacting with the environment. Change, thus, comes from maturational processes determined by organistic factors rather than the environment.

The mechanistic model, associated primarily with B. F. Skinner (1938), alleges that changes across age result from alterations of antecedents and consequences; developmental explanations are then derived from principles of learning. This latter model asserts that the child of any age is a relatively passive responder to increasingly more complex and varied stimuli. Skinner argued that "all organisms were subject to the *same law of effect* (i.e., principles of reinforcement), and could be studied in the *same basic manner*" (1938, p. 27). Consequently, many behaviorally orientated clinicians viewed developmental processes as relatively unimportant (Ollendick & Vasey, 1999; Ollendick, King, & Muris, 2004).

MODELS FOR EMOTIONAL AND BEHAVIOR DISORDERS

We focus here on the following models for emotional and behavior disorders:

- Biopsychosocial model
- Transactional model
- Interaction model
- Constructivist model
- Nature–nurture model
- Environmentalist model
- Behavioral model

The Biopsychosocial Model

The current view that many factors interact to result in an emotional or behavior disorder may be traced to the work of George L. Engel who proposed the biopsychosocial model of disease (Engel, 1977). His comprehensive model provides a basic framework for understanding disordered behavior, asserting that biological factors alone are not sufficient to explain mental disorders and that biopsychosocial factors are involved in the causes, manifestation, course, and outcome of mental disorders. The relative importance of any single factor—be it biological, psychological, or social—may vary by individuals as well as by age and stage of development. This could account for different etiologies for the same condition—for example, depression from exposure to stressful life events versus depression caused by genetic predisposition. An understanding of certain terms—*correlation*, *causation*, and *consequence*—is important to fully understand the biopsychosocial model.

• •

Correlation: A measure of the strength of the relationship between two variables. It is used to predict the value of one variable given the value of the other. Note that correlation does not imply causation.

Causation: A relation that holds between two temporally simultaneous or successive events when the first event (the cause) brings about the other (the effect). An example would be fire causing smoke.

Consequence: The logical or natural outcome that follows from an action or condition. (Based on information obtained from Wikipedia [ed.wikipedia.org/wiki].)

• •

A correlation simply means that events are linked together in some way. For example, stress and depression may be correlated, but causation may be an unidentified third factor. If stress usually precedes depression, stress might be called a "risk factor" (cause) for depression. Risk factors (causes) may be biological, psychological, or sociocultural. Establishing causation may be very difficult as random assignment to experimental and control groups may be impossible ethically and/or financially. Consequences are defined as later outcomes of a disorder. For instance, in the case of depression, a consequence may be suicide or illness (Frasure-Smith et al., 2000). In short, the biopsychosocial model holds that biological, psychological, and social factors may be causes, correlations, and/or consequences regarding the development of mental disorders. The biopsychosocial perspective is thus essential in assessing and planning intervention strategies for children with behavior problems.

Berkley's (1990) biopsychosocial model is shown in Figure 2.2, which uses concentric circles to clarify

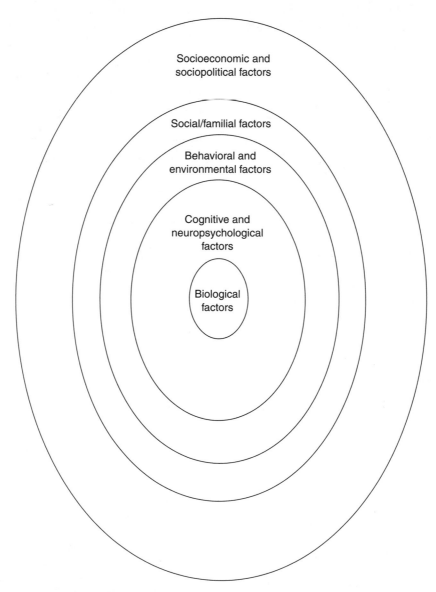

FIGURE 2.2 The biopsychosocial model of assessment and functioning.

Source: Adapted from Engel, G.L. (1980) The Clinical Application of the Biopsychosocial Model, *American Journal of Psychiatry*, 137: 535–544. Reprinted with permission from The American Journal of Psychiatry (Copyright, 1980) American Psychiatric Association.

multiple levels of functioning and suggests possible interactions. Such interactions among levels can radiate both inward and outward, thereby affecting different levels. This model is thus invaluable when assessing behavior planning as well as behavioral/educational assessments for students who demonstrate problem behavior.

Biological Factors: The Core   Biological factors form the innermost circle of the biopsychosocial model, which includes "physical integrity and genetic predispositions toward various behavioral classes, such as depression, anxiety or ADHD" (Barkley, 1990). This level deals with the basic physical/biological integrity of the individual and especially with the central nervous system (CNS) or brain. The CNS is affected by genetic predispositions as well as by external environmental factors such as lead toxins (Lamphear, et al., 2005; Woodruff et al., 2003). In addition, alcohol use during pregnancy (Streissguth et al., 2004; Shaywitz et al., 1980), smoking by the mother (Matthews, 2001) and prenatal anoxia can all affect the integrity and subsequent development of the CNS (Barkley, 2002). It is in this innermost core that one might find evidence of neurological dysfunction at the cortical or subcortical level of the brain; the influence of neurotransmitters (or a deficit thereof) in the brain that affects attention and/or impulsivity/hyperactivity; or the combined effect of neuroanatomical and neurotransmitter effects. More knowledge is being accumulated about these biological factors in several behavior problem diagnostic categories, such as ADHD.

Cognitive and Neuropsychological Factors   The second concentric circle involves cognitive and neuropsychological patterns directly related to how the CNS functions (Castellanos et al., 1996). Combinations of difficulties in fine and gross motor skills, visual-motor and visual-spatial skills, and difficulty with central auditory processing can all influence the child and result in manifestation of deficits and inappropriate behaviors. Such combinations of deficits may result in unique impairments where only one academic skill may be affected. Multiple deficits may be clearly associated and define a diagnostic problem or may be multifactorial and contribute to the association of two or more problems.

Behavioral and Environmental Factors   The third circle in the biopsychosocial model deals with behavioral and environmental interactions of various problem behaviors. These interactions typically occur in the child's natural environment and might involve teachers, parents, and others who communicate expectations or place demands on the child. Information about whether the child can perform better in some situations and not others will be important. For example, the degree of structure provided in a learning environment may affect how the child adjusts and whether disordered or acceptable behavior is forthcoming.

In addition to physical environmental interaction, the child's social interactions with parents, teachers, peers, and siblings are important. In many cases, there are social skill problems that are characteristic of the disorder (e.g., with conduct disorder [CD], ADHD, or autism). Social skill deficits as well as other difficulties such as talking and listening, taking turns, following rules, and transitioning from one social setting to another may all elicit some problematic behavior.

Social and Familial Factors   In the fourth circle, the focus is on interactions within the family or in more general social situations. Familial problems such as alcoholism, depression, anxiety, and occupational issues may significantly affect the child at many levels. Attempts to modify the problem behavior may thus require examination of the most intimate family contexts within which the problem occurs. Modification of how others react to the child (the primary identified person) is critical in helping the child.

Socioeconomic and Sociopolitical Factors   The fifth circle involves factors such as parental education, socioeconomic status, and occupation, along with other parenting habits—good or bad. Geographic factors can partially determine what resources are available to the child for assessment and treatment (Barkley, 2002). The level of resources may thus indirectly affect the outcome of the treatment (and the prognosis) regarding how the child will or will not be able to function. It is also important that theories of development be culturally dependent, and that cultural factors be included here. Miller and colleagues (2003) have pointed out that such factors have often been ignored in developmental psychology.

DEVELOPMENTAL ISSUES

Deviant Versus Normal Child Development

All children develop differently, and in this section we make a distinction between typical patterns of child development and those deviant patterns that result in behavior disorders, mental health problems, and disturbed patterns of attention and learning. Deviance from the norm will refer to specific (deviant) patterns of academic and/or psychosocial behavior that do not coincide with what is expected of the child at various developmental stages.

Expressions such as "deviant," "maladaptive," and "antisocial" were commonly used in the 1980s and before; today "challenging" is most often used to describe behaviors that differ significantly from the expectations of others (Jackson & Panyon, 2002). Such shifts in language also reflect two key changes: (1) knowledge about the origins and causes of behavior, and (2) the ethical standards that govern the treatment of those who appear different.

In typical patterns of development, a child may reach certain developmental milestones at the average age at which most children attain the skill. It is estimated that about 3 percent of children will experience *developmental delay*—delayed achievement of one or more of a child's milestones, which may affect speech and language, fine and gross motor skills, and personal and social skills. Approximately 15 to 20 percent of these children will actually show abnormal development. The rest will eventually catch up and develop normally over time—just a little later than expected.

Forehand and Wierson (1993) have delineated the role played by developmental factors in both behavior and cognitive behavior therapy with children, especially disruptive children. After reviewing developmental changes from preschool through adolescence, they present a model that shows the sequence of the development of disruptive behaviors. The steps through which such behavior develops are proposed to occur hierarchically and emerge at certain age levels. It is argued that the tasks faced at each developmental transition, taken in combination with behaviors learned in earlier developmental stages, pose challenges for individuals that may result in disruptive behavior.

Developmental Psychopathology

Developmental psychopathology bridges a gap between development and clinical child psychology (Cicchetti & Toth, 2006). Rutter (2005) has defined the concept as "the study of the origins and course of individual patterns of behavioral maladaption, whatever the age of onset, whatever the cause, whatever the transformations in behavioral manifestations, and however complex the course of developmental pattern may be" (Rutter & Sroufe, 2000). Thus, developmental psychopathology is organized around developmental milestones, transitions, and sequences in physical, cognitive, and social-emotional development (Ollendick, Grills, & King, 2001).

Viewed as a series of reorganizations, development is determined by genetic, constitutional, physiological, behavioral, psychological, environmental, and sociological factors in dynamic transaction with one another (Cicchetti & Cohen, 2006; Cicchetti & Rogosch, 2002). Pathological development represents a lack of integration among systems that contribute synergistically to adaptation at specific developmental levels.

Development at one level does not necessarily affect later behavior, since the process of both typical and deviant behavior development appears to result from distinct and unique transactions between the child, who is always changing, and his or her changing environment. There are multiple pathways that produce behavioral outcomes. It is, therefore, important to identify and understand characteristics, both internal and external to the child, that promote or inhibit deviations and that maintain or disrupt early adaptation and development. Developmental psychopathology is most concerned with the origins and course of disorders, its precursors and sequelae, its variation and manifestation with development, and its relations to typically developed behavior patterns (Cicchetti & Walker, 2003; Rutter, 2005). Developmental psychopathology does not endorse or replace a particular theory of child behavior; it simply enhances awareness about various phenomena that may appear unrelated.

DEVELOPMENTAL ACQUISITION OF BEHAVIOR DISORDERS

Many psychiatric disorders of childhood once thought to be mental or functional in nature (Yudofsky, Hales, & Stuart, 2002) and behavioral disorders presumed to be learned or related to environmental factors (Gresham & Gansle, 1992) have been found to have a neurodevelopmental or neurochemical basis, as noted by Teeter and Semrud-Clikeman (1997). Attention to the scope and sequence of development of cortical structures and related behaviors that emerge in the child is important to ascertain the intactness of the child's development, and to assess further the impact of the environment (i.e., enrichment, instructional opportunities, and intervention strategies) on this process.

Gaddes and Edgell (1994) have noted that all behavior (including cognitive processes) are mediated by the brain and central nervous system and their supporting structures. Behavioral approaches have been utilized in assessing and treating disorders of childhood and adolescence (Prins & Van Manen, 2005; Shinn et al., 2002). Analysis of antecedents and consequences has been an essential feature of functional behavioral analyses where there is an ongoing assessment and treatment (Kratochwill, Sladeczek, & Plunge, 1995). Behavioral interventions are often found to be an integral part of the treatment program for disorders with a central nervous system basis, including learning disabilities (Shechtman & Pastor, 2005), ADHD (Flick, 1998), and traumatic brain injury (Warschausky, Kewman, & Day, 1999). In sum, the brain and CNS may affect behavior *and* behavior may affect the brain and CNS.

THE TRANSACTIONAL MODEL

The limitations of the early child development theories led to the development of the *transaction model*—a theory asserting that developmental changes result from continuous and reciprocal interactions or transactions between the active child and his or her environment (Sameroff, 1995; Mundy & Neal, 2001). Current theorists generally agree that development involves systematic, successive, and adaptive changes across all life periods in the structure, function, and content of the child's mental, behavioral, social, and interpersonal characteristics (Sameroff, 1995). Since changes are successive and systematic, changes at one point in time will influence subsequent events.

According to Teeter and Semrud-Clikeman (1997), the transactional model "assumes a dynamic interaction among the biogenetic, neuropsychological, environmental, cognitive, and psychosocial systems." As the child becomes more independent, influences from the social and cultural environment will be experienced. Although parental temperament and caretaking may not change the basic biological characteristics of the child, they may serve as a buffer and affect how the child's biological vulnerabilities are manifested. Appropriate interventions, along with changes in the child's home, school, and social environment, can reduce the negative effects of many neuropsychological or biogenetically-based disorders (Teeter & Semrud-Clikeman, 1997). For some disorders, a medication regime may also be beneficial.

It is important to recognize that all of these interactions are complex and that brain–behavior relationships are dynamic and fluid within this neurodevelopmental framework. Various learning disorders (Rourke, 2005), traumatic brain injuries (Bigler, Clark, & Farmer, 1997), and psychiatric disorders with CNS involvement (Lipkin & Hornig, 2004; Charney, Nestler, & Bunney, 2004; Penza, Heim, & Nemeroff, 2003) may be assessed and treated. Interventions for many behavioral and psychiatric disorders often require a combination of medication as well as behavioral, academic, and psychosocial strategies; an integrated transactional assessment–intervention paradigm is thus crucial.

THE INTERACTION MODEL

• •

The *interaction model* refers to a dynamic changing sequence of social interactions between individuals who change their reactions and responses as a result of the interaction. Social interaction provides a basis for all social relations.

• •

Before parents and teachers can obtain a fundamental understanding of how to manage problem behaviors, there must be a general understanding of the nature of the parent–child or teacher–child interaction process, as well as an understanding and acceptance of the basic nature of the problem behavior.

Some early research studies in clinical psychology suggested that more aggressive children tend to have parents who are more punitive, more negative, and less affectionate. There was clearly a correlation, but these studies erroneously concluded that there was causation, that aggressive children are aggressive because of the punitive style of their parents. In early clinical practice, many clinicians tended to look either for what the parents may have done wrong or for what they failed to do in order to account for the child's problems. As happened then and still occurs today, many parents are often blamed and held responsible by others for their child's problems. It is not unusual for parents to report these comments: "His teachers say I just need to be more firm with him," or "My mother tells me I spoil her—she thinks I should not let her get away with all the things she does." Parents also tend to blame themselves: "I know it must be something that I've done. My child is not like others in the neighborhood." Such comments frequently lead parents and even some teachers to feel guilty, inadequate, and depressed and to have low self-esteem regarding how they manage children at home or in the classroom.

Bidirectional pattern

Undirectional pattern

Some of these early beliefs reflected a *unidirectional pattern* in the parent–child or teacher–child interaction, a belief that placed the responsibility for a child's inappropriate behavior solely on the parent or on the teacher. Parents were more often than not viewed as lacking in one or more aspects of parental competence and as deficient in their interactional behavior. Today, we realize that a bidirectional view of the parent–child or teacher–child interaction is more accurate. Both unidirectional and bidirectional views are two facets of the interaction model.

For example, families with a bipolar parent differ from the average family in having less cohesion and organization, and certainly more conflict (Chang, Blasey, Ketter, and Steiner, 2001). Despite such differences, it does not appear that the environment of families with a bipolar parent alone determines the outcome of psychopathology in the children, or that the psychopathology of the children determines the family environment. Both influence each other.

In this interaction model, the child may have just as much of an effect upon what discipline is used as does the parent or teacher (i.e., a bidirectional pattern). Interactions are reciprocal and complex; a bidirectional view is obvious. Within this model, which was originally proposed by Barkley (1990), we can at any time view the outcome of the interaction as a function of several factors—of constitutional, genetic, emotional, environmental, and learning—that abide in each parent, teacher, and child. For example, parents of children with ADHD are more likely to show characteristics of genetically based ADHD. Consequently, when a child acts impulsively, there may be a tendency for the parent to react impulsively with discipline; or just the opposite may occur if the parent is aware of these impulsive tendencies (i.e., he or she may take "too much time" to react or not react at all). In either case, this pattern may be detrimental to the child.

There may be many factors outside the parent–child interaction that may not affect this interaction, as has been noted by Barkley (1981). On the parent/teacher side, financial, marital, stress, and health problems may affect how the adult functions. For example, adults with ADHD are more prone to stress-related emotional problems (Flick, 1998b). Such difficulties may modify (or lower) the parent's threshold for discipline. When parents and teachers are stressed or drained, they may be less tolerant of a child's misbehavior, which will affect their reaction to such behavior. On the child's side, school problems, peer problems, and health and stress problems will affect their behavior in the parent–child or teacher–child interaction. For example, children who have experienced a fight in school or have been criticized in a class because of their behavior may come home with a heightened level of suppressed anger (i.e., with a chip on their shoulder) that may be more easily displaced within the parent–child interaction, or perhaps the sibling–child interaction.

DYNAMICS OF EMOTIONAL AND BEHAVIOR PROBLEMS

Understanding the underlying dynamics of emotional and behavioral problems is critical for both teachers and parents if they are to deal effectively with such behavior. First, it is important to understand that the basic behavior is, in many cases, driven by a child's neurophysiology. This understanding can alleviate much guilt and faultfinding—of self and others—which often occurs as parents and teachers attempt to deal with problem behaviors.

Second, it is essential to understand that the most consistent finding about problem behaviors is their *inconsistency*. Thus, a child's good days will be followed by bad days, which may be puzzling to both teachers and parents but may become more readily accepted. It is not at all unusual to hear this comment from parents: "His teacher said he did all of his work yesterday, but none today. If he did it one day, she knows he can do it." This inconsistency frequently sets children up for unreasonable expectations that result from a lack of understanding about the causes of a child's inconsistent work or behavior patterns. The child's neurophysiology may change from one day to the next, affected by stress events, food and drink intake, sleep patterns, environmental changes,

interpersonal encounters, as well as both prescription and over-the-counter medications. Whatever affects the child's neurophysiology also affects his or her behavior.

Hierarchy of Responses

The interactions that occur between parent and child or between teacher and child represent a hierarchy of responses designed to manage the child's behavior (Barkley, 2006). These parent/teacher–child dynamics occur in the following sequence:

1. Ignoring
2. Restrictive commands
3. Negative affect and commands
4. Physical discipline
5. Acquiescence
6. Learned helplessness

This sequence is also shown graphically in Figure 2.3.

In short, an adult may begin with ignoring a child's misbehavior and then proceed to restrictive commands such as "Stop that!" The adult may then add a negative affect with these commands (e.g., looking angry or stern, frowning). The next step may be physical discipline where the child is slapped or spanked. When successful control is still not forthcoming, the adult may acquiesce or "give up." The final state is learned helplessness as the parent admits failure: "It's hopeless—I give up. I'll just let him do whatever he wants."

It is of paramount importance for the parent or teacher to learn to distinguish which behaviors are functions of an underlying neurophysiology and which are not. For instance, if a directive is given by an adult to a child (e.g., "Pick up your toys and put them in the closet."), and the child fails to do it, the parent or teacher may simply ask the child to repeat the request. If the child is able to repeat it, then refusal certainly may be an example of outright noncompliance, not inattention.

Older children and adolescents frequently have many additional problems to deal with, including poor self-concept, associated with a long history of failure in school, depression, and at times "acting out" of aggressive behavior. Ultimately, this may result in the child dropping out of school or necessitating some type of residential placement to impose limits and control behavior. Early understanding, acceptance, and intervention for the child's emotional and/or behavior problems will

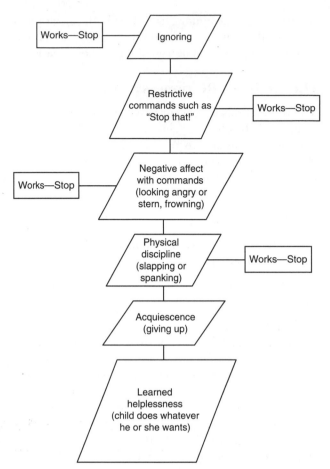

FIGURE 2.3 Hierarchy of responses in adult–child dynamics.

clearly have a greater effect on the success of treatment and the prognosis. It is critical to know that, at this time, there is no "cure" for some of these disorders. However, the behaviors associated with these conditions, once recognized, can be managed, understood, and accepted.

THE CONSTRUCTIVIST MODEL

According to the constructivist model, learning and development occur when young children interact with their environment and the people around them (Hunt, 1996). Basically, constructivists view young children as active participants in the learning process. Because such active participation is necessary for learning, the constructivists believe that children are ready for school when they can initiate many of the interactions with the environment and the people around them. Kindergarten classrooms are carefully structured, being divided into different learning centers that are equipped with developmentally appropriate materials for these young children. Children move from one activity center to another, and daily activities are made meaningful by incorporating the children's experiences into the curriculum. At home, parents encourage reading and storytelling activities as well as the child's participation in household activities that introduce concepts of counting and the use of language. Pictures of goals and toys that stimulate interaction may be provided. When young children encounter difficulties in the learning process, the constructivist will neither label them nor restrain them. Instead, children will be given individualized attention, and their classroom curriculum will be customized to address these difficulties.

Cognition includes a broad range of human abilities such as memory, perception, problem-solving, and attention to name just a few. Development is viewed as the gradual acquisition of a widening range of abilities. Piaget formulated a theory of cognitive development that has many applications to developmental neuropsychology and the way(s) learning occurs. According to Piaget, there are four stages of learning or development:

1. *Sensory-motor stage (birth to about 2 years):* The primary mode of learning for children at this stage occurs through the five senses, by touching, holding, looking, listening to, talking, and feeling things. They bang and shake everything in sight, and their sense of time is "now" and the sense of space is "here." When they add motor skills (e.g., crawling, walking), their environment expands dramatically. This sensory-motor mode of learning, which then involves both senses and movement, may continue through age 12.

2. *Preoperational stage (ages 2 to 7):* These children are busy gathering information (learning) and trying to figure out ways to utilize what they have learned to solve problems. They will think mostly in specifics and have difficulty generalizing anything, constantly asking "why" questions. They judge everything by how it affects them, and how they like it.

3. *Concrete operations stage (ages 7 to 11):* Children begin to manipulate information mentally, trying to define, compare, and control it. Their thinking, however, remains concrete. Concrete operational children are capable of logical thought. They still

learn through the senses but now think as well. During this stage, teachers may begin a lesson at a concrete level and move toward a more generalized one. For example, in approaching the concept of kindness, they may begin by talking about a kind thing someone did and then move to talking about being kind. The last step would then involve a discussion of kindness as a concept. Because 7- to 10-year-olds are very literal in their thought processes, they may take everything they hear at face value.

4. *Formal operations stage (beginning at about 11 years of age)*: At this time, children begin to think more abstractly. They no longer restrict thinking to time and space, and they begin to reflect, hypothesize, and theorize. They also start to develop the following cognitive abilities: (a) *knowledge of facts and principles* (e.g., memory of dates, names, definitions, vocabulary); (b) *comprehension of facts and ideas*; (c) *application* (i.e., knowing rules, principles, and procedures and how to use them); (d) *analyzation* (i.e., breaking down concepts into parts); (e) *synthesization* (putting together information or ideas); and (f) *evaluation* (judging the value of information).

THE NATURE–NURTURE MODEL

The nature–nurture model is a controversial theory that views *nature* as one's genetic inheritance and *nurture* as one's environment. The two interact—nature can influence nurture and nurture can influence nature—and each can contribute to the development of mental disorders (Plomin, 1996). Studies have found that various forms of learning (nurture/environment) can even lead to changes in brain structure and function. With schizophrenia, identical twins are found in only 46 percent of cases; if both twins are diagnosed as schizophrenic some environmental factors may thus protect against the development of schizophrenia even in identical twins (Plomin, 1996). Clearly, there is an interplay of nature and nurture in any result and outcome.

THE ENVIRONMENTALIST MODEL

The environmentalist model—characterized by the work of John Watson, B. F. Skinner, and Albert Bandura—believes that the child's environment shapes

learning and that behavior, development, and learning are all seen as reactions to the environment. Thus, readiness for kindergarten will occur whenever children (at whatever age) can respond appropriately to the environment of the school and the classroom, which would include rules and regulations, curriculum activities, exhibiting positive behavior in group settings, and comprehending instructions from teachers and other authority figures. The ability to respond appropriately to the environment is essential if children are to engage in teacher-initiated learning activities. Success depends on a child being able to follow instructions.

Many theorists adhering to this viewpoint believe that children may learn best through rote activities such as reciting the alphabet over and over, copying letters, and tracing numbers. They are expected to sit in desks arranged in rows and listen attentively to the teacher. At home, parents may provide activity workbooks on coloring or tracing numbers—things that require little interaction between parent and child. The young child who has difficulty in this classroom and school environment may be labeled with a learning disability and then followed in a special education classroom with curriculum designed to control his or her behaviors and responses.

THE BEHAVIOR MODEL

The behavior model is primarily concerned with all overt activity that a child exhibits and what intervention can be used to change that observable and measurable behavior. Behavior theorists view the causes of the child's behavior as events outside the child and in the immediate environment. Consequently, the child's behavior is seen as primarily determined by external forces.

Because of current technology, certain internal physiological factors may be made observable and thus modifiable within the constraints of a behavioral format—for example, brainwave (EEG) activity coming under conscious control and thus capable of being shaped and developed. For the most part, due to the expense and rarity of such equipment, the main focus will be on those clearly obvious behaviors that are readily observable and modifiable by teachers or parents.

Proponents of the behavioral model assume that all behavior, both appropriate and inappropriate, is a consequence of the application of the following principles of reinforcement: (1) reinforcement follows behavior;

(2) behavior should be reinforced immediately after it occurs; (3) reinforcement must be appropriate—that is, rewarding (to strengthen the preceding behavior) or punishing (to weaken the preceding behavior); and (4) frequent, small rewards are more effective than a few big rewards. These principles reflect the belief that behaviors can be controlled and manipulated by the control and manipulation of environmental stimuli.

The behavior model has roots in the works of Wolpe (1958), Bandura (1969), and Skinner (1971, 1974) to name just a few, but behaviorism has most often been associated with the work of Skinner, where humans, like any other organisms, are regarded as entirely the product of their environment, responding in a deterministic way to the external conditions to which they are exposed. In Skinner's work, all reference to subjective states of mind are considered irrelevant and perhaps even counterproductive with regard to scientific inquiry.

While there have been variations in the conceptualization of behavioral constructs, the basic principles of behavior theory have been consistently applied. There have been many applications of behavioral techniques to various childhood behaviors including ADHD, autism, anxiety, and speech problems. Many such behavioral interventions have been used in school settings.

The educational context for behavioral intervention in the classroom for children with behavioral problems has been noted by Hewett (1967), who says that the basic goal for behavior specialists is "the identification of maladaptive behaviors which interfere with learning and assisting the child in developing more adaptive behaviors." Every child is considered a candidate for learning regardless of his or her degree of psychopathology and other problems. Basic behavior such as sitting quietly in a chair may represent only a starting point and may be but a small part of eventual goals such as reading that the teacher hopes to accomplish. Care will be taken to ensure its mastery before more complex goals are introduced.

There are many behavioral interventions that may be applied to change behavior. These are discussed in detail in Chapters 10 and 11 with emphasis on specific applications in Chapter 12. A teacher or parent wanting to apply such behavioral interventions in the classroom, school, or at home would follow a general sequence of steps: (1) observe and describe the behavior to be changed, (2) select developmentally appropriate and effective reinforcers at a specified point in time, (3) design and plan to consistently use the behavioral intervention along with the basic principles of reinforcement, (4) monitor and evaluate the effectiveness of the intervention, and (5) revise and implement alternate interventions as needed and warranted according to the effectiveness of the prior intervention. Each step will be reviewed in more detail in Chapter 11, which discusses behavioral techniques and interventions.

SUMMARY

This chapter focuses on the understanding of emotional and behavior disorders. After looking at the origins of such disorders, it covers the development of psychopathological issues targeting risk and protective factors. Following a brief discussion of the major theories of child development, the primary focus is on models for emotional and behavior disorders, beginning with the biopsychosocial model. Various developmental models are viewed (including the biopsychosocial model, the transactional model, the interaction model, the constructivist model, the nature–nurture model, the environmentalist model, and the behavioral model) with a primary conceptualization of the behavior model emphasized.

DISCUSSION QUESTIONS

1. Discuss the origins of emotional and behavior disorders.
2. What are risk and protective factors?
3. Explain the concept of "plasticity."
4. What are some of the theories of child development?
5. Explain the biopsychosocial model. What are some of the core factors and how might these relate to the development of a behavior disorder?
6. Explain the hierarchy of responses in the interaction model.
7. Who are the theorists commonly associated with the behavior model?

CHAPTER 3

Educational Outcomes of Students with Emotional and Behavior Disorders

Overview

- Praise and opportunity to respond
- Current educational outcomes for students with emotional and behavior disorders
- Current employment for students with emotional and behavior disorders
- Improving post-school outcomes for students with emotional and behavior disorders
- Current social relationships for students with emotional and behavior disorders
- Major recommendations from the President's Commission on Excellence in Special Education
- Service delivery for special education
- The learning-centered classroom
- Researched interventions for behavior problems

Case History

Allen is an excessively active 8-year-old student in a regular class who has been diagnosed with attention-deficit/hyperactivity disorder (AHDH) and is on 10 mg of Ritalin twice a day. He is disruptive in class, shows inappropriate verbalization, refuses to remain seated, and tears up and throws materials. Allen's behavior is interfering with his learning and that of the other students. *What would you do?*

During the mid-1980s, researchers attempted to answer basic questions about special education students when they leave the public school system. A number of follow-up studies found high dropout rates, low employment, and social isolation, suggesting that special education had not been effective (Edgar, Levine, & Maddox, 1986; Hasazi, Gordon, & Roe, 1985; Mithaug, Horinchi, & Fanning, 1985). A poll by Harris and colleagues (1986) also found that unemployment for prior special education students was higher and wages lower than for any other group. The outcomes for these students do not appear to have improved since the mid-1980s. Data from the National Longitudinal Transition Study (NLTS) in August 2006 are consistent with previous studies (Thurlow, Ysseldyke, & Anderson, 1995)

With the advent of inclusion, a greater number of students with emotional and behavior disorders (EBD) are being educated in general education classrooms by teachers who are not special education teachers. It is important that these teachers know the characteristics of the students they are teaching. Numerous researchers have pointed out that students with EBD have the lowest grade point average, high dropout rates (Sutherland, Wehby, & Yoder, 2002), and high unemployment rates. Salmon (2006) has offered the following strategies to help improve the education of students with EBD: (1) increasing praise or encouragement and opportunities to respond to academic requests, (2) improving the organization of the classroom, and (3) improving the training and education that regular education teachers receive.

PRAISE AND OPPORTUNITIES TO RESPOND

Teachers can improve the education of EBD students through the use of praise and opportunities to respond (OTR) in the general classroom setting. OTR not only promotes greater active participation in class but also results in fewer behavior problems and improved retention of information for EBD students. Clearly, teachers who praise students more often provide higher rates of OTR (Sutherland et al., 2002). Increasing OTR also gives teachers more occasions to praise EBD students. Both OTR and praise appear to be effective in helping students. If teachers fail to respond, students will experience frustration in the learning process.

CLASSROOM ORGANIZATION

Teachers can also implement specific management strategies to increase the rates of success for EBD students (Gunter et al., 2002). These strategies include (1) establishing and posting rules (no more than five) and consequences, (2) facilitating interaction between student and teacher, and (3) the use of general behavior management strategies. The use of self-monitoring and peer tutoring has also been found to increase on-task behavior and academic production (Cook et al., 2003). Simple worksheets rather than packets also result in sustained effort on independent work (Gunter et al., 2002). After new material is taught directly by teachers, independent seat work will allow each student time to practice learned skills on assigned work that is within the student's capability but still challenging.

TEACHER PREPARATION

In 2008, few educators use such strategies (originally outlined by Wehby et al., 2003). Without teacher preparation, EBD students are not properly managed, and there is a high rate of teacher burnout that seems clearly related to this lack of teacher preparation during the preservice years. There are also questions as to why teachers persist in using techniques that lack effectiveness and fail to use some of the more successful evidence-based practices. Many preservice teachers receive instruction on managing behavior problems but not on effective academic techniques, and sometimes the reverse is true: Teachers have not been taught how to manage behavior problems and how to implement effective strategies.

Due to time constraints and the difficulties of accommodating the various needs of preservice teachers, most receive minimal training on special education topics such as EBD (Salmon, 2006). In general, the goal of teacher training needs to combine classroom management strategies with academic instruction that is conducive to learning for all students, including EBD students in the general education classroom. In addition, preservice training of teachers should include interventions that may enhance the probability of success for EBD students with regard to their postschool outcomes.

IMPROVING POSTSCHOOL OUTCOMES FOR EBD STUDENTS

According to Jolivette and colleagues (2000), students with EBD have the least favorable outcomes in education, employment, and social relationships of any disability. Jolviette and colleagues also present some school-based strategies to improve outcomes for students who have trouble with social relationships, academic problems, and chronic behavior problems, which include noncompliance, aggression, and disrespect toward authority. Long-term problems clearly affect postschool outcomes.

When such students are placed in the most restrictive settings, this often exacerbates their characteristics. The use of "zero tolerance" may further distance EBD students from educators who might be able to help them. However, inclusive placement is clearly not effective either.

Educational Outcomes

Learning disabilities often coexist with EBD and may result in problems mastering academic content (Coleman & Vaughn, 2000), thus proving that the relationship between academic and social behaviors appears reciprocal; failure in one portends failure in the other. Because EBD students have few interactions with teachers, they get less exposure to academic content. Such students do poorly in basic skills such as reading and math; more than 50 percent of these students drop out of school (Chesapeake Institute, 1994) and many do not finish high school. Few students who do graduate pursue further education.

Current Employment

EBD job seekers take longer to find employment and many experience lower percentages of employment and lower rates of employment (Malmgren et al., 1998). Most EBD workers hold multiple short-term jobs rather than full-time steady employment. Consequently, students with EBD show long-term poor employment activity.

Current Social Relationships

Emotional and behavior disorders generate problems with social adjustment and may make it difficult for individuals to form relationships with those who can help them become independent. They are more likely to have poor experiences in their interactions with others and they are also more likely to be arrested and/or incarcerated.

There are several ways in which postschool outcomes can be improved (Jolivette et al., 2000):

■ *Social skills training:* Most skills, including social skills training, require individual planning (Scott & Nelson, 1998) and this is one of the most effective interventions for helping EBD students, especially when it provides *direct instruction* (to identify the special social skills needed) and *teacher mediation* (to prompt and reinforce appropriate behavior). Goals might include allowing EBD students to develop positive social relationships, to improve their ability to cope with daily behavioral expectations, and to provide effective self-determination.

■ *Peer mediation and conflict resolution:* Students without a disability can be trained to interact with EBD students, which allows positive behavior to be naturally rewarded. After training, students meet for various social activities where the trained peer models reinforce and prompt appropriate social responses from the EBD students. Thus, the adult (teacher) is removed from the interaction loop.

■ *Positive behavioral support:* Positive behavioral support (PBS) is based on the assumption that schools address the full range of behavioral issues and needs of students concerning strategies for preventing behavior problems and intervening when inappropriate behavior occurs (Sugai et al., 2000). PBS interventions stress the teaching of appropriate replacement behaviors that serve the same function as the undesirable behavior.

■ *Vocational training:* The School to Work Opportunities Act (1994) facilitates vocational training—the coordination of school and community efforts to provide the Individual Education Plan (IEP) in the least restrictive environment with the goal of moving EBD students from the school environment to the work environment. EBD students are provided specific job training, work placement, and job coaching while still in school

■ *Transition planning:* In accordance with P.L. 105-17, schools must write and implement a transition plan for all EBD students aged 14 years and older. This plan contains details of each student's and family's goals for employment and independent living.

Some of the following goals and needs may be included:

1. Enlisting community agencies to help financially
2. Placement in multiple work sites to aid decision-making after graduation
3. Identifying counseling centers
4. Exploring all subgoals to help the student with employment and finances

■ *Wrap-around planning:* Wrap-around plans match individual and family needs with community agencies and opportunities. Services might include (1) counseling, (2) financial advice, (3) job training, mentoring, or coaching, and (4) health services (Karp, 1996). Appropriate community supports and contacts must be in place while the student is in school to achieve postschool success.

A NATIONAL AGENDA FOR EDUCATING SED STUDENTS

A study of the National Agenda for Achieving Better Results for Children and Youth with Serious Emotional Disturbance found 14 successful programs that have several shared characteristics: (1) a common set of values, (2) staff agreement about these values, (3) operationalization of values and organizational policy, and (4) a set of practices that implement these values (Osher & Hanley, 2001). Students with serious emotional disturbance (SED) are mostly identical to EBD students and consistently received lower grades, failed more courses and minimum competency exams, and were retained more often at grade level. Only 42 percent of students with SED earn a diploma, while 50 percent of all youth with disabilities and 75 percent of youth in the general population do so. About 48 percent of students with SED drop out in grades 9 through 12, as opposed to 30 percent of all students with disabilities, and only 24 percent of general education students. Students with SED miss more days of school and are arrested at least once before they leave school, as opposed to 9 percent of students with disabilities and 6 percent of all students. For a more comprehensive discussion of the drop-out rate for students with emotional or behavioral disorders, see Cook and colleagues (2003); for a discussion of specific outcomes for those with serious emotional disturbances, see Wagner (1995).

Seventy-three percent of SED students who drop out are arrested within 5 years of leaving school.

Compared to all students with disabilities, students with SED (1) are more likely to be placed in restricted alternative settings or drop out of school, (2) are more likely to have their families blamed for their emotional problems and to have great financial expenditures for their condition, and (3) are more likely to have teachers and aides who seek reassignment or leave their positions.

The Office of Special Education Programs (OSEP) (Koyanagi, 1994) participated in the planning process and identified seven strategic targets:

1. *Expand positive learning opportunities and results.* Foster the provision of engaging, useful, and positive learning opportunities, which should be result-driven and should acknowledge as well as respond to the experiences and needs of children and youth with serious emotional disturbance.

2. *Strengthen school and community capacity.* Foster initiatives that strengthen the capacity of schools and communities to serve students with serious emotional disturbance in the least restrictive environments appropriate.

3. *Value and address diversity.* Encourage culturally competent and linguistically appropriate exchanges and collaborations among families, professionals, students, and communities. These collaborations should foster equitable outcomes for all students and result in the identification and provision of services that are responsive to issues of race, culture, gender, and social and economic status.

4. *Collaborate with families.* Foster collaborations that fully include family members on the team of service providers that implements family-focused services to improve educational outcomes. Services should be open, helpful, culturally competent, accessible to families, and school- as well as community-based.

5. *Promote appropriate assessment.* Encourage practices ensuring that assessment is integral to the identification, design, and delivery of services for children and youth with SED. These practices should be culturally appropriate, ethical, and functional.

6. *Provide ongoing skill development and support.* Foster the enhancement of knowledge, understanding, and sensitivity among all who work with children and youth with and at risk of developing serious emotional disturbance. Support and development

should be ongoing and aim at strengthening the capacity of families, teachers, service providers, and other stakeholders to collaborate, persevere, and improve outcomes for children and youth with SED.

7. *Create comprehensive and collaborative systems.* Promote systems change resulting in the development of coherent services built around the individual needs of children and youth with and at risk of developing serious emotional disturbance. These services should be family-centered, community-based, and appropriately funded.

In order to implement these seven targets (Office of Special Education Programs, 2005), a flexible and proactive continuum of services must be constructed around the needs of children with SED and their families. Services must also be sustained and comprehensive, and they must engage families, service providers, and SED students. As diversity increases, the needs of such children will require interactive and community-based relationships characterized by mutual respect and accountability.

PRESIDENT'S COMMISSION ON EXCELLENCE IN SPECIAL EDUCATION

In 2001, President George W. Bush created the Commission on Excellence in Special Education, an organization charged with the responsibility to continue the president's educational vision "where every public school reaches out to every single student and encourages every child to learn to his or her full potential." In order to recommend reforms for the special education system, the commission heard from hundreds of families, educators, and communities through public hearings and written comments. On July 1, 2002, *A New Era: Revitalizing Special Education for Children and their Families* (Wehman, 2002) was published based on that input. This report sets forth recommendations addressing each of the nine findings. The commission's following three recommendations are excerpted from the report:

Major Recommendation 1: Focus on Results— Not on Process.

The Individuals with Disabilities Education Act (IDEA) must return to its educational mission: serving the

needs of every child. While the law must retain the legal and procedural safeguards necessary to guarantee a "free appropriate public education" to children with disabilities, IDEA will only fulfill its intended purpose if it raises its expectations for students and becomes results-oriented—not driven by process, litigation, regulation, and confrontation. In short, the system must be judged by the opportunities it gives and the outcomes achieved by each child.

Major Recommendation 2: Embrace a Model of Prevention Not a Model of Failure.

The current model guiding special education focuses on waiting for a child to fail, not on early intervention to prevent failure. Reforms must move the system toward early identification and swift intervention, using scientifically based instruction and teaching methods. This will require changes in the nation's elementary and secondary schools as well as reforms in teacher preparation, recruitment, and support.

Major Recommendation 3: Consider Children with Disabilities as General Education Children First.

Special education and general education are treated as separate systems, but in fact share responsibility for the child with disabilities. In instruction, the systems must work together to provide effective teaching and ensure that those with additional needs benefit from strong teaching and instructional methods that should be offered to a child through general education. Special education should not be treated as a separate cost system, and evaluations of spending must be based on all of the expenditures for the child, including the funds from general education. Funding arrangements should not create an incentive for special education identification or become an option for isolating children with learning and behavior problems. Each special education need must be met using a school's comprehensive resources, not by relegating students to a separately funded program. Flexibility in the use of all educational funds, including those provided through IDEA, is essential.

The Commission believes that the same principles of the No Child Left Behind Act should be the driving force behind the reauthorization of IDEA. These principles are results-oriented accountability; flexibility; local solutions for local challenges; scientifically based programs and teaching methods; and full information and options for parents. It is hoped that reauthorization of IDEA will have a strong influence on moving IDEA towards reform. Parents and professionals involved in the special education system should become more familiar with the President's Commission on Excellence in Special Education's report in order to continue to influence how IDEA is implemented. (Bellah, 2002).

MODELS OF SERVICE DELIVERY FOR SPECIAL EDUCATION

IDEA mandates the inclusion of special needs students and identifies three basic models of service delivery for special education: (1) full inclusion, (2) conservationist, and (3) conciliatory (Pruslow, 2000).

Full Inclusion Model

This student grouping is characterized by its commitment to accommodate the needs of all students through the services of an adaptive instruction team (AIT), which consists of a regular education teacher (or discipline specialist), a special educator, and a teaching assistant. This is based on work by Lipsky and Gartner (1998), Roach et al. (1995), and Villa and Thousand (2003)

Conciliatory Model

This modified inclusion model questions the viability of full inclusion for all special education students (Audette & Algozzine, 1997; Deno, Foegen, Robinson, & Espin, 1996). It replaces the three-person adaptive instruction team characteristic of the full inclusion model with an inclusion team that consists of a regular education teacher and a special education teacher (Pruslow, 2000). Viewed as a demonstration of fiscal responsibility, this two-person team models the approach most often used in early inclusion attempts (Villa & Thousand, 2003). Another compromise in this model is the provision for resource rooms to support integrated special education students who would normally be in a self-contained classroom in the conservationist model (traditional) approach.

Conservationist Model

This model represents arguments for the perpetuation of traditional special education, which may include the regular classroom, resource room, and the self-contained classroom. Services then might target several different sources (Kauffman & Hallahan, 1995). It also argues for the application of a "continuum of services" to placement (Pruslow, 2000). A more recent approach focusing on improvement of service delivery was presented by Wohlstetter and colleagues (2004).

In the conservationist model, there are three submodels of special education services delivery: (1) the self-contained classroom, (2) the pull-out program, (3) the plug-in program.

The Self-Contained Classroom Students with special needs have their own classroom, special education teacher, and perhaps an aide. The maximum size is eight or fewer students (one to two or four for more severe disabilities). All students are treated the same and have access to school programs.* The following advantages and disadvantages are associated with the self-contained classroom.

Advantages

Classes are small.
Curriculum is geared to meet students' needs.
Students receive most teaching time with a special education teacher.
Students who cannot achieve in a regular education class may do well in this setting.

Disadvantages

Students are isolated from the rest of the school.
Being in a "special class" carries a stigma.
Students fail to receive social benefits of being with peers.
Assigning one teacher to a few students is expensive.

The Pull-Out Program Students with special needs spend part of their day in general education classes, and they are "pulled out" by the special education teacher for small group instruction. It is sometimes difficult to schedule these sessions without removing students

---

*Material in the following section has been adapted with permission from Flora Kuferman, a special education consultant at the Bureau of Jewish Education.

from general education classes at times when they would miss interesting or important lessons. It may also require more communication between the special education teacher and general education teacher when there are materials to work on in the general class. The following advantages and disadvantages are associated with the pull-out program:

Advantages

Students experience the social benefits of being included with peers in a general education class.

Individual or small group instruction is tailored to the specific learning needs of students.

All students and teachers learn about diversity and accommodating special needs.

Disadvantages

Students sometimes miss interesting or important lessons.

Being pulled out carries a stigma.

Scheduling is difficult.

Sometimes students cannot keep up with the work of the general education class.

The Plug-In Program   Students with special needs are in the general education class all the time, but the special education teacher goes into the class to work with one or more students. Scheduling for this option may also be difficult. The following advantages and disadvantages are associated with the plug-in program:

Advantages

Students benefit by being included with their classmates in a general education class.

Students receive individual or small-group instruction geared to their specific learning needs.

All students and teachers learn about diversity and accommodating special needs.

All students benefit from the special education teacher being in the classroom.

Disadvantages

Some teachers have difficulty sharing their classrooms with another teacher.

Scheduling time to meet with special needs students in classes can be difficult.

Some children need more than brief visits from a special education teacher.

It is also possible to mix models within any school. But in all cases, the special education teacher must formulate realistic goals for students in special education.

Much research has focused on the student's understanding of various aspects of the service-delivery setting: (1) self-contained classroom versus mainstream classroom, (2) pull-out model versus in-class model, (3) general classroom teachers versus specialists, and (4) awareness of what special education placement involves.

Padeliadu and Zigmond (1996), among others, found that students seemed to enjoy getting their instruction in the resource classroom. There were also significant differences as a function of age, placement, and service-delivery preference. Older students seemed to be more accurate in explaining the purpose of the resource (i.e., pull-out) room (Padeliadu & Zigmond, 1996) and were more likely to choose to spend time in a resource room (Vaughn & Bos, 1987). Also, younger students chose an in-class (versus pull-out) model as their preferred service-delivery setting (Jenkins & Heinen, 1989).

••

A *resource classroom* is a classroom, which is sometimes smaller, where a special education program can be provided to a student with a disability. Such students receive individualized instruction in this setting for part of the day. The child will receive individualized instruction (defined by the IEP) along with accommodations in the regular classroom.

••

Lerner (1997) noted that instruction in strategy intervention does improve the likelihood that a learning disabled student can succeed in a general education class. However, the Joint Committee on Teacher Planning for Students with Disabilities (1995, p. 5) found that "educators need to think in terms of supported inclusion, not simply inclusion." Mercer and Mercer (1998) have summarized the criteria that are needed to implement a successful model of supported inclusion:

Teachers must be philosophically committed to meeting the needs of all students in the general education classroom. Teachers must have time to plan and think about the needs of diverse learners. Teaching practices that meet the needs of all students must be incorporated into the instructional program. General education teachers must collaborate with special education teachers to assess, teach, and monitor student progress. Short-term, intensive instruction from a special education teacher needs to be available for some students with disabilities. Sustained instruction in basic skills or learning strategies that cannot be provided in general education classes must be available to some students with disabilities. (p. 23)

TYPES OF CLASSROOMS

Postschool outcomes may also be influenced by the type of classroom in which a student with EBD is placed. We compare two options here: the learner-centered classroom and the curriculum-centered classroom.

Learner-Centered Classrooms

Learner-centered classrooms focus primarily on individual student's learning. The teacher's role is to facilitate growth by utilizing the interest and unique needs of students as a guide for meaningful instruction. Because such classrooms are goal-based, students' learning is judged by whether they achieve predetermined, developmentally oriented objectives. In theory, every student can earn an A by mastering the material. The method by which learning occurs is oftentimes experiential.

Curriculum-Centered Classrooms

Curriculum-centered classrooms focus essentially on teaching the curriculum. Teachers determine what ought to be taught as well as when, how, and in what time frame they should teach it. The curriculum that must be covered throughout the year takes precedence. These classes often require strict discipline, and children's interests are considered only after curriculum requirements are met. In this framework, students are compared with one another, and individual success is judged according to how well others do. A fixed standard of achievement is not necessarily in place, and classroom grades may resemble the familiar bell curve.

Many teachers are not strictly learner-centered or curriculum-centered, and they may fall in the middle of this continuum. Many simply use what works for them based on their fundamental belief structure, which may be reflected in the way the learner-centered

teacher makes time to collaborate with others to deal with challenges as they evolve and to research new ideas and learn about key concepts that students must acquire. Evaluation of students is ongoing in this type of learning context. In contrast, the curriculum-centered teacher works mostly alone, with collaboration taking place primarily in team meetings where all teachers involved may agree to teach the same lessons.

RESEARCHED INTERVENTIONS FOR BEHAVIOR PROBLEMS

....

Researched interventions refers to the use of the most effective interventions for behavior problems. They are one that have the best success or best outcomes.

....

Clearly, there are many approaches that schools can use to prevent behavior problems and to address them when they do occur. Effective behavioral interventions require collaborative efforts from the school, home, and community agencies. Helping children and youth must be a shared responsibility. The following points have been summarized from research conducted by the National Dissemination Center for Children with Disabilities (2003):

- Assessment of a student's behavior must be linked with interventions that follow the student through whatever placements the student has.
- Multiple interventions are necessary for improving the behavior of most students. Any positive effect of a single strategy, especially when the intervention is short-term, is likely to be temporary. Just as behavior problems and risk factors come in packages, so too should interventions.
- To produce lasting effects, interventions must address not only the behavior that led to disciplinary action but a constellation of related behaviors and contributing factors.
- Interventions must be sustained and include specific plans for promoting maintenance over time and generalization across settings. Focusing on the student's behavior while placed in any short-term setting, such as an interim alternative educational setting, is not sufficient. Interventions need to follow the student to his or her next placement (and elsewhere).

■ A combination of proactive, corrective, and instructive classroom management strategies is needed. Interventions must target specific prosocial and antisocial behaviors and the "thinking skills" that mediate such behaviors. Such a combination provides an atmosphere of warmth, care, support, and necessary structure.

■ Interventions must be developmentally appropriate and address the strengths and weaknesses of the individual student and his or her environment.

■ Parent education and family therapy are critical components of effective programs for antisocial children and youth.

■ Interventions are most effective when provided early in life. Devoting resources to prevention reduces the later need for more expensive treatment.

■ Interventions should be guided by schoolwide and districtwide policies that emphasize positive interventions over punitive ones.

■ Interventions should be fair, consistent, culturally and racially nondiscriminatory, and sensitive to cultural diversity.

■ Interventions should be evaluated as to their short-term and long-term effectiveness in improving student behavior. Both the process and outcome of each intervention should be evaluated.

■ Teachers and support staff need to be well trained with respect to assessment and intervention. Staff working with students who have behavior problems will require ongoing staff development and support services.

SUMMARY

The education of students with emotional and behavioral disorders is the prime focus of this chapter. A discussion of praise and opportunities to respond is followed by an emphasis on structural issues in the classroom and basic foundations for teachers. The objective is to improve postschool outcomes as well as to improve factors that impinge on teacher training. Major recommendations of the President's Commission on Excellence in Special Education are discussed as well as the varied methods of service delivery to special education students. The basics of the learner-centered and curriculum-centered approaches are discussed, with the primary focus on those general interventions that are recognized as the best practices for dealing with and preventing behavior problems.

DISCUSSION QUESTIONS

1. Describe what is meant by OTR.
2. How does classroom organization affect behavior?
3. What kind of teacher preparation is needed to deal with students having behavior disorders?
4. How can postschool outcomes be improved for students with behavior disorders?
5. What are the three major recommendations from the President's Commission on Excellence in Special Education?
6. List the seven strategic targets that were developed for the national agenda for children and youth with SED.
7. Describe the three models of service delivery for special education.
8. Discuss the advantages and disadvantages of the self-contained classroom.
9. Compare and contrast the learner-centered and the curriculum-centered classrooms.
10. Describe some of the general procedures for preventing challenging problem behavior.

PART II

Recognizing Emotional and Behavior Disorders

There are a number of diagnostic conditions that a teacher may face whether in a regular class, in an inclusive setting, or in a self-contained class for special education. Some of these disorders will present major challenges for teachers but some will require little behavior management. While this book focuses on externalizing disorders—those forms of behavior disorders that are most difficult to deal with—it also describes and explores less challenging diagnostic conditions. For example, most any one of the *externalizing* conditions (i.e., attention-deficit/hyperactivity disorder [ADHD], conduct disorder [CD], oppositional defiant disorder [ODD], etc.) will frequently present a management challenge. However, most of the disorders within the category of internalizing disorders will present very little challenge. A child with one of these conditions (i.e., generalized anxiety disorder [GAD], obsessive-compulsive disorder [OCD], posttraumatic stress disorder [PTSD], etc.) may cause little disturbance in a class room. In fact, many teachers may not even know that the child has any problems. Should there be cognitive interference due to anxiety, learning performance problems may often be attributed to laziness or lack of effort. Thus, even though there may be no significant behaviors to cope with, it will be important for the teacher to be able to recognize the conditions. Other emotional disorders may present a variety of problems; the main problem behaviors will be addressed in various chapters of this book.

The chapters that follow describe the incidence rates, explore etiologies and developmental factors, and review some associated conditions of individual emotional and behavioral disorders. It should be emphasized that while all of these conditions are important and deserve attention with regard to the curriculum adjustments involved, only some will be the focus of behavioral intervention due to a student's disruptive behavior. Because conditions involving anxiety, learning problems, and some forms of depression may not present any disruptive behavior in the classroom, only their symptoms and characteristics, not behavioral interventions, will be discussed. It is possible, however, that these disorders may be associated with (i.e., comorbid with) others that do present a disruptive behavior—for example, attention-deficit/hyperactivity disorder with mild depression. It will therefore be helpful to know something about such associated conditions and to understand what activities and strategies, when appropriate, might be beneficial.

Problematic behavior may be associated with some of the more disruptive conditions and would thus be a target for behavioral interventions. The focus will therefore be on targeted symptomatic behavior. It is the behavior problems that are addressed, not the diagnoses. While diagnostic impressions will determine what classification children may be given, it is their problem behavior that is the focus of the targeted interventions that will be discussed. Behavior interventions are commonly used in class and school settings by teachers, school psychologists, and counselors. In addition, clinicians in private practice may also employ these techniques conjointly with those in the school setting.

CHAPTER 4

Externalizing Disorders

Overview

- Attention-deficit/hyperactivity disorder
- Oppositional defiant disorder
- Conduct disorder
- Interventions for externalizing disorders
- Tics and Tourette's syndrome

Case History

Aston is a 12-year-old seventh grader who has a full scale IQ of 98 on the WISC-III and shows much off-task behavior. He also has exhibited yelling out, playing with objects, excess talking, and making funny faces and some inappropriate gestures. He is taking 20 mg of Ritalin twice daily. Aston's off-task behavior has led to many office referrals. He has verbalized many times that he hates to write and often makes this comment whenever he is asked to do a task that requires "writing." *What would you do?*

The externalizing disorders include attention-deficit/hyperactivity disorder (ADHD), oppositional defiant disorder (ODD), and conduct disorder (CD). There is generally some degree of overlap among these disorders, but ADHD appears to be the most common and will be the focus in this chapter. This chapter also includes information on tics and Tourette's disorders, because these are frequently associated with ADHD. The primary difficulty with all of these disorders is that children experience conflict with their environment (Quay & Hogan, 1999). Garland and colleagues (2001) noted that the rates of ADHD and disruptive behavior disorders are extremely high in public sectors of care (e.g., child welfare, mental health, juvenile justice, and public school services for youths with serious emotional disturbance).

ATTENTION-DEFICIT/ HYPERACTIVITY DISORDER

The symptoms of attention-deficit/hyperactivity disorder appear as a cluster of symptomatic problems rather than as a unitary abnormal behavior condition (Nigg et al., 2002). The most common teacher complaints involve ADHD, and children with this condition comprise about 40 percent of referrals to special education and mental health centers (Webb & Myrick, 2003). There are two core characteristics of this disorder: (1) inattention—the child has difficulty focusing and maintaining attention, misses critical details, and frequently shifts from one activity to another; (2) hyperactive-impulsive behavior—the child fidgets, blurts out answers, and may have difficulty remaining seated in the classroom or at home (for example, at the dinner table). According to the DSM-IV (American Psychiatric Association [APA], 1994), six symptoms out of the total number of symptoms (from either of these two groups) must be present to make a diagnosis, and the severity of symptoms must result in functional impairment. So it is possible for a child to have ADHD but not experience any impairment of academic performance or in social skills. Additionally, symptoms must be present for at least six months, the age of onset must be less than seven years of age, and there must be impairments in both home and school settings. The DSM-IV lists three diagnostic subcategories: (1) primarily inattentive type; (2) primarily hyperactive-impulsive type, and (3) combined type (the most prevalent type).

Incidence ADHD is estimated to affect 3 to 5 percent of school-age children. However, more recent studies have estimated that the incidence can be up to 10 percent and perhaps even higher (Flick, 2000). In our fast-paced society, there may be evidence of a higher incidence of ADHD (Schmidt-Neven, Anderson, & Godber, 2002; Flick, 2000). Both the diagnostic incidence and medication usage have increased since 1985 (Safer, Zito, & Fine, 1996); ability tests indicate that children have become more impulsive and less attentive (Wechsler, 1991). Alternative explanations for the apparent increase in this diagnosis may reflect an increased awareness about ADHD symptoms as well as more subtle forms being diagnosed (e.g., among girls and adults with ADHD). There may also be a small group of cases that represent an actual increase that may be associated with acquired ADHD characteristics;

Case Study

Attention-Deficit/Hyperactivity Disorder

Dylan is an 8-year-old third grader in a regular education classroom. Although his grades have been average and above, his behavior has constantly interfered with his achievement. Dylan has much trouble staying in his seat to complete assignments. He gets bored quickly and is often caught playing with his pencil, a piece of paper, or a little toy that he has brought from home. Dylan rushes through his work and makes many careless mistakes. He is quite impulsive, frequently blurts out answers before raising his hand, and interrupts his teacher as well as his classmates with comments. Dylan often gets in fights and frequently blames someone else for starting them. Although he loves to play soccer, arguments often ensue because he does not play by the rules of the game. Dylan often gets in trouble for not completing his work and for not returning homework even when he says he has done it.

these may be due to the influence of various organic factors (e.g., lead poisoning, head trauma, and ear infections with high fevers), as noted by Flick (2000).

Etiologies   There is strong evidence for a genetic basis in ADHD. Biederman and colleagues (1990) have presented data where about 65 percent of children with ADHD have had at least one relative with ADHD, compared with 24 percent for psychiatric and 15 percent for normal groups. Fisher, Francks, and McCracken (2002) have noted that molecular genetic studies of ADHD have previously focused on examining the roles of specific candidate genes, primarily those involved in dopaminergic (neurotransmitter) pathways. They find, however, that there is not likely to be a major gene involved in ADHD susceptibility. Some authorities have noted that genetics sets the stage for risk (Ingersoll & Goldstein, 1995). Life experience then determines whether an individual ultimately receives a diagnosis of ADHD. Several environmental toxins—including lead poisoning, food additives (salicylates), food dyes, along with cigarette smoking and alcohol use during the pregnancy, fluorescent lighting, and brain injury—have been reported to be etiologic or to contribute to ADHD. There is little substantial evidence that fluorescent lighting is a factor that causes ADHD or triggers it. However, there is support for other events and substances in the etiology of ADHD. In short, ADHD may be either inherited or acquired (Flick, 1998b).

Medications   A complete listing of medications for ADHD is found in Appendix A. Several of these medications are also used in the treatment of other comorbid disorders; all medications are described in full.

Developmental Issues   During the preschool years, children with ADHD exhibit overactive and impulsive behaviors, as there are increased demands for them to follow directions and modulate social behaviors. About 60 to 70 percent of children later diagnosed with ADHD could have been identified by symptoms during preschool (Flick, 1998b). Young children who have ADHD symptoms are also more likely to have language problems (Purvis & Tannock, 1997; Cohen et al., 2000); this group may also develop a wide range of behavior problems (Tomblin et al., 2000; Flick, 1998b) compared with children who do not have ADHD symptoms.

During elementary school, symptoms include distractibility, difficulty with sustained attention, low-frustration tolerance, and fidgeting. The core symptoms of ADHD (i.e., inattention, impulsivity, and hyperactivity) persist into adolescence and beyond (Robin, 1998; Wolraich et al., 2005; Weiss & Hechtman, 1993); however, both hyperactivity and to some extent inattention may decrease during adolescence or before.

In a large school-based sample of children in the first to the fourth grades, August, Braswell, and Thuras (1998) conducted screenings for disruptive behavior problems during a 5-year period. According to parent observation, both inattention and hyperactivity/impulsivity symptoms declined from year 1 to year 4, with hyperactivity showing a more significant decline. According to teacher observations, attention problems declined from year 1 to year 3 and then stabilized; the hyperactivity ratings were stable during the first three years and declined thereafter. Of the children diagnosed with ADHD in the first year, 69 percent met the criteria in year 4 or 5. Those children who persisted with the ADHD diagnosis were also more likely to have CD or ODD. Currently, ADHD is seen into adulthood for 50 to 60 percent of children with this condition. ADHD has also been related to other forms of behavior and emotional problems in the adult years (Ingram, Hechtman, & Morgenstern, 1999; Weiss & Hechtman, 1993).

Associated Conditions   Many children frequently meet the criteria for ADHD and oppositional defiant disorder, or ADHD and conduct disorder (Barkley, Edwards, & Robins, 1999). The presence of ODD, and especially of CD, results in a much more guarded prognosis (Hansen, Weiss, & Last, 1999). The risk for more serious acting-out behaviors is increased when ADHD is combined with ODD and particularly so with CD. In one hypothesized pathway or trajectory, if ADHD appears first and is then combined with environmental familial risk factors such as marital discord and poor parenting, the probability for ODD and CD is enhanced. When more serious behaviors such as aggression appear in early childhood, there is a poorer prognosis for later development. About 50 to 70 percent of adolescents with ADHD also develop ODD during their youth and a significant number might develop CD, which appears to be a more severe form of ODD. Basically, the issue that separates CD and ODD is safety. This means that children with CD may present danger to self, others, and personal property, while those with ODD might annoy others but are not especially dangerous (Barkley et al., 1990; Barkley & Murphy, 2006).

Biederman and colleagues (1996) have noted that there appears to be two subtypes of ODD associated with ADHD: one that develops into CD and another that is not likely to develop into CD in later years. Spencer and colleagues (2001) have indicated that a comprehensive approach to diagnostic evaluation is the key to establishing an effective treatment program as the response to treatment may differ with individual disorders. For example, a cluster of symptoms that is considered to be resistant to treatment of ADHD—resulting in oppositionality, aggression, and conduct disorder—may better respond to medications along with behavioral interventions following mood stabilization. Weller, Weller, and Dogin (1998) have noted that children who exhibit behavior more characteristic of a mood disorder than oppositionality along with their ADHD may respond to Ritalin with dysphasia—impairment of the ability to speak or understand language—but exhibit frank visual hallucinations on Dexedrine. In the presence of a significant family history of mood disorder, it is appropriate to consider an early-onset bipolar disorder. Bipolar disorder is often considered to evolve from or develop alongside ADHD.

Kim and Miklowitz (2002) examined whether early onset bipolar disorder may be mistakenly attributed to ADHD or CD or whether ADHD and CD may be misdiagnosed as "mania." While reliable diagnoses can be made despite symptom overlap, children with bipolar disorder and ADHD may have a distinct subtype of bipolar disorder. Some authors also suggest that manic symptoms may represent "noise" that simply reflects the general severity of the psychopathology (Flick, 1998b). Prospective studies have focused on whether early onset bipolar disorder can be successfully differentiated from ADHD or CD, whether all three types of disorders can be recognized in comorbid cases, and whether comorbid cases represent a distinct subtype of bipolar disorder. So, the verdict is still out on bipolar disorder as it is difficult to diagnose it when confounding disorders are present. It is also questionable whether there is a distinct type of bipolar disorder when characteristics of ADHD and/or CD are present. Carlson and Meyer (2000) found that boys with ADHD along with symptoms suggesting childhood bipolar disorder do not respond differently to Ritalin than boys without such symptoms; there is no evidence that Ritalin precipitates young adult bipolar disorder in susceptible individuals. Children with ADHD have much difficulty adjusting to situational demands (Nixon, 2001), and the impulsive quality of their behavior appears to be primarily responsible for placing them at higher risk for social difficulties (Frankel & Feinberg, 2002). For example, sociometric studies and evaluation of play behavior indicate that children with ADHD may not be chosen as often by peers in partner activities (Frankel & Feinberg, 2002). Clearly, children with ADHD have much difficulty with social skills (Mrug, Hoza, & Gerdes, 2001).

About 20 to 30 percent of ADHD children may also have a reading disability. The combination of ADHD with LD causes the child to appear even more inattentive (Rutherford, Quinn, & Mathur, 2004), which may lead to significant underachievement during the middle elementary grades since many reading problems typically may not be diagnosed until third grade or beyond. Geffner (2006) reports findings of significant expressive language problems with older children (9–10 years old) having greater difficulties than younger children (6–8 years old). These deficits in language ability were related to issues in social competency. Adolescents with ADHD continue to have problems, and about a third may be suspended from school at least once (Robin, 1998). Teenagers with ADHD are at greater risk for developing internalizing problems including depression (Biederman et al., 1995) and anxiety (Pliszka, 1992). Mick and colleagues (2000) investigated sleep problems associated with ADHD and found that together with anxiety, behavior disorders such as ADHD were significantly associated with sleep disturbances. In short, while sleep difficulties are common in ADHD youth, they are frequently accounted for by associated anxiety, other behavior disorders, and inappropriate medication usage. They also note that the lack of association between a positive family history of ADHD and sleep difficulties suggests that ADHD is not a misdiagnosis of the consequences of the disruption of normal sleep.

Symptom Pattern   In addition to the use of psychological testing to rule out or rule in other disorders (or to define comorbid condition), a detailed history, accumulated background information (e.g., report cards, medical test results, and work samples) along with traditional parent, teacher, and (when self-report is appropriate) child rating scales are all useful in assessing ADHD.

Activities and Strategies for ADHD   The following activities and strategies may be used with ADHD students (Shore, 1998; Flick, 1998a):

1. Praise ADHD students whenever they display appropriate behavior. Many students with disruptive behavior disorders have had a deficiency of positive strokes or reinforcement, either because they show more inappropriate behavior in general or they receive fewer strokes even when they do show appropriate behavior because the teachers and parents may be reluctant to provide positive strokes when the child's ratio of negative to positive behavior is so high. Basically, this philosophy states that "they don't really deserve positive strokes."

2. Structure situations so that rules are clearly understood. Teachers and parents can help the child by writing down rules, reviewing them periodically, and developing predictable routines.

3. Place students with ADHD in locations that minimize distractions. This does not mean that they are always seated near the teacher. In some cases, it may be best to seat them near another student who can serve as a good model.

4. Monitor students to help maintain their work activity, reinforcing them for starting work, continuing to work, and extending their work span (extent of work time *before* they get off task). Continue monitoring until work is completed to reinforce work completion. Develop a private signal so ADHD students can let you know when they need help without alerting others to their need.

5. Allow movement. For overactive children, the need to move is akin to physiological requirements such as the need for food or water. This movement activity may be used to reward the child for work completed. If the expectation for this work activity is reasonable (i.e., one with which the child can comply), the child may be allowed to go to a designated place in the room for a book or other activity when the assignment has been completed.

6. Teach students ways to organize and to develop a routine place for homework, important assignments, and test papers. Use color-coded folders, assigning similar colors for folders and notebooks in a given subject. Review these procedures on a regular basis.

7. Reorganize assignments into shorter tasks and work periods. Thus, two 15-minute assignments may allow more productivity than one 30-minute task.

8. Show students how to break up assignments for homework into shorter segments. Shorter assignments may be especially appropriate for children with dysgraphia, a handwriting disorder.

9. Manipulate the child's attention span with novel dynamic presentations. The use of an overhead projector and color to emphasize words can help the child to focus. Reveal only limited material at any one time.

10. Create assignments that do not rely on handwriting all the time. Use more oral assignments or perhaps allow the child to use computer skills.

11. Exercise has been found to help children with ADHD. Try to incorporate some brief physical exercise or at least some stretching in the academic day's routine. You can also sometimes allow standing to do those tasks (math facts, spelling bee, etc.) that do not require the student to be seated.

12. Encourage special projects that utilize a child's special interest or talent (e.g., performing magic tricks). Allow students to demonstrate these to the class. This is a great way to enhance self-concept and to counteract some of the frustrations encountered in doing routine daily work.

13. Help students master social skills. For children who blurt out inappropriate comments, teach techniques that will allow them to delay such impulsive behavior (for example, by counting to 10 or repeating the question to themselves silently). Deliver positive reinforcement and praise when appropriate behavior occurs.

14. Emphasize the *quality* of a student's work, not the *quantity*. Stress that understanding and accuracy are the goal. If a child has poor writing, teach the self-instruction technique of verbalizing letter formation while writing. This form of self-talk is a slow down technique that minimizes careless errors. Always praise improvement.

15. Use resources and the staff (e.g., an aide) at school to assist with various problem behaviors. A child may be quite motivated to work in a particular situation or with a special person as a reward for improved

Case Study

Oppositional Defiant Disorder

Julie is a 13-year-old female in the seventh grade whose parents are divorced and who currently lives with her father and two younger brothers. She rarely sees her mother and has a generally poor relationship with her. Julie presents a striking appearance in school. She is physically well developed for her age and, on most occasions, appears well groomed; she has her ears triple-pierced, a nose ring, and a small snake tattooed on her left ankle. She is pleasant on most occasions and shows no significant impairment of cognitive processes. However, Julie has been in legal trouble, having been arrested twice for shoplifting. She seems to habitually get in trouble at school and often blames others for her problems.

Julie has trouble following rules at school. Disobedient and argumentative with little tolerance for frustration, she has stolen things from other students and, at times, destroyed property. She has admitted to some use of alcohol and has smoked marijuana. She denies being sexually active, although she is very flirtatious with male students.

Julie has told others that she doesn't get along with her younger brothers and is reportedly "mean to them." They too have had problems similar to Julie's. While she seems to have many friends, her friendships are "fleeting" and do not last long. She is bossy even with friends and quick to anger. Struggling academically, she argues with teachers, sometimes refuses to do her work, and annoys classmates. She in turn becomes annoyed with students who like to tease her and see her "get in trouble." She often retaliates and seems spiteful and vindictive in returning the teasing. Julie argues with everyone—classmates, teachers, and her father. He states that "she often does exactly the opposite of what I tell her to do."

work or behavior. Note that the emphasis is on *improvement*. It is best to avoid setting arbitrary goals that may be too difficult for the student to achieve. Let the student's behavior be your guide.

16. Keep parents informed and involved. Cooperative home and school programs can be very effective. (Note that this does not mean that children who have unproductive days should be punished at home.) Both teachers and parents must focus primarily on *positive* behavior. Send home notes on good behavior or improvements. Call parents to report such behavior—not just when there is a problem (Shore, 1998; Flick, 1998b).

OPPOSITIONAL DEFIANT DISORDER

Oppositional defiant disorder (ODD) refers to a pattern of inappropriate behavior that is characterized by hostility, defiance, temper outbursts, and argumentative behavior. According to DSM-IV criteria (APA, 2004), there must be at least four symptoms (out of the total)

occurring over a six-month period to make this diagnosis. Related behavior problems can include temper tantrums, arguing with adults, active defiance, noncompliance with rules, and deliberately annoying others and blaming them for mistakes. Children with ODD are also easily annoyed and touchy, and they can be vindictive.

Incidence   The prevalence or incidence rate of ODD is estimated to range from 2 to 16 percent; it is more frequent in boys.

Etiology   There has been little research on the etiology of ODD.

Developmental Course   Although the majority of children with ODD do not develop CD, 90 percent of children and teens with CD do have a history of symptoms associated with ODD (Rowe et al., 2002).

CONDUCT DISORDER

Conduct disorder (CD) is a condition that includes the acting-out of aggression, destruction of property, and violations against authority (e.g., lying, cheating, or

Case Study

Conduct Disorder

Rachael is a 15-year-old girl who has been suspended from school for assaulting a teacher. She was in the eighth grade. She reports to the pediatrician that she needs a psychological evaluation before she can go back to school. Over the past 2 years, Rachael has had seven suspensions for fighting, bringing a knife to school, smoking pot, and stealing things from others. She has frequent conflicts with her mother (who gets on her nerves), which results in Rachael running away for several days. Her mother explains that her daughter has had a long history of aggressive and destructive behavior over the years: pulling the cat by its tail, breaking dishes and furniture, and starting a fire when she was playing with a small gas stove. She reportedly loved to play with matches when she was younger. In school, Rachael has poor grades and is always in trouble. She has few friends and all of them have problems similar to hers. Rachael's mother reports that her father, who is currently in jail for stealing cars and bodily assault, has been frequently away from home when not in jail. Rachael's mother sometimes works in a bar and leaves Rachael and her 9-year-old brother unsupervised overnight.

breaking other school rules). Children with CD violate the basic rules and rights of others. Their behaviors may include bullying or threatening classmates, starting fights, using a weapon, stealing, and being physically cruel to people and animals. With adolescents, these behaviors may also include forced sex, staying out overnight, fire setting, repeatedly running away from home, frequent truancy from school, and breaking into someone's house, a building, or a car. At least one of these problem behaviors is required within the past year for diagnosis. Again, some functional impairment must be noted. The destruction or disturbance must also be significant and such behaviors must occur in more than one setting. These severely disordered behaviors can occur frequently and have an impact on the child's academic and social functioning. Two CD subtypes have been noted: (1) childhood onset, and (2) adolescent onset. The prognosis is poorer for childhood onset CD. ODD appears to be a significant risk factor for individuals with CD (Eddy, 2003; McGee, Williams, & Feehan, 1992).

Incidence   Although prevalence or incidence rate of CD varies, estimates range from about 2 to 9 percent for girls and 6 to 16 percent for boys. Costello (1989) estimated the incidence at 3 to 7 percent in the general population. Similar findings were reported by Ehrensaft and colleagues (2003).

Etiologies   While there are few genetic studies on CD, having a biological parent with antisocial behaviors definitely increases the risk of having the disorder

(Lahey, Waldman, & McBurnett, 1999). Physiological factors such as resting heart rate, nasal tone, and skin conductance have shown differences between children with CD and their normal peers. Families having a high frequency of poor relationships and few social supports appear to be a risk factor for CD (Webster-Stratton & Reid, 2004; Waschbusch & Willoughby, 2007). However, parental interactions appear to be the most central factor causing CD (Webster-Stratton & Dahl, 1995; Holmes, Slaughter, & Kashani, 2001). Parents of children with CD are generally more violent, more critical in their discipline, and more inconsistent, often failing even to monitor their child's behavior; they may even ignore or punish appropriate social behaviors (Sanders, 1999). Slee (1996) investigated mothers' perceptions of the family climate in families with a child who exhibited CD compared with families with a normal child. Mothers with a child having CD perceived the family climate as less cohesive, less encouraging of the expression of feelings, and more conflictual than their normal counterparts. These mothers were also more control-oriented. In addition to parental factors, there is increasing evidence for an association between mood disorders and externalizing disorders (Biederman et al., 1996). Twin studies revealed a greater incidence and relationship between criminality and antisocial behavior in monozygotic twins (Mayer et al., 2000; McCartan, 2007). Also, impact of the influence of biological parents is most pronounced on antisocial behavior (Herndon & Iacono, 2005). Although genetics play a role, the environment also contributes a significant influence (Reinke & Herman, 2002; Friedman, 2004). Clearly, there is a sufficient interplay of genetics and environment.

Developmental Issues Conduct disorder has an onset age of 6 years. From elementary school through adolescence, there is a general escalation of the presence and severity of CD symptoms. Children with CD move from conflicts with parents and teachers to aggression with peers, lying and stealing, truancy at school, delinquency, physical violence, and substance abuse. Although from 25 to 40 percent of older children with CD also develop antisocial behaviors in adulthood (Johnston and Ohan, 1999), historical data from adults with antisocial or aggressive behaviors almost always includes CD in their background.

Medications Medications for CD and ODD are discussed in Appendix A.

Activities and Strategies for ODD and CD The following activities and strategies may be used with students who have ODD/CD (Shore, 1998; Flick, 1998b).

1. Provide good models for appropriate social behavior.
2. Discuss, clarify, and review how each student is expected to behave during a new activity.
3. Post clearly stated rules for classroom behavior and review them on a regular basis. Praise compliance with each rule.

4. Quickly intervene when behavior problems escalate. Use questions to elicit what appropriate behavior is expected.
5. Use soft reprimands for inappropriate behavior. Avoid lectures, threats, sarcasm, belittling, etc.
6. Look for antecedents of a student's misbehavior. By changing or modifying an event that elicits misbehavior, that misbehavior may be avoided altogether.
7. Develop private, nonverbal signals to give feedback on when the student needs to change a misbehavior.
8. Provide immediate feedback with praise on appropriate behavior. Be very specific in giving praise. Instead of just saying, "good," say, "I really liked the way you did exactly what I asked."
9. Ignore those disturbances that you consider to be minor. In many cases, inappropriate behaviors are designed to get attention—even negative attention—from teachers or peers. When this is not forthcoming, the behavior will in time become weaker and then extinguished.
10. Provide a time-out place (e.g., a chair at the back of a classroom) where students can go to cool down or chill out when they become upset. If caught early enough, children can learn to self-monitor upsetting behavior and move to the cool down area by themselves. Do not label this as time-out; it should be developed as a self-imposed self-control procedure, or chill out.

Case Study

Tic Disorder and Tourette's Syndrome

Gordon is a 13-year-old seventh grader who has experienced a variety of facial movements and tensing of muscles in the upper body since he was 5 years of age. These initially consisted of facial grimacing, blinking, and puckering of the lips. At age 8, he started to make various sounds such as hissing, throat clearing, clucking, and grunting. By 10 years of age, he began to shrug his shoulders and make sudden jerky head turns; he would sometimes scream. Most of these movements would occur at home rather than in school. At age 12, these movements started to decrease. There is no family history of neurological problems. Gordon reports that his symptoms seem to increase in frequency and severity when he is under stress, after physical exercise, and after drinking anything with caffeine. Gordon has also been diagnosed with ADHD, predominated inattentive type. He thus has many difficulties in school with impulsive behavior, poor concentration, and poor school work performance. However, he is most upset when others observe his symptoms of Tourette's syndrome and often laugh at him. Even though his symptoms appear less frequently at school, when they do appear they are the most upsetting to him.

11. Use humor and interesting novel activities to prevent boredom and to make some lesson plans more palatable to students who already may be "turned off" to academic activities.

12. Use various behavior techniques such as behavior contracts, token/point programs, and a home-school daily report card to utilize some of the more powerful reinforcers at home to reward appropriate behavior in school.

TICS AND TOURETTE'S SYNDROME

Georges de la Tourette, a French neurologist, first described Tourette's syndrome (TS) in 1825. The onset of this disorder occurs before 18 years and the symptoms typically diminish during adolescence, sometimes disappearing by early adulthood. In most cases, the symptoms are relatively mild; many wax and wane or may even be replaced by other TS-type behaviors. Although the behaviors are involuntary, control, albeit limited, is not impossible. For instance, a child may be able to suppress a tic for a short time, but the delay may cause the expression of the tic to be stronger.

The DSM-IV identifies numerous motor tics and one or more vocal tics as the distinguishing symptoms of TS (APA, 1994). Such symptoms result in significant problems in classroom behavior, both for the child—whose self-esteem and peer acceptance may suffer—and for the teacher—who has to manage such disruptive behavior and still teach.

A tic is a recurrent, nonrhythmic, stereotypical, brief motor movement or vocalization that occurs without warning. The tics seen in Tourette's syndrome manifest as uncomplicated behavior, such as eye blinking, mouth twitching, or more complex and descriptive behaviors that include touching others and involuntary vocalizations.

Motor tics may involve a variety of movements identified in the DSM-IV (APA, 1994):

- Rapid eye blinking
- Body rocking
- Jerking of head
- Eye rolling, wide eye opening
- Twitching of mouth
- Shuddering
- Grimacing
- Kicking
- Nose twitching
- Jumping
- Touching others

Vocal tics can include the following:

- Grunting
- Coughing
- Repeated throat clearing
- Sniffing
- Yelping or vocalizing other meaningless sounds and noises
- Coprolalia (the utterance of obscenities and other socially inappropriate and offensive language)

Oftentimes children with TS also have learning and attention problems that affect school performance. A student with TS may have a low tolerance for frustration and can quickly lose his temper. Aggressive, socially inappropriate acts often result in peer rejection; the social and emotional problems that often accompany TS may cause greater distress than the physical displays or the academic difficulties. About 50 percent of those with TS also meet the criteria for ADHD, often being wrongly diagnosed as having ADHD. However, stimulant medications (which help with ADHD behaviors) are contraindicated for Tourette's syndrome as they may actually exacerbate tics.

Lack of knowledge and understanding about this syndrome complicates and worsens many already aggravated situations. Some teachers see TS children as just "nervous." Others believe that they are obnoxious children deliberately engaging in attention-getting behaviors, whose main purpose in life is to make the teacher's life miserable! Even parents of TS children may view their behaviors as strange and often deliberately oppositional and thus may treat them in a punitive manner. But possibly the most devastating things for TS children are the painful ridicule and rejection of their peers, especially during late childhood and early adolescent years. TS is thus associated with significant social impairment often interfering with normal school behavior and adjustment (Mather & Goldstein, 2001).

Incidence Although the prevalence of TS is fairly low, the incidence of other tic disorders is much higher, estimated at 5 to 24 percent of children (Singer, 1997). More recent estimates of the prevalence of TS is 5 to 10 per 10,000 (Zohar et al., 1999) and more frequent in boys (1.1 percent) than in girls (0.5 percent) (Kadesjo & Gillberg, 2000). Kurlan et al. (2002) classified tic disorders on a continuum from least severe to most severe, where the more severe the tic disorder, the more severe the functional impairment. By gender, TS is estimated at 1 to 8 per 1,000 males, and 1 to 4 per 1,000 females (Burd et al., 1986). These rates may not accurately reflect the true sex ratios due to various sampling biases or complex cases.

Etiologies   In a comprehensive review of tics and TS, Guggenheim (2004) suggested that TS is a familial syndrome and that the identified child shows a real genetic vulnerability for TS. Research shows that 8 percent of relatives of children with TS also meet the criteria for the disorder (Comings et al., 1996), a rate significantly higher than the general population. However, the mere presence of an implicated gene is often not sufficient to produce the disorder (Peterson, 1995). Nevertheless, researchers are now looking for a specific single gene responsible for the expression of the TS disorder, rather than multiple genes.

Medications   Medications for TS are discussed in Appendix A.

Associated Conditions   Children with TS may have one or more of several comorbid (associated) conditions, including obsessive-compulsive disorder (OCD), ADHD, and learning disabilities (LD). Other psychiatric disorders that can coexist with TS include ODD and CD, which frequently occur with ADHD (Barkley, 1998) and are also commonly associated with TS (Pierre et al., 1999). Thus, children with TS may also exhibit problematic behaviors (such as lying, stealing, and fire setting), as well as interpersonal difficulty. TS has also been found to be associated with depression (Robertson, 2000). Additionally, children with TS may have a high frequency of anxiety disorders such as phobias (Pierre et al., 1999), as well as reading and speech deficits, motivation problems, sleep disorders, and motor coordination problems (Comings, 2001).

Symptom Patterns   TS can range from mild symptoms to severe tics with associated behavior deficits. Diagnosing TS requires careful history taking and behavioral descriptions. As Comings (1990) noted, and supported by Chowdhury (2004) and Kushner (2000), TS may often be misdiagnosed for several reasons, but mostly due to the misunderstanding that the child must swear. Clearly, the child does not need to swear in

order to receive the diagnosis. The neuropsychological (NP) evaluation can help to identify frontal lobe deficits as well as speech, language, memory, and learning problems. The NP evaluation may also help to rule out visual-field defects often found in TS patients (Sturm, 2007).

Activities and Strategies for Tics and TS   Since the tic behaviors of a child with TS are not under voluntary control, teaching may be difficult. However, Flick (1998a) offers some suggestions for helping the child to feel a part of the class and be accepted more readily by others.

1. Become familiar with the TS child's particular problem behaviors. Children differ on many aspects of their typical TS behaviors; no one should assume that all children with TS have the same symptoms or that symptoms are of the same severity. Likewise, children with TS will differ in their associated conditions; each child with TS should be treated in a unique fashion.

2. Once general information is obtained from parents, speak privately with the child and let him know that you are aware of his medical problem. Ask the child for suggestions about what might help to make him feel more comfortable in class and assure him that perhaps working together will improve the situation.

3. Obtain information from the Tourette's Syndrome Association (www.tsa.org), which offers a brochure entitled "Matthew and the Tics" that is designed for teachers to read to students or for students to read themselves. It is essential, of course, to get permission for such a presentation from the child's parents, who may also wish to be involved in the presentation. Knowing more about the medical condition should help classmates understand that the child with TS may have behaviors that are difficult to control. Classmates who tease and make noise that may be perceived as "making fun" can be handled on an individual basis.

4. Try to avoid making TS children self-conscious about their disorder and so sensitive that they create social barriers between themselves and classmates. Remember that, the most appropriate response to tics (from teacher and students) is "no response." When tics are disruptive, try to redirect attention and

activities at that time. (For example, suggest that this would be a good time for exercise or a relaxation break.)

5. Prearrange a private signal with TS students that they can use when they have the urge to emit a tic. This will give them automatic permission to leave the classroom and go to the bathroom or the nurse's office, or perhaps to have a space in the corner of the room for "chill out" and "recover." However, TS and tics are neurological in nature and should be viewed as basically uncontrollable.

6. Allow children with TS to move around periodically. For example, ask them to distribute materials in the classroom or to serve as messengers to the school office, or allow them to go to the bathroom when needed. Routine exercise breaks help with the attentional focus of a TS child as well as for many other children with and without disabilities.

7. Do not overprotect children with TS; expect them to abide by the class rules just as others would. Unless there are other medical problems that restrict activities, they should be eligible to participate in field trips, school plays, and sporting events.

8. Capitalize on the talents and special interests of TS children. These skills will allow them to build self-confidence and be successful in the classroom and to receive recognition and acceptance from peers. For example, a student could give a presentation using his skills and knowledge about his baseball card collection.

9. Allow children with TS who have difficulty expressing their knowledge in one modality (for example, in handwriting), to communicate by other means. Allow them to give oral reports, tape-recorded reports, and reports presented using computer skills. Or perhaps you may allow them to copy notes from others. Also allow extra time when there are minor problems with impaired handwriting.

10. Incorporate routine relaxation techniques in the class to help TS children deal with the increased stress associated with frustration over work and the tension surrounding possible emission of the tic. Varying these techniques (e.g., muscle tension and/or relaxing, deep breathing, visualization, and positive self-statements and self-talk) can counteract boredom and expectations while at the same time provide a variety of techniques that may be useful to a group of classmates who have different needs and preferences.

SUMMARY

This chapter has focused on externalizing disorders: ADHD, ODD, and CD, as well as tics and Tourette's syndrome. There is a brief overview of each condition as well as information on the incidence, etiology, biological basis, medications, developmental issues, and associated conditions. In addition, there is a listing of useful activities and strategies that may be employed in the classroom. There is an emphasis on behavioral interventions for externalizing disorders in general, and some emphasis on specific behavioral applications.

DISCUSSION QUESTIONS

1. What are the primary types of ADHD?
2. What are some of the "associated conditions" for ADHD?
3. What are some of the symptoms of ODD?
4. How are ODD and CD different?
5. Discuss some of the interventions used with externalizing disorders.
6. What is Tourette's syndrome?
7. What might stimulant medication do for someone with Tourette's syndrome?
8. What are some of the associated conditions for Tourette's syndrome?
9. Discuss possible interventions for Tourette's syndrome.
10. How are simple tics different from Tourette's syndrome?

CHAPTER 5

Mood Disorders and Other Behavior Disorders

Overview

- Depression
- Bipolar disorders
- Medications
- Interventions
- Traumatic brain injury
- Fragile X syndrome
- Fetal alcohol syndrome

Case History

Lauren is an 11-year-old female who has been diagnosed with ADHD and functions at about the second-grade level. When she was 4 years old, Lauren was placed in the care of a foster family because of both physical maltreatment and neglect by her biological parents. She has gone from one foster home to another and has had much difficulty making an adequate adjustment. She was eventually adopted when she was 8 years old by a family with no other children. Her social interpersonal relations with peers are poor; she is generally uncooperative and often disruptive in group settings. Several months after she enrolled in elementary school and was placed in a self-contained special education EBD class, she was involved in stealing. Lauren has frequently stolen small items such as candy or cookies, and personal items such as pencils or erasers, taken either from other students or from the teacher. These objects have been found either on her person or in her desk. *What would you do?*

MOOD DISORDERS

Mood disorders in the pediatric population can fall into three categories: (1) depression, (2) bipolar disorders, and (3) mood disorders that are related to a medical condition or to the use of some substance. This chapter focuses on depression and bipolar disorders.

Depression

Everyone may occasionally feel "blue or sad," but such feelings may pass within a couple of days. Depression is a mental health disorder that can impair the ability to eat or sleep as well as how you think and feel about yourself. It is normal to respond to losses in life with sadness and gloom. However, when depressive feelings prevent a person from performing everyday activities, they may be considered symptoms of a depressive disorder.

The two subcategories of depression are major depression and dysthymia. The symptoms for these two conditions are difficult to discriminate. Initially, weight or appetite changes, somatic complaints, anxiety, disturbed sleep, reduced energy, and difficulty functioning in school are all common symptoms of both conditions (Birmaher et al., 1996a,b). In general, children do not discuss feelings at all, much less depression. Instead, they communicate their depression through temper outbursts, low frustration tolerance, peer problems, mood swings, and other behavioral problems, all of which are often signposts for depression (Marsh & Barkley, 2006).

In school and at home, the following are some of the warning signs of childhood depression: (1) less interest or pleasure in activities, (2) change in appetite, (3) an apparent change in weight, physical agitation, or visible fatigue, (4) comments of worthlessness or guilt, (5) an increase in difficulty with concentration, (6) reports of thoughts about death or suicide (National Institute of Mental Health [NIMH], 2000). Also, school performance has been noted to be a sensitive indicator of sudden onset of depression (Forsterling & Binser, 2002). Despite many recent advances regarding the nature and causes of depression or mood disorder, a common problem during childhood continues to be largely unrecognized and misunderstood (Ghaemi, 2003).

Incidence   Approximately 2 percent of children 2 to 12 years of age and 8 percent of teenagers may experience depression (Cicchetti & Toth, 1998). For children, there are equal numbers of males and females; for teenagers, the male to female ratio is 1 to 2 (Lewinsohn et al., 1994). During any period of childhood, between 2 to 3 percent of children may experience significant depression; 20 percent of children and/or teenagers will experience a significant episode of depression along with suicidal ideation.

Etiologies   Genetic factors can account for 50 percent of depressive disorders (Cox et al., 1989). Few studies have been conducted on children, but the data generally support a genetic influence (Thapar & McGuffin, 1994). Parents who are depressed are more likely to have children who are depressed. Clearly, genetic factors contribute to the risk of being depressed, as do experiences within the family context (Ingersoll & Goldstein, 1995). Todd and colleagues (1996) have also found increased prevalence of alcoholism in relatives of depressed and bipolar children. While researchers note that mood

---

Case Study

Depression

Jeb is a 9-year-old boy in the third grade who has a history of depressed mood. For about three months, he has shown decreased interest in activities he once enjoyed, low energy, and poor concentration. He often argues with his teachers about his work and has numerous fights with peers for minor disagreements. He reportedly has had many arguments with his parents, who are recently divorced, and has told several teachers that he would like for his parents to "get back together." Jeb has been an honor student but now is barely passing subjects like math and science. He has been known to have temper tantrums and once while flailing his arms about hit another child. He denies any responsibility. Jeb was quite a social student but has now withdrawn from most social activities. He has been quite critical of himself and has talked about killing himself so that "everyone would be better off."

disorders and maternal alcoholism appear to be independently transmitted, paternal alcoholism clearly increased the risk for a mood disorder in offspring. They point out that the potential psychosocial and genetic effects of familial alcoholism need to be considered in the clinical management of childhood-onset mood disorders.

Associated Conditions   Depression in young people often co-occurs with other mental disorders (most commonly anxiety, disruptive behavior, and substance abuse disorders) and with physical illnesses such as diabetes (Kovacs, Goldston, et al., 1997). When a child is depressed, school performance deteriorates. The child also loses interest in extracurricular activities and may drop out of school. Complaints of headaches and stomachaches can be frequent, especially before entering a new situation. Phobias can also develop. School-age children are cognitively able to internalize environmental stressors such as family conflict, criticism, and failure to achieve academically; and they might exhibit low self-esteem and perhaps guilt. Much of their inner turmoil may be expressed in somatic complaints (e.g., headaches and stomachaches), anxiety (e.g., school phobia or excessive separation anxiety), and irritability (e.g., temper tantrums or other behavioral problems) (Birmaher et al., 1996).

In research studies depression has been reported to co-occur with anxiety disorders (Lewis & Waschbusch, 2007), conduct disorders (Biederman, Mick, & Faraone, 1998), and ADHD (Biederman et al., 1998). The combination of multiple disorders results in a more severe clinical disorder with an even poorer prognosis (Wozniak et al., 1995). Followed over time, 20 to 30 percent of children with depression have exhibited symptoms of bipolar depression (Waterman & Ryan, 1993).

Bipolar Disorders

Bipolar disorders have been underdiagnosed for a long time (Weller, Weller, & Fristad, 1995). Mohr (2001) noted that bipolar disorder in children has been unrecognized for many reasons, including lack of awareness, diagnostic confusion, and the different clinical picture in children. In prepubertal childhood, bipolar disorder is a nonepisodic, chronic, rapid cycling mixed manic state that may mimic and be associated with ADHD and CD. Two indicators of a bipolar disorder in children are (1) a family history of bipolar disorder, and (2) the onset of hypomania after administration of an antidepressant medication (Geller et al., 1998).

Case Study

Bipolar Disorder

Jason is a 9-year-old boy who has always been small for his age. When he was about 3, he used to scream and hit his head and would aggressively hit, bite, and kick others at his preschool. He often had temper tantrums over little things (like not getting a Coke). It has been like walking on eggshells, and no one knows when he will fly into a rage over nothing. Jason also complains of headaches, stomachaches, and frequent diarrhea, and he has trouble swallowing. He was referred to a psychiatrist at age five and was diagnosed with ADHD and ODD. Psychological testing revealed that he was of average ability and scored high on "math." His Individual Education Plan (IEP) was primarily focused on anger management and the development of appropriate behavior, especially cooperation. Jason has much difficulty with timed tests, especially in math, and frequently screams and bangs his head on the wall. He worries about his grades, is bossy on the playground, and has few friends. Jason talks almost constantly and is quite creative, making up stories about monsters and "flowing in the world." Because of his stories, there have been concerns about physical abuse and he has been placed in a foster home. He has repeatedly run away and has threatened to kill the family cat. He boasts that if he had a gun, he would kill everyone and himself. Observed over time, he has been noted to show a vacillation of moods called rapid cycling. It was also discovered that the child's father has been diagnosed with bipolar disorder and his mother with major depression. Considering Jason's ability to focus on projects, his rapid mood changes, and his family history, his diagnosis has been changed to early-onset bipolar disorder.

Children seldom exhibit the symptoms of bipolar disorder that adults show—irritable mood, flight of ideas, or excessive engagement in pleasurable activities that may have painful consequences (Lewinsohn, Klein, & Seeley, 1995). Pediatric bipolar disorders are basically characterized by psychomotor agitation, increased verbalizations, elevated or expansive mood, distractibility, inflated self-esteem, and a decreased need for sleep (Lewinsohn et al., 1995). Reports of hypersexuality or precocious sexuality have been noted (Geller et al., 2000). Rapid cycling between mania and depression is most often seen as a hallmark of childhood bipolar disorder (Cogan, 1996). The age of onset is variable but generally appears to be around puberty (Lewinsohn et al., 1995). There are generally poor outcomes for bipolar disorder, as indicated by the low recovery and high relapse rates for this disorder (Geller et al., 2000). However, there is apparent stability of the bipolar diagnosis over a 6-month period as reported by Geller and colleagues (2000).

Incidence   As yet, no national or international study of pediatric bipolar disorder is available. However, some data suggest a prevalence rate of about 1 percent for adolescents, a percentage comparable to adult rates (Chang et al., 2003; Lewinsohn et al., 1995). Different than in depressive disorders, the male–female ratio in bipolar disorder remains equal through the life span (APA, 1994).

Etiologies   The evidence for a genetic influence is substantial for bipolar disorder. Investigators (Torrey, 1994; Wildenauer et al., 1999) have suggested that bipolar disorder and schizophrenia share similar genetic suggestibility in their genetic linkage studies. However, the mode of transmission is not clear, and transmission through multiple genes or a single recessive gene interacting with environment risk factors are hypothesized (Meltzer, 2000). Researchers are investigating various locations on chromosomes X, 4, 12, 13, 18, 21, and 22 as a probable site for the gene of bipolar disorder (Hyman, 2000). Whereas unipolar depression appears related to both genetic and environmental factors, bipolar depression is most likely a genetically based disorder (Althoff et al., 2005; Neves-Pereira et al., 2002). In a review of research, DelBello and Geller (2001) cited studies suggesting that children of bipolar parents are at increased risk for developing

mood and other disorders such as anxiety. However, Cooke and colleagues (1999) noted that specific family attributes (i.e., environment) do not contribute to the development of bipolar disorder.

Associated Conditions   Hyperactivity may be the first developmentally age-specific manifestation of prepubertal-onset bipolar disorder (Geller & Luby, 1997). When the children are seen initially because of bipolar symptoms, about 90 percent of prepubertal and 30 percent of adolescents with bipolar disorder also have ADHD. Roberts and colleagues (2000) discuss bipolar disorder in ADHD children who are grown up. The similarity of symptoms was also noted by Giedd (2001). Sachs and colleagues (2000) observed that the presence of ADHD in children having a family history of bipolar disorder could identify these children at highest risk for the development of bipolar disorder. Faraone and colleagues (1997) report that ADHD comorbid with bipolar disorder may be distinct from other forms of ADHD and can be related to what others term childhood-onset bipolar disorder. In a longitudinal study (Wozniak et al., 1999), bipolar disorder was found to be a risk factor for trauma or post-traumatic stress disorder, but ADHD was not. While trauma was associated with the development of major depression, this was independent of ADHD status. Conduct disorder occurs in about 22 percent of bipolar children and 18 percent of bipolar adolescents (Geller et al., 1995). About 33 percent of children and 12 percent of adolescents with bipolar disorder may also manifest anxiety conditions (Geller et al., 1995). Spencer and colleagues (2001) have reported that what was previously considered refractory ADHD, oppositionality, aggression, and conduct disorder may respond after mood stabilization (e.g., with medication).

Medications   Medications for depression and bipolar disorder are discussed in Appendix A. Depakote may be more effective with "rapid cyclers." Note that the following medications have no documented efficacy with children who have mood disorders: Amitriptyline (Elavil, Etrafon, Limbitrol, Triavil), Desipramine (Norpramin), Imipramine (Tofranil), Nortriptylene (Pamelor), and Venlafaxine (Effexor).

Activities and Strategies for Mood Disorders   Not all suggestions will be applicable to all forms of depression because of the dramatic way depression and bipolar disorders may be manifested behaviorally. The teacher must select the best strategies for each child. Many of the suggestions for activities and strategies for ADHD, ODD, and CD may also be more applicable to bipolar disorders. The following strategies can be useful in dealing with depressive disorders (Flick, 1998b):

1. Create a climate in the classroom that supports and nurtures self-esteem. An important part of this strategy is to communicate that mistakes are expected and are a part of the learning process.

2. Take time during each day to focus on some aspect of relaxation that will alleviate the stress that is often associated with frustration and the commission of errors. Abdominal breathing, imagery, and positive visualizations may all be helpful for the depressed child as well as other students.

3. Develop positive feelings and cognitions by offering praise that is specific and genuine. This may be done on a regular basis (e.g., through a recognition program that focuses on improvement, not just A+ grades). Write positive notes to praise good work; avoid negative comments.

4. Restructure the work assignments of students functioning at a lower level than expected as a result of a depressive disorder. This will make it more likely that they will be successful. A gradual return to their former, expected level of performance may be planned as success continues.

5. Show children who are critical of their own work or behavior how to convert negative self-statements into positive ones. If a child says or writes "nobody likes me," this may be just the "tip of the iceberg" with regard to negative self-statements. Help the child learn to replace negatives with positive self-statements—for example, "they all voted to have me help with the class party—I must be liked."

6. Show children who may be unaware of their status in a certain class the evidence that documents their progress. Showing an improvement in grades or daily work such as penmanship over time may thus be helpful feedback.

7. Exhibit some of a child's work to demonstrate to others and to the child that the work is worthy of recognition. Some special artwork or a collection in which some expertise is demonstrated would be examples.

8. Ask students who appear withdrawn questions and reinforce any sharing of information with them. Offer specific feedback to the child: "I'm really glad you were able to tell me about your experience at your last school—that helps me a great deal").

9. Engage the student in some activity that may be helpful to you and to the class as a whole. This might involve taking care of a class pet, handing out or collecting papers, running errands, coaching another student, or explaining a computer activity.

10. Build some physical exercise into the class's daily routine. Exercise is not only effective in addressing some components of ADHD, it is also useful in helping to counteract some forms of depression.

11. Avoid using a red ink pen to correct papers and mark only those answers that are correct.

Case Study

Traumatic Brain Injury

Tommy is a 7-year-old boy who was injured when his bicycle collided with a car. Thrown in the air and hitting his head on a brick fence, he was found unconscious by another driver and was taken by ambulance to the hospital, where he was operated on to remove a large subdural hematoma (blood clot). A 60-day IEP was written to help him reintegrate into school. A teacher and peer tutors were assigned. After 2 months in rehab, Tommy went to a second-grade classroom with a full-time tutor. Each year his IEP has been reviewed and changes are made as needed. Tommy has had much difficulty with math and science, and he specifically has trouble remembering his assignments and following through on independent work. Counseling has helped him with social skills and his relationships with peers. Tommy's IEP team continues to meet every 6 months to develop preventive strategies or to modify his educational plan.

12. Emphasize that students should compete only with their own past performance as opposed to competing with others. Then, when students better their own performance, they are successful.

13. When addressing a behavior problem, express concern about the behavior, not the person. Explain how the behavior may affect others: "John, when you make noise, it's difficult for me to teach and for others to hear what I'm saying. If you try to be quiet, it will help all of us."

14. Keep close contact with a depressed student's parents and let them know more about their child's successes than about failures and problems. Point out to parents how they can reinforce at home what successes the child has at school.

OTHER BEHAVIOR DISORDERS

Traumatic Brain Injury

Traumatic brain injury (TBI) is relatively common during childhood because of the greater risk for accidents (Keenan, Hooper, & Wetherington, 2007; Hawley et al., 2004). About 500,000 children incur head injuries due to bicycle accidents alone (Semrud-Clikeman, 2001). Car accidents involving teenagers, accidents in the home, and falls are also common. Child abuse is the most common source of TBI for infants and young children (Semrud-Clikeman, 2001). Sports can also increase the risk of TBI in football (Powell & Barber-Foss, 1999) and in soccer (McCrory, 2003).

Individuals with Disabilities Education Act (IDEA) offers the following definition of TBI:

> An acquired injury to the brain caused by an external physical force resulting in total or partial functional disability or psychosocial impairment, or both, that adversely affects a child's educational performance. The term applies to open or closed head injuries resulting in impairments in one or more areas: cognition; language; memory; attention; reasoning; abstract thinking; judgment; problem solving; sensory; perceptual and motor abilities; psychosocial behavior; physical functions; information processing; and speech. The term does not apply to brain injuries that are congenital or degenerative or brain injuries induced by both. [34 Code of Federal Regulations, 300]

Brain dysfunction caused by genetics, disease, or birth trauma would thus need to be ruled out.

Incidence   More than 1,000 children from birth to 21 years of age are hospitalized each year for head injuries, some of them developing persistent behavior problems; some researchers have found that more than one-third of the injuries result in lifelong disabilities (National Distribution Center for Children with Disabilities [NICHY], 2006). About one-half of the children with TBI require special education; others in regular classes need modifications in their curriculum or in the classroom in order to function more effectively.

Etiologies   Accidents in the home account for the majority of head injuries in preschool children; child abuse is a close second (Wetherington & Hooper, 2006). Falls, pedestrians in car accidents, bicycle accidents, and sporting injuries are major sources of mild TBI in school-aged children (Kemich, 2004). Motor vehicle accidents cause the majority of severe TBI cases in older children (Bowley et al., 2002). Older teens seem to incur more severe head injuries secondary to high-speed car accidents. A TBI from a fall may develop intracranial hematomas while a TBI from a car accident is more likely to result in a concussion (Ewing-Cobbs et al., 1998).

Anderson and colleagues (2004) indicated that estimates of initial severity of the head injury may not always predict long-term outcome. A study noted that many children with mild head injuries had significant behavioral problems, but other children who had severe head injuries were doing relatively well (Prasad et al., 2002). Regular follow-up assessments are thus important in monitoring and tracking progress or decompensation. The time or developmental stage of the head injury also appears relevant to prognosis. In general, early TBI may result in greater impairment than later injuries (Limond & Leeke, 2005). Significant impairment of brain function with a TBI prior to 1 year of age was supported by Ewing-Cobbs, Barnes, and Fletcher (2003). Between 1 to 5 years of age, there may be reorganization of brain functions and language recovery. However, after 5 years, TBI may result in significant loss of function. With later TBI, there is not only damage to specific brain regions but also interference with the normal sequence of brain development. When a child has a TBI, family adjustment may influence the outcome. Boyle and Haines (2002) found that when a family member suffers a severe TBI, depression can be elevated, along with decreased ability to express feelings, impaired social activities, and increased control. Their study suggested that, overall, caregiver families coped adequately. Rivara and colleagues (1996) noted that while pre-injury functioning was the best predictor for a child with TBI over a 3-year period, families at risk for poor outcomes should be identified early to provide support and encouragement for the development of new coping resources.

Associated Conditions   Children with severe head injuries have an increased risk for psychiatric disorders regardless of their age, sex, or social class; mild head injuries do not appear to be associated with such an increased risk. However, the risk for those with severe injuries is heightened among those children who have histories of pre-accident (i.e., premorbid) behavior disorders, as well as those experiencing various psychosocial adversities in their homes—these effects being additive rather than interactive.

Investigators have noted that selected risk factors may influence the course of TBI. Certain children appear to have a higher risk for brain injury. Some of these preexisting (premorbid) conditions include ADHD and behavioral problems (Norris, 2007), learning disorders (Sullivan & Knutson, 2000), and reading problems, impulsivity, and overactivity (Luis & Mittenburg, 2002); increased risk-taking behavior may result in an increased risk of accidents. Taylor (2004) also noted an increased number of problems reported by the teacher, including hyperactivity, depression, and antisocial behavior that predated the child's TBI. Behavioral interventions have been primarily used to address externalizing behaviors, whereas there has been only a paucity of work on internalizing behaviors and prosocial behaviors such as assertiveness (Warschausky et al., 1999). These authors also note that the systematic study of psychological intervention lags far behind the rapidly increasing knowledge of the neurobehavioral sequelae to TBI in childhood. Anderson (2006) has reported that most studies on brain injury in children have used single subjects or only a small number of subjects. Larger numbers of subjects or use of meta-analyses might be beneficial.

Meta-analysis: An analysis that statistically combines the results of several studies that address a shared research hypothesis. Just as individual studies summarize data collected from many participants in order to answer a specific research question (in which each participant is a separate data-point in the analysis), a meta-analysis summarizes data from individual studies that concern a specific research question (in which each study is a separate data point in the analysis).

Premorbid (before injury) developmental difficulties along with specific learning problems (Landry et al., 2004), language problems (Bates & Roe, 2001), and lower academic achievement (Kesler et al., 2003) have also been noted. In addition, Solomon and Sparadeo (1992) have indicated that an individual who sustains a TBI is at increased risk for sustaining a second brain injury. This risk is age and sex related. Children under 14 had a twofold risk, those from 15 to 24 a threefold risk, and those over 25 a fivefold risk. Males had twice the likelihood of a second TBI as females. These data were supported by more recent findings (Max et al., 2006).

When children with TBI have been in a coma for more than 24 hours, there are more significant and chronic intellectual deficits according to Arroyos-Jurado and colleagues (2006), who also relate visual and visual-spatial deficits to the severity of injury; memory deficits are also commonly noted. Furthermore, attention (Konrad et al., 2000) and executive control functions are impaired, especially with severe TBI (Catroppa et al., 2007). The Neurobehavioral Rating Scale (NRS) may be used to assess the behavioral manifestations of TBI. There are four factors (scales) on this 27-item scale:

1. *Factor I:* Items evaluating cognition, memory, motor retardation, and emotional withdrawal;

2. *Factor II:* Self-appraised planning and disinhibition;

3. *Factor III:* Physical complaints, anxiety, depression, and irritability; and

4. *Factor IV:* Expressive and receptive language.

More recently, there was a report on the pediatric behavior scale used to evaluate ADHD symptomology following a TBI. The pediatric behavior scale is not part of the NRS.

Activities and Strategies for TBI   The following activities and strategies may be used with students who have TBI.

1. Teach TBI students how to write homework assignments in an assignment book or planner.

2. Provide students with an outline to follow with regard to assignments, projects, etc.

3. Use mnemonic strategies or visual cues (pictures, rhymes, etc.) to remember lists.

4. Provide TBI students with notes from lectures.

5. Ask questions to cue recall of material. Don't assume the student knows the material.

6. Ask a class aide to help student stay on task and help with organization and planning.

7. If a TBI student looks confused, ask another student to help explain the material.

8. Use frequent repetitions. TBI students may have poor short-term memory.

9. Teach verbal rehearsal and self-talk to aid student in performing the expected behavior.

10. Use shorter assignments to help student focus. Increase length if a student maintains success.

11. Give specific and frequent positive feedback so that students are aware of when they are correct.

12. Avoid raising expectations too quickly. Be aware that TBI students may have good days and bad days.

13. Know that change is especially difficult for TBI students. Provide structure.

14. Prepare TBI students for transitions. Give them advance warning of what is coming and what the expectations are.

15. Use simple and short sentences, keeping directions clear and limiting them to only a few steps.

16. Be sure to communicate with parents of TBI students about what strategies work best and things that deserve more focus.

Fragile X Syndrome

The occurrence of a "fragile" site on the long arm of the X chromosome (at Xq27) was first described by Lubs (1969). However, the clinical manifestations of what has come to be called fragile X syndrome disorder were not studied in detail until the 1980s. In addition to some distinguishing physical features (e.g., enlarged testes in males, prominent ears and a long, narrow face), the disorder includes mental retardation and a wide range of psychological defects, such as behavior problems, hyperactivity, short attention span, learning disabilities, and aggressiveness. There may also be unusual hand movements. Crawford, Acuna, and Sherman (2001) reported that only one of 40 autistic children had fragile X syndrome.

The developmental delays and physical features associated fragile X syndrome are clearly not obvious at birth. At around 8 to 10 months of age, the parents typically become concerned over the child's inability

---

Case Study

Fragile X Syndrome

Michelle is a 14-year-old eighth grader with academic problems related to emotional difficulties she is having. Michelle doesn't get along with other students. She is bossy, always talking fast, and arguing with others about the "rules of the game." When she is not angry, she shows evidence of depression. She has used learning strategies to help remediate her learning deficits. Easily distracted, Michelle requires a low distraction environment and has preferential seating close to a study carrel and a place where she can work independently or in a small group. She has been also seated near a student who shows appropriate in-class behavior and good work. Michelle is also impulsive, often blurting out answers before raising her hand and frequently beginning work before the teacher has finished explaining what to do. As a result, she often does the wrong assignment or has used the wrong things to do her work. Because of her apparent "need to move," she, along with the whole class, engages in physical activity breaks, breaking up an assignment by standing and doing some activity. Since Michelle is so poor in estimating time, a timer is used to provide cues as to how much time she has left on an assignment. She clearly has a short attention span and is very distractible.

to cuddle, lack of regular routines, fussiness, or delayed development of walking and talking. It is not until about 22 to 24 months that such a child is diagnosed as developmentally delayed. During the early school years, most of these children are placed in self-contained classrooms. By age 8, many of them are still challenged by learning even basic functional skills. Slightly more than half may be able to dress and bathe themselves, care for toileting needs, identify selected letters of the alphabet, count three objects, and sight-read at least 10 words. Few may be able to write their first and last names or to state their telephone number. Unlike Down syndrome with mental retardation, the cognitive retardation in fragile X may not be apparent until later developmental stages; marked deterioration in intellectual functioning can occur between 10 to 15 years of age (Cornish et al., 2005). In addition to intellectual loss, there are significant impairments in visual and sequential processing skills (Dew-Hughes, 2004), along with hypersensitivity to some sounds, interest in some odors, and tendencies to self-injury. Kuo and colleagues (2002) found that while family environment contributed significantly for normal girls, there was little contribution to cognitive abilities in girls with fragile X syndrome. However, for this latter group, there was a suggested relationship between socioeconomic status and a measure of intellectual functioning. They also looked at early behavior signs in preschool males with fragile X syndrome. This group showed deficits in motor skills, increased initial avoidance, decreased social withdrawal, deficits in attention, increased hyperactivity, and positive mood. They were different from control subjects in all areas except hyperactivity and attention. However, Hessel and colleagues (2001) linked the fragile X gene on the X chromosome to behavior. For boys, they were able to predict internalizing and externalizing types of problems based on educational and therapeutic problems, while the quality of the home environment predicted autistic behavior. For girls with fragile X, social withdrawal and anxious or depressed behavior were predicted. Home and school-based environmental variables were noted to be important (Kuo et al., 2002).

Incidence   The estimate of incidence varies; it is thought that fragile X affects about 1 of 4,000 girls and 1 of 2,000 boys.

Etiologies   Fragile X syndrome is caused by a full mutation in the FMR-1 gene on the X chromosome. Since boys have only one X chromosome, they are more likely to develop symptoms than girls. A girl's normal X chromosome may compensate for her fragile X chromosome. The characteristic physical traits noted in boys may be either totally absent or less noticeable in girls.

Associated Conditions   Fragile X syndrome may be associated with numerous problem behaviors that may need to be addressed. These include autistic-like behavior, behavior problems, hyperactivity, and ADHD symptoms. Other medical problems such as seizures and mitral valve prolapse may also develop and require treatment.

Activities and Strategies for Fragile X   The following activities and strategies may be used with students who have Fragile X:

1. Use a whole word approach to coding and spelling.
2. Use illustrations to explain subject matter.
3. Utilize high interest and concrete examples.
4. Space learning over time; have a written schedule.
5. Emphasize modeling for academic and behavioral goals.
6. Use highly structured routines with visual cues demonstrating change.
7. Practice relaxation and stress management during the classroom routine.
8. Explain the use of a personal organizer.
9. Employ activities that require organization, planning, and judgment.
10. Demonstrate how a new idea or new information is derived.
11. Do exercises on time estimation (e.g., have the student estimate the time needed to complete a task).
12. Provide an outline of planned activities.
13. Use a minimum number of options to reduce choices.
14. Set clear-cut goals and quiz students to be sure that their goals are understood.
15. Use questions to promote independent thinking and to communicate understanding of a task.

Case Study

Fetal Alcohol Syndrome

Lacie is a 10-year-old fourth grader who was born premature, weighing only four pounds, and was diagnosed with fetal alcohol syndrome. After being placed with several foster homes, she was eventually adopted. She suffers petit mal seizures on occasion and is on medication. She is small, has a diminished vocabulary (more than 2 years below her age level), and poor math skills. Lacie is easily distracted, has a short attention span, and rarely completes her assignments. She might be able to sit in her seat by herself; although she has no close friends, and plays alone much of the time. When she does play with someone, it is usually a younger child. Although she does not hit other students, she does things that annoy them, such as pinching or patting them, which often escalates to the point of aggression. Lacie shows poor recognition of personal space and often invades the boundaries of her classmates by coming too close to them.

Fetal Alcohol Syndrome

Fetal alcohol syndrome (FAS) is a disorder caused by maternal exposure to alcohol during pregnancy. FAS children may show developmental delays, hyperactivity, motor incoordination, attentional problems, learning disorder, and perhaps retardation and seizure disorder. According to Streissguth (1997), children born with this disorder show growth deficiency, facial anomalies, and CNS dysfunction as reported by Teeter and Semrud-Clikeman (1997).

Incidence   Fetal alcohol syndrome is estimated to occur in 1 to 3 per 1,000 births (National Institute on Alcohol Abuse and Alcoholism, 1991). Variation in incidence may be associated with community, ethnic, and cultural factors as well as geographic area (May & Gossage, 2001).

Medications   The medications used to treat FAS are symptom specific, meaning that each medication selected should target specific symptoms. For example, a stimulant medication for ADHD symptoms of distractibility and overactivity may be considered. Other medications may be selected as needed to target other specific symptoms such as anxiety or depression.

Etiologies   The nature and severity of FAS appears to be directly related to when, how much, and how frequently the mother drank, as well as the mother's age (Maier & Weist, 2001; Jacobson et al., 2004). The frequency of alcohol use is significant for neurobehavioral problems between 7 to 28 drinks per week in early and midpregnancy (Jacobson et al., 2004). However, even moderate exposure to alcohol in utero can result in distinguishable problems on the first day of life that continue throughout the child's development. It is believed that nutritional and metabolic effects of alcoholism in the mother, along with the teratogenic effects of the alcohol on the fetus, affects development (Lieber, 2000).

Associated Conditions   Perhaps the most frequent co-occurring condition is ADHD (Steinhausen et al., 2002). These same authors also noted a high incidence of mental retardation. Specific problems were observed in adaptive behavior—especially social skills. Math skills (Hill et al., 1999) and language skills (Rogers, Wehner, & Hagerman, 2001) have also been found to be deficient. Severe behavior problems are also frequently found in FAS children. Many of these deficits seem to be related to executive control and impulse control, particularly in social contexts. It is sometimes difficult to sort out what may be primary factors and what may be secondary because most FAS children come from chaotic home environments where alcohol and drugs are freely used. In one longitudinal study (Streissguth et al., 1991), researchers reported that only 9 percent of the children remained with both parents; 3 percent lived with the biological mother. Also, 69 percent of the biological mothers were dead 5 to 12 years after the child was initially seen. These same researchers noted that 33 percent of FAS children were given up for adoption or abandoned in the hospital. Similar findings were obtained in other longitudinal studies (Autti-Ramo, 2000; Steinhausen, Williams, & Spohr, 1993).

Activities and Strategies for FAS The following activities and strategies may be used with students who have FAS:

1. Show the child how choices can provide opportunities for independent thinking and decision-making skills.
2. Minimize auditory and visual distractions by organizing and simplifying bulletin boards and bookshelves and by keeping the door closed to reduce hallway distractions.
3. Develop routines by maintaining consistency in the classroom—for example, by asking students to sit in the same seats every day.
4. Signal transitions with a visual signal such as a raised hand, again, maintain consistency.
5. Limit the number of rules you ask students to follow. Keep them simple and repeat them regularly.
6. Show how assignments can be grouped to make them more manageable.
7. Redirect misbehavior when possible.
8. Always focus on positive prosocial behavior.
9. Keep rewards interesting by changing them to avoid boredom and predictability.
10. Use worksheets with no more than three or four problems and a lot of white space.
11. Encourage students to use the computer to complete tasks whenever possible.
12. Give directions one step at a time. Wait for students to complete a step before going to the next one.
13. Show students how to indicate that an assignment has been completed.

SUMMARY

This chapter covers mood disorders and other behavior disorders. The primary depressive disorders are *depression* and *dysthymia*. Some characteristic warning signs are listed; bipolar disorder may be characterized by rapid cycling between mania and depression. The prominent characteristics of TBI, fragile X syndrome, and fetal alcohol syndrome are also reviewed. Some general activities and strategies for dealing with these conditions are suggested.

DISCUSSION QUESTIONS

1. What are the two major subcategories of depression?
2. What are some of the warning signs of childhood depression?
3. Bipolar disorders may often be confused with which other conditions?
4. Discuss the genetic basis for bipolar disorder.
5. What are some of the factors that often result in TBI?
6. What is fragile X syndrome?
7. What is the basis for FAS?

CHAPTER 6

Pervasive Developmental Disorders and Psychotic Disorders

Overview

- Autism
- Asperger's syndrome
- Psychotic disorders
- Childhood schizophrenia

Case History

Madison is an 8-year-old third grader who has been classified as learning disabled (LD) and a child with emotional and behavior disorders (EBD). She has been seen by the teacher as a child with "behavior problems." Her medications include Ritalin and guanfacine. Whenever a teacher fails to pay attention to Madison, she gets off task and engages in either crying, playing with small objects, singing, or walking around the room. *What would you do?*

PERVASIVE DEVELOPMENTAL DISORDERS

According to DSM-IV, pervasive developmental disorders (PDD) include autism, Asperger's syndrome, and PDD not otherwise specified in the DSM-IV(APA,1994). Autistic disorder and Asperger's syndrome are discussed here as is childhood schizophrenia, a psychotic disorder.

Autism

According to Roberts (2004), autism is one of the most severe forms of the childhood psychiatric disorders. A hallmark symptom, termed social reciprocity by Schultz (2005), is evident just after birth. The important clinical features of this condition include a marked abnormal or impaired development in communication and social interaction. There is also a marked restrictive repertoire of activities and interests along with cognitive deficits (Zilbovicius et al., 1995). These symptoms vary with age. Studies of long-term outcomes show that only 5 to 10 percent of autistic children may become independent as adults; 25 percent make progress but require close supervision; the remainder are severely impaired (Kaplan, 1998). About 70 to 75 percent have IQ scores below 70 (Gillberg, 1993) with major deficits in verbal skills (especially language comprehension). High-functioning autism, which assumes an IQ of 70 or more, may not be as rare a condition as previously thought and both its difference from and similarity to Asperger's syndrome, the highest functioning PDD subtype, appears to need further clarification (Kurita, 2001). Children with autism can exhibit hyperactivity and impulsivity and have a short attention span. A high threshold for pain along with oversensitivity to touch or sound is also not unusual. Likewise, there may be a preoccupation with the smell or feel of objects. Mood and affect can be abnormal along with inappropriate reactions to dangers. Children may show temper tantrums, apprehension, and an array of self-injurious behaviors (e.g., head banging, self-biting, or poking various body orifices). A review of the autistic syndrome is provided by Schuler (2001).

Zwaigenbaum (2001) notes that autism disorders are characterized by impairments in social interaction and both verbal and nonverbal communication, along with preferences for repetitive interests and behaviors. About 20 to 40 percent of children with autism have lost

---

Case Study

Autism

Jude is an 8-year-old third grader. He is bright and has an excellent memory. He rarely initiates conversations, but he does answer when asked direct questions. Jude reacts with aversion when touched by others and, at times, even exhibits "tantrum-like" behavior. He is also sensitive to loud sounds; when a buzzer sounds to indicate the end of a period, he seems to cringe. When there is a siren from an ambulance or fire engine, he may put his hands over his ears. Jude does not get good grades, especially in subjects that require abstract thinking; he is also very inattentive regarding dress and personal hygiene. Peers are superficially friendly, mainly because he is able to draw pictures of superheroes for them. On most occasions, he is a social outcast. Nevertheless, Jude appears to be a happy child, and is particularly fascinated by shiny objects that spin. Jude shows most of the characteristics of autism, including difficulty with communication and restricted play and activity interest. Jude also has trouble with changes in routine or transitioning from one place to another. He often exhibits repetitive movements. For example, to avoid peer interaction when entering the classroom, he circles around the desks along the wall until he reaches his seat; he never goes directly to his seat. Jude often rocks back and forth in a kind of self-stimulation pattern, although this is not as prominent as it was when he was younger. When he fell down during recess recently and skinned his knee, he did not cry. Jude becomes quickly aggravated with minor sources of frustration and "loses his temper." When he does express his anger, he often apologizes but then will do the same thing again. Because Jude loves to work on the computer, his teacher has adopted assignments in several subjects that he can complete this way. He also likes predictability and uses a picture schedule to help with routines.

meaningful words by the age of two years and display autistic symptoms thereafter (Kurita, 2001). Early signs that distinguish autism from other atypical patterns of development include poor use of eye gaze, lack of gestures to direct other people's attention (particularly to show things of interest), diminished social responsiveness, and lack of age-appropriate play with toys (especially imaginative use of toys in play). Additional characteristics are noted in the American Academy of Neurology's guidelines (1949) for early identification.

Watling, Deitz, and White (2001) describe sensory-based behaviors of young children with autism. Results on the Sensory Profile Questionnaire (Dunn, 1999) indicate that children with autism were different on eight of the ten scales; the most significant were sensory seeking, emotionally reactive, low endurance/tone, and oral sensitivity, inattention/distractibility, poor registration, and fine motor/perceptual functions. Much research needs to be done on this interesting area of sensory deficits.

Incidence   The estimates on incidence range from 4 or 5 cases per 100,000 (Rutter, 1978) to 10 or 11 cases per 10,000 (Wing & Potter, 2002). Figure 6.1 presents more recent statistics, showing that the number of reported cases of autism has increased dramatically over the past decade. The ratio of females to males is about 3 or 4 to 1 (Rutter & Lockyer, 1967). Reports (Fombonne,

1999) suggest a minimum estimate of 18.7 per 10,000 for all forms of PDD based on 1996–1998 data. Prevalence rates have increased, reflecting changes in case definition as well as improved recognition. The average male/female ratio was 3.8:1. Wing and Potter (2002) have also reported that the rise in incidence and prevalence may be due to changes in diagnostic criteria and increasing awareness and recognition of autistic spectrum disorders. Autism is considerably more common (Yeargin-Allsopp et al., 2003). The prevalence of autism has been estimated at about 0.05 percent in the United States and in many European countries; although it was reported to be 0.1 percent or higher in Japan and in some other European countries, though the reasons for this difference is unclear (Kurita, 2001).

Etiology   The genetic basis for autism is supported by two findings: (1) the incidence of autism in siblings is about 50 times greater than that in the general population (Smalley et al., 1988; Rutter, 2005), and (2) there is a high concordance with dyzygotic twins (Maestrini, Monaco, & Bailey 2000; Korvatska et al., 2002). There is also a higher incidence of autism from prenatal and perinatal complications involving meconium in the amniotic fluid, bleeding during pregnancy, and the use of some prescribed hormones (Jick, Beach, & Kaye, 2006; Croonenberghs, Deboutte, & Maes, 2002). Purcell,

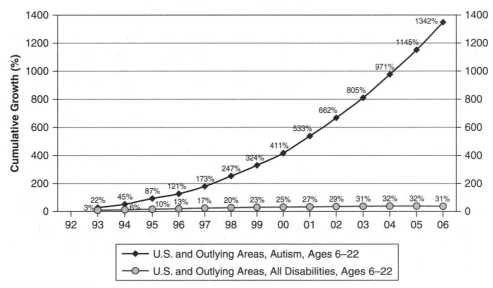

FIGURE 6.1   Growth of the number of cases cumulative for U.S. school years 1992–2006.

Jeon, and Pevsner (2001) believe that autism is caused by mutations in one or more genes. However, Hultman, Sparen, and Cnattingius (2002) have found that intrauterine and neonatal factors related to deviant intrauterine growth or fetal distress may be important in the pathological development of autism as well as genetic factors. The etiology of autism is now considered mostly genetic for reasons such as the significantly higher concordance rate of autism in identical twin pairs (60 to 80 percent) than in fraternal twin pairs (0 to 10 percent) and a 3 to 5 percent incidence of autism among siblings of an autism proband, 30 to 100 times higher than in the general population (Kurita, 2001). A proband is an individual or family member who is being studied in a genetic investigation. For example, a proband might be a child with autism.

Associated Conditions   Many children with autism also exhibit retardation, epilepsy, attention deficits, and aggressive and impulsive disorders. Comings (1990) believes those with autism have overlapping symptoms with Tourette's syndrome. Eating disorders such as pica, sleep problems, and mood/affect disorders have been associated with autism (American Psychiatric Association [APA], 1994). Gillott, Furniss, & Walter (2001) also found that children with autism were more anxious with hyperanxiety on scales reflecting separation anxiety and OCD.

Social Stories   Perhaps the best-known method of helping teach social concepts and skills is found in Carol Gray's *Social Stories: Comic Strip Conversations and Thinking Stories.* Written according to specific guidelines that describe a situation in terms of relevant cues and common responses (Gray & Garland, 1993), the stories convey the underlying goal to understand the student's perspective, to give social information, and to present information so it is understood. Consequently, stories address a wide range of topics (Exkorn, 2005). While lacking research support, these stories are theorized to be most effective with mid- to higher-functioning students. At times, these stories are written for specific students by their parent or a member of the educational team. The box below presents one of Gray's first Social Stories. According to Gray, this story may be subdivided into several shorter stories, with each paragraph standing on its own to teach one concept at a time.

Who Is Line Leader?

My name is Andrew. I am in the first grade. Sometimes, the children in my class form (one, two, three, etc.) lines.

The children in my class stand in a line when we are getting ready to go to another part of the school. Children do move a little when they stand in a line. Children may move to scratch, or fix their shirt, or their shoe. Sometimes because they are standing close together, children may touch one another. Many times, it is an accident when children touch one another in line. They were not planning to touch another child.

The children in my class walk in a line to move safely in the halls. Walking in a line keeps children in order, too. If another group of students are walking in the hall going in the opposite direction, the two groups can pass one another easily. That's why teachers have asked children to walk in lines for many, many years. It is a safe and organized way to move many children. Usually, children stand and walk in lines for a short period of time. Once the children reach their destination, their teacher often doesn't need them to stay in the line anymore.

Sometimes, I may be the line leader. This means that the other children in my class will walk behind me. Sometimes, I may be second, or third, or fourth, or another position. Many children in my class like to be the line leader. My teacher knows who should be first in line. Teachers know about being fair, and try to make sure each child is line leader now and then. It's important to follow directions about who is line leader. My turn to be line leader again gets closer every time the children in my class walk in a line.

Source: Adapted from http://www.thegraycenter.org/socialstories.cfm.

At times, comic strip conversations may incorporate the use of simple drawings and color to illustrate an ongoing communication (Gray, 1994). Such an approach helps the student understand the quick exchanges of information in conversations.*

Students with autism clearly have difficulty with what others are thinking and feeling (Baron-Cohen, 1990; Dawson & Fernald, 1987). Thinking stories (a variant of Social Stories), which can be used with high functioning autistic students, demonstrate the variety of possibilities regarding what other children or teachers might be thinking when they make certain statements or when they behave in a certain way. These stories follow a specific format that uses visual symbols from comic strips to illustrate the concepts they are trying to convey.

Using Social Stories, Scattione and colleagues (2002) observed a decrease in disruptive behavior with the autistic children in their study. Likewise, Thiemann and Goldstein (2001) used Social Stories to study five students with autism. They found an improvement in social communication, supporting the use of visually cued instruction to guide the social language development of autistic students. Using a musically adapted

version of Social Stories, Brownell (2002) found that treatment was viable as well as effective when Social Stories are either read or sung.

Hagiwara and Myles (1999) developed an intervention that used Social Stories in a computer-based format to improve social and behavioral problems. The intervention increased the skill levels of some of the participants in certain settings, and some students did show generalization of their newly acquired skills to other settings.

Asperger's Syndrome

The essential features of Asperger's syndrome are severe and sustained impairment in social interaction and the development of restricted, repetitive patterns of behavior, interests, and activities. In contrast to autism, there are no clinically significant delays in language, cognitive development, or age-appropriate self-help skills, adaptive behavior, and curiosity about the environment. There must, however, be clinically significant impairments in social, occupational, or other important areas of functioning.

Incidence   Estimates of Asperger's syndrome suggest that it is rare and occurs only in about 2.6 percent of the population (Gillberg & Billstedt, 2000). While

---

*Many thanks to Carol Gray for her personal comments and assistance with Social Stories™.

Case Study   **Asperger's Syndrome**

Jarret is an 8-year-old boy who has been diagnosed with Asperger's syndrome by a child psychiatrist. Jarret does not show expressions of emotion (except anger) and has much difficulty showing reciprocal love even to his parents. He seems to prefer being alone and playing by himself. In meeting with Jarret's parents, the psychiatrist noted that their son's problems were not due to poor parenting. Jarret's mother thought that she too might have Asperger's syndrome. She explained this to the psychiatrist. As a child, she cried frequently and, like Jarret, was overly sensitive to loud sounds.

Jarret does not like to be cuddled and often plays with toys that are shiny or with things that "spin around" like a top. At home, Jarret is overly aggressive toward his brother (even cruel at times); on one occasion he tried to choke him. His mother pulled him off and asked Jarret how his brother might feel being choked; Jarret had great difficulty making eye contact with her and said nothing. Later, he was seen with his arm around his little brother. At school, Jarret appears to be of average ability and does not have a reading problem. He does have a good visual memory, but this has not helped him with school subjects. When Jarret runs, he is noticed to have unregular movements; he avoids contact with peers and often sits with a masklike facial expression. When engaged in conversation, he speaks quickly and in an adult manner, not changing his communication whether he is speaking to an adult or child.

some initial estimates suggested an equal ratio of males and females, more recent information indicates that the condition is more common among males (APA, 1994).

Etiology Although the source of autism and Asperger's syndrome is unclear, these disorders are certainly neurologically based, affecting the way the brain interprets sensory information. Researchers are also looking for genetic factors. Despite abundant research on autism, there is surprisingly little academic research on Asperger's syndrome. However, there does appear to be an increased frequency of Asperger's syndrome among the family members of those who have the disorder (APA, 1994).

Associated Conditions Asperger's syndrome may be associated with some medical conditions. In many cases, evidence of Tourette's syndrome may be present. Differential diagnosis may focus on ruling out schizophrenia disorder, obsessive-compulsive disorder, and schizoid personality disorder.

Medications Medications for autism and Asperger's syndrome are discussed in Appendix A.

Social Stories The social skill intervention techniques of the Social Stories and Comic Book/Strip Conversations of Gray (1994) can be effectively used with students who have Asperger's syndrome (Attwood, 2006; Neihart, 2000; Rogers & Myles, 2001). Because changes in routine can create particular anxiety for students with Asperger's syndrome, Social Stories written at the child's reading level can help students understand such transitions and provide information as to when to expect a change and how to react to it (Safran, Safran, & Ellis, 2003). Initially, story scripts can be followed closely and then "faded" as the student develops competence in a situation (Gray & Garland, 1993). Both Social Stories and Comic Book/Strip Conversations hold promise as useful techniques that can guide the student with Asperger's syndrome to engage in more functionally appropriate social behavior. It is clear that the most effective school-based approaches in treating those with Asperger's syndrome appear to include a combination of early identification, family involvement, and individualized treatment (Dempsey & Foreman, 2001).

Guidelines for Educational Activities According to Williams (1995) the following classroom strategies can be used to address each of the seven defining characteristics of Asperger's syndrome (AS):[*]

1. *Insistence on sameness:* Children with AS are very sensitive to change. Much stress and worry result when they not know what to expect. The following strategies may be helpful:
    a. Establish a reliably predictable environment.
    b. Minimize transitions and/or practice dealing with them.
    c. Establish a daily routine.
    d. Avoid surprises; prepare the child for any necessary changes in routine.
    e. Expose the child to any change in activity or situation as soon as possible (e.g., transitions).

2. *Impairment in social interaction:* Children with AS are unlikely to understand complex rules of social interaction. They do not like physical contact, talk *at* people instead of *to* them, and do not understand jokes. Their speech may be in a monotone, and they are sometimes labeled "little professor" because of the adultlike pedantic style of their verbalizations. The following strategies may be helpful:
    a. Be alert to bullying and teasing of the AS child.
    b. Explain to classmates that the AS child's social problems are a true disability.
    c. Praise peers who treat the AS child with compassion.
    d. Focus on the AS child's academic skill assets.
    e. Teach the AS child what to say and how to say it via modeling and role play.
    f. Show AS children that they can learn social skills *intellectually* without social instinct or invitation, despite their lack of understanding the emotions of others.
    g. Use a buddy system to help educate classmates, pairing an AS student with a normal student. Seat these two next to each other in the classroom and ask the other child to look out for the AS child on the bus, at recess, etc.

---

[*]Much of this section has been adapted with permission from Sage Publications from William (1995).

h. Encourage group activities; limit the time spent in isolated interests.

3. *Restricted range of interests:* Children with AS may be preoccupied with odd or unusual things; they may talk excessively about their area of interest and have difficulty shifting to another topic. The following strategies may be useful:

   a. Designate times when the AS child can talk about his or her specific interests.

   b. Use positive reinforcement to help shape a desired behavior (Flick, 1996; 1998b; 2000)—for example, praising students who pause to allow others to speak.

   c. Allow AS students to pursue their own interests, but make them aware that they must follow rules and do assignments outside of their area of interest.

   d. Initially try to give assignments that involve the AS child's area of interest.

   e. Use the AS child's fixation to broaden his or her repertoire of interests (e.g., if there is interest in studying animals that live in the rain forest, learning about their home in addition to other features or characteristics of these animals).

4. *Poor concentration:* Often off-task, distracted, and disorganized, AS children have difficulty in the classroom because they are unable to figure out what is relevant (Farrell, 2004). The following strategies may be useful:

   a. Create structure by breaking down assignments and giving frequent feedback.

   b. Use timed work sessions. This helps with organization and shows that compliance with rules (i.e., structure) pays off. This motivates the AS child to be productive.

   c. Lighten the amount of homework and class work; provide ample time in a resource room where the assignment can be completed.

   d. Use a nonverbal signal such as pointing to an eye to get child focused.

   e. Establish a buddy system pairing a normal student with an AS child.

   f. Encourage AS children to refocus on the real world and to leave behind irrelevant thoughts and fantasies.

g. Create structure for AS students even during play activities.

5. *Poor motor coordination:* Children with AS may be clumsy and awkward and have stiff gait, which means they may have difficulty with games involving motor skills and are also likely to have motor problems that affect handwriting and drawing skills. The following strategies may be useful:

   a. Refer AS students to physical ed if their gross motor problems are severe.

   b. Involve AS students in noncompetitive sports and exercise programs.

   c. Establish a highly individualized cursive writing program, guiding the child's hand through letter formations and using a verbal description of letter formations to reinforce learning by accessing both sides of the brain in writing and to minimize careless errors.

   d. Use more structure in developing appropriate letter size. Start with large graph paper and reduce the size of the squares to shape smaller formations of letters and numbers.

   e. Consider the AS child's work speed when assigning timed units of work.

   f. Conduct tests in an area such as a resource room where the AS child can have more time and access to teacher redirection when needed.

6. *Academic difficulties:* Although AS children have average to above average intelligence (especially in verbal skills), they lack high-level thinking and comprehension skills. They also tend to be quite literal and concise with poor abstraction ability. AS children may have excellent rote memory but they may respond verbally in a pedantic, mechanical style. Problem solving is poor. The following strategies may be useful:

   a. Provide a challenging academic program that rewards learning.

   b. Remain cognizant that parroting information does not reflect understanding of academic material.

   c. Give extra explanations and simplify abstract concepts.

   d. Capitalize on the child's exceptional rote memory regarding factual information.

e. Avoid emotional nuances or multiple levels of meaning and relationship issues.

f. Don't assume that what the AS student reads is understood.

g. Communicate to the AS child that there are firm expectations that will be established for the quality of work and that poorly executed work must be corrected.

7. *Emotional vulnerability:* While the AS students may have the academic abilities, they do not have the emotional resources to cope with the demands of the classroom. Easily stressed and prone to low self-esteem, they may become very self-critical about mistakes. Adolescents are especially prone to depression, and rage reactions are common responses to stress and frustration. Coping with people requires a monumental effort. The following strategies may be useful:

a. Prevent outbursts by maintaining consistency and routine and preparing the child for any changes or transitions.

b. Teach stress management techniques. Review deep breathing, counting, requests to visit the special ed teacher. Include a ritualized behavior that the child finds comforting.

c. Remain calm and matter-of-fact in interactions with the child. Psychiatrist Hans Asperger (1991) noted that "the teacher who does not understand that it is necessary to teach children (with AS) seemingly obvious things will feel unimportant and unrelated." Such children cannot perceive their own feelings or the feelings of others and so may cover up depression or deny it.

d. Behavior reflecting greater disorganization, inattentiveness, and isolation may indicate depression. Don't accept comments such as "I'm ok" from an AS child you suspect is depressed.

e. Ask a staff member to check on adolescents with AS daily.

f. Provide assistance with academic problems promptly. AS children can easily be overwhelmed and they exhibit serious acting-out behaviors.

g. Provide access to a highly structured special ed classroom for those AS students who also are very fragile emotionally. Such children need to see themselves as competent and productive. Frustration with academic work may significantly affect self-concept and increase withdrawal and depression.

Case Study **Childhood Schizophrenia**

Ryan is a 14-year-old eighth grader whose condition has progressively deteriorated. Tests for drugs and other medical conditions have been negative. He refuses to eat because even food that he once liked tastes "funny." He has lost much weight and is beginning to "zone out" for hours at a time. During these periods, he sometimes laughs uncontrollably or stares at his hands, saying only that they are different than they used to be. Ryan's grades went from C's and D's to all F's. His teachers say that he does little work and often just gets up and walks out of class, roaming the halls. He has become very aggressive with others at times, talking to himself and laughing. His mother reports that he sometimes gets very upset with her and runs out of his room. Although he has never said that he hears voices, it has become apparent that he does and he finally has admitted that God talks to him. Ryan has now started to talk in a "word salad"—nonsensical speech that sounds like a foreign language. He is beginning to say that other students are from a different planet. He has also said that his mother is going to kill him and that his brothers are there to protect him. Ryan often comes out of his room, screams, and says that everyone is going to die. He listens to the same music over and over, paces constantly, or just doesn't get out of his bed. When Ryan started to hallucinate, imagining that there were "bugs on the wall," he was admitted to a psychiatric hospital.

PSYCHOTIC DISORDERS

Psychiatric disorders in childhood (childhood psychosis) have been around for some time, but its definition has been subject to change (Campbell et al., 1997). While psychosis in adults may focus on delusions, hallucinations, impaired reality testing, and disorganized bizarre speech (APA, 1994), many of these functions are still under development in children. Thus, for schizophrenia and other psychotic disorders in children, the age of 7 years has been established as the lower limit for diagnosing these psychotic (thought) disorders.

Childhood Schizophrenia

Childhood schizophrenia—a term reserved for diagnosis in a person under 15 years of age—is a mental illness that involves the child's affect, perceptions, thoughts, behaviors, speech, and communication. For at least 6 months, the child must have symptoms that seriously interfere with the ability to function in school, at home, or in social situations. Some of the following primary symptoms may be present:

■ *Hallucinations:* false perceptions (e.g., hearing a voice or seeing a person when no one is there).
■ *Delusions:* false beliefs (e.g., believing that a monster is going to do some harm).
■ *Disorganized speech:* incoherent words, getting off the topic.
■ *Flat affect:* showing no emotion.
■ *Alogia:* little or no speaking.
■ *Avolition:* difficulty starting or maintaining a task.

Of course, many things need to be considered when evaluating children for schizophrenia, including their age, consistency of symptoms, other medical and/or psychological conditions accounting for strange behavior, prior immediate experience (e.g., exposure to alien creatures and monsters in a movie), and even their own creative imagination. When these factors are considered and a child persists in having many of the key symptoms, a diagnosis may be rendered. Typically, this diagnosis is made by a psychologist or psychiatrist; special assessments or tests may also be needed prior to arriving at a final diagnosis.

The Individuals with Disabilities Education Act (IDEA) defines *serious emotional disturbance* as follows:

A condition exhibiting one or more of the following characteristics over a long period of time and to a marked degree that adversely affects educational performance:

■ An inability to learn that cannot be explained by intellectual, sensory, or health factors;
■ An inability to build or maintain satisfactory interpersonal relationships with peers and teachers;
■ Inappropriate types of behavior or feelings under normal circumstances;
■ A general pervasive mood of unhappiness or depression; or
■ A tendency to develop physical symptoms or fears associated with personal or school problems [Code of Federal Regulations, Title 34, Section 300.7(6)(9)].

As defined by IDEA, the category of emotional disturbance does include schizophrenia, but this inclusion does not apply to children who are just socially maladjusted unless it is documented that they also have a serious (i.e., psychotic-emotional) disturbance. Because the federal government is now reviewing how a serious emotional disturbance is defined, this definition may be revised.

Incidence   It is known that from 6 to 10 percent of all school-age children exhibit persistent emotional and/or behavioral problems; however, only about 1 percent are identified as having a serious emotional disturbance. Childhood psychosis (in those children less than 12 years of age) is rare. Current prevalence is about 1.4 per 10,000 (McKenna et al., 1994). Fewer than 1 percent of all psychotic disorders are manifested prior to age 10, and only 4 percent appear before age 15 (Remschmidt et al., 1994).

Etiologies   There is much evidence for a significant genetic contribution to the etiology of schizophrenia (Cloninger et al., 1998; Van Os & Marcelis, 1998). A multifactorial (i.e., many factors) mode of genetic transmission is also indicated (Freedman et al., 1997; Gershen, 1998; Guidry & Kent, 1999).

Associated Conditions   There is considerable symptom overlap and shared symptomology between childhood schizophrenia and severe speech and language impairment along with pervasive developmental disorders (e.g., autism, Rett's disorder, and Asperger's syndrome), ADHD, and stereotypic movement disorder (APA, 1994).

Medications   Medications for psychotic disorders are discussed in Appendix A.

Strategies for Childhood Schizophrenia

The following activities and strategies may be used with students who exhibit childhood schizophrenia (Brophy, 1996):

1. Don't diagnose—just describe the problem behaviors.
2. Check with students who are prone to daydreaming by saying their name (not calling on them).
3. Assist students in developing social insight (e.g., explaining that teasing doesn't mean someone doesn't like you; that it takes time to make new friends) and support how these students can respond more effectively.
4. Assign designated roles to provide more structure in social situations.
5. Teach students how to greet each other and provide suggestions on assertive requests.
6. Provide general ideas on how students can be more assertive and role-play (practice) these suggestions.
7. Assign another student as a partner, especially one who is popular, to facilitate more frequent contacts with others and to provide a model for the behavior.
8. Make time to talk with students for a few minutes and to respond clearly to what they are trying to communicate.
9. Display work done by students or present it in class when appropriate.
10. Find out what special interests students have and talk about them.
11. Role-play suggestions from above.

SUMMARY

This chapter focuses on the characteristics of pervasive developmental disorders such as autism and Asperger's syndrome, and psychotic disorders such as childhood schizophrenia. Gray's (2003) Social Stories provide an excellent format to teach social skills not only to children with autism or Asperger's syndrome but also to any child who has deficits in social skills.

DISCUSSION QUESTIONS

1. What is the hallmark symptom of autism?
2. What are the impairments in autistic disorders?
3. What is the most effective treatment intervention for autistic children?
4. Describe how Social Stories are used with higher functioning autistic students.
5. How is Asperger's syndrome different from autistic disorders?
6. What is the main problem in defining psychosis in children?
7. Describe some of the primary symptoms of childhood schizophrenia.
8. How does IDEA define a serious emotional disturbance?
9. Which strategies can be adapted for use with older children who manifest schizophrenic disorders?

PART III

Identifying and Assessing Behavior Disorders

There are several reasons a clinician may wish to formulate a diagnostic impression to assess a child who presents academic and/or behavior problems: (1) to determine whether the child might benefit from medication, (2) to decide whether to include the child in a general education class *or* to educate the child in a special setting, (3) to fulfill the request of an insurance provider, and (4) to gather statistical information. The current trend in education has emphasized inclusion, which means that children may be separated from their typical peers only if educating them in that setting would be detrimental to the students themselves or to classmates. In most cases, a child's disorder would need to be judged quite severe to prevent him or her from being included with their typical classmates. Diagnostic evaluations are primarily designed to ascertain the child's strengths and weaknesses and to determine eligibility for special resources and special clinical programs outside of the school setting. Aside from the assessment of strengths and weaknesses, the diagnostic or traditional evaluation may point to appropriate accommodations that may help the child adapt to the school programs and curricula while specific skill deficit areas are addressed.

In contrast to traditional assessment procedures, a functional behavioral assessment (FBA) focuses on specific problematic behaviors and the setting events, antecedents, and consequences of that behavior. The focus is entirely on problematic behavior with the goal of determining the function of the inappropriate behavior concerning what triggers it and what maintains it, so that specific behavior interventions may be used to change its occurrence and/or frequency. It is evident that both traditional assessments and functional behavioral assessment are necessary; however, there has and there will be less emphasis on the use of traditional assessments for categorical purposes. Instead, the FBA will be used most frequently to deal with problematic behavior.

Chapter 7 focuses on the assessment of students for possible classification and placement in special education. Various tests and procedures are discussed, with an emphasis on the use of a neuropsychological approach to assessment. Chapter 8 focuses on alternative assessment—namely, functional behavioral assessment. This type of assessment is essential and allows for the development of a behavioral intervention plan (BIP) where students are taught alternative behavior that may substitute for the problem behavior. In addressing the problem behavior, the needs of students are met by providing them with the same reinforcing function as did the problem behavior. Competing behaviors thus replace the problem behavior with a functional substitute that is more effective, more efficient, and most importantly, more acceptable. A case study provides an example of the FBA. In Chapter 9, there is an extension of the process from the FBA to the behavioral intervention plan which ultimately is included in the Individualized Education Plan (IEP). The major focus is on how the IEP of students with a behavior disorder is affected by the 2004 Individuals with Disabilities Education Act (IDEA).

CHAPTER 7

Assessment of Behavior Disorders

Overview

- Making a differential diagnosis
- Background and developmental history
- Behavioral observations
- Selected basic psychological tests
- Rating scales
- Projective tests
- Special inventories
- Psychometric terminology
- Psychological/neuropsychological assessment
- Rationale for neuropsychological assessment
- Symptom overlap
- The neuropsychological approach
- Specific tests versus test batteries
- A multidisciplinary evaluation
- Components of the neuropsychological assessment
- The diagnostic process
- Interpretation of test data

Case History

Chris is a 6-year-old first grader in a general education program who does not receive special services for speech. His teacher has noted that his social interactions are poor and inappropriate on many occasions during both classroom and free play. In the class, Chris often engages other students in conversations that get them off task, or he makes noises by humming. During free play, he sometimes calls students names and hits or kicks them. Although his teacher has used verbal reprimands and has sometimes removed him from the classroom, he continues to engage in inappropriate behaviors. The teacher decides to work on getting Chris on-task during a 15-minute reading period. *What would you do?*

The first step in dealing with children having behavior disorders is to better understand their condition(s) and to know both general and specific procedures to cope effectively with their problems. (Note that the term "condition" is shown as either singular or plural since several disorders tend to cluster together.) In some cases, it may be difficult to separate and delineate the primary, secondary, and tertiary components. Many of today's young children meet the criteria for multiple disorders, making it difficult to treat such cases with a single intervention. Nevertheless, each component of every disorder must be treated with appropriate interventions—encompassing medical, behavior, and educational factors.

Ideally, special education, in conjunction with appropriate medical treatment, selectively enhances the instructional interventions used to improve the overall education and the successful social adjustments of children with various physical, mental, and emotional conditions that are manifested in the classroom as learning and behavioral difficulties.

In all modern schemes, the defining criteria for nearly all psychiatric diagnoses are purely descriptive and phenomenological (Dilling, 2000). No causal mechanisms are implied. Research will determine these. This is a major step forward from earlier classification schemes that identified untestable causes such as a "dcfcctivc cgo" to cxplain a student's disorder.

What the Law Says About Eligibility

The parents of a student with a history of behavior problems have been told that their daughter was found to be not eligible for special education. Following a due process hearing, new evaluations have found that the student meets the criteria for services under the emotionally disturbed label and has been found eligible for special education and related services by another school district. Evidence was admitted to determine whether the student qualified for special education at the time of the due process hearing when she was classified as emotionally disturbed. The question now is whether the parents are entitled to tuition reimbursement for the private school year following their request to the school district to evaluate their daughter. Reimbursement for the independent evaluation was denied pending submission of evidence proving that the evaluation complied with the school district's guidelines.

What IDEA Says About Evaluations

The following are items that relate to what IDEA says about psychological evaluations.

- Regarding the request for evaluation—the bill clarifies that a parent may initiate a request for an initial evaluation to determine if a child has a disability.
- Regarding the special rule for eligibility, expanding provision precludes schools from finding that a child has a disability if the determinant factor is lack of appropriate instruction in reading, as included in the essential components of reading instruction as defined in No Child Left Behind.
- With regard to minorities, a new provision requires states to have policies and procedures that are designed to prevent the inappropriate overidentification or disproportionate representation by race and ethnicity of children as students with disabilities.

IDEA 2004 on Assessment

There are new requirements to address overidentification of children, particularly minority children, for special education. Based on numerous reports, Congress concluded that some students are being inappropriately identified as having a disability or being placed in the wrong disability category, largely due to their race or ethnicity. IDEA now requires states to develop policies and procedures to prevent the overidentification or disproportionate representation by race and ethnicity of children as having a disability or having a particular disability. States can review their policies and procedures and updated evaluation and referral procedures, and potentially require school districts to use early intervening funds to address their problem. For example, states can examine historical trends in districts and review records to ensure that a pattern of overidentification does not inappropriately place a larger number of students of a particular ethnic or racial background in special education.

INTRODUCTION TO ASSESSMENT

For many years, psychological testing has been a primary function for many school psychologists and clinical psychologists when presented with a child who demonstrates some form of academic or behavior problems. While this clinical activity has served a useful function in diagnosis and classification of such disorders, there have been several problems associated with such assessment procedures.

The first is that there has been little relationship demonstrated between the results of these evaluations and ultimate interventions. This does not mean that knowing whether a child meets the diagnostic criteria for ADHD or has visual-spatial difficulty is not helpful information. Such information can be used to address the identified deficits by implementing specific training programs. Determining the most appropriate diagnoses can indicate which medications may be most helpful (information for the physician) and which psychosocial interventions (information for the school psychologist and teacher) might be used in conjunction with medications or alone as a solo program. In some cases, a comprehensive psychological assessment can identify factors that may modify a treatment approach either medically or psychologically. In general, however, there has not been a prescriptive approach to treatment and, as a result, many children with varying disorders may be provided the same intervention, regardless of their diagnosis.

The second problem is that arriving at an appropriate diagnosis may not be in the best interest of the child—for example, when children meet the criteria for special education placement but are instead put in general education classes. Essentially, such children should be put in special classes if they meet the criteria for special educational classification. Alternatively, some children who do not meet the criteria for special education may actually be able to profit from placement in a special class.

Despite the problems associated with assessment, the clinical activity of testing and evaluation may continue until reforms are implemented. Although some readers may wish to skim this chapter for information, it may provide teachers, parents, and students with useful information about psychological reports and testing. While the test procedures discussed are commonly used in psychological evaluations, specific procedures may be noted in addressing each category of disorders. This will provide the readers with information on the central core of evaluation procedures, and some specific test procedures that can be employed with each diagnostic category.

Both traditional and alternative assessment procedures may be helpful in designing an optimal program for a specific child. Typically, the more formal assessment (traditional testing) is conducted first; the functional behavioral assessment (FBA) is usually completed at a later point, prior to the development of the behavioral intervention plan (BIP) and the Individualized Education Plan (IEP).

ARRIVING AT A DIFFERENTIAL DIAGNOSIS

Many professionals believe that the diagnosis of a behavior disorder should be made solely from DSM-IV criteria. Based on information supplied by a child's parents, a comprehensive developmental history is obtained by a private professional or by the school psychologist. As part of that history, current behavioral characteristics are noted and integrated with the developmental history to form the basis of a diagnostic impression. Most children with behavior problems, however, present such a complex array of symptoms that they often meet the criteria for an additional diagnostic classification as well. Consequently, the clinician must consider several sources of information besides the developmental history from parents to piece together the puzzle and sort out which characteristics are primary and which ones may be secondary or tertiary problems. Such a multi-level analysis will frequently lead to a multicomponent treatment program that addresses each significant component. This process may be likened to the story of the three blind men who encounter an elephant and are asked to describe it. Each one focuses on a different part of the elephant, and three different pictures of the same animal emerge. Too narrow a focus on the child with behavior problems may simply result in an inadequate description, diagnosis, and treatment.

In general, the evaluation process begins by obtaining information from more than one source—for instance, from the child's parents and teachers, and if age-appropriate from the child himself. Children being evaluated may also be placed in different testing situations and given tasks to determine how they cope to determine whether they have associated learning problems or behavioral and emotional problems, or both. A comprehensive evaluation of this type provides a complete description of the child's abilities, achievements, specific visual-motor, memory and auditory skills, language skills and executive control skills as well as behavioral/emotional characteristics. The sections that follow explore each component that contributes to the overall differential diagnosis.

Background and Developmental History

Family medical history, including psychiatric conditions (both diagnosed and undiagnosed) on both sides of the family, is clearly important to consider along with the child's unique medical history. For example, a child whose parent has ADHD could also have experienced the cumulative effects of lead poisoning, and thus have a dual etiology for a disorder. Many disorders have a genetic as well as a psychological basis. The child's birth history may include indicators of neonatal distress, anoxia, maternal smoking and drug use during pregnancy as well as other risk factors. Studies of effects during pregnancy have reported that nicotine from cigarette smoking and alcohol from drinking during pregnancy have been shown to cause significant abnormalities in the development of the caudate nucleus and the frontal regions of the brain in children (Barkley, 1998; Linnet et al., 2005; Wilens & Biederman, 2006). It has been noted that the greater the number of complications during pregnancy, the greater the risk of ADHD as well as other disabilities. A history of ear infections, especially with high fevers, may also be a contributing factor. Other possible significant medical conditions for the child include asthma, thyroid dysfunction, hypoglycemia, hearing defects, sleep apnea, encephalitis (brain infection), mild brain damage (head trauma), and seizure disorders. Therefore, a comprehensive assessment of the child's *background and developmental history* along with *parental and family history* are all essential.

Behavior Observations

In addition to the background and developmental history, three sets of observations are obtained about the child with behavior problems during the assessment process:

1. Parents present their observations, which often seem to be mostly in the form of complaints regarding behavior difficulties and behavior differences (e.g., how their child is different from others).

2. Teachers provide general behavioral descriptions from their viewpoint at the same time that the behavioral ratings are obtained. In addition, parents and teachers both typically complete more formal rating scales that entail norm-referenced comparisons to other children the same age as the identified child. These ratings may provide information about various types of behaviors that can be helpful not only in diagnosis but also in planning interventions.

3. Observations are obtained during testing from the psychological examiner. These observations serve as a context for the interpretation of the test results and provide basic information about how the child deals with "assigned tasks." Many of the tasks presented in the testing session are similar to the cognitive activities inherent in school subjects. Thus, a kind of "micro classroom" context is created so that the child's adaptive skills can be assessed within the test session.

Information from these rating scales can be most helpful, especially those ratings from the child's teacher. Teachers may in fact be in the best position to rate a child as they have more information on behavior at various developmental levels; this information can be compared with that of other peers, in general, or of others in the child's class. These ratings not only help in the diagnostic process but also serve as baseline observations to which the child's progress will be compared. Thus, these initial ratings may be periodically repeated to monitor the child's behavior during and after various treatment modalities, since there will be increasingly more complex demands and rules with which the child can be compared across time. Such monitoring will aid in determining additional needs for either medications or specific interventions to deal with changing rules and expectations that are experienced by the child.

Clearly, the way the child feels during testing will also affect test scores—illness, lack of sleep, fear, depression, resentment, and lack of understanding of the purpose of the evaluation can all affect the results. All of these observations must be considered as the context of the evaluation.

Behavioral observations during the assessment tell the examiner much about how children approach tasks, what strategies they may have used, and how they feel about their performance. Awkward pencil grip, blocking on verbal responses, eye contact, long pauses, facial expressions, counting on fingers to solve math problems, word-finding difficulty, restless behavior, excessive talking, and looking around at each noise and distraction are observations that the examiner may record. Most of these behaviors may be no surprise to the experienced examiner, but some may be unique, conveying highly individual information about a child.

Basic Psychological Tests

The assessment of any child is a key factor in planning a program of treatment. For example, the child with ADHD often does well in a one-on-one situation; this performance on psychological tests with the examiner may be viewed as one that would be manifested in an ideal situation. Thus, the assessment reveals more about how the child might function in an ideal situation with maximum academic performance and assessment of

abilities within the context of the child's natural physiological tendencies. Some children who are not yet on medication may essentially be untestable. Others may have little trouble with the test situation, especially because of its novelty (i.e., its stimulation value). For those children who are already on medication, an attempt may be made to also see the child off the medication and later to compare his or her performance while on medication. Although it is usually recommended that children be tested off medications, it does depend on the type of medication the child is taking. Since it may be risky to stop some medications abruptly, this issue must be discussed in detail with the child's pediatrician. In general, it is better to test the child before medications are prescribed; conducting the psychological evaluation first will help to delineate all of the components of the child's problems. Medications, when appropriate, can then be used to target specific issues.

Although it is more desirable to evaluate children at-risk with a neuropsychological test battery, they are more frequently tested with a brief battery of specific psychological tests. Typically, these tests will consist of measures of cognitive ability and verbal achievements along with specific assessments to rule out suspected conditions. The most common psychological tests used are presented in Table 7.1. Additional tests might include measures of visual-motor/visual-spatial skills and some clinical measures of social-emotional functions, such as the Draw-A-Person (DAP) and the Kinetic Family Drawing (KFD); children may also be queried about their understanding of problems. Additional checklists, rating scales, and other inventions and projective procedures may be given to address the suspected at-risk disability. Some background information will be needed to learn more about the child's parents and relatives as well as to obtain a medical history in chronological time sequence. It is only through such background information as well as behavior ratings by teachers, and direct observations and performance by the child that a reliable and valid diagnosis can be given. The use of different test procedures and information from parents and teachers along with a view of problems from the child's perspective can supply appropriate information to contribute to an acceptable diagnostic impression.

Rating Scales   There are several rating scales of behavior/emotional problems that may complement

TABLE 7.1 Basic Psychological Tests

Measures of Ability and Achievement		
Test[a]	**Measure**	**Age Range**
WISC-IV	Cognitive ability	6–16.11
KBIT-2	Cognitive ability	4–90
Stanford-Binet	Cognitive ability	2–85
WRAT-4	Achievement	5–75
WIAT-II	Achievement	6–16.11
PIAT-R	Achievement	6–22.11
WJ-R (Ach)	Achievement	2–95
Measures of Language		
Test	**Measure**	**Age Range**
PPVT-IV	Receptive/expressive language	5–75
TOKEN	Receptive language	3–12.5
TOLD-I:2	Language	4–12
Measures of Visual-Motor/Visual Spatial Skills		
Test	**Measure**	**Age Range**
Berry VMI	Visual motor/visual spatial	3 +
Bender-Gestalt	Visual motor/visual spatial	4 +

[a]The complete names of these tests are found in Table A.3 in Appendix A.

individual evaluations, depending on the suspected conditions. Some of the more commonly used ones are described in Table 7.2.

The following checklists and rating scales are also used:

● Pediatric Symptom Checklist (PSC)
● Revised Behavior Problem Checklist (RBPC)
● Systematic Screening for Behavior Disorders (SSBD)
● Behavior Rating Profile (2nd ed.—BRP-2)
● Autism Screening: Instrument for Educational Planning (2nd ed.—ASIEP-2)
● Burk's Behavior Rating Scales (BBRS-R)
● Emotional and Behavioral Problem Solving Scale (EABPS)
● Social Skills Rating System (SSRS)
● Piers-Harris Children's Self-Concept Scale
● Multidimensional Self-Concept Scale
● Vineland Adaptive Behavior Scales (2nd ed.—Vineland-II)

Projective Tests Those assessment procedures that are basically *unstructured* where students can give an almost infinite variation of responses are termed *projective tests*. Some of the more commonly used ones are described in Table 7.3.

Special Inventories Special inventories are test instruments that are administered to parents, teachers, or the identified child. Some of the more commonly used ones are described in Table 7.4.

Psychometric Terminology

It is important to become familiar with the psychometric terminology related to tests that are used to classify students and describe their behavior. There are two key terms that reflect the adequacy of any objective test: reliability and validity.

Reliability refers to the consistency of measurement in a test—how much error is involved in that measurement or how much the obtained score varies from the

TABLE 7.2 Rating Scales for Behavioral/Emotional Problems

	BASC-2	CBCL/6–18	CARS	ASDS	AETeRS
Authors	Reynolds and Kanphon	Achenbak and Rescarla	Schopha, Ruchler, and Renner	Myles, Tones-Bock, and Simpson	Ullmann, Sleator, and Sprague
Date Published	2004	2001	1988	2000	1986–1991
Forms/Items	Teacher form Parent form Self-Report Student observation Developmental history	Parent form Three competence scales Eight cross informant syndromes Internalizing problems Externalizing problems	15 items	50 items from five areas: 1. Cognitive 2. Maladaptive 3. Language 4. Social 5. Sensorimotor	Teacher/parent forms 24 items in 4 factors 1. Attention 2. Hyperactivity 3. Social skills 4. Oppositional behavior
Age Range	2–21	6–18	2+ years	5–18	6–14
Use	Identifies problem behavior required by IDEA to develop FBA, BIP, and IEP	Diagnoses of specific DSM categories	Diagnoses autism	Diagnoses Asperger's syndrome	Identifies specific areas where child has difficulty

TABLE 7.3 Projective Tests for Behavioral/Emotional Problems

	Rorschach	CAT	DAP	ATP	KFD	FSD
Authors	Rorschach	Bellak and Bellak	Machover	Buck, 1948	Kaufman	Prout and Phillips
Date Published	1921	1949	1948		1970	1974
Forms/Items	Ten inkblots Responses scored for location or type No reading required	Ten pictures of animals or humans (for older kids) Child tells story about the picture and how characters are feeling.	Drawings of a whole person	Drawing of house, tree, and person	Child asked to draw picture of family doing something	Child asked to draw picture of self and classmates
Age Range	5 + years					
Use	Assesses personality dynamics and underlying motivations	Reveals interpersonal conflicts, emotions, and aggressive tendencies	Reflects on anxieties, self-esteem, and personality of child	*House:* feelings toward family *Tree:* feelings of strength/weakness	Targets child's attitude and feelings toward whole family and their dynamics	Elicits attitudes toward others at school and how child functions there

TABLE 7.4 Special Inventories for Behavioral/Emotional Problems

	MMPI-2	M-PACI	PIC-2	CDI
Author	Butcher, Dahlstram, Graham, and Tellegon	Millon, Tringone, Millon, and Grossman	Lachar and Gruber	Kovacs
Date	1989	2005	2001	1992
Items	478 true/false items	97 true/false items	Parents complete 275 true/false items to assess behavioral, cognitive, and interpersonal adjustment	27 items, each with three statements Child selects statement that best describes feelings for past two weeks
Age Range	14–18	9–12	5–19	6–17
Uses	Identifies problem behavior and facilitates diagnoses	Detects early signs of Axis I or Axis II behavioral/emotional disorders	Provides integrated picture of child's adjustment in home, school, and community	Quantifies a wide range of depressive symptoms

true score (Domino & Domino, 2006). One subtype of reliability is *internal consistency*—whether a test measures a related set of characteristics (e.g., spatial ability). If this measure is high, it means that the items on the test are highly correlated. Another subtype of reliability is *test-retest reliability*—how well the score would correlate if the test were administered again to the same persons. Obviously, the length of time between testings would be important. If the tests are given close in time, the scores should be quite similar. If the test times are far apart, the scores might reflect changes in whatever is measured.

Validity refers to whether the test measures what it is supposed to measure, assuming that the items are representative of what is measured and that the test is reliable (Domino & Domino, 2006). *Content validity* refers to whether the test addresses material it is supposed to cover. *Criterion-related validity* compares the test score with some independent criterion or outcome. The degree to which the test score predicts the outcome is termed *predictive validity*. *Construct validity* refers to how well a test measures a specific psychological construct (e.g., intelligence). This measure may thus be determined by seeing how well a test correlates with other tests that purport to measure the same thing.

Other factors can also affect the validity of a test: rapport with the examiner, a handicap such as blindness, motivation (e.g., a student intentionally tries to look bad, and an unsettling intervening event such as a big fight with parents before the test. Some tests may be reliable but not valid (Kenny, Holden, & Santilli, 1991; Moss, 1994), but a test cannot be valid if it is not reliable. The term *standardized test* means only that there are a specific set of procedures for the administration and scoring of a test and that there is a group of children on which the test was established (standardized). Neil (2004) discusses how to choose instruments (tests) for research and evaluation.

There are some additional terms that anyone using a test should be familiar with. *Age equivalent* refers to the age where a child's test score would be average. Defined by comparing a raw score to standardized age norms, the term is often used in developmental assessments to provide an age standing. *Grade equivalent* is the grade level at which a child's test score would be considered average. This score is determined by comparing a student's score to grade norms. A grade equivalent of 3.5 means that the student's score is identical to one obtained by students in the fifth month of the third grade (or mid-third grade). *Deviation IQ* compares scores across ages to estimate the student's intelligence. (It is a "standardized score" so that two individuals with IQ scores can be compared.)

Lastly, it is important to consider the *standardization sample*—the group on which a test is developed, which must be comparable with the group to which the test is being applied. For example, a test that was standardized only on white students may not be valid for use with black students. For a test to be valid, the standardization sample, on which norms are developed, should be comparable in breakdown by race and show similar means and standard deviations (a measure of variability around the mean) to the population on which the test is used. In most cases, the standardization sample is determined by the breakdown of the most recent census in the geographic area that the test is utilized.

It is regrettable that measurement issues are often viewed with distaste, or disinterest, given that diagnoses, placement decisions, and goals are based on test scores. An awareness of and consideration of these issues is thus a key factor in assessment.

Psychological/Neuropsychological Assessment

There is no single test for diagnosing behavior problems, as noted by Flick (1998b, 2000, 2002). Clinical observation—combined with the results of the child's performance on specific psychological and neuropsychological tests measuring verbal, nonverbal, visual-motor, gross-motor, memory, executive control, and attention skills—are essential for the psychologist and/or neuropsychologist to describe the pattern of behaviors that the child presents and to formulate a diagnosis (Flick, 2004). Children who are mentally retarded or who experience brain injury may have basic difficulties with attention and concentration that generate test results that differ dramatically from children of average or above-average intelligence with externalizing disorders. Because of the complexities of the evaluation, a neuropsychological rationale must be considered (Flick, 1998b, 2000).

Rationale for Neuropsychological Assessment

An underlying assumption in the field of neuropsychology is that the brain mediates behavior and that the behaviors that are part of a typical clinical picture are quite complex. For example, it is highly unusual for the child being evaluated for ADHD to have only that disorder. In most cases, the pattern may consist of secondary or even tertiary problem areas, in addition to the primary disorder. A frequently diagnosed condition such as ADHD may also spawn or be associated with several other conditions—for example, learning disabilities, bipolar disorder, oppositional defiant disorder, conduct disorder, stress problems (such as posttraumatic stress disorder), depression, and anxiety.

SYMPTOM OVERLAP

A few of the overlapping symptoms for disorders such as conduct disorder, anxiety, and depression that are frequently associated with ADHD are shown in Figure 7.1. This figure illustrates that there are many symptoms that overlap, which makes it difficult to arrive at a diagnostic impression. Symptoms may mimic various disorders (e.g., anxiety or depression may mimic ADHD). Thus, while the symptoms may "look like" ADHD, they may really reflect anxiety or depression (Flick, 1998b). We may conclude, for example, that the boy who does not finish his work, becomes distracted, and gets off-task may have ADHD. However, he may in fact have a learning disability, which causes him to have difficulty with the assigned task and in order to avoid it, he engages in some distraction, gets off task, and fails to finish the work. Overt behavior may thus not be the best guide (Flick, 1998b).

THE NEUROPSYCHOLOGICAL DIAGNOSTIC APPROACH

The usual approach for neuropsychologists is to orchestrate a complex battery of tests to measure an array of symptoms. Then, through a process of ruling-in specific conditions and ruling-out others, the initial symptom picture becomes clearer. Since the behavior of children in their natural environment is of prime concern, the goal is to present neuropsychological tasks similar to those on which each child must ultimately function. In the case of any child with a disability, measures of attention—both simple and complex—are essential. As noted by Barkley (1990, 2000), "attention plays a critical role in the neuropsychological assessment of children with developmental, learning, or other neuropsychological problems because it underlies the very capacity of children to undergo any form of psychological

testing." In addition, measures of behavioral response inhibition would also be needed to document the child's impulsive style. Estimates of activity level, organizational skills, cognitive flexibility, social-emotional development, visual-motor skills, and a general capacity to adapt to situational changes are all important in documenting behavior problems.

Various forms of organic brain dysfunction may also involve attentional and behavioral response systems, which means that we may see ADHD-like behavior in neuropsychological cases of epilepsy, head injury, structural brain lesions, and other conditions.

Several research reports outlined by Flick (1998b) have been written on the use of specific neuropsychological test batteries to evaluate children with behavior problems. These studies have focused on assessment of frontal lobe functions and other neuropsychological skills using simple measures such as the Wisconsin Card Scoring Test, verbal fluency tests, and attentional (continuous performance, or CPT) tests. In one study, a battery of tests was used that not only looked at frontal lobe (anterior brain) functions but also included a variety of other measures of IQ, reading skill, and verbal memory, as well as an assessment of attentional and impulsivity factors. The idea that disturbances in frontal lobe functions may be related to impulse control and may be responsible for the kind of cognitive impairments noted with ADHD was supported. The conclusion was that inability to control, direct, and sustain attention appears as a core deficiency of ADHD but not of impulsivity. However, others believe that behavioral inhibition reflects the core difficulty, not attention problems. Barkley (1997) suggests that the problems of self-control may warrant renaming ADHD as a "developmental disorder of self-control." A study supporting Barkley's theory was conducted by Nicpon, Wodrich, and Kurpius (2004).

SPECIFIC TESTS VERSUS TEST BATTERIES

As Barkley (1997) has noted, "over the past 50 years, the view of attention as a single, unitary construct has given way to theories of attention as being multidimensional." Tests such as the Bender-Gestalt quickly became accepted as diagnostic instruments for "organacity," but with an abundance of research studies, it became clear that a simple test such as the Bender-Gestalt should not be used as a screening instrument for organic

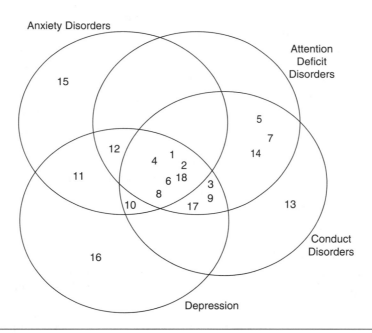

Symptomatic Behavior Characteristic	Attention Deficit	Anxiety Disorder	Depression	Conduct Disorder
1 Poor concentration	X	X	X	X
2 Restless	X	X	?	X
3 Fails to complete tasks	X		X	X
4 Day dreams	X	X	X	X
5 Impulsive	X			X
6 Poor sleep	X	X	X	X
7 Aggressive	?		?	X
8 Mood disturbance	X	X	X	X
9 Poor self concept	X		X	X
10 Quiet and withdrawn	?		X	
11 Guilt over transgressions		X	X	
12 Memory problems	X	X	X	
13 Stealing/lying				X
14 Poor social skills	X			X
15 Fearful/avoidance	?	X	?	
16 Crying	?	?	X	
17 Sensation seeking (high risk)	X		?	X
18 Difficulty focusing on task	X	?	?	?

Note: X = symptom usually present; ? = symptom possible; Blank = symptom not usually present.

FIGURE 7.1

Source: Flick (1998b). Reprinted with permission.

dysfunction. It was, however, found to be a useful addition to a battery of tests where each test would assess a specific brain-behavior relationship. In the evaluation of complex organically based problems, test batteries such as the Reitan-Indiana Neuropsychological Test Battery and the later-developed Luria-Nebraska Neurological Test Battery may be more useful than single tests alone. Many variations of these batteries as well as numerous other very specific batteries have been developed. For example, one battery has been proposed to evaluate patients exposed to toxic materials. To date, however, no specific battery has been developed for the assessment of ADHD or any other behavior disorders (Flick, 1998b). Various tests to measure attention have been discussed by Barkley (1997, 2000); Baron, Fennell, and Voeller (1995) have suggested basic domains of function that are typically assessed in a child neuropsychological examination, and they then listed commonly used neuropsychological tests in the evaluation of attention-deficit disorder within a broader context of a learning disability.

Many problems have been discussed with regard to the traditional static test batteries, which may be lacking in theory-based constructs as well as being poorly referenced to real-life criteria. Consequently, neuropsychological test batteries that cover a broad range of functions and have sufficient flexibility to include assessment of the many varied associated conditions are preferred.

Neuropsychological intervention with children has been reviewed in depth by Hunter and Donders (2007). A review of the NEPSY by Ahmad and Warriner (2001) describes a developmental neuropsychological assessment that provides a flexible approach to evaluating the neuropsychological development of children ages 3 to 12. The NEPSY is divided into five "functional domains," which include a pool of tests that describes (1) attention and executive functions, (2) language, (3) visual-spatial processing, (4) sensorimotor, and (5) memory/learning. Korkman (1999) notes that the NEPSY was developed by integrating Luria's concepts of functional (brain) systems and the principle of specifying primary and secondary deficits along with contemporary views on child neuropsychological traditions. Korkman, Kemp, and Kirk (2001) review studies on learning disorders (including dyslexia), developmental language disorders, attention disorders, and comorbidity problems. Korkman and Peltomoa (1991) used the patterns of NEPSY test results to predict attention problems for

children at school, as did Fahey (2006); Till and colleagues (2001) found that children (ages 3 to 7 years) of mothers exposed to organic solvents during pregnancy showed a poorer outcome on the NEPSY on those tests reflecting receptive and expressive language and graphomotor ability. In general, the NEPSY has been shown to be sensitive to a wide range of neuropsychological impairment of the brain.

A MULTIDISCIPLINARY EVALUATION

The many variations of attention-deficit/hyperactivity disorder (i.e., ADHD) provide an example of a disorder that involves multidisciplinary evalation. It is clear that any neuropsychological evaluation that attempts to assess the characteristics of this disorder must take into consideration the following factors:

1. ADHD is a complex disorder that has, in itself, many facets or variations.
2. ADHD has more basic subtypes than those described in DSM-IV.
3. The concept of attention has several subcategories; the concept of behavioral inhibition may likewise be subdivided.
4. ADHD is a developmental disorder that changes over the life span. Thus, for comparative purposes and in order to utilize the deficit approach to neuropsychological assessment, we must be familiar with normal neuropsychological and general behavioral development.
5. ADHD also involves situational components in which some of the variations are manifested—for example, when behavior problems appear only in school or the reverse.
6. Knowledge of comorbid conditions as adjunctive problems frequently associated with ADHD is essential.

Although the focus has been on the evaluation of ADHD, other behavior disorders could easily be substituted.

As Strauss, Sherman, and Spreen (2006) so eloquently pointed out, the current emphasis on neuropsychological evaluations (especially for the learning disabled child) is not concerned with localization issues or even with determining that there is demonstrable brain dysfunction. The primary concern in the evaluation of the child with LD, as it would be for the child with any behavior problem, is to document strengths and weaknesses as they relate to the real-life issues of learning or adapting to the environment. The patterns thus obtained on neuropsychological testing would shed some light on the direction and overall thrust of treatment intervention and habilitation for the child.

The sections that follow present many of the currently accepted neuropsychological and psychological tests administered to children. Those used by a particular school may, however, vary and might not be included.

Components of the Neuropsychological Assessment

The various tests that typically comprise the neuropsychological test battery to assess children with behavioral/emotional problems may depend upon each clinician's choice. A comprehensive guide is provided by Vanderploeg (1999). In this book, various categories of functions are emphasized in the test battery. These specific functions relate to the numerous deficits and problems associated with various disorders. A single diagnosis or multiple diagnoses can thus be rendered. A wide range of functions are assessed to allow the psychologist to not only rule in the primary disorder, but also rule out associated disorders and/or mimic syndromes. F-Foldi (2004) has suggested the use of neuropsychological evaluations for environmental interventions with school-aged children who have behavior and learning disorders. It was also suggested that the assessment of the child's abilities, related to brain functions, be integrated with behavioral data gathered in the home (by parents) and in school (by teachers).

The following categories of functions are generally addressed by the neuropsychological assessment: (1) ability, (2) achievement, (3) executive control, (4) visual-motor skills, (5) motor skills, (6) memory, (7) attentional skills, (8) self-concept/self-esteem, (9) social skills, (10) visual-spatial skills, (11) language skills, and (12) behavioral-emotional assessment specific for each disorder. Table 7.5 presents a list of tests commonly used in the diagnosis of various behavioral/emotional disorders. This list is not exhaustive, and clinicians may wish to use other procedures, about which they may have greater familiarity, as well as other clinical proce-

dures such as projective tests to evaluate emotional and behavioral factors.

For a more in-depth discussion for most of these tests, see other references in testing such as Aylward (1994) and Domino and Domino (2006) or specific test manuals for additional technical information. Educators may wish to consult a resource reviewing norm-referenced tests used in the assessment of ability, achievement, and behavioral assessment of children (McCauley & Swisher, 1984). For a more detailed discussion of the tests listed for attention-deficit disorder, see Flick (1998b).

The Diagnostic Process

The complex diagnostic process that is used to make a complete and accurate evaluation of a child's presenting problems (at school and/or home) and then to formulate a comprehensive individualized therapeutic program for clinical management of the child's behavior is shown in Figure 7.2 (Flick, 1998b, 2000). There may be one or more presenting problems that significantly affect the child's performance and behavior in school and, perhaps, the behavior at home. While an important objective of this process is formulation of the primary, secondary, and tertiary diagnosis, the evaluation process also gives the clinician an overall picture of the child's strengths and weaknesses, which are incorporated into the individualized treatment program of behavior management and other clinical procedures. This treatment program will most likely have behavior modification components; it may or may not include a medication regimen (which would be coordinated by the child physician); it will include mechanisms to monitor and evaluate progress. Specific problem areas and symptomatic behaviors become targets for change.

It should be noted that this diagnostic process centers around a clinical evaluation of the child outside of the school setting, typically conducted by a private clinical psychologist or neuropsychologist. It is often completed independent of any assessment coordinated by the child's school. Thus, medical and psychosocial treatments are frequently conducted through private practitioners with the goal of including home and school behaviors in the treatment program. It should also be noted that this evaluation, in contrast to evaluation by schools, is designed for clinical purposes on which clinical treatment will be based.

TABLE 7.5 Selected Tests Used to Assess Behavior Disorders

Test[a]	Assessment Time (minutes)	Content Area	Age Range	Diagnostic Targets
WISC-IV	50–85	Cognitive ability	(6 to 16–11)	General
WASI*	15–30	Cognitive ability	(6–89)	General
WPPSI-R	30–60	Cognitive ability	(3 to 7–3)	General
WRAT-4*	15–30	Cognitive—achievement in reading, spelling, and math	(5–75)	General
PPVT-IV*	10–15	Listening comprehension	(5–75)	General
LDDI	10–20	Intrinsic processing	(8 to 17–11)	General
Berry VMI*	10–15	Visual-motor, visual-spatial, nonverbal abilities	(3+)	ADHD, general
SSRS	15–20	Social skills, problem behaviors, academic competence (parent/teacher forms)	(5–12)	BD, CD, ODD, PDD
RCDS	10	Depression	(8–12)	D, BD
RADS	5–10	Depression	(6–19)	D, BD
RCMAS	5–10	Anxiety	(7–17)	A, OCD
CAFAS	10	Aggression, conduct problems	(7–17)	PDD, BD
CBCL*	10–17	Internalizing/externalizing disorders—parent	(4–18)	ODD, BD, PDD, A/D
TRF*	10–17	Internalizing/externalizing disorders—teachers	(4–18)	ODD, BD, PDD, A/D
K-SADS*	30–40	Broad spectrum of psychiatric disorders except PDD and LD	(6–18)	Affective, psychotic, anxiety, and behavior disorders
CRS*	15–20	ADHD symptoms (parent and teacher forms)	(3–17)	ADHD, LD, PDD
BASC-2	10–20	Maladaptive behaviors	(8–11)	ADHD, ODD, CD, A, D
ADDES	15–20	ADHD-I, I, & H (parent and teacher forms)	(4–20)	ADHD
DBRS	10	Symptoms of ADHD, ODD, CD	(5–10)	ADHD, CD, ODD
PHCSCS	30	Self-concept	(9–18)	General
WRAML	45–60	Memory	(5–17)	General
WJ-R(Ach)	50–60	Academic achievement in reading, reading comprehension, math, and written language	(2–95)	General
TOPS-R	45	Problem solving	(6–12)	General
TOKEN	20–30	Language, following direction	(3–12.5)	General
DSI	15–20	Dyslexia	(6–21)	General
BRIEF	25–35	Executive functions	(5–18)	ADHD, CD, TS, TBI, PDD
TGMD-2	15–20	Gross motor skills	(3 to 10–11)	LD, ADHD
TAP	5–10	Auditory processing skills	(5–10)	LD, ADHD
GADS	5–10	Asperger's behavior problems	(3–22)	AS, PDD
CARS	10–15	Autistic vs. DD	(2+)	PDD, Autism
ABI*	20–25	MR adaptive behavior	(6 to 18–11)	General
CDS	5–10	Severe behavior problems	(5–22)	CD
PKBS-2	8–12	Social skills/problem behaviors	(3–6)	General

TABLE 7.5 Selected Tests Used to Assess Behavior Disorders (continued)

Test[a]	Assessment Time (minutes)	Content Area	Age Range	Diagnostic Targets
THS	30–43	Handwriting skills	(5–11)	LD, ADHD
ABS-Si2	15–30	Coping skills/social adaptation	(3 to 18–11)	General
Vineland	20–60	Functional daily living skills, classroom and interview forms	(3 to 12–11) Classroom	General
NEPSY	45–120	Neuropsychological development of attention/executive language, sensorimotor, visual-spatial, memory and learning functions	(3–4 to 5–12)	LD, ADHD, TBI, PDD
SCAN-C	20–45	Auditory processing perception	(5 to 11–11)	LD, ADHD
ADD-H*	10–15	Attention, hyperactivity, social skills, and oppositional behavior ratings by teacher and parent	(5–12)	ADHD, LD, TBI, BD, ODD, CD
ACPT	25	Auditory vigilance	(6–11)	ADHD
Conners CPT-II	14	Visual problems	(6+)	ADHD, LD, TBI, BD, ODD, CD
Conners K-CPT	7.5	Visual attention problems	(4–5)	ADHD, LD, TBI, BD, ODD, CD
TOVA	25	Distractability and impulsivity	(4–19)	ADHD, LD, TBI
TOVA-A	25	Attention and auditory processing problems	(6–19)	ADHD, LD, TBI
IVA	13	Auditory/visual CPT	(6+)	ADHD, LD, TBI
CMDQ	30–60	Developmental questionnaire	(3–17)	ODD, CD, A, D, TS, BD

[a]The complete names of these tests are found in Table A.3 in Appendix A.
*Screening battery (total time: parents (2 3/4 hours); teachers (about 45 minutes); clinical (1 1/2 hours).

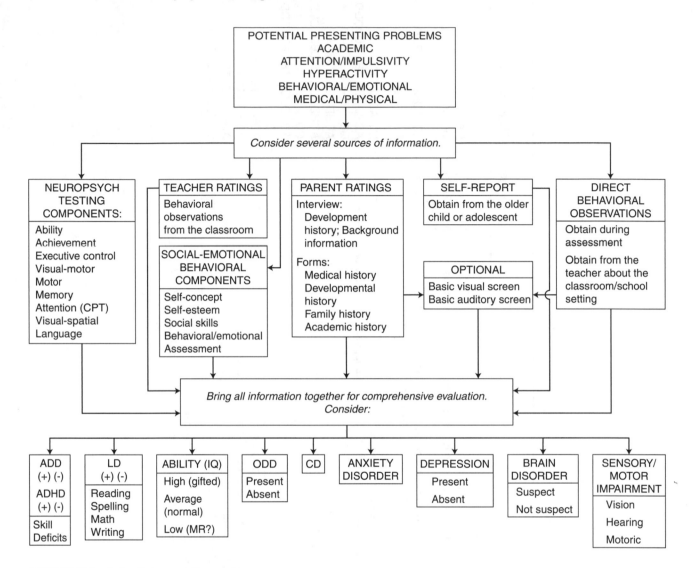

FIGURE 7.2 Potential presenting problems.
Source: Flick (1998b). Reprinted with permission.

To begin, it is essential for the clinician to obtain information from several sources, including the child's parents and teachers (at school, at music lessons, in Sunday school), as well as coaches for sports activities, and, of course, through self-ratings from older children. Observations during a direct interview and rating forms completed by the parents provide parental input. This information will include the child's medical history (e.g., seizures, head trauma, medications), devel-opmental milestones, family medical history (e.g., regarding possible familial genetic disorders), and the child's academic history. All of this information can be invaluable in raising suspicions about certain diagnoses or in making hypotheses to be considered and ruled in or out with test procedures. Then, combining this information with results from a wide range of test procedures, the clinician is able to formulate a pattern of strengths and weaknesses as well as assets and deficits that either support or negate a "suspected" diagnosis. Independent observations in the classroom (or other schoollike settings) would certainly help to diagnose and document behavior disorders because those settings tend to elicit many of these types of problematic behaviors.

Note that the self-reporting data and one-on-one interview of the child are especially critical when evaluating older children or adolescents. As they get older, children can provide more valid and reliable information about their behavior, especially about externalizing (acting-out) problems. Direct behavioral observations during the testing session provide a wealth of information about how the child copes with easy or difficult material, whether a basic visual or hearing problem may exist, and information about many other issues related to general maturation, language, communication, self-concept, attitudes toward academic tasks, coordination problems, arousal level, and potential neurological problems.

Assessment of behavioral/emotional characteristics provides the last component; such an assessment reflects whether the child presents evidence of externalizing problems (e.g., aggression, defiance, conduct disorders) or internalizing problems (e.g., anxiety, obsessive-compulsive tendencies, depression).

Once all the data and evidence have been gathered, a number of diagnostic conditions may be considered based on several factors: the general background information; parent, teacher, and self-ratings; behavior observations at home, school, and in assessment situations; and, of course, the neuropsychological test data. Typically, more than one diagnostic condition is present; for example, with ADHD, it is the exception for a child to manifest only that disorder. Thus, the implication for treatment is almost always that a multimodal program will be needed to deal with a complex pattern of symptoms and problems. This would be consistent with the problem-oriented treatment intervention approach adopted in this book.

Each separate component of the behavior/problem pattern must be addressed. While medications are often very helpful, they are generally ineffective with the aggression problems related to oppositional deficit disorder (ODD) and conduct disorder (CD). Likewise, medications have little effect on learning disabilities (as we're reminded by the rhyme, "Pills do not teach skills"), and many children with ADHD or other behavioral-emotional problems almost always need basic skill development through training. Specific behavioral training procedures (for parents and sometimes teachers as well as for the child) will be used to address some of these skill deficits.

An individualized, multimodal treatment program may thus be developed to focus on the child's deficits (perhaps including organizational skills, learning strategies, training in following directions, and development of social and study skills) and to evaluate progress periodically. This program will also include the use of appropriate and targeted medications when needed, as well as appropriate targeted behavioral interventions in school. Inappropriate problem behaviors may be the primary targets for behaviors that need to be addressed in the home situation.

INTERPRETATION OF TEST DATA

Much information is often collected in the evaluation of a child. The first step in the interpretation of this data is to list all of the tests given with their respective standard scores or percentile ranks. This will allow for a direct comparison of the strengths and weaknesses across a variety of dimensions assessed, and the development of a profile for this child.

FUNCTIONAL IMPAIRMENT

Once the overall pattern has been determined and the clinician arrives at a diagnosis, there is the question about whether or not there is functional impairment. This means that even though a child carries a specific diagnostic label (i.e., a DSM-IV diagnostic number), this does not mean that the student may show impairment in school or elsewhere. The degree of functional impairment is critical and this may be assessed with an instrument such as the Brief Impairment Scale (BIS) by Bird et al. (2005). Thus, while a clinical assessment may provide a diagnostic label, the degree of impairment must be considered. This score will reflect how well the student has adapted to the demands of school. It also points to the importance of considering which problematic behaviors are of prime concern and must be addressed in the school or classroom environment. Again, this approach would be consistent with a specific behavior problem orientation in the school setting.

SUMMARY

It is important for teachers to know basic information about psychological/neuropsychological testing: the components of this assessment are discussed with a selected review of tests and rating scales that may be employed. Obviously, it is not possible to cover all of the procedures that might be used. However, basic test characteristics such as reliability and validity are described, and a rationale is provided for using the neuropsychological assessment. While the evaluation is important for clinical purposes (in private practice) and for classification (in schools), the prime function of the behavior intervention will involve utilization of symptom patterns and specific problem behaviors. There is considerable symptom overlap and typically there is evidence of multiple diagnoses, which usually means that a multicomponent treatment program is needed.

DISCUSSION QUESTIONS

1. What is the first step in dealing with difficult to manage children?
2. What are some of the things that IDEA 2004 says about evaluations?
3. How is a differential diagnosis made?
4. How is a family medical history important in the diagnostic process?
5. What should a brief battery of psychological tests measure?
6. What are some of the commonly used rating scales?
7. What are some of the commonly used projective tests?
8. Which two measures reflect the adequacy of any objective test?
9. Can a test be valid if it is not reliable? Explain.
10. Why must symptom overlap be considered when diagnosing a behavior disorder?
11. Test batteries that evaluate behavior problems have focused primarily on which area of the brain?
12. The five functional domains of the NEPSY include tests that describe which areas?
13. The diagnostic process may provide not only a multicomponent breakdown but also a picture of which functions of the child that may be incorporated in his or her treatment program?

CHAPTER 8

Functional Behavioral Assessment

Overview
- The functional behavioral assessment approach
- Conducting a functional behavioral assessment
- Formal versus functional behavioral assessment
- Functional behavioral assessment model
- Do's and don'ts of functional behavioral assessment

Case History

Kevin is a 7-year-old second grader with a full scale IQ of 107 who has been referred because of his avoidance of academic tasks, especially paper and pencil tasks. Classified as EBD, Kevin also shows problem behaviors such as aggression, critical verbalizations to peers and teachers as well as destruction of property and "playing with his work materials." Kevin has told his teacher that he has some difficulty seeing letters that are too small and too close together. He refuses to do his work. *What would you do?*

The functional behavioral assessment approach (FBA) is a multifaceted process that focuses on the function or purpose of the problem behavior in relation to the environment. Sometimes the same behavior may have functions that are quite different. For example, Britney and Mark may both blurt out answers in math class without raising their hand. The function of Mark's behavior might be to gain attention from the teacher, but Britney may wish to escape the written work that follows the math questions. Sending each child out of the room would have different effects: Mark would be deprived of the teacher's attention (withdrawal of a positive reinforcer), while Britney would be allowed to escape the written math work (avoidance of the unpleasant written work). While Mark would be punished for blurting out, Britney would be reinforced for it. This would not take into consideration the novel and stimulating reinforcement each child may receive when sent out of the room.

The FBA can provide the structure needed to get at the function of a behavior and to help devise a behavioral intervention plan (BIP) to change the inappropriate behavior into one that is more appropriate and desirable. The FBA can be an informal process that may be employed by the classroom teacher to assess and intervene proactively when the challenging behavior first appears (Scott & Nelson, 1999b), or it can be a formal process that is used by the Individual Educational Plan (IEP) team to design interventions for students who exhibit severe behavior problems that either impede their own learning or that of their classmates, or that pose a threat to themselves or others (Chandler & Dahlquist, 2002; Crone & Horner, 2003).

THE FBA AND BIP PROCESS

Whether used formally or informally, the FBA facilitates the planning of the BIP. The following seven steps are involved in conducting the FBA:

1. IEP team is sent a letter or e-mail inviting them to an FBA meeting.
2. IEP team meets to define the identified student's target behavior and an FBA. Parent completes referral and gives permission for the process.
3. IEP team does FBA, analyzes data, and begins BIP.
4. IEP team meets to review FBA and to finalize BIP.
5. IEP team reviews FBA and finalizes BIP.

6. BIP is implemented; behavioral data are collected.
7. Teacher and staff meet to review data and modify BIP if necessary.

The ultimate goal is to formulate and test a hypothesis about the function of the student's inappropriate behavior. This hypothesis should generate a BIP that aims to replace inappropriate behaviors with appropriate ones that serve the same function. For example, when Dustin receives negative attention for defiant behavior such as refusing to do his work, his teacher may respond by withholding attention and might instead teach him how he can get positive attention in a more appropriate way. Dustin's teacher may then construct some situations to facilitate successful outcomes so that Dustin's newly developed behavior may be strengthened through reinforcement (Crone & Horner, 2003). Although teachers may find it difficult to withdraw attention to inappropriate behavior, the plan would be to minimize negative attention to inappropriate behavior (refusal to work) and initially lavish attention for appropriate behaviors. This plan can be complex as there may be more than one reason for resistance or refusal to work.

Special education teachers, as well as those in general education, are often confronted with students who deploy challenging behaviors. An efficient way to address these problem behaviors and to maintain continuity of instructions is through a five-step informal FBA procedure that can be used to develop a BIP for those students whose behavior is problematic. This process allows either teachers or the IEP team to gather and record information that will help to develop a theory about the function of the student's misbehavior and ultimately help to maximize the effectiveness and efficiency of the BIP.

The problem-solving components of an FBA will have clearly defined outcomes that allow educators to view the situation from the student's perspective. Five steps are involved:

1. Define the problem behavior.
2. Identify specific events, times, and situations as triggers.
3. Obtain background information.
4. Identify consequences.
5. Develop a theory/hypothesis about the misbehavior.

Sample forms documenting the five steps in the FBA are found in Appendix C. Now, let's look at each step in more detail.

Defining the Problem Behavior

Clear, observable, and specific terms must be used so that the problem behavior is recognizable to all and not subject to any misinterpretations. Ask specific questions: What is the problem? What are the details? If there are several problems, prioritize them and their target behaviors. For example, stating, "Joe is aggressive and runs away" is vague and unclear. For the BIP, it would be better to say "Joe runs out of the classroom, snatching and destroying materials." The outcome should be a clearly written specific description of the problem behavior. A sample form is included in Appendix C to record this information.

Before an FBA can be implemented, it is important to have a precise description of the behavior that is causing learning and/or discipline problems and to define and write about that behavior in concrete terms that are easy to communicate and simple to measure and ultimately to record. If descriptions of behavior are vague, it is difficult to determine appropriate interventions. Some examples of precise and specific description of problem behavior are as shown below.

It may be necessary to observe carefully the student's behavior in different settings (classes, recess, lunchroom, etc.) and during different types of activities. This can be done by conducting interviews with the student's teachers and other staff to make a precise list of those situations in which the problem behavior occurs. Once the problem behavior has been adequately defined and precisely described, a plan may be developed to conduct an FBA in order to determine the functions of the student's behavior. This can then lead to formulating a BIP and then implementation of the BIP.

Identifying Specific Events, Times, and Situations

Look for patterns that may indicate what triggers or sets-off the problem behavior. This can help to identify the circumstances surrounding the misbehavior, indicating when it does and does not occur. These circumstances might include the physical environment, time of day, subject matter, or other trigger events. When challenging problem behavior does not appear to occur consistently under the same circumstances, the educator may need to investigate the situation more thoroughly using the Antecedent-Behavior-Consequence (ABC) form or the scatter plot to formally record basic data. Other supporting data may include interviews, ratings, and checklists. Some key questions may be asked:

Who was there?

What was going on at the time?

What happened just before the behavior occurred?

When and where does the behavior occur?

Information on the resultant outcome should then reveal when the problem behavior is most likely to occur and when it is least likely to occur in the student's daily schedule. A sample form is provided in Appendix B to record this data.

Obtaining Background Information

This component should take into consideration medical, physical, and social issues as well as diet, sleep patterns, stressful events, and prior interventions. Such factors may clearly contribute to the occurrence of the behavior and need to be recorded. A sample form is shown in Appendix C. The outcomes should then specify the biological/physiological, psychological, and environmental/social factors that may be associated with the problem behavior.

Problem Behavior	Precise and Specific Description
Allen is aggressive.	• Allen hits other students during history class and at recess.
Mark is disruptive.	• Mark tells inappropriate jokes during math class that results in classmates laughing.
Robert is hyperactive.	• Robert is out of his seat in most of his classes. • Robert blurts out answers in most of his classes. • Robert completes about 50 percent of his assigned seatwork.

Source: Adapted with permission from http://cecp.air.org/fba/ problembehaviorconducting.htm.

Identifying the Consequences

When the consequences of a problem behavior are identified, it becomes possible to determine what appropriate behavior may be used as a replacement and what the desired consequences might be. Consequences maintain behavior as well as what happens after the behavior to increase the probability of the occurrence of the problem behavior. This process will help to promote a positive behavior change. For example, Dylan may impulsively blurt out questions and answers to obtain the teacher's attention; this may be noticed especially when the teacher is giving out assignments. The teacher's plan is to ask Dylan to help pass out materials when she assigns work so that he can gain the attention he desires without blurting out. A sample form is included in Appendix C to record this information, which documents the function of the problem behavior and identifies some of the potential strategies and interventions that may be used to deal with it.

Developing a Theory or Hypothesis

After identifying the behavior and the events occurring before and after it, the teacher may be able to make an educated guess about what the student is getting from the problem behavior. One or more summary statements describe why the student engages in the challenging problem behavior. Some questions might be asked: What is the purpose or intent of the behavior? What does the student get out of the behavior? A sample form in Appendix C may be used to describe the purpose or function of the behavior—from attention or escape to some tangible reward. Educators need to look at what is actually happening following a consequence, not what they think is happening. What might be a punishment for one student may be a positive reinforcement for another. For example, if Dylan is only reprimanded for blurting out, his frequency of blurting out may stay the same or even increase, thereby supporting an attention factor maintaining or reinforcing the problem behavior. When attention is removed and his blurting out decreases, this may confirm the attentional consequence as reinforcing. Even though it may be negative or unpleasant attention, it is still attention, and it can maintain or even increase the inappropriate behavior. The outcome here is that one or more hypotheses

may be generated that describe specific behaviors that occur in specific situations with the consequences that maintain the problem behavior in that situation.

The information that is compiled in this five-step FBA may be recorded on the FBA summary form in Appendix C. This process may help the classroom teacher to formulate a BIP regarding what changes can be made in the classroom to facilitate the occurrence of more appropriate student behavior (Ruef et al., 1998).

Teachers who know how to use the five-step FBA can facilitate classroom management for students with problem behaviors. For students with identified disabilities, the FBA and BIP forms may be included in each student's IEP. Formal FBA and BIP are generated by a team that may include teachers, parents, medical professionals, counselors, therapists, and others from the community.

The typical five-step process may vary with each student and no single procedure or assessment tool will provide for all of the outcomes in a valid and reliable way. Assessment methods may therefore vary on a continuum from *low-end techniques* (e.g., interviews) to *high-end techniques* (e.g., direct manipulation of variables) as in test instruments. The IEP team members may be in the best position to decide which assessment methods may be sufficient to gather and record information in order to develop a theory or hypothesis about the function of a particular problem behavior. The IEP team can therefore identify those methods that will clarify the pertinent factors or variables that affect the student's behavior. Perhaps this process will involve starting at the lowest levels of assessment methods and working up to arrive at a point where factors or variables that influence behavior can be changed to produce socially acceptable behavior. This assessment process can be repeated until a positive behavior change has been sustained over a sufficient period. With this procedure, improvement in behavior may therefore be facilitated.

As illustrated by this case study, not all students who present problems in the classroom need to receive psychological evaluations and not all of them need a functional behavioral assessment. Some students may respond to simple behavioral techniques that may allow a teacher to avoid going through the process of referring and evaluating a student for special education. However, the use of functional behavioral assessment remains an

Case Study

General Behavioral Problems

Marvin is a 9-year-old third grader who presents no serious behavior problems but annoys his teacher, Ms. Hicks, when he consistently "forgets" to bring his homework back to school. Ms. Hicks has tried several things to help him. She has checked Marvin's understanding of the work assigned, has tried to determine whether he dislikes writing, and has even enlisted his mother's help in getting him to put the homework in a special folder so that it will always get back to school. Marvin explains that he just forgets to do the work, even though he has written down the assignment and knows how to do the work. Ms. Hicks was about to refer Marvin for a psychological evaluation and FBA when another teacher suggested a motivation technique. Ms. Hicks would allow Marvin to get a token each day that he brings his completed homework back to school. At the end of the week, the entire class would get a popcorn party and no homework if Marvin has at least three tokens. The first week he brought in his homework on 4 days. All of his classmates excitedly congratulated him and provided much encouragement for the next week as they enjoyed their popcorn party. The next 2 weeks, Marvin was again successful on 4 days. The criterion was gradually increased (i.e., with progressive increased demands for percentage of homework completed) as Marvin got better at completing his homework. His classmates would remind him each day about the popcorn party, and Marvin now had to return homework for all school days. He met the criterion and seemed to enjoy getting the tokens each day, earning a party for the whole class, and receiving compliments from his classmates as well as from Ms. Hicks. Although he was not a student in special education and did not have a "disability," Marvin's response to this motivational approach was positive.

important tool to use for many students. Now, the important thing about functional behavioral assessment is the problem behavior and its characteristics.

Challenging behavior is particularly common among young children, both with and without disabilities. These problem behaviors may include aggression, self-injury, repetitive movements, destruction of property, screaming, general noncompliance, fidgeting, withdrawal, and inattention. Many of these behaviors are actually similar to those of typically developing children except that the frequency, intensity, and persistence are well beyond what is considered part of normal development (National Research Council, 2001). Such behaviors can become a serious problem when they interfere with learning, affect the development of social skills, or become harmful to the child or to others (Chandler & Dahlquist, 2002).

UNDERSTANDING THE FUNCTION OF BEHAVIOR

Functional behavioral assessment is based on the understanding that all behaviors, whether appropriate or inappropriate, serve a *function* for the child. For example, when Mark grabs a ball from John, it does

What the Law Says

The Individuals with Disabilities Education Act (IDEA) is a federal law that was passed in 2004 and today serves as a guide for all state special education regulations. Schools are thus obligated by law to provide functional behavioral assessment (FBA) for students whose problem behaviors interfere with their education or the education of others.

not necessarily mean that he is "aggressive" or that his parents do not discipline him at home. These are possible misunderstandings of behavior (Chandler & Dahlquist, 2002). FBA assumes that the problem behavior is *learned*—as is all behavior—and that it occurs and persists because it serves some function for the child. In our example, Mark grabs the ball because it got him the desired object, the ball. Such problem behavior can now be addressed with the ultimate goal of teaching Mark appropriate ways to get the ball.

Many interventions used in today's classrooms are selected because they are familiar or popular. *Punitive* interventions such as the time-out or the removal of

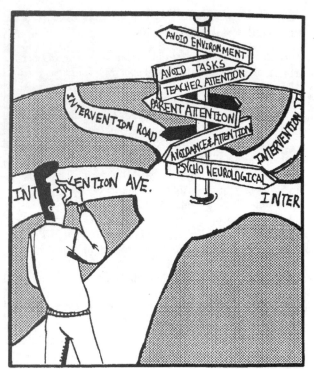

WITHOUT A FUNCTIONAL ASSESSMENT MAP TO GUIDE HIM, MR. SMITH IS UNSURE OF WHICH ROAD TO TRAVEL.

information will lead to the development of positive interventions designed to prevent and remediate the problem behavior (March & Horner, 2002).

The Basic Functions of Behavior

The two basic functions of any problem behavior are (1) positive and (2) negative reinforcement, as shown in Figure 8.1. In the case of positive reinforcement, positive outcomes might include attention from others, control of a situation, getting food or other tangible objects as well as getting access to some individuals, activities, or materials. However, it is important to note that reinforcement is highly individualized and that what is punishing for one child may be reinforcing for another.

---

*Recently, this FBA with interventions has been termed positive behavioral support (PBS) (Buschbacker & Fox, 2003; Lucyshyn et al., 2002). The main goal of PBS is to prevent and change the inappropriate behavior and to provide support for the appropriate behavior.

privileges are two examples (Chandler et al., 1999). The use of such procedures may actually cause the inappropriate behavior to be either maintained or become worse because they do not address the underlying "function" of the inappropriate behavior. Horner and colleagues (2002), in reviewing research where FBA was used prior to intervention, noted that nonpunitive interventions were more positive and significantly reduced problem behavior.

Functional behavioral assessment is a proactive and positive tool that assesses and predicts problem behaviors. Subsequently, intervention strategies implemented can be based on the assessment information (Horner & Carr, 1997).* If behavior problems can be anticipated, they can be prevented by implementing strategies that address such behavior problems *before* they become an established pattern (Horner et al., 2002). The primary purpose of FBA is to identify the function, or reason, for the problem behavior; this

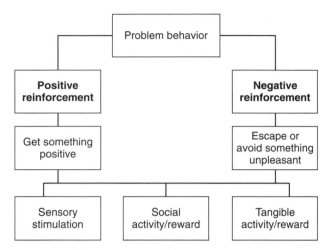

FIGURE 8.1   The two basic functions of problem behavior.
Source: Information from the Wisconsin Department of Public Instruction (2009).

For example, a verbal reprimand may serve as positive reinforcement for one child while being aversive reinforcement for another child.

A second function, negative reinforcement, occurs when the problem behavior results in escape or avoidance of something that is unpleasant. For example, Michael learns that screaming or slamming his books on the desk will remove him from a math class that he neither likes nor understands. Such misbehavior, which results in Michael being sent to the office, is exactly what he desires and this results in the problem behavior being reinforced. Thus, it is more important to pay attention to the *function* (getting out of math) of the behavior than its *form* (screaming/book slamming) when developing behavior intervention to control and replace the problem behavior.

However, another function of behavior is sensory stimulation or sensory regulation. This function is especially important when working with children who have ADHD or autism (Flick, 1998b), and it may also be a component in other disorders as well. The goal of sensory stimulation is to regulate (by increasing or decreasing) the level or type of sensory input in the environment, or to produce sensory stimulation. For example, if a boy with autism rejects touching or anything that is "gooey" like finger paint or whipped cream, he might act out aggressively when asked to touch such

substances. If he hits his teacher or pulls her hair, the teacher may move away, thus reinforcing the student for his aggressive behavior. By not having to touch the finger paints, he is reinforced and a reduction of tactile input is established. The problem behavior may then reoccur whenever the teacher tries to get him to use the finger paints.

This function might usually be subsumed either under positive or negative reinforcement functions. However, it might be considered a separate function since the child's behavior might result in an internal nonobservable change. According to some theories, behavior that serves the function of increasing stimulation (e.g., as it does in ADHD) may be more understandable. The sensory regulation or sensory stimulation function might occur when there is a difference between the type or amount of sensory input in the environment and the child's internal sensory needs. Such a disparity may occur within any sensory system—tactile, visual, olfactory (smell), auditory (hearing), gustatory (taste), proprioceptive (the relative position of parts of the body), and vestibular (sense of movement) (Emmons & Anderson, 2005). For example, some children with autism (or even ADHD) may act out—maybe by rocking back and forth or making vocal noises—during quiet time or a quiet activity such as reading. This behavior would serve the function of increasing stimulation during an activity (reading) that is basically passive and "quiet."

The sensory regulation or stimulation function might also occur when children have sensory stimulation problems where they are unable to correctly interpret and respond to sensory input (O'Riordan & Passetti, 2006; Walker, Colvin, & Ramsey, 1995). Such children may be hypersensitive to noise and may cover their ears when a siren is heard. In autism, behaviors such as "eye gouging" or "head banging" may be automatically reinforcing as they produce endorphins or other physiological stimulation of the nervous system (Berkson & Tupa, 2000; Shore & Iwata, 1999).

Thus, when a child's behavior regulates sensory input or produces sensory stimulation, the interventions must address that child's sensory needs. For example, in the case of the autistic child who finds touching finger paints aversive, the child might wear protective gloves or might use a crayon for drawing. Mueller, Moore, and Sterling-Turner (2005) note that conducting an FBA in the classroom can present a challenge regarding which environmental variables to evaluate. There have been no published studies that have looked at combinations of variables (e.g., escape *and* attention), compared to those being presented separately.

Some time ago, Carr (1977) suggested that interventions should address the function of behavior by teaching students to communicate their needs, thus allowing them to achieve the same function through more appropriate behavior. In short, their problem behaviors can be thought of as a form of communication as well as a way to control their environment. Interventions that teach children more appropriate ways to communicate their needs has been called *functional communication*, with its goal being to teach functionally equivalent appropriate behavior in place of the problem behavior (Newcomer & Lewis, 2004).

FBA prior to interventions that replaces problem behavior with more appropriate behavior has been well documented (Goldstein, 2002; Walker et al., 1998). It has also been used with children who have a variety of disabilities as well as with normal children (Kern & Dunlap, 1999). In fact, Horner and colleagues (2002) noted that the success of changing problem behavior was directly related to whether or not FBA was conducted first, thus suggesting an intervention plan that matched the function of the behavior.

Primary Functions of Problem Behavior

It is important to be familiar with the following possible functions of behavior when performing FBA:

- *Escape or avoidance*—avoiding a particular activity such as a class, an interaction with a specific person or group, or an unpleasant situation.
- *Justice or revenge*—getting back at a person or group for a real or imagined slight, sometimes on behalf of a friend or family member.
- *Acceptance and affiliation*—belonging or gaining acceptance to a group; seeking to impress members of a peer group the student hopes to gain.
- *Power or control*—wishing to dominate, be in charge, control the environment; refusing to follow rules or directions; refusing to participate in some activities.
- *Expression of self*—seeking to announce independence and/or individuality, to express a self-image.

- *Access to tangible rewards or personal gratification*—behaving so as to get tangible reinforcement (an item, money, or privilege); seeking to feel good or get immediate feedback or reward.
- *Sensory stimulation or sensory regulation*—wanting to increase or decrease level or type of sensory input to environment, or to produce sensory stimulation.
- *Play*—engaging in play activity instead of an assigned task; combining both escape and stimulation, such behavior may occur repeatedly with others or alone.
- *Seeking attention*—the desire to gain positive or negative attention from peers or teachers; this is the most commonly identified function.

Note: A behavior can have more than one function for two different students. Many behaviors have attention as a secondary function in addition to some other function. Identifying *attention* too frequently may lead to an inaccurate hypothesis if it is the only function considered.

The Functional Behavioral Assessment Components 1 through 5 shown in Appendix B can be used to assess the function of the behavior that will contribute to the development of a theory or a hypothesis about the behavior. Remember that any specific behavior may have more than one function. Teachers need to use this form to organize problem behaviors and their functions.

THE FUNCTIONAL BEHAVIORAL ASSESSMENT PROCESS

According to O'Neill and colleagues (1997) FBA is a "process for gathering information that can be used to maximize the effectiveness and efficiency of behavioral support." It not only reveals when a problem behavior might occur but also clarifies the consequences that have maintained that behavior. This is quite important. The U.S. Department of Education (1999, p. 45) identified five steps for conducting FBA:

1. Define the problem behavior and the conditions under which it occurs.

2. Gather information about the environment and the behavior. This might entail using interviews, questionnaires, review of records, rating scales, checklists, and direct observation to determine the events that precede and follow the behavior problem.

3. Develop a hypothesis about the function of the behavior.

4. Develop a behavioral intervention plan that will teach an appropriate behavior that serves the same function as the problem behavior. This will involve arranging the environment to prompt the desired behavior and to develop a plan to provide consequences for both desirable and undesirable behaviors.

5. Monitor the behavior to verify the hypotheses and to validate the intervention. The FBA is complete when the intervention is successful. If unsuccessful, return to step 2 and continue gathering information to develop another hypothesis about the function of the problem behavior.

Conducting a Functional Behavioral Assessment

A comprehensive review of the several components that make up the functional behavioral assessment was conducted by Fox and Gable (2004). There must be identification of the antecedents and consequences for the problem behavior. Antecedents serve as triggers for the problem behavior or set the stage for it. Consequences that are positive will increase and/or maintain the problem behavior; those that are aversive will decrease it. Among the factors that can influence a child's behavior are *setting events*—motivational and situational variables that can often determine how a child responds to antecedents and consequences (Chandler & Dahlquist, 2002). Setting events might include fatigue, being sick, having a fight, or having a change in routine. In general, setting events can be grouped into three factors: (1) biological, (2) environmental, and (3) social-emotional and situational factors. A setting event checklist can be found in Appendix B.

We next focus on the strategies and tools used to find the setting events, antecedents, and consequences that trigger and maintain both appropriate and problem behavior.

The Methods and Tools Needed to Conduct an FBA

There are two basic methods that are available to the IEP team to gather information: (1) indirect assessment and (2) direct assessment. Let's look at each one.

Indirect Assessment   The first step in a formal assessment is to accumulate indirect information. This may involve assessing a student's environment to better define the problem behavior and to identify the current supports for that behavior. Information is obtained about the conditions under which the behavior is and is not observed, as well as defining the target or desirable replacement behavior (Sugai et al., 2000). Typically, the initial referral will contain demographic information about the student, such as age, grade, and placement as well as a description of the problem behavior and the strategies that have been used in past attempts to deal with it (Chandler & Dahlquist, 2002).

The IEP team conducts interviews with individuals who have observed the problem behavior or who are familiar with the student. This may include teachers, aides, and other school personnel, as well as family members, therapists, counselors, and social workers. This information might better describe the problem behavior along with other factors that are never associated with it. For example, if Thomas never exhibits any of his problem behaviors while working on the computer, this would be important information. Such information, however, should also list the student's preferred activities (e.g., reading motorcycle magazines, playing computer games, and participating in sports), strengths (e.g., sense of humor, developing friendships, and knowledge of science), and skills (e.g., playing sports, drawing). These pieces of information may be useful in the establishment of motivation for the IEP (Chandler & Dahlquist, 2002).

It is important to obtain interview information from those who have observed the child's behavior problem, including parents, teachers, therapists, and others who know the child. These individuals can identify a different perspective on antecedents and setting events that occur before the behavior, and the consequences that follow it. Some instruments can be administered as well to get interviews with others. An example of a functional assessment interview is shown in Figure 8.2.

The functional analysis interview (FAI) is an interview protocol designed to obtain information about a child's problem behavior (O'Neill et al., 1997). This includes variables associated with the presence or absence of the problem behavior, the function of that behavior, and general information about the child, as well as those who interact with him/her. The interview takes about 45 to 90 minutes and has adequate reliability and

FUNCTIONAL ASSESSMENT INTERVIEW FORM

Interviewer(s) _Mr. Church_   Date _10/3_

Student(s) _Trish_

Respondent(s) _Ms. Pasillas_   Title _Paraprofessional_

1. Describe the behavior of concern: _Trish gets mad on playground and yells at other kids. She sometimes hits other students or kicks them. None of the kids want to play with her._

2. How often does the behavior occur? _It seems like every day._

2a. How long does it last? _Not long. I keep my eye on her and stop her before it gets out of hand._

2b. How intense is the behavior? _I don't think she has drawn blood, but she hits and kicks so hard I bet she bruises kids_

3. What is happening when the behavior occurs? _Trish wants to play with others who are already involved in a game._

4. When / where is the behavior most / least likely to occur? _It happens everywhere._

5. With whom is the behavior most / least likely to occur? _Usually with other girls. I don't think I remember her fighting with a boy._

FIGURE 8.2   Functional assessment interview form.

Source: Adapted with permission from http://cecp.air.org/fba/problembehavior2/appendixc.htm.

6. What conditions are most likely to precipitate ("set-off") the behavior? _When Trish doesn't get her way._

7. How can you tell the behavior is about to start? _She usually yells before she hits._

8. What usually happens after the behavior? Describe what happens according to adult(s), peers, and student responses. _When she starts yelling I usually make her stand by me for a while. If it is a major hit, I send her to the office. If it is a shove or something like that I usually just have her stand by me._

9. What is the likely function (intent) of the behavior; that is, why do you think the student behaves this way? What does the student get or avoid? _I think she does it to get her way._

10. What behavior(s) might serve the same function (see question 9) for the student that is appropriate within the social/environmental context? _She needs to learn to wait her turn, ask nicely, and control her temper. She needs to learn to make friends, too. Nobody wants to play with her._

11. What other information might contribute to creating an effective intervention plan (e.g., under what conditions does the behavior _not_ occur)? _She's pretty good when she is talking with me or when she is playing games that I supervise._

12. Who should be involved in planning and implementing the intervention plan? _I think I should. I'm the one out here with her. Also, Mr. Church seems to keep her under control while we're in the lunchroom._

FIGURE 8.2 (_continued_)

validity (O'Neill et al., 1997). A sample of this interview form is found in Appendix B.

The Questions About Behavioral Function (QABF) is a 25-item checklist where the rater indicates the frequency of the problem behavior across situations and addresses the message that is communicated through the problem behavior (Paclawskyj et al., 2000). Studies have documented the reliability and validity of the QABF (Paclawskyj et al., 2000).

The Functional Assessment Checklist for Teachers and Staff (FACTS) presents a series of questions that guide observations and are used to develop support plans following identification of the function of the behavior (March et al., 2000). A sample of this checklist is found in Appendix B.

The Problem Behavior Questionnaire presents a series of questions about the student to determine when the behavior occurs and which behavior is more troublesome. It also provides a profile that will assist the teacher in the formulation of an FBA and BIP (Scott & Nelson, 1999b). A sample of this questionnaire and the profile form is found in Appendix B.

The Motivation Assessment Scale (MAS) is a 16-item questionnaire that attempts to discover the function or motivations of the problem behavior (Durand & Crimmins, 1988). It is organized into four categories of reinforcement: (1) attention, (2) tangible, (3) escape, and (4) sensory factors. The MAS asks questions about the likelihood of a behavior occurring in a variety of situations (e.g., when presented with math problems). This scale has been noted to have poor interobserver reliability and limited utility (Paclawskyj et al., 2001).

These indirect methods are basically for screening; they are a good first step in conducting the FBA but they should not be the only step. These instruments will help to develop hypotheses about the things that trigger and support the problem behavior, as well as to suggest the function of the problem behavior. However, these hypotheses need to be verified with direct observation of the child in his or her natural environment.

Indirect Assessment Summary　After all of the information has been gathered, there are typically four factors that emerge. First, the setting events or establishing operations occur—those factors that can either facilitate the problem behavior or make it worse; such factors may include lack of sleep, diet, fatigue, social conflicts, and medical conditions. The setting events checklist in Appendix B provides guidelines.

Second, there are antecedent events that precede and appear to "trigger" the problem behavior. These may include (1) task demands (e.g., excessive homework, insufficient time), (2) instructional situations (e.g., work that is too hard, confusing instructions), or (3) peer or adult requests (e.g., "John, please complete that assignment before you go out to recess").

Third, the outcome of the problem behavior can fall into three categories: attention, escape/avoidance, or attempts to get something tangible.

Fourth, there is concern over the consequences for the problem behavior or an event that follows the behavior and reinforces or maintains it. After gathering such information, *direct observation* is needed to formulate the BIP.

Direct Assessment　While indirect assessment is an important tool to assess inappropriate problem behavior, direct assessment, or *direct observation*, is essential to ascertain the function or purpose of the problem behavior (Scott & Nelson, 1999b). Using direct assessment, educators try to obtain the "big picture" of the events or social interactions in the student's environment that both precede and follow the problem behavior.

The information obtained from direct assessment is obtained through observation and may come from several instruments. The two that are most commonly used are the ABC observation form (see Figure 8.3) and the scatterplot (see Figure 8.4). Educators have noted that such tools are invaluable for either formal or informal behavioral assessments.

The ABC observation form is typically divided into three columns: (1) the preceding events (*antecedents*), (2) the problem behavior (*behavior*), and (3) the events that follow the behavior (*consequence*). For example, during an observation period using the ABC form, an educator might note in the behavior column Terrance slams his math book and pencil on the desk and refuses to complete the assignment. The antecedent event was that the teacher asks students to open their math books and to complete problems 1 to 30 on page 18. The consequence was that Terrance was sent to the office. In this case Terrance escaped the demand of doing math problems and gave some indication as to his behavior problem. In this case it was hypothesized that Terrance

ABC OBSERVATION FORM

Student: _Cindy Adams_
Date(s) _Oct. 10 & 15, 2010_ Grade: _2_ School: _M.L..King Elementary_
Observer: _Janet Hoffman, Special ed. teacher_
Behavior of Concern: _Mars/destroys school property_

	Date: 10/10/10 Time: 9:25–10:10	Date: 10/10/10 Time: 1:05–1:45	Date: 10/15/10 Time: 9:25–10:10
CONTEXT OR CIRCUMSTANCES	Cindy is in Reading Group from 9:25–9:45, then working independently at a table with two other students.	Cindy is in Math Class. The teacher is giving examples of 2-digit subtraction on the board.	
ANTECEDENT (what happens just prior)	The students take their books and materials to the table. Students are to share a bucket of crayons.	The teacher asks for a volunteer to come to board and solve the problem. Cindy jumps out of seat and says aloud "Ooh, me, please."	
BEHAVIOR	Cindy dawdles a bit, then takes a crayon and begins to scribble on the desk. Another student calls out to the teacher about it.	When the teacher does not select Cindy, she scowls and throws her math book on the floor, wrinkling several pages.	
CONSEQUENCE (what happens right after)	The teacher stops her lesson and goes to the table. She asks Cindy why she did that. Cindy says she doesn't know.	The teacher gives Cindy a stern look but does not stop the lesson. Cindy makes a face and picks up the book.	
COMMENTS OR OTHER OBSERVATIONS	Though negative, Cindy seems pleased to have the teacher's attention. Cindy's "answer" only encourages more questions.	Cindy seems to not be able to handle times when the teacher is not attending directly to her.	

FIGURE 8.3 A sample of a completed ABC observation form.

Source: Information from the New Mexico Public Education Department "Addressing Student Behavior—A Guide for Educators" (2003, 2005). Some information in this guide was adapted from "Addressing Student Problem Behavior" (1998, 2000) which is a copyright-free document, prepared by the Center for Effective Collaboration and Practice.

SCATTERPLOT

Student: _Carl Clark_

Date(s) _10/6-10/10/10_ Grade: _5_ School: _Barton Elem._

Observer: _Mr. Dennison (principal)_

Behavior of Concern: _verbal outbursts of anger and protest followed by refusal to respond to directions by teacher/adult authority_ Additional relevant information: _Carl is with Ms. Wills in the a.m. for Reading/Lang. & with Mrs. Bryant in p.m. for Math/Sci./Soc.Si._

Code used (if any): _tally mark for each observed instance_

Setting or Class	Times or Intervals	Day/Date M. 10/6	Day/Date T. 10/7	Day/Date W. 10/8	Day/Date Th. 10/9	Day/Date F. 10/10	Total Times Observed
Reading	8:45–10:00	//	///	/			
Transition	10:00–10:10		/		/	///	10
Language	10:10–11:50	///					1
Transition	11:50–12:00		//	///	//	///	13
Lunch	12:00–12:30	/	/				1
Transition	12:30–12:40			/			1
Recess	12:40–1:00						1
Transition	1:00–1:10			/	/	/	1
Math	1:10–1:55	/		//		/	2
Transition	1:55–2:00		/		/		3
Sci./Soc. Si.	2:00–2:40	/	//		/		2
						/	4

Observation Notes

(e.g., specific circumstances under which the behavior occurred, particular antecedents that triggered the behavior, times/conditions during which the behavior does not occur, patterns observed, etc.)

Carl acts out more frequently in Read./Lang., which are in the a.m. and with Ms. Wills. Though he may like the p.m. subjects better, his behavior could be a reaction to the subjects, the teacher, or the time of day. I suggest observing Carl when there is a substitute for Ms. Wills, Mrs. Bryant, or both, and/or interviewing him about these classes.

FIGURE 8.4 A sample of a completed scatterplot form.

Source: Information from the New Mexico Public Education Department "Addressing Student Behavior—A Guide for Educators" (2003, 2005) Some information in this guide was adapted from "Addressing Student Problem Behavior" (1998, 2000) which is a copyright-free document, prepared by the Center for Effective Collaboration and Practice.

not only disliked math and writing but was able to escape from this situation using his inappropriate behavior.

Another variant of direct observation is the *scatterplot*—a form that looks something like a day planner and breaks up a student's day in gridlike notes in 10-minute segments. Behavior to be recorded is written on the form, and the time during which the behavior occurs is either circled or crossed out. The scatterplot therefore gives the *frequency* of the problem behavior, along with the *time of day* that it is most likely to occur. Patterns may emerge when looking over several days of data. For example, when the RBP team reviews a scatterplot of Kaitland's problem behavior of noncompliance to the teacher's requests, it was noted that her behavior occurred at various classroom times. In further consultation with Kaitland's teacher, it was found that Kaitland's noncompliance was directly related to situations where she was asked to read in front of her classmates. On some occasions, this noncompliance occurred during the process of reading, but it also occurred during times when she anticipated being asked to read. Because Kaitland is in several classrooms, this pattern may have been difficult to discern without the use of a scatterplot. Clearly, collecting data using the *ABC observation form* and the scatterplot is time consuming, yet the information obtained can help to isolate both environmental and contextual variables that maintain a student's problem behavior and provide a basis for developing a theory or hypothesis about the problem behavior.

Another form that can be used to summarize data is the data triangle chart (see Figure 8.5). The data triangle is just another way to view and summarize the data. It is not used as much as the other two primary observation forms (i.e., the ABC and scatterplot). Appendix B includes additional examples of the ABC observation form, the scatterplot, and the data triangle chart.

There are no rules or guidelines about how much data must be collected through direct assessment prior to developing a hypothesis about the problem behavior. Consequently, these numbers may range from one session to several weeks (Chandler & Dahlquist, 2002). No matter how much time is involved, the use of direct observation is considered the best way to identify setting events, antecedents, and consequences of the problem behavior and to ultimately discover the function of the behavior. However, "the ultimate test of the validity or success of functional assessment is the effectiveness of the interventions derived from that assessment" (Chandler & Dahlquist, 2002, p. 81).

Using the Assessment Information   Clearly, the assessment information obtained from FBA should provide the basis for the development of positive behavior interventions and supports (Sugai, Lewis-Palmer, & Hogan-Burke, 2000). The following factors should be considered in developing intervention plans: (1) selection of the appropriate replacement behavior, (2) selection of the positive intervention strategies and the individual reinforcers, (3) selection of strategies that match the problem behavior, (4) provision of plans that are able to manipulate antecedents and consequences, and (5) intervention implementation procedures.

However, generalization across teachers is difficult to obtain when attempting to teach the format for implementing the FBA. Wallace and colleagues (2004) found only limited use of FBA procedures by teachers who were instructed on how to use it. Future studies must use a larger number of teachers and a more varied presentation of the mechanics of conducting an FBA.

Functional Assessment Checklist   The functional assessment checklist helps to sequence the operations needed to complete a functional behavioral assessment. It provides a step-by-step guide in formulating the FBA for use in developing the behavioral intervention plan. A sample of this checklist is shown in Appendix B.

THE GOALS OF INTERVENTION

It is important to remember that children engage in problem behavior because it helps them achieve some goal—it serves a function. There are two basic goals for any intervention:

- *Goal 1*: Select the appropriate behavior that serves the same function as the problem behavior, arrange for that behavior to be triggered, and then reinforce it when it appears (McEvoy & Reichle, 2000).
- *Goal 2*: Teach the child how to communicate with others about what they need.

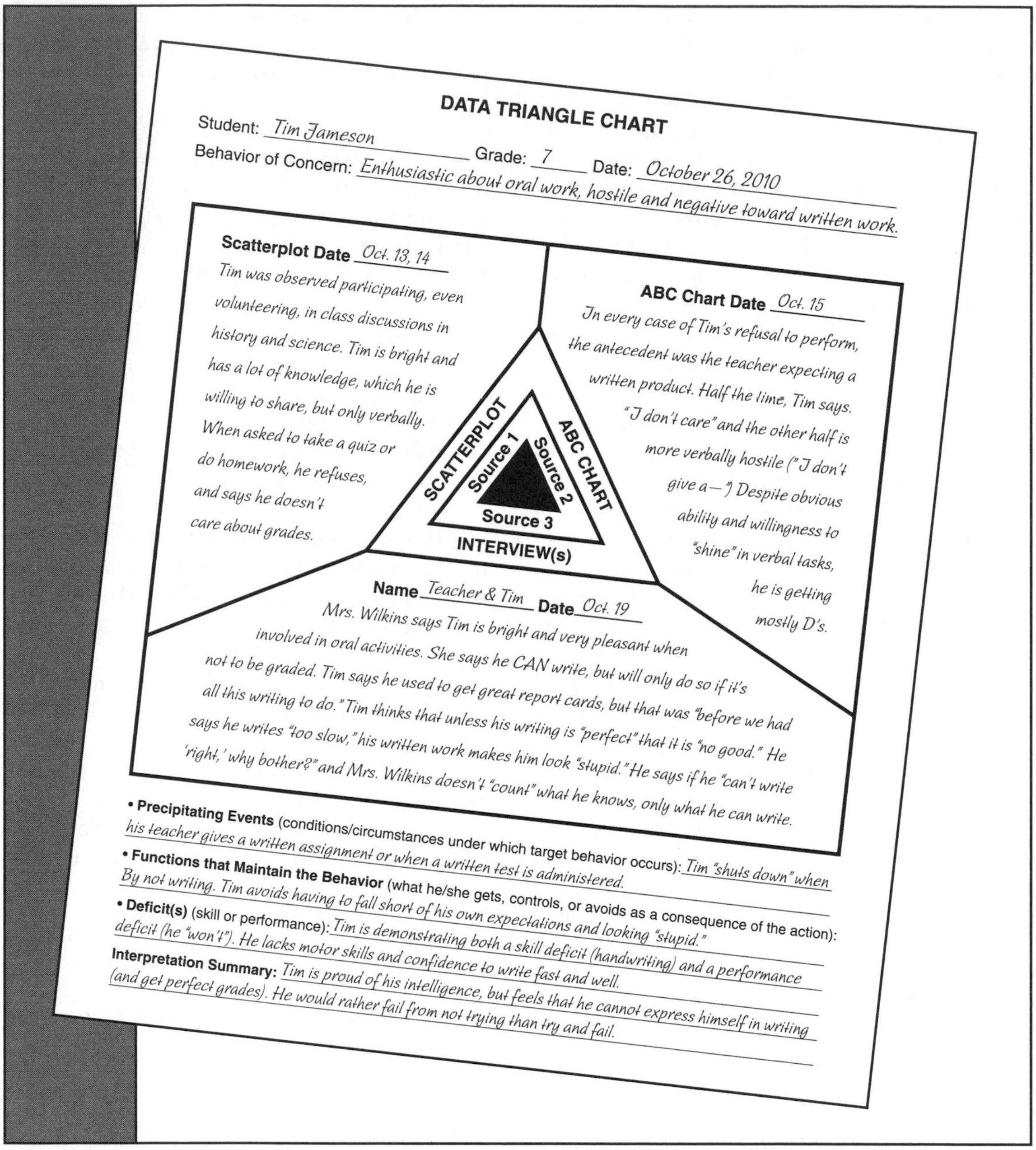

DATA TRIANGLE CHART

Student: _Tim Jameson_

Behavior of Concern: _Enthusiastic about oral work, hostile and negative toward written work._ Grade: _7_ Date: _October 26, 2010_

Scatterplot Date _Oct. 13, 14_

Tim was observed participating, even volunteering, in class discussions in history and science. Tim is bright and has a lot of knowledge, which he is willing to share, but only verbally. When asked to take a quiz or do homework, he refuses, and says he doesn't care about grades.

ABC Chart Date _Oct. 15_

In every case of Tim's refusal to perform, the antecedent was the teacher expecting a written product. Half the time, Tim says, "I don't care" and the other half is more verbally hostile ("I don't give a—") Despite obvious ability and willingness to "shine" in verbal tasks, he is getting mostly D's.

SCATTERPLOT Source 1

ABC CHART Source 2

Source 3

INTERVIEW(s)

Name _Teacher & Tim_ **Date** _Oct. 19_

Mrs. Wilkins says Tim is bright and very pleasant when involved in oral activities. She says he CAN write, but will only do so if it's not to be graded. Tim says he used to get great report cards, but that was "before we had all this writing to do." Tim thinks that unless his writing is "perfect" that it is "no good." He says he writes "too slow," his written work makes him look "stupid." He says if he "can't write 'right,' why bother?" and Mrs. Wilkins doesn't "count" what he knows, only what he can write.

• **Precipitating Events** (conditions/circumstances under which target behavior occurs): _Tim "shuts down" when his teacher gives a written assignment or when a written test is administered._

• **Functions that Maintain the Behavior** (what he/she gets, controls, or avoids as a consequence of the action): _By not writing, Tim avoids having to fall short of his own expectations and looking "stupid."_

• **Deficit(s)** (skill or performance): _Tim is demonstrating both a skill deficit (handwriting) and a performance deficit (he "won't"). He lacks motor skills and confidence to write fast and well._

Interpretation Summary: _Tim is proud of his intelligence, but feels that he cannot express himself in writing (and get perfect grades). He would rather fail from not trying than try and fail._

FIGURE 8.5 A sample of a completed data triangle chart.

Source: Information from the New Mexico Public Education Department "Addressing Student Behavior—A Guide for Educators" (2003, 2005). Some information in this guide was adapted from "Addressing Student Problem Behavior" (1998, 2000) which is a copyright-free document, prepared by the Center for Effective Collaboration and Practice.

Meeting the Intervention Goals

It is important not only to formulate these basic goals of intervention but also to know that these goals have been met. Figure 8.6 outlines this process.

When problem behavior is maintained by negative reinforcement, this process becomes more complicated. Although children can be taught some appropriate behavior that allows them to escape or avoid the situation, it may not be good for them to escape or avoid some tasks or activities. For example, if they show the problem behavior to avoid the dinner table, it may be more important to reduce the aversiveness of eating at the table. In this way they learn an appropriate social skill that will be needed in future situations (for example, in the school cafeteria). This problem might be addressed by either having other students sit at the table one at a time so that the child with problem behavior can gradually habituate to the increasing numbers of people through a kind of desen-

sitization process, or the child can also be reinforced for sitting at the table longer periods of time through a shaping process.

Replacing Behavior Problems

It is important to identify the appropriate behaviors that will replace problem behaviors. The box below summarizes the characteristics of appropriate replacement behavior:

1. It is acceptable to the child.
2. It is appropriate to the setting.
3. It is a behavior that the child has or can easily learn.
4. It promotes independence and maximizes participation.
5. It is incompatible with the problem behavior. (Chandler & Dahlquist, 2002)

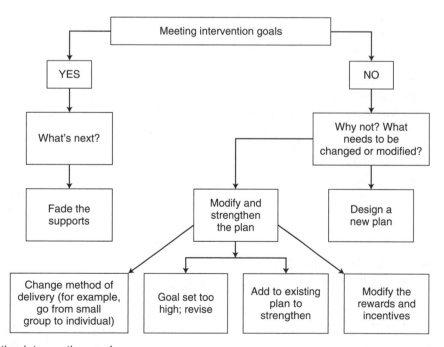

FIGURE 8.6   Meeting intervention goals.

Source: Adapted with permission from *Functional Behavior Assessment: A Study Guide*, Wisconsin Department of Public Instruction, 125 South Webster St., Madison, WI, 53703, 1-800-243-8742. Downloaded 9/08 from http://dpi.wi.gov/sped/doc/tba-study.doc

In general, these new behaviors should be better at achieving the identified function(s) than the problem behavior. They should also be more efficient and effective than the problem behavior (Sugai, Lewis-Palmer et al., 2000).

Selecting Positive Interventions and Individual Reinforcers

A core assumption of functional behavioral assessment is the focus on positive interventions that support appropriate replacement behavior. The disadvantages of punishment have long been documented (Skinner, 1953; Walker & Shea, 1999). In addition, IDEA 2004 has specified that intervention plans be based on positive behaviors and supports.

With regard to individual reinforcers, it can sometimes be difficult to identify the ones that effectively motivate children. Edible reinforcers can be effective for a short period, but children satiate on these very quickly.

Nature and Type of Reinforcers   There are several techniques that may be used to get at the nature and type of reinforcers that may be effective with an identified child. Based on several questionnaires and rating scales, the teacher can develop a list of things that the child likes and dislikes (Flick, 1998b).

There are a number of activity or social reinforcers that can be used. Reinforcers that consist primarily of edibles have to be selected carefully, and it is important to avoid candy and undesirable edibles that may foster other problems. A copy of the Children's Classroom Reinforcement Survey for Teachers may be found in Appendix B. Likewise, a copy of the Student Reinforcement Survey can also be found in Appendix B.

Social Rewards   Social rewards may include the following nonverbal and verbal reinforcements:

Nonverbal Reinforcement

Pat child on shoulder	Smile
Wink	Give OK sign
Give a thumbs-up sign	Hug child
Pat child on head	Place arm around child

Verbal Reinforcement

Good for you!	You're doing fine.
Great!	That's the right way.
Terrific!	You remembered!
Nice going.	You're getting better every day.
Exactly right.	Much better!
You're learning fast.	You've got it made.
I'm very proud of you.	That was beautiful.
Fantastic!	You're a joy.
You're really learning a lot.	Tremendous!
You really make my job fun.	That's better than ever.
Right on!	It's such a pleasure to work with you.
You haven't missed a thing.	You've got your brain in gear.
I like that.	You've got that down pat.
Good work!	Super!
You're really improving.	Congratulations—you did it!
Congratulations!	You're on the right track.
Now you have the hang of it.	Good job.
Super good!	That's it!
Outstanding!	You must have been practicing.
Keep working on it. You're improving.	That was first class work.
Way to go!	Keep on trying.
You're doing much better today.	That's right!
Superb!	That's the best ever.
Sensational!	That's much better.
I've never seen anyone do it better.	You did that very well.
That's good.	I'm happy to see you working like that.
You're really going to town.	Marvelous!
You're really working hard today.	Couldn't have done it better myself.
Well, look at you go!	Wonderful!
Now you have it!	You're very good at that.
Keep it up!	Now that's what I call a fine job.
Extraordinary!	That's the right way to do it.
You certainly did well today.	Perfect!
Now you've figured it out.	You did a lot of work today.
That's wonderful.	One more time and you have it.
Wow!	That's how to handle it.

That's really nice.

You've just about got it.
Fine!
That's coming along nicely.
Good going.
You did it that time.
I think you've got it now.

Nothing can stop you now.
Good remembering!
You figured that out fast.

Keep up the good work.
That kind of work
    makes me happy.
That's better.

I'm proud of the way
    you worked today.

That's the best job you've
    ever done.
That's great.
I knew you could do it.
You're doing beautifully.
Nice going.
You outdid yourself today.
You've just about
    mastered that.
Good thinking.
Excellent!
You're making real
    progress.
That's the way to do it.
You're doing a good job.

That's quite an
    improvement.

The previous list of social rewards is certainly not exhaustive, and there may be many individualized verbal and nonverbal forms of communication that you can use to convey your approval to a child. There are a number of both examples of social praise (social rewards) to give a child.

If you are not accustomed to using these positive verbal and nonverbal reinforcements, it will take some personal preparation, rehearsal, and practice before becoming comfortable using these expressions. Eventually they will become automatic when you "catch" the child in some appropriate behavior, or when using a reinforcer in a behavioral intervention program. In addition, stickers, tokens, and tickets appear to be generally reinforcing for most children.

Mechanism of Rewards   This refers to the process of giving a reward (i.e., how to give it; when to give it; how to be specific, positive and sincere). It is critical to do the following:

1. Make positive comments immediately after observing the good (i.e., appropriate) behavior.
2. Be very specific about what you like—for example, "I like it when you follow my instructions."
3. Remember to give the positive feedback without any negative component. Additional statements

like, "Why can't you do that all the time?" diminish the reward value of the compliment.

4. Be sincere.

It may be important at this time to think about some of the possible negative thoughts, verbalizations, or actions that you may have said or done, or even thought of saying or doing, and to guard against using them in the future. It is always important to listen to yourself and to be aware of any such negative comments.

FAILURE TO SHOW APPROPRIATE BEHAVIOR

Students may not show appropriate classroom behavior for two reasons: (1) they do not know how to perform the skill or behavior because they have a *skill deficit*, or (2) they know how to perform the skill but do not consistently show this skill because they have a *performance deficit*.

Skill Deficits

If a student does not know how to perform a certain skill, the intervention plan should include instruction about that skill. For example, a student who is unable to handle the aggressive verbal behavior of a classmate may need to be taught to recognize the words or actions that typically lead to aggression and to be able to tell whether the behavior is or is not provoked by the student. A series of role-play sessions could then teach the student how to defuse such situations by avoiding any critical comments as well as when to walk away from confrontational peers.

Example of a Skill Deficit

Paul recognizes a problem situation but doesn't have the self-control needed to regulate his behavior. He may benefit from the following approach: (1) his teacher demonstrates modeling of self control, (2) behavioral rehearsal is used by the teacher to review self-control techniques, and (3) his teacher initiates discussions about when to use these learned strategies as well as how to use them.

Performance Deficits

A performance deficit occurs when a student knows how to perform a behavior but does not do it consistently. In such cases, the intervention plan should target those techniques and strategies that will help students increase their use of the appropriate behavior. However, students might think that acting quickly is desirable because resolution is valued. The teacher might counter this belief by having students list all of the additional problems that might result from a quick but faulty solution or action. Another reason for not performing a behavior is that a student may not see any value in doing it.

Example of Performance Deficit

If Rachel can avoid being ridiculed by threatening her classmates on the playground, she may not see any advantage to interacting positively with them. Here the intervention plan may focus on increasing her use of already learned skills to interact appropriately with her peers. Because of Rachel's aggressive behavior, it may also be important to prompt her classmates to play with her so that both she and her classmates can be reinforced for engaging in positive and appropriate social behavior.

COMPREHENSIVE INTERVENTION PLANS

In general, a comprehensive intervention plan involves decreasing the student's problem behaviors while increasing the appropriate replacement behaviors. This plan entails arranging the setting events and antecedents so that they no longer trigger the problem behavior and it no longer occurs. If the problem behavior does occur, it will no longer get the desired result (Buschbacker & Fox, 2003; Horner & Carr, 1997). For example, if Mark takes the ball from Eric, the ball is returned to Eric so that Mark's aggressive behavior is no longer reinforced. A review of the entire process of addressing student behavior through an FBA that leads to a BIP is shown in Figure 8.7.

Family Involvement

Whenever problem behavior is addressed, family involvement becomes an important issue in the development of interventions. Families can provide valuable information that might focus on the child's strengths, characteristics, and needs that relate to the problem behavior (Walker et al., 1998). Families may also provide information about setting events such as sleep problems or emotional issues and, of course, preferences for reinforcers.

Families can help by implementing interventions at home that may be similar to the ones used in school (Kaiser, Hancock, & Nietfeld, 2000). However, the reality is that some families may not have the interest, time, ability, or resources to give. In any case, they should be supported for any involvement, from providing information in interviews to implementing a behavioral program at home that reinforces the more appropriate replacement behaviors (Chandler & Dahlquist, 2002; Lucyshyn et al., 2002).

FORMAL ASSESSMENT VERSUS FUNCTIONAL BEHAVIORAL ASSESSMENT

While the FBA is typically used after the student's eligibility for special education classification has been determined, it will be enlightening to look at how the FBA is different from that of formal assessment. There are a number of tests that comprise the formal assessment, but there are only a few interviews, rating scales, and checklists that are used in the FBA. Formal assessment is used to determine eligibility and typically comes prior to the use of the FBA; however, the FBA can be used at any time to develop intervention plans targeting specific areas of problem behaviors.

Most special education eligibility procedures are based on a traditional model of formal assessment such as psychological testing where the primary purpose is classification, not intervention. In contrast, functional behavioral assessment seeks to identify and assess the functions of behavior. These two approaches have been extensively compared in Goldfried and Kent (1972) as well as Cone (1988) and Nelson and Hayes (1979). More recent publications by Mash and Hunsley (2005) and Watkins and Pacheco (2000) have focused on similar issues. Both formal and functional

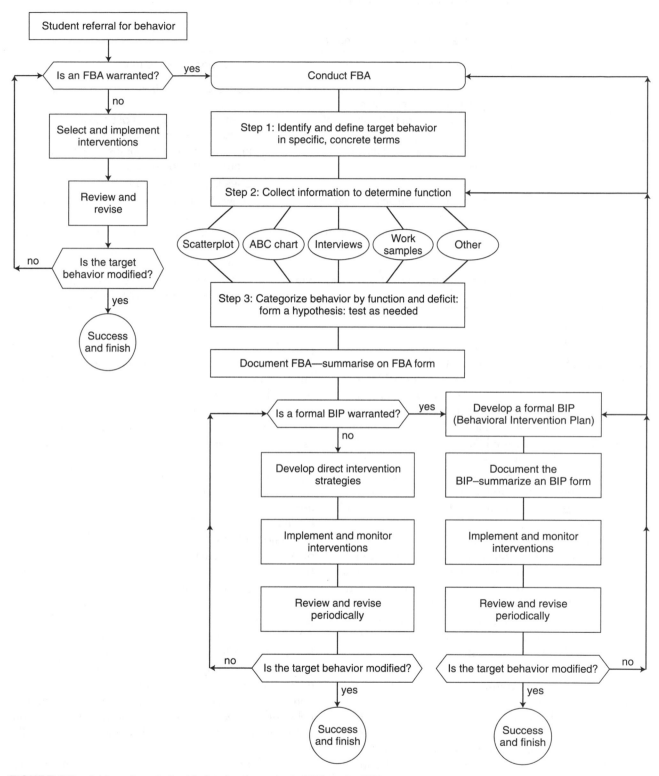

FIGURE 8.7 Addressing student behavior through an FBA and a BIP.

Source: Information from the New Mexico Public Education Department (Addressing Student Behavior) (2005).

TABLE 8.1   A Comparison of Formal and Functional Behavioral Assessment

Dimension	Formal Assessment	Functional Assessment
Cause(s)	Identifies some underlying physiological traits that account for the condition.	Lists a sample of behavior in a specific situation.
Outcome	Identifies the causes of behavior problems.	Identifies the functions of behavior problems—what elicits or maintains them.
Purpose	Diagnoses a condition and provides classification.	Identifies the reason for the behavior and suggests intervention.
Process	Uses inference.	Uses little or no inference.
Employment or use	Draws from tests, rating scales, interview data.	Draws from rating scales, interview data, and observation.
Approach	Follows the nomothetic-trait approach.	Follows the idiographic-behavior approach (i.e., the comprehensive study of an individual).
Features	Uses global assessment of behavior at one point in time.	Uses repeated measures of behavior in specific situations over time.

behavioral assessment are compared and summarized on a number of factors, as shown in Table 8.1.

With regard to the causes of behavior, formal assessment may view behavior as a sign of some underlying physiological or personality trait or "intrapsychic process," while functional behavioral assessment interprets behavior as just a sample of behavior in a specific situation. Regarding outcome, formal assessment tries to identify the causes of behavior within the individual while functional behavioral assessment targets the external environment for causes (i.e., what elicits or maintains the behavior).

With regard to purpose, formal assessment tries to classify or diagnose a condition, whereas functional behavioral assessment identifies the function or reason for that behavior and tries to implement intervention procedures. Msall and Tremont (1999) note that functional behavioral assessment provides families and clinicians with a common language for describing a child's strengths and limitations in self-care (feeding, dressing, grooming, bathing, continence), mobility, and communication/social cognition. Functional assessment relies on little or no inference while formal assessment usually adopts a high level of inferential reasoning.

Some experts have distinguished between functional behavioral assessment and functional behavioral analysis (Carr, 1994; Horner & Cell, 1997). Functional behavioral assessment utilizes a full range of assessment

procedures such as interviews, rating scales, and direct observation to identify the antecedents and consequences associated with the occurrence of the troublesome behavior. Functional behavioral analysis, however, refers to the systematic experimental manipulation of environmental events, usually in simulated situations to assess their impact on the occurrence of the behavior in question.

Formal and functional assessments adopt one of two contrasting approaches center align: (1) the *nomothetic-trait approach* or (2) the *idiographic-behavior approach* (Cone, 1988). The primary focus in the nomothetic-trait approach is on the assessment of syndromes or characteristics such as emotional disturbances, attention deficit disorders, or learning disability using indirect norm-referenced tests (e.g., ability tests, executive function tests, achievement tests, and personality tests). This approach is useful in describing differences among individuals but it is flawed in identifying behavioral functions. The idiographic-behavior approach emphasizes the direct assessment of specific behavior of individuals and measures these behaviors repeatedly over time. While the idiographic-behavior approach adopts an intraindividual comparison, the nomothetic-trait approach model uses interindividual comparisons.

A key distinguishing feature of functional behavioral assessment is the repeated measurement of specific behaviors in specific settings or situations over time for a specific individual. A functional assessment model assumes that behavior is situationally or setting specific. It can be characterized as an active model of assessment where the student's baseline level of performance (in a specific setting or situation) is used as the criterion against which treatment effects are compared and evaluated. This intrasubject variability can also be used as a basis for functional behavioral analysis. This variability may relate to physiological and/or environmental events and can be identified, isolated, functionally analyzed, and perhaps controlled. In contrast, formal assessment states and provides global measures of behavior typically at only one point in time. In the typical triennial reevaluation, students may be retested only to find that they are still having academic and/or behavioral problems, offering virtually no useful information regarding interventions. An overview of the stages encountered in conducting functional behavioral assessments and developing behavioral intervention plans is shown in Figure 8.8.

FUNCTIONAL BEHAVIORAL ASSESSMENT MODEL: ASSESSMENT

The functional behavioral assessment model was first proposed by Cone (1978); it is an extension and modification of the behavioral assessment grid, and it is based on five aspects of functional behavioral assessment: (1) type of behavior problem, (2) dimension of behavior, (3) assessment methods, (4) the quality of data, and (5) social validation. Let's consider each aspect.

Type of Behavior Problem

In formal assessment, "students" are classified instead of their behavioral excesses or deficits. In functional behavioral assessment, it is acknowledged that some behavior problems may not necessarily be excessive or deficient but are situationally inappropriate. Thus, these excessive, deficient, or situationally inappropriate behaviors provide multiple targets for intervention.

Dimensions of Behavior

The functional behavioral assessment model stresses the importance of assessing "objective features" of behavior such as frequency, temporality (duration, latency, and interresponse time), intensity, and permanent products (labels for the assessment process). Objective dimensions are assessed using observation-based assessment methods. Event-based recording measures the frequency of behavior and is best used with discrete behavior (i.e., behaviors that have a clear beginning and end, such as the number of times a child hits another child). An example based on Tieghi (2003) is shown in Figure 8.9.

Interval-based methods refer to the recording of behaviors that either occur or fail to occur within a specified time. For example, off-task behavior might be recorded for 5 minutes in 30 intervals of 10 seconds. The rate of off-task behavior of a student who is off-task for 15 of the 30 intervals will be 50 percent. This type of recording would best be used with behaviors that are "continuous"—i.e., having no specific beginning or end. A complete description of the whole

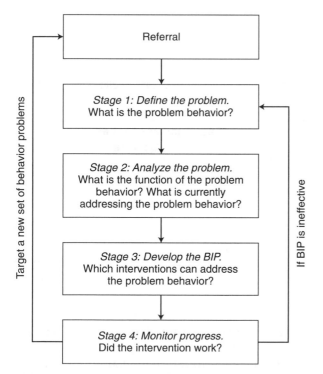

FIGURE 8.8   The stages for conducting an FBA and developing a BIP.

Assessment Information: Event Recording (i.e. Frequency/Behavior Count)—Description, Procedures, and Example

When the behavior that you are looking at can be easily counted, event recording may be the best method to use, as it does not require too much effort and may not interfere with ongoing activities. A behavior can be easily counted when:

■ The behavior has a clear beginning and end so that you can easily tell when the behavior starts and when it ends, *and*
■ It does not happen at such a high rate that it is hard to keep track of.

There are several ways to keep track of behaviors as they occur: You can use a wrist counter; put paper clips, pennies, or buttons in one pocket and move them to a different "target" pocket as each behavior occurs; or make tally marks on a piece of paper. To obtain the total number of times that the behavior occurred, at the end of your observation time, you would either look at your wrist counter or add up the number of items in the "target" pocket, or the number of tally marks. This form uses tally marks. However, you can choose a different method to keep track of behaviors as they occur.

Examples of behaviors that you can measure by counting include leaving one's seat, raising one's hand, yelling out an answer, asking to go to the bathroom, being on time.

Procedures

■ Write down the behavior that you will be looking for and its definition.
■ Every time that you are "on the look out" for the behavior
  ■ Write down the date.
  ■ Write down the time.
  ■ Make a tally mark every time that the behavior occurs. (If the behavior does not occur, make sure to enter a zero.)
  ■ At the end of your observation period, total the number of tally marks for that day. (If you are using a different method to keep track of behavior, enter the number in the total column.) **(This is what you graph.)**

Example

Behavior: Leaving seat during class time

Behavior Definition: Being at least one foot away from desk/seat during class, anytime after tardy bell rings. Includes times when student has asked for permission to leave seat.

Date	Time	One Tally for Each Time the Behavior Occurs	Total Number of Times Behavior Occurred
11/5	1–2 PM	ǀǀǀǀ ǀ ǀ	7
11/6	1–2 PM	ǀ ǀ ǀ ǀ	4
11/7	1–2 PM	ǀǀǀǀ ǀ	6
11/8	1–2 PM	ǀǀǀǀ	5
11/9	1–2 PM	ǀǀǀǀ ǀǀǀ	8

FIGURE 8.9

Source: Information from Tieghi (2003). Reprinted by permission.

interval, partial interval, and momentary sample recording is shown in Figures 8.10 through 8.12.

Time-based recording refers to the measurement of the temporal aspects of behavior such as duration, latency, or interresponse times. *Duration* refers to how long a behavior lasts (measured in seconds, minutes, or hours). An example is shown in Figure 8.13.

Latency refers to the time elapsed between an environmental event and the start or end of a specific behavior (e.g., the end of teacher directions and

---

Assessment Information: Whole Interval Recording—Description, Procedures, and Example

If you are interested in knowing that the behavior continues without interruption, you can measure the behavior by counting the number of intervals in which the behavior occurred throughout the entire interval. In order to keep track of the time intervals, note that you will need some timing instrument such as a wall clock, wristwatch, or stopwatch.

Examples of behaviors that you can measure using whole interval recording include writing, reading, and working on a given assignment.

Procedures

■ Write down the behavior that you will be looking for and its definition.
■ Write down how long you will be observing every time—the total observation time.
■ Divide the total observation time into same-length intervals (here we included 10 intervals); write down the length of each interval. Intervals can be from a few seconds to a few minutes long.

Note: Total observation time and length of intervals need to be the same each time that you observe.

■ Enter the date of your observation.
■ Make sure that you have your timing instrument available prior to beginning your observation.
■ Keep an eye on your timing instrument to keep track of the intervals.
■ **During each time interval:**
  ■ Look to see if the behavior occurs **throughout the entire interval.**
  ■ If the behavior stops at any time, place an X for that interval.
  ■ If the behavior is still occurring at the end of the interval, place a checkmark (✓) for that interval.
■ At the end of your observation time, total the number of checkmarks. **(This is what you graph.)**

Example

Behavior: On-task behavior

Behavior Definition: **Looking at the teacher while she is talking; talking to the teacher; or looking at assignment**

Total Observation Time: 10 minutes   *Length of each interval*: 1 minute

Date: 12/5				Interval								**Total Number of Times Behavior Occurred (✓)**
Time: 1:10–1:20 PM	1	2	3	4	5	6	7	8	9	10		
✓ or X	X	✓	✓	✓	X	✓	X	✓	✓	X		6

FIGURE 8.10
Source: Information from Tieghi (2003). Reprinted by permission.

beginning of compliance). An example is shown in Figure 8.14.

Interresponse time refers to the time elapsed between instances of the identical behaviors. *Permanent products* involves the measurement of the actual physical by-products of behavior. Torn papers, graffiti on school property, and written notes all would be pertinent. An example is shown in Figure 8.15.

Once a decision is made regarding which measurement would be appropriate to record, it must be graphed. Figure 8.16 provides information on how these measures may be displayed and graphed.

Assessment Information: Partial Interval Recording—Description, Procedures, and Example

When the behavior that you are looking at is not easily counted, you can measure the behavior by counting the number of time-intervals in which the behavior occurred. A behavior is not easily counted when

- It is difficult to tell exactly when the behavior begins or when it ends, *or*
- It occurs at such a high rate that it is difficult to keep a count on it.

If this behavior happens so quickly that it is hard to catch (the behavior itself does not last for a long time), use the partial interval method to measure this behavior: Look to see whether or not the behavior occurs at some point in each time interval (the behavior does not need to occur throughout the entire interval). Note that you will need some timing instrument such as a wall clock, wristwatch, or stopwatch in order to keep track of the time intervals.

Examples of behaviors that you can measure using partial interval include praising others, making a particular comment, making a certain gesture, walking by a particular place.

Procedures

- Write down the behavior that you will be looking for and its definition.
- Write down how long you will be observing every time—the total observation time.
- Divide the total observation time into same-length intervals (here we included 10 intervals); write down the length of each interval. Intervals can be from a few seconds to a few minutes long.

Note: Total observation time and length of intervals need to be the same each time that you observe.

- Enter the date and time of your observation.
- Make sure that you have your timing instrument available prior to beginning your observation.
- Keep an eye on your timing instrument to keep track of the intervals.
- **During each time interval:**
    - Look to see if the behavior occurs.
    - Once the behavior occurs, place a checkmark (✓) for that interval.
    - If the behavior did not occur at the end of the interval, place an X for that interval.
- At the end of your observation time, total the number of checkmarks. **(This is what you graph.)**

Example

Behavior: Saying something nice

Behavior Definition: Making a statement to a peer or a teacher during class time, in a pleasant tone, which includes either praise or politeness—for example, saying "you did well" or "excuse me."

Total Observation Time: 20 minutes   *Length of each interval*: 2 minutes

Date: 11/5	Interval										Total Number of Times Behavior Occurred (✓)
Time: 9:10–9:30 PM	1	2	3	4	5	6	7	8	9	10	
✓ or X	✓	X	X	✓	X	X	X	✓	X	X	3

FIGURE 8.11

Source: Information from Tieghi (2003). Reprinted by permission.

Assessment Information: Momentary Sample Recording—Description, Procedures, and Example

When the behavior that you are looking at is not easily counted, you can measure the behavior by counting the number of time-intervals in which the behavior occurred. A behavior is not easily counted when

- It is difficult to tell exactly when the behavior begins or when it ends, *or*
- It occurs at such a high rate that it is difficult to keep a count on it.

If a behavior such as reading or writing tends to last for a while, use the momentary sample method: Simply look at the end of each interval to see if the behavior is occurring at that particular moment. Since the behavior lasts for a while, you do not need to be looking throughout the entire interval. Note that you will need some timing instrument such as a wall clock, wristwatch, or stopwatch in order to keep track of the intervals.

Examples of behaviors that you can measure using the momentary sample method include writing, reading, working on the given assignment, talking.

Procedures

- Write down the behavior that you will be looking for and its definition.
- Write down how long you will be observing every time—the total observation time.
- Divide the total observation time into same-length intervals (here we included 10 intervals); write down the length of each interval. Intervals can be from a few seconds to a few minutes long.

Note: **Total observation time and length of intervals need to be the same each time that you observe.**

- Enter the date and time of your observation.
- Make sure that you have your timing instrument available prior to beginning your observation.
- Keep an eye on your timing instrument to keep track of the intervals.
- **At the end of each time interval:**
  - Look to see if the behavior is occurring at that particular moment—not before, not after.
  - If the behavior is occurring at that moment, place a checkmark (✓) for that interval.
  - If the behavior is not occurring at that moment, place an X for that interval.
- At the end of your observation time, total the number of checkmarks. **(This is what you graph.)**

Example

Behavior: Talking to peers

Behavior definition: Talking to a peer anytime when the teacher is talking or when should be performing individual work during class time.

Total Observation Time: 50 minutes   *Length of each interval:* 5 minutes

Date: 11/5	Interval #	Total Number of Times Behavior Occurred (✓)
Time: 10:10 – 11 AM 1 2 3 4 5 6 7 8 9 10		
✓ or X X ✓ X ✓ X ✓ ✓ ✓ X X		5

FIGURE 8.12

Source: Information from Tieghi (2003). Reprinted by permission.

Assessment Information: Behavior Duration—Description, Procedures, and Example

If you are interested in measuring how long a behavior lasts, you can do that by using the duration recording method. However, in order to do so, you need to make sure that the behavior that you are looking at has a clear beginning and a clear ending so that you can tell exactly when the behavior starts and when it finishes. You will also need some timing instrument such as a wall clock, wristwatch, or stopwatch.

Examples of behaviors that you might want to measure the length of include crying, being out of the classroom, being in a particular location, and engaging in a particular activity.

Procedures

■ Write down the behavior that you will be looking for and its definition.
■ Make sure that you have your timing instrument available prior to beginning your observation.
■ Each time that you are observing for the behavior, write down the date and time.
■ Each time the behavior occurs
  ■ Write down the time when the behavior began.
  ■ Write down the time when the behavior stopped.
  ■ Calculate the length of time that the behavior lasted and write it in minutes and/or seconds. (**This is what you graph.**)

Example

Behavior: Working individually

Behavior Definition: Sitting at desk, with an assignment on the desk, looking at assignment, not talking to peers. Once student looks up (not looking at assignment any more), the behavior has stopped. If student begins talking to peers while looking at assignment, behavior has stopped.

Date	Time	Time When Behavior Began	Time When Behavior Stopped	Number of Minutes Behavior Lasted
11/5	9:30 – 10:30 AM	9:55 AM	10:06 AM	11
11/5	9:30 – 10:30 AM	10:19 AM	10:28 AM	9
11/6	9:30 – 10:30 AM	9:43 AM	9:51 AM	8
11/7	9:30 – 10:30 AM	10:04 AM	10:19 AM	15
11/7	9:30 – 10:30 AM	10:13 AM	10:23 AM	10

FIGURE 8.13

Source: Information from Tieghi (2003). Reprinted by permission.

Teachers and others conducting objective assessments must decide how many behaviors should be observed, a decision that will be influenced by the nature and severity of the students' problematic behaviors and the degree of concern about each behavior. Some behaviors may be part of a larger response class. Specifically, noncompliance may take many forms, such as open defiance, cursing, refusing to complete work, or throwing paper. These behaviors may be independent and unrelated. If all of these behaviors cannot be targeted, they may be rank ordered with regard to their importance.

Assessment Information: Latency Recording (i.e., Time to Respond)—Description, Procedures, and Example

If you are interested in measuring the time that it takes for the person to respond, you can measure just that by using the latency recording (time to respond) method. However, in order to do so, you need to make sure that the behavior that you are looking at has a clear beginning so that you can tell exactly when the behavior starts. To measure how long it takes to respond, you will need some timing instrument such as a wall clock, wristwatch, or stopwatch.

Examples of behaviors where you might want to measure latency include how long it takes to go sit at one's desk, how long it takes to take out materials, and how long it takes to begin writing.

Procedures

- Write down the behavior that you will be looking for and its definition.
- Make sure that you have your timing instrument available prior to beginning your observation.
- Each time that you are looking for or expecting the behavior to occur, write down the date and time.
  - Write down the time when the instruction to do the behavior is given.
  - Write down the time when the behavior starts.
  - Calculate the length of time (i.e., latency) that it took for the behavior to begin and write it in minutes and/or seconds. (**This is what you graph.**)

Example

Behavior: Time it takes to start working

Behavior Definition: Time it takes for the student to begin writing on assignment paper after instruction to start working on assignment is given to the whole class.

Date	Time	Time When Instruction Is Given	Time When Behavior Starts	Number of Minutes for Behavior to Start
11/5	8:30 – 9:30 AM	8:46 AM	8:52 AM	6
11/5	1:30 – 2:30 PM	1:46 PM	1:48 PM	2
11/6	8:30 – 9:30 AM	8:32 AM	8:35 AM	3
11/6	1:30 – 2:30 PM	1:41 PM	1:46 PM	5
11/7	8:30 – 9:30 AM	8:55 AM	9:02 AM	7
11/7	1:30 – 2:30 PM	1:45 PM	1:46 PM	1
11/8	8:30 – 9:30 AM	8:44 AM	8:49 AM	5
11/8	1:30 – 2:30 PM	1:40 PM	1:43 PM	3
11/9	8:30 – 9:30 AM	8:37 AM	8:41 AM	4
11/9	1:30 – 2:30 PM	1:43 PM	1:46 PM	3

FIGURE 8.14

Source: Information from Tieghi (2003). Reprinted by permission.

Assessment Information: Permanent Product Recording—Description, Procedures, and Example

When the behavior that you are looking at results in a lasting product, permanent product may be the best method to use because you don't have to be "on the lookout" for the behavior to happen, as you can measure it afterward by looking at its product. However, you do have to be careful that only the target person's target behavior, and not someone else's or some other behavior, results in the product that you have chosen to look at.

Examples of lasting products to look at include having a bed made, having a clean room, written assignments, papers thrown on the floor, items left on the table, and the way someone is dressed. In these examples, the behaviors that you might be looking for could be, cleaning, answering questions correctly, number of completed assignments, number of assignments turned in, dressing skills, and self-help skills.

Procedures

■ Write down the permanent product that you will be looking at.
■ Write down the behavior that you will be looking for in that permanent product, and its definition.
■ Do the following for each permanent product that you look at:
  ■ Enter the date when the permanent product was completed.
  ■ If the permanent product that you are looking at could occur several times during the day, also enter the time.
  ■ If there are different types of permanent products that you are looking at, enter the label of that permanent product.
  ■ If the behavior that you are measuring could occur more than once in that permanent product (for example, you are looking at correct answers in homework assignments), write down the number of times that the behavior occurred and the number of opportunities in which the behavior could have occurred. If the behavior did not occur, make sure to enter zero.
■ Calculate the total percentage of times that the behavior occurred per day. (**This is what you graph.**)

Example

Behavior: Answering questions correctly on homework assignments turned in.

Behavior Definition: Answer on homework questions is complete and accurate (excludes partially answered items). Excludes any written assignments performed in class.

Permanent Product Looked at: Homework assignments turned in.

Date	Time	Permanent Product Label	Number of Times Behavior Occurred (Number of Correct answers)	Number of Opportunities	Total % of Times Behavior Occurred
11/5	2 PM	Homework Section I	12	20	(12/20) × 100 = 60
11/6	2 PM	Homework Section II	4	10	(4/10) × 100 = 40
11/7	2 PM	Homework Section III	25	40	(25/40) × 100 = 63
11/8	2 PM	Homework Section IV	12	30	(12/30) × 100 = 40
11/9	2 PM	Homework Section V	14	30	(14/30) × 100 = 47

FIGURE 8.15

Source: Information from Tieghi (2003). Reprinted by permission.

Assessment Methods

Functional behavioral assessment attempts to ascertain the relationship between environmental events and behavior so that these environmental events can be manipulated to effect changes in behavior. There are three types of assessment methods: (1) *indirect methods*—which may employ interviews, behavior rating scales, and review school records; (2) *direct (descriptive) methods*—which consist of systematic behavioral observations of antecedents, behaviors, and consequences in natural settings; and (3) *experimental methods*—which involve standardized experimental manipulations designed to identify the contingencies that control the problematic behavior. The only disadvantage of experimental procedures is that they are conducted almost always in simulated instead of naturalistic settings.

Rarely used in schools, experimental methods are typically used with those who present self-injurious behavior along with severe or profound mental retardation. Kern and Vorndran (2000) examined the use of functional behavioral assessment for "transition difficulties" with an 11-year-old girl with mental retardation and attention

---

Some Procedures and an Example of Graphing

In addition to measuring a behavior, a graph allows you to have a visual image of the status of the measurements that you gather at any point in time: On average, how often the behavior of interest occurs, times when the behavior is lower, and times when the behavior is higher. By looking at a graph, you can tell right away if the behavior is increasing or decreasing, when it peaks, when it plummets. You can then follow up on this information by examining the situations surrounding times when the behavior has changed. Every time that you collect information, enter it on your graph.

- ■ *Procedures for preparing a graph*
  - ■ ① Label the horizontal axis with the time component.
  - ■ ② Label the vertical axis with the behaviour.
  - ■ ③ Number the vertical axis.

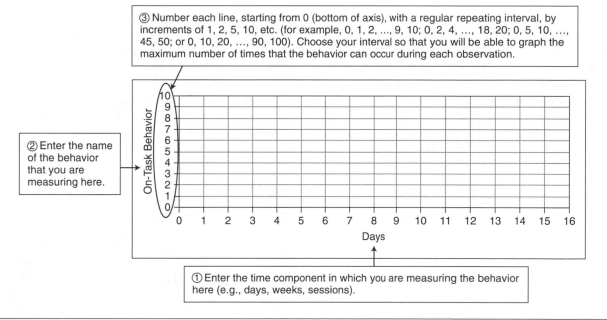

③ Number each line, starting from 0 (bottom of axis), with a regular repeating interval, by increments of 1, 2, 5, 10, etc. (for example, 0, 1, 2, …, 9, 10; 0, 2, 4, …, 18, 20; 0, 5, 10, …, 45, 50; or 0, 10, 20, …, 90, 100). Choose your interval so that you will be able to graph the maximum number of times that the behavior can occur during each observation.

② Enter the name of the behavior that you are measuring here.

① Enter the time component in which you are measuring the behavior here (e.g., days, weeks, sessions).

FIGURE 8.16

Source: Information from Tieghi (2003). Reprinted by permission.

Placing points on a graph

- ■ Ⓐ Look at the first column on your measurement form. On the *horizontal axis*, find the time component that represents *when* you collected the information—for example, Day 3.
- ■ Ⓑ Look at the last column on your measurement form. On the *vertical axis*, find the *value of the measurement*—for example, 6.
- ■ Ⓒ Place a dot where the horizontal and vertical lines cross; ✐ connect each dot to the previous one with a line.

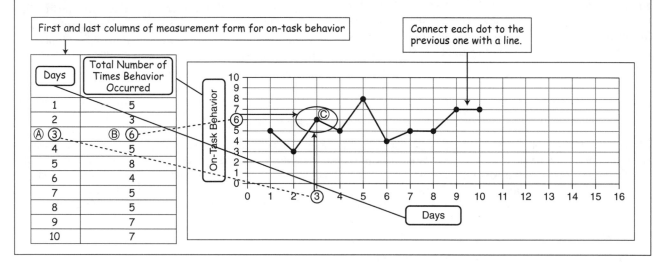

deficit. Hypotheses implicated access to preferred activities and access to social interaction as potential functions for flopping to the ground during transitions. Scheduling social interaction *after* appropriate transitions markedly reduced her rates of flopping behavior.

School records often have a great deal of information for functional behavioral assessments. A useful procedure is the School Archival Record Search (SARS) by Walker and Shea (1991). The SARS has information regarding demographics, special education status such as placement, school attendance, achievement test results, retentions, disciplinary incidents, Title I services, and perhaps some narratives. Information on the number of suspensions, accommodations, interventions, curriculum adjustments, and parent conferences for the identified student can also be found through SARS.

Functional behavioral assessment interviews may identify and define target behaviors and even provide some hypotheses regarding the function of behaviors. These interviews are more structured and systematically focus on possible functionality of behavior. An example of the functional assessment interview, adapted from the work of O'Neill and colleagues (1997), appears on page 111–112.

Behavior rating scales and checklists can be used for briefly identifying target behaviors. These rating scales evaluate specific behaviors and their functionality; standard published rating scales may be used.

Direct observation of antecedents, behaviors, and consequences is the most important aspect of functional behavioral assessment and may be used as support and confirmation for information obtained from rating scales. The ABC observation form discussed earlier in this chapter (page 114) would be useful here. Another useful method is the scatterplot assessment (see page 115), which was discussed by Easton and McColl (1997). In this procedure, the target behavior may be related to specific times of the day indicating a need for a temporal analysis. The systematic recording of behavioral data might involve frequency counts (e.g., number of times a student yells out) or interval-based recordings of the number of time intervals the student is doing academic work. Measurement across time will ensure that the data are representative (i.e., that they have content validity).

Quality of Data

Quality refers to the reliability and validity of obtained data. Sasso and colleagues (2000) have reviewed the literature concerning the promise and practice of functional assessment, especially concerning the area of emotional and behavioral disorders. Reliability in functional assessment refers to agreement among different observers viewing the same behavior (Newcomer & Lewis, 2004). The educator might use the same time interval (*interobserver agreement*) or the same observer viewing the same behavior at different times (*intraobserver agreement*) (Chandler & VanLaarhoven, 2004; Suen, 1990). Again, reliability in functional assessment reflects the degree that two observers act like equivalent measuring instruments (Lewis et al., 2002). Whereas traditional reliability is concerned with variation across a group of individuals, functional behavioral assessment reliability is concerned with one individual's behavior over time (Suen, 1990).

Validity in traditional psychology is defined as the quality of inferences drawn from test scores (Meyer et al., 2001). There are three types: (1) *content validity*—referring to the content domain, (2) *criterion-related validity*—referring to the prediction of behavior, and (3) *construct validity*—referring to the meaning of hypothetical constructs. Functional behavioral assessment mainly involves content, convergent, or treatment validity. There is no concern with hypothetical constructs because only observable behaviors are assessed. There is also little concern with predictive (or criterion-related) validity. Functional behavioral assessment validity can be defined as the representativeness of behavior measured in a specific situation, at one point in time, and by one observer. Each type of validity appropriate for RBA involves various aspects of assessment.

Content validity represents the most important, salient, and relevant type of validity. The fundamental question is how well the measurement of behavior in a particular situation at a given point in time by a particular observer represents that same behavior measured in other situations, at other times, and by different observers. One may compare samples of behavior during baseline with samples during treatment, where both assessments depend on content validity (Newcomer & Lewis, 2004; Gresham, 2004).

Convergent validity involves assessment by more than one method that yields equivalent information. It can be defined as agreement between two attempts to measure the same behavior using different methods (Paclawskyj et al., 2001). However, the lack of agreement would not invalidate the data assessment. Such disagreement among methods may reflect situational specificity of behavior, not the invalidity of the method of measurement. A good example can be found in the study by Cruse and colleagues (2002).

Treatment validity refers to the degree to which assessment information contributes to or is useful in producing beneficial treatment outcomes (Shapiro & Heick, 2004). This form of validity is basic to all functional behavioral assessment. If an assessment procedure is to have treatment validity, it must lead to a clear specification of target behaviors, then result in effective treatments and also be useful in evaluating treatment outcomes. The results of a study by Nielsen and colleagues (1999) demonstrated that functional behavioral assessment and comprehensive intervention implemented during typical preschool activities decreased the challenging behavior of the participants. Three observations were made: First, data obtained from the functional behavioral assessment identified two functions of challenging behavior: to obtain tangibles and attention. Second, the results of the comprehensive interventions showed a significant decrease in challenging behavior, an increase in appropriate requests, and maintenance or increase in engagement. Third, these teachers learned to implement the comprehensive interventions. Now, it's important to next look at the sequence of behaviors that are involved in RBA.

Antecedent events refer to events that precede the identified problem behavior. The antecedent event is also described as a discriminative stimulus, for it occurs immediately prior to and in the presence of the behavior that is reinforced. For example, if a teacher's instruction regarding an assignment is followed by noncompliance, and if the student avoids the work assigned, then whatever behavior that allowed the student to avoid the work would be reinforced (i.e., successful avoidance). The avoidance behavior might involve acting-out (e.g., throwing an object and hitting another student) and it may be followed by the student being sent to the office (and being unable to do the assignment). Recently, more attention has been put on antecedent events in the design of behavioral intervention (Smith and Iwata, 1997). In another example, Mueller and colleagues (2001) found that teacher-delivered task demands (an antecedent event) were functionally related to hand flopping (an inappropriate behavior) in a 5-year-old boy with autism, although this behavior (hand flopping) initially appeared to be maintained by social consequences (e.g., attention).

Setting events are another form of antecedent events that are removed in time and place from the occurrence of a behavior but are related to the occurrence of that behavior. Some experts distinguish between setting events and *establishing operations*—an antecedent event that changes the effectiveness of the reinforcer (Iwata, Smith, & Michael, 2000). For example, if a student has eaten several bags of candy to the point of being satiated, it is unlikely that candy would be a future potential reinforcer at the time. Being satiated (the setting event) would thus change the reinforcing properties of the candy. A setting event such as getting into a fight at home before going to school could set the stage for later aggressive behavior at school. According to Forehand and McMahon (1981), parent training programs were successful in reducing oppositional behavior at home. This work was later supported by Webster-Stratton, Reid, and Hammond (2001). Setting events could involve changes in routine, curriculum, or internal changes in the child (e.g., headaches, medication effects). One may also discover that a child's inappropriate behavior occurs in the presence of one teacher but not another, despite the fact that the child is equally capable of doing the work for either one.

A functional behavioral assessment might indicate that a behavior functions to (1) bring about a specific consequence, or (2) avoid or escape from a specific consequence. In short, a behavior may result in the student obtaining something desirable or avoiding something undesirable. The framework model for such functions of behavior have been noted by O'Neill and colleagues (1997). The two broad categories are subdivided into obtaining or avoiding socially mediated internal stimulation, attention, or objects and activities. One factor not considered in this framework is when students do not have a skill in their repertoire (i.e., a skill deficit rather than a performance deficit). For example, a handwriting skill deficit would be a plausible explanation for a student to act out during a lengthy written assignment.

Social Validity

Social validity refers to the assessment of the social significance of the goals of an intervention (i.e., the target behavior selected); the social acceptability of intervention procedures to reach these goals; and the social importance of the effects produced by the intervention (Wolf, 1978). A more recent discussion of social validity can be found in Hojnoski and colleagues (2006). In general, three questions are posed by social validity: (1) What needs to be changed? (2) How do we do it? (3) How can we assess effectiveness? Fox and McEvoy (1993) reviewed the progress in and barriers to accessing and enhancing generality of social behavior change and its relationship to social validity.

Social Significance of Goals The selection of target behaviors is one of the most important decisions in functional behavioral assessment. For example, getting all math problems correct may be more important (i.e., socially significant) than being on-task all the time. If there is consensus about what is most important, this can suggest a target behavior. The term *habilitative validity* (a variation of social validity) refers to the degree to which the goals, procedures, and outcomes of an intervention maximize the benefits and minimize the costs to an individual and to others (Austin, 2004). Noell and Gresham (1993), however, use the term *functional outcome analysis* for the same process. According to this theory, intervention goals are socially valid when the benefits (both objective and subjective) outweigh the costs.

Treatment Acceptability of Procedures Kazdin (1982) referred to *treatment acceptability* as a judgment regarding whether a specified treatment as outlined is fair relative to a specific problem and is reasonable and nonintrusive, and it is also consistent with what a treatment should be. Krain, Kendall, and Power (2005) indicated that treatment acceptability is a primary issue in treatment selection and use. If a treatment is deemed acceptable, its use will probably be high. Gresham and Lopez (1996) stated that a more direct index of treatment acceptability would use the concepts of *integrity* and *use* as direct behavioral measures of acceptability. Integrity (where some aspect of treatment may be unacceptable) or use (where a treatment may be rejected by most) may serve as behavioral markers for treatment acceptability. There is a current controversy over the validity and applicability of assessment FBA procedures with students who show emotional and behavioral disorders (EBD). In a comparison of results and acceptability of FBA procedures with a group of middle school students with EBD, there was 64 percent agreement between teacher/student interviews and classroom observations. In general, social validity was deemed adequate.

Social Importance of Effects   The social importance of effects establishes the clinical or practical significance of behavior changes. A key question must be answered: Does the outcome of the intervention represent a significant improvement or a relevant behavior change? Jones and Lungaro (2000) suggested evaluating the achievement outcome interventions at several levels: (1) *proximal effects*, which may be assessed by visual inspection or counting (e.g., noting the increase in sight word vocabulary or the number of math problems completed); (2) *intermediate effects*, which may involve changes in collateral behaviors (e.g., reading fluency, higher grades in math); (3) *distal effects*, which may represent long-term changes in behaviors or outcomes (e.g., more friendships or reading more books that are not part of the assignments).

USING FUNCTIONAL BEHAVIORAL ASSESSMENT TO CHANGE BEHAVIOR

After sufficient data have been collected through functional behavioral assessment, information must be summarized in order to make decisions about how to change behaviors. Hypotheses about target behaviors and alternate behaviors need to be written. For example, a student might engage in inappropriate behavior such as aggression when faced with a boring or difficult task such as math homework. It will be important to determine what behavior is desired of the student instead of the inappropriate behavior (i.e., what appropriate behavior

could result in the same consequences). The first consideration in planning such an intervention is to focus on changing antecedent events that will make the problem behavior less likely to occur. Numerous changes in antecedent events have been described by Sprague, Sugai, and Walker (1998): (1) changing the schedule of activities, (2) altering the size or composition of groups, (3) shortening the tasks, (4) mixing easy tasks with more difficult ones, and (5) adaptation of the curriculum.

O'Neill and colleagues (1997) also described two strategies for altering consequences: (1) increase the value of the payoff for appropriate behavior, and (2) decrease the value of the consequence for inappropriate behavior.

Teaching alternative appropriate behaviors is based on a replacement model (Gresham, 1998). Some appropriate behaviors may be lacking in the student's repertoire (i.e., there may be a skill deficit). The problem behaviors might then occur because the student "has no alternative." The use of modeling, coaching, and behavioral rehearsal may be helpful in dealing with such cases. Once these behaviors are taught, they can be reinforced in various situations to promote not only continuity but also generalization. Kern and colleagues (2001) examined the efficacy of using self-management procedures to reinforce both behavior that was incompatible with the target behavior and appropriate replacement behavior that was functionally equivalent to the undesirable target behavior. These self-management procedures resulted in lower rates of problem behavior. An example of an FBA with function based behavioral supports is found in the section that follows.

DEVELOPMENT OF A POSITIVE FUNCTION-BASED BEHAVIOR SUPPORT PLAN

There are several steps involved in creating a positive function-based behavior support plan (BSP):

Step 1:   Function-based summary statement—This comes from the FBA and should include the following:
  A. *Operational definition* of the problem behavior that is observable and measurable.
  B. *Information* on its frequency, duration, and intensity.

C. Antecedent *trigger*.

D. Description of any *setting events* that increase the probability of occurrence for the trigger of the problem behavior.

E. Description of any *setting events* that decrease the probability of occurrence for the trigger of the problem behavior.

F. *Hypothesis* regarding why the student continues to engage in the problem behavior and its maintaining consequences.

Example

In math class, Vince gets into arguments with the math teacher when she asks him to correct his mistakes. He makes verbal objections and states that he doesn't want to redo the work, and/or he becomes very critical of his teacher. These behavior problems occur several times per week and are of moderate intensity. However, his behavior problems are more likely to occur if he has had a conflict with another student, or if he has less than 90 percent of the problems wrong. His behavior problems are also less likely when his math teacher provides verbal praise before discussing corrections or if he has less than 10 percent of math problems wrong. Overall, his behavior helps to avoid correcting his work.

Step 2: *Replacement behaviors*—Describes the appropriate replacement behavior that can meet the same function (or delay) as the problem behavior.

Step 3: *Competing behavior pathway*—Create a chart from available information.

Step 4: *Identify intervention strategies*— Brainstorm (and select) strategies for each area that follows that will make the problem behavior less effective, less efficient, and less relevant than the replacement or desired behavior.

A. *Intervening prior to the problem behavior*— strategies and interventions that will

1. Make the triggering antecedents less likely to trigger the problem behavior.

2. Minimize setting events so they will have less of an impact on triggering antecedents.

3. Teach replacement behavior that is more acceptable, easier to do, and more likely to be reinforced.

4. Reinforce and strengthen replacement/ desired behavior.

Be specific about types of reinforcers and their schedule, specific teaching interventions, social and affective skill programs, and how triggers and setting events can be manipulated to increase the likelihood of replacement behavior and decrease the likelihood of problem behavior.

B. *Intervening after problem behavior*—Again emphasize making the problem behavior inefficient (less reinforcing). Specify the consequences, strategies, etc., that can be used to decrease the occurrence of the problem behavior.

Step 5: *Plan to monitor progress*—This must include

A. Outcomes of the plan that address changes in problem behavior or replacement behavior along with the criteria for success.

B. Data collection form to monitor progress.

C. Schedule to assess progress (optional).

D. Emergency procedures if behavior escalates.

Step 6: *Plan for a behavior support plan (or BIP)*—This must include

A. Who, what, and when.

B. How plan will be shared with other team members, staff, and family.

C. Training needed.

D. Name of the plan coordinator.

Step 7: *Implement/evaluate the Behavior Support Plan (also called the BSP)*—Be sure to

A. Implement the plan.

B. Assess progress.

C. Celebrate success and continue monitoring.

D. If implementation fails, review implementation.

E. If implementation is OK, reassess hypothesis on function of problem behavior.

F. If OK, modify plan and reassess periodically.

G. If hypotheses inaccurate, modify FBA and redesign support plan.

A copy of a typical FBA summary report with a behavioral intervention plan (BIP) is shown in Appendix B. The box on the next page presents a list of do's and don'ts to follow when conducting functional behavioral assessment.

Do's and Don'ts of Functional Behavioral Assessment

Do...	Don't...

Do...

- Use several different types of data; review records and permanent products, conduct interviews and observations, use rating scale checklists.

- Interview the people who know the child best— parents, teachers, paraprofessionals, peers, siblings, friends of family.

- Be aware of the child's environment. Remember that even subtle things such as changes in seating location, time of day, or lighting have the potential to influence the child's behavior.

- Consider the problem relative to the child's skills. Is it a "can't do" or a "won't do" problem?

1. Does the child have a grasp of the skills required to complete the task?

2. Does the child have the skills but is not choosing to use them for some reason?

- Consider the impact of tasks and activities upon the child's behavior.

1. Pay attention to the types of responses required (e.g., verbal or nonverbal, written or oral).

2. Review any relevant curricular materials.

- Observe the child as much as possible. The more information that is collected, the more valid and accurate the assessment.

- Describe the child's behavior as thoroughly as possible (i.e., who, what, when, where, why).

- Observe the child at different times of day.

- Get feedback from others—make functional assessment a team effort! This helps ensure both an accurate assessment and the identification of good intervention strategies.

- Be respectful. Keep in mind that children sometimes feel uncomfortable when they are observed.

Don't...

- Make it too obvious that the child is being observed because this may change behavior.

- Be disorganized. Keep complete notes, with full names of people, dates, etc. This will help collect data that are more accurate and valid.

- Forget to observe the child during both structured activities such as lessons and unstructured events such as transitions.

- Give up, especially when a child reacts to an intervention plan. This is often a direct indication that the intervention plan is working. Be consistent, and make decisions with data that are collected over a period of time.

- Forget to consider the potential influence of the child's eating and sleeping patterns (e.g., night terrors, food allergies, whether or not the child had breakfast earlier in the day).

- Ignore the influence of cultural factors—some behaviors are considered more socially acceptable in some cultures than others.

- Assume that the purpose of the child's behavior holds true across settings (i.e., what may be true in one setting may not be true in another).

- Forget to identify the child's strengths and preferences; knowing these will make intervention much more successful.

- Just pay attention to issues surrounding a behavior when it occurs; remember that it is just as important to learn about when a behavior DOES NOT occur.

- Get discouraged! It often takes time to correctly identify the function or purpose of a child's behavior.

Source: Information from http://myweb.usf.edu/naheindel/PBSsection3c-DosDonts.html, University of South Florida website.

SUMMARY

The focus here is on functional behavioral assessment—a process that determines the primary function of a problem behavior and then develops a hypothesis about that behavior and an intervention plan to change it. This assessment may be done independently of the evaluation used to determine classification and eligibility. The various components of functional behavioral assessment are addressed, and some of the major tools used are discussed. The intervention plan is discussed in detail, as are ways to monitor whether or not the plan is effective and efficient.

DISCUSSION QUESTIONS

1. What are the primary functions of behavior?
2. What is a functional behavioral assessment?
3. What are the five steps in conducting an FBA?
4. What are setting events? Why are they important?
5. What are the two basic methods or tools used to gather information for the FBA?
6. Who should conduct the interview with a student who shows problem behavior?
7. What is negative reinforcement? Are there any problems with negative reinforcement?
8. Name five things that would be characteristic of appropriate replacement behavior.
9. What is the importance of positive reinforcement in the support of appropriate replacement behavior?
10. Is candy a good positive reinforcer? If not, how would you select appropriate reinforcers for a child who is exhibiting problem behaviors?
11. Discuss the importance of social rewards.
12. How is the FBA different from a formal (psychological) assessment?
13. Compare and contrast the nomothetic-trait and idiographic-behavior approaches for formal and functional behavioral assessment.
14. What is treatment validity and how is it important to FBA?
15. Describe the social validation of the goals of intervention. Why is this important?
16. What is the first consideration in planning an intervention?

CHAPTER 9

The Behavioral Intervention Plan and Development of the IEP

Overview

- Developing a behavioral intervention plan
- Evaluating and monitoring the BIP
- Managing dangerous behaviors
- Motivational considerations
- Manifestation determination
- Alternative manifestation determination
- Introduction to the IEP
- The IEP process
- Deciding placement
- Modifying the IEP

Case History

Jordan is a 14-year-old eighth grader who is eligible for special education due to his behavior disorders but is now in a regular education class. While testing has not revealed problems with his cognitive skills (academic functioning), he consistently fails to complete his homework assignments and is frequently absent (truant) from school all day. He has also been seen in juvenile court for vandalism. His social relations with peers are generally poor. Over the years, Jordan has been seen by a clinical psychologist and by several counselors and carried many labels such as ADHD, OCD, paranoid schizophrenia, tic disorder, Tourette syndrome, as well as ODD. He has received medication off and on for these conditions and has shown a positive response to past treatment. He has just been given a new label of conduct disorder (CD). Jordan and his parents are cooperating with the school and psychologist to work on a coordinated program. *What would you do?*

A functional behavioral assessment (FBA) and a behavioral intervention plan (BIP) are part of a positive behavioral support process. According to IDEA 1997 and the revision in 2004, the FBA is mandated for students with disabilities whose behavior either causes a change in school placement or constitutes a pattern of misbehavior. The FBA serves to improve the quality of behavioral interventions and behavioral planning (Sugai et al., 2000).

When disciplining actions result in the removal of a student with a disability for ten or more cumulative school days or when a change in educational placement occurs, the IEP team must review all pertinent data on the student. The team can then decide whether to conduct an FBA and develop a BIP, or determine whether the student's BIP needs to be modified. Based on the FBA, a BIP may be developed and included in the IEP. This plan must consist of positive intervention strategies and behavioral supports that target the behavior and needs of the student. A BIP may reduce the need for extreme disciplinary measures of suspension and expulsion, which have both been shown to be ineffective. Figure 9.1 illustrates the decision-making points in a process conducted by the Massachusetts Department of Education.

IDEA 2004 AND BEHAVIOR DISORDERS

The original Individuals with Disabilities Education Act (IDEA) of 1997 has been modified in IDEA 2004 to implement changes that affect all children with disabilities but some children who have an emotional or behavior disorder may experience certain specific applications. While it is not possible to address each one of the changes that might affect an individual child, some of the more general changes might affect the IEP process, due process, or discipline. These changes are listed as follows:

IEP Process (1) Short-term objectives or benchmarks are no longer listed by the IEP team. Such objectives are now only required for those students who must take an alternate assessment (generally less than 1 percent of all students with disabilities). However, even though IDEA 2004 no longer requires that short-term objectives be listed, it still requires a listing of how progress will be measured and reported. (2) Level of

performance must be measured using the student's present levels of academic achievement as objective assessment data. (3) Educational progress describes any advances that the student is making toward annual functional goals that include the short-term objectives. (4) Individual appropriate accommodations and alternate assessments must be included in the student's IEP. This must include a statement of any accommodation needed to measure the academic achievements and functional performance of the student. A student who is involved in alternate assessment cannot participate in regular assessment; the alternate assessment selected must be an appropriate one. (5) Transition services were eliminated for students 14 years of age; however, students 16 years and older were included. Under IDEA 2004, such students must have their IEP updated yearly and should include an appropriate measure of goals along with any services needed to assist students in reaching these goals. (6) Educational placement decisions cannot be made until the IEP team develops a consensus concerning the student's needs, program, and goals. IDEA 2004 emphasized that unilateral placement by the school based on the child's disability classification is not acceptable and not legal. (7) Reviewing/revising the IEP must occur at least once per year to see if the students are achieving their annual goals. The IEP team needs to revise the IEP to deal with lack of progress, updated evaluation or additional information that is provided to the team, along with any change in special needs.

Due Process (1) Statute of limitations allows a two-year period that parents can exercise their due process rights. (2) Due process without complaints is a new provision for the school district to file a response within 10 days (unless the state hearing office is notified within 15 days) challenging the parents' due process claim. The state hearing offices have five more days to offer a finding. The parents' claim typically involves the idea that their child's educational rights are being compromised. (3) A resolution session is scheduled for parents who file a due process complaint. The school then has 30 days to resolve their complaint; following this a due process hearing can be set up.

Discipline (1) Student rights for a *stay put* in the current educational placement is eliminated for *any* violation of the school's code of conduct. This action

- This chart should be read in conjunction with discipline procedures in state law, M.G.L. c. 71, §§ 37H & 37H1/2, and district-wide and school-wide student codes of conduct.
- Protections in the IDEA apply to students who have been found eligible for special education and to students for whom the school is deemed to have knowledge that the child might have a disability (i.e., students who have not yet been found eligible but the school had a basis of knowledge of a disability, including students who have been referred for initial evaluation). 34 CFR § 300.354
- Beginning on the 11th school day of a student's disciplinary removal during the school year, and if removal is a change in placement, the student must be provided free appropriate public education (FAPE) services during the period of removal to allow him/her to continue to participate in the general education curriculum and progress towards IEP goals, even if in a different setting. 34 CFR § 300.530(b) & (d).
- If the conduct that the student is being disciplined for involves the "special circumstances" of weapons, illegal drugs, controlled substances, or serious bodily injury, school personnel may remove the student to an interim alternative educational setting (IAES) for up to 45 school days, regardless of the manifestation determination. 34 CFR § 300.530(g). The IEP Team must determine the IAES.
- Although the following flowchart lays out the steps that a school district must take when disciplining a student with a disability, it is important to remember that at any point the parent and school district can agree to change a student's placement for disciplinary reasons. Agreements should be in writing, and signed by the school personnel and the parent.

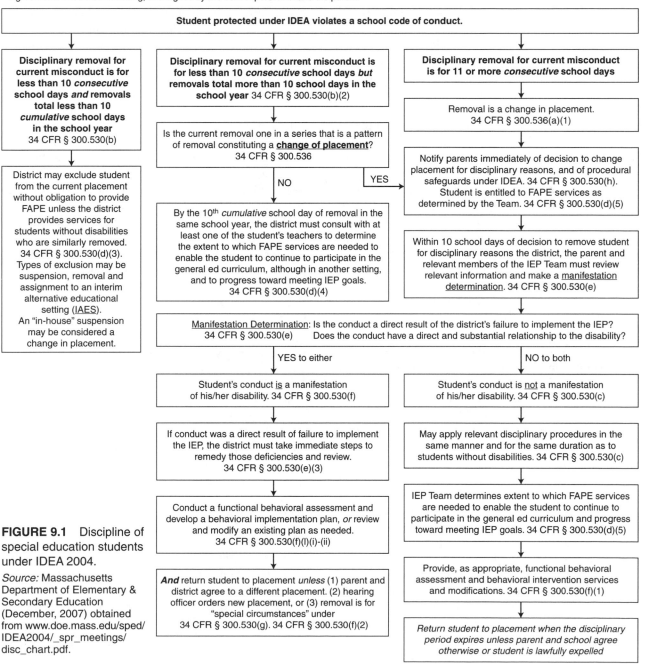

FIGURE 9.1 Discipline of special education students under IDEA 2004.

Source: Massachusetts Department of Elementary & Secondary Education (December, 2007) obtained from www.doe.mass.edu/sped/IDEA2004/_spr_meetings/disc_chart.pdf.

may result in students being removed from their current placement for 10 days. The stay put allows students to remain in their current placement while the parents challenge the placement or the manifestation determination—an important change permitting the student to have access to a Free and Appropriate Education (FAPE) in the Least Restrictive Environment (LRE). (2) Services in an alternate educational setting are important in getting a FAPE. Under IDEA 2004, the student must receive services to continue to be involved in a general education curriculum while moving toward the IEP annual goals. It is noteworthy that all students with disabilities must receive services that are needed for a FAPE, even when a specific student is removed from the current educational placement. (3) A manifestation determination review is needed for a student who seriously violates a code of conduct. Under IDEA 2004, the burden of proof is now on parents to prove that their child's behavior was a direct manifestation of his or her disability. The segment of IDEA 2004 that requires the IEP team to consider that students' disabilities improved their control or understanding of the consequence of their behavior has been deleted. The school will now have an easier time removing students who present dangerous behavior because parents who are involved in the IEP must carefully attend to the behavioral needs of their child. (4) The time limit on removal for 45 calendar days has been changed to *45 school days*. Students must now be held accountable for their actions. The time limit is now a total of 9 weeks instead of 6 weeks. (5) Assessment/interventions plans have not changed. The FBA and BIP are still required for students with disabilities who receive an IEP. The FBA and BIP are still needed in evaluating students to determine the function of their acting-out behavior(s) and to propose the most effective treatment. (6) Individual care determination will be the key in determining any change of placement or evaluation needs for the student who violates a school code of conduct. This provision will be quite helpful to parents who wish to prove that their child's behavior is a manifestation of the disability.

The case-by-case (individual) method of looking at specific violations of the school code of conduct may reveal that, under IDEA 2004, the school may provide early intervention to young students who are "at risk." These students clearly need additional academic and/or behavioral services in order to succeed in a general education classroom. However, they may not need to be in special education. There are three circumstances that are applicable: (1) the child's parents had expressed concern (in writing) that the child may need special education prior to discipline attempts, (2) the parents request an evaluation, and (3) the teacher may refer the child for evaluation. If the request for evaluation is made during the time period of disciplinary action, the school must complete the evaluation as quickly as possible. At the time, they remain in an interim alternative educational placement.°

The information obtained from the FBA may help to clarify why problem behaviors occur and reoccur. An FBA may be needed for an initial evaluation or reevaluation of the student during the initial development of or review of the IEP. While conducting the FBA, it will be important to document previous interventions or teaching strategies that have had either a positive or negative impact on the student's behavior. However, all other information on environmental, medical, or psychological factors must also be gathered. This may include changes in the family (e.g., being assigned to a new foster family), a medical problem (e.g., a head injury), or a psychological issue (e.g., how others respond to the student). Conducting an FBA and developing a BIP may be fairly simple or complex, depending on the specific concerns of the student.

DEVELOPING A BEHAVIORAL INTERVENTION PLAN

A behavioral intervention plan (BIP) consists of strategies designed to increase or decrease a pattern of behaviors exhibited by a student. These strategies may include preventive techniques, the teaching of replacement behaviors or skills, and recommendations on how to respond to problem behaviors.

BIP Components

A BIP uses a problem-solving approach and is based on information obtained through the FBA process. Possible behavioral interventions, environmental

---

°For additional information on the IEP for students with behavior disorders under IDEA 2004, see *Wrights Law: Special Education Law* (2nd ed.), or go to www.wrightslaw.com/idea/art/iep.roadmap. htm or www.schwaylearning.org. You may also contact Candice Cortella, Director of the Advocacy Institute, Washington, DC.

manipulations, and teaching strategies are formulated and based on appropriate alternative behaviors, antecedent events, consequences, and setting events in the environment. Here the actual BIP is developed and specified. The plan is typically multidimensional and should address not only reactive manipulation of consequences such as behavioral contracts but also the following three points:

1. *Instruction*: Teaching appropriate and desirable replacement behaviors.

2. *Preventive measures*: Reducing or even eliminating the conditions that trigger the problematic behaviors.

3. *Environmental arrangements*: Making the appropriate changes in the setting where problematic behavior occurs.

For example, when Serena was asked to redo her written work to correct errors in spelling and grammar, she refused to comply and used offensive language, becoming visibly upset. A review of past infractions revealed that there were similar episodes in the past, all occurring following a request to redo and correct her work. This was interpreted as an attempt to avoid rewriting and was based on several observations of similar situations. A BIP was developed using the multiple observations and the suggested hypotheses of refusal to do written corrections (avoidance). The BIP will ask for the following to happen:

1. Serena is to be instructed on the appropriate way to ask for help and when to alert the teacher (or parent at home) when a task is too difficult.

2. Serena is to keep a record (self-monitor) of times when she either "stayed calm" or "lost control."

3. Serena's teachers will review correction strategies and provide an answer key for her work along with assisting her in how to review her work and how to make corrections.

4. Serena's teachers will reinforce her with specific verbal praise when she cooperates on the first three steps and also (a) when she starts a task, (b) while she is working, and (c) when she completes the task.

5. If a verbal conflict ensues, Serena will be given an opportunity to problem solve and to complete a simple task before attempting corrections.

A successful BIP clearly depends on the accuracy of the hypotheses (i.e., reason for the misbehavior) and on the IEP team's ability to match strategies of reducing or eliminating problem behavior and increasing the student's appropriate behavior to his or her skill level. A change in behavior is more likely to occur when the IEP team finds a way to make the inappropriate behavior ineffective, inefficient, or irrelevant and to make the replacement alternative behavior more reinforcing for the student. The flow chart in Figure 9.2 illustrates *the positive behavior support (PBS) process*.

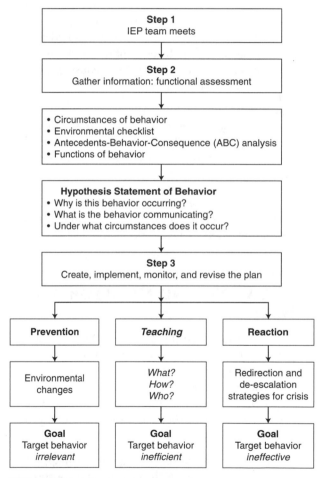

FIGURE 9.2 The positive behavior support (PBS) process.

Source: Information from Fodor (2002) An Introduction to Positive Behavioral Supports (PBS) in School Settings, University of Idaho: Center on Disabilities and Human Development. Obtained online at pbs.idahocdhd.org/files/PBS%20Manual%2006.pdf.

The BIP should again include the following steps:

1. Define the target behavior in measurable terms.
2. Prepare a prevention plan that changes identifiable events, times, situations, and any other factor that may trigger the target behavior.
3. Make plans to teach an alternative replacement behavior or a skill that can compete with the problem behavior and that can accomplish the same purpose with similar effort and immediacy but in a more acceptable way (i.e., through a more acceptable function).
4. Make sure that a plan is in place to respond to the student's problematic behavior so as to reinforce appropriate behavior. The IEP team should specify ways of avoiding reinforcement of the student's inappropriate behavior and thus causing greater stress and emotional upset.
5. Include specifics on how to manage a crisis situation.
6. Collect data to measure progress toward the desired goals to identify when interventions need to be changed if progress falls below expectations.
7. Set a date to review the BIP.

Sample BIP forms are located in Appendix C. The BIP can be included in the student's IEP along with the corresponding goals, benchmarks, and objectives.

EVALUATING AND MONITORING THE BIP

In order for the BIP to be effective, there should be ongoing evaluation and monitoring when necessary. In fact, a strategy to evaluate and monitor the effectiveness of the BIP should be included with the initial conceptualization of the plan. According to Crone and Horner (2003), the BIP should include the following:

1. A method for measuring changes in the inappropriate behavior as well as the desired and appropriate replacement behavior.
2. A means to assess the practicality of the plan.
3. A way to evaluate the satisfaction of others (parents, teachers, and the student) with the program.

There must be regularly scheduled IEP team meetings to evaluate data, including frequency counts of targeted behavior, the ABC Observation forms, scatterplots, and other student data. The following four questions should be asked:

1. Were the goals of the BIP achieved?
2. Did the implementation of the BIP go as planned?
3. Is there a need for additional assessment?
4. Does the BIP need to be modified in any way?

Once the goals of the BIP have been achieved, there should be a maintenance plan implemented that can provide continuing support for the student.

EFFECTIVENESS OF THE FBA AND BIP

The effectiveness of the FBA and BIP can be compromised in several ways:

1. The IEP team fails to evaluate, monitor, and adjust the BIP.
2. The assessment is incomplete.
3. The problem or alternative replacement behavior may not be adequately defined and specified.
4. There may be lack of training and support from key personnel as well as a poor understanding of the plan.
5. There may be a failure to determine whether the problem behavior significantly interferes with the physical, emotional, or academic well being of the student.
6. The primary person implementing the intervention (usually a teacher) may lack the needed skills.
7. There may be a lack of understanding of cultural, home, or family issues.

Any breakdown in the FBA or BIP procedures may cause the plan to be less effective and successful. Teachers who are confronted with students who have special needs provide critical input toward the effectiveness of the BIP and ultimately to the IEP team. Being involved with the BIP will thus allow teachers to contribute to positive and successful outcomes for their students.

Case Study

FBA Needed

Steven is an 8-year-old second grader in a regular class who has been referred by Ms. Chin, his teacher, because of disruptive behavior that has labeled him the "class clown." When Ms. Chin walks away from him, he "falls out of his chair," which result in laughs and giggles from his classmates. He also walks around the classroom, talking to and distracting students from their independent work. During transitions and changes in activities, such as going to lunch, he often pushes others to be first in line. Steven teases others and wrestles with them while in line. As a result, Steven has received numerous office referrals for his inappropriate behavior, yet the problem behavior continues. Steven has been recommended for an FBA.

It is clear in this example that a general model is needed to plan interventions for Steven. The competing behavior pathway diagram (Condon and Tobin, 2001) as shown in Figure 9.3 shows three ways for Steven to respond: (1) with ideal behavior (a desired alternative), (2) with inappropriate behavior (i.e., problem behavior), or (3) with an alternate behavior that can achieve the same outcome. (i.e., acceptable alternative). Thus, Figure 9.3 shows the three ways that Steven can respond.

• •

Competing behavior pathway: This involves the use of a chart that creates a link between the FBA and the BIP. Competing behaviors are behaviors that are mutually exclusive. An individual cannot concurrently engage in two competing behaviors. For example, screaming and talking softly are competing behaviors. When applied to the BIP, target behaviors and desired behaviors are competing behaviors. A child cannot simultaneously ignore the teacher and follow directions at the same time. The purpose of the competing behavior pathway chart is (1) to enforce the importance of building the behavior intervention plan around the hypothesis statement; (2) to recognize competing behavior alternatives (desired or acceptable behaviors) to the target behavior; and (3) to determine approaches for making the target behavior ineffective, inefficient, or irrelevant through changes to the routine or environment.

Note: O'Neill et al. (1997) show the basic paradigm; Condon and Tobin (2001) give the specifics.

• •

The intervention strategy planning chart shown in Figure 9.4 provides guidelines to develop and write a specific plan for Steven.

The FBA indicated (from interviews and direct observation) that Steven's most problematic behaviors— being off-task and exhibiting inappropriate physical contact—were initiated and/or maintained by attention from his classmates and the teacher.

Steven's diagram and planning charts for inappropriate physical contact behavior are shown in Figure 9.5 and for off-task behavior in Figure 9.6. Following construction of these planning charts, the next step would involve implementation of the plan. This refers to the *who, when*, and *how* for each component of the plan.

Since Steven seemed to be highly reactive to observation when it was used as part of the FBA process, he was taught to use the self-monitoring sheet. Steven thus learned to monitor his own behavior and to check with his teacher three times a day to see if she agreed with him on his ratings (accuracy). This not only resulted in more appropriate teacher attention (from the feedback) but also garnered appropriate attention from his classmates upon achieving a goal (i.e., doing an activity with a classmate).

POSITIVE BEHAVIORAL INTERVENTION PLAN

A positive behavioral intervention plan has been created for Thomas Jones, a student with Tourette's syndrome who has been disrupting his class with aggressive acting-out behavior. The planning form shown in Figure 9.7 presents an example of how an IEP team can develop a program. A blank planning form can be found in Appendix C.

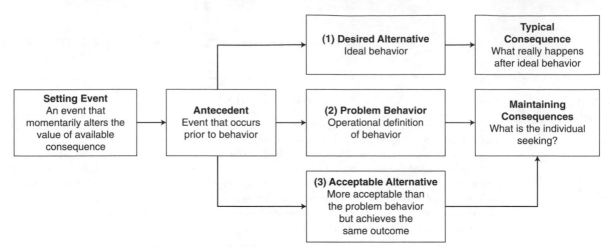

FIGURE 9.3 A competing behavior pathway diagram.

Source: Information from Condon and Tobin (2001, pp. 44–50). Reprinted by permission.

Setting Events	What are ways to minimize the likelihood or neutralize the effect of the setting event?	• Remove interruptions or distractions • Provide food • Provide rest • Other
Antecedent Strategies	What are ways to change the context to make the problem behaviors unnecessary?	• Clarify rules and expected behavior for whole class • Write a contract with the students • Change seating arrangements • Change schedule • Other
	What are some ways to prevent the problem behavior?	• Provide reminders about behavior when problem behavior is likely • Provide extra assistance • Modify assignments to match student skills • Other
Teaching Strategies	What can be done to increase expected behaviors or to teach a replacement behavior?	• Teach new behavior • Practice expected behavior in class • Follow a self-management program • Other
Consequence Strategies	What should happen when a replacement behavior occurs?	• Eliminate whatever was the maintaining consequence for the problem behavior such as peer attention, teacher attention, or break from work.
	How can maintaining consequence for the problem behavior be eliminated or reduced?	• Minimize negative attention • If safe, allow a 10-second delay before responding • Teach peers how to concentrate on their work and ignore distractions • Other
	What should happen when a desired behavior occurs?	• Establish a reward program • Praise student for good behavior • Other

FIGURE 9.4 Intervention strategy planning chart.

Source: Information from Condon and Tobin (2001, pp. 44–50). Reprinted by permission.

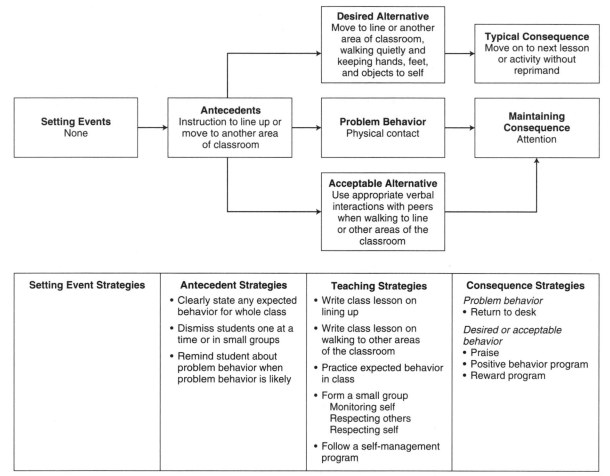

FIGURE 9.5   Steven s diagram and planning chart for inappropriate physical contact behavior.
Source: Information from Condon and Tobin (2001, pp. 44–50). Reprinted by permission.

Additional Thoughts on the BIP Process

First, prior to implementation of the BIP, all staff who have involvement and responsibility with the plan must be adequately trained to implement the plan in a consistent manner. A timeline for all procedures must be established, with specific tasks given to certain individuals. Decisions must be made regarding whether to implement the plan on a partial or whole-day basis. It might be decided, for example, to implement the plan in part of the day and then to expand it to the whole day, contingent upon the success of the plan. Again, the IDEA– Functional Behavior Analysis form in Appendix C may be used to help the IEP team record what is needed prior to implementing the plan.

Second, the BIP must be implemented consistently by the school staff, informing each person of his or her responsibility in providing specific services for the student.

Third, the plan may be implemented for a period of two weeks before checking on how it is working. At this point, there must be an evaluation of (1) how successful the staff was in implementing the plan correctly and consistently, and (2) how successful the BIP was in preventing the target problem behavior and/or increasing new and more appropriate behaviors. The sample planning form in Appendix C can be used to help the IEP team record the successes and problem areas of the BIP following implementation.

Fourth, when procedures are ineffective, alternative interventions may be developed or the IEP team may consider further assessments to obtain additional relevant information. Other factors may therefore affect the occurrence or frequency of the problem behavior. The form *Reconsidering the Behavioral Intervention Plan* may be used; a sample form is found in Appendix C.

Fifth, when interventions are repeatedly found to be ineffective, it must be determined whether the conditions of the BIP were consistently applied and were appropriate or whether a different placement and alternative strategies may be needed. Thus, the BIP may be tweaked rather than be considered a failure. A feedback form called the Behavior Support Plan Feedback form used to assess areas of difficulty in implementing the BIP with behavioral supports may also be found in Appendix C.

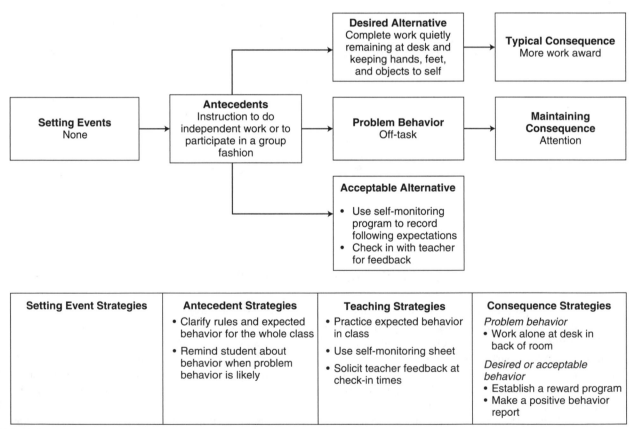

FIGURE 9.6   Steven's diagram and planning chart for off-task behavior.
Source: Information from Condon and Tobin (2001, pp. 44–50). Reprinted by permission.

Positive Behavioral Intervention Plan Planning Form

IEP teams can use this form to guide them through the process of developing the Positive Behavioral Intervention Plan.

Student _____Thomas Jones_____ Age ___13___ Sex ___M___

Teacher(s) _____Ms. Gilbow / Team B_____ Grade ___6___

Case Manager _____Ms. Brantley_____ Date(s) ___4/17/10___

Reason for intervention plan: *Tom's behavior often disrupts class. Yesterday he threw a dictionary across the room, knocked over his desk, kicked it, and began yelling obscenities at the teacher and the other students in the LD resource room. The teacher had to call for help from his ED resource room teacher to calm him down and safely remove him from the classroom.*

Participants (specify names):

(X) student ___Tom___   ( ) special education administrator_____

(X) family member ___Mrs. Jones___   (X) general education administrator ___Mr. Scott___

(X) special educator ___Ms. Gilbow___   ( ) school psychologist _____

( ) general educator_____   ( ) other agency personnel _____

( ) peer(s)_____

( ) other (specify) _____

Fact Finding

1. **General learning environment:** Describe the student's school class schedule, including any special programs or services.
   Tom receives special education to provide support for his emotional difficulties and learning disability in two resource rooms. These classes provide instruction in math, language arts, reading, social skills, and social studies. He is in the regular classroom for specials, lunch, and science. He rides a special bus with a paraprofessional to school.

2. **Problem behavior:** Define the problem behavior(s) in observable, measurable, and countable terms (i.e., topography, event, duration, seriousness, and/or intensity). Include several examples of the behavior.
   Thomas has Tourette's syndrome, a learning disability that manifests itself in reading and language arts, and an emotional disturbance. Symptoms of Tourette's lead him to display distracting tics and vocalize curses during the usual course of the day. This sometimes causes his classmates to make uncomplimentary comments. His emotional and learning disabilities often lead to frustrating academic and social situations. When he becomes frustrated, he often throws objects (books, backpacks, pencils), turns over furniture (chairs and tables), and curses obscenities at the adults and other students present in the classroom.

3. **Setting events:** Describe important things that are happening in the student's life that may be causing the behavior(s) of concern.
   Thomas recently started to be mainstreamed more often in the regular classroom. He has begun to take science (an area of strength and interest) in the general education setting.

4. **Review existing data:** Summarize previously collected information (records review, interviews, observations, and test results) relevant to the behavior(s).
   An examination of Tom's medical records and interviews with his parents and teachers all reveal that due to Tourette's syndrome he has uncontrollable tics that cause his head to jerk to the side. Often during these tics he curses, a behavior that has never been observed in isolation.

   A review of his IEP, test results, and interviews with his parents and teachers reveal that he has learning problems that keep him from realizing success in the mainstream classroom and causes him a lot of frustration. He

FIGURE 9.7

Source: Adapted from Addressing Student Problem Behavior (Part III) by the Center for Effective Collaboration and Practice. Reprinted with permission of CECP. Obtained online at http://cecp.air.org/fba/problembehavior3/appendix61.htm.

also is frustrated by the many rude comments made by his classmates regarding his tics. During unstructured time (recess, before school, between classes), other students have been observed teasing him. His parents and teachers report that this really bothers Tom and makes it difficult for him to make friends. He spends most of his spare time with his 4th grade sister who walks him to and from class in the mornings and afternoons.

Possible Explanations

5. **Identify likely antecedents (precipitating events) to the behavior(s):** *Academic frustration, social ridicule by peers.*
6. **Identify likely consequences that may be maintaining the behavior(s):** *When Tom acts out, he is removed from the situation. We believe that this behavior allows him to escape a frustrating situation.*
7. **Identify and describe any academic or environmental context(s) in which the problem behavior(s) does *not* occur:** *This problem has never occurred in the resource room for students with emotional disturbance. Parents report that it rarely occurs at home and that Tom did not have the same problem in his 5th grade class. They also report that Tom was asked not to return to the local YMCA because of his acting-out behavior.*

Validation

8. **Functional assessment:** Do you already have enough information to believe that the possible explanations are sufficient to plan an intervention?
   a. If yes, go to Step 9; if no, then what additional data collection is necessary?
      ( ) Review of IEP goals and objectives
      ( ) Review of medical records
      ( ) Review of previous intervention plans
      ( ) Review of incident reports
      ( ) ABC (across time and situations)
      ( ) Motivational analysis
      (X) Ecological analysis
      (X) Curricular analysis
      ( ) Scatterplot
      ( ) Parent questionnaire/interview
      (X) Student questionnaire/interview
      (X) Teacher questionnaire/interview (specify who) <u>*Mr. Elliott—5th grade teacher*</u>
      (X) Other (explain) <u>*Talk with director of the YMCA*</u>
   b. Summarize data. Attach additional sheets if necessary.
   Tom does not seem to have problems in environments that are well supervised and where he is not expected to perform tasks that are more difficult than his skill level.
■ *The YMCA director reported that the other kids teased Tom and that Tom would just "explode." He said that he knew the other kids antagonized Tom, but he was afraid someone would get hurt if Tom was permitted to continue to come to the Y. He told Tom that when his behavior was under control he was welcome to return.*
■ *Mr. Elliott, his 5th grade teacher, said that at the beginning of the school year he had his class study Tourette's syndrome and had guest speaker come in to discuss the effects of Tourette's. Tom even led some of the discussion. He felt that once the other students understood what was happening they were more comfortable with the tics and soon they began to ignore them.*
■ *Tom is about 2 years behind his grade-peers in reading and written language ability. He is intelligent and can understand grade-level tasks that are presented orally. When he is permitted to respond orally rather than writing an answer, he performs on grade level. If he is asked to read aloud or silently or is asked to fill out worksheets without assistance, he becomes frustrated or distracted and does not complete his work.*
■ *Tom does better in structured environments where there is adult supervision. Adults in these environments seem to deter the teasing of his peers and provide him with individual help in academics. Ms. Gilbow, his special education resource teacher, reports that he does well when given independent work on his grade level. He also does well in structured cooperative learning groups where he is permitted to respond orally and other team members do the writing and reading aloud. His teacher also reports that Tourette's syndrome was thoroughly discussed at the beginning of the school year and reviewed when new students are placed in her class.*

(continued)

9. **Formulate hypothesis statement:** Using the table below, determine why the student engages in problem behavior(s), whether the behavior(s) serves single or multiple functions, and what to do about the behavior(s).

	Internal	External
Obtain Something		
Avoid Something	*Expectation of ridicule about his tics and embarrassment associated with school failure.*	*Avoiding ridicule by avoiding social situations in which peers tease him.*

10. **Current level of performance:** Describe problem behavior(s) in a way the team will recognize onset and conclusion of behavior.
    Tom becomes noticeably frustrated and tics increase in response to peer taunting or difficult academic assignments. He hangs his head down low and focuses intently on one thing before a big outburst of aggressive behavior. He becomes nonverbal except for the obscenities associated with Tourette's syndrome.

11. Describe replacement behavior(s) that is/are likely to serve the same function as the behavior(s) identified in Step 10.
    Tom will approach the adult in charge of the setting when he notices himself getting agitated and ask to have assistance—either academic help or counseling. This will allow him to escape the situation without using inappropriate behavior.

12. **Measurement procedures for problem behavior(s) and replacement behavior(s):**
    a. Describe how (e.g., permanent products, event recording, scatterplot), when, and where student behavior(s) will be measured.
    Using event recording, Tom will be taught to count the number of times he becomes frustrated and the number of times he has outbursts versus how often he asks for help. He will be given a checklist to record this on.
    b. Summarize data by specifying which problem behavior(s) and replacement behavior(s) will be targets for intervention.
    Problem behavior: out of control anger—throwing things, hitting or kicking, using unacceptable language, or making threatening remarks or actions.

    Replacement behavior: appropriately dealing with anger—(1) asking for help from an adult or peer when feeling angry and wanting to leave a situation; (2) using self-talk and anger management skills to independently deal with anger.

13. **Behavioral intervention plan:**
    a. Specify goals and objectives (conditions, criteria for acceptable performance) for teaching the replacement behavior(s).
    Working with Ms. Gilbow, the ED resource room teacher, Tom will verbally identify and describe the physical signs that he experiences when he is becoming angry.
    Tom will recognize when he is becoming angry and will seek the assistance of an adult rather than acting-out 100 percent of the time.
    Tom will contact the director of the local YMCA and report his progress at controlling his temper, and discuss the technique that he uses to manage this. He will ask if he can return to the YMCA and use his skills with the adults that supervise after-school activities there.
    b. Specify instructional strategies that will be used to teach the replacement behavior(s).
    The ED resource room teacher will model thinking aloud using a role-play situation in which she becomes angry. She will identify why she thinks she is angry and will discuss all the possible ways to deal with her anger. She will model choosing an option that helps her reduce her anger in acceptable ways.
    Tom will role-play situations in which he has a history of becoming angry (e.g., during recess, in the classroom, in the hall while passing others) with the ED resource room teacher and other students. He will model his self-talk

(continued)

and will discuss ways of dealing with his anger in acceptable ways (e.g., enlist the help of an adult or trusted peer). He will choose a time when he usually encounters anger and frustration to practice this technique and will report back to his teacher and the class the outcomes of this technique. If the technique is successful, he will identify other situations in which it could be used. If it is unsuccessful, he will work with his teacher and peers to identify reasons why it did not work and suggest modifications.

Tom will use the technique in other school and nonschool settings.

c. Specify strategies that will be used to decrease problem behavior(s) and increase replacement behavior(s).

The adults that work with Tom will be told the signs to look for that indicate that Tom is beginning to feel frustration. They will approach him and ask him if he needs to talk. Anytime he asks them if he can speak with the counselor or to them about the way he feels, they will comply immediately or send him to an environment with an adult who can talk with him if they are busy.

d. Identify any changes in the physical environment needed to prevent problem behavior(s) and to promote desired (replacement) behavior(s), if necessary.

Tom will be given the opportunity to respond to academic questions verbally (either aloud or on a tape recorder). Tom will never be asked to read aloud in class unless he asks to. He will be given audiotapes with the written materials read aloud on them, or work in cooperative groups in which other students read the written materials aloud. Tom's classmates will be taught about Tourette's syndrome and will be given the opportunity to ask questions of experts (including Tom, if he feels comfortable) about the syndrome.

e. Specify extent to which the intervention plan will be implemented in various settings; specify settings and persons responsible for implementation of plan.

This plan will first be implemented in the ED resource room and then in the LD resource room. Once Tom has identified the physical signs that he is becoming angry, he will share them with his teacher in science class and his parents. The intervention plan will then be implemented in those settings as well. Once Tom has gone for 2 weeks without having a behavior incident in which he loses control, he will contact the director of the YMCA (with adult support, if he feels it is necessary) to discuss the possibility of his return.

14. **Evaluation plan and schedule:** Describe the plan and timetable to evaluate effectiveness of the intervention plan.

a. Describe how, when, where, and how often the problem behavior(s) will be measured.

For the first 3 weeks, Tom and his ED resource room teacher will discuss and chart his progress daily (the percentage of appropriate reactions to his anger). They will compare it to the number of outbursts during the previous 2 weeks. If after 3 weeks Tom's behavior has not decreased by at least 50 percent, the team will meet again to discuss possible changes in the intervention. If after 6 weeks, Tom's behavior has not decreased by at least 90 percent, the team will meet again to discuss possible changes in the intervention. At 8 weeks Tom should have no incidents of outbursts at school.

b. Specify persons and settings involved.

Initially it will be the responsibility of the ED resource room teacher. The intervention will then be initiated in the LD resource room and Tom's science class and at home. Once Tom has had no outbursts for 2 weeks, the intervention will be extended to the YMCA (with the director's agreement).

c. Specify a plan for crisis/emergency intervention, if necessary.

If Tom has a behavior outburst, the ED resource room teacher will be called in to help.

d. Determine the schedule to review/modify the intervention plan, as needed. Include dates and criteria for changing/fading the plan.

May 8, 2010 Review/modify if the behavior has not reduced by 50 percent.

May 29, 2010 Review/modify if the behavior has not been reduced by 90 percent.

June 12, 2010 Review/modify if the behavior has not reached 0.

15. Describe plan and timetable to monitor the degree to which the plan is being implemented.

Each Friday the ED resource room teacher will contact Tom's other teachers and the recess supervisors to discuss the implementation of the plan. Anytime Tom has a behavior outburst, the ED resource teacher will conduct an out-briefing with the adult in charge to discuss the situation and to determine whether the plan was followed as written.

USING EXTRAORDINARY DISCIPLINE PROCEDURES

Typically, initial interventions are low level and non-aversive in managing problem behavior. Aversive discipline is usually avoided but when needed must be used with extreme caution. Such procedures generally include seclusionary timeouts, physical restraints, and room clears. The use of these procedures can be managed by the IEP team, who must document the usefulness of the procedure, the need for it, and the specific training of the staff who will undertake it.

Managing Dangerous Behaviors

Students who become dangerous to themselves, to other students, or to adult staff may need to be confronted. The primary goal of this intervention should be the safety of all involved. These dangerous behaviors may include pulling chairs out from others, lashing out to engage in self-destructive head banging or self-mutilation, and verbal threats. A swift and professional response may avoid physical injury as well as any legal repercussions. It is important to minimize mistakes whenever possible.

There are five steps that should be followed when dealing with violent and potentially dangerous behavior:

1. Ensure the safety of all using room clears and physical intervention only when needed.
2. Notify the student's parents/guardians.
3. Have an established format to record and report the procedures used.
4. Determine the most appropriate referral or placement.
5. Teach those students who can remain at school the appropriate adaptive skills.

Now, let's look at each step in more detail.

Step 1   "Clearing the room" and directing other students to move away from the student are essential when a student begins to act dangerously in the classroom. There are many advantages to this procedure, including minimization of potential injury to the adult or student as well as the removal of a "peer audience."

The following points are important to note:

■ There must be a specific prearranged place for students to go (e.g., hallway, auditorium, another classroom).

■ The teacher needs a prearranged signal for help. The assistants who will aid the teacher must be identified in advance and must receive specific training on how physical restraint should be employed if and when it is needed. Of course, it would not be a bad idea to have all teachers and staff receive such training.

■ Consequences must be predetermined for dangerous student behavior. Although it is obvious that students with behavior disorders would receive far greater benefit from a skill development or coping orientation rather than any type of punishment, educators must also consider whether they have a special educational classification that would cause them to be viewed differently to avoid possible placement change without due process, which would be a violation of federal law.

Note: Educators must consult the section on the prevention of escalation of violence prone interactions. Prevention is far superior than dealing with dangerous acting-out behavior.

Step 2   When severe acting-out behavior occurs, it is especially critical to consult with parents about developing a comprehensive plan in order to avoid future acting-out behaviors. It will also be essential for the school to determine if such episodes occur in other situations (e.g., at home), and if there are clear antecedents for the behavior. This may be sometimes determined through the interview process with all involved (parents, teachers, staff, etc.) or through a functional behavioral assessment.

If the student has not already become involved in an anger management program, this option may be discussed. Parents must give their consent for such a program and their participation as well as the student's involvement will be essential.

Step 3   Complete records of the incident may be helpful in arriving at the most appropriate interventions, and they will also provide data for any future legal actions, especially if injuries have resulted from the student's behavior and possible assault charge may be filed. If the student is injured, a suit of negligence may be filed by the parents. Additional complications may occur when an ethnic or racial minority is involved. Records should clearly demonstrate that school staff not only provided help but made every effort to ensure the safety of the identified student and other students.

The administrator keeping records on these events should also include a description of all antecedent events leading up to the incident, the student's behavior, and any action taken to minimize injury. There should also be a description of how the student's behavior must be addressed to prevent future acting-out.

The student's behavior should also be monitored over time to reflect the number of incidents, severity, and/or the number of minutes of acting-out behavior along with records of the effectiveness of the intervention procedures documented.

Step 4   This stage basically involves appropriate referral and placement to meet the needs of the student based on records that have been kept. With sufficient monitoring, a decision can be made about whether a student has been correctly placed and is receiving the necessary help. For those students whose behavior has been severe and continues to present a danger to themselves or others, the administrator should contact police and juvenile authorities or perhaps refer the students for evaluation regarding an inpatient setting. The involvement of a school psychologist and/or outside mental health consultants would be a necessary component of this process.

Step 5   Students who are kept within the school setting should be encouraged to participate in an anger management program that will allow them to learn sufficient self-control to continue their current regular class placement. This part of the BIP plan is essential in helping students to learn and develop strategies that will prevent future violent or physically aggressive behaviors. A sample crisis emergency plan is shown in Appendix C.

MOTIVATIONAL CONSIDERATIONS

What will motivate students to cooperate, follow rules, and make changes in their behavior? Essentially, the school must determine the relevant factors for each individual student.

In many situations, students may not have other options. That is, many students who are already engaging in problematic behavior may be put in an anger management program. How well students cooperate with the requirements of such a program may be based on the dynamics of the teacher. Skilled teachers will show students that there are alternatives to strict academics and that the material in class does not need to be boring. Students will also receive much individual attention and positive support for their participation in an anger management program, without the negative criticism to which they are accustomed.

MANIFESTATION DETERMINATION

Manifestation determination: A decision made by the IEP team to evaluate whether a child's disability is related to misconduct that could result in suspension or expulsion.

Whenever a change in educational placement results from disciplinary action, the IEP team needs to conduct a manifestation determination reviewing the relationship between the student's disability and the problem behavior that resulted in the disciplinary action. The IEP team must then ask several questions: (1) Were the student's IEP and classification appropriate in consideration of the problem behavior? (2) Did special education services and a BIP use strategies consistent with the student's IEP? (3) Could the student understand the impact and consequences of his or her behavior?
(4) Could the student control that behavior? Of course, all these questions are difficult to answer and certainly involve some subjective judgment. Zilz (2006) provides a legal history of the logic that underlies manifestation determination.

The following forms are used in the manifestation determination:

1. Manifestation of handicapping condition decision—used in determination of whether or not the student's behavior was impacted by or independent of his disability
2. Manifestation determination review
3. Manifestation determination

Sample forms for manifestation determination are shown in Appendix C.

DECISION-MAKING GUIDELINES

The following are decision-making guidelines for the IEP team in processing an individual child:

1. *Functional behavioral assessment results:* Either before or no later than ten days after an educational placement change, a functional behavioral assessment must be planned and reviewed with a behavioral intervention plan. The results will help the IEP team when conducting a review in a manifestation determination.

2. *Results of eligibility evaluations/reevaluations:* During any evaluation or reevaluation, assessment tools and strategies should provide relevant information to determine the individual student's needs, not just those typically associated with the student's disability. If an FBA has been conducted, a manifestation determination review will be facilitated.

3. *Special considerations by the IEP team:* During the development of any IEP, the IEP team should take into consideration any behavior that impedes the student's learning, as well as that of others, and to have had positive intervention strategies and supports to address the problem behavior when appropriate. If a BIP plan has been incorporated into the IEP and implemented, a manifestation determination will be facilitated.

ALTERNATIVE MANIFESTATION DETERMINATION

An alternative to the usual approach to conducting a manifestation determination was proposed by Katsiyannis and Maag (2001). This approach is based on the social skills literature of the 1980s (Gresham & Elliot, 1984; Maag, 1989). As an example, a student might engage in an aggressive act. The IEP team asks a series of questions to determine the nature of specific deficits (Maag, 1989):

1. Does the student have the requisite skills to engage in appropriate alternate behavior? Such a role-play can help determine if the student has the requisite skills to act properly instead of violently.

2. Can the student analyze the problem, generate solutions, evaluate their effectiveness, and select one solution? Interviewing the student can determine if the student can (a) identify the problem, (b) establish realistic and concrete goals, (c) generate a number of alternate courses of action, (d) imagine what others might do in similar situations, and (e) evaluate the pros and cons of each proposed solution as well as order them from least to most practical and desirable. The biggest problem here is that the interview is retrospective, reducing validity of this approach; the student's answers will probably be biased and distorted over time (Segal & Shaw, 1988).

3. Does the student interpret the situation factually or distort it to fit some bias? This can determine whether the student displays any cognitive distortions related to the situation, which may occur when the student does not factually interpret some aspect of the situation.

4. Has the student been taught to self-monitor his behavior? Is the student able to use this skill and has a positive change in the target behavior occurred?

This approach is empirically sound and may result in more functional information being obtained. However, there is no evidence that it would produce a more realistic outcome than the conventional method.

OVERVIEW OF THE INDIVIDUALIZED EDUCATION PROGRAM

Every public school student who receives special education and related services must have an Individualized Education Program (IEP), an individualized document designed for one student that creates an opportunity for teachers, parents, school administrators, related services personnel, and students (when appropriate) to work together to improve the educational results for children with disabilities. The IEP is therefore the cornerstone of a quality education for children with disabilities.

To create an effective IEP, parents, teachers, other school staff—and often the student—must

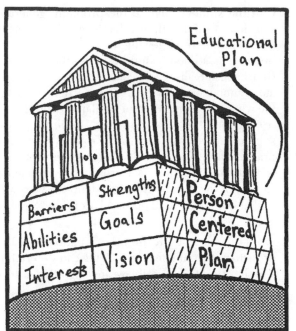

Educational Plan

Strengths
Barriers
Goals
Abilities
Person Centered Plan
Vision
Interests

A PERSON CENTERED PLAN PROVIDES A STRONG FOUNDATION FOR INDIVIDUALIZED EDUCATIONAL PLANS.

come together to look closely at the student's unique needs. These individuals pool knowledge, experience, and commitment to design an educational program that will help the student be involved and progress in the general curriculum. Without a doubt, writing—and implementing—an effective IEP requires teamwork.

The development of educational goals (i.e., long-term objectives) and behavioral goals (i.e., short-term objectives) for students needing special education was included in the Education for All Handicapped Children Act of 1975 and the Individuals with Disabilities Education Act (IDEA) of 1990.

The 1997 amendments to IDEA clarify what is required of the IEP team addressing behavioral problems of children with disabilities. The recent IDEA changes must now be included in the contents of a student's IEP.

What the Law Says About the IEP

The Individual Education Program (IEP) must contain measurable annual goals and a description of how a child's progress toward meeting those goals will be evaluated and reported through documents such as quarterly reports to parents. In addition, special education and related services and supplementary aids and services must be based on peer-reviewed research to the extent practicable. Appropriate measurable postsecondary goals must be included in the IEP beginning no later than the first IEP to be in effect when the child is 16. Any transition services needed to assist the child in reaching those goals must be included. Additional new provisions encourage districts to consolidate IEP meetings with reevaluation meetings and to use alternative means of meeting participation when conducting IEP team meetings, such as conference calls and video conferences. Changes to IEPs can in effect be made without convening the IEP team if both the school district and parent agree.

What the Law Says About Procedural Safeguards

Schools must distribute a copy of the procedural safeguards once a year, upon initial referral or request for evaluation, upon filing of a complaint, and upon request by a parent. Procedural safeguards provide for protection of the rights of children with disabilities and their families. They include the right to participate in all meetings (parents), to examine all educational records, and to obtain independent evaluation of the child. Procedural safeguards are the checks and balances of the system. They provide recourse for parents who disagree with decisions made and provide for mediation, due process hearings, and other complaints.

Source: "A Guide to The Individualized Education Program," Office of Special Education and Rehabilitation Services, U.S. Department of Education, July, 2000.

■ Assign primary responsibility for the IEP.

Gather Information

■ Review the student's records (including the previous IEP).
■ Consult with the student and parents as well as school staff and other professionals.
■ Observe the student.
■ Review the student's current work.
■ Conduct further assessments, if necessary.
■ Consolidate and record information.

Set the Direction

■ Establish a collaborative approach that includes the student and parents.
■ Establish roles and responsibilities.

Develop the IEP

■ Identify and record the student's strengths and needs.
■ Identify goals and expectations.
■ Determine strategies and resources.
■ Develop a transition plan.
■ Establish a monitoring cycle.

Implement the IEP

■ Share the IEP with the student and parents as well as school staff and other professionals; provide a copy to parents and to the student, if 16 or older.
■ Put the IEP into practice.
■ Continuously evaluate the student's progress.
■ Adjust goals, expectations, and strategies as necessary.

Review and Update the IEP

■ Update the IEP periodically (at least once per reporting period).
■ Review and update the IEP at year-end or when the student transfers to another school.
■ Store the IEP in the student record folder.

FIGURE 9.8   The IEP process checklist.

Source: Information from *Individual Education Plan (IEP): Resource Guide,* 1998, (ISN 077879212) published by The Ministry of Education and Training in 1998. Obtained online at www.edu.gov.on.ca/eng/general/elemsec/speced/iepenq.pdf.

Special Education Process under IDEA

The special education process under IDEA requires that certain information be included in each child's IEP. It is useful to know, however, that states and local school systems often include additional information in IEPs in order to document that they have met certain aspects of federal or state law. The flexibility that states and school systems have to design their own IEP forms is thus one reason why IEP forms may look different from one school system to another.

The writing of each student's IEP takes place within the larger framework of the special education

process under IDEA. Before taking a detailed look at the IEP, it may be helpful to look briefly at how a student is identified as having a disability and needing special education and related services. Figure 9.8 illustrates the IEP Process Checklist, an overview of what is involved in the IEP.

The following is the sequence of steps involved in processing a student for special education:

Step 1: Child Is Identified   Through a process called "Child Find," the state must identify, locate, and evaluate all children with disabilities in the state who need special education and related services. To do so, states conduct Child Find activities that identify children and ask parents if the system can evaluate their child. Parents can also call the Child Find system and ask that their child be evaluated. A referral or request for an evaluation can then be submitted.

What the Law Says About Request for Evaluation

New IDEA legislation from 2004 clarifies that a parent may initiate a verbal or written request for an initial evaluation to determine if a child has a disability. Parental consent is needed *before* the child can be evaluated. The evaluation also needs to be completed within a reasonable time after the parent gives consent. A school professional may also ask that a child be evaluated to see if he or she has a disability.

What the Law Says About Consent for Services

Schools must obtain informed parental consent before providing special education and related services to a child. Should a parent refuse to consent to the provision of services, the school district may not use procedures such as mediation and due process in order to provide services.

Step 2: Child Is Evaluated   The evaluator must assess the child in all areas related to the suspected disability. The results of the evaluation will decide the child's eligibility for special education and related services and help make decisions about an appropriate educational program for the child. If the parents disagree with the evaluation, they have the right to take their child for an Independent Educational Evaluation (IEE), which they can ask the school system to pay for.

What the Law Says About a Time Frame for the Evaluation

A new provision of IDEA (2004) requires that an initial evaluation be completed within 60 days of receiving parental consent for the evaluation unless the state has established a time frame within which the evaluation procedure must be completed.

What the Law Says About Eligibility

An expanded provision of IDEA (2004) precludes schools from determining that a child has a disability if the determinant factor is lack of appropriate instruction in reading, including the essential components of reading instruction as defined in No Child Left Behind.

Step 3: Eligibility Is Decided   A group of qualified professionals and the parents look at the results of the child's evaluation. Together they decide if the child has a disability, as defined by IDEA. Parents may ask for a hearing to challenge this eligibility decision.

What the Law Says About Dispute Resolution

Changes allow the use of mediation without first requiring the filing for a hearing, and they also introduce a new "preliminary meeting" that can be used to seek a resolution prior to a due process hearing. In addition, new provisions substantially change the awarding of attorney's fees.

Step 4: Child Is Found Eligible for Services   A student who is found to be a "child with a disability" as defined by IDEA is eligible for special education and related services. Within 30 calendar days after a child is determined eligible, the IEP team must meet to write an IEP for the child. Steps 5 and 6 summarize what is involved in writing the IEP.

Step 5: IEP Meeting Is Scheduled   The school schedules and conducts the IEP meeting. School staff must do the following:

- Contact the participants, including the parents.
- Notify parents early enough to make sure they have an opportunity to attend.
- Schedule the meeting at a time and place agreeable to parents *and* the school.
- Tell the parents the purpose, time, and location of the meeting.
- Tell the parents who will be attending.
- Tell the parents that they may invite people to the meeting who have knowledge or special expertise about the child (e.g., relatives or a school counselor).

Step 6: IEP Meeting Is Held and IEP Is Written
The IEP team gathers to talk about the child's needs and to write the student's IEP. Parents and the student (when appropriate) are part of the IEP team. If the child's placement is decided by a different group, the parents must be part of that group as well.

Before the school system may provide special education and related services to the child for the first time, the parents must give their consent. The child will begin to receive services as soon as possible after the meeting.

If the parents do not agree with the IEP and placement, they may discuss their concerns with staff members of the IEP team and try to work out an agreement. If they still disagree, parents may ask for mediation, or the school may offer mediation. Parents may file a complaint with the state education agency and may request a due process hearing, at which time mediation must be available.

Step 7: Services Are Provided   The school makes sure that the child's IEP is being carried out as it was written. Parents are given a copy of the IEP. Each of the child's teachers and service providers has access to the IEP and knows his or her specific responsibilities for carrying out the IEP, including the accommodations, modifications, and supports that must be provided to the child as outlined in the IEP.

Step 8: Progress Is Measured and Reported to Parents   The child's progress toward the annual goals is measured, as stated in the IEP. Parents are regularly given progress reports and informed of their child's progress and whether that progress is enough for the child to achieve the goals by the end of the school year.

Step 9: IEP Is Reviewed   The child's IEP is reviewed by the IEP team at least once a year, or more often if requested by parents or the school. If necessary, the IEP is revised. Parents, as team members, must be invited to attend these meetings, and they can make suggestions for changes, and agree or disagree with the IEP goals and with the placement.

If parents do not agree with the current IEP and placement, they may discuss these concerns with the rest of the IEP team and try to work out an agreement. There are several options at this point, including additional testing, an independent evaluation, or asking for mediation (if available) or a due process hearing. They may also file a complaint with the state board of education.

Step 10 Child Is Reevaluated   At least every three years the child must have an evaluation, often called a "triennial." Its purpose is to find out if the child continues to be a "child with a disability" (as defined by IDEA) and if the child's educational needs are being met. The child must be reevaluated more often if conditions warrant this or if the child's parent or teacher asks for a reevaluation.

What the Law Says About IEP Paperwork as Defined by IDEA

New provisions call for pilot programs in not more than 15 states to carry out activities designed to reduce paperwork burdens, enhance educational planning, improve positive outcomes for children with disabilities, promote collaboration between IEP team members, and ensure satisfaction of family members. In addition, up to 15 states can apply to take part in the pilot program focused on the development of a comprehensive, multiyear IEP.

WRITING THE IEP

To facilitate a decision about what special education and related services are needed by a student, the IEP team will look at the child's evaluation results (e.g., classroom tests, individual tests given to establish the student's eligibility, and observations by teachers, parents, paraprofessionals, related service providers, administrators, and others). This information will assist the team in determining how the student is currently doing in school. Knowing this will help the team develop *annual goals* to address those areas where the student has an identified educational deficit.

The IEP team must also discuss specific information about the child, including the following:

■ Child's strengths
■ Parents' ideas for enhancing their child's education
■ Results of recent evaluations or reevaluations
■ Results on state and district-wide tests.

In addition, the IEP team must consider any "special factors" that will best help the child meet certain objectives:

■ Advance toward annual goals
■ Be involved in and progress in the general curriculum
■ Participate in extracurricular and nonacademic activities
■ Be educated with and participate with disabled and nondisabled children through a process of inclusion.

What the Law Says About Medication

A new provision requires states to prohibit state and local school district personnel from requiring a child to obtain a prescription for a substance covered by the Controlled Substance Act as a condition of attending school, receiving an evaluation, or receiving services under IDEA.

Special Factors to Consider

Depending on the needs of the child, the IEP team needs to consider the following special factors:

■ If the child's behavior interferes with his or her learning or the learning of others, the IEP team will consider strategies and supports to address the child's behavior.
■ If the child has limited proficiency in English, the IEP team will consider the child's language needs in relation to the IEP.
■ If the child is blind or visually impaired, the IEP team must provide for instruction in braille or the use of braille.

■ If the child has communication needs, the IEP team must consider them.
■ If the child is deaf or hard of hearing, the IEP team will consider language and communication needs, including opportunities for the child to communicate directly with classmates and school staff in an alternative method of communication such as sign language.
■ If the child lacks certain skills, the IEP team must consider the need for assistive technology devices or services.

The IEP team will then write the child's IEP, including services and supports the school will provide for the child. If the IEP team decides that a child needs a particular device or service (including an intervention, accommodation, or other program modification), the team must write this information in the IEP. For example, if a child's behavior interferes with learning, the IEP team would need to consider positive and effective ways to address that behavior and to discuss the positive behavioral interventions, strategies, and supports that the child needs in order to learn how to control or manage behavior. If the team decides that the child needs a particular service (including an intervention, accommodation, or other program modification), they must include a statement to that effect in the child's IEP.

Placement Decision

A child's placement decision—where the IEP will be carried out—will be made by a group that includes the parents and others who know the child with consideration of the evaluation results, and what placements are appropriate for this child. In some states, the IEP team serves as the group making the placement decision. In other states, this decision may be made by another group. In all cases, the parents have the right to be members of the group that decides the educational placement of the child.

Placement decisions must be made according to IDEA's least restrictive environment (LRE) requirements, which state that, to the maximum extent appropriate, children with disabilities must be educated with children who do not have disabilities through the process of inclusion.

The law also clearly states that special classes, separate schools, and other removal of children with disabilities from the general educational environment may occur only if the nature or severity of the child's disability is such that education in general education classes, with the use of supplementary aids and services, cannot be achieved satisfactorily.

What types of placements are there? Depending on the needs of the child, the IEP may be carried out in the general education class (with supplementary aids and services as needed), in a special class (where every student in the class is receiving special education services for some or all of the day), in a special school, at home, in a hospital, institution, or in another setting. The school must ensure that the child has an appropriate placement by

- providing an appropriate program for the child on its own (i.e., the school);
- contracting with another agency to provide an appropriate program; or
- utilizing some other mechanism or arrangement that is consistent with IDEA for providing or paying for an appropriate program for the child.

The placement group will base its decision on the IEP and which placement option is appropriate for the child. Can the child be educated in the general education classroom, with appropriate aids and supports? If the child cannot be educated in such a classroom, then the placement group will talk about alternative placement.

Distributing the Written IEP

According to IDEA regulations, when the IEP has been written, parents must receive a copy at no cost, and everyone who will be involved in implementing the IEP must have access to the document. This includes the child's

- regular education teacher(s);
- special education teacher(s);
- related service provider(s) such as speech therapists; and
- any other service provider (such as a paraprofessional) who will be responsible for a part of the child's education.

Each of these individuals needs to know what his or her specific responsibilities are for carrying out the child's IEP. This includes the specific accommodations, modifications, and supports that the child must receive, as stated in the IEP.

Implementation of the IEP

Once the IEP is written, it is time to provide the student with the special education and related services listed in the IEP. This includes all supplementary aids and services and program modifications that the IEP team has identified as necessary for the student to advance appropriately toward the IEP goals, to be involved in and progress in the general curriculum, and to participate in other school activities. An example of a complete IEP is shown in Appendix C.

Reviewing and Revising the IEP

The IEP team must *review a student's IEP* at least once a year to see whether the child is achieving his or her annual goals. The team must revise the child's individualized education program, if necessary, to address

- the child's progress or lack of expected progress toward the annual goals and in the general curriculum;
- information gathered through any reevaluation of the child;
- information about the child that the parents share;
- information about the child that the school shares (for example, insights from teachers based on their observation of the child or the child's classwork); and
- the child's anticipated needs.

Although the IDEA requires this IEP review at least once a year, the team may review and revise the IEP more frequently. Either the parents or the school can ask to hold an IEP meeting to revise the child's IEP. For example, the child may not be making progress toward the IEP goals, and the teacher or parents may become concerned. On the other hand, the child may have met most or all of the goals in the IEP, and new ones need to be written. In either case, the IEP team would meet to revise the IEP.

When the IEP team is meeting to conduct a review of the child's IEP (if necessary to revise it), members must again consider all of the factors discussed under the section Writing the IEP.

Parental Disagreement with the IEP

Sometimes parents may disagree with the school's recommendations about their child's education. Under law, parents have the right to challenge decisions about their child's eligibility, evaluation, placement, and services that the school provides. If parents disagree with the school's actions, they may pursue a number of options through agreement with the school, mediation, due process, and filing a complaint with the state board of education.

What the Law Says About Complaints

According to a new provision of IDEA (2004), a complaint must be limited to a violation that occurred not more than two years before the date the parent or school district knew or should have known about the alleged action.

Transferring Schools New provisions in IDEA (2004) direct school districts to provide services to students with IEPs who transfer into a new school, including services comparable to those described in the previously held IEP. The new school must take steps to promptly obtain the child's records from the previous school, and that school must respond promptly to such requests. For students who did not have an IEP in effect but for whom an evaluation has begun, districts are required to complete the evaluation promptly.

SUMMARY

After the functional behavioral assessment has been completed, a behavioral intervention plan as well as the child's IEP are developed. The BIP should include (1) instruction, (2) preventive measures, and (3) environmental arrangements. It should also be evaluated and monitored. Failure to do so may compromise the effectiveness of both the FBA and BIP. The development of the competing behavior pathway is essential.

DISCUSSION QUESTIONS

1. What are the three points the BIP should address?
2. According to Crone and Horner (2003), what should the BIP include?
3. Why should the BIP be monitored?
4. What are the five steps used in dealing with violent and potentially dangerous behavior?

OSEP MONITORING

The U.S. Department of Education's Office of Special Education Programs (OSEP) regularly monitors states to determine their compliance with IDEA. Every two years OSEP requires that states report progress toward meeting established performance goals that, at a minimum, address the performance of children on assessments, drop-out rates, and graduation rates. As part of its monitoring, the department reviews IEPs and interviews parents, students, and school staff to find out

- whether, and how, the IEP team made the decisions reflected in the IEP;
- whether those decisions and the IEP content are based on the child's unique needs, as determined through evaluation and the IEP process;
- whether any state or local policies or practices have interfered with decisions of the IEP team about the child's educational needs and the services that the school would provide to meet those needs; and
- whether the school has provided the services listed in the IEP.

Educators can use this information to write effective IEPs that comply with IDEA, an important first step in improving educational results for children with disabilities, including those with emotional and/or behavioral problems.

Because teachers must be prepared to deal with violent and potentially dangerous behaviors, some basic procedures are discussed. In addition, manifestation determination is explained, and the ten essential steps of the IEP review the process of dealing with a child who has a behavior disorder or other disability. Issues or problems following the IEP are also discussed.

5. When there is a change in educational placement that results from a disciplinary action, what does the IEP team need to do?
6. How is the alternative manifestation determination (MD) different from the usual MD approach?
7. What is the function of the IEP?

8. Briefly describe the 10 steps in the IEP process.
9. What does the law say about medication?
10. What guideline(s) are used in deciding on placement for a child with behavioral problems?
11. Who should get a copy or have access to the IEP?
12. How often should the IEP team review a child's IEP?
13. What options do parents have if they disagree with the IEP?
14. Who monitors states for compliance with IDEA?

PART IV

Managing Behavior Problems in the Classroom

This section focuses on the management of behavior problems in the classroom. It is primarily based on the use of behavioral strategies that have been proven to be effective in dealing with problem behaviors.

Chapter 10 begins with a focus on the effective classroom environment—from the physical environment of the classroom to the characteristics of effective teachers and the type of instruction they use. Communication factors, rules, and classroom conflicts are all significant issues that can affect the performance of students. Another important issue concerns homework. The section on the use of physical punishment discusses the general impression that all punishment may be ineffective, especially with students who have behavior disorders. This book adopts a general perspective that emphasizes positive techniques. Punishment techniques are discussed as secondary techniques but they vary in their degree of aversiveness and their use should be minimized. The chapter concludes with a discussion of Section 504 accommodations as well as a listing of some commonly used procedures.

Chapter 11 outlines various positive interventions and supports. There is a basic discussion of positive and negative reinforcement with techniques of modeling, shaping, and chaining that might be used in many interventions. Various techniques of behavior change are described, including token economy, instrumental behavior, behavior momentum, the positive response program, and contingency contracting. The chapter also considers the important issue of generalization—the hope that behavior that changes in one class will generalize to other classes. Precorrection—a major technique used in working with students who have behavior disorders—is covered in detail. Other issues such as auditory and visual attention, the use of self-talk, and consequences are also discussed. The process of self-monitoring, which allows students to function more independently, is further reviewed. Mildly aversive techniques such as ignoring, time-out, overcorrection, and behavior penalty are also presented.

Chapter 12 explains specific proactive behavioral interventions along with their application to typical problem behaviors such as aggression, social skill deficits, inattention, inability to follow instructions, impulsivity, and noncompliance. There is also a case example of functional behavioral assessment with a behavioral intervention plan.

Chapter 13 focuses on teaching students with behavior disorders. A general context is presented first with emphasis on the No Child Left Behind law. Some of the major issues derived from this law include progress, use of evidenced-based practices, accountability, and highly qualified teachers. There is emphasis on the primary issues in instructional strategies and how to incorporate evidence-based practices in the curriculum. The use of the more substantial curriculum-based assessments is suggested, as well as techniques of self-monitoring to promote greater independence of students. The chapter concludes with information on the Morningside Model as an example of effective educational programs that can be used with challenging students.

CHAPTER 10

Establishing an Effective Classroom Environment

Overview

- Physical environment of the classroom
- Least restrictive environment
- Effective teachers
- Transitions
- Type of instruction
- Communication
- Classroom rules
- Classroom conflicts
- Peer confrontation
- Homework policy
- Corporal punishment
- Section 504 accommodations

Case History

Tyler is a 6-year-old first grader in a general education program who receives speech therapy. His teacher has noted a high rate of inappropriate behavior during both academic and free-time activities. Tyler engages classmates in off-task conversations, makes noises, and sometimes resorts to name-calling, kicking, and biting peers. The teacher has used verbal correction and, at times, Tyler has been sent out of the classroom. On-task behavior was emphasized during reading. However, nothing seems to work. *What would you do?*

Some interventions may not rely on behavioral strategies but might use plain common sense techniques. The following is such an example.

> A middle school in Alabama has been encountering a unique problem. Several of the girls have begun to use lipstick and after putting it on in the bathroom, several of them would press their lips to the bathroom mirrors, leaving dozens of lip prints. The principal decides that something has to be done. She calls all of the girls into the bathroom, along with the custodian. She explains that all of these lip prints are causing extra work for the maintenance crew who has to clean the mirrors every night. To demonstrate how time-consuming it is to clean the mirrors, she asks the custodian to clean one of the mirrors. He takes out a long-handled squeegee, dips it into a toilet, and then cleans the mirror. Since then there have been no lip prints on the mirror, and the principal has demonstrated that not all interventions require complex behavioral techniques; there are often simple solutions to problems.

There are many factors to consider when attempting to maximize the probability of success for all students in a classroom—those with various academic and behavioral problems but also those who are the most academically capable, well behaved, and emotionally stable students. A well-structured classroom will thus improve academics and behavior for all students (Walker, Colvin, & Ramsey, 1995). The classroom environment also sends an important message to students about what the teacher values in academics and behavior (Savage, 1999). Some of these environmental factors include the physical aspects of the classroom, classroom rules, homework policy, communication, discipline policies, conflict resolution procedures, types of instruction used, accommodations, and various characteristics of the teacher. The first area to consider is physical environment.

THE PHYSICAL ENVIRONMENT OF THE CLASSROOM

The teacher must arrange the classroom environment to improve learning and to prevent problem behaviors before they occur. The physical environment, which can affect the behavior of both teacher and students (Savage, 1999), is perhaps the easiest to manipulate. How students are seated is an important factor related to the spatial structure of the classroom. Flick (1998a) suggests that students should be seated close to the teacher for ease of providing help and giving

reinforcement. The goal, however, will be to allow students to be able to work independently.

Students who have disruptive behavior problems should be seated at a distance from classmates who may be easily provoked. The ideal arrangement would be seat the student with behavior problems next to someone who will not be distracted by problem behavior and who may provide a good role model for the student. In general, the classroom should be organized to accommodate a wide variety of instructional programs and activities throughout the day (Savage, 1999). If any changes need to be made, it is easier to change the seating arrangement for students than to change student behaviors. It is clear that on-task behavior improves for older children with learning disabilities or behavior problems when desks are arranged in rows rather than clusters. In fact, Wheldall and Lam (1987) note that the rate of disruptions is about three times higher when desks are arranged in clusters. This finding was also supported by Kern and Clemens (2006). Marx, Fuhrer, and Hartig (1999) reported that the greater the distance between student desks, the greater the frequency of on-task behavior. Thweatt and McCroskey (1996), with additional support provided by Rose and Church (1998), found that the more time the teacher walked around the room, the fewer the number of behavior problems. When the teacher remained in front of the class, interactions occurred primarily with students in the front and center areas of the class; students on either side of this so-called T-zone did not interact as frequently.

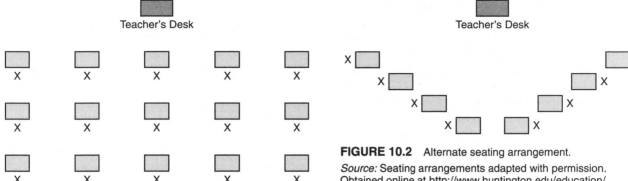

FIGURE 10.1   Possible seating arrangement.

Source: Seating arrangements adapted with permission. Obtained online at http://www.huntington.edu/education/lessonplanning/seating.html.

Seating Arrangements

Traditional seating arrangements seat students in rows all facing the same direction (see Figure 10.1). This is the optimal arrangement for general lectures and individual seatwork. The X indicates the student; the box represents the desk.

For discussion-type sessions, students may best be seated in the semicircle or "horseshoe" arrangement shown in Figure 10.2.

For small group activities, desks and chairs can be arranged so that students face one another. Plan A or Plan B in Figure 10.3 are options.

Depending upon teacher involvement or direction, tables or desks may be arranged so that students never have their backs to the teacher. Whatever arrangement is used, it is important to arrange the seating so that (1) students who are tempted to behave negatively will have minimal interaction with other students by keeping desks far

FIGURE 10.2   Alternate seating arrangement.

Source: Seating arrangements adapted with permission. Obtained online at http://www.huntington.edu/education/lessonplanning/seating.html.

enough apart, and (2) the teacher has enough room between desks to walk around the room. Seating students in rows may be important when focusing on specific tasks and academic learning, but seating arrangement in clusters may facilitate greater social exchanges among students (MacAulay, 1990; Walker & Walker, 1991). The classroom should also be arranged to limit student contact in "high traffic" areas (e.g., near the pencil sharpener or wastebasket) and to seat distractible students a distance from these areas (Quinn et al., 2000; Walker et al., 1995). All students should have a clear view of the teacher, and the teacher should be able to see all students (Quinn et al., 2000; Wolfgang, 1996; Stewart & Evans, 1997). The teacher should have access to those students with behavior problems at all times (Wolfgang, 1996). The physical environment of the classroom can serve as a significant setting event to provide students with effective instruction and to facilitate the use of proactive techniques for dealing with inappropriate behavior. It is also good to have a classroom that is well organized and allows the teacher to have quick access to those students who may have disruptive problem behavior (Bettenhausen, 1998; Stewart & Evans, 1997).

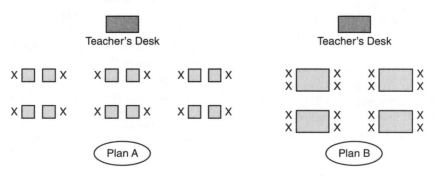

FIGURE 10.3   Alternate seating arrangement.

Source: Seating arrangements adapted with permission. Obtained online at http://www.huntington.edu/education/lessonplanning/seating.html.

Classroom space is also a critical factor that facilitates a teacher's ability to praise, monitor, and supervise students. There should be clearly defined spaces in the classroom, and students should know, through rules, what is appropriate behavior in each area (Walker et al., 1995; Quinn et al., 2000). Paine and colleagues (1983) noted eight components of space allotment in the classroom: (1) placement of student desks, (2) placement of teacher's desk relative to students, (3) movable class partitions, (4) teaching station placement, (5) stations for independent work (or self-control), (6) materials station, (7) activity station, and (8) bulletin boards. Classrooms should also include a quiet space where students can go to use "chill out" techniques to cool down (or calm down) and regroup whenever they are upset or overstimulated. This can also serve as a place where students can go when they need a distraction-free environment (Quinn et al., 2000; Walker et al., 1995). This is not a "time out" space, but the procedure is similar; the space should be positively labeled as a place to "chill out" and to regain self-control.

Class Size

There is extensive research on the effects of class size and school size on academic and behavioral outcomes. Over the past 20 years, researchers have looked at dropout rates, academic achievement, behavioral problems, attendance, and attitudes associated with the size of the educational setting. Some evidence supports the benefits of small school size and small class size (Wasley, 2002). There is not only increased achievement in smaller schools; there is also greater participation in extracurricular activities, better attendance, and positive outcomes for ethnic minorities and students of low socioeconomic status (SES).

Students in small classes show higher achievement in academic classes, and minority students have better outcomes. Most importantly, students in smaller classes display less disruptive behavior compared to those in regular-sized classes. In fact, reducing class size to fewer than 20 students results in higher achievement at every grade level. Dropout rates are higher in larger schools too. Smaller classes allow teachers more time to focus on individual students and to use innovative instructional strategies.

It has also been noted (Jimerson, 2006) that smaller schools have fewer incidences of inappropriate student behavior, and their students experience a greater sense of belonging in their schools. However, there is a body of research (Allen, 2002) that suggests greater cost savings and curriculum selections for students in larger schools while there are higher costs per student in smaller schools.

It has also been found that affluent students often do better academically in larger schools. Never-the-less, the preponderance of evidence suggests that smaller classes and smaller schools are the most beneficial to all students, but especially to low-income and minority students (Boss, 2000).

At times, it is not feasible to provide students who have various disabilities with all that is needed within the identified classroom. For these students, different classroom environments may facilitate the development and learning of specific skills. As Mercer (1995) and Alexander, McKenzie, and Geissinger (1998) have noted, the educational program needs to provide the *most enabling environment* (and not necessarily the "least restrictive" one). While this may require a decision about whether to place the student in a general or in a special education class, it may involve a combination of both to decide which placement would be most beneficial for a given academic area or behavioral context. The general emphasis is inclusion of students with disabilities with those students without disabilities.

What the (IDEA) Law Says About Least Restricted Environment

To the maximum extent appropriate, children with disabilities . . . should be educated with children who are not disabled and . . . special classes, separate schooling or other removal of children with disabilities from the regular educational environment should occur only when the nature or severity of the disability is such that education in regular classes with the use of supplementary aids and services cannot be achieved satisfactorily.

Source: Douvanis, G., & Husley, D. (2002). The Least Restrictive Environment Mandate: How Has It Been Defined by the Courts? Retrieved on 10/1/09 at http://www.ericdigests.org/2003-3/courts.htm.

Least Restrictive Environment

As part of Individuals with Disabilities Education Act (IDEA), the least restrictive environment (LRE) is identified as one of the principles that govern the education of students with disabilities. This means that students with disabilities should have the opportunity to be educated with nondisabled peers as much as possible and that they should have access to the general education curriculum, extracurricular activities, and any other program that a nondisabled peer would be able to access. Students with disabilities should also be provided with supplementary aids and services needed to achieve their academic goals when placed in a setting with nondisabled peers. If the nature or severity of the disability prevents a student from achieving these set goals in a regular class, the student may be placed in a more restrictive environment. The fewer opportunities students have to interact and learn with nondisabled peers, the more the setting is considered restrictive. By law, teachers are required to provide a free appropriate public education (FAPE) in the least restrictive environment for those students with disabilities. The case below illustrates an example of legal contesting of placement.

Clyde K vs. Puyallip 35F, 3d 1396 (9th Cir. 1997)

The court found that the student was not receiving academic benefits in the general education classroom and actually had regressed academically. Although appropriate aids and services had been provided, the student was socially isolated, and therefore nonacademic benefits were minimal. The court acknowledged that the student's presence in the classroom had negative effects on the teacher and the student's peers. The language of the court's decision included the statement, "Disruptive behavior that significantly impairs the education of others strongly suggests a mainstream placement is no longer appropriate."

The overriding emphasis on LRE has put placement decisions in the foreground of debate rather than the determination of how each student's assessed individual needs can best be met, and the best educational setting for the student. The intent of LRE is maximum integration, but this should be balanced by the overriding emphasis on the most appropriate placement (Curry & Hatlen, 1988) or the most enabling placement (Huebner, 1989).

The most appropriate placement is defined as "the environment in which all the needs of a student are best met where the student acquires the greatest benefits from the educational program" (Curry & Hatlen, 1988, p. 420). The most enabling placement is defined as an environment "in which the student has the opportunity to fully participate in all aspects of the school experience including acquisition of special skills, thereby providing an academic, social, and emotional environment that encourages a complete development in preparation for life. The issue is the quality of education provided within a particular placement as measured by the degree to which specific, unique needs of a student as appropriately assessed and identified in his/her IEP" (Huebner, 1989). Unfortunately, findings in the past indicate that placements have often been determined by availability of space, transportation, required related services, or category of disability, not by the unique educational needs of the individual student (Will, 1986).

EFFECTIVE TEACHERS

Teachers who are effective exert a significant influence on their students' academic achievement, emotion, and behavior as well as on their overall development. According to Jones and Jones (2001), the effective teacher must carefully determine instructional goals and plan learning activities that will provide the necessary materials to get students actively participating in the learning process. While monitoring their students' progress, the effective teacher gives frequent feedback regarding each student's progress and accomplishments. Because students have difficulty learning from teachers they do not like or respect, teachers must also be likeable. As Walker and Shea (1991) have stated, effective teachers are authentic teachers.

What the Law Says About Teachers

The No Child Left Behind, (NCLB) law calls for highly qualified teachers in every public school classroom. NCLB with IDEA (2004) shows how special education teachers can meet the "highly qualified" standard by being certified in special education. New special education teachers teaching multiple subjects must meet the NCLB standard in at least one core subject area (language arts, math, or science) and will have 2 years from the date of employment to take advantage of certain NCLB provisions to demonstrate competence in other core subject areas.

Park, Turnbull, and Turnbull (2002) used qualitative data to focus on the quality indicators of professionals who work with children who have behavior problems. They organized their analysis according to three themes: (1) respect for children, (2) skills to meet special needs, and (3) commitment.

Effective teachers employ a reasonable and limited set of classroom rules and respond quickly and consistently to problem behaviors and situations. They are also familiar with behavioral techniques and know how to use them. Before these techniques are reviewed, teachers or teachers in training are urged to take the nonstandardized Survey of Teacher Behavioral Practices, which is found in Appendix E. This assessment may be repeated following the completion of this book to see how answers may change. A handout for teachers covering general behavior management procedures may also be found in Appendix E.

Effective teachers structure the classroom to maximize academics and to minimize disruptive events. They also provide clear instructions and expectations for academic performance, keep instruction fast-paced, and maintain an interactive teaching style while eliciting students' responses. Effective teachers must consider the goals of seatwork and render immediate feedback to students. Furthermore, it has been generally found that teachers who spend more time away from the front of the room and away from their desks encounter fewer behavioral problems.

Typically, only about half of the school day is devoted to actual direct instruction, according to Strother (1984). Much time may be wasted dealing with transitions, coping with misbehavior, and responding to requests for help in addition to the time it takes to organize instruction (Sprick, Garrison, & Howard, 1998). When students spend an inordinate amount of time doing seatwork, they show less productive learning since there is little interaction with the teacher (Parmar & Cawley, 1991). According to Reid and Lienemann (2006), the effective teacher focuses on instruction and learning by fostering academic learning time. To do this, interruptions must be minimized, transitions should run smoothly with little or no disruptions, and teachers should find ways for students to be more punctual.

TRANSITIONS

The effective management of transitions in the classroom—those times when teachers tell students to end one task or activity and begin another—can assist teachers in minimizing disruptions and behavior problems and maintaining optimal learning conditions for effective instruction (Cangelosi, 2000; Smith et al., 2004).

Transitions are times when students can be disruptive (Burden, 2003). Effective, smooth transitions require both adequate behavioral management and time management (Stainback & Stainback, 1996). They are done quickly and have a clear beginning and a clear end (Burden, 2003; Rosenberg et al., 1997; Cangelosi, 2000). Thus, the amount of downtime between tasks or activities is reduced (Harman et al., 2004). There are a number of strategies that promote rapid transitions, including preventive measures and the use of situational behaviors to make transitions smooth (Ferrer, Fugate, & Rivera, 2007).

Teachers can plan ahead to organize management strategies, lesson plans, schedules, and their classrooms to make successful transitions. First, they should have a clearly stated routine for daily tasks and activities—for example, entering the classroom, taking attendance, and collecting homework (Cangelosi, 2000; Smith et al., 2004; Burden, 2003). The greater the routine in tasks, the less disruption these routines may cause students (Cangelosi, 2000). Also, when class rules and expectations are clear, the likelihood of inappropriate behavior during transitions is minimized (Rosenberg et al., 1997; Stainback & Stainback, 1996). Second, if transitions are problematic because students do not know what to expect during the school day, teachers can post and adhere to a daily or weekly schedule; they should also inform students of any changes in the schedule ahead of time (Burden, 2003; Olsen & Platt, 2000; Ayers & Hedeen, 1996). It is also helpful if the schedule incorporates times for transitions, especially those that bridge active and quiet activities as well as those that involve preferred and less preferred activities (Sainato, 1990; McIntosh et al., 1998). Teachers and students must be prepared for each new lesson or activity to minimize disruptions (Burden, 2003; Stainback & Stainback, 1996). Third, teachers should make materials readily accessible so that students can reach them easily and rapidly (Olsen & Platt, 2000). Fourth, when students are required to move around the room between activities or lessons, teachers can arrange the setting to facilitate the flow of transitions so they can run smoothly. Likewise, when changes are made in other areas of the school grounds, teachers should be aware of that setting (Cangelosi, 2000; Burden, 2003; Rosenberg et al., 1997; Stainback & Stainback, 1996).

While teaching or when transition times arise, there are several strategies teachers can employ to encourage the smooth movement from one lesson or activity to another. Just like teaching any new skill or new behavior, teachers can model the appropriate way for students to make the transition and then allow students to practice it, providing feedback as they go (Olsen & Platt, 2000; Smith et al., 2004). Consequently, once students know *what* to do, it is important for them to know *when* to do it (Tompkins & Tompkins-McGill, 1993).

One highly effective option is to give a specific visual or auditory signal or verbal cue to announce that a transition is soon needed (Burden, 2003; Cangelosi, 2000; Rosenburg et al., 1997; Smith et al., 2004). This signal needs to be given with sufficient notice so that students may finish what they are doing and get prepared for the next activity (Ayers & Hedeen, 1996; Tompkins & Tompkins-McGill, 1993). A teacher might, for example, signal students five minutes ahead of time and again close to the end of the activity. This would be especially important for those students who may have trouble with self-monitoring (Ayers & Hedeen, 1996). Many students with behavior problems have a poor

appreciation of time and might feel rushed or surprised, yet helped to prepare, by the announcement of the transition (Flick, 1998b).

Once having given the cue for the transition, teachers should provide sufficient time for students to complete what they were doing and get prepared for the next activity or lesson. At this time teachers might circulate among students during transition times, attending to individual needs and questions as well as helping them prepare for the next task. Positive comments should be given to those students who do the right thing as this can serve as a model for other students to emulate (Flick, 1998b; Burden, 2003; Olsen & Platt, 2000). Remember, too, that teachers can always provide incentives and other reinforcers to those who make successful transitions (Olsen & Platt, 2000; McIntosh et al., 2004). This may include rewards such as free time, use of a computer, and tokens or points if such a system is used. Also, it is especially important to reward students who show improvement in their ability to handle transitions.

For any student with learning and/or behavioral problems, such measures can support appropriate classroom behaviors by making and setting clear expectations, focusing on the prevention of disruptive behaviors, and placing limits on sources of frustration that can sometimes make inappropriate behavior more likely. The hope is that teaching students how to make more effective transitions in school may generalize and aid in coping with changes and functioning more independently in other environments.

Nearly 20 percent of the students' day can be spent in transitions. To adequately manage these transitions, the effective teacher provides clear signals for the beginning and end of activities and prepares students for the changes by reviewing what is to be expected of them. The teacher can then actually model appropriate transitions with the class—providing reinforcement for transitions that are quick and nondisruptive.

Effective teachers must also establish and maintain good relationships with students, which will increase the likelihood of student compliance with requests. Mather and Goldstein (2001) offer several suggestions for developing and maintaining a good relationship with students: (1) avoid direct confrontation of provocative behavior, (2) use genuine praise or encouragement for each student and ensure some success for that student each day (i.e., catch them being good), (3) use humor, (4) arrange opportunities for students to be successful, make a contribution, and feel important each day, (5) find ways to give students unconditional positive attention, and (6) work on developing a positive attitude and expectation for every student in the class.

Effective teachers utilize positive communication in their interactions with students. As a result, there is less noncompliant behavior. In contrast, teachers who use punitive, harsh methods are likely to experience greater noncompliance in the form of passivity, oppositionality, and open defiance. As Straus and Donnelly (2001) point out, corporal punishment should absolutely never be used with students.

TYPE OF INSTRUCTION

There are many different types of instruction, besides the often-used multisensory techniques. Multisensory techniques utilize all of the senses to improve learning. Thus, a child might see a word (visual), hear a word (auditory), and write a word (kinesthetic) to enhance the learning of spelling words. All of the senses work together (hands, eyes, ears, and voices) to help organize and retain learning. Traditional teaching has involved the phrase "Listen to me." However, only a small percent of learners process information through the auditory sense. Many are visual learners, and some are kinesthetic learners (i.e., learn through activity). Professional educators have developed a variety of models of instruction where each is designed to produce classroom learning (Joyce, Weil, & Calhoun, 2003). Two of these educational approaches are discussed here: direct instruction and small-group instruction.

Direct Instruction

Direct instruction, also referred to as *active teaching*, is a proactive approach to minimizing or preventing classroom disruption. Rosenshine (1995) has developed considerable research support for direct, or explicit, instruction over the past 25 years. Several principles of direct instruction, such as more teacher direction and student-teacher interaction, are the foundation of this approach. Based on the work of Good and Brophy (2008), along with Rosenshine and Stevens (1986), the following suggestions are offered: (1) involve all students, (2) seat students with academic difficulty close to the teacher or near center of learning activity, (3) present lessons in a well-organized sequence, (4) review previously learned materials before starting a new lesson, (5) begin by stating clear, concise goals and explanations of what is to be learned, (6) present new material in small steps, integrating practice and demonstration with each step, (7) offer frequent opportunities to practice and generalize skills, (8) ask students questions to check their understanding, and (9) emphasize academic rather than behavioral achievement. Many studies have shown that when students are performing well academically, there are fewer behavioral problems.

Small-Group Instruction

Small groups may vary, but generally consist of 10–15 students. The groups may be set up within a regular class or may be separated from it.

Small-group instruction, while effective for learning, may present problems for the teacher as some students may be disruptive to the rest of the class while the teacher works with the small group. Periodic praise directed at the remaining class can be helpful to keep those students on task. Rice (1999) and Paine and colleagues (1983) offer the following suggestions for the teacher to manage this split-classroom: (1) move about the room, stopping only briefly in one place, (2) scan the room to be aware of what the whole class is doing, (3) praise students for doing the appropriate thing, and (4) use follow-up with the groups. Use praise or encouragement often and specifically, addressing the student by name and describing the behavior to be praised. Praise should be delivered in a dynamic, enthusiastic voice rather than in a mechanical fashion. Since the use of praise generally decreases in the higher grades, teachers must be aware of the need to use more positive behavioral support and give less negative attention such as reprimands and criticisms.

The use of praise by teachers has been found to be rather low (i.e., one statement per hour) with students who have behavior disorders (Copeland, Sutherland, & Wehby, 2000). Praise is most effective when it is used across many different environments (Berner, Fee, & Turner, 2001). The appropriate amount of praise often depends on the student's age and personality (Copeland et al., 2000). Developmentally, a young child may require praise every 10 minutes, whereas the older students may require far less praise. It is, however, important as praise has been shown to increase not only the student's motivation and appropriate behavior but also time on-task.

There are basically two types of praise: specific and nonspecific. Specific praise, which has been shown to be most effective, identifies the behavior that is desired, whereas nonspecific praise does not. Specific praise can be used to reinforce both academic and social type behavior (Sutherland & Wehby, 2001). Unfortunately, specific praise has been estimated to be used as little as 5 percent of the time (Copeland et al., 2000). Teachers may also encourage students to praise each other (Fee, Holloway, & Seay, 2003). In all cases, praise should be sincere and varied (Copeland et al., 2001), and enthusiastic (Filcheck, Greco, & Herchell, 2002). It is likewise important to praise students who are improving but not yet completely successful (Janas, 2002).

Praise should be given immediately after the desired behavior (Copeland et al., 2000) and then faded as the student improves. Thus, the teacher should initially offer praise every time a desired behavior appears and then praise intermittently thereafter, perhaps shifting the attention to another target behavior that needs to improve.

Most teachers who work with students who have emotional and/or behavior disorders praise either ineffectively or inconsistently (Copeland et al., 2000). Praise was found to occur at a rate of about one statement per hour and to be specific in only about 5 to 17 percent of cases. Furthermore, the rate of praise was found to decrease as the seriousness of the behavior disorder increased (Sutherland, 2000). For those students who were at mild risk for behavior problems, the ratio of reprimands to praise was about 2 to 1; for high-risk students the ratio was 4 to 1. Even if the behavior improved, there was little change in teacher praise. Reprimands were given for both academic and social behavior problems (Sutherland et al., 2002).

Observation and feedback techniques have been found to increase praise by teachers in the classroom (Copeland et al., 2000). In this method, the teacher is initially observed (by an outsider) and feedback is given on the use of praise. Self-evaluation is a variation of this method: the teacher records behavior using an audiotape or video recording, then the tape is reviewed (by the teacher) and student reactions as well as the general class environment can be monitored. *Teachers may use Post-it notes around the classroom to remind themselves about praising students* (Copeland et al., 2000). Students can also prompt teachers to use praise when they inform teachers that they have finished their work. When students fail to receive praise for appropriate behavior, they will seek attention for inappropriate behavior (Flick, 1998b). Praise is an intervention that requires little time but perhaps some training to implement.

Joseph is frequently reinforced by other students and by his teacher when he talks inappropriately about other students during quiet work time. The teacher decides to ignore these comments and then begins to praise Joseph at those times when he is working but not talking inappropriately. He eventually increases time on-task while not making fun of other students. Joseph still has trouble with self-control and talks impulsively, but now he wants to earn the teacher's praise. This desire for specific praise has now created a different focus or target behavior.

It is clear that nonspecific or generic praise has little or no effect on students. Although training teachers to give specific praise may need funding, it will be well worth the investment in the long run. Once trained, teachers may use this technique many times in the future without costs to the school.

COMMUNICATION

Teachers who interact with students frequently and use positive communication are more likely to have students who are compliant to requests. Conversely, teachers who use punitive techniques such as yelling at students are likely to encounter greater oppositional defiance or elicit more passive-aggressive behaviors. When ineffective, negatively oriented communication is the norm, there is often a pattern of escalating disruptive behavior. McMahon and Forehand (2003), along with Webster-Stratton (1996), have noted that when positive communication patterns are lacking, students are more likely to have a negative perception of requests and thereby resist compliance. Unfortunately, many teachers respond negatively to noncompliance with timeouts, response costs, and other punishments rather than using positive consequences and focusing on the manipulation of antecedents. Preventive interventions are recommended because they reduce the frequency of negative interactions with students. As McMahon and Forehand (2003) have noted, the efficient management of antecedent events is the key to maintaining compliance by students.

Communication issues not only involve student-teacher interactions but also apply to the teacher's relationship with parents, which should ideally begin at the start of the school year and continue throughout the year. Being accessible to parents through personal meetings as well as by phone or e-mail may deter problems early. Especially for students with disabilities, a daily note may be an effective way to communicate about problems before they escalate. The goal for communications with parents should be a positive focus on the child's appropriate behavior. Encouraging parent involvement is also essential in developing home-school programs that may provide teachers with access to some of the more potent reinforcements available to the child only at home.

CLASSROOM RULES

Classroom rules should be clear and concise, providing students with the teacher's expectations regarding both academic policies and behavior. These rules should also be few in number (about four to five), briefly stated, and worded positively (for example, say "keep your hands to yourself" instead of "don't hit"). The content should focus on key classroom issues: (1) punctuality, (2) movement around the class, (3) talking with other students, (4) permissions, (5) following directions, (6) academic work policy, and (7) participating in group activities.

These rules are best reviewed at the beginning of the school year and periodically thereafter (Flick, 1998b). Classroom rules should also be posted where all students can see them. Modeling and role-play may be used to help students learn the rules. In reviewing rules that may need daily attention, the teacher may

randomly call on students in the class to cite the rule. Selecting students who know the rules and can cite them may provide good models for children who show problematic behaviors; the teacher does not need to query students with problem behaviors in order for them to learn the rules (Flick, 1998b). Sometimes reviewing class rules in this way is more acceptable to students with behavior problems.

Good rules are definable, reasonable, and enforceable (Michaelsen, 1998). Those rules that cannot be enforced may be of little use. According to Berkowitz and Martens (2001), it is the use of reinforcement for appropriate behavior and the ignoring of inappropriate behavior in accordance with the rules that is most effective in improving overall classroom behavior. In essence, the rules are necessary but not sufficient by themselves for the development of acceptable classroom behavior. Students not conforming to classroom rules may cause significant disruptions that clearly interfere with academic learning (Kerr & Nelson, 2006).

Some Examples of Classroom Rules	
• Attend to personal needs before class.	• Use appropriate language in class.
• Remain seated during work periods.	• Follow teacher instructions.
• Bring required material home.	• Keeps hands and feet to self.
• Bring required material to school.	• Begin work after instructions given.
• Remain quiet unless talking is permitted.	• Be on time for class.
• Use inside voice in class.	• Complete homework.

The list above is not exhaustive, and other rules can be added. The most effective classroom rules are stated positively and communicate what needs to be done—not what should not be done. Teachers should choose a maximum of four to five rules that are most important with regard to the students in the class. Some teachers may initially start with one or two rules and then add others as they learn more about the students.

CONFLICTS IN THE CLASSROOM

Conflicts between students and teachers—more commonly found in upper elementary classes as children approach adolescence—may arise over disagreements and misperceptions. Rigid teachers who believe that students should "do as they are told" are more likely to be faced with conflicts than teachers who practice conflict resolution and make use of the so-called "teachable moment." The way a teacher responds to conflict is critical. According to Kreidler (1997), there are five effective ways to manage classroom conflict:

1. *No-nonsense approach:* The teacher does not give in but attempts to be fair and honest while providing firm guidance in learning what is acceptable behavior.

2. *Problem-solving approach:* The teacher avoids power struggles with the students and uses a group problem-solving process. The result is more creative ideas and stronger interpersonal relationships.

3. *Compromising approach:* The teacher listens to the students and helps them listen to each other. Each side may then be approached to "give a little" and to compromise.

4. *Smoothing approach:* The teacher encourages all involved to stay calm. Since most conflicts involve relatively unimportant issues, students' attention may simply be redirected to other matters.

5. *Ignoring approach:* The teacher sets limits and allows students to work things out within these boundaries.

Depending on circumstances in the classroom, any one of these approaches may be used at different times. Sometimes the ignoring approach may work best; at other times, and especially when safety is a concern, the no-nonsense approach may be best. Kreidler (1997) has offered some additional strategies for dealing with conflicts, also supported by Weinstein, Tomlinson-Clarke, and Curran (2004) and shown in Figure 10.4. There are also some effective strategies for dealing with conflicts between individual students, including "chilling-out" (in a kind of time-out), meditation, reflective listening, role-playing, and role rehearsal. Some of these issues are discussed more completely in the section on conflict resolution. However, it is important that mediation strategies be practiced and monitored for all students during nonconfrontational times. When mediation skills are learned in this manner, they may become more automatic and will be employed more spontaneously during actual conflict situations. The use of reflective listening may also be helpful. Students are shown how to listen actively by paraphrasing and reflecting back on what they hear as other students tell their side of the story without interruption. For recurring problems, students can review some possible solutions and choose one to consistently implement. For problems that occur less frequently, the students discuss more effective ways of coping with the problem should it ever recur.

By the rules: Most conflicts between students and teachers relate to class rules. Rules must be clearly stated, posted, verbalized, and reviewed with clear definitions of the consequence for violating or breaking the rule.

One-on-one: Confront a student who balks at the consequence one-on-one (not in front of the class) and determine the reason for the resistance.

Conflict resolution: Focus on the *problem*, not the student. (i.e., talk of how to solve the problem).

Third party: Ask another teacher to serve as a mediator if the conflict resolution produces no satisfactory results.

Higher authority: Ask the principal or the childs parents to help find a resolution.

Note: It is important to model appropriate behavior in resolving such conflicts. Rational use of problem solving, conflict resolution, and behavioral contracts may be important in teaching the child to control emotions and to use logical thinking.

FIGURE 10.4   How to solve student versus teacher conflicts.

Source: From *Creative Conflict Resolution* by William J. Kreidler. Copyright © 1984 by William J. Kreidler. Used by permission of Good Year Books, Tucson, AZ. Order online at www.goodyearbooks.com or call toll free (888) 511–1530.

PEER MEDIATION

Peer mediation: A form of conflict resolution where disputing parties converse with the goal of finding a mutually satisfying solution to their disagreement, and a neutral third party facilitates the resolution process. The salient feature of peer mediation as opposed to traditional discipline measures and other forms of conflict resolution is that, outside of the initial training and ongoing support services for students, the mediation process is entirely carried out by students working with their classmates.

In peer mediation, a person trained as a mediator helps two (or more) people resolve a conflict or disagreement. The conflict being resolved might be as simple as who should pay for a damaged locker. Or it might be complex, involving two students who are seriously fighting. In either case, mediation attempts to solve the dispute through peaceful means. The mediator, however, does not simply listen to the conflict and draw up the terms of a solution; the students experiencing the conflict (the participants or disputants) do that. In addition, it is the participants, not the mediator, who enforce the agreed-upon solution.

Mediators in peer mediation play a special role. They do not decide what is right or wrong or find people guilty or innocent, as a judge would in a courtroom. Instead, they try to help the disputants find and agree upon a peaceful way to resolve their conflict.

Preventing and Reducing Aggression Through Mediation

As we all know, conflict is an unavoidable part of life. And there are many types of conflict that may occur in school: a fight or disagreement between classmates, friends arguing over who is to blame for a broken possession.

Conflicts are not always minor and harmless. Assaults or threatened assaults often happen between people who know each other and, in many of these cases, start off with small arguments or disagreements. The mediation process provides a way for students to resolve their disagreements before either party resorts to violence. It also helps them reach agreements without feeling they have had to "give in." In this way, both sides in a mediation come out as winners. Figure 10.5 illustrates what might happen in a mediation session.

- ■ **Step 1. Introduction:** The mediator's role is to make the parties feel at ease and explain the ground rules. It is not to make a decision but to help the parties reach agreement. The mediator explains that he or she will not take sides.
- ■ **Step 2. Telling the story:** Both parties will have a chance to explain what happened. One person tells his or her side of the story first, with no interruptions allowed. The other party then explains his or her version of the facts, again with no interruptions allowed. Any of the participants, including the mediator, may take notes during the process. The mediator's notes are thrown away at the end of the session to ensure confidentiality.
- ■ **Step 3. Identifying the facts, issues, and interests:** The mediator next attempts to identify any agreed-upon facts and issues and the issues that are important to each person. The mediator listens to each side, summarizes each party's view, and checks to make sure each party understands the other view.
- ■ **Step 4. Identifying alternative solutions:** Participants (with help from the mediator) think of all possible solutions to their problem. Because the opposing sides to the dispute probably arrived at the mediation session with a desired outcome in mind, it is often difficult for them to consider other solutions. The mediator makes a list of solutions and asks each party to explain his or her feelings about each one.
- ■ **Step 5. Revising and discussing solutions:** On the basis of feelings expressed by each party, the mediator revises the list of possible solutions and tries to identify a solution that *both* parties may be able to agree on.
- ■ **Step 6. Reaching an agreement:** The mediator helps the parties to reach an agreement by choosing a solution that has been discussed and that both parties agree on. After the parties have decided on a solution, an agreement should be put in writing. The written agreement should be as specific as possible, stating exactly what each party has agreed to do and when he or she will do it. The agreement should also explain what will happen if either disputant breaks the agreement. The parties themselves are responsible for enforcing the contract by bringing examples of breached agreements to the attention of the mediation program. Once it is finalized, the agreement, which usually takes the form of a contract, is signed by both parties.

FIGURE 10.5 A sample mediation session.

Source: Adapted from psychology.jrank.org/pages/478/peer.mediation.html.

Peer Mediation Skit

Conflict: Thomas bumps into Ronnie in the school hallway.
Ronnie: Don't you know how to walk? What is your problem?
Thomas: I'm sorry!
Ronnie: You SOB!
Hunter: Hey guys! What's going on? I help run a peer mediation program. You have a choice, either go into the program or go to the office. What's your decision?
Ronnie: You really messed up.
Thomas: I didn't do anything! But I'll choose to do the program.
Ronnie: I'll do the program, too.
Hunter: Come with me. We need to fill out some papers.
The guys complete the papers and an appointment was set up for the Peer Mediation Program (PMP).
Ms. Bunn: Welcome to the PMP. My name is Ms. Bunn. I am one of the teacher advisors for the program. Some senior peer mediators will coordinate the program; each person (or group) will have a peer mediator. Let me introduce you to Bob and Glenn.
Bob: Each person here has been involved in a conflict. These can be resolved in the office or through detentions. Peer Mediation is an organization to help you deal with conflict in a better way. In the future, you might be able to avoid other conflicts or trouble.
Glenn: Let's first introduce ourselves and talk about something we like. This way, you can be more comfortable in opening up and sharing something about yourselves.
Introductions are made.
Bob: Ok. Now, let's go over the rules:
1. Always be honest
2. Be quiet when someone else is speaking until it's your turn
3. Listen and understand why the conflict happened
4. Say what's on your mind
5. Sign the contract to complete PMP
6. Always respect each other
Glenn: Here are some of the steps in PMP:
1. Tell the whole story
2. Describe the facts of the conflict and how you feel
3. Offer some opinions
4. Make an agreement
Any questions?
Hunter: Ok. Now let's start the program. Thomas will speak with Glenn; Ronnie will speak with Bob.
Glenn: Ok. Now Thomas, tell your side of the story. Ronnie is to be quiet and just listen to what you have to say.
Thomas: I was at my locker and Ronnie walked by me. As I turned away from my locker, Ronnie bumped into me. He started calling me names and I thought he was going to start a fight with me.
Glenn: Are there any incidents of prior hostility between the two of you?
Thomas: Well, in the seventh grade we went to the same elementary school. We didn't get along. He used to pick on me so he could look tough.
Bob: Ok. Ronnie, now tell your side of the story.
Ronnie: During elementary school, he used to try to be like me. Now I just try to avoid him, but when he bumped into me, I snapped and cursed him out.
Bob: So, both of you guys have had problems in the past. Mostly, these problems and anger were suppressed. So when Thomas bumped into you, the tension broke and you said some inappropriate things to him.

(continued)

Glenn: Is that all?

Thomas: Yeah, I guess so.

Ronnie: Yeah.

Bob: Do you both understand what happened? Do you understand how each one of you sees the conflict?

Ronnie: Yeah. What happened goes back to things that occurred in elementary school.

Thomas: I know that Ronnie doesn't like me from things that started in the past, but is there a good reason for his anger?

Glenn: Ok. Let's go back to your stories. Tell your feelings and each one needs to listen to the other.

Thomas: I really get angry about how you treat me. I changed, but I guess you didn't.

Ronnie: I still don't like you. Maybe you changed, but I don't know.

The Peer Mediators will now ask the students about a) I think b) I feel and c) I want statements to resolve the conflict. The Peer Mediators will ask questions and even switch roles.

Bob: Thomas, I get the feeling that you feel hurt. You changed yourself and it hurts when you are not accepted.

Thomas: Yeah, that's right.

Glenn: Ronnie, it's scary to think of Thomas different. Switch roles and think what would have happened in the conflict.

Thomas: Well, I think I would have forgiven Ronnie for bumping into me. It's no big deal.

Ronnie: I could have said sorry and just walked away.

Bob: Both of you need to work out some of the issues of the past. Aggression is inappropriate. Thomas feels hurt and Ronnie is not forgiving Thomas for bumping into him.

The mediators will now ask Thomas and Ronnie how they think the conflict can be resolved.

Glenn: How can you solve this problem?

Ronnie: I guess we could both talk to each other more.

Thomas: Maybe we could talk during lunch and maybe you (Ronnie) could see me differently.

Glenn: Great! Now, each one of you should write down as many solutions that you can think of.

Bob: Read each solution and see if both of you agree to them. The object is to find the best solution.

Glenn: So you both agree to these solutions? Now, each one needs to write a contract about the solutions.

Contracts are written.

Bob: Fine, now all you have to do is follow up on those solutions. Let's meet again in one week, here.

Thomas: Ok.

Ronnie: Ok.

Glenn: See you both then.

Thomas and Ronnie say goodbye.

Training of Peer Mediators

The training programs for peer mediators vary: in some schools all students are trained to act as mediators; in other schools only selected students are. Selected students may be used initially with the intention of including more students later. Mediators either volunteer or are nominated by teachers or other students; often, students who are "troublemakers" turn out to be the best mediators. Many programs have a required conflict resolution course sometime during the middle school years. Training conducted by teachers, counseling staff, or outside consultants may range from a semester-long course (15 to 20 hours of training), to a two-day workshop for middle or high school students, to a three-hour workshop for elementary students. Through discussion and role-playing, students learn conflict resolution skills such as active listening, cooperation in achieving a goal, acceptance of differences, problem-solving, anger management, and methods of maintaining neutrality as a mediator. Students also practice the structured mediation process they will be following in an actual dispute resolution. The peer mediation skit in the box above presents an example of this process.

HOMEWORK POLICY

Generally, teachers should first consider management of the classroom environment *before* focusing on the student. When students are actively engaged in learning, follow class rules, and can effectively communicate with the teacher as well as other students, it is likely that the classroom environment will have been effective and optimal.

Few teachers have ever had coursework or specific training related to homework issues, yet this activity encompasses a significant percentage of time in the education of all students. In the elementary grades, homework is perceived as a critical activity that helps students develop more independent learning skills, self-direction, and self-management skills, and the ubiquitous concept of responsibility. Students with various disabilities may struggle in school and have impaired homework skills due to the increased stress of homework assignments. These children are being turned off and feel stressed out. If the child has a learning or behavior disorder, the stress is even greater (Epstein et al., 1990).

According to Roderique and colleagues (1994), most school districts do not have a formal homework policy. There is also great variation in the underlying reasons teachers have for assigning homework: the kind of homework assigned and the amount, frequency, and approach used by students (Flick, 2000). Once established, a homework policy should be reviewed periodically and revisions made as the curriculum changes (Roderique et al., 1994). Lack of a homework policy in the elementary grades might not show up in academic performance until students reach high school. About 25 percent of students in regular classes and over 50 percent of those with disabilities have trouble completing homework assignments (Polloway, Foley, & Epstein, 1992). Some students have trouble turning in homework even though it has been completed (Flick, 2000).

While homework should be designed to gradually promote greater independence from parental assistance, for many students with disabilities it is a struggle to finish it. For students who experience writing difficulties or dysgraphia, teachers may need to adjust the amount and perhaps type of homework expected of them. Failure to make such adjustments may mean that students will have negative experiences and unpleasant reactions to homework that can escalate to the point of developing maladaptive behaviors around homework. For many students with disabilities, it is a struggle to complete homework even with assistance from parents. The issue of homework may actually bridge the gap between general education and special education.

As the child progresses to junior and senior high school, homework becomes a cost-effective way of providing instruction. In the elementary grades, it is important for teachers to provide high levels of feedback such as constructive comments, and considerable supervision so that assignments may be correctly done. For middle school and high school students, assignments can actually facilitate the acquisition of knowledge in specific academic areas. In elementary school, homework has been shown to have no clear effects on learning, but by high school homework leads to a higher level of achievement (Cooper et al., 1998; Black, 1997). While homework may not show conclusive evidence of learning in elementary school, a good foundation is established for later academic success in higher grades.

According to Cooper (1989), school districts need to clearly indicate their rationale for homework, explain why it is sometimes mandatory, and state the general time requirements for it. There is a clear correlation between time spent on homework and measures of achievement. Homework has been shown to boost academic achievement. It can help to develop good study habits (Cooper et al., 1998) along with independent work and study skills. Some students believe that homework can actually assist them in acquiring new learning and improving grades (Checkley, 2003). The problems that students encounter may begin when assignments are given in class, continue when completing the assignments at home, and end when completed homework is returned to the teacher (Flick, 2000).

Giving assignments to students in class — the first step in the homework procedure — may involve some issues. When teachers put up an assignment at the end of the class (or day), students rushing to copy it may make errors (Black & William, 1998). Also, teachers might poorly estimate how much time an assignment will take. There are many ways to improve the accuracy and acceptance of homework assignments. Teachers should clearly state assignments in writing on the board, provide students with a printed copy, and review the assignments orally. They can also model how students may repeat the directions of the assignment mentally (i.e., subvocally) in their own words. This basically involves teaching self-talk to the student. Also, to confirm that students understand what to do, teachers should provide some time for them to begin the assignment; if there is any trouble or confusion, the assignment may be clarified before students leave the class.

Equal importance should be given to the content and length of the assignment. Too much homework may interfere with free time (Tabor, 1996). Students may be involved in some extracurricular activities that conflict with completing homework (Cooper, 1989). Students who perceive assignments as meaningful and only reasonably difficult are more likely to complete the assignment. When homework is individualized with options and is meaningful to the student's class work, students will do it more willingly and tend to be more successful (Black, 1997).

In general, homework has to be meaningful and should complement learning in the classroom. Polloway and colleagues (1994) have noted that the most frequent incomplete assignments are those involving unfinished classwork or practice tasks. Boredom is a typical complaint from all students, especially from those with ADHD. Homework that provides reinforcement of previously learned material in class may serve to counteract such complaints of boredom. An essential point is to keep repetition to a minimum. Nicholls, MacKenzie, and Shufro (1994) have noted that fewer homework problems are encountered by students who are able to see how their classwork and homework relate to their own skills, interests, and experiences. Some homework problems for students with disabilities can be minimized by giving assignments that relate to something of interest and importance to the student. Many teachers continue to assign useless, counterproductive homework that duplicates but does not reinforce work covered in class (Begley, 1998). The level of difficulty of the material is also important. Kohn (2006) has noted that students must have some understanding of the material to be able to independently complete the relevant homework assignment at home. Lack of understanding can create frustration, and ultimately lead to avoidance of the work. Homework help, online or by phone from a classmate, can be beneficial. Familiarity with homework can also help a parent get involved in their child's educational process, which

raises the student's level of academic achievement. To accomplish this, there is a strong need for good communication between parents and teachers (Jayanthi & Sawyer, 1995). Homework fosters improvement in the bond between home and school. A helping parent needs to understand the nature and methods of homework. Some parents may lack enthusiasm for their child's homework in the early grades as it can significantly interfere with family life as well as the student's involvement in other activities (Cooper et al., 1998). Many accommodations can be made by teachers around homework, such as reducing the length of the assignment (e.g., assigning every other math problem), or changing the format it takes (e.g., a model or project instead of a written narrative).

Completion of homework in a quiet environment must be stressed by the teacher. Watching TV, talking on a cell phone, or listening to music may all result in homework being poorly done (Cooper, 1989; Nathan, 1998). Nevertheless, research has shown that some background music (no vocals or TV) can be beneficial for those students who need to prime their nervous system to be productive—for example, children with ADHD and perhaps some other disorders as well (Flick, 1998b).

Communicating that completed homework is valued, expected, and will be rewarded is essential (Rosenberg, 1989; Margolis & McCabe, 1997). *Homework should never be used as a punishment.* Providing positive comments and constructive feedback can motivate students to complete future assignments. The teacher must clearly convey a sense of importance about homework consistently so that the message of overall significance is received by the student. Grades for homework, when given, should not only reflect the student's abilities but also the effort that the student has expended.

If turning in completed homework is an issue for some students and assignments are not completed, it is important to query the student about this problem. Assignments that are too long or too difficult, or that involve the student's disability (e.g., a handwriting disorder) should be avoided. Learning the reasons for the incomplete homework is essential. Some students do need to be more closely monitored and parental involvement is crucial. Again, most experts agree that homework, as part of the learning process, should not be used as punishment.

Parents are best involved as homework "consultants," and they should not be manipulated into doing the assignments for the child. When parents assume responsibility for the child's work, this encourages the child to become excessively dependent upon the parent. Such dependency may extend into the school environment as the child will harbor expectations of teacher assistance similar to that provided by the parents (Flick, 1998b, 2002).

PHYSICAL OR CORPORAL PUNISHMENT

Research and clinical experience regarding the use of physical punishment such as spanking is that it is generally ineffective since it never tells the child what to do, only *what not to do* (Flick, 1998a). In addition, there are several undesirable "side effects" that may result from physical punishment (Gershoff, 2002):

1. A general tendency to withdraw from social contacts.
2. Aggression turned back toward the punisher—either active (hitting), or passive (resistance or tuning out).
3. Modeling of aggressive behavior (often as inappropriate solutions to problems), which teaches that hitting is a solution to problems and that people can hit if they are big enough and in a position of power.
4. Disruption of the social relationship with the authority figure who imposes the punishment (typically a tendency to distance oneself from that authority person).
5. A failure of the control imposed by the punishment to generalize to other situations.
6. Selective control where an inappropriate behavior is inhibited only in the presence of the authority figure who punished the child. This is similar to the criminal who avoids robbing a store where a policeman is standing by.
7. Stigmatizing the self-concept with feelings of being worthless and deserving of such treatment.

The use of corporal punishment in the home (see Bauman & Friedman, 1998) and in school has been widely debated. Some believe it is a means of discipline while others call it abuse. One has to wonder what would account for the widespread use of corporal punishment as a form of discipline. One reason may be that corporal punishment often provides immediate, but only temporary, suppression of the undesirable behavior (Goldstein, 1988); however, it is clear that *it does not have long-term effect,* and it creates all kinds of side-effects. Corporal punishment is harmful to children and can lead to emotional as well as physical problems. It has also been associated with a variety of psychological and behavioral problems in children such as anxiety, depression, increased aggressiveness, modeling of the punishing behavior, social withdrawal, delinquency, substance abuse, and impaired self-concept (Straus, Sugarman, & Giles-Sims, 1997). Corporal punishment is so readily at hand that it discourages some educators from trying alternatives.

Educators often discount systematic evidence of the ineffectiveness of corporal punishment in the research literature. Such evidence is often scorned as impractical and theoretical. They ignore their own practical evidence that corporal punishment does not have the desired effect on discipline in a school or at home. There is no evidence that discipline is better when corporal punishment is used, and in many places the schools and homes with the most corporal punishment have had the worst discipline. Brenner and Fox (1998) have reported that parents who use verbal and corporal punishment were more likely to have children with behavior problems. According to Flick (1998b), in many cases the child's behavior may elicit more restrictive and more punitive responses from the parent or educator. In essence, the interaction between the child and adult may escalate to the point where physical punishment is used more frequently.

Corporal punishment in the home and at school is banned in a number of countries, including Austria, Cyprus, Denmark, Finland, Italy, Norway, and Sweden. Bans are currently being debated by the governments of Germany, Ireland, Poland, Spain, and Switzerland. Since Sweden banned corporal punishment, Durrant (1999) noted that identification of children at risk has increased, child abuse mortality is rare, and prosecution rates have remained steady; social service intervention has now become increasingly supportive and preventive.

In the United States, about 20 states prohibit corporal punishment in public schools. However, 30 states continue to authorize corporal punishment in their schools. Although there are estimates that this problem has been underreported by two to three times, there were over 1 million occurrences identified in the 1986–1987 school year with 10,000 to 20,000 students requesting subsequent medical treatment. The highest incidence tends to be in the south and southwest (particularly Florida, Texas, Arkansas, Alabama, Mississippi, Tennessee, Oklahoma, Georgia, and Kentucky), while the lowest is in the northeast, where a number of states have outlawed corporal punishment. Current studies indicate that physical punishment is more common in the elementary grades (versus high school), in rural schools (versus urban), with boys (versus girls), with disadvantaged children (versus middle-class and upper-class Caucasians) (Dietz, 2000), and with clinic-referred children (Mahoney et al., 2000).

ACCOMMODATIONS AND SECTION 504

Accommodations are individualized modifications that are made to make learning easier for children with various disabilities. If children are in a special education program, accommodation may be part of the Individualized Education Plan (IEP), but may also be in effect in any general school classroom in which they are placed. Another option is that the child may receive accommodations under Section 504 of the Rehabilitation Act of 1973. Typical 504 accommodations are presented in Appendix D. Accommodations may also be made by many general education teachers for students who are struggling. Accommodations should focus on the child's primary needs. Some of the most frequently used accommodations are large print booklets, extended time on tests, reading questions aloud, small groups, one-on-one instructions, the use of computers in lieu of handwriting, bilingual books in math, and bilingual dictionaries. Sometimes it is important to consult with the identified child as to what may or may not be helpful in class. With the help of the child, two or three accommodations can be initially selected; others may be added as needed. Typically, five accommodations could eventually be tried. Accommodations are made with regard to the physical environment of the classroom, issues around instruction, factors associated with testing, the mechanisms of grading/grades, homework issues, and communication with parents. A complete list of accommodations can be found in Appendix D.

The Fairness Issue

Many teachers still pose questions about the fairness of providing accommodations for some children, making the argument that other students in class would perceive such modifications as "unfair." It is good to remember that many of these children with disabilities have been different from birth; they are literally born with a different nervous system, different neuroanatomical brain structures, and different physiological mechanisms. It would thus be difficult to treat such children the same as their normal counterparts. One of the major problems is something that has been called the invisible handicap—the view that disabled children who generally look like everyone else and do not exhibit any dramatic change in physical appearance are not in need of accommodations. Children with obvious disabilities such as cerebral palsy or other orthopedic handicaps are often more readily accepted and provided appropriate modifications in their physical and/or learning environment without question. Fairness should therefore be based on what is known about the unique makeup of each child. If it is not, such children may be unable to meet the expectations about their ability to function in the classroom and may thus experience excessive criticism and perhaps continued failure.

Dealing with the Fairness Issue

One approach to the fairness issue is for the teacher to discuss individual differences among students. For example, cognitive skills may be addressed by a wide range of observations: (1) some students are better in reading than in math, (2) some students learn more rapidly than others, (3) some students have better handwriting than others, or (4) some students are better at sports than others. This type of discussion may sensitize students to individual differences and hopefully result in greater tolerance for those students who struggle. However, even in cases where a child struggles, there is often some "island of competence"—some area in which the child excels. In light of the differences discussed, the teacher can explain how there may be different expectations regarding the amount and kind of work that can be done by students with various disabilities. Or the teacher could focus on how the work may be done (e.g., by the use of a tape recorder or computer rather than handwritten).

Timed Tests

Timed tests are generally an area of difficulty for disabled students, either due to slowed cognitive processes or fine motor incoordination resulting in poor and labored handwriting. The obvious question is why is there such a need for timed tests? A related question is why is it essential to do 20 math problems in 30 minutes? If education is to prepare students for the "real world," many of these educational expectations are certainly questionable. While every person is confronted with deadlines, it is generally well known that there is greater flexibility encountered as an adult with regard to work expectations.

SUMMARY

This chapter deals with the universal factors that will impinge on the environment of all students. First, there is the physical environment, including the student's seating arrangements and class size. While laws dictate that students need to be educated in the least restrictive environment, the most enabling or appropriate placement is of primary concern. All students should, of course, have effective teachers, so that academic achievement is maximized. One of the most important things teachers must deal with is the effective management of transitions, a process that can minimize classroom behavior problems. The type of instruction can also be important. Direct instruction (or active teaching) is proactive and can prevent class disruptions. Small-group instruction can, however, be disruptive. No matter what type of instruction is used, praise is essential; specific praise is most effective. Communication is likewise critical for all interactions with students and with parents. Classroom rules provide basic structure for students. They should be few in number, briefly stated, clear, and worded positively. Class conflicts are often dealt with using peer mediation, an approach that primarily involves group problem-solving. A teacher's homework policy is also an important factor. Student problems with homework can involve one or more levels of intervention beginning with copying (or getting) assignments, doing them, and returning the completed work to the teacher. Physical or corporal punishment is also addressed and deemed generally inappropriate for all students, both at home and at school. Lastly, we focus on accommodations and how these may apply to students who have emotional and/or behavioral disorders.

DISCUSSION QUESTIONS

1. What is the advantage of arranging student seating?
2. How can "chill out" techniques be facilitated? Why are they important?
3. What is the effect of class and school size on academic and behavioral outcomes?
4. How is size beneficial to low-income and minority students?
5. What are some of the characteristics of effective teachers?
6. Why is it important for teachers to effectively manage transitions?
7. What are some suggestions for managing transitions?
8. Discuss the various types of instruction and their relationship to classroom disruption.
9. Discuss the two types of praise and some of the factors that affect praise. Make specific reference to students with emotional and/or behavior disorders.
10. What type of interventions are recommended because they reduce the frequency of negative interactions with students?
11. What are some of the guidelines for the use of classroom rules?
12. Discuss the five effective ways that Kreidler says can be used to manage classroom conflicts.
13. What are the six major parts of the peer confrontation strategy?
14. What are some of the possible sources of homework problems? Are there any solutions to these problems?
15. What are some general problems with corporal punishment? Why should this procedure not be used in schools?

CHAPTER 11

Positive Behavioral Interventions and Supports

Overview

- Orientation
- Basics of reinforcement
- Positive versus negative reinforcement
- Variations in reinforcement
- Modeling rules
- Planning to change behavior
- Developing new behavior
- The use of shaping
- The token economy
- Instrumental behavior plans
- Behavior momentum
- Contingency contracting
- Generalization
- Precorrection approach to problem behaviors
- Direct instruction
- Punishment
- Ignoring
- Monitoring behavior
- Time-out
- Overcorrection
- Behavior penalty

Case History

Justin is an 11-year-old fifth grader who has a full scale IQ of 119 on the WISC-III and is in a special education program for students with EBD. He is functioning at or above grade level in all academic areas and his performance on standardized school tests is also at or above grade level. Justin's social skills are weak but adequate and he has shown a fair ability to interact with peers and teachers. However, Justin is frequently off-task and rarely completes assignments. When requested to hand in his work at the end of each session, he is often reprimanded for failure to complete an assignment. He immediately cries, yells, and on occasion inflicts self-injury by either banging his head on the desk or biting his arm. *What would you do?*

In order for teachers to profit from the use of positive behavioral interventions and supports, some background information is necessary. To begin with, it is clear that about 90 percent of students in schools are unlikely to present significant behavioral problems during the school year (Horner et al., 2004). For these students, some form of a schoolwide system of rules, expectations, and consequences may be useful to maintain order (Sugai, Sprague, et al., 2000). These basically compliant students may respond to internal controls that may be independent of any school policy. Also, the typical response of teachers and administrators to students with behavioral problems is to remove them from school via suspension, expulsion, or placement in either special education or some alternative program. Such actions clearly do not work.

The most likely reaction to conduct disorders, according to Horner and colleagues (1986), is some combination of punishment and removal. Milofsky (1974) has noted that special education programs have often been used by public schools as repositories for students with discipline problems. This has been supported by the Council for Children with Behavioral Disorders (established in 1963). Many researchers have also supported the idea that behavioral interventions should be an educative process promoting the use of social and adaptive alternatives to problem behaviors through learning, not just through focus only on behavior problem reduction (Koegel, Koegel, & Dunlap, 1996; Scotti & Mercer, 1999).

In the past, corporal punishment has been endorsed and supported as a primary means of enforcing behavior standards in schools. However, even in recent times only 27 states have banned corporal punishment (Evans & Richardson, 1995), and according to a survey by Brown and Payne (1988), teachers still believed that corporal punishment was necessary to maintain discipline. Others have commented on the use of alternate techniques (Kostelnik et al., 2002).

MRS. JONES GAMBLES JENNY'S EDUCATION ON A HUNCH.

FACULTY EXCUSES

TABLE 11.1 Comparison of Traditional Behavior Management with Positive Behavior Support

Traditional Behavior Management	Positive Behavioral Support
1. Views individual as "the problem."	1. Views systems, settings, and skill deficiencies as "the problem."
2. Attempts to "fix" individual.	2. Attempts to "fix" systems, settings, and skills.
3. Extinguishes behavior.	3. Creates new contacts, experiences, relationships, and skills.
4. Sanctions aversives.	4. Sanctions positive approaches.
5. Takes days or weeks to "fix" a single behavior.	5. Takes years to create responsive systems, personalized settings, and appropriate empowering skills.
6. Is implemented by a behavioral specialist, often in atypical settings.	6. Is implemented by a dynamic and collaborative team using person-centered planning in typical settings.
7. Is often resorted to when systems are inflexible.	7. Flourishes when systems are flexible.

Source: Information from Lombardo (1997). Reprinted by permission.

Even though the term *positive behavioral support* (PBS), whose inception dates back to the 1980s, uses such procedures, they have been intermittent at best. During this time, problem behavior was viewed as more of a systems issue than a sign of individual pathology. The development of problem behavior was seen to reside within a dynamic interaction between the child's responses to the environment and the environment's reaction to the child. In short, many experts agreed that there was no place for punishment in the discipline of students in schools (Glasser, 1992). The use of time out and other forms of "punishment" was also de-emphasized. Instead, the emphasis turned to positive behavioral support, a form of behavioral intervention different from traditional behavior management, as illustrated in Table 11.1.

ORIENTATION

It has been often noted that most students behave appropriately at certain times during the school day. However, it is at these times that teachers often ignore students when they are doing what they are supposed to do. Reinke, Lewis-Palmer, and Martin (2007) indicate that there is little evidence to suggest that teachers, universally and systematically, deploy contingent praise as positive reinforcement; praise for appropriate classroom behavior is rarely observed. In short, students should be reinforced when they engage in appropriate behavior, and they should not receive attention only when they misbehave. Students learn very quickly that they can get more attention by behaving inappropriately and do so to get attention (Reinke, Lewis-Palmer, & Martin, 2007; Maag, 2001). The use of simple positive techniques by classroom teachers can have a significant influence on the entire school (Tolan, Gorman-Smith, & Henry, 2001).

REINFORCEMENT BASICS

Reinforcement is defined as any stimulus that maintains or increases a behavior that occurred immediately prior to the reinforcing stimulus (Keyes, 1994). If the behavior is maintained or increased in rate, duration, or intensity, the stimulus is a reinforcer. According to Zirpoli (2007), there are many factors that are associated with the effectiveness of reinforcement, as noted in the box on the following page.

THE "I DON'T KNOW WHY HE DOES IT" GLASSES PREVENT MRS. SMITH FROM SEEING WHY TIM THROWS TANTRUMS AT THE STORE.

Key Points About Reinforcement

- *Immediacy:* As the interval between the behavior and the reinforcement increases, the relative effectiveness of the reinforcer decreases. This is especially true initially; later on the interval may be increased.

- *Verbal praise:* Reinforcement should describe exactly what the student did that was appropriate so that an association is developed between the behavior and the reinforcer. The association of verbal praise with the reinforcer will increase the reinforcement properties of verbal praise.

- *Schedule of reinforcement:* Reinforcement should be given every time initially, to establish the behavior. Continuous schedules should then be faded to an intermittent one.

- *Types of reinforcement:* It is important to allow students to select reinforcers that they think will "work" for them, not reinforcers that the teacher selects.

- *Quality/quantity of reinforcement:* Teachers should strive to use reinforcers that are fresh and deliver just enough to reinforce but not satiate the child.

- *Who delivers the reinforcement:* Reinforcers are more effective when the student likes or admires them.

- *Consistency:* Teachers should maintain consistency in delivering the reinforcement. Inconsistency results in confusion and detracts from the effectiveness of the program.

Source: Information from Zirpoli (2007). Reprinted by permission.

Positive Versus Negative Reinforcement

Positive reinforcement, as shown in Table 11.2, involves the presentation of a reinforcing stimulus (e.g., a no-homework slip) following a target behavior (i.e., what the teacher is attempting to develop) to maintain or increase the frequency, duration, or intensity of the target (i.e., antecedent) behavior. Giving extra time on the computer after completing assigned work would be another simple example of positive reinforcement.

Negative reinforcement, also shown in Table 11.2, on the other hand, involves the removal of an aversive stimulus following a target behavior that results in the maintenance or increase in the frequency, duration, or intensity of the target (i.e., antecedent) behavior.

Clearly, negative reinforcement is not punishment. However, it has played a significant role in the development of many problem behaviors (Zirpoli & Melloy,

1993; Bowen, Jenson, & Clark, 2004). For example, a student who has trouble doing the work in math class may act out by yelling, hitting another student, or being disrespectful to a teacher. The result is that the student gets to leave the room and go to the office or a time-out room—thus avoiding the dreaded math assignment. This punishment involves either the presentation of an aversive (unpleasant) stimulus, or the removal (withdrawal) of a positive (pleasant) stimulus.

Table 11.3 presents some examples of how specific behaviors are developed and maintained by positive or negative reinforcement.

Reinforcers can range from food and drinks to activities and verbal statements. Teachers quickly find that children may satiate on reinforcers such as food or drink and they will lose their effectiveness over time. Candy in particular is not only discouraged by dentists

TABLE 11.2   Strength of Antecedent Behavior

Stimulus	Increased	Decreased
Present	Positive reinforcement	Punishment
Positive/adversive	(Positive stimulus presented)	(Aversive stimulus presented)
Remove	Negative reinforcement	Punishment
Aversive/positive stimulus	(Aversive stimulus removed)	(Positive stimulus removed)

TABLE 11.3   Examples of Problem Behavior Maintained by Positive or Negative Reinforcement

	Positive Reinforcement Occurring Immediately After a Problem Behavior, Resulting in its Increase	Negative Reinforcement Occurring Immediately After a Problem Behavior, Resulting in its Increase
Attention	Receiving a reprimand after screaming, or receiving any attention to inappropriate behavior.	Running away to escape negative attention by others.
Tangible Objects	Getting a toy (or food) after hitting another child.	
Demands/Task		Having a tantrum, which results in unpleasant or difficult task being removed.
Sensory Stimuli	Sucking on fingers or head banging due to sensations it produces.	Hitting oneself to relieve pain or general avoidance/escape of sensory stimuli through inappropriate behavior.

Source: Information from Zirpoli (2007). Reprinted by permission.

MR. THOMPSON FAILS TO SEE THAT JON PREFERS THE ISOLATION BOOTH TO MATH CLASS.

TABLE 11.4   Potential Primary and Secondary Reinforcement

	Primary Reinforcers	Secondary Reinforcers
Positive Stimulus	Food	Money
	Water	Tokens
	Sleep	Grades
	Sensory stimulation	Approval
Aversive Stimulus	Shock/pain	Ridicule
	Written work	Exclusion
	Extreme temperatures	Violation of personal space
	Loud noise	Gestures
	Physical pressure	

but may certainly contribute to hyperactivity and obesity in some children. As recommended by McVey (2001), more attention should be given to the use of praise or encouragement—a reinforcer that is easy to give and less subject to satiation.

There are two types of reinforcers (as shown in Table 11.4). These are primary and secondary reinforcers.

Types of Reinforcers

Primary reinforcers are naturally reinforcing because they meet a basic physiological need such as food or water. Secondary reinforcers are not naturally reinforcing but can become so when paired with a primary reinforcer. Verbal praise is an excellent example. A good example of a secondary reinforcer is *money*. It has no intrinsic value except when it is associated with something that can be bought. A child may respond to a primary reinforcer, which can be faded out and replaced by social praise given a sufficient number of pairings (or associations). High preference activities such as computer time, free time, or extra recess can also serve as reinforcers. Some students respond well to secondary reinforcers such as tokens or tickets. Another strategy to consider is the *Premack principle*, the theory that a low frequency activity can be reinforced when followed by a high frequency activity (Flick, 1998b). Keyes (1994) reviewed evidence of this when fourth and fifth graders were reinforced by increasing amounts of computer time after they had completed increasing levels of academic tasks. Table 11.5 lists some of the types of reinforcers that can be used with students (Zirpoli, 2007).

Two points should be emphasized here: (1) these are not the only reinforcers a teacher might use, and (2) reinforcers might differ with regard to their desirability. For example, "stars"—a tangible but secondary reinforcers—are not necessarily reinforcing to all students. It should also be noted that reinforcers can be combined (e.g., verbal praise along with another reinforcer such as points).

High preference reinforcers have been shown in research to be the most effective (e.g., popcorn or pizza) (Piazza et al., 1996). However, a trial and error method might identify a specific set of reinforcers for certain students. Piazza and colleagues (1996) found that a choice preference was the preferred way to identify reinforcers. In this study, each potential reinforcer was paired with every other reinforcer until the high preference stimuli are found. Green and colleagues (1988) found that such trial and error assessment results did not always correlate with items selected by teachers.

Varying the Types of Reinforcers

A simple reinforcer may quickly lose appeal. However, having a variety of reinforcers to select from allows teachers to keep the reinforcer free from satiation effects. According to Zirpoli (2007), teachers might prevent satiation in the following ways:

■ Vary the reinforcer or use a different reinforcer for each target behavior.
■ Monitor the amount of reinforcement, using just enough to reinforce the target behavior.
■ Avoid edible reinforcers, or use them as infrequently as possible.
■ Move from constant to intermittent reinforcement as soon as possible.
■ Move from primary to secondary reinforcers.

TABLE 11.5 Types of Reinforcers

Tangible	Social	Activities
Stars	Verbal recognition	Choice time
Rubber stamps	Verbal praise	Time with teacher
Check marks	Student of the day	Read a story
Points	First in line	Pass out materials
Toys	Leader of day	Feed class pet
Edibles	Phone call home	Use computer
Magazines	Note home	Run errand
Puzzles	Activity leader	Listen to tape

Source: Information from Zirpoli (2007). Reprinted by permission.

Classroom Reinforcement

Teachers need to be specific with students about which behaviors are expected or acceptable and which ones are not. For example, when a teacher says "respect others," students must understand exactly what "respect" means. Behavior can be reinforced only when it is specific and observable. Examples of classroom rules might be "keep your hands and feet to yourself" or "say excuse me" before interrupting others. These are behaviors that can also be modeled by the teacher, who can show what "keeping hands and feet to self," looks like. When classroom rules state what the student cannot do (e.g., don't hit others) then the focus is negative and the result involves punishment. When the rules are stated in a positive frame, the emphasis is on reinforcement and students are told what to do and which behavior will earn reinforcement. As also stated in Chapter 10, the rules of the classroom should be posted and reviewed regularly.

Modeling Rules Teachers need to be consistent in following their rules modeling appropriate behavior. For example, if "please" and "thank you" are some of the social behavior that is encouraged in students, then such behaviors should also be exhibited by teachers. In short, teachers need to model the behavior that is expected of their students.

Giving Reinforcements When choosing among the numerous ways to give reinforcers, teachers should remember to (1) be consistent, and (2) show some emotion or excitement in their delivery. It is important to give reinforcers immediately after the appropriate behavior. Students, and especially those with disabilities, will be more stimulated by a dynamic verbal expression of praise (or encouragement) that may be combined with some other reinforcer. Some students have greater need for stimulation and will seek it out.

BEHAVIOR CHANGE

There are many ways teachers can approach behavior change. The following example illustrates the series of steps that may be involved:

Step 1 Describe the behavior to be changed in positive terms—for example, increasing a student's in-seat behavior.

Step 2 Collect some baseline data on how long this student can remain seated. Record in-seat behavior for 30 to 60 minutes per day for 5 days and calculate an average.

Step 3 Establish a program goal—for example, 15 minutes of in-seat behavior. The student should understand what this increase means.

Step 4 Compare the gap between the student's ability to remain seated and the program goal. If the difference is significant, the student may have to be reinforced for gradually increasing the time for in-seat behavior. For example, Rob might be initially reinforced for sitting for 1 minute. After he is able to do this, he might be expected

TABLE 11.6 Examples of Problem Behaviors and Their Alternative Appropriate Behaviors

Problem Behavior	Alternative Appropriate Behavior
Constantly moving	Remains still
Talks excessively	Remains quiet
Ignores peers	Greets peers
Shows anger with peers	Works/plays cooperatively with peers
Curses peers	Communicates appropriately with peers
Defies authority	Respects authority, speaks courteously with adults

to sit for 5 minutes, then 10, and finally 15 minutes. How fast students can move from one criterion to the next will vary. There needs to be a performance criterion. For example, Rob might be told that he needs to remain seated for 1 minute over two observation periods before he moves to the next level (i.e., 5 minutes). He may be given increasing amounts of computer time for each reinforcement. Because students who have a hard time remaining seated may have a "need to move," reinforcement for seatwork might be permission to get up and move to the computer or to go get a book in the back of the room (Flick, 1998b, 2002).

Developing New Behaviors

Many students will need to develop a new behavior either (1) to replace an old problem behavior, or (2) because the new behavior is a skill deficit. In either case, it will be important to look at those behaviors that are alternatives—more appropriate behaviors that can replace the problem behavior.

For every problem behavior, there is an alternative appropriate behavior that can be developed (Flick, 1998b). Table 11.6 provides some examples.

Behavioral programs that focus solely on punishing behaviors may work only for a short time. Focusing on developing more appropriate behavior through a positive orientation is essential. If interrupting others is the problem behavior, then waiting one's turn to talk is the appropriate behavior on which to focus.

Modeling In many cases, the appropriate behavior may not seem clear, and the student may not know what to do. It will thus be important for teachers to initially model the appropriate behavior to be established.

Shaping Shaping is another technique that can be used to develop new behaviors through successive approximation—any intermediate behavior that gets closer to the reinforcement of a desired behavior. Shaping may also be used to modify the frequency, duration, or intensity of a current behavior. For example, in the case of Rob who was gradually taught to remain seated for an increasing number of minutes, shaping was used.

Shaping has also been used to improve language, handwriting, and many other skill behaviors. It is often combined with other procedures such as modeling to develop the new behavior. This process is used to basically save time, as it might take a very long time for the student to demonstrate a closer approximation to a desired behavior. The simplest thing is to show a student the desired behavior and allow time for the student to imitate it. At first, the behavior may not look exactly like it should but reinforcement can be withheld until improvement occurs. Shaping can also be used to decrease the frequency, duration, or intensity of a current behavior. In this case, students are learning to express a behavior differently, not learning a new response. For example, when a student talks too loud in class, shaping can be used to encourage the student to talk in a more acceptable speaking voice— what teachers might describe as "using your inside voice." Again, modeling can be used to demonstrate what an acceptable voice is.

Chaining Chaining is a process that refers to the performance of a sequence of behaviors rather than just one behavior. For example, Zirpoli (2007) points out that chaining might be used if a teacher wishes to have students walk into the classroom, place backpack by their desk, put lunch in their lockers, and then sit at their

---

The Fairness Issue Regarding Reinforcement

Many teachers say that they find it difficult to provide tokens or any positive reinforcement program to a child with a disability because it isn't "fair" to the other children. Riffel (2005) offers a good analogy in response. Let's say you are in a meeting and someone starts to choke and to turn blue. Are you going to say, "I'm sorry, I don't have time to give the Heimlich maneuver to everyone else in the room, so it wouldn't be fair if I only gave it to you. I'm so sorry." Although this is an unlikely scenario, it does drive the point home. If you use the "It's not fair" rule, Riffel notes that you are functioning at the emotional level of a 7-year-old. Students will understand procedures that are explained clearly, and they will soon agree that each of us needs different things in life.

Source: Information from Riffel (2005). Reprinted by permission.

---

desks. In this case, four behaviors are taught together as one behavior chain. Each of the behaviors are connected to one another like the links in a chain. Each link will then serve as a discriminative stimulus (i.e., a prompt) for the next behavior in the chain. The development of this chain is called a *task analysis* (Zirpoli, 2007).

Initially, teachers need to reinforce students for each correct completion as well as to reinforce them for completing each behavior in the correct sequence. After the student has learned the sequence, reinforcement can be intermittent and faded. It should be noted, however, that students may complete this chain at different times; some may require more days to learn the sequence. After reinforcement is faded, it will still be important to review the steps and to give occasional reinforcement; remember that social praise is one reinforcement that is always available.

Token Economy Point System

A *token point system* may be used with children 6 through 12 years (Flick, 1998b). Keep in mind that these systems are simply rough guidelines. Some very effective programs have been conducted with immature adolescents (and older children); some children younger than 6 years have also used the point system (or more likely tokens). Some early references to the use of such token/point systems may be found in Ayllon and Azrin (1968) and Kazdin and Bootzin (1972).

Token economy point systems are classified as positive behavior interventions because only appropriate behaviors are included. An example of a token economy point system that can be used for children ages 6 to 8 is shown in Figure 11.1.

Comment on Token Point System for Ages 6 to 8

There are several things to note about a token point system for ages 6 to 8:

1. There are only six items to receive points.

2. Points assigned are marked on the chart with slash marks; most desired behaviors receive 4 points for each observation per class. Thus, on any single day a student may receive 4 points more than once in each class. Behaviors that the teacher wishes to reinforce more strongly may receive more points (e.g., get along with peers may receive 6 points if the teacher wishes to emphasize that item).

3. A student who has the points needed for a privilege may get it that day. Some items—for example, purchasing a store item or getting a homework pass—may be restricted to Fridays only.

4. *Daily points used* are then subtracted from *daily points earned* (i.e., total cumulative points); this gives the *daily net points*.

5. It is important that the teacher give privileges only when the student has the required points and that no credit be allowed (i.e., giving the privilege before the points are earned).

6. There is only one basic criterion for all token point systems and that is it must be designed to be successful (Flick, 1998b), which is in fact the ultimate criterion for *all* behavioral interventions. In short, it is important that the program be challenging but not so difficult that the student always fails.

Name __John_____ Age _____ Date _____

Behavior	Points	M	T	W	Th	F	Total
Follows instructions	4/class	//	/		/	//	24
Completes work	4/class	//	/		/	//	24
Obeys class rules	4/class	/	/		/	//	20
Gets along with peers	4/class	/		/	//	/	20
Completes homework	4/class	//		/	//		20
Works on-task	4/class	//	/		/	//	24
Bonus Points	2/Class	/	//		/	///	14
Total points		42	20	8	34	42	138
Total cumulative points			42	30	66	88	138
Points Used		20	20	20	20	50	130
Net points		22	22	32	46	38	104
Privilege	**Points Used**	**M**	**T**	**W**	**Th**	**F**	**Total**
First in line	10	/	/	/	/		40
Class helper	10	/	/	/	/		40
Store item (Fridays only)	50					/	50
Homework pass (F)	20						
Popcorn party for class (F)	100						
Totals		20	20	20	20	50	130
Savings	Based on 4 classes						38 points remaining
Rules	• Follows instructions (starts work after instructions). • Obeys class rule (raises hand to answer). • Gets along with peers (works and plays cooperatively, shares).						

FIGURE 11.1 Teacher point system (ages 6–8).

Source: Information from Flick (1998b). Reprinted by permission.

7. The teacher should not try to include more than *one to three students* in such a program. For the novice teacher, it may be better to begin with only one student and perhaps add students as the teacher feels more comfortable with the system and becomes more experienced with it.

8. Students should be told that points may be exchanged only at the end of the day.

9. Students should understand what is expected of them (i.e., the desired behaviors), and what each privilege means. An individual session with the student prior to implementing the program would help to clarify thus.

10. If other students ask to be included in this program, teachers may answer as follows: (a) the student is doing well and may not need the points program; (b) all students will benefit when the identified student is able to purchase a "popcorn party" for the whole class; or (c) if the student making the request is not doing well, the teacher

Name John_____ Age _____ Date _____

Behavior	Points	M	T	W	Th	F	Total
Followed instructions	5/class	///	//	///	//	///	65
On-task	5/class	////	//	///// /	/	////	85
Completes work	10/class	//	/	///	/	///	100
Obeys class rules	5/class	/		/		//	20
Works/plays cooperatively	10/class	/		/		/	30
Completes homework	20/class		/	/		/	60
Bonus Points	2/Class	//		///	//	/	16
Total points		74	50	116	29	107	
Total cumulative points			124	120	149	256	
Points used		0	120	0	0	250	
Net points (savings)		74	4	120	149	6	(s) 6
Privilege	**Points Used**	M	T	W	Th	F	Total
Store item (Fridays only)	300					/	300
Homework pass (F)	150					/	150
Extra computer time	130						
Free time	120			/			120
Totals				120			570
Rules		• Follows instructions (starts work after instructions).					
		• Obeys class rule (raises hand to answer/keeps hands and feet to self).					
		• Works and plays cooperatively, shares, and helps.					

FIGURE 11.2 Teacher point system (ages 9–12).

Source: Information from Flick (1998b). Reprinted by permission.

may say that such a program may be considered. It will, therefore, help for other students to give *encouragement* to any student in the point program. This will not only provide involvement for other students but will give support to the student in question (on the point system). Since an edible reinforcer is used, the popcorn party may be relegated to Fridays only; (d) the teacher can offer verbal praise to all students for the same behaviors as the identified student. Teachers also need to be *very specific* and tell the student exactly what he/she liked about his/her behavior. For example, "You really did a good job on that assignment—you worked hard and you completed it."

A sample program for children ages 9 through 12 is found in Figure 11.2.

Token Point System for Ages 9 to 12

The token point system for ages 9 to 12 is very similiar to the program for ages 6 to 8. The number of desired behaviors may vary as do the number of privileges. With older students, the teacher may also give more bonus points. These points are given for any appropriate behavior that is not on the list or any behavior that a teacher wishes to reinforce that is close to a behavior on the list. For example, a student who does not complete an assignment but finishes 80 percent of it may receive a bonus; the student will get another bonus the next day by completing 90 percent of an assignment. It may take several days and a few more bonuses to complete 100 percent of an assignment (i.e., assuming there are no other factors operating).

Teachers wishing to reinforce closer approximations to the desired behavior (via shaping) may thus do so with bonus points. It is also important for the teacher to give

	Week 1	Week 2	Week 3	Week 4	Week 5
Total points	138	152	157	180	182
Savings	8	20	25	30	33
Cumulative savings	8	28	53	83	116

Student ___John___   Teacher _Mrs. Blake_   Age _8_

Monitoring period 10/01   Number class 4

Goal ___Entire class goes on a special field trip___

Points required ___100___   Date met _____

FIGURE 11.3   Summary of point totals across weeks.

verbal praise along with the bonus points—for example, saying something like "John, you've been working very hard on that assignment. You didn't complete it, but you're very close. I'd like to give you a bonus for that."

At the end of each week, all unused points will go into savings for that student (see Figure 11.3).

See the summary in Figure 11.3 for all points. A goal can be set for use of these points and will demonstrate to students how they are progressing. A *sample form* is shown in Appendix E. In this example, the goal was met because John saved enough points to earn a special field trip for the whole class. He may also be instrumental in selecting the place where the class will go on their field trip. In this system, the identified student thus has the support of the whole class (because they all want the field trip).

Steps to Establish a Token Economy   Again, there are several steps teachers should follow when setting up a token economy. A review of these steps follows:

Step 1   Select one to three students for the program. Note that each program may be individualized. This means that different behaviors and/or privileges may be selected.

Step 2   Select the appropriate behaviors that are to be reinforced for each student (Flick, 1998b). Table 11.7 presents a partial list of suggestions.

Step 3   Select the privileges to be used for each student. It is important to work with the student on this listing. Table 11.8 offers some suggestions.

Step 4   Explain the program to each student, using language that is developmentally appropriate.

Step 5   Begin the program on a Monday, so that it can be monitored week to week.

Step 6   Keep a record of points earned and develop a goal for using leftover points kept in savings.

Step 7   When a student is being monitored, remember to give verbal praise for successful behaviors.

Step 8   If a behavior is weak or nonexistent, teachers must use shaping (along with bonus points) or model the behavior and allow the student to imitate it. The student may need to review this behavior periodically. Also, if the student rarely gets points for a specific behavior, additional motivation may be given by increasing the number of points for that behavior; note that infrequent points may be a red flag that other factors are operating.

Step 9   Monitor behaviors closely. Use the point totals across time to compare how many points are received for each behavior and how many

TABLE 11.7   Some Appropriate Behaviors for a Token Economy

■ Raises hand to answer or to ask a question	■ Turns in homework
■ Follows instructions	■ Works cooperatively with others
■ Remains seated	■ Plays cooperatively with others
■ Begins work immediately	■ Shares materials
■ On-task for seatwork	■ Keeps hands/feet to self

Note: Individualize for each student.

TABLE 11.8 Potential Reinforcers for a Token Economy

■ Store item (Fridays only)	■ Tickets
■ First in line	■ Good behavior card
■ Class helper	■ Favorite magazine (with permission)
■ Homework pass (Fridays only)	■ Favorite book (with permission)
■ Extra computer time	■ Popcorn party (for class)
■ Free time	■ Pizza party (for class)
■ Token	■ Stickers

points are received each day. By inspecting point totals over several weeks, patterns may emerge regarding which behaviors are easy or more difficult, which days are better, and which privileges are preferred.

Step 10   Monitor a student's progress over several weeks. Changes may be made in the program— for example increasing or decreasing point totals or selecting new privileges. As mentioned earlier, the single most important criterion is for any program to be *successful*. Programs that are too difficult, where the student receives no reinforcer (i.e., no points), should be stopped immediately.

Step 11   When a student is exhibiting a specific behavior as often as possible, replace that behavior with a substitute behavior. For example, if John completes all of his seatwork, over several days or weeks, the teacher might drop this behavior and add "raising hand to answer," or "keeping hands and feet to self." The teacher will continue to give verbal praise (but no points) for any behavior that is dropped: "John, you did a good job of completing your work. I'm really proud of you."

Step 12   Remember that the token system, as with any behavioral program, is designed for short-term use. When the student achieves success, it may be time to terminate the program, but to continue giving verbal praise for the identified behavior. Point systems are not meant to be continued indefinitely. The blank forms needed for students point systems ages 6–8 and 9–12 are shown in Appendix D.

Alternatives to Punishment

The purpose of *discrete trial training* (DTT) is to teach positive behaviors. Consequently there should be no need for punishment when involved in a DTT session.

The fact that problem behaviors are not being reinforced should be enough to discourage them in favor of the behaviors to which reinforcement is being given. However, it may be necessary to minimize or lessen particular problem behaviors outside of the discrete trial session. The first step in this process is to ascertain the motivation behind the current behaviors (i.e., to conduct a functional behavior analysis). Once the function of the behavior has been determined, a plan can be created to teach better ways to meet those needs.

•••••••••••••••••••••••••••••••••••••••

Discrete trial training (DTT) is a teaching technique that incorporates the principles of applied behavior analysis (ABA), some of which include positive reinforcement; reinforcement schedules; shaping, prompting, differential reinforcement; etc. It is not in itself ABA. DTT is a strategy used to teach a child new behaviors in a one-to-one setting. In DTT, larger concepts are broken down into smaller concepts. (Adapted from http://autismed.com/glossary.html, retrieved 10/31/09.)

•••••••••••••••••••••••••••••••••••••••

There are four basic alternatives to punishment for reducing difficult behaviors and encouraging more appropriate behaviors:

■ Differential reinforcement of other behaviors (DRO) is the reinforcement of *any* behavior other than the problem behavior.

■ Differential reinforcement of alternative behaviors (DRA) is the reinforcement of behaviors that serve as alternatives to the problem behavior, especially alternative means of communication. For example, a child can be taught to present his teacher with a picture known as a *PECS symbol* instead of having a tantrum to escape from work. PECS is a nonverbal communication system developed by Bondy and Frost (2001) to help children with autism quickly acquire a functional means of communication. The PECS procedure is briefly outlined in the box on the following page.

A Brief Guide to PECS

The PECS manual guides readers through the six phases of training and provides examples, helpful hints, and templates for data and progress reporting:

Phase 1: Teaches students to initiate communication by exchanging a single picture for a highly desired item.

Phase 2: Teaches students to be persistent communicators, to actively seek out their pictures, and to go to someone to make a request.

Phase 3: Teaches students to discriminate pictures and to select the picture that represents the item they want.

Phase 4: Teaches students to use sentence structure to request something.

Phase 5: Teaches students to respond to the question "What do you want?"

Phase 6: Teaches students to comment about things in their environment both spontaneously and in response to a question.

Source: Information from http://www.pecs.com/whatsPECS.htm. Permission granted by Pyramid Educational Consultants, Inc., for the Picture Exchange Communication System (PECS).

■ Differential reinforcement of incompatible behaviors (DRI) is the reinforcement of behaviors that are incompatible with the problem behaviors and behaviors that the child cannot be doing simultaneously. For example, children who are constantly touching their neighbors during circle time could be reinforced for keeping their hands in their laps, or sitting on them (both incompatible behaviors).

■ *Differential reinforcement of lesser rates of behavior (DRL)* is the reinforcing of periods of time in which the child exhibits the behavior at a predetermined lesser rate. For example, children who currently talk out approximately 10 times every 5 minutes when they are in the library with their class could be reinforced if they only talk out five times during that same 5 minutes.

POSITIVE VERSUS NEGATIVE STIMULUS EVENTS

A comparison of positive and negative stimulus events is presented in Table 11.9.

TABLE 11.9   Comparison of Positive and Negative Stimulus Events

	Presentation	Withdrawal
Positive stimulus	*Positive reinforcement* (increases behavior)	*Extinction/response cost* (decreases behavior)
Aversive stimulus	*Punishment* (decreases behavior)	*Negative reinforcement* (increases behavior)

Reinforcement is a function of whether a stimulus event is presented or removed (withdrawn) after a response is made, and whether the child's responding increases (i.e., the behavior is strengthened) or decreases (i.e., the behavior is weakened). Any stimulus event that increases (strengthens) responding is called reinforcement; any stimulus event that decreases (weakens) responding is called punishment. The stimulus event may be positive—something pleasant and desirable—or negative—something aversive and seemingly undesirable. In general, the child will work to get more positive stimulus events and will most likely wish to avoid or escape aversive ones.

While rewards or reinforcers may be phased out over a period of time following successful behavior change, it is always appropriate to continue the use of social reinforcers or praise. While both praise and the more tangible rewards are presented at first on a fixed schedule (i.e., every time the target behavior occurs), it is essential to proceed to a stage where social praise continues but the tangible reward is presented on a variable schedule (i.e., not every time but almost randomly). At some later point, the social praise may go to a variable schedule.

WRITING INSTRUMENTAL BEHAVIOR PLANS

Behavior that leads a person to obtain a specific reinforcement (reward) is termed *instrumental behavior*. The simplest example of instrumental behavior is illustrated when a parent offers a reward to a child: "First you eat your dinner, then you get your dessert." This has also been called *Grandma's Rule*. Eating dinner is thus "instrumental" in getting "dessert." Instrumental behavior plans should meet two basic criteria:

1. They should be stated in a positive framework—for example, "When you finish your math assignment, you may go to the back of the classroom and get a book" instead of "If you don't finish your math assignment, then you can't go to the back and get a book."

2. They should use *when* instead of *if*, leaving no doubt that the work will be done—for example, "when you do your class work, then you can have free time." Consequently, there is no option for *if* it will be done, only *when* it will be done. These *when—then* plans can be used equally well in the home or school setting (Flick, 1998b).

Note that children should not be allowed to have what they want based on a promise to complete the desired behavior at a later time. Teachers who say, "You can have free time, but you have to promise to complete your assignment" will discover too late that the assignment will not be completed. It is also important to note that children with attention-deficit/hyperactivity disorder and certain other behavior disorders experience some difficulty with "delay of gratification." Typically such a child would prefer to do a small amount of work for a small "immediate" reward than a larger amount of work for a much larger reward at some later time. Large rewards offered for good grades at the end of a semester or year will thus be ineffective.

Teachers should remember that the when–then paradigm is the basis for most behavior management programs. It is both simple to use and effective. Here are some examples to follow:

1. *When* you finish your math assignment, *then* you may have some computer time.

2. *When* you clean out your desk, *then* you may have a treat.

3. *When* you raise your hand to ask a question, *then* you can have a token.

4. *When* you finish work on your group project, *then* you can have a homework pass.

5. *When* you talk in a normal tone, *then* you can have a ticket.

6. *When* you finish your reading assignment, *then* you can have free time to select a book in the back of the room.

BEHAVIORAL MOMENTUM

A behavioral approach to studying the allocation of behavior under changed environmental constraints is termed *behavioral momentum*. Asking noncompliant students to complete tasks they would be likely to do is an example of a behavioral momentum procedure that can be used to increase the likelihood of these students doing something that they have previously resisted (Mace & Belfiore, 1990; Zarcone et al., 1994). A more recent application of behavioral momentum for students with autism can be found in Ahearn and colleagues (2003) and for children with developmental disabilities in Dube and colleagues (2003). The model of behavioral momentum was originally proposed by Nevin, Mandell, and Atak (1983), and it has surfaced more recently in Plaud and Gaither (1996), which focuses on the use of high probability requests as a proactive procedure to reduce noncompliance. Behavioral momentum has also been used to improve medication-taking behavior and attempting hard tasks and to discourage self-injury and aggressive behaviors.

The underlying principle of behavioral momentum is similar to a technique that experienced sales people have used for years. The salesperson asks a series of questions posed so that everyone would answer in the positive. Once they have answered "yes" several times, there is a positive agreement momentum that makes it more likely that everyone will answer yes to the last question. Once there is momentum, there is thus an increased likelihood of getting students to give a positive response. In recent studies (e.g., Lee & Laspe, 2004), it was found that getting compliance with "give me five" and "give me a hug" (high probability requests) increased the probability of getting developmental delayed subjects to "put a lunchbox away" (a low probability request).

Implementation of Behavioral Momentum

In order for behavioral momentum to be implemented, the following steps are suggested:

1. Parent or teacher first selects a series of behaviors that a student would like to do at least 75 percent of the time (a high probability behavior).

2. Parent or teacher then asks the student to do several of the high probability behaviors before asking him or her to complete the low probability behavior. Asking for two or three of the likely behaviors will increase the probability that the student will complete the unlikely behaviors. This procedure is ideally suited for noncompliant students in any age group.

3. If behavior momentum is used at home, parents may start with two or three simple requests before making a request that may be normally rejected: "Please go get my purse or wallet over there so I can give you some money," or "Please bring me that homework pass so that I can give you one." In school, teachers may arrange the order of activities in their classroom so that two or three easy activities are completed before asking students to complete a more difficult one. Such a classroom procedure would be essential in a class where there are several students who are typically noncompliant. Teachers may say, "Bring me that folder over there so I can give you a homework pass." When the student complies, say, "Very good, you did exactly what I asked you to do." Any completion of a compliance request may likewise be followed by verbal praise. For some students, it is necessary to begin at a low level and to expect more at some future time.

POSITIVE RESPONSE PROGRAM

One of the main problems with noncompliant students is that they rarely respond to requests. If a response can be trained, the positive reponse program may function very much like the behavioral momentum program. The teacher must instruct the student regarding how to make any positive response to a request. Students may even choose which response they would like to use—anything from "sure" and "okay" to "yes, I will" and "no problem." These responses can be modeled by the teacher and reinforced when imitated by the student. Any other response can be accepted as long as it is not inappropriate in some way. Students are asked directly to give one of the agreed-on responses when a request is made of them. This procedure is adapted from one described by Rhode, Jenson, and Reavis (1996). Initially, each time the student replies with one of the selected responses, the response is verbally reinforced by the teacher. After an initial period of 1 to 2 weeks, the response is reinforced randomly. The effect of saying the response appears to cue or help start the requested behavior and typically reduces noncompliance. In general, the teacher must be aware of the developmental appropriateness of the procedure when considering it. This means that it will more likely work better with younger students.

This program can also be used to utilize peer support and encouragement to motivate students for increased compliance. Teams can be formed to compete with one another, with each team selecting a different response. One team may be the "OK team," another may be the "No problem team," and so on. Teams compete for some payoff (e.g., the team with highest number of responses gets no homework).

The teacher's method of dealing with the younger child who shows problematic behavior in the classroom and other school settings is, in general, similar to those employed with older children. However, some adjustments are needed for (1) the use of reinforcers that are appropriate to the child's age (or mental age), (2) some developmental changes that occur in the manifestation of the behavioral problem patterns over time, and (3) employment of specific techniques of discipline that are more commonly used with older students. This does not mean that those procedures that have been used for younger students do not work with older students; the teacher is simply given a wider range of procedures from which the most useful, acceptable, and effective ones may be selected.

Positive Behavioral Orientation

A *positive behavioral orientation* is a technique that communicates to students what behavior is important and desired in school, work, play, and family settings. The general focus is on what are appropriate expectations—the "do" as opposed to the "don't" rules. In summary, it is important to view classroom management of children (young or older) with behavior problems across two dimensions: (1) the ABC sequence of antecedents, behavior, and consequences; and (2) the focus of modification on the environment (e.g., the classroom), the child's skill deficits, or the teacher's response to the child. The ABC sequence and the focus of modification has been previously discussed.

In a *positive behavioral orientation*, the focus is on antecedents (i.e., ABC) and modification of the

AFTER ATTENDING PBS TRAINING, MRS. JONES RECOGNIZES HOW TO USE THE POWER OF ADULT ATTENTION.

environment both deal with the establishment of structure in the classroom. Children with behavioral problems need continuing emphasis on structure, whether it is imposed by others or requested by the child. In many cases the child must depend on the teacher or other school personnel to provide these adjustments or accommodations. Such accommodations, together with the structure of effective communication with the child who has behavioral problems, comprise the antecedents in the behavioral sequence.

CONTINGENCY CONTRACTING

A contingency contract is an agreement between a student and teacher that states the behavioral and/or academic goals for the student and the reinforcers or rewards that the student will receive contingent upon completion of these goals.

Contract Goals

Behavioral or academic improvement should be part of the contract. Each contract, however, should have only one stated goal. Contracts are not appropriate for behaviors that may be dangerous to the student or to others, such as aggression or self-injury; such behaviors should therefore not be included in contracts.

Establishing a Baseline   In order to set a goal, teachers must first establish a baseline assessing the student's present level of performance with regard to the identified problem behavior. For example, if the goal is that a student must learn to raise his hand instead of "blurting out," then the teacher must know how often the student raises his hand. For example, does he raise his hand five times per class or five times per day, or perhaps not at all? If the goal is for the student to complete more math problems, the teacher must likewise determine how much the student completes at present. Is it one worksheet per class or perhaps none? This baseline level of performance should be assessed over a one-week period.

Defining Goals

The goal must be clearly defined for the student by the teacher. For example, the teacher might talk to the student about raising his hand, with the goal defined as raising his hand five times without blurting out. It is important that expectation be in line with baseline and that there is a realistic expectation of what the student is able to do. The following should be done when preparing the contract:

1. Decide where the contract is to be in effect—for example, in math class or social studies class.

2. Describe the level of performance needed. For example, does the behavior need to be exhibited only once or does it need to be maintained over some time period? Perhaps the student will need to complete 60 percent of math homework over a 2-week period.

3. Specify in the contract what reward the student will receive when completing the contract. This should be negotiated with the student according to age and preferences. It is best to avoid edibles and instead use rewards such as computer time, free time, and no homework pass. This reward should be given right after the student completes the contract.

4. Review contracts periodically to determine progress, or to renegotiate the contract. Perhaps the goal may be set too high or the rewards might be inappropriate. The student might need to work for a privilege at home (in which case, parents should be consulted and their cooperation requested). Each contract should have a starting date and a date for goal completion.

5. Write contracts in simple, clear language that the student will easily understand. For example, use *reward* in place of *reinforcer*. It is also important that *both student* and *teacher* sign the contract. It may also be useful to have the contract signed by a witness (e.g., another student, parent, or teacher).

Practicing with a Shorter Contract

If the student is unfamiliar with contracts, the teacher may practice with a shorter contract to demonstrate how the system operates. Something very easy should be selected so that the student will immediately achieve success within a few days. Subsequently, the real contract can be discussed along with the student's observations about accepting a contract.

Contract Considerations

The following items should be considered when implementing a behavioral contract:

1. Deliver positive consequences (reward) right after completion.

2. State contract goals in a positive way. For example, "the student will raise his hand and wait for the teacher" instead of "the student will not crumple and mess up his paper and throw it away."

3. If there is no progress, renegotiate the contract without blaming the student.

4. Allow students to work for rewards at home. This is possible if students and parents are willing and able to cooperate.

5. Vary the duration of contracts. Some may be achieved in the short term (2 to 3 days); long-term contracts may require 1 to 3 weeks and a greater investment of effort and energy.

Remember that contracts focus on giving positive consequences for appropriate behavior. They encourage teachers to communicate realistic expectations clearly in writing and specify exactly what the student will receive upon completion of the contract. It is important to establish the baseline measure of current performance and to make the contract needs consistent with what the student is capable of doing, not what a teacher might *think* that the student can do. Contracts can always be made more difficult when the student achieves success. Contracts can also be used with an entire class or with a single student. Some sample contracts are shown in Appendix D.

GENERALIZATION

Any behavior change or behavior program will also entail *generalization*—the hope that behavior changes in one place will generalize to another and that one behavior change will facilitate change in another behavior. There are two types of generalization that are of interest: (1) response generalization, and (2) stimulus generalization.

THE "I KNOW WHY HE DOES IT" GLASSES PREVENT MR. THOMPSON FROM SEEING WHY JEFF WON'T STAY SEATED.

Response Generalization

Response generalization is a process that occurs when a behavior is more likely to occur in the presence of a stimulus as a result of another behavior having been reinforced and strengthened in the presence of that same stimulus (Kazdin, 2001). Response generalization assists in changing behaviors, other than the target behavior, in the same direction (i.e., an increase or a decrease) as the target behavior. For example, the teacher may work on decreasing physical aggression and the student may also show a decrease in verbal aggression. In another situation, the teacher may work on developing one social behavior (e.g., sharing) and notice that a second one (e.g., cooperation) improves as well. The teacher might also observe a decrease in one inappropriate behavior (e.g., blurting out) can result in an increase in an appropriate behavior (e.g., increasing time on task). It is not unusual for teachers to observe that improvement in one area of behavior also results in improvement in another.

Teaching for Generalization

Generalization is the process that is involved when teachers seek to have students improve their completion of academic work and also to develop better self-control or to become more competent socially. Facilitating this goal is the aim of planned generalization (Stokes & Baer, 1977).

Generalization was characterized by Stokes and Baer (1977) as occurring when the effects of educational or therapeutic behavior change programs are exhibited across a variety of times, people, and settings without the need of active intervention in the situations. Generalization should be planned from the beginning of any teaching or behavioral program and integrated into the first phase of teaching (Weiss & Harris, 2001; Liberty & Billingsley, 1988). There are several methods to accomplish this goal:

1. Teach in a natural setting. According to Dowd and Tierney (2005), the ideal place would be where the behavior is most likely to occur (e.g., in the classroom). Pull-out programs may fail to generalize (e.g., to teaching social skills) and would not be recommended.

2. Use natural antecedents that will act as a natural cue for the target behavior (Carter, 2003). Sometimes artificial projects must be used in the initial stage of teaching appropriate behavior. For example, a chime might be sounded to teach in-seat or on-task behavior and later paired with a natural cue. The artificial cue should then be faded out as soon as possible. A *natural cue* may be the teacher's voice or a mannerism; for example, touching her finger to her ear/a cue to listen). This sequence encourages students to stop talking and begin work when they hear the teacher's voice, a natural stimulus for this behavior.

3. Use natural reinforcers to develop appropriate behaviors (Riley-Tillman et al., 2005). Thus artificial reinforcers such as tokens need to be faded to verbal praise, just as schedules of reinforcement need to change from continuous to intermittent. Natural classroom reinforcers might be a good grade, a positive comment from the teacher, or

putting a student's work on the bulletin board. In addition, teaching students self-management skills not only promotes generalization but also helps students maintain appropriate behaviors.

4. Try to generalize behaviors from one setting to another (e.g., from class to class or class to playground) when the target behaviors are reinforced in other settings (Riley-Tillman et al., 2005). For example, behaviors such as sharing and cooperation that are learned in the classroom may be reinforced outside. The classroom generalization is complete when the appropriate behavior appears throughout the whole school as the student demonstrates sharing and cooperation in the lunchroom, on the playground, in the gym, etc.).

Stimulus Generalization

Stimulus generalization—the increased probability of a response being emitted in the presence of a stimulus as a result of being reinforced in the presence of another stimulus (Kazdin, 2001)—is of greater concern than is response generalization to educators (Martin & Dear, 2000). The teacher may start in a target situation such as a classroom and then reinforce the behavior in other situations such as the lunchroom.

One way to promote stimulus generalization of a behavior to other situations is to train the behavior "loosely"—a process that has also been called incidental teaching, naturalistic teaching, nonintrusive teaching, and minimal intervention (Alberto & Troutman, 1999). When there is variation (different teachers, different situations, slightly different instructions, etc.) in the way a behavior is taught, there will be increased likelihood of generalization to other situations.

Another procedure is to train students under the same conditions in which they will need to perform. For example, if the goal is to have students be able to stay "on task" in the classroom, then initial training for on-task behavior should first take place under ideal conditions (no distractions). Gradually, these distractions may be introduced during the second phase of training. Making the conditions under which the student will perform more like those in which the student trains allows for the incorporation of as many common stimuli as possible in the training condition. In short, there will be improved generalization when the training conditions are as similar as possible to the performance conditions in which the student will show the behavior. For example, classroom noise can be recorded and used to train students in other situations (Flick, 2000), or noise in other situations can be recorded for transfer of training to occur there. Students can thus practice appropriate behaviors within the context of noise in the lunchroom or in a small group in a classroom. It may then be easier to reinforce the appropriate behavior in the lunchroom (Flick, 2000).

Precorrection Approach to Problem Behaviors

A precorrection is simply a reminder to students that takes the form of a prompt before problem behavior occurs. For example, a teacher might say, "Remember, before you go to homeroom, collect all your materials, put your work on my desk, and quietly line up."

Source: Adapted with permission from Colvin, Sugai, & Patching (1993).

Teachers must manage a variety of problem behaviors in a wide range of settings—from the playground and lunchroom to the classroom. The use of *reactive techniques* (after an inappropriate behavior has occurred) may be ineffective in handling the problem. Teachers can, however, become *proactive* instead of *reactive* in solving behavior problems. According to Colvin, Sugai, and Patching (1993), there are two basic assumptions underlying the use of precorrection. The first is that all behavior, whether appropriate or inappropriate, is learned; thus, more appropriate behaviors can be taught. The second is that students can learn behavior through the systematic manipulation of teacher input (antecedents) and teacher output (consequences).

TABLE 11.10 Correction and Precorrection Procedures

Correction	Precorrection
■ Procedure is reactive.	■ Procedure is proactive.
■ Consequences are manipulated.	■ Antecedents are manipulated.
■ May lead to negative interactions between teacher and student.	■ May lead to positive interactions between teacher and student.
■ Focuses on inappropriate behavior.	■ Focuses on appropriate behavior.
■ May lead to escalating behavior.	■ May lead to appropriate behavior.
■ Focuses on immediate events.	■ Focuses on future events.

Source: Information from Colvin, Sugai, and Patching (1993). Reprinted by permission.

Just as teachers adjust instruction when academic errors are made, they can also arrange instruction to correct errors in behavior.

Colvin and colleagues (1993) have noted the similarity between academic correction and behavior correction. Precorrection is a preventive management approach to problem behaviors. Instructional precorrection may involve teaching a student who use offensive language the classroom rules until a level of understanding is reached regarding the rule. Correction and precorrection procedures are compared in Table 11.10.

According to Colvin and colleagues (1993), there are seven steps in the precorrection process:

1. *Identify the context and the predictable behavior.* The context may be any event, task, condition, circumstance, or antecedent that is associated with the behavior. The context can be identified formally through functional analysis, where an observer takes notes on the antecedents (e.g., when the teacher is giving directions), the behaviors (e.g., student makes faces at neighbor), and the consequences (e.g., other student yells and disrupts the class). However, the context of the behavior and consequences may be identified informally through observations and discussions with other staff or by a review of the child's records.

2. *Specify the expected behavior.* It is important to give an objective, observable description of the behavior. For example, instead of saying "pay better attention" say "watch the teacher" (the latter instruction being more observable than the former). Try also to select a behavior that is incompatible with the problem behavior—for example, students

who are watching the teacher cannot also be watching their neighbors—and select expected behaviors that are functional replacements for the problem behavior—for example, watching the teacher versus going to the office.

3. *Modify the context.* Adjust instructions, activities, seating arrangements, etc., in order to increase the likelihood that the appropriate behavior will occur and decrease the likelihood that the inappropriate behavior will occur. Colvin and colleagues (1993) suggest using the least obtrusive modifications before resorting to more restrictive ones.

4. *Conduct behavioral rehearsals.* These should occur just prior to the student entering the target situation. Rehearsals may include (a) recalling the appropriate behavior, (b) modeling that behavior, or (c) keeping a checklist of the behavior as a reminder (a self-management procedure).

5. *Provide strong reinforcement for expected behaviors.* New behaviors are weak and this may require stronger reinforcement to replace the old behaviors, which have existed for some time and so may be more difficult to change. All of this argues for early intervention.

6. *Use prompts to encourage expected behavior.* While students will need to receive immediate feedback when an expected behavior is exhibited, there may also be a need for the use of a prompt, reminder, or cue within the context where the expected behavior is to occur. For example, the teacher may say, "Who can raise your hand and tell me the capital of Mississippi?" Correction procedures may also be used. The teacher may ignore

the first occurrence of the inappropriate behavior, and then use a prearranged signal to communicate what appropriate behavior is expected (e.g., putting finger on lips to signal quiet or raising hand while talking out is occurring). For the third occurrence of an inappropriate behavior, the teacher can demonstrate a new signal. (For example, after a student talks out, say, "If you have a comment or question, please let me know by raising your hand.") Instead of direct visual cues as reminders, the teacher can also use a form of cognitive (verbal) mediation to cue the correct behavior. For example, the teacher may say, "What is the correct procedure when you want to make a comment or ask a question?" Students who respond appropriately can be reinforced with praise and repetition of the appropriate procedure: "That's correct—when you wish to make a comment or ask a question, please raise your hand."

7. *Monitor the plan.* It is important to check on whether the precorrection procedure is working—whether the inappropriate behavior is decreasing and the appropriate behavior increasing. This task may be assigned to an aide, practicing student, volunteer, or even class peers.

A summary checklist for the above precorrection procedures is shown in Figure 11.4.

In general, precorrection has been demonstrated to be effective in targeting both academic and behavioral problems.

Colvin and colleagues (1997) used precorrection procedures to improve transition behaviors in elementary students. Baseline data suggested high rates of problem behaviors, especially running, hitting, and yelling. An increase in the use of precorrection during targeted transitions of entering the school building, moving to the cafeteria for lunch, and exiting the school building resulted in a general decrease in problem behaviors.

A functional analysis of noncompliance, aggression, and disruptive behavior during instruction was conducted with a 10-year-old boy with severe disabilities (Reid et al., 1999). These researchers showed that unresponsiveness before difficult instruction was associated with higher rates of problem behavior, negatively reinforced by termination of that instruction.

Precorrection was then applied before difficult instruction when the student was rated as nonresponsive. Results showed that precorrection increased responsiveness and reduced problem behavior during difficult instruction.

DIRECT INSTRUCTION OF EXPECTATIONS AND ROUTINES

Teachers often mistakenly assume that students know how to line up, listen in groups, walk in the hall, hand in papers, and so on. Unfortunately, for some students "just knowing" what is expected is not enough. It is only through direct instruction that teachers can be sure that their students might learn and master the desired behaviors and expectations in the classroom. Teachers must also provide opportunities to practice these behaviors and give reinforcement to students for correct behavioral responses (Carpenter & McKee-Higgins, 1996).

As discussed earlier, teachers can use precorrections—reminders that provide students with opportunities to practice or to be prompted for expected behavior before they are faced with those situations where problem behaviors often occur (Colvin, Sugai, & Patching, 1993). For example, if students experience difficulty in line formation, they can be asked to recall the four expectations for acceptable behavior in line before they line up: (1) use "walking" feet, (2) use resting (quiet) mouth, (3) keep hands and feet to self, and (4) walk behind the person in front of you. A second-grade teacher's outline of the precorrection approach is shown in Figure 11.4.

THE USE OF PUNISHMENT

There are many behavioral techniques that might be effective but involve punishment or a negative approach to behavior management. These procedures can be listed in order of their degree of aversive stimulation. Of course, physical punishment, which was discussed, could top the list, but will not be discussed here and is never recommended as an option. The following are other variations of punishment that may need to be used with the more positive techniques, already discussed. These techniques that follow are listed from least unpleasant to most unpleasant punishments.

Three Objectives for Second-Grade Students

1. State the four behaviors for walking in line properly.
2. Identify the reason why walking in line properly is important in promoting a positive learning environment in school.
3. Perform the four behaviors for walking in line properly, using role-play and actual real-life situations.

Materials Used

Pictures or graphic visuals (drawings) of the four behaviors for walking in line properly.

Procedures

1. Ask students the following question: "What would happen if there were no laws about how cars drive on the streets of our city?" Students will probably answer lots of accidents, people getting hurt, property damage, etc. Explain that while lives are not at stake in school (as they are when you drive a car), rules about how students move through school hallways is important.
2. Use instruction and modeling to talk to students about rules for walking in line:
   a. Students must walk through the halls so as to not disturb students in other classrooms who are involved in learning.
   b. By following the rules students can get to lunch and recess in a timely manner.
   c. Walking rather than running in the hallways helps to keep students safe by making accidents less likely to happen.
3. Present visuals for the four rules; show and demonstrate (model) each one.
   a. Keep hands and feet to self.
   b. Use walking feet.
   c. Make sure you have a resting (quiet) mouth.
   d. Stay behind the person in front of you.
      Guided Role-Play Practice: Students in small groups role-play a rule violation. Students then role-play walking in line following the four rules.
      Independent Practice: Review the rules for walking in line properly (reminder); as students walk around properly, reinforce correct behavior with verbal praise.
4. Begin the closure process. Return to classroom and ask students to describe what they did well, and what needs work. Tell students that you will be starting an incentive chain. Each time the class is in the hall walking properly without supervision or redirection, a link will be added, starting from the ceiling. When the chain reaches the floor, a 15-minute recess will be given. Also, if a student is redirected more than once each day, this student will need to practice (overcorrection) the rules during a scheduled recess. This practice is given as the teacher must assume that the student has forgotten the rules. Students may also review the rules in a homework assignment that describes and illustrates the four rules. This can be done either at home or in a free class period. These rules should be posted and reviewed daily, especially just before students are expected to use them.

Source: Information from Otten and Tuttle (2004). Reprinted by permission.

FIGURE 11.4 Outline of precorrection.

■ Ignoring
■ Time-out
■ Overcorrection
■ Response cost

Remember that our emphasis here will always be on the use of positive behavioral interventions and supports.

Ignoring Behaviors

If attending to a behavior rewards and strengthens that behavior, then ignoring a given behavior (and paying attention to something else) is mildly punishing and weakens the behavior in question. Chance (1999) views this process as the extinction of a behavior that ceases to exist due to a lack of reinforcement. Similarly, Pierce, and Epling (1995) state that extinction is the permanent removal of the source of reinforcement for a behavior. In other words, ignoring a behavior helps to extinguish or eliminate that behavior.

A teacher's attention has quite a powerful impact on students, especially young children. Unfortunately, this generally does not not hold true for adolescents, although many of them still crave attention, especially if an early pattern of "attention to appropriate behavior" was developed and maintained over the early years. Of course, many children with problem behaviors have a history of receiving a substantial amount of attention for their inappropriate behaviors—the class clown is a classic example—such attention will have to be modified. However, the fact that a child is responsive to any kind of attention will be an asset in behavior management.

Before a teacher can decide which behaviors should be ignored, it is helpful to look at the general category of those behaviors that will best respond to the ignoring procedure. Generally, these behaviors are (1) behaviors that are annoying, (2) behaviors that do not involve acting out of anger, and (3) behaviors that interfere with the achievement of a goal.

Table 11.11 presents a sample list of behaviors to be ignored. Ignoring does not imply avoiding dealing with the behavior. It is instead a viable technique to weaken and remove these behaviors. Once again, it is important to consider the developmental appropriateness of each behavior; many of these behaviors are more frequently and generally noted in younger children.

THE PRESENTER FAILS TO PENETRATE HIS LISTENERS' PROTECTIVE BUBBLE.

TABLE 11.11   Sample Behaviors to Be Ignored

1. Whining	11. Swearing (for reaction)
2. Pouting	12. Inappropriate noises
3. Repetitive demands	13. Repetitive questions
4. Repetitive requests	14. Clowning
5. Burping	15. Inappropriate eating (occasional noise)
6. Passing gas	16. Rolling eyes (when punished)
7. Screaming	17. Stamping feet (after being punished)
8. Temper tantrums	18. Baby talk
9. Crying (demanding)	19. Complaining
10. Sulking	20. Begging

Note also that this listing is not meant to be exhaustive. There may be many behaviors (some unique to the classroom) that are quite annoying and are not included here.

In most cases, ignoring behaviors on a consistent basis will weaken them sufficiently so that eventually the unacceptable behavior becomes extinct. The key words are *consistent* and *ignoring*, and teachers must monitor the behavior to determine if the frequency (i.e., the strength) does actually change.

During the actual process of ignoring the behavior, teachers may expect that the behavior will get worse before it gets better. This process is called an *extinction burst*, and it is frequently accompanied by an increase in the frequency, duration, or intensity of the inappropriate behavior (Pierce & Epling, 1995). It is important to continue to be consistent and focus on the procedure itself over a reasonable period of time—from 2 to 8 weeks, depending on how strong the behavior is initially. A teacher who "gives in" to the child will often not only reinforce the behavior at an even higher level of intensity but also reinforce a pattern of persistence that will make it even more difficult to change the behavior in the future. To avoid giving in and attending to the inappropriate behavior, teachers must consistently use self-talk, a process described in the box below.

An Example of the Self-Talk Procedure for Teachers

Okay, I know this is going to get worse, but I can handle it. It's important for me to keep my attention on the work on my desk. I know I won't be able to concentrate very well, so I'm not concerned about getting anything accomplished—I just need to keep my attention on these materials. . . .

Okay, I know his behavior is getting worse now. I expected that so it's no surprise to me. I need to relax through my deep breathing and bring my attention back to my materials. I'm prepared for this to continue for a while and to get even worse. I can handle this. I can continue to allow my muscles around my neck and shoulders to relax and let go. I can imagine the relaxation spreading to other muscles in my body. I'll just have to wait this out. I know that if I give in, he'll just be more persistent next time—and even more intense. I can handle this. I can remain calm and relaxed.

It is also recommended that the teacher pick an appropriate time to use the ignoring approach, a time when the procedure can be carried to completion.

In all behavioral programs, there must be an ongoing analysis and evaluation of how well the program is working. If the behaviors to be ignored have already become too well established to be handled with the ignoring technique alone, an alternative option here is to reinforce the opposite, appropriate behaviors while using the ignoring procedure.

MONITORING PROBLEM BEHAVIOR

Sometimes rather surprising effects can be obtained by simply monitoring or counting the occurences of a behavior, an almost universally acknowledged but poorly understood method. The sample chart in Table 11.12 illustrates this process. Counting (monitoring) inappropriate behavior may result in decreases in such behavior while counting (monitoring) appropriate behavior may result in *increases* in appropriate behavior. Even

TABLE 11.12 A Chart for Monitoring Problem Behavior

	M	T	W	Th	F	Totals
9:00–9:10	/		/	/	/	4
9:30–9:40	//	/	//	//	/	8
10:00–10:10	//	///	/	/	/	8
10:30–10:40	///	/	///	///	/	11
Total for the day	8	5	7	7	4	31

when counting is the only consequence, there is very often a change. For example, VanAcker (2002) monitored a school and classroom climate that promoted desired behavior and academic achievement.

Behavior Should Be Monitored

The information obtained through monitoring behavior is crucial in an ongoing analysis of a behavioral program to determine what, if any, changes may be needed. A baseline measure can be used to determine when behavior does or does not change and whether the behavior in question has improved or gotten worse.

Specific Behavior Selected to Change

There are two options for the occurrence of any behavior:

- There may be an increase in the frequency of its occurrence.
- There may be a decrease in the frequency of its occurrence.

The first option, a desired behavior, would be an appropriate though weak behavior; the second option, an undesirable behavior, would be an inappropriate behavior of mild strength.

Although these behaviors may not be of primary concern, they clearly need to be dealt with at some point in the overall behavioral program. Dealing with secondary behavior problems early on may make some of the more significant problems actually easier to handle at a later time.

Record Selected Behavior

How do you decide what interval (observation unit) to select when monitoring a problem behavior? If a behavior occurs frequently, you may wish to select a daily recording or even a specific period of the day—for example, from 2 p.m.–3 p.m.

If the behavior occurs infrequently, you may wish to use a 2-day observation period. However, a typical starting point might be to record information daily. The behavior must be clearly defined, observable, and countable. That way, for example, it will be clear how many times the child engages in an appropriate behavior such as saying "please" when making a request

or in an inappropriate behavior. In either case, the selected behavior can be seen or heard and, therefore, counted each day (or according to any other designated interval).

When beginning to use these behavioral techniques, only one behavior at a time should be monitored. When data have been accumulated for at least 1 week, they may be plotted as shown in Figure 11.5.

The sample graph shows the following information:

1. There is probably some finite limit to the improvement (e.g., you have only so many chances to say "please" in 1 day).
2. There is general improvement (e.g., the number of times "please" is verbalized increases over 14 days).
3. There may be some variation in the number (e.g., at the end of 1 week there is actually a decrease).

This behavior monitoring procedure simply shows that by observing and keeping a record of a behavior, the frequency and underlying strength of that behavior can change. This occurs without any formal consequences.

TIME-OUT PROCEDURE FOR MISBEHAVIOR

Much like ignoring, the time-out procedure for misbehavior removes the child from any potential positive reinforcement (Cross & Goldberg, 2005); in the case of ignoring, positive reinforcement is withheld from the child. Time-out operates on the same principle as the old "go sit in the corner" punishment. Students reportedly hate such punishment and want to get it over quickly because it is boring; many ask for some other punishment rather than be put in time-out.

What is time-out like? A child who just hit a classmate might be told by his teacher, "No hitting; go to time-out, now!" He then goes to the designated time-out location—usually a boring hallway or room. The time-out place should be devoid of all positive reinforcements (toys, TV, games, etc.) and it should not be a place where a student could easily fall asleep; either of these consequences would not be punishing. The number of minutes in time-out can be set according

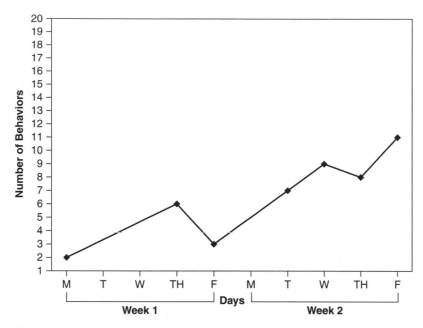

FIGURE 11.5 Monitored behavior over 2 weeks.

to the child's age (i.e., 1 minute for each year) on a kitchen timer. This and other criteria are in accordance with recommendation by experts (e.g., Clark, 1996), who also recommend that the teacher use no more than 10 words or 10 seconds to get the child to time-out.

Once in time-out, the child is basically ignored until the timer rings. It is important that a student never be told to come out of time-out when he can behave. No teacher or other students should pay attention to, talk to, or otherwise provide reinforcement for the child in time-out. The child cannot take a toy to time-out, and the teacher should not get hooked into paying attention to the behavior of a child while in time-out. Some children are quite adept at getting into a hassle, particularly with a teacher, while in time-out. In such cases, it is not surprising to hear the teacher later say, "Time-out does not work; he misbehaves even more now." If time-out is used incorrectly, the misbehavior may become worse, as the child may actually be getting rewarded (by teacher attention) for getting into the time-out. One teacher reported that a small child was put in a large appliance type box. The child could only see forward but would poke a finger through a hole in the box. This attracted more attention, laughs, and giggles from the class, and the "time-out" was deemed useless.

Immediately after the timer rings, the time-out is over, and the teacher can ask the child, "Now Jimmy, can you tell me why you were sent to time-out?" If Jimmy says, "Because I hit my classmate," the teacher says, "That's right." If he says, "I don't know," the teacher gives him the correct answer and he is allowed to go back to class. It is best to avoid giving attention just after time-out and, of course, it is not recommended that children receive a hug, pat on the back, treat, or anything special that will give them the impression that time-out really pays off! Students also should not receive a lecture after time-out, and they should not be asked to promise never to exhibit inappropriate behavior again. However, it is not unusual for some children to engage in some more appropriate behavior after time-out. Anytime behavior changes in a more positive direction, the appropriate behavior should not be ignored. Do reinforce this change and point out to the child that you are pleased to see this behavior. It is also useful to state the process that changed: "You really have much better control over yourself; I like the way you are now sharing that toy with your classmate."

Listing Behaviors for Time-Out

In order to understand the *time-out procedure*, it is important to consider when to use time-out—and for what inappropriate behavior. The following acting-out behaviors would justify the use of a time-out:

Hitting others, or threats to hit	Hostile teasing
Temper tantrums	Sassy talk, or back talk
Angry screaming	Spitting, threatening to spit
Grabbing toys	Persistent interrupting:
Throwing toys	Adult conversation
Destroying toys	After a warning
Throwing objects at others	Dangerous acts
Mistreating or hurting pets	Cursing
Obnoxious, loud crying	Pushing others (hard)
Slapping	Damaging property
Pinching	Mocking teachers
Scratching	Loud complaining or making demands
Kicking others	Name calling
Biting, or threats to bite	Making faces at others
Hair pulling	Disobeying a command to stop misbehavior
Choking others	

Time-out is best used for behaviors that would be classified as aggressive, or acting-out behaviors. Whining and pouting as well as fearful, seclusive, timid, irritable, and grumpy behaviors, for example, would not be appropriate for time-out. Passive behavior such as failing to perform some assignment or forgetting to do something is not appropriate for the time-out procedure. Not doing something is *not* an acting-out behavior.

Developing a Time-Out Plan

It is important for teachers to understand and practice time-out before actually using it. This means that they must review some critical issues and develop a plan to deal with any problems encountered in time-out. The following guidelines will help implement the process:

1. *Select target behaviors.* It is important to use time-out for specific acting-out behaviors and to avoid using it for every misbehavior. Teachers who use the time-out procedure for everything will find that this reduces its effectiveness and the punishment may become a prime source of getting attention. Also, to be effective, time-out depends on the presence of a generally positive environment to which the student can return.

2. *Select a place for time-out.* Use any place that is boring, where the child will not receive attention from those passing by and where there is no access to rewards. A special room, hallway, or corner will suffice. Do not lock the child in the time-out area or use a location that may generate fear. Separating or segregating the child in isolation is not advisable. A quiet section of the classroom may be set aside and designated as a time-out zone—a place for calming down and regaining control.

3. *Determine how many minutes should be spent in time-out.* This is usually determined according to the child's age (i.e., 1 minute for each year), which means that a 10-year-old would receive a 10-minute time-out. When several children are involved, especially in a school setting, a specific number of minutes may be used. No time-out should exceed 12 minutes.

4. *Measure the time consistently, using a kitchen timer.* This avoids having a child continually asking, "Can I come out now?" The timer cannot be manipulated, rushed, or avoided. Students need to know that they can come out of time-out only when the timer rings. This structure allows them to know what to expect and avoids troublesome situations; responsibility is not placed on the teacher or the child to decide when enough time is spent in time-out.

5. *Withdraw attention while the child is in time-out.* This cannot be emphasized enough. Teachers often make the mistake of lecturing or continuing to hassle with the child, which simply makes time-out ineffective. A child may yell, "This isn't going to work" or try screaming, crying, complaining of pains, or even pleading to use the bathroom. All of these behaviors should be ignored, unless a real physical danger is obvious. Any destructive behaviors during

time-out may result in added punishment, such as a behavior penalty, and having the child "clean up" or "pay up" for any mess or damages incurred.

6. *Establish the connection after time-out by asking, "Why were you sent to time-out?"* The child who answers correctly is allowed to go back to class. The child who answers incorrectly or doesn't know is informed of the behavior that precipitated the time-out. It is especially important to make students aware of the "cause–effect" sequence when there is a lack of awareness and weak internal cognitive recognition about which behaviors will bring about negative consequences. They must know what the consequences will be for certain misbehaviors. They will learn this for the behaviors selected but only after much practice and review.

7. *Do not lecture after a time-out or force a child to promise never to do something again.* Such promises do not result in improvement, and entrap the child for any future transgressions.

> When you spend an inordinate amount of time with a child immediately after time-out, the child gets the message that certain behaviors can really get you upset or excited. When the child needs to "stir up some excitement," she will certainly know which buttons to push!

8. *Rehearse the time-out before using it.* Do a "dress rehearsal" to ensure there will be no surprises when the time-out actually occurs, and to allow both participants—child and teacher—to review their roles. You can present the time-out in the following way: "For some time now, we have had hassles over name calling. This is not much fun for you or me. So, when you 'name call' you will be sent to time-out." A general explanation should be given regarding the sequence of events in time-out, appropriate for the child's age, then run through the procedure privately, saying, "Ok, now let's suppose you have just name-called; that's a time-out for name calling—go now!" The child knows where to go and that a timer will be set for a specific number of minutes; it will be situated where the child can hear it.

The child comes out of time-out and you ask, "Why were you sent to time-out?" If the child correctly states the reason, say, "That is exactly right." If not, the child is told. This rehearsal is quite important and ensures the teacher and child are ready. Be aware that, as Goldstein (1988) has noted, the first few times that a child is placed in time-out, there may be a "time-out burst" where a heightened degree of aggressiveness may occur. These outbursts will usually subside, especially if the teacher adds to the duration of the time-out the number of minutes that the outburst lasts. The rehearsal is best done when the child is by him/herself in the classroom and not in front of the whole class.

It is important to note that time-out, like many other forms of punishment, is often overused but usually slightly less so by teachers. So much emphasis has been placed on dealing with behavior that is inappropriate, that very little time is spent focusing on which behaviors a parent or teacher wishes to see more often. Remember, *punishment never tells the child what to do—only what not to do*. Balance reward and punishment techniques. (This does not necessarily mean an equal number of rewards and punishments.) Focus on using positive reinforcements for appropriate behavior as much as, or even more than, using aversive consequences for inappropriate behaviors. Skill development through reinforcement for appropriate behavior is crucial for the survival of the child.

Time-Out at Home and at School

In general, time-out will be used more frequently at home. There has been much *controversy* over its use in school and it has generally been difficult to set up a time-out place in the school setting. Because of such difficulty, time-out has not received as much emphasis in overall behavior management programs in schools. It can also backfire when a child is sent outside the classroom and it often becomes rewarding, not punishing. Consider the girl who is having difficulty doing a task and becomes easily distracted, engaging in aggravating behavior such as pinching her neighbor. Should she be sent out of the room? If she is, she may actually be taken out of an unrewarding and boring task and therefore rewarded for acting out, and she will probably repeat the behavior in the future. In normal discipline programs, when this occurs a number of times, she may be suspended and forced to leave school—not a particularly undersirable punishment. Suspension from school may work for normal children who would, for varying reasons, find it unpleasant to be sent out of the class or to be sent home. It would not, however, be effective for most children with chronic behavior problems.

There are variations in time-out. These must be considered here and are discussed as follows:

1. *Modified time-out* is a time to "calm down," "refocus," or "redirect" activities to a different situation.

2. *Time-out for two:* Frequently, when peers fight, rather than playing detective to discover who started the problem, both children go to time-out. Either an average of their ages or a preset number of minutes may be chosen. Whenever you can avoid the option of "getting to the bottom of this fight," the effectiveness of time-out is enhanced. Remember that it is important to deliver consequences of behavior *immediately* following the behavior. If you delay, there may be confusion about what started the fight and the students win. Punish both by saying, "Both of you have a time-out for fighting—go now." When they come out of the time-out, ask both why they were sent to time-out, then more importantly, ask them, "Now, can you think of another way you could have solved your problem without fighting?" Here both students will compete for a "good answer" and this process will aid in the development of problem-solving skills. Both students are now learning to develop cognitions that may mediate aggressive behavior in the future. When the child knows other options and is reinforced for using them, coping skills can improve. Impulse-oriented children learn cognitive mediating techniques that essentially involve "thinking before acting" as a means of controlling their impulses.

3. *Chill-out procedure:*. This is a useful variation of the time-out where students may decide to withdraw from a situation so that they can calm down and get control. Instead of losing control when they become frustrated and angry over doing some difficult work, and perhaps being removed from the class (which can be rewarding), they can be taught

to ask for the teacher's permission to allow them to sit in a special chill-out chair (e.g., a bean bag or a special desk) so that they can calm down and then return to their assigned work. At this point, there may, of course, be a need for special assistance and instruction on the material that caused the initial upset. Chill-out is time-limited, and there is a limit to the number of times it can be used. This procedure will also need to be reviewed and practiced (through a behavioral rehearsal) so that it can be used almost automatically by the student.

Problems with Time-Out

Some children comply immediately with time-out; others resist. The easiest way to deal with resistance to time-out is to add additional minutes. The young child may be held in the chair; no excessive force should be used. The child should be told that when he calms down and the timer rings he can come out of time-out. It is important not to let the child out if there is severe misbehavior. No lecturing or scolding should be given. It is also important to withdraw visual attention and not to look at the child who is in time-out.

With an older child, simply add additional minutes to the time-out for each instance of resistance (i.e., failure to go) as suggested by Clark (1996), but this should not exceed 5 minutes. If the resistance continues, a behavior penalty such as the withdrawal of a privilege may be given.

Basic Time-Out Principles

In theory, time-out is by definition a punishment where students are withdrawn from potential positive reinforcement when they are segregated from the rest of the classroom. Procedures may vary from an in-class strategy of placing the student in a time-out corner to relocation of the student to a hallway, another class, or a school time-out room. Many schools do not condone the use of time-out as a punishment for inappropriate behavior as the procedure does not meet the intent of IDEA. There must be positive (or rewarding) implications where the student can return to the in-class setting.

What the Law Says About Time-Out Rooms

The courts have noted that putting John in a locked time-out room might be excessively intrusive and could be labeled as "unreasonable seizure." An unreasonable seizure may also occur when John is not properly informed of the purpose of the time-out area or the reason for removal from class. The courts must consider two issues: (1) whether the student established that he was "seized" according to the Fourth Amendment or was he sent to the time-out room, (2) whether the time-out was reasonable.

Consult *Rasmur v. State of Arizona, 24 IDELER, 824 (D. Ariz. 1996)* and *Hayes v. Unified School District, No. 377, 559 IDELER, 249 (D. Kan. 1987)* for additional details.

The following questions should be answered regarding the use of time-out procedures for students with mental and physical disabilities:

- *District policy on time-out:* Does the school district have a policy on time-out for all students? Is placement in a time-out room reasonable and part of a well-documented set of interventions designed to improve the student's behavior in the classroom?
- *Nature of the misconduct:* Can the student's behavior problem be addressed with a less intrusive strategy? Does the student need to be removed from the classroom?
- *Location of time-out room:* Does the problem behavior justify the transfer time to and from the time-out room?
- *Size of the time-out room:* Can the time-out room accommodate the student and a staff person (who supervises the student)?
- *Interior of the time-out room:* Is the interior "punitive" or does it allow for de-escalation and return to class?
- *Safety considerations:* Is the room safe? Have all dangerous objects been removed? Does it meet state, local, and fire code requirements?
- *Number of minutes in time-out isolation:* Does the time correspond to student's age and cognitive ability (mental age)? In most states, time is equal to the student's age but should not exceed 10–15 minutes.
- *How student spends time during time-out:* Is there a written plan (in the IEP) about what to do when the student is in time-out?
- *Written permission from parents (or legal guardians):* Have parents authorized the use of the time-out room as part of the student's BIP and IEP?

This procedure, as with all punishment techniques, must be used carefully, if at all.

Time-Out in the Classroom

The general consensus seems to be that time-out rooms are controversial, difficult to manage, and costly, and they open the school for litigation. Other procedures are best used. Those schools that do elect to use time-out rooms should do the following:

- Develop policies around time-out rooms, put these in writing, and always obtain parental permission to use them.
- Avoid isolation in time-out rooms if problems can be better managed within the classroom. Not all behavior problems require a student's removal from class.
- Ensure that time-out rooms have adequate heating, lighting, and ventilation and that they are safe and have no dangerous objects.
- Never lock the time-out room.
- Make staff available to supervise or monitor the student during a time-out.
- Notify parents when a time-out is used.
- Keep students in time-out only until they have adequate self-control.
- Permit student to use the restroom within reason.
- Make a student's time-out consistent with the BIP and IEP guidelines so that it will not be considered denial of a free and appropriate education.
- Keep records on each time-out—date, time, basis for time-out, and the teacher who made this determination.
- Follow Section 504 guidelines governing the use of time-out for students with disabilities. The district's policy should be the same for disabled and nondisabled students.

OVERCORRECTION

Overcorrection is a punishment technique that provides for positive practices contingent on the behavior, as described in detail by Flick (1998b, 2000). This procedure appeals to teachers because the overcorrection technique relates directly to the misbehavior. There are two forms of overcorrection: (1) restitutional overcorrection and (2) positive practice overcorrection.

Restitutional Overcorrection

Restitutional overcorrection is a procedure that requires the student to restore the environment to a state that is vastly improved compared to the one that existed prior to the occurrence of the problem behavior. For example, a student who dumps a drink on the floor of the lunchroom might need to clean the floor on that day as well as the days after. A student who writes a curse word on a classroom wall may have to not only clean the wall of the classroom but also the walls of the hallway.

Positive Practice Overcorrection

Positive practice overcorrection is a procedure that follows mild punishment, with an educative opportunity to engage in appropriate behavior. Examples are abundant, beginning with the common practice of teachers requiring students to write misspelled words correctly five times. Another example might involve a teacher asking the student who comes into the class and slams the door to go out of the room and come back closing the door appropriately and then, to repeat that appropriate behavior several times. The teacher might then say, "Now, that's the right way to enter the classroom. I don't know if you've really learned this behavior, so you may have to practice it again." Such an intervention is best practiced when only one student is involved. If more students are involved there are some benefits to modeling appropriate behavior in front of the class, but this procedure can backfire and some problems might result: (1) the procedure will be difficult to apply and monitor, (2) it may take more of the teacher's time, and (3) student resistance may be difficult to deal with.

WRITING A BEHAVIOR PENALTY PLAN

A *behavior penalty plan* or *response cost* involves taking a privilege away from a child for a short period of time. There are some advantages to the use of this penalty. Unlike the time-out, which may be more difficult to employ, a behavior penalty does not require a special place, and it can be administered anywhere, anytime. In addition, any misbehavior can easily be dealt with using a behavior penalty.

The following general guidelines apply to the behavior penalty plan:

1. Make a list of a maximum of three behaviors that may be difficult to deal with using other techniques.
2. Inform the child which behavior will result in a behavior penalty.
3. Make a list of privileges that can be taken away for a behavior penalty.
4. Remember to review with the child the consequences for one of these misbehaviors, as well as to note the rewards for appropriate behavior. The child is informed which privilege will be lost should the misbehavior occur and what the reward will be should the child show alternative appropriate behavior instead. This technique, called *priming*, will increase the effectiveness of the consequences and provide some cognitive link of past consequences to present behavioral control. There will be some internalization of what consequences will follow either misbehavior or appropriate behavior. It is also assumed that, given a choice, the child will prefer the positive consequence (reward) for appropriate behavior.
5. Give the child some predetermined signal (preferably nonverbal) to serve as a warning and to allow the child to develop self-control, which may subsequently be rewarded. One signal might be to hold up two fingers for the child to see. This will serve as a signal for the child to decide either to change the current misbehavior, or to accept the consequences. Review all of this with the child prior to being in these situations. You can even have a rehearsal similar to the one previously discussed for a time-out (see page 214).

6. Once the signal is given, say, "Children, look here" (while holding up two fingers), and allow students a few seconds to respond. The hope is that children will develop and gain control over their behavior and thereby avoid loss of a privilege.

7. If control is achieved, you may say, "John, I'm very proud of the decision you made to stop teasing (annoying, hitting, or anything else) your classmate. I like the way you are sitting quietly with him. As I said, for your good behavior you have earned a homework pass." If you have set up a point system, then points may be given instead of the homework pass. John should, however, be reminded that you will be pleased to see good behavior continue and disappointed if he loses the reward for any misbehavior that might surface. Remember, the last behavior prior to a reward is the one that is strengthened. If John misbehaves just prior to getting the reward, such misbehavior would then (erroneously) be rewarded.

8. Be consistent and follow through with the procedure. If not, the child will see that you often say things you don't mean. It is important to provide the reward as soon as possible. Any significant delays may result in frustration and perhaps some angry, acting-out behavior.

Using Response-Cost and Behavior Penalty

Response cost and behavior penalty are two terms that are used interchangeably. This procedure is especially effective for young children up to adolescence. It was first described by Justen and Howerton (1993), but more recently by De Paul and Stoner (1994), Mather and Goldstein (2001), and Tiano and colleagues (2005). (Please note that this procedure is not negative reinforcement, but rather a creative twist on positive reinforcement.) Rather than doling out positive reinforcement one by one, in this procedure (i.e., response cost) *all reinforcements* (e.g., points or tokens) are given initially (i.e., up front). The child's goal is to end with a prespecified minimum number of points or tokens in order to earn his reward. Inappropriate behavior results in points or tokens being taken away. This procedure has already been described McCain and Kelley (1994); in the school situation, the focus is on several variations:

The Individual Case   As described by Kendall and Braswell (1993), a child might initially be given 20 points or tokens. Whenever the student makes a mistake, such as going too fast, omitting a step, or giving a wrong answer, a point or token is taken away as a cue for the child to stop and think before answering. The teacher briefly explains why the point or token was taken away so that the child may learn and respond differently in the future.

The Individual Within a Group   In this situation, the child begins with a set number of points determined by the range of a particular inappropriate behavior—for example, during a one-week period, blurting out answers up to a maximum of four times each day. Using this frequency as a guide, a teacher can establish the criteria for success on a daily or weekly basis. (This depends on the age of the children and their need for immediate reward. For ages 8 or younger, a daily program may be sufficient. However, each child's program should be designed individually according to need.) If a daily program is acceptable, the child may receive six points or tokens in advance. Each time the child speaks out of turn, one point or token is subtracted. A 3 × 5 inch card may be placed on the desk with either the words, "Raise your hands to answer," or a drawing or picture of a child with hand raised (Figure 11.6), or both. When the child "blurts out," a slash mark, deleting one point, is put on the card. The child knows that the goal is to keep at least one point in order to receive some prearranged reward. A record is kept each day so that the criteria may be adjusted down to accommodate the child's improvement (e.g., when she blurts out only two times per day maximum). A teacher may then give only four points or tokens. Of course, this procedure is always combined with immediate verbal praise when the child raises her hand, and praise for successful completion. Various behaviors may be selected that involve adherence to class rules in addition to the example given. Children who are able to work on more than one behavior or those who have prior experience working with individual behaviors (e.g., using the picture cards described in Figure 11.6) may profit from the use of a more complex response-cost system, monitoring several of these behaviors. A complete graphic depiction of rules is shown in Appendix D.

Name:	Response cost card					
Date:	M	T	W	Th	F	Total
 Raises hand						
Rule above	Points lost					

FIGURE 11.6   A graphic depiction of rules. A horizontal line may be used to divide each card so the upper portion may record points earned for compliance with the rule while the lower part may record points lost for noncompliance.

Source: Adapted with permission from Flick (1998b).

The Response-Cost Lottery According to Wielkiewicz (1986) and Witt and Elliott (1982), the response-cost lottery involves a small group of children within a class who compete only with others who have similar problems and so may allow for an increased probability of success. In this procedure, a 3 × 5 inch card is taped on each student's desk, with a specific number of slips (a different color for each child) tucked under the card. Again, let's use the example of blurting out; it is determined that the child with the worst frequency of blurting out does so a maximum of up to four times per day. Then a total of six slips per child may be given, and each time a child blurts out, one slip is removed from under his card. At the end of the day, the slips remaining for each child are put in a box. At the end of the week, one slip is randomly drawn from the box, and the winner receives the predetermined reward. Students know that every time they lose a slip of their color paper, there will be fewer chances of their color paper being drawn. This provides an interesting variation of response-cost and introduces the concept of probability.

SUMMARY

This chapter begins with a discussion of positive and negative reinforcement, providing a basically positive orientation for positive behavioral interventions and supports. There are essentially three types of reinforcers: tangible, social, and activities. It is important to vary reinforcers and to have a few classroom rules that emphasize what students should do. To develop new behaviors, the student must learn the appropriate behaviors that are to replace the problem behavior. Teachers may use modeling and shaping to establish these behaviors. In addition, a token or point system may be used. While the teacher can address behaviors that are appropriate but weak, often an instrumental behavior plan is useful. In other words, teachers may use Grandma's Rule or a "when–then" format. Behavioral momentum is frequently used to deal with noncompliance. Contingency contracting is often useful with older students; both response and stimulus generalization have fostered improved behavior in addition to the target behavior. While corrective measures are often employed as a reactive procedure, precorrection serves as a proactive technique. Whenever a behavior is targeted for change, it is important to monitor it. There are a few punishment techniques that are less aversive. Ignoring the problem behavior is one; while this technique is often difficult, the use of self-talk can facilitate this process. Time-out is another but it must be done correctly *and* must be rehearsed privately. Likewise, overcorrection and behavior penalty are forms of punishment that focus on getting rid of an unwanted behavior.

DISCUSSION QUESTIONS

1. What is the best definition of reinforcement in the classroom?
2. According to Zirpoli (2007), what are some of the factors associated with the effectiveness of reinforcement?
3. What is the difference between positive and negative reinforcement?
4. What is the problem with using candy or popcorn as reinforcers? What is the solution to this problem?
5. Give examples of each of the three categories of reinforcers.
6. Why should reinforcers be varied?
7. Why is it important to maintain a positive focus in using reinforcements?
8. Why should teachers model the behavior they expect from their students?
9. Would students prefer a dynamic (expressive) teacher? Why?
10. What are some of the essential steps in behavior change?
11. Give some examples of alternate appropriate behaviors for each problem behavior.
12. What is the purpose of modeling and shaping in developing new behaviors?
13. Explain how chaining can be used to develop a sequence of behaviors.
14. Explain some of the sequential steps essential to a token economy (point) program.
15. Explain the function of verbal praise.
16. Describe the use of the "when–then" format.
17. How would you use behavior momentum procedures with a student?
18. Explain the "positive response program" in dealing with noncompliance.
19. What is a contingency contract?
20. What are the two types of generalization? Explain each.
21. How can teachers "teach" for generalization?
22. Compare and contrast precorrection and correction procedures.
23. Explain the types of punishment and their hierarchy from least aversive to most aversive.
24. What kind of behavior can be ignored?
25. Explain the various types of punishment.
26. Why should behavior be monitored?
27. Is time-out the best procedure you can use to eliminate problem behaviors? Explain.

CHAPTER 12

Specific Proactive Behavioral Interventions for Problematic Behaviors

Overview

- Aggression
- Social skill problems
- Inattention
- Following directions
- Self-monitoring
- Impulsivity
- Noncompliance
- Inappropriate verbalizations
- Complete case study

Case History

Dylan is an 8-year-old third grader who has been diagnosed with ADHD. He is taking Ritalin, which helps with his impulsive behavior, but he still shows many disruptive behaviors—making facial or hand gestures, talking with classmates seated nearby, walking around the classroom when he should be seated, and tapping his pencil, fingers, and other objects on his desk. This has prompted a re-evaluation to change placement. In Dylan's school, there are three third-grade teachers who work together, each with one area of academic specialty—social studies, language arts, and math. Each teacher also has an assistant. The teachers have developed a program that involves self-monitoring and tokens for appropriate behavior that will redirect Dylan's disruptive behavior. Teachers and staff now report that the program is not working. *What would you do?*

Most teachers spend a great deal of time dealing with inappropriate and disruptive problem behaviors. Due to various factors such as time constraints, inconsistencies in application, and a lack of understanding of behavioral principles, their attempts to modify behavior may often fail. We have reviewed some of the basic principles of behavioral techniques but have not discussed specific application of these techniques so far in this book. While we have also briefly discussed interventions for various diagnoses, we have not focused on some of the common problematic behaviors that cut across diagnoses. It is the following problem behaviors—not diagnoses—that will be the focus of this chapter: (1) aggression, (2) social skill problems involving cooperation and sharing, (3) impulsivity, (4) hyperactivity, (5) inattention, (6) on-task behavior, (7) noncompliance, and (8) inappropriate verbalizations. In addition to providing general behavioral intervention strategies, we discuss some cases that involve children who present the aforementioned problem behavior in the classroom. These children will vary in age and types of problems, and the strategies or programs addressing the problematic behaviors will be reviewed.

A few of the basic tenets of our approach should be reviewed.

1. *Behaviors* are controlled by the antecedents, behaviors, and consequences (ABC) approach. Expanding the simple ABC model to a four-term contingency would add setting events, which changes the dynamics of the antecedents, behaviors, and consequences. For example, a student may not complete an assignment for a teacher who just gave him extra homework, while the student does complete an assignment given by a second teacher who gave only a small amount of homework (the two teachers differ in *setting events*).

2. All behavior—appropriate or inappropriate—is learned. Proactive behavioral techniques involve helping students learn more appropriate skills through positive intervention while avoiding aversive consequences.

3. The least restrictive and least intrusive and the most parsimonious and effective interventions should be used. For example, it may be easier to offer verbal praise to a student rather than to implement a complex token economy. Behavioral interventions may vary across the following dimensions: (a) *restrictiveness*—the extent to which the student has limited access to basic human freedoms like privacy, movement, and leisure (Cooper, Peterson, & Meier, 1987); (b) *intrusiveness*—the extent to which behavioral interventions are obtrusive and affect bodily or personal rights (Erchul & Martens, 2002)—Wolery, Bailey, and Sugai (1988) list pain, discomfort, and social stigma as factors; (c) *effectiveness*— the extent to which the procedure produces the least harm while achieving its goal.

4. A positive programming approach will provide the student with more choices while obtaining the same consequence. It is important to remember that a student's problem behavior may be the only behavior that was learned to bring about a desired consequence such as attention.

5. It is the child's *behavior*—not the child—that may be troubling. This "people first" orientation will help the teacher working with students who have autism or ADHD and present problematic behaviors. An appropriate description of such a child might be a "student with ADHD who exhibits defiance and verbal aggression," and not an "aggressive ADHD student."

The cases that follow in this chapter will show that not all problematic behavior is difficult to manage. The cases will describe a variety of ages and types of problem, while covering some of the basic annoying and sometimes more serious behavior problems of students with different disabilities. Remember that cases will reflect behavior problems, not diagnoses. The case on the following page involves a 7-year-old girl with a persistent thumb-sucking problem. These interventions reflect characteristic problem behaviors and may not flow smoothly from one behavior to another. The next problem behavior to be addressed is aggression.

AGGRESSION

We discuss here the four types of aggression: (1) defiance and verbal aggression, (2) hostile-aggressive behavior, (3) behaviors requiring physical restraint, and (4) passive-aggressive behavior.

Defiance and Verbal Aggression

Students who are verbally aggressive use words to get what they want, to gain attention, or to avoid doing some task. According to Wolfgang and Glickman (1986)

Case Study

Case 1: Using Self-Monitoring and Habit Reversal for Thumb Sucking

Beth is a 7-year-old second grader who demonstrates excessive, although not severe, thumb sucking in the classroom. Beth's classmates ridicule and tease her, which disrupts the class and embarrasses Beth. She is progressively being rejected by her peers.

Assessment

Baseline data were collected over a 7-day interval in order to count the number of times Beth sucked her thumb during two 1-hour periods. The teacher collected this baseline data. Observations were made during different classes. During the two 1-hour periods, Beth averaged 8.1 instances of thumb sucking, a clearly high-frequency inappropriate behavior.

Self-Monitoring and Habit Reversal

Beth's teacher decided to use the habit reversal technique, which meant that Beth would clench her fist with her thumb inside her hand whenever she felt the urge to suck her thumb. The teacher also asked Beth to keep track of thumb sucking during successive 30-minute intervals by marking a sheet of paper indicating whether she did or did not suck her thumb during the previous 30-minute interval. Beth self-monitored her thumb sucking throughout the day. If she met criteria of 75 percent or 9 out of 12 intervals without thumb sucking, she would earn a reward from a menu of choices.

The graph below shows how Beth reduced her frequency of thumb sucking from 8.5 to about 0.5—a reduction that also improved her relationships with other students.

The teacher prepares the graph. Its purpose is to provide feedback to the teacher regarding the effectiveness of the intervention. The intervention may be carried out for a longer period or simply replaced with social praise when the child does the right thing.

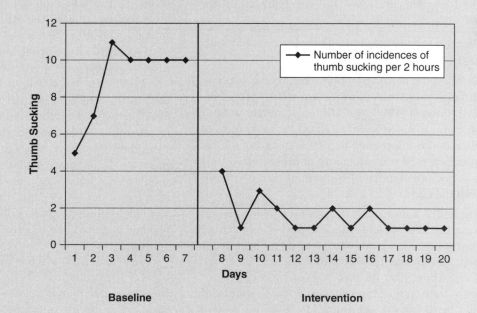

and more recently by the Center for Mental Health in Schools at UCLA (1999), this kind of behavior includes making fun of or teasing others, swearing, yelling out, joking or laughing (especially when others are reprimanded), and being sarcastic or disrespectful with teachers (Jimerson & Brock, 2004); physically aggressive behavior is rarely involved.

The first step in dealing with defiance and verbal aggression is to avoid confrontations with the student. In most cases, ignoring or not attending or responding to the outburst may prevent further escalation. It is usually nonproductive to attempt to reason with a student who is upset. It is best to withdraw attention, not respond, and even turn away from the student. If the behavior is short-lived or weak, this procedure may be sufficient; if it strengthens and reoccurs consistently, then other interventions may be warranted.

To address such problems, it is essential that a *functional behavioral assessment* be completed before a proactive behavioral intervention is selected. This will determine the function that the aggressive behavior serves and what circumstances may trigger it. For example, Marcus and colleagues (2001) found that the self-injurious aggressive behavior of some children was maintained by both positive and negative reinforcement. For one child, aggression was found to be sensitive to peer attention. If the annoying behavior is designed to gain attention, the following steps are needed:

1. Weaken the inappropriate behavior by not attending to it.

2. Develop the more appropriate behavioral response through positive reinforcement when it is exhibited. Porrata (1998) was able to eliminate temper tantrums in a 4-year-old child by getting parents to elicit and reinforce incompatible behavior, a form of differential reinforcement of other behavior. It is especially important to note any improvement with the child.

3. Model the appropriate response if students do not have the appropriate response in their behavioral repertoire. This kind of training might best occur in private to avoid any embarrassment to the child. Then when it is time to use it, provide a signal or cue—for example, tapping your finger to your head may be the prearranged signal to "use your head—think of what you need to do." Of course, this is a

learning paradigm that may require several training sessions (in private) along with constant differential reinforcement—praise (reinforcement) of the appropriate behavior, especially when the student does not exhibit the inappropriate behavior in situations that previously gave rise to (triggered) the inappropriate behavior.

Hostile-Aggressive Behavior

Students who display hostile-aggressive behavior are understandably dreaded by teachers (Bushman & Anderson, 2001). Capable of dominating and controlling others with often explosive actions, such students have the intent to do harm, whether it be physical or emotional, through physical aggression—kicking, hitting, spitting, throwing materials at a person or at property, and biting (Bohnert, Crnic, & Lim, 2003). Typically, such behavior may be triggered by frustration, and ultimately results in gaining negative attention from others, especially teachers. Any reprimand may lead to an escalation of defensiveness and verbal lashing out toward the teacher: "You always pick on me! Leave me alone, I didn't do anything." This interchange may escalate until the teacher, wanting to reestablish control, ends the cycle, usually by sending the child to the principal's office. When the interchange ends, the teacher is often left with feelings of failure, confusion, and negative feelings toward the student. This situation will probably sensitize the teacher to respond more angrily and quickly to future problems and to label the student as a "troublemaker" (Spoth, Redmond, & Shin, 2000).

There are two common ways that teachers may attempt to deal with hostile-aggressive behaviors: by either acting as an authoritarian (giving ultimatums), or by attempting to reason with the student. In the former case, the student might adopt a position of "you can't make me do anything," resulting in ineffective management. In the latter case, much time is wasted talking with the student who is generally unable to explain the reasons for being upset or losing control. Again the teacher may feel like a failure, and be frustrated and confused.

Teachers using a behavioral approach should first identify the problematic behaviors and then conduct a functional behavioral assessment, which will help to identify the specific situations that can trigger outbursts (Crone & Horner, 2000). It will also be essential to

<table>
<tr><td>Case Study</td><td></td><td colspan="3">Case 2: Strategies to Cope with Spitting and Biting in Preschool</td></tr>
</table>

Case Study

Case 2: Strategies to Cope with Spitting and Biting in Preschool

Barbara is a 4-year-old who is being seen for behavioral intervention because she frequently spits and bites both her classmates and the staff at her preschool. An ABC analysis has been conducted.

Results of ABC Analysis
Name: Barbara
Description of behavior(s) of interest: Spitting and biting

Date	Time	Antecedent	Behavior	Consequence	Comment
1/19	3:00	Told it was time to get ready for the bus	Tried to bite TA	"no biting"	
		Told "no biting" after attempt	Tried to bite again	Eye contact, firm "no biting"	TA helped with her coat and boots
1/20	1:00	Peer's turn to share	Spit at TA	"No spitting"	
	2:00	Teacher assisting another child with difficult toy	Called for attention to her project	Ignored	
		Ignored when calling for attention—teacher still engaged with another student	Spit at teacher	Told she was "all done" and taken from the tower she had built	
1/22	1:00	Attention to peer	Bite attempt	Full eye contact—firm voice, "no, do not bite. That hurt me."	Barbara grinned after being reprimanded
	1:30	Finished puzzle activity	Bit peer	"No biting! It's not nice to bite your friends. Johnny doesn't like it when you bite him. You'll need to come over here and sit by me."	

Baseline/Intervention Data for Barbara

The ABC analysis indicated the function of both behaviors was to gain attention. Based on this hypothesis, intervention strategies have been implemented. The use of collaboration prior to challenging behavior provided attention and an opportunity for the staff to determine the need to teach new skills. A schedule of differential reinforcement of other appropriate behaviors (DRO or differential reinforcement of other behavior) was implemented. [Note: DRO is a technique of rewarding a child if an undesired behavior is *not* shown during a specified time.] Ongoing data confirmed that the challenging

(continued)

behavior was decreasing. Barbara has also needed assistance with various skills, indicating that some of her attention seeking may have been a request for assistance. Collaborative activities focused on providing opportunities to increase Barbara's fine motor skills, such as zipping her coat or working on art projects. Request for assistance was also added to the interventions in her positive support plan. In the future, tolerance for delay will also be used to gradually increase her level of independence in the absence of inappropriate behaviors.

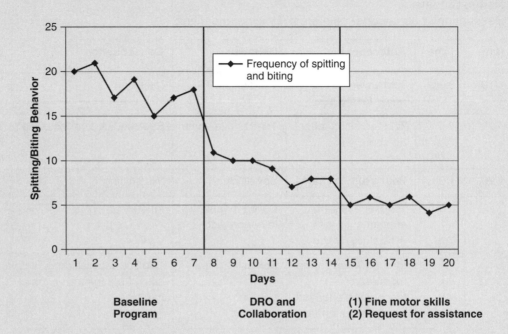

Behavior during the 7 days of baseline indicated that Barbara engaged in challenging behavior an average of 19 times each day. After 7 days of implementing DRO and collaboration, challenging behavior was decreased to 8 times each day. Fine motor skill building and request for assistance were implemented. Challenging behavior remained the same for the first 6 days of learning those new skills.

Source: Case adapted from http://ceed.umm.edu/CEED/projects/preschoolbehavior/case.htm. Case description reprinted with permission from West Virginia University Press, from *Education & Treatment of Children*, 22, 171–178.

meet with the student (and parents) to discuss which behaviors are acceptable and which ones are not and to identify whatever consequences the student might receive for problem behaviors. It is always possible that such behaviors may be triggered by academic work or tasks that are beyond the student's capabilities or may be difficult to perform (e.g., labored handwriting that slows down academic work). If the student receives positive reinforcement for the outburst and then is allowed to escape from the unpleasant work assignment, these reactions may reinforce the behavior problem by the attention it receives as well as by negative reinforcement—being allowed to escape from an unpleasant task, even if it means being sent to the principal's office (Miller, Tansy, & Hughes, 1998).

In developing proactive plans, the teacher may let students know when their behavior is escalating by using a signal or cue—for example, holding up a fist to signal that students need to get control or close up. When students stop the escalation they can receive positive feedback; if they then go on to exhibit additional appropriate behavior, they may receive more positive feedback. It is important to remember that a student's unacceptable behavior did not develop overnight and that it will take some time to establish replacement behavior. Backup reinforcers can be used for those times when the student behavior changes—for example, giving the student some job as a special reward for improved control. It is, of course, not only important that students learn appropriate replacement behaviors but also that they learn some problem-solving procedures centering around what they can do when they become frustrated and angry. This not only provides some options regarding replacement behavior but may also help students generalize improved self-control to other situations. In short, it is important that students be able to demonstrate their replacement behaviors in all classrooms, with all authority figures, teachers as well as parents. During the generalization and maintenance phase, change will be more rapid and more extensive when all authority figures handle the problem behavior in the same manner. As suggested by Flick (1998b, 2000, 2002) and Petermann and Petermann (1997), school behavior programs must also involve parents to be more effective. When aggression is determined by multiple features, treatment may need to be more complex. Lalli and Casey (1996) report that the aggression of a young boy with developmental delays occurred more frequently when he was asked to pick up his toys, a request that ended a period of play and social interaction. Treatment consisted of praise, a break, and access to his toys, all contingent on compliance. These researchers found that aggression decreased only when someone interacted socially with the child during the break. It is also important to recognize that when a child is asked to stop play to pick up toys, a punishment is in effect. Compliance is also a problem, and this child needs more reinforced compliance type behaviors.

To develop a long-term proactive behavioral intervention plan, the teacher needs to consider many factors:

1. The teacher must feel a sense of competency in dealing with problem behaviors, perhaps through the use of self-talk and affirmations. Many students with hostile problem behaviors are not aware that frustration and anger are escalating so quickly, and they are unable to react appropriately in time. This means that the teacher will need to continue reinforcing the appropriate alternative replacement behavior and to avoid giving attention to the inappropriate behavior.

2. Teachers should practice proximity control—decreasing unwanted behavior by positioning themselves next to the student who frequently shows misbehavior (Kerr & Nelson, 1998; Zirpoli & Mellow, 2001). This procedure also helps in "catching the child being good" (Allen & Cowdery, 2004; Gootman, 2001).

3. Teachers should establish a quiet spot in the classroom where students can go to calm down and get control. In essence, this type of "chill-out" or "calm-down" place is simply a variation of time-out. While time-out is technically a withdrawal from all positive reinforcement, it also allows children to calm down and get control (before they are released from time-out), an important requirement.

4. It is essential that teachers prevent conflicts from escalating to the point of losing control. If two students are in the process of escalating a conflict, they must be separated and reminded that it takes two to have a fight and if one student is inappropriately threatened, a fight can be avoided. When a student escalates a conflict but then exhibits self-control, the teacher should give positive reinforcement for that self-control behavior.

5. If the teacher needs to deal with a second phase of defensiveness, a simple re-direction procedure may be appropriate (Reimers & Brunger, 1999). This will involve avoiding confrontation, giving attention to the second-line defensive behavior, simply focusing instead on what needs to be done using redirection, Questions such as "What is it that you need to be doing at this time?" allow the student to shift from a feeling mode to a thinking mode—the latter of course will facilitate greater cognitive control.

There are two teacher reactions that are not advised when dealing with hostile-aggressive behavior: (1) Do not corner a student who is emotionally out of control, and leave sufficient personal space for the student to leave the classroom, and (2) Do not argue with such a student. Give choices to the student for the present situation, and for older children the option to discuss it at some later time. Any attempt to discuss the student's behavior during emotional upheavals may simply reinforce the escalation process.

Case Study

Case 3: Cursing, Hitting, and Spitting in a Mentally Retarded 10-year-old

Susan is a 10-year-old girl with mental retardation who has presented numerous problem behaviors—including hitting, spitting, and cursing—in the classroom and at home. Susan's teachers have tried a variety of techniques to change problem behaviors. Ignoring was employed with some of Susan's negative behaviors (i.e., aggressive but not dangerous); passive restraint was used in response to hitting or spitting; and verbal praise was provided for positive, appropriate behaviors exhibited in lieu of the inappropriate ones. There was an initial increase in cursing but this then rapidly declined. After passive restraint, the teacher used time-out, which was associated with maintenance of the three inappropriate behaviors at low levels. Time-outs were brief and consisted of withdrawal of attention, withdrawal from a favorite activity, or withdrawal of something used in an activity. Attention was also focused on positive behavior (DRO) at the same time as time-outs given. Behavioral improvements were maintained until the end of the school year. Whenever Susan behaved appropriately, she was reinforced with praise and touch (such as a pat on the back).

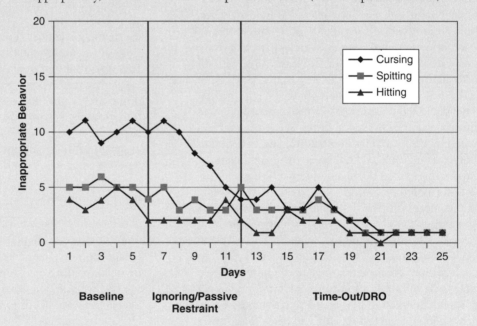

Source: Information from Kee, Hill, and West (1999). Reprinted by permission. "School-Based Behavior Management of Cursing, Hitting & Spitting in a Girl with Profound Retardation," *Education & Treatment of Children,* 22, 171–178.

Physical Restraint

Physical restraint is a procedure where a teacher uses his or her body to immobilize a student to protect the safety of staff or other students. Morgan and Jensen (1988) noted that this procedure has been overused and sometimes even abused, and has led to lawsuits over violation of the student's constitutional rights. Thus, it is important for teachers to evaluate the risk and to use the procedure judiciously (McAfee, Schwilk, & Mitruski, 2006). It should be used only as a last resort to protect students from hurting themselves or others or from damaging property.

Schloss and Smith (1987) provide some guidelines for use of physical restraint:

1. Verbally instruct the student to engage in nonaggressive behavior.

2. If the student remains in an aggressive posture 3 seconds after the verbal prompt, provide a gentle manual prompt (e.g., softly press against the student's shoulder) and repeat the verbal prompt.

3. If after 3 additional seconds the student is still in an aggressive posture, physically direct him or her to a safe area using accepted manual restraint techniques.

4. Once restrained in the safe area, provide frequent verbal cues such as, "I can let go of you when you are relaxed."

5. Once the student has remained relaxed for 3 minutes, gradually relinquish physical control and proceed to the educational and therapeutic aspects of the behavior management program. If the student's behavior escalates so rapidly that waiting 3 seconds between steps would be hazardous, manual restraint should be used immediately.

6. If a student reacts violently or with discomfort to physical touch, avoid any physical touch.

It is important to note that all of these procedures are contingent upon the age and size of the student involved and this technique should be used only by trained staff. The only exception might be for preschool children who may be more effectively restrained by a teacher. In all cases, physical restraint should not take the place of appropriate behavioral planning. Violent behavior will only be changed when students learn those behaviors that are appropriate and effective for meeting their needs.

There are three prominent risks associated with using physical restraint: (1) there is the possibility of injury, (2) being restrained may cause anger to escalate or it may be reinforced by the attention the student receives, (3) there is the possibility of legal recourse.[*]

Passive-Aggressive Behavior

A student might show passive-aggressive behavior either to get attention or to express anger (Macciomei & Ruben, 1999; Shapiro & Kratochwill, 2000). Sometimes, such

[*]Teachers can learn more about formal training in using physical restraints by contacting the school district or special education office about in-service training. They can also contact the National Crisis Prevention Institute (www.crisisprevention.com)

students may deal with anger and frustration by eliciting similar passive-aggressive feelings in others. Students exhibit typical passive-aggressive behaviors by hearing only what they want, moving slowly when asked to do something, purposefully forgetting, being accidentally destructive, complaining excessively, and not completing work. Of course, there can be other reasons for such behaviors but their frequency and pervasiveness make them stand out. It may appear that students are attempting to avoid or escape from some activity, but it is the manipulation or conflict that results from such behaviors that drives them and provides the attention they are seeking. Once the behaviors are reinforced by attention, a cycle begins that periodically reinforces the behaviors and prevents the student from shifting to engage in more appropriate behaviors. These students also lack self-esteem since their complex manipulative behaviors often prevent them from realizing any success with task completion. These students are also deficient in their ability to express feelings of frustration and anger, which leads them to vent their feelings indirectly by manipulating and controlling the emotions of others.

The first step in dealing with a passive-aggressive student is to again conduct a functional behavioral assessment. If attention does not appear to maintain the behavior, it is questionable whether the student really displays passive-aggressive behaviors. The second step involves examining how the teacher has been dealing with the behavior. The teacher's emotional state must be appraised after confrontation with the student. If there is a feeling of helplessness and anger, then the methods used are not working. The teacher should first make a list of three to five of the student's behaviors that are most annoying and then find alternative behaviors for each one. It is important at this point for the teacher to withdraw attention to the student's inappropriate manipulative behaviors, and to reinforce any spontaneous exhibition of alternative behaviors. If the student is not showing any of the alternative behaviors, then these behaviors can be modeled for the student. For example, the student can be engaged in role-playing where the more appropriate alternative behaviors are exhibited in place of the inappropriate behaviors. When these behaviors are exhibited in the natural environment of the classroom, they can be reinforced either by verbal praise or perhaps through the use of a token or point system. Cooperative learning is yet another behavioral intervention that can be used where the student works

Case Study

Case 4: Using Positive Strategies to Cope with Avoidance in a Preschooler

Mark is a 4-year-old preschool student who refuses to pick up toys at the end of activities. When the teacher repeats the request, Mark laughs and runs off to hide. Although Mark has been told that he will not get to play with the toys the next day, he still refuses to cooperate. A time-out was tried, but his teacher quickly realized that this was inappropriate as Mark appeared happy to go to time-out where he could watch the other children pick up the toys.

A functional behavioral assessment revealed that Mark's behavior was instrumental in avoiding the task of picking up the toys. The time-out simply allowed him to successfully avoid clean-up. Mark was then asked to collaborate with his teacher on clean-up activities. Rather than asking him to complete the task by himself, the teacher would work with him, collaborating and modeling the appropriate behavior. She might say, "OK, I'll pick up the red blocks—you pick up the green ones. After you do this, we can go to the art table to draw." As Mark picks up the blocks, he is reinforced with praise: "That's the way to go. You're doing a good job." After praising him in order to sustain his work behavior, the teacher may praise him again at the end: "You did a good job of picking up these blocks. I'm proud of you." The teacher may also reinforce Mark by mentioning another fun activity such as drawing that he can do after completing their task. This procedure may be repeated, gradually allowing Mark to pick up more and more blocks. A competitive strategy may also allow the teacher to reinforce him for picking up the most blocks: "That was great—you picked up a lot more than I did!" The ultimate stopping point will be when Mark picks up all the blocks. The teacher then reinforces him again: "That was fantastic! You picked up all the blocks. I didn't have to pick up a single one."

Source: Information from: http://cehd.edu/CEED/projects/preschoolbehavior/case.htm.

with another student who already shows appropriate behaviors.

The student will also need to learn more acceptable ways of expressing anger. If a problem-solving approach is used, the student may be asked, "What else could you do when you feel frustrated and angry?" The teacher might then list the student's appropriate and inappropriate behaviors. In fact, this may be an excellent exercise to conduct with the entire class. Through observation, the identified student may learn other options to replace the problematic behavior. In addition, it is important to build self-esteem by giving tasks that the student is entirely capable of performing and by reinforcing them as they are completed. The teacher might say, "You did an excellent job on that project I gave you. I'm really proud of you." Of course, if there is an underlying problem with the completion of some simple academic tasks, this may represent some type of learning impairment, attentional problem, or even a neurologically based dysfunction such

as a handwriting disorder caused by impaired fine motor or visual-spatial functions; such conditions must be ruled out.

SOCIAL SKILLS PROBLEMS

Fitting into today's society is a challenge for many children, especially for those with behavioral and emotional disabilities. Many students may show aggressive behavior in some situations when they do not know how to behave (Fox & Boulton, 2005; Cook, 2003). This section will focus on two essential social skills that are especially important for all children: sharing and cooperation.

Sharing

At some point, everyone has had an experience of having to share with others. It is normal to share as part of developing friendship, and certainly siblings often share food, toys, and time with their parents. Children with disabilities may develop a sense of being the less favored child—or even the "black sheep" of the family. Often feeling victimized, such children will at times resent having to share, resent being second, and ultimately resent their siblings. This situation generates conflict and leaves parents or teachers frustrated and frazzled in seeking peaceful solutions to hassles at home and in the classroom. It is at times quite difficult to know where to begin.

In the case of young children, competition often involves difficulties with sharing toys. Training on this social skill can begin with an exercise aimed at teaching the concept of sharing to one or more siblings or playmates in class. Although conflict over a toy with subsequent fighting may, of course, result in placing the toy in time-out (i.e., stopping the training session), this will not teach the child about sharing or playing cooperatively; it may only serve to discourage fighting. What is needed is the prosocial approach, which might involve the following steps in a dispute over sharing toys:

1. Explain to both children that you have noticed that there is difficulty in playing with a toy and that you expect them to share this toy, then say, "I'd like to show you what I mean by sharing."

2. *Model* sharing behavior by saying, "I can play with the toy for a while and then I can offer it to you." Depending on the age of the children, the time spent with the toy may vary, using briefer periods for younger children.

3. After modeling sharing behavior, say, "OK, now I'd like to see each of you share this toy. I'm going to use a kitchen timer so that you both can play with this toy for 1 minute."

4. Set the timer for 1 minute (time is subjective and depends on age of child), and when the bell rings say, "OK, I like the way you played with the toy" and (to the other child) "I like the way you played with something else while you were waiting for this toy."

5. Allow the other child to play with the toy, again setting the timer for 1 minute. Praise the second child as you did the first child.

6. If there is any hassle while the first child plays with the toy, warn the second child that fighting over the toy will mean that the first child will have the toy for an additional minute.

7. If there are more hassles about the toy, explain that the toy will go into time-out: "OK, we'll need to try this another time. This toy goes in time-out for 15 minutes." (The time may be varied. For something really desirable, 15 minutes may be sufficient; 1 hour or 1 day may be used for other, less desirable toys.)

As with most programs, the really important factor is not the time-out, but rather the opportunity to develop more appropriate prosocial skills. Return to this training quickly and often for the most efficient learning to occur.

There are fewer opportunities in school to observe and reinforce sharing or taking turns, but some occasions can be found—especially for younger children. Often youngsters working on projects together at a table may be faced with the problem of taking turns with materials. This behavior may be monitored by the teacher, reported to parents, and directly reinforced in the classroom, on a form such as the recording sheet for social skills (shown in Figure 12.1). A copy of this form is also shown in Appendix D. The teacher may use this form to demonstrate sharing to the child: "When I see you sharing and taking turns, I'm going to mark this paper so that you can show your parents at home how well you can do with this behavior." If a fight breaks out in the classroom, the teacher may cue students with the question, "What should you be doing instead of fighting over that game?" This allows the child to develop some cognitive awareness of appropriate behavior such as sharing. When the child changes his behavior and begins to share, the teacher may give praise and a pat on the back, saying, "I'm going to put a good mark on your report." As with other skill training, this information may be used equally well in the classroom and at home in a behavior (point) system.

The blank form may be used to monitor the social skills for any student. Rewards may be established especially for improvement (e.g., going from two

Name _____   Teacher _____   Date _____

Social Skill	M	T	W	Th	F	Totals
Listening						
Following rules						
Sharing						
Working/playing cooperatively						
Solving problems						
Controlling anger						
Totals						

FIGURE 12.1   A recording sheet for social skills.

Cooperation Problems

Cooperation problems have been of prime concern to parents of children with various disabilities (Phillips, Schwean, & Saklofske, 1997). As with other appropriate behaviors, it is not possible for the child to play cooperatively and fight at the exact same time. Thus, more frequent reinforcement of cooperative behavior should result in a decrease in fighting or aggressive behavior. Teachers should have a plan for dealing with fighting through priming, a method that reminds students of what to expect for appropriate as well as inappropriate behaviors. The teacher thus states what the consequences will be for appropriate behavior: "You'll get a token for your cooperation." Inappropriate behaviors (e.g., grabbing or monopolizing a toy) will result in loss of time with the toy. These reminders can be directed in general toward all students. Although this procedure is technically not bribing, there are similarities: A person is offered a reward (e.g., money or a toy) to not perform some behavior (e.g., writing a ticket/fighting with classmate).

To develop social skills related to cooperation, a teacher might suggest that the identified child and her classmate play a game where the identified child will not be at a disadvantage. For example, checkers is not a good choice for this as there are too many chances for the identified child to make impulsive and poorly planned responses. A better choice would be a game such as Candyland where success is more dependent upon chance. This will ensure more opportunities to reinforce cooperative behavior. Once the game is selected, the teacher can use the behavior check card shown in Figure 12.2 to record data. She can then explain its purpose to both children: "You know that it has sometimes been difficult for you two to play together without fighting. I'm going to be looking for times when you two get along in play without fighting. When I see this, I'll let you know, but I'll also put a mark on this card. When you two reach 10 marks we will have a celebration by going somewhere (or doing something) that you both like." A blank behavior check card may be found in Appendix D. The following behavior check card may be used in school, at home (include Saturday and Sunday), or both. The teacher may put slash marks on each category (working cooperatively or playing cooperatively) when he/she catches the child engaged in cooperative play or work.

This is an example of a *structured token economy*, a method in which neither child will know when the teacher will be observing them; this kind of random check results in far greater consistency in exhibiting

Name _____   Teacher _____   Date _____

Behavior	M	T	W	Th	F	S	S
Working cooperatively							
Playing cooperatively							
Cumulative totals							
Date	Point total goal this week						

FIGURE 12.2 Behavior check card.

appropriate cooperative behavior. For behaviors that are weak and especially those that are in the initial states of development, it will be important to reinforce students positively for nearly every time the appropriate behavior is exhibited. Later on, a leaner schedule of reinforcement may be used. If necessary, the teacher can use a game to model cooperative behavior and even show the child which behaviors would be inappropriate and what will happen if inappropriate behavior occurs. Signals such as holding out two fingers can be used to warn the child when such behavior occurs. This communicates that the child has two choices: change the inappropriate behavior, or accept the consequence for that behavior. Both children are told that if inappropriate behavior occurs, the game will be stopped. However, by giving children a chance to change behavior by themselves, the responsibility for the consequence is shifted totally to them. Remember that it is far better to promote positive, prosocial behavior than to simply punish an inappropriate behavior. Punishment never tells the child *what to* do. As children get better at earning points for cooperative behavior and the point totals increase, the teacher can set higher goals for the same payoff. This is very much like training someone to jump hurdles. The object is to start low, reinforce success, and then raise the expectation. Conditions are never raised to some prearranged expectation, or extended to a point where the child consistently fails. Failure, especially continual failure, teaches nothing. If children voice complaints over the increase in expectation, the teacher might lessen their concerns by stating, "Yes, you do need a greater

number of points to get the reward, but you are getting so much better at cooperation that it's much easier for you to get the points; you know I'm really proud of the progress you've made."

INATTENTION

Inattention may be either *visual* (not paying attention to what the teacher does) or *auditory* (not paying attention to what the teacher says). A critical element of "paying attention" involves *listening*—hearing and then processing auditory input from others. Listening skills are vital for academic work (gathering information, following directions, understanding assignments, etc.), and being able to really listen to others also contributes to effective social interactions as well. Often, when a child misinterprets something said by another child and acts or responds based on this misunderstanding, the stage may be set for negative interactions, conflict, and aggression. Such situations most often occur within a group (peer) context—not in a one-on-one situation. Peers see only the overt response—usually aggressive behavior—and quietly record this as another bit of evidence to avoid this child. Following such incidents, even if children are told accurately what was initially said to them (as contrasted to what they "heard"), they may still appear confused and may even develop the belief that they are "misunderstood" by others.

After listening skills have been learned and practiced in a small group setting, these skills can be generalized to the classroom setting. The teacher can follow the same process to verify that communications

Case Study

Case 5: Auditory Attention (Listening) in a Young Child

Zach is a 6-year-old boy who is having trouble with the regular school kindergarten program. Basically, he does not listen to oral instructions. After being initially given some simple things to process, his teacher asked him to write letters of the alphabet, numbers, or his name, and then immediately asked him to repeat what she had said. Zach was reinforced with specific verbal praise or a pat on the shoulder for each time he was able to correctly recall what he had been instructed to do. The teacher also read some simple stories to him and asked him to repeat in his own words what was said. Zach showed general improvement over time.

In another exercise, Zach was asked each day to recall 10 items from those presented to him by the teacher. Baseline data shown in Figure 12.3 reveal that he could recall very few in the beginning.

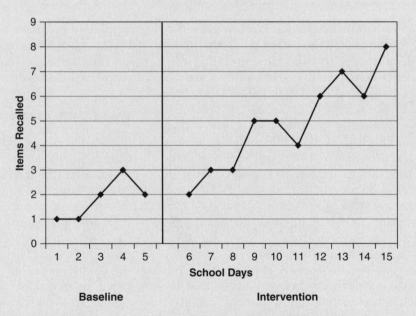

FIGURE 12.3 Recall of items presented orally (young child).

Over a 2-week period, he recalled more items of the 10 presented. He was simply maintained by social rewards of specific praise and pats on the shoulder.

are heard accurately by asking a student, "What did I just ask you to do?" The teacher gives immediate feedback (verbal praise) to the child for accurate response statements. Parents should also be given this information on a daily or weekly basis, including a record of the number of requests and the number of the child's accurate responses. Of course, learning occurs much faster when parents at home follow the same procedures and reinforce their child for correct

processing of information. The teacher might even suggest this positive approach for home use. Remember that children will make better progress when they know what to do. Short-term record keeping may allow for back-up praise and reward at home and is needed only for about 2 weeks. In the future, this may be replaced by frequent praise from the teacher. When formal reports are given to a parent, any listening skills that are improving may be listed

Case Study

Case 6: Auditory Attention (Listening) in an Older Child

Branden is an 8-year-old second grader who has much difficulty with listening behavior. He is often lost while reading and fails to listen to his teacher when she gives instructions that are more complex. There are three components to the instructions that Branden receives: (1) correctly responding to questions such as, "What should you be doing at the present time?" (2) correctly responding to complex instructions such as, "Put your books in your desk, take out a pencil and paper, open your book to page 17, and do the odd-numbered problems." and (3) correctly responding by rephrasing what is said in a story that has been just read to the class. Each day, there were 20 items to be recalled from the story. Baseline and intervention data appear in Figure 12.4.

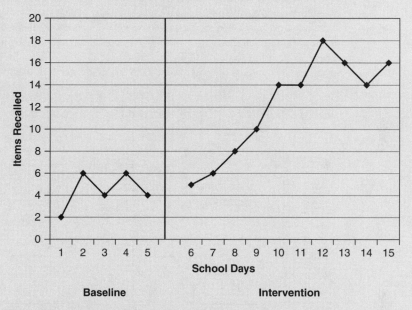

FIGURE 12.4   Recall of items presented orally (older child).

Although Branden had a few poor days during the intervention, he generally improved and showed a higher percentage of items correctly recalled. He was maintained using special verbal praise and nonverbal pats on the shoulder.

on the child's behavioral (point system) program. It is extremely important to keep any feedback to parents very positive. If classroom listening performance stays at 90 percent correct or better, the child should receive some agreed-upon reward from the teacher. The parent's or teacher's use of priming each morning, to remind the child of the potential reward, often results in faster learning of these listening skills.

Visual Attention

Visual attention is another important skill that students must learn in order to maintain on-task behavior, especially during written work. Visual attention is trainable; it can be modified and maintained through behavioral modification. The following case is an example of a student who was distractible by attending to things other than her work. She was often off-task and this, of course, prevented her from completing many tasks.

**Case
Study**

Case 7: Visual Attention in an Older Child

Tiffany is a sixth-grade student who likes to stare out the window and often fails to pay attention. Her teacher planned a simple intervention using a momentary time sampling procedure of 15-second intervals. Tiffany was deemed to be on-task when she was oriented to the teacher and responding verbally, which showed that she was following the teacher's instructions with evidence of attention to task or if she just raised her hand for information. Data intervals being on-task were then divided by the total number of intervals. She was observed 2 days per week for 6 weeks during math period using a multiple baseline design.

During a baseline of 1 week, the teacher did not greet students at the door but followed the normal routine. During intervention the teacher greeted Tiffany by name and gave some positive statement such as, "I really like your hairstyle" or "You really look good." The basic idea would be to use something positive that may be unrelated to school work. Comments about appearance like hair style, dress, etc., may be appropriate, or the student's smile, or attitude. The teacher was allowed to vary the statement without specific instructions by the teacher from day to day. Figure 12.5 illustrates the results.

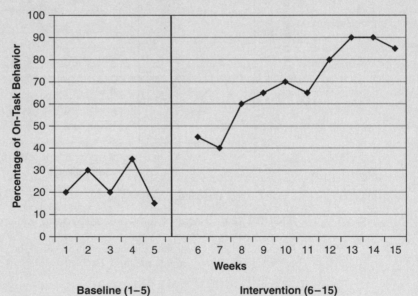

FIGURE 12.5   Change to appropriate situations.

As a result of this simple teacher greeting at the door in the morning, Tiffany's attention to the teacher and on-task behavior improved significantly. Remaining on-task was maintained over time with periodic positive verbal praise for beginning a task, remaining on task, and completing her work. She was also provided reinforcement when she was clearly paying attention to the teacher and was able to repeat directions or explain a procedure in math.

On-Task Behavior

Perhaps one of the most difficult behaviors to deal with is on-task behavior—the ability of students to focus on assignments so that they may be completed. There are many reasons why students may have trouble staying on-task. Some of these factors may have physiological causes such as ADHD, and others may be simply learned or they may be behaviors that are associated with another disorder. Whatever the reason, the behavior of remaining on-task may be shaped and developed. The following case is an example of on-task behavior that is associated with autism. While some specific approaches may be used, the underlying behavior problem may respond to behavioral intervention.

Case Study

Case 8: On-Task Behavior in an Autistic Boy

David is a 7-year-old boy with autism who has been in a general education kindergarten class with pull-out services once a week along with special education services in class. He requires a one-on-one aide in order to learn new skills. Risperdal is administered at home both in the morning and in the evening. There are nine students in his class. David makes annoying and distracting bomb noises and sometimes either puts his head down or hits or pushes staff. He leaves tasks before completing them and also engages in inappropriate talk such as yelling noises and making comments on some television programs.

Behavioral interventions for David have consisted of a token program with positive behavioral supports. The general instrumented format was work followed by play. During baseline, David completed work then chose a play activity. Data were collected on (1) the number of noises, (2) inappropriate physical contact (with staff), and (3) inappropriate talking. In his positive support plan, David was shown a picture of work activity (e.g., a student working) then a picture of play activities (e.g., a student playing) he could earn. His rewards consisted of playtime, appropriate edibles such as popcorn, and a picture book. The plan was in effect for 2 weeks.

The results showed a decrease in his disruptive and inappropriate behaviors along with a significant increase in his productivity, as shown in Figure 12.6.

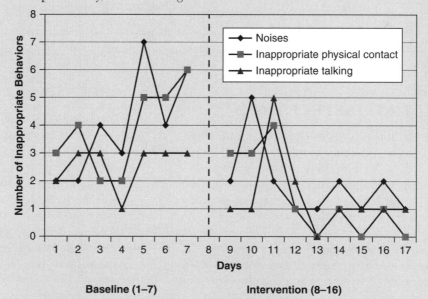

FIGURE 12.6   Disruptive inappropriate behaviors.

(continued)

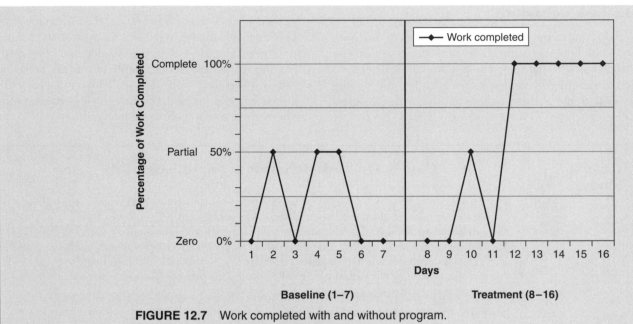

FIGURE 12.7 Work completed with and without program.

As David's inappropriate behavior decreased, his work output increased and he was able to stay on-task for longer periods to complete his assigned work. In order to increase his appropriate behavior, specific praise was delivered for completing his work partially or completely. Of course, he was required to complete his work before engaging in play—a simple instrumental procedure. David could also earn tokens for suppressing his inappropriate behavior. At the end of each day, he could trade his tokens or accumulate them and trade them in after a week. Reinforcers were primarily things he enjoyed, such as time on the computer, popcorn, or a McDonald's certificate.

FOLLOWING INSTRUCTIONS

Only after children have well-established listening skills can they be expected to follow instructions well (DuPaul, 1991). Training in the two skill areas of listening and following instructions can even be done together. Complying with requests or following directions is something children are expected to "do" as compared with things they "should not do." As such prosocial skills become stronger and more frequent, there is a corresponding reduced probability of inappropriate behavior. When children are doing what they are supposed to—following directions or rules—they cannot be doing what they are not supposed to do.

You may use many other tasks for this type of exercise. Remember, any request given may bring about a reward for listening (i.e., knowing what to do), and for carrying out the request(s) (i.e., doing it). Completing the task may thus result in additional praise and touch (i.e., a pat on the back). Both skills (listening and following directions) may also be included in a behavioral point system.

When such behaviors are rated on a home–school note, it will facilitate learning of the skill and enhance generalization of the skill. As children are reinforced for their use of compliance in more situations, compliance becomes stronger and more "generalized." Following rules in class, on the playground, in the lunchroom, and on the school bus are all situations in which compliance

Case Study

Case 9: Following Instructions

Five kindergarten girls (ages 4 to 6 years) were asked to follow a daily routine where the following 10 instructions were given: (1) pick up the toys, (2) sit down, (3) come and get a pencil and paper, (4) write your name on the paper, (5) fold your paper, (6) bring the pencil and paper to my desk, (7) put your chair on the table, (8) get your mat out, (9) lie down, and (10) be quiet. This was a multiple baseline design using the typical routine during the day; teacher attention in the form of specific praise was the single consequence. Data were recorded on a sheet indicating who correctly followed instructions. Figure 12.8 shows the mean percentage of instructions followed each day; correct responses were checked if the child did what was requested within 15 seconds.

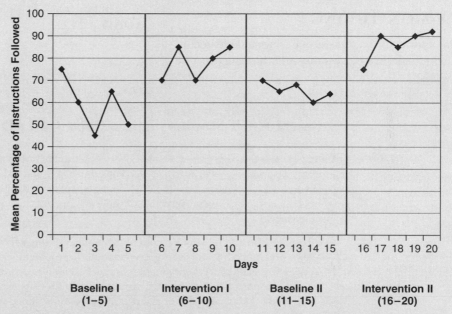

FIGURE 12.8   Instructions followed across baselines and interventions.

Several obervations are apparent. First, there is much variability in the first baseline. Second, there is general improvement from baseline to the second intervention. Third, when attention and specific praise are not forthcoming for each task, the percentage of correct appropriate behavior (i.e., following instructions) is lower. Each child did improve with appropriate attention and regressed without it. Attention as specific praise (e.g., "I like the way you picked up your toys as soon as I said to do it") was essential. Of course, timing each student would help but this was done even in the second baseline II (where correct responding dropped). The most important thing was the specific verbal praise given by the teacher for those who did the requested behavior (Schutte & Hopkins, 1970).

may become generalized. Successfully generalizing this compliance behavior does, however, require the cooperation of teacher, bus driver, and others, along with consistency of consequences to strengthen the skill. Inappropriate behaviors such as breaking rules may be reinforced when children are able to manipulate attention from the bus driver or the person monitoring the lunchroom. Predictable consequences must be in place for misbehavior—as well as recording and relating of appropriate behavior such as following the rules. Keep in mind that it is far more important to teach children prosocial skills that emphasize what they need "to do" rather than what they "should not do." Reminding children (through priming) of what the rules are in different situations and stating the consequences for adhering to or violating them will further improve the child's ability to be successful.

SELF-MONITORING

Self-monitoring is the process of having students record data about their own behavior in order to change its rate

(Coleman & Webber, 2002). Self-monitoring has been used with children who vary in age (Agran et al., 2005) and who show a wide array of handicapping conditions. There has been considerable variation in procedure, which may account for its underutilization by teachers (Agran et al., 2005). Self-monitoring has been used for both academic and nonacademic behavior problems (Shapiro & Cole, 1994). One of the easiest programs to use is the self-regulation program created by Parker (1992), for both individual students and the whole class. The following case describes a self-monitoring program to facilitate on-task behavior in a child with both ADHD and LD.

Case Study

Case 10: Self-Monitoring in a Child with ADHD and LD

Justin is a 12-year-old sixth grader who has been diagnosed with LD and ADHD. He has difficulty attending to instructions, following rules, and completing assigned tasks (mostly because he gets off-task). When Justin stays on-task, he is more likely to complete an assignment. A self-monitoring program has been set up for Justin consisting of three components: (1) baseline, (2) intervention, and (3) maintenance.

During baseline, the teacher kept a record of the number of times he was on-task or off-task during a 20-minute work period. Justin also kept a record during each of these periods for each day during math. A page was marked with either a plus (+) for being on-task or a minus (–) for being off-task each time a tone sounded. The tone was given at varying intervals played with an endless loop tape (i.e., a tape used to play material over and over). The baseline period was in operation over a period of 5 days. The percentage agreement between student and teacher was low.

During intervention, Justin was told that he would receive a point each time he was on-task when the beep sounded but only when his mark agreed with the teacher. There were 20 possible marks during each work period. When there was agreement between his mark and the teacher's, he got a bonus. Thus, Justin got double points for being on-task and an additional point if his mark agreed with the teacher. His score for each work period could thus range from 20 to 40 points. He was also given positive verbal feedback when his score matched that of the teacher. His reward was arranged with his mother as a trip to McDonald's. He received this after 200 points were earned. His mother also agreed to not allow him to go or to take him to McDonald's at any other time.

During the maintenance phase, Justin was still given verbal praise when his ratings matched that of the teacher but was not earning trips to McDonald's. Such trips were now random and not always linked to his performance in school. Thus, he had to do well in school to go to McDonalds (reward), but he was not rewarded for not doing well in school (being off-task). Data are presented in Figure 12.9 for the three periods of this program; the number of sessions appears at the bottom. Justin's rating agreement with the teacher varied from 20 percent in baseline to 95 percent during the intervention phase and 83 percent during maintenance. The form used in the program for each work period is shown in Figure 12.10.

(continued)

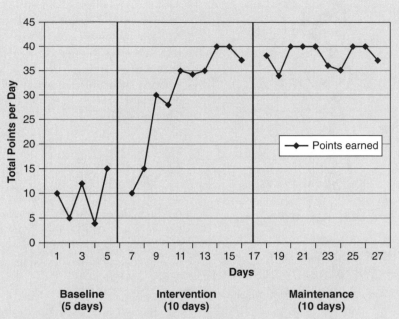

FIGURE 12.9   Justin's performance: points for being on task.

Name _____   Class _____

Put a plus (+) when on-task and a minus (–) when off-task for each period assessed.

1. _____   11. _____
2. _____   12. _____
3. _____   13. _____
4. _____   14. _____
5. _____   15. _____
6. _____   16. _____
7. _____   17. _____
8. _____   18. _____
9. _____   19. _____
10. _____   20. _____

FIGURE 12.10   A self-monitoring form.

Justin's on-task behavior improved significantly. In a follow-up assessment, he was found to have maintained his ability to stay on-task as he completed 90 percent of his work and his teacher's rating was at an average of 36 over a 3-day period. Also, Justin's work improved in other areas as well as he learned to stay on-task during his work in other subject areas. Because of his LD in reading, he did require special remedial tutoring in that area, and he continued to have problems with reading assignments. This self-monitoring procedure used with Justin could have been used with the whole class and other target behaviors could be selected to monitor.

**BY THE TIME I THINK ABOUT WHAT
I SHOULDN'T DO – I'VE ALREADY DONE IT !**

Reprinted by permission of Wiley/Jossey-Bass (Flick, 1998b)

IMPULSIVITY

Impulsivity is often used interchangeably with other descriptive terms such as "lack of self-control" or "behavioral disinhibition." They all generally imply acting without thinking. There are many possible situational contexts related to impulsivity in children, which vary in severity and in the nature of consequences. For example, the impulsive child might blurt out answers or talk without permission. This might only be considered annoying and may disturb the class to a mild or moderate degree. On the other hand, when impulsivity is combined with other problems such as aggression or depression, the results may have dire consequences. Acting-out aggression with impulsivity may create many disruptive situations in and outside of the classroom (Dupaul & Stoner, 2003). Likewise, when impulsivity is combined with depression, consequences may cause great concern for self-harm.

There may be different forms of impulsivity (Flick, 2000. According to Robin (1998), it is possible to divide impulsivity into three areas: (1) *behavioral impulsivity* (i.e., poor judgment and acting rashly), (2) *cognitive impulsivity* (i.e., sloppily rushing through academic tasks

with careless mistakes), and (3) *emotional impulsivity* (temper control problems and emotional overreactions). At present, however, there are no good data on the pattern of these subtypes of impulsivity across various disorders, the nature of developmental factors, nor whether such a breakdown would predict different outcomes for various disorders and, most importantly, whether each subtype would be sensitive to treatment effects. Nevertheless, such a breakdown appears heuristically useful. A copy of the impulsivity scale (Flick, 2000) appears in Appendix E.

There appears to be some relationship among measures of impulsivity across situations, yet this has not been determined with research support. Classroom teachers will still benefit from dealing with the most frequent expressions of impulsivity. Therefore, the following general steps may be used to control blurting out (Flick, 1998b):

1. Review and post rules regarding raising one's hand and being called on to obtain permissions (e.g., to answer a question, get assistance, go to the bathroom). In addition to posting written rules or verbalizing them, you may tape a card on the child's desk depicting the rule. Examples of picture cards that can be used to demonstrate rules are found in Appendix D.

2. Ignore students who blurt out answers and fail to raise their hands.

3. Praise students who do raise their hands, and use them as models. Remember, never compare one student with another; simply praise the one who does the right thing: "Charles, you followed the rule and raised your hand to answer—very good. Now what is . . .?"

4. When children who have blurted out before do the right thing, direct attention to them immediately.

5. Monitor the number of times each day that the child raises his or her hand to answer. A simple count may be kept from week to week. The count from the first week before the problem is addressed is used as the baseline. The intervention may start in the second week. Reward weekly improvement over each child's baseline levels and then over the previous week's performance. You can also tape a card on the child's desk with a

picture of a student raising her hand. Individual cards illustrating various rules are shown in Appendix D. In addition to counting the number of appropriate behaviors, give verbal praise along with some back-up reward when a specific goal is reached.

As with most behavioral programs, a combination of (1) ignoring blurting out (extinction), and (2) positive reinforcement for the appropriate response (i.e., raising hand to answer) will result in a more powerful behavior change program. If this response is poorly developed in the child's behavioral repertoire, then the teacher may model the correct response for answering questions. This would be very important, especially for younger children who may have had more limited experience with this procedure. Remember that a nonverbal modeling of a behavior can have a more powerful influence on a student's behavior.

In situations where excess talking is "against the rule," the student may be exhibiting a combination of (1) lack of self-control, and (2) a need to engage in excess vocal-motor activity. Some aspects of this impulsive behavior is also typical of hyperactivity. Many of the same suggestions may apply to excessive *talking*.

The following guidelines may be useful in dealing with vocal-motor hyperactivity:

1. Review the rules about which situations and which times are be appropriate for talking.

2. Ignore talking that is minimal.

3. Praise and give attention to those students who remain quiet at the appropriate time.

4. When students remain quiet in those situations where they would have talked before, immediately point out this behavior change and the student.

5. Ask the identified child or another student, "What is it that you should be doing now?" Reinforce all correct answers.

6. Establish a random variable schedule of recording/monitoring whether or not the child was talking during the recording interval. This is preferable to a predictable recording schedule, which allows children to know when they are being recorded and thus inhibits talking. If every incident of talking is noted, the student may actually enjoy receiving attention and would thus be reinforced by the teacher's attention.

Like other behavior problems, excess talking may possibly reflect some academic problem, and students who have difficulty with some academic material may talk to escape from or avoid doing a task. A teacher who sends such a child out of the room is doing exactly what that child desires—complete avoidance of the difficult material, even on a temporary basis. While excess talking may reflect an underlying physiological need such as vocal-motor stimulation or a focus of neurologically based hyperactivity, a learned component will be added after the repeated experience of being sent out of the room. Because of this, it is important for the teacher to obtain a functional behavioral assessment for any of the behavior problems that are incorporated in a behavioral intervention plan.

Dixon and Cummings (2001) used a progressive-delay of reinforcement schedule to increase self-control and decrease disruptive behavior in children with autism. When initially given a choice between an immediate smaller reinforcer and a larger delayed reinforcer, all children chose the smaller (immediate) reinforcer. When access to the larger reinforcer required either no activity or engaging in a concurrent task during the delay, all children demonstrated self-control; disruptive behavior decreased during delays that required a concurrent task compared to sessions without an activity requirement. Similar findings were reported by Vollmer and colleagues (1999), who also found that self-control was displayed when the delay of reinforcement was signaled (with a hand gesture or timer). This issue has also been discussed in detail by Luman, Oosterlaan, and Sergeant (2005).

In a study by Neef and colleagues (2005), children with ADHD were most influenced by the immediacy and quality of a reinforcer; least by its rate and effort—suggesting impulsivity. Children of typical development (a non-ADHD group) were most influenced only by the quality of the reinforcer; the influence of immediacy (relative to other factors) was not statistically significant.

**Case
Study**

Case 11: Impulsivity

Ms. Chin is generally considered to be a good teacher. Her second-grade classroom is well organized, and she has posted just a few class rules that are important. Most children know these rules because they are reviewed daily. Two 8-year-old students in the class—Brian, who is white, and DeMarcus, who is African American—routinely have trouble with the "raising your hand to answer" rule. Although they know the rules, they blurt out answers, typically in math class. Brian and DeMarcus have both been diagnosed with ADHD and are on medication. Both boys also show much evidence of hyperactive behavior: tapping their pencils, humming, walking around the room, talking to other students, and sometimes tapping others on the shoulder or head. Their classmates have been clearly annoyed, and some have reacted aggressively to these annoyances.

One problematic behavior for Ms. Chin is that both boys have trouble with the rule "raise your hand to ask or answer questions." They blurt out answers and act very competitively, trying to be the first one to get the correct answer. Both boys are getting C grades in math, and both scored within the average range with regard to math facts. They basically know the material but they just respond impulsively and cannot follow that one rule.

Ms. Chin has decided to use a behavioral intervention with both boys. She identified the target behavior—*raise your hand to answer*—and proceeded to the first step—getting baseline data during the 30-minute period each day that was devoted to "math facts." It was during this time that impulsive behaviors would be counted. Thus, both boys were subjected to a review of the rule prior to each 30-minute session where behaviors were to be counted. The results of the baseline data appear in Figures 12.11 and 12.12. Data were obtained for 1 week; Brian averaged 5.4 for raising his hand while DeMarcus averaged 7.4. The number of math facts reviewed was kept constant—that is, Ms. Chin asked 50 math fact questions each day.

The intervention would consist of two parts: (1) a cue or visual reminder of the rule, and (2) reinforcement of correct responses. A response was considered correct when the student raised his hand to answer without blurting out. This was always reviewed prior to the 30-minute session. The cue or visual reminder

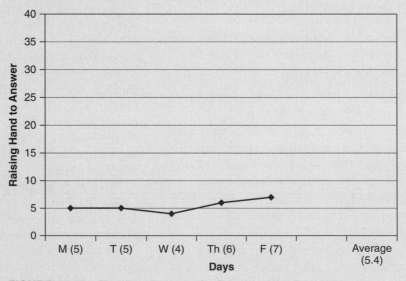

FIGURE 12.11   First baseline data for Brian—raising hand to answer.

(continued)

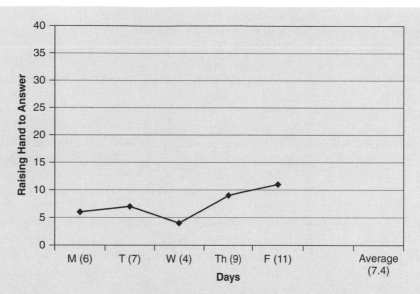

FIGURE 12.12 First baseline data for DeMarcus—raising hand to answer.

was a cartoonlike picture of a boy raising his hand. This picture was attached to a stick so that it could be easily held up before each question. Both boys sat in the front row but apart from each other.

A differential reinforcement of lower rates of responding (DR-LR) was used for the second part of the reinforcement. The targets were 10 percent below baseline data. In the beginning, this was considered to be 10 percent below the average determined at baseline. Each student knew his own target behavior each day. When a student reached the target behavior, he was given a mark on a card that was taped to his desk. He was also given verbal praise at that point by Ms. Chin: "Very good, Brian! You raised your hand and will get a mark now." Figures 12.13 and 12.14 show the accumulation of points for each boy. Brian averaged 10.6 (exceeding the criterion target), while DeMarcus averaged 29.7 during the intervention phase.

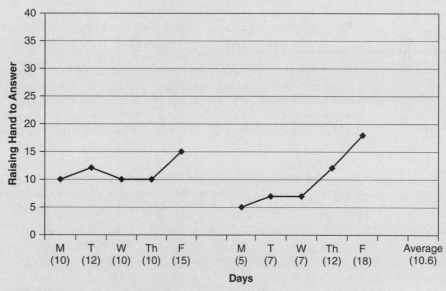

FIGURE 12.13 Intervention data for Brian—raising hand to answer using DR-LR at 10% below the last target.

(continued)

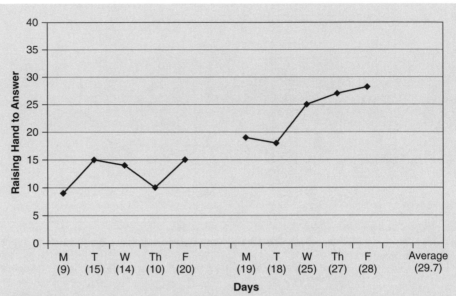

FIGURE 12.14 Intervention data for DeMarcus—raising hand to answer using DR-LR at 10% below the last target.

Both boys had preselected some backup reinforcers—either some tangible rewards such as a small toy car or extra computer time—to get when they each accumulated a sufficient number of points. When both boys accumulated a target number of marks, the class would have a popcorn party. The experimental period lasted for 2 weeks.

In addition to making progress, each boy showed some improvements in other areas as well. For example, the amount of time on-task, completion of work, and in-seat behavior all improved although these were not officially monitored. After completing the intervention, each boy seemed to maintain his appropriate behaviors with continued verbal praise. There were some minor increases in blurting out, but overall their problem was much improved. Ms. Chin has been quite satisfied with the results and intends to continue the use of verbal praise for correct behavior (i.e., following the rule) and also will periodically use the visual reminder. Both Brian and DeMarcus are satisfied with their newly developed behavior, which has generalized to other subject areas such as reading.

At the end of this intervention, Ms. Chin recorded a second baseline to see how much had changed. Figures 12.15 and 12.16 illustrate the following data: While Brian improved some (postintervention average = 6.7), DeMarcus improved more (postintervention average = 8.0), compared to the first baseline.

(continued)

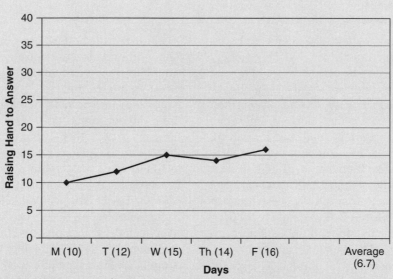

FIGURE 12.15   Second baseline data for Brian—raising hand to answer.

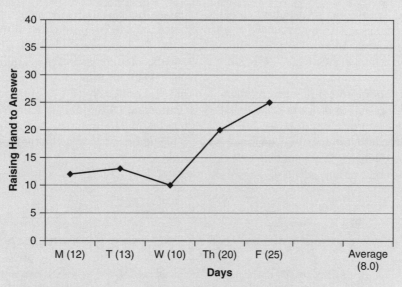

FIGURE 12.16   Second baseline data for DeMarcus—raising hand to answer.

NONCOMPLIANCE

Noncompliance occurs, when the child fails to comply or follow directions given by the teacher. *Compliance* is a key goal of healthy early child development and is linked to children's social and emotional competence (Hamre & Pianta, 2001). Compliance that is invariant is neither expected nor desired, and some noncompliance is therefore normal and may even promote the development of autonomy and prosocial independence (Boyd & Richardson, 1985). Using direct observation, studies across 12 different cultures showed that compliance to parental requests ranged from 72 percent for children 2–3 years old to 79 percent for children 4–5 years old, and up to 82 percent for children 6–8 years old (Weiss, Caspe, & Lopez, 2006). However, excessive noncompliance appears as the most frequent reason for psychiatric referral of young children (Forehand & McMahon, 1981). Longitudinal investigations showed a progression from noncompliance to tantrums to physical attacks on up to stealing and conduct problems (Chamberlain & Patterson, 1995). Such data suggest that excessive noncompliance can be a precursor to more serious behavior problems (Drabick, Strassberg, & Kees, 2001; Kalb & Loeber, 2003).

Teachers and parents more frequently complain about what some children fail to do rather than what they do. Although some of these children are bright, they come to class unprepared, often resist doing homework, and make excuses such as, "I thought that assignment was due next Monday." Many of these children promise to "do better" but continue to noncomply. Anger often underlies oppositional behavior, and noncompliance over assignments, chores (at home), and direct requests suggest a passive form of anger. Noncompliant students are clearly distinct from children who do "forget" or become confused over instructions, fail to write them down, or just misinterpret them. Patterson and Guillon (1968), among the earliest behaviorists to work with children and families, noted that noncompliance was an underlying problem that must be addressed in working with difficult to manage children.

Research with aggressive children and children seen in clinics has emphasized the dysfunctional nature of noncompliance (Patterson, 1982). Excessive noncompliance is a frequently encountered conduct problem and a prime reason for early psychiatric referral of young children (Kalb & Loeber, 2003; McMahon & Forehand, 2003). Patterson (1982) has conceptualized noncompliance as a coercive response that is maintained by parental mismanagement of their child's behavior. He proposed that the early appearance of noncompliance puts children at risk for a series of events, including coercive family interactions, poor peer relations, impaired academic performance, possible delinquency, and more problems in later life (Patterson, DeBaryshe, & Ramsey, 1989). According to his view at that time, when noncompliance is addressed, it facilitates working with other aspects of behavior disorders.

Case Study

Case 12: Noncompliance to Requests in an Elementary School Student

Tommy is a 7-year-old child who frequently ignores requests and directions. His passive-aggressive, oppositional behavior makes it difficult to maintain continuity in teaching. A functional behavioral assessment and review of academic records indicates that (1) Tommy does not lack the ability to perform the tasks requested, and (2) his resistance does not appear to be an attempt to escape or avoid tasks. He does not seem to respond well to directions that prompt cognitive mediation ("What are you supposed to be doing now?" or "What did I just ask you to do?") Generally, Tommy was able to answer most of these questions—however, he did appear to enjoy the manipulate control inherent in these situations as well as some of the attention received as a result of noncompliance (i.e., not doing what he was supposed to be doing).

(continued)

Positive responses of children like Tommy who exhibit challenging oppositional behavior may be increased by making easily achievable, high-probability requests initially. Before making a request that Tommy has been known to ignore or that has caused him to act out, his teacher decided to make high-probability requests and give positive reinforcement after each one. For example, Tommy was asked to take something to the office for his teacher. Upon his return, she praised him immediately: "I'm glad I can count on you to take care of important matters." This initiated the momentum of positive behavior. Five seconds after giving the positive reinforcement (praise) for the last high-probability request, his teacher made a low-probability request. If Tommy did not comply, she gave him another higher-probability request rather than a reprimand.

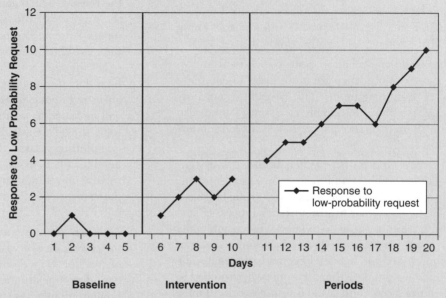

FIGURE 12.17   A graph showing Tommy's response to requests.

During days 1–4, Tommy's responses to low-probability requests were consistently low. On days 6–10, he showed a steady increase in positive responses to low-probability requests when these came after a high-probability request. Tommy's response to low-probability requests steadily increased on days 11–20 to a point of more than 80 percent compliance.

Source: Information from http://special.edschool.virginia.edu/information/ints/disrupt.html.

Most parents and teachers have found that ignoring, pleading, and attempts at negotiations do not work; get-tough approaches and physical discipline may only make the problems worse. While behavioral interventions are essential to changing noncompliance, they are not the only tools available to parents and teachers. Some of the following approaches can be used:

1. *Encourage assertiveness:* For example, when a difficult assignment must be completed within a limited amount of time, some students will comment on the difficulty and ask for extended time. A teacher may praise such students for being assertive as a model for other students.

2. *Offer choices:* When students can chose from two or three options, they are more likely to complete the chosen assignment. This procedure not only empowers them in making decisions, it may also allow them to choose a topic that holds more interest for them.

3. *Structure homework:* When homework assignments are complex and may require a comprehensive approach in dealing with problematic behavior, it will be important to structure this process (Flick, 2001). Parents will need to know what assignments are given, teachers will need to know that the assignments got home along with the materials needed to complete them. Parents will also need to structure a time and place for homework. Finally, completed assignments will need to be checked by the teacher. This structure must be developed and reinforced at every step until homework becomes an automatic process (Flick, 2001).

4. *Adjust expectations:* If a parent or teacher expects too much of the child, there may be resistance to work completion. Many students will avoid or simply fail to do some tasks, saying that there is too much work or it is too difficult, Giving more reasonable work assignments and reinforcing their completion can be helpful.

5. *Reinforce compliance:* There are three points at which reinforcement may be given: (a) when the child begins the task, (b) while the child is working on a task, and (c) when the child completes the task. This process is most effective when all three

events are reinforced. A student may signal avoidance of a task when he gets up to sharpen a pencil each day that a specific task is scheduled. He may even talk, disturb others, and eventually be sent out to the office, all of which reinforces exactly what he desires—task avoidance. The teacher may adjust the task difficulty and announce that all students who are "caught" working on the assigned task when a bell rings will earn a computer break. Most likely the child will be in his seat working to earn the reward. The teacher may also keep a record of the number of times a child complies on assignments. After recording a week of baseline information, the child may be told that he will first earn a ticket for each compliance. After 1 week, this may be reduced to getting a ticket every other compliance, and then every third time. In other words, he will be asked to perform the assignments and get fewer tickets. Basically, as the child gets better at completing tasks, fewer reinforcements are needed. Of course, tickets (rewarding in themselves) may sometimes be traded for some other desirable reward such as no homework or computer time.

6. *Reinforce improvement:* A variation of reinforcing compliance, it will be important for any parent or teacher to give positive feedback when a child complies in a situation where there was previous noncompliance. Any improvement in compliance includes a change in frequency of compliance or, as in the latter case, compliance is substituted for a prior noncompliance (i.e., a change in compliance). Nordquist and McEnoy (1983) used a combination of differential attention (where attention was given to compliance and time-out was given for noncompliance) in two 4-year-olds who were highly oppositional to instructions (from parents, teachers, and other service personnel). More recently, this approach was supported by McNeill and colleagues (2002).

7. *Repeated request:* A request may be repeated over and over until that request is recognized and completed by the student. It is a variant of the "broken record" procedure used to deny a request by the student. In this case, a positive

request is made by the teacher until compliance is achieved.

8. *High probability requests:* There are some requests that may carry a high probability of compliance, even in a child who is predominately noncompliant to most requests. For example, it would be most unlikely for a child to refuse to go get a homework pass or computer time so that the parent or teacher may reward him. However, young children may require use of an edible reinforcer. Similarly, it may be easy for a teacher to get compliance on a simple task: "Go get that roll of tickets so

Case Study

Case 13: PDD with Multiple Challenging Behaviors

Brittany is a 10-year-old girl who has been diagnosed with Pervasive Developmental Disorder (PDD). Her cognitive and language skills are moderately developed but her functional use of language and social skills is significantly impaired. She shows a high rate of challenging behavior, including hitting, kicking, swearing, and throwing objects. She attends a child care program 1 hour before school and 2 hours after school every day. Problem behavior has been noted during this school program as well as on the bus ride. Several previous punishment/reward programs were unsuccessful, and she has received several bus citations threatening her bus-riding privileges.

Intervention began in the school environment, but it was clear that multiple interventions (that would also include the bus driver) would be needed. A functional behavioral assessment revealed that the frequency of Brittany's problem behavior increased when she was asked to stop engaging in a fun activity to perform a task. Also, her running away and hitting others (even during group time or play) was thought to represent an attempt to gain attention. Overall, Brittany's problem behavior appeared to be maintained by *attention* and *access to preferred activities.*

Typically, Brittany developed problem behavior during group activities where she was required to wait and attend to directions and in the presence of new task demands. She performed best when there was a structured schedule and when school staff sat next to her. The conclusion was that Brittany engaged in problem behavior (1) to gain attention from adults, (2) to gain access to preferred activities that were not provided as a choice, and (3) to escape tasks that were not part of the routine.

The first intervention was to reduce the frequency of Brittany's swearing and aggression. However, her communication problems also appeared to represent a primary reason for many of these behaviors. Thus, an alternative communication system was devised using single line drawings (e.g., a figure drawing, or house tree person), to request items or express feelings. A time-out component was also added to the communication program, even though it would be only a small part of this plan. Daily 1-hour interventions were established to help Brittany acquire communication, choice making, leisure, and conversational skills. Before being prompted to choose an activity, she was asked to first state two rules related to (1) friendly talking, and (2) keeping hands and feet to self to maintain access to the activity. Britany was then asked whether she wished for the staff member to stay and talk or to go. A timer was set for 3 minutes. When it rang, she was asked whether she wanted to continue or to choose a new activity. If there was any problem behavior, the activity was stopped and Brittany was placed in time-out for 1 to 3 minutes. A staff member tightly held Brittany's arms to her side to keep her in time-out but provided no other attention. As Brittany's communication skills improved, the need to hold her in time-out decreased, and she no longer tried to escape. At the end of the time-out, she was allowed to return to pick another activity. Again, she was to rehearse the two rules before gaining access to her choice.

(continued)

During the first week, the time-out was needed 10 times during each 1-hour session. By the second week, this dropped to three to five times per 1-hour session. By the third week, time-out was not needed. This was maintained for the rest of the intervention. After about 2 months, some academic tasks were added to her choices. When she worked on an academic task, she was prompted to either touch the "I'm done" icon or just say "I'm done" whenever she wished to take a break or engage in a fun activity of her choice. To improve social skills, conversation scripts were developed by Brittany's mother, who provided details of activities such as shopping or trips to a restaurant in which Brittany had participated outside of school. Brittany was first asked questions while she engaged in preferred activities. After 2 months of intervention, the rate of Brittany's problem behavior decreased from an average of 60 occurrences per hour to an average of 3 per hour. Communication skills improved and she began to initiate choice making. She would then use the timer and set it to control her interactions, an important component in her improved behavior.

After several months of intervention, it was necessary to train others (such as aides, or her parents) to work with Brittany during the day rather than just during the 1 hour of the school day and to involve more school staff in her treatment program. Also, Brittany's mother used a modified procedure that included preferred home activities such as watching videotapes, cooking projects, and water play. Sessions were shortened to 15 minutes per day but incorporated the same demands, choice making, and consequences for problem behavior that were used at school. The teacher developed conversational scripts about preferred activities similar to the ones that were developed by Brittany's mother for use at school. Even the bus driver could be involved and become familiar with the use of Brittany's communication system or a web board system as described by Hong & Jun (2004).

In general, this case demonstrated some important principles. First, it is essential to be persistent. If something doesn't work at first, try something else. Second, it demonstrates that many people need to be involved in the child's program so that others use the same procedure. The child will learn faster when all involved (e.g., teachers and parents) use the same system. Third, there is often a need for several behavioral strategies and the use of several different components (e.g., figure drawings, time-out, stories, pictures, etc.).

Case Study

Case 14: Group Program for Dylan, Chris, and Roger

Dylan, Chris, and Roger are three 8-year-old boys with problem behaviors who are creating most of the disturbances in Ms. X's third-grade class. Dylan has the most difficulty with anger, engaging in frequent name calling, making disruptive noises, and occasionally displaying a full temper tantrum. Chris has difficulty raising his hand to answer questions, and often blurts out answers, talks loudly, and laughs inappropriately with little control. Roger also has trouble with self-control and often yells out answers, makes inappropriate noises, and hits others.

A functional behavioral assessment for each boy revealed that some of these disruptive behaviors were related to the inability of all three boys to perform or have difficulty doing assigned tasks. Most of the tasks that precipitated disruptive behaviors involved lengthy written assignments. In fact, some of the boys had already learned how to get out of doing the tasks by being sent to the office for

(continued)

inappropriate aggressive behavior. While some adjustments in assignment expectations were made, acting-out behaviors were reduced just slightly. It was as if they had developed a life of their own.

Two behavioral interventions have been initiated on an individual and a group basis:

1. All temper tantrums are ignored by the teacher, and the class has been instructed to ignore any temper outbursts. When Dylan, Chris, or Roger exhibit self-control (i.e., stop the tantrum) or cope with a situation differently (i.e., do not show a tantrum in a situation where tantrums were previously shown) then verbal praise and recognition are given.
2. Individual point systems have been established for Dylan, Chris, and Roger. Dylan receives points for talking to others appropriately, remaining quiet during work activity, and coping with frustration without temper outbursts. He loses points for name calling, making noises, and temper outbursts. After receiving a specified number of points, he may choose a small toy from the reward menu. Chris receives points for raising his hand to answer questions, talking in an appropriate voice, and controlling laughter; he loses points for the opposite inappropriate behaviors. Like Dylan, he can choose a small toy with a specified number of points. Roger receives points for raising his hand, remaining quiet, and controlling aggression; he loses points for his inappropriate behaviors. After accumulating a specified number of points, he can select a small toy.

It is important to remember that the one major criterion in setting up such programs is that they be successful. At first, there must be liberal distribution of points and a conservative fine (loss of points) system. A simple signal system is used to assign (+) or (−) points that convey information on the child's behavior that is (1) immediate, (2) least intrusive on others, and (3) least embarrassing. Ms. X keeps the record at her desk. There are daily systems at first; later, points are exchanged every 2 days, then only once per week. However, praise is also delivered along with each positive reinforcement (point) and when the points are exchanged for a toy. During the day, verbal praise may also be given to let the three boys know how they are doing. Providing such praise also serves as a model for other students regarding what appropriate behaviors pay off. In general, a positive approach to managing behavior is emphasized. Based on the total net points earned by all three boys, group reinforcement for the entire class is also made available. The three boys are thus able to earn special privileges for their classmates through their positive behavior. This group program has several benefits:

1. It encourages classmates to ignore inappropriate behaviors of the identified boys.
2. It allows classmates to encourage and help the identified boys to engage in more appropriate behaviors.
3. It improves the acceptance and peer status of the boys with a history of acting-out behaviors.
4. It generally enhances the personal self-concept of the identified boys.

I can give one to you to place in the jar that will be used to pick a winner of Pokeman cards."

Many *oppositional behaviors* are learned and developed very early within parent–child interactions. Such behaviors must also be addressed through parent training, as well as in-school programs in order to be maximally effective.

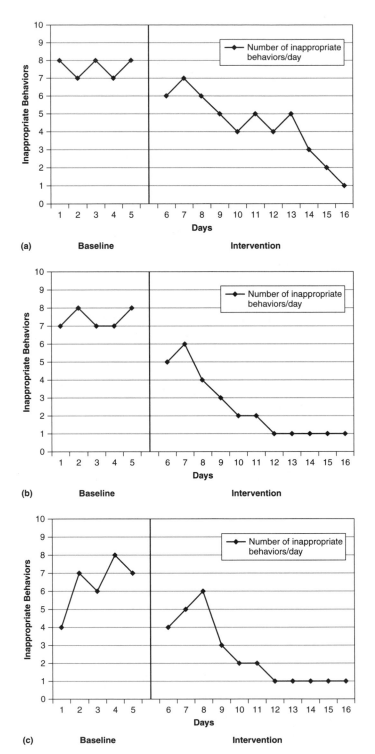

FIGURE 12.18 Data plates for three problem behaviors: (a) Dylan's name calling, (b) Chris's yelling out, and (c) Roger's inappropriate noises. Note that there is a dramatic reduction following each of the interventions. It is possible to plot each behavior over time to see the rate of improvement for each boy.

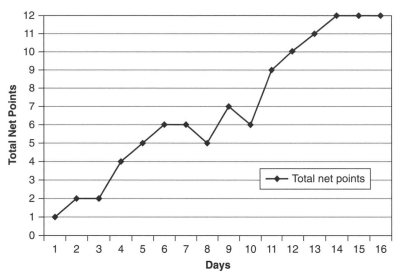

FIGURE 12.19   Plotting the improvement of total net points for Dylan, Chris, and Roger over a period of time.

INAPPROPRIATE VERBALIZATIONS

Inappropriate verbalizations are a category of problem behaviors that includes cursing, gestures, disrespectful talk, name-calling, and any other inappropriate verbalizations directed toward peers, teachers, or other adults. It is a common problem reported by many teachers and is addressed now using a self-monitoring approach.

Case Study

Case 15: A Self-Monitoring, Self-Management Approach

Chris is a 14-year-old boy who has been diagnosed with conduct disorder. He engages in a high frequency of obscenities, talking in a disrespectful manner, and making obscene gestures. Because these behaviors are becoming more frequent, he has been referred for a behavioral intervention that is based on a self-monitoring, self-management approach.

Chris receives reinforcements for making appropriate verbalizations, including any positive response to directions or conversations where positive words or appropriate tone of voice and facial expression are exhibited. During baseline, episodes of these appropriate verbalizations were counted by the teacher with a counter recorder that clicks each time it is pressed. Events were recorded during random 15-minute periods each day in the classroom, lunchroom, and gym as well as and during recess. Each day, there were ten 15-minute periods that contributed to Chris's score.

During intervention, Chris was instructed to make a mark on a card each time he engaged in an appropriate verbalization. An example is shown in Figure 12.20. After these verbalizations were noted, a review was conducted each morning to determine how familiar Chris was with the appropriate verbalizations. Each one remembered correctly received verbal praise. He was then given the card. At the same time, either the teacher or an aide tallied the number of appropriate verbalizations that occured during each 15-minute recording period. Chris was not directly aware of when these random periods occurred—only that there were 10 15-minute periods each day. At the end of the

(continued)

| Name | | | | | | | Date | | |

Target behaviors: (a) positive response to directions, (b) positive words used in conversation, (c) appropriate tone of voice, (d) appropriate facial expression.

(1)	(2)	(3)	(4)	(5)	(6)	(7)	(8)	(9)	(10)
TOTALS									

FIGURE 12.20   Data recording card.
The recording card used by Chris to show each time he engaged in one of the target behaviors. He was given examples of each and might be asked to role-play (act out) each one. Correct role-plays were praised; incorrect ones received comments and appropriate ones were modeled.

day, if there was 90 percent or better agreement between his recordings and those of the aide, he was allowed to leave school 5 minutes earlier than normal. Each day, his self-monitorings were recorded and compared with the baseline. The results are shown in Figure 12.21.

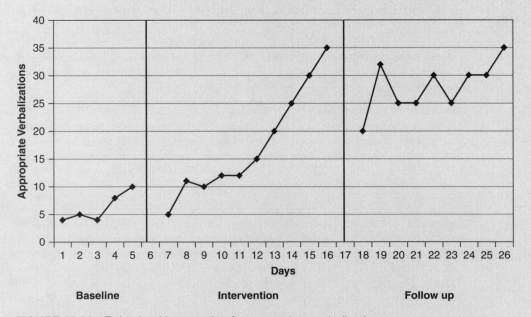

FIGURE 12.21   Behavioral intervention for appropriate verbalization.

(continued)

During intervention, Chris received a no-homework pass when his total number of appropriate verbalizations exceeded the previous day by 5 points. His performance was plotted on a graph, and he was given verbal praise for success (e.g., "You really did well today! You've exceeded your previous day's points by 5 points—Congratulations! You get a homework pass for one subject."). After 2 weeks of intervention, Chris showed success on 7 out of 10 days (see follow-up).

During the follow-up maintenance phase, Chris continued to receive verbal praise, but he no longer earned the homework pass. On 3 out of 5 days, his performance equaled that of his best performance during the intervention phase. Overall, his teacher commented that the program has been a success and Chris continues to give appropriate verbalizations, which have been maintained with verbal praise by the teacher.

Case Study

Case 16: Summary of FBA and BIP Procedures

John is a 10-year-old ED student who has problems fighting with other students, primarily during morning sessions that involve partner activity. Fighting is more likely to occur when his attempts to gain teacher attention fail. However, fighting also occurs when John is provoked by his peers, and it seems to serve the function of his need to control his peers. Although there is a hierarchy of disciplinary actions in place of deal with such behaviors, behavioral interventions are being used to avoid moving up to suspension, and reduce further escalation of John's problems.

Two functions are attributed to John's behavior:

1. *Attention seeking:* John is frustrated when the teacher does not pay attention to him. Frustration leads to anger and increases the likelihood of a fight. Fighting then brings about attention, albeit attention for his inappropriate behavior.

2. *Needing to control peers:* This need seems directly related to John's deficit in social skills, especially his ability to work cooperatively with others.

The following intervention strategies are being developed:

1. Focus attention on John prior to his becoming emotionally upset. This may help to clarify any problems with the work or to specify the role of each student in their cooperative effort.

2. Develop a signal that John can give if there is a misunderstanding or if there is some question about the work assigned. This signal for John may be as simple as raising his hand to get the teacher's attention.

3. Provide John with training in social skills, including a special emphasis on interactive cooperative behavior.

4. Use a token (point) system to monitor John on the following behaviors: (a) following instructions, (b) completing assignments, (c) requesting assistance, and (d) cooperating with peers. This behavioral program will have a positive orientation, and John will work to earn additional computer time.

As indicated by the plots in Figure 12.22, John has shown significant improvement in all positive appropriate behaviors. His episodes of verbal aggression have also significantly decreased. Over the course of 2 weeks, John's verbal aggression has decreased from a baseline average of about four

(continued)

(a) Baseline

Behavior	Points	M	T	W	Th	F	Total
Follow instructions	1	//	/	///	/	/	8
Complete assignments	1	/		/		/	3
Request assistance	1	/		/	//		4
Cooperate with peers	1	/	//	/	/	///	8
Total		5	3	6	4	5	

(b) Sample Token (Point) System

Behavior	Points	M	T	W	Th	F	Total
Follow instructions	1	/////	///	////////	////	/////////	29
Complete assignments	1	//	///	/	//	////	12
Request assistance	1	//	//	/	/////	//	12
Cooperate with peers	1	/////	///// ///	///	////////	////	25
Total		14	13	13	19	19	

FIGURE 12.22 Baseline and sample token system.

outbursts during baseline to an average of about three outbursts during the first week, and about one during the second week. The program will continue until the verbal outbursts are down to zero. During this time, John will do the following:

1. Continue in the social skills program.

2. Work with those students who serve as excellent models and are instructed to withdraw attention from John when he escalates emotional behavior.

3. Continue to signal the teacher when there are questions about the work or when some difficulty is encountered.

SUMMARY

This chapter focuses on specific interventions for children with behavior problems such as aggression, social skill problems, inattention, impulsivity, noncompliance, and inappropriate verbalizations. The use of self-monitoring is discussed. Physical restraint is also explored as a consequence for physically dangerous behavior. Lastly, a complete case study concerning a 10-year-old student, who had problems fighting, was presented.

DISCUSSION QUESTIONS

1. What are the four types of aggression? Explain each.
2. Explain two basic things that teachers should not do when confronting a student who is "out of control."
3. When should teachers use physical restraint?
4. What are the risks in using physical restraint?
5. What are the dynamics involved in passive-aggressive behavior?
6. How would you develop cooperation and sharing among classmates?
7. How would you train an older child to improve attentional skills?
8. How would you improve a child's compliance with your requests (i.e., following directions)?
9. Explain why self-monitoring is useful.
10. What are the different forms of impulsivity? Explain each.
11. How would you train students to raise their hands to answer questions, rather than blurting out?
12. Discuss the work of Gerald Patterson, one of the earliest behaviorists. Why was this work important? What was his philosophy?
13. When a child is severely noncompliant, what can the teacher do?
14. Why should teachers focus on improvement?
15. Can self-monitoring be used to deal with inappropriate verbalizations? Explain.

CHAPTER 13

Teaching Students with Behavior Disorders

Overview

- No Child Left Behind
- Scientifically based instruction
- What is scientifically based research?
- What works in classroom instruction?
- Curriculum-based assessments
- Effective practice to educate EBD students
- Opportunities to respond
- Self-monitoring for transitions
- Reducing problem behavior through academic management
- The Morningside Model

Case History

Crystal is a 7-year-old first grader in an EBD class. She shows a number of problem behaviors, including aggression when asked to do an assignment and playing with work materials, especially her papers, which she either tears up or crumples, and pencils. Despite these problems, she is generally attentive and shows appropriate behavior during discussion groups or when she can participate in hands-on learning. Crystal is being raised by her grandparents and reportedly does various simple chores around the house. However, in class, she is disruptive and frequently off-task, and she usually tries to destroy her meager work. *What would you do?*

Students with emotional and behavior disorders present both behavior problems and achievement problems in school, because behavior problems interfere with academic achievement (Nelson, Benner, Lane, & Smith, 2004; Severson & Walker, 2002). Such students have lower graduation rates and are less likely to pursue further education (Kauffman, 2001). Spencer, Scruggs, and Mastropieri (2003) reported that a sample of second-graders functioned well below normal in vocabulary, listening comprehension, spelling, social studies, and science, and had academic deficits in all areas. Anderson and colleagues (2001) also found reading achievement scores of EBD students did not improve over time when compared with LD students. Thus, EBD may have more of an adverse effect on academic achievement than does LD.

The rates of academic achievement deficits of EBD students have been found to range from 25 to 97 percent (Mattison, Hooper, & Glassberg, 2002). Greenbaum and colleagues (1996) found the percentage of EBD students (ages 12–14) performing below grade level was 97 percent. It is noteworthy that many researchers used grade equivalent scores from grade-level group administered tests as indices for determining academic achievement deficits (Nelson, Benner, & Gonzales, 2004). The ordinal nature of such scores would make it problematic to use them as indicators of performance (Martella, Nelson, & Marchand-Martella, 2003), and especially for use of grade-level, group-administered achievement tests.

When Greenbaum and colleagues (1996) followed a group of students over time, the percentage of those reading below grade level on first assessment (ages 8–11), 4 years later (ages 12–14), and 7 years after intake (ages 15–18) was 54 percent, 83 percent, and 85 percent, respectively. For math, the percentages were 93 percent, 97 percent, and 94 percent, respectively. Mattison and colleagues (2002) found that the rates of academic achievement deficits were initially 64 percent and 62 percent (average age 11.5 years) 3 years later for EBD students. In general, these rates either remained stable or got worse over time. Mattison and colleagues (2002) found that conduct disorder (CD) and oppositional defiant disorder (ODD), based on DSM-III diagnoses, were negatively related to academic achievement (i.e., the more CD/ODD present, the lower the achievements). Likewise, Abikoff and colleagues (2002) found that comorbid ADHD and disruptive behavior

disorders were more closely related to academic achievement deficits than other psychiatric disorders alone or in combination in a multimodal treatment study.

A cross-sectional study of a random sample of 155 kindergarten through twelfth-grade students with EBD was conducted by Nelson, Benner, Lane, and Smith (2004). Using standardized scores from individually administered achievement tests, this study provides a more accurate estimate of academic achievement of EBD students across content areas and ages, when compared with other research that uses grade equivalent scores from grade-level, group-administered achievement tests.

•••

Dimensional classification: A measure of the degree to which children exhibit particular behavioral symptoms on a continuum. Dimensional classification assumes that a number of behavioral traits exist and that all children possess them to a degree (Mash & Wolfe, 1999). In contrast to psychiatric classification, dimensional classifications are more a judgment and are based on empirically derived categories (Kauffman, 2001).

•••

Using a dimensional classification system to examine problem behaviors that are related to academic achievement, this study produced three basic findings:

■ Both male and female students with EBD experienced large academic deficits when compared with a typical group.

■ Academic achievement levels remained stable in reading and written language while deficits in math seemed to broaden over time. Just as behavior patterns became increasingly more stable and resistant to interventions (Walker & Severson, 2002), academic deficits also became increasingly more stable (O'Shaughnessy, Lane, Gresham, & Beebe-Frankenberger, 2003). Such academic deficits did not seem to be a function of a complex interaction between the behavior problems associated with EBD students and the educational programs that are available to them.

■ Externalizing behaviors (e.g., attentional problems, aggression, and other acting-out behaviors) were clearly related to academic achievement in all content areas.

The findings for this study were consistent with earlier studies (Abikoff et al., 2002; Lane, Gresham, MacCilan, & Bocian, 2001), regarding conduct and attention problems being related to EBD. A recent review by Mooney and colleagues (2005) noted that there have been only 55 studies conducted over the past 36 years on effective academic interventions for EBD students. As has been observed in several studies, it is essential that EBD students be identified early, so that more focused interventions can be provided (Lane and Wehby, 2002; Severson & Walker, 2002). Without such support, these students are likely to have academic deficits persist throughout their school years, making intervention at a higher grade even more challenging. The identification of students who have problems learning (and individual behavior disorders) is highlighted by No Child Left Behind (NCLB).

NO CHILD LEFT BEHIND

The NCLB Act of 2001 is a comprehensive and powerful law that has changed the way public school students are educated in the United States. The law represents dramatically increased federal mandates and requirements for states, school districts, and public schools, generally holding states and public schools accountable for improving student achievement in both reading and math. The primary purpose of NCLB is to ensure that all students achieve important learning goals while being educated in safer classrooms by well-prepared teachers. It also requires that educators use scientifically based strategies and instruction methods.

To increase student achievement, NCLB requires that school districts assume responsibility for all students to reach 100 percent proficiency levels on tests of reading and math. The law also requires that schools close academic gaps between economically advantaged students and disadvantaged students who are from diverse economic, racial, and ethnic backgrounds, as well as students with disabilities. To measure progress, NCLB requires that states administer tests for all students. If a school district does not meet the required standards of proficiency, the law mandates that corrective action will be applied.

The following have been the primary goals of NCLB:

■ All students will achieve high academic standards by attaining proficiency in reading and mathematics by the 2013–2014 school year.

■ Highly qualified teachers will teach students.
■ All students will be educated in schools and classrooms that are safe, drug free, and conducive to learning.
■ All limited English-proficient students will become proficient in English.
■ All students will graduate from high school.

Although we could debate how realistic the goals are, it is clear that change or reform is needed in (1) how students are taught, and (2) how progress is measured. However, public schools will need to be responsible for improving the achievement of all students. One of the best ways to instruct students is the use of evidence-based programs that determine what materials and/or interventions work well with students.

SCIENTIFICALLY BASED INSTRUCTION

States must use evidence-based programs to improve the academic achievement of all students. Too often schools have used programs that are based on fads or personal bias and have proved to be ineffective. Evidence-based programs have been demonstrated, through research, to be generally effective with students.

Although it may not be possible to cover effective educational practices for all disabilities (especially the behavior disorders), Iovannone and colleagues (2003) have published an important analytic review of the six core elements of effective educational practices geared toward students with autism spectrum disorder (ASD). These core elements are described in Table 13.1.

The Challenge

Both teachers and administrators may be challenged by NCLB to use scientifically based research (SBR) in deciding which programs and practices will be implemented to improve student achievement. In fact, funding may even depend on whether programs have a scientific base (Beghetto, 2003). The use of SBR also challenges schools seeking to implement reform strategies through Comprehensive School Reform (CSR), a program that is usually initiated when school improvements are unsuccessful and students are not meeting standards.

TABLE 13.1   Core Elements of Effective Educational Practices

Core Element	Description
Individualized supports and services	Must be tailored to meet the unique individual needs and family characteristics of each student. Individualized programming includes (1) considering family preferences when selecting curriculum, (2) developing programming that reflects a student's preferences and interests, and (3) determining the appropriate intensity and level of instruction on the basis of the student's strengths and weaknesses.
Systematic instruction	Must be based on identifying desirable learning outcomes, developing specific and focused teaching strategies to achieve these outcomes, consistently implementing the teaching strategies, and using information about students, performance to guide daily instructional decisions.
Comprehensible and structured learning environments	Must allow students to predict their daily routine and respond appropriately to behavioral expectations during different activities.
Specific curriculum content	Must include and emphasize language and social interaction, because these are the primary challenges for students with ASD.
Functional approach to problem behavior	Must represent a movement away from punishment-based approaches that emphasize obedience and compliance and toward instruction that emphasizes useful skill development.
Family involvement	Improves programming because family members know their child best, spend the most time with him or her, and have an immense influence on their child. It is crucial that they are active participants in developing and implementing their child's educational programming.

Source: Information from Iovannone, Dunlap, Hunter, and Kincaid (2003). Reprinted by permission.

Understanding SBR

According to the No Child Left Behind Act of 2001, the term *scientifically based research* involves the application of rigorous, systematic, and objective procedures to obtain reliable and valid knowledge relevant to education activities and programs. In addition, it includes research that has the following characteristics:

1. It employs systematic, empirical methods that draw on observation or experiment.

2. It involves rigorous data analyses that are adequate to test the stated hypotheses and justify the general conclusions drawn.

3. It relies on measurements or observational methods that provide reliable and valid data across evaluators and observers, across multiple measurements and observations, and across studies by the same or different investigators.

4. It is evaluated using experimental or quasi-experimental designs in which individuals, entities, programs, or activities are assigned to different conditions and with appropriate controls to evaluate the effects on the condition of interest, with a preference for random-assignment experiments, or other designs to the extent that those designs contain within-condition or across-condition controls.

5. It ensures that experimental studies are presented in sufficient detail and clarity to allow for replication or, at a minimum, offer the opportunity to build systematically on their findings.

6. It has been accepted by a peer-reviewed journal or approved by a panel of independent experts through a comparably rigorous, objective, and scientific review (Title IX, Part A, Section 9101 [37]).

Source: Information from NCLB Act (www.ste.state.ok.us/NCLB/pdf.sbr.pdf).

Scientifically Based Research

While the definition in the box on the previous page challenges researchers to provide better evidence of what works in order to make sound decisions in the classroom, few studies in education can meet this definition (Feuer, Towne, & Shavelson, 2002).

The American Institutes for Research (AIR), founded in 1946 as a nonprofit organization, is a carefully designed institution motivated by the desire to enhance the human experience. It is committed to contributing to the science of human behavior and the development of man's capacity and potential.

In 2002, AIR introduced two standards as follows: (1) the gold standard, which meets all requirements of SBR, and (2) the silver standard, which meets all requirements except for "random sampling" (AIR, 2002). One very important component of SBR is the use of randomized controlled trials, as explained below.

The Iowa Department of Education has identified the range of possibilities in education research, as illustrated in Figure 13.1. The following categories relate to the strength of the empirical evidence and their definitions:

- *Gold standard:* NCLB criteria; most rigorous research designs; research-proven programs/strategies.
- *Strong evidence:* Research-based programs and strategies; strong evidence but lacking one or two design elements present in the gold standard.

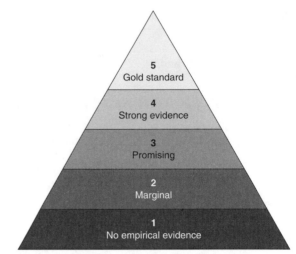

FIGURE 13.1　The gold standard for reviewing research studies.

Source: Information from the Iowa Department of Education (www.iowa.gov/educate/prodev/definitions.html).

- *Promising:* Research-related programs with one or more proven strategies but untested as a whole and needing systematic study.
- *Marginal:* Programs with one or two promising practices but little supporting empirical evidence.
- *No empirical evidence:* Untested programs or theories, with no empirical evidence reported; reports are anecdotal, testimonial, etc.

Randomized Controlled Trials

Although a number of research designs can be used to determine the effectiveness of a prevention program (i.e., programs designed to prevent behavioral problems), the randomized controlled trial (RCT) is widely considered the most scientifically rigorous. In a RCT, a target population is divided and randomly assigned either to receive the preventive intervention or to be assigned to a "no-treatment" comparison condition or to an alternative intervention. The combined use of both random assignment and a comparison group is intended to control for selection bias as well as extraneous variables that may cause postintervention differences. A less rigorous alternative is the quasi-experimental study, in which the assignment to intervention or comparison conditions is not random. Because analytic methods allow researchers to adjust for pretest differences in the intervention and comparison conditions, the quasi-experimental study is still considered a fairly rigorous form of evaluation.

Source: Information from Kyler, Dumborger, and Greenberg (2005). Reprinted by permission of the Pennsylvania State University Prevention Research Center.

A New Vocabulary for SBR

To research the effectiveness of programs that focus on students with behavior disorders, teachers must look at the research evidence to date.

In order to become a critical consumer of research, it is important to understand at least these basic terms:*

■ *Evidence-based education*: "The integration of professional wisdom with the best available empirical evidence in making decisions about how to deliver instruction" (Whitehurst, 2002).

■ *Professional wisdom*: "The judgment that individuals acquire through experience. Increased professional wisdom is reflected in numerous ways, including the effective identification and incorporation of local circumstances into instruction" (Whitehurst, 2002).

■ *Control group*: A group of individuals whose characteristics are similar to the experimental group except that they do not receive any of the program services or products being evaluated. Slavin (2003) suggests that, in a good study, several schools (at least five schools in each group is desirable) using a given program are compared with schools who are not using the program but meet the same demographic criteria.

■ *Empirical research/evidence*: Research conducted for the purpose of collecting measurable data in terms of attitudes, behavior, or performance. Empirical research is designed to generate projectable, numerical data on a topic.

■ *Randomized experiment*: The most convincing form of a control group comparison in which students, teachers, or schools are assigned by chance to a group. Such comparisons are very rare in education but very influential (Slavin, 2003). Some educational researchers contend that even though this method is used in the medical field, it is difficult to conduct in educational contexts and may be potentially harmful to children (Mid-Continent Research for Education and Learning, 2002; Shavelson & Towne, 2002). This is part of the criteria to reach the gold standard of SBR.

*Adapted from pages 11–12 of "The Challenge & Hope of Scientifically Based Research" by Margaret A. Trybus in *Improving Student Achievement and Teacher Effectiveness Through Scientifically Based Practices* (View Points Hall). Available online at http://mcrel.org/policy/pubs/pdfs/up11.pdf. Copyright © 2004 by North Central Regional Educational Laboratory. Reprinted with permission of Learning Point Associates.

■ *Statistical significance*: The difference between the achievement of students in the experimental and the control group. According to Slavin (2003, p. 14), "a usual criterion is <0.05, which means that the probability is less than 5 percent that an observed difference might have happened by chance."

⸱⸱⸱

The **effect size** is a standardized measure of the effect of an intervention (treatment) on student outcomes. The effect size represents the change (measured in standard deviation) in an average student's outcome that can be expected if that student is given the treatment. Basically, the effect size is a measure of the strength of relationship between two variables.

⸱⸱⸱

■ *Effect size*: Studies should be reviewed to determine the number of schools involved in the research and whether the effect size is higher than +0.20 (Slavin, 2003; Marzano, 2003). The more schools involved in a study done by more than one researcher, the more confident you can be that the program's results are valid.

As you become familiar with the terminology and concepts that underlie SBR, you can select those evidence-based programs that are appropriate and most useful for the teaching and management of students with behavior disorders. This will require a combination of professional wisdom and the use of empirical evidence to evaluate programs that depend upon experience and the use of empirical information along with scientifically based research and the consensus of experts. The flowchart in Figure 13.2 describes this process.

What Works in SBR   The What Works Clearinghouse (WWC), an organization created in 2002 by the U.S. Department of Education, identifies appropriate research practices that may be used in replication studies in schools. It is also a resource that assists in educational decision making regarding the scientific evidence for programs and practices (Beghetto, 2003). The WWC's ambitious agenda includes four key goals:

■ Establishing standards for research aiming to draw causal inferences and to establish the validity of tests and other assessments.
■ Creating an independent group of technical advisors.
■ Selecting topics to focus research.
■ Conducting syntheses of research studies (WWC, 2002).

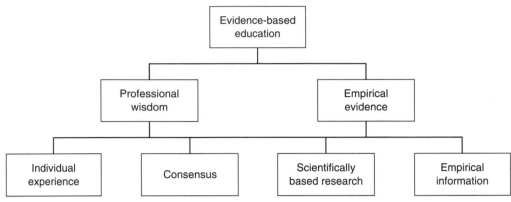

FIGURE 13.2 Evidence-based education.
Source: Information from Whitehurst (2002).

Practically Speaking: How Might Practitioners Put Scientifically Based Research to Work?

When a school learns that it is on the academic early warning list because some subgroups have not met standards on the state assessment for mathematics, a school improvement committee must be formed to write a school improvement plan (SIP) that meets state criteria. (For an example of this type of plan, see the SIP from the Illinois State Board of Education at www.isbe.net/sos/improvement/SIPRUBRIC.pdf.)

The committee must then create an "action plan" that designates activities "supported by scientifically based research with a theoretical base," as mandated in the state criteria. The state rubric (and this applies to all states) specifically asks how the activities cited in the plan are supported by SBR, and what types of measures will be used to determine if the activities meet the needs of the low-achieving students.

The following steps are taken by the improvement committee to address this mandate:

1. *Analyze school data.* The school improvement committee does an extensive analysis of school information, including attendance, truancy, mobility, expulsion, and retention rates. Committee members also analyze data on the demographics of the school population, breaking it into economically disadvantaged, limited-English-proficient, white, African American, Hispanic, Native American, and Asia/Pacific Islander students.

2. *Generate a hypothesis.* The data analysis leads committee members to generate a series of hypotheses to provide possible explanations for why some students are not meeting state standards. They discuss the primary causal factors that contributed to low achievement, and select the factors within the school's capacity to change or control. The four factors they choose to address are (a) homework completion, (b) mathematics problem solving, (c) algebra skills, and (d) parental involvement.

3. *Create an action plan.* The school improvement committee begins its search of scientifically or evidence-based research, looking for instructional activities that would fit the factors identified. Committee members can search the What Works Clearinghouse to find relevant research and read articles from the National Council of Teachers of Mathematics in order to understand the theoretical base of best practices in mathematics.

4. *Evaluate research.* The committee reviews the research, investigating the plausibility of replicating it in the school improvement plan. To evaluate the research, the committee frames its questions around the following major themes:
   a. *Theoretical framework:* What was the theoretical basis of the program being considered? Is it related to learning theory and best practices in the field of mathematics?

b. *Research design:* Did the study have a control and an experimental group that were randomly assigned? If not, what was the research method? What was the sample size? What was the study's hypothesis? What were the researchers trying to test or prove?

c. *Research methodology:* What was the treatment for the experimental group? What activities were implemented? How many schools were in the study? In what settings did the research take place? Was the context similar to our school demographics?

d. *Implementation and replication:* Is the treatment program understandable so that it can be replicated in our school? What kinds of resources were used in the study, and do we have the capacity to provide them?

e. *Evidence of results:* What assessment data were used to measure the treatment? If achievement testing, how comparable is this to our assessment system? Has the hypothesis been adequately tested in order to justify the conclusions? What statistical measurements were used, and do we have the capability to replicate them?

f. *Approved research:* To what extent has the research been accepted by a peer-reviewed journal or approved by a panel of independent experts? Is the research considered rigorous, objective, and scientific to meet the SBR criteria?

After completing these processes, the school leaders make a commitment to translate specific, applicable research into practices in their own setting. With these steps, the school has begun to incorporate research into its culture and to increase the likelihood of strengthening teaching and improving learning.

Source: Information from Trybus (2004). Reprinted by permission.

An important issue in this process is how practitioners might put scientifically based research to work, a topic discussed in the box above.

Research on Classroom Instruction   Educators need to know what will help to evaluate programs for assessment and instruction in schools. The first research technique is *meta-analysis*, a strategy that combines results from a number of studies to determine the net effect of an intervention. When conducting a meta-analysis, the researcher translates the results of a given study into a unit of measurement termed the *effect size (ES)*. Most special education interventions revealed an ES below 0.5 and thus represent less advantage than one-half of 1 school year's worth of schooling. The special education interventions demonstrated effects that primarily ranged from negligible to small, and at best, medium. The effect size expresses in standard deviations (a measure of variability around the mean) the difference between the increased or decreased achievement of an experimental group (the group getting the instructional strategy) with that of the control group (the group getting something other than the instructional strategy). This means that if the effect size computed for a certain study is 1.0, the average score for students in the experimental group is 1.0 standard deviation higher than the average score of students in the control group. Another way of saying this is that a student at the 50th percentile in the experimental group would be 1.0 standard deviation higher than a student at the 50th percentile in the control group.

Figure 13.3 shows that student achievement scores are distributed in a bell curve or normal distribution with a range of about three standard deviations above and below the mean(0).

One of the most useful aspects of the effect size is that it can easily be translated into percentile gains. In many studies and reports, the research is reviewed in terms of both effect sizes and percentile gains. For example, if a review of 14 studies reveals that the effect size is 0.73, this means that the average student who was exposed to the instructional strategy scored 0.73 standard deviations above the score of the average student who was not exposed to that instructional strategy. This difference is shown by the shaded area in Figure 13.4. By consulting a conversion table that allows for translation of effect sizes into percentile gains, the effect size of 0.73 represents a percentile gain of about 27 points.

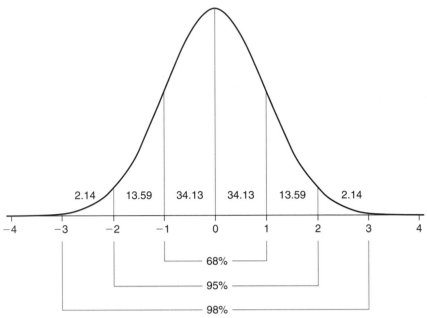

FIGURE 13.3   A normal distribution showing the percentage of scores distributed around the mean.

Source: Information from Marzano, Pickering, and Pollock (2001). Reprinted by permission.

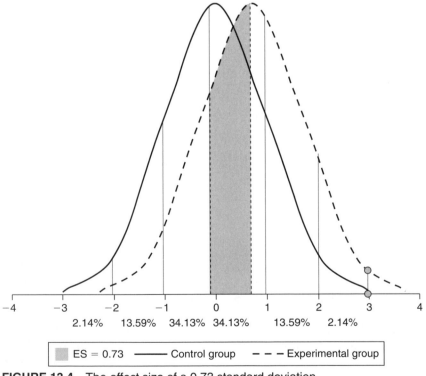

ES = 0.73   ——— Control group   – – – Experimental group

FIGURE 13.4   The effect size of a 0.73 standard deviation.

Source: Information from Marzano, Pickering, and Pollock (2001). Reprinted by permission.

TABLE 13.2   Categories of Instructional Strategies that Strongly Affect Student Achievement

Category	Average Effect Size	Percentile Gain[a]	Number of Effect Sizes (N)	Standard Deviation (SD)
1. Identifying similarities and differences	1.61	45	31	0.31
2. Summarizing and note taking	1.00	34	179	0.50
3. Reinforcing effort and providing recognition	0.80	29	21	0.35
4. Homework and practice	0.77	28	134	0.36
5. Nonlinguistic representations	0.75	27	246	0.40
6. Cooperative learning	0.73	27	122	0.40
7. Setting goals and providing feedback	0.61	23	408	0.28
8. Generating and testing hypotheses	0.61	23	63	0.79
9. Activating prior knowledge	0.59	22	1,251	0.26

[a] The maximum percentile gains possible for students currently at the 50th percentile.
Source: Information from Marzano, Pickering, and Pollock (2001).

Another way of interpreting effect size is in terms of a year's growth. Experts on meta-analysis explain that an effect size of 1.0 can be interpreted as about one year's growth in achievement (Lipsey & Wilson, 2001).

A study conducted by the Mid-Continent Regional Educational Laboratory (McREL) identified nine categories of instructional strategies for K–12 classroom teachers that have the highest probability of enhancing student achievement for all students in all subject areas and at all grade levels. These categories, shown in Table 13.2, represent the most effective strategies derived from meta-analysis together with experience in the field of thousands of educators over the past 30 years.

As indicated in Table 13.2, the average effect size (unique and specific to each category) of these strategies ranges from 0.59 to 1.61. If we look at one category—*reinforcing effort and providing recognition*—we see that the average effect size for this category is 0.80 with a standard deviation of 0.35. There were 21 studies (N) that were used to compute this average effect size of 0.80, some with an effect size as high as 3 standard deviations above the mean of 0.80, and some were 3 standard deviations below the mean of 0.80. The range was from a high of 1.85 [0.80 + 3(0.35)] to a low of 0.25 [0.80 − 3(0.35)]. Thus, reinforcing effort and providing recognition resulted in a gain of 0.80 years' growth in student achievement. Some strategies resulted in a (positive) high of 1.85 years' growth; others resulted in a (negative) loss in achievement of 0.25 years. A negative effect size means that the experimental group (i.e., the instructional strategy) performed worse than the control group.

Overall we can see that no instructional strategy works equally well in all situations. The effectiveness of a strategy depends on the student's current level of achievement, how well the strategy is applied by the teacher, and some other contextual factors such as grade and class size. Because these instructional strategies are just tools, some judgment in their use is required as they may not work equally well with all students and in all situations, even when they are implemented adequately.

INSTRUCTIONAL STRATEGIES THAT WORK

Let's now look at each of the nine instructional strategies that are most likely to improve student achievement across all content areas and grade levels. These strategies are explained more fully in Marzano, Pickering, and Pollock (2001). The materials that follow have been adapted from that book, and discussed in Varlas (2002). Permission granted by The Association for Supervision and Curriculum Development (ASCD) to reproduce these materials.

1. ***Identifying similarities and differences***: The ability to break a concept into its similar and dissimilar characteristics allows students to understand (and often solve) complex problems by analyzing them in a more basic way. Teachers can either directly present similarities and differences, accompanied by a deep discussion and inquiry, or simply ask students to identify similarities and

differences. While teacher-directed activities focus on identifying specific items, the research shows that student-directed activities encourage variation and broaden understanding. Graphic forms are a good way to represent similarities and differences.

Applications

- Use Venn diagrams or charts to compare and classify items.
- Engage students in comparing, classifying, and creating metaphors and analogies.

---

2. ***Summarizing and note taking***: These skills promote greater comprehension by asking students to analyze a subject to expose what is essential and then put it in their own words. This requires substituting, deleting, and keeping some things and having an awareness of the basic structure of the information presented.

Applications

- Provide a set of rules for creating a summary.
- When summarizing, ask students to question what is unclear, clarify those questions, and then predict what will happen next in the text.

Taking more notes is better than fewer notes, though verbatim note taking is ineffective because it does not allow time to process the information. Teachers should encourage and give time for review and revision of notes; often notes are the best study guides for tests.

Applications

- Use teacher-prepared notes.
- Stick to a consistent format for notes, although students can refine the notes as necessary.

---

3. ***Reinforcing effort and providing recognition***: Effort and recognition address the attitudes and beliefs of students, and teachers must show the connection between effort and achievement. Although not all students realize the importance of effort, they can learn to change their beliefs to emphasize effort.

Applications

- Share stories about people who have succeeded by not giving up.
- Have students keep a log of their weekly efforts and achievements, reflect on it periodically, and even mathematically analyze the data.

Recognition is most effective if it is contingent on the achievement of a certain standard. Also, symbolic recognition works better than tangible rewards.

Applications

- Find ways to personalize recognition. Give awards for individual accomplishments.
- Remember to pause, prompt, praise. If a student is struggling, *pause* to discuss the problem, then *prompt* with specific suggestions to help him or her improve. If the student's performance improves as a result, offer *praise*.

---

4. ***Homework and practice***: Homework provides students with the opportunity to extend their learning outside the classroom. However, the amount of homework assigned should vary by grade level and parent involvement should be minimal. Teachers should explain the purpose of homework to both the student and the parent or guardian; teachers should also try to give feedback on all homework assigned.

Applications

- Establish a homework policy with advice—such as keeping a consistent schedule, and setting a time limit that parents and students may not have considered.
- Inform students whether homework is for practice or a preparation for upcoming units.
- Maximize the effectiveness of feedback by varying the way homework is delivered.

Students should adapt skills while they are learning them. Speed and accuracy are key indicators of the effectiveness of practice.

Applications

- Assign timed quizzes for homework and have students report on their speed and accuracy.
- Focus practice on difficult concepts and set aside time to accommodate practice periods.

5. *Nonlinguistic representations*: Knowledge is stored in two forms: linguistic and visual. The more students use both forms in the classroom (i.e., the more they follow a multimodal approach), the more opportunity they have to achieve. Recently, the use of nonlinguistic representation has proved to not only stimulate but also increase brain activity.

Applications

- Incorporate words and images using symbols to represent relationships.
- Use physical models and physical movement to represent information.

6. *Cooperative learning*: Organizing students into cooperative groups yields a positive effect on overall learning. When applying cooperative learning strategies, keep groups small and do not overuse this strategy. Try to be systematic and consistent in approach.

Applications

- When grouping students, consider a variety of criteria, such as common experiences or interests.
- Vary group sizes and objectives.
- Design group work around the core components of cooperative learning—positive interdependence, group processing, appropriate use of social skills, face-to-face interaction, and individual and group accountability.

7. *Setting objectives and providing feedback*: Setting objectives can provide students with a direction for their learning. Goals should not be too specific; they should be easily adaptable to students' own objectives.

Applications

- Set a core goal for a unit, and then encourage students to personalize that goal by identifying areas of interest to them. Statements such as "I want to know . . ." and "I want to know more about . . ." get students thinking about their interests and actively involved in the goal-setting process.
- Use contracts to outline the specific goals that students must attain and the grade they will receive if they meet those goals.

Feedback generally produces positive results. Teachers can never give too much; however, they should manage the form of that feedback.

Applications

- Make sure feedback is corrective in nature; tell students how they did in relation to specific levels of knowledge. Rubrics are a great way to do this.
- Keep feedback timely and specific.
- Encourage students to lead feedback sessions.

8. ***Generating and testing hypotheses***: Research shows that a deductive approach (using a general rule to make a prediction) to this strategy works best. Whether a hypothesis is induced or deduced, students should clearly explain their hypotheses and conclusions.

Applications

- Ask students to predict what would happen if an aspect of a familiar system, such as the government or transportation, were changed.
- Ask students to build something using limited resources. This task generates questions and hypotheses about what may or may not work.

9. ***Cues, questions, and advance organizers***: Cues, questions, and advance organizers help students use what they already know about a topic to enhance further learning. Research shows that these tools need to be highly analytical, should focus on what is important, and are most effective when presented before a learning experience.

• •

An ***advance organizer*** is information that is presented prior to learning and that can be used by the learner to organize and interpret new incoming information (Mayer, 2000).

• •

Applications

- Pause briefly after asking a question. Doing so will increase the depth of your students' answers.
- Vary the style of advance organizer used: Tell a story, skim a text, or create a graphic image. There are many ways to expose students to information before they "learn" it.

IMPLEMENTING EVIDENCE-BASED PRACTICES IN SCHOOLS

Consider the following example of how evidence-based practices might or might not be implemented in schools:

Teachers from one school have just attended a workshop on the use of red pens in promoting student achievement. It has been found that when students use red pens the result is an increase in their overall achievement. The workshop presenter noted that 12 children initially tested (on the average) 2 standard deviations below the mean in basic achievements of reading, spelling, and arithmetic. These students were given red pens to use in their work and after only 2 months gained, on average, 5.7 standard score points on all achievements combined, and individually in reading (6.3), spelling (3.7), and arithmetic (1.75). Critics might question the results as no control group was described. Also, researchers were the ones who obtained these

Effectiveness Versus Efficacy

Although evidence-based programs are considered in common parlance to have demonstrated "effectiveness," the scientific community further delineates programs as being "efficacious." In research terms, programs that have been evaluated in a study in which the researcher artificially controls the study environment are said to have demonstrated efficacy—that they can produce positive outcomes when all conditions are right. Generally, once a program has demonstrated efficacy, it is then evaluated in more naturally occurring, "real-world" conditions. Although evidence-based programs have demonstrated positive outcomes in a controlled study, not all have demonstrated true "effectiveness" by being evaluated in more natural conditions. This is another facet of evidence that should be considered when selecting a preventive intervention.

Source: Information from Pennsylvania State University, Prevention Research Center from Kyler, S., Bumbayer, B., and Greenberg, M. (2005). Evidence-Based Programs (Technical Assistance Fact Sheet #2). University Park, PA.

results and only standardized measures of achievement were used. Furthermore, there was no peer review of the study and, on theoretical grounds, there is no reason to believe that using a colored red pen could make a difference in the students' achievement test scores. What do you think?

This example illustrates the necessity of using *evidence-based practices* (*EBP*) when making decisions about instructional programs for schools. The use of EBP allows educators to select those practices that have been formally researched in the field (i.e, in school settings), and now form part of a generally accepted knowledge base. The discussion that follows centers around contextual factors involved in EBP, with a major focus on accountability and scaling up of research regarding EBP as an indicator of school reform.

Accountability

The No Child Left Behind Act of 2001 is an example of a new direction in education toward accountability—the need for educators to select instruction and interventions that have demonstrated effectiveness and efficacy.

When one looks at the proliferation of workshops and commercial products on effectiveness and efficacy, it appears difficult to decide what is "good" and "bad" information (Stanovich & Stanovich, 2003). The peer review process in journals and meetings may be the best source for objective information on what works and what does not.

Scaling Up

••

Scaling up: The process of replicating innovations on a larger scale. The term is used in many fields, including business, engineering, and medicine. Although the particular details will vary from field to field, the goal is the same—taking an innovation that works on a small scale and making it work in more places and for more people.

••

Scaling up is a term that is often used to describe efforts to minimize or eradicate the *research-to-practice gap*—the length of time between the conduct of research and its application to educational practices in schools (Steiner, 2000). The scaling up process involves (1) the accumulation of research evidence, which relates to the building of a knowledge base using varied tools and research designs, and (2) the preponderance of research evidence, which refers to an established knowledge base that is derived from the outcomes of accumulated research. New knowledge means an improvement in instructional practices and potential solutions to pressing problems. Applications of the scaling up concept to evidence-based practice in schools requires two cooperative processes (Bodilly, 1998): (1) the scaling up of research to ultimately implement the results in schools, and (2) the scaling up of practices or removing barriers that affect the translation of research findings to educational settings. There must be cooperation between the research community (in accumulating evidence) and those who evaluate the evidence to make the best decisions about how to implement EBP in schools.

ESSENTIAL ORGANIZATIONAL NEEDS FOR PUTTING EBP IN SCHOOLS

Evidence-based practice involves more than just getting educators to study research publications. It is a decision-making paradigm that concerns the importance of accountability and the need to differentiate between good and bad information. There is also a need to accumulate a knowledge base that addresses real-life problems and to translate this essential knowledge to implement it in schools.

Educators must use the best designed and highest quality research evidence to make informed decisions, and they must be skilled at integrating this evidence into the school curriculum. Likewise, researchers must increase the quantity and quality of research that is relevant to educational real-life decisions. Education must make some dramatic changes to achieve the level of evidence-based practices that seems both necessary and sufficient to maximize educators' roles in meeting the needs of all children in school.

Comprehensive Meta-Analysis—Need I

A comprehensive meta-analysis is needed to provide a description of the available evidence concerning assessments and interventions used in schools. Such a document is critical in scaling up education to provide contemporary analyses of how well knowledge is being accumulated concerning specific practices and, most importantly, to describe which practices are supported by a preponderance of the evidence.

The U.S. government published such a document through the National Reading Panel (NRP, 2000), summarizing the available evidence on interventions and instruction regarding reading in five areas: vocabulary, fluency, phonic awareness, comprehension, and phonics. This document (available at www.nationalreadingpanel. org) is an important resource for reading teachers, elementary school teachers, special educators, and others who need to select treatments or instructional interventions in reading for academically challenged students.

Guidelines and Systematic Research Reviews—Need II

Teachers must judge the wealth of evidence that relates to a specific diagnostic or treatment approach. For example, the American Psychological Association (APA) organized a task force to develop guidelines to determine when a childhood intervention reached an acceptable level of evidence for demonstrated effectiveness (Lonigan, Elbert, & Johnson, 1998). To be classified at this level, an intervention must have accumulated evidence that includes two or more well-conducted group-design studies by different and independent researchers showing that the treatment/intervention is better than an alternative intervention or at least equivalent to an already established intervention.

There must also be a plan to disseminate systematic research reviews. In comparison to the use of evidence-based practices in school, the medical field may use media outlets that are geared specifically to the provision of accessible and easily digestible practice guidelines that are based on the most recent studies; such literature must be made available to busy educators. One example of an organization that converts bodies of research into usable guidelines for clinical practice is the Campbell Collaboration (www.campbellcollaboration.org), which focuses on social, behavioral, and educational interventions. The What Works Clearinghouse of the U.S. Department of Education's Institute of Education Sciences (IES) follows a similar path to provide reports on educational interventions and behavioral intervention reports. The U.S. Department of Health and Human Services' Agency for Healthcare Research and Quality (www.ahcpr.gov) is another resource to access evidence-based practice guidelines along with regular updates on clinical-outcome research that is related to healthcare.

Research Infrastructure—Need III

A critical value in the use of EBR in schools is the role of the researcher. There is a critical need for people with research training who can competently ask questions about school-based services and who can objectively evaluate research. Of course, studies of students in real life situations are different from studies conducted in a laboratory where there is often control over many extraneous variables. Adequate numbers of researchers must focus on applied research in the school settings, targeting issues that are directly relevant to the challenges that are faced by students.

Curriculum-Based Assessment

Curriculum-based assessment (CBA) is a research-based technique that can facilitate student achievement by aligning the instruction with a student's learning needs (Fuchs, 2004). It assesses student progress using materials taken directly from the school curriculum, and it also helps educators modify instruction based on measured learning rates (Shaprio & Eckert, 1993).

CBA is also a performance-based technique that involves direct and repeated measurement of a student's performance in core subjects such as reading, mathematics, spelling, and written language. The following are primary features of CBA:

- It is brief.
- It can be frequently administered.
- It is cost effective.
- Its results are sensitive to changes in skill development.

A teacher may use a brief measure (a probe) to score and chart a student's progress on a graph, which is compared to a goal. The visual display of results includes the acquisition and retention rates of learning, and these are then used to select which educational interventions are effective and which ones need to be altered.

The control measure of this instrument is the student's fluency in a subject area—the speed with which the student is able to produce correct answers on an academic test. For example, in reading the fluency measure might be the number of correct words read per minute.

In math, it could be the number of problems correct on a worksheet within a 2-minute time limit. The primary reason that fluency is used is that students need to show the acquisition of basic skills that track their movement through the curriculum sequence. If the student does not exhibit fluency on a certain academic skill, that skill will need to be taught on the student's instructional level in order for the student to advance up the curriculum. Often, such mastery may result in increased motivation and a reduction of frustration and the frequency of behavioral problems. Fluency also provides information on the rate of learning. When instruction is given at a rate faster than the student can maintain, frustration occurs and there is difficulty in mastering the academic content. However, once the rate is known, the teacher can adjust the pace of instruction to the student's level, increasing the likelihood of progress through the curriculum sequence.

USING EFFECTIVE PRACTICES TO EDUCATE EBD STUDENTS

Greater numbers of students with emotional and behavior disorders are being educated in general education classrooms taught by general educators. These students may have the lowest grade point averages, and about half are failing one or more classes each year (Sutherland & Wehby, 2001); these students also have higher dropout rates and higher unemployment when they do exit school (Sutherland & Wehby, 2001).

There are several strategies that may help students with EBD become more successful. These include (1) increasing praise and providing more opportunities to respond to academic requests, (2) setting up an organized classroom, and (3) improving the training and education that teachers receive in educating students with EBD.

Wehby, Lane, and Falk (2003) point out that students with EBD exhibit an inability to establish acceptable relationships in both home and school environments, inappropriate behavior under normal circumstances, and perhaps a persistently depressed mood. They are likely to act out, get off task, disobey rules, and present problematic behavior to their teachers. They also spend an inordinate amount of time doing independent work (Good & Brophy, 2008) Teachers of students with EBD become frustrated and, because of these students' disruptive behavior, often provide less instruction to them (Wehby et al., 2003). As other researchers have noted, with greater misconduct there is generally less instruction (Sutherland & Wehby, 2001).

Opportunities to Respond

A significant amount of research in educating students with EBD has focused on opportunities to respond (OTR) to academic requests (Sutherland & Wehby, 2001; Duffy & Forgan, 2005). Generally, when students are provided more opportunities to respond to questions, there is greater active participation in class, fewer behavior problems, and enhanced learning. However, research indicates that most teachers of students with EBD rarely provide adequate opportunities to respond (Sutherland & Wehby, 2001); when more opportunities to respond were provided, there were increased educational outcomes, increased task management, and less inappropriate/disruptive behavior. Another study found that teachers who praise students often provide high rates of opportunities to respond (Sutherland, Wehby, & Yoder, 2002); low rates of praise were likewise associated with fewer opportunities to respond. These two strategies can be effective in helping students with EBD achieve academically while at the same time minimizing their disruptive behavior. Educators thus need to implement these strategies into their classrooms to increase the probability of success for EBD students.

Teachers can also institute specific management styles in the classroom that lead students with EBD to success (Gunter, Coutinho, & Cade, 2002). These strategies include (1) the posting of rules (with consequences) in highly visible places, (2) facilitating student–teacher interactions, and (3) using token economies in behavior management. Positive results can enhance success for all students (Cook et al., 2003; Gunter, Coutinho, & Cade, 2002). The use of self-monitoring and class-wide peer tutoring can lead to both greater on-task behavior and academic success (Cook et al., 2003). However, neither group of authors provides suggestions regarding the implementation and the establishment of these strategies. The example on the following page is a case study involving student monitoring of transitions.

In general, *self-monitoring* is defined as the practice of students observing and recording their own academic and social behaviors (Hallahan & Kauffman, 2003; Vaughn, Bos, & Schumm, 2000). It is an important step that they can take in becoming more independent by assuming responsibility for their own

Case Study

Student Monitoring of Transitions

Tyler is a 12-year-old seventh grader in a self-contained class for students with behavior disorders. He experiences much difficulty whenever the teacher changes or transitions to a new academic subject. Tyler has been receiving many verbal reminders to help him to begin a new assignment.

Upon assessment, three target behaviors were identified: (1) getting materials needed for the next class subject, (2) remaining in his seat, and (3) exhibiting no disturbing behavior in the class (i.e., moving quickly and quietly to the next subject). During baseline, the teacher recorded these three behaviors as present or absent over a 5-day period between 8:00 a.m. and 2:00 p.m. When it was determined that Tyler showed appropriate behavior during transitions only about 65 percent of the time, a self-monitoring intervention was planned.

Figure 13.5 illustrates the recording sheet that was used. Beneath the three rules, Tyler was told to mark a plus (+) if he followed the transition rules and a minus (−) if he did not. His recording grid was divided into 7 subject periods over 5 school days.

Each day, Tyler could receive 7 tokens. His teacher recorded a similar chart to match against Tyler's chart to determine agreement, which was recorded at 85 percent.

The rules of transition were reviewed each morning during the intervention phase. Role-play was conducted so that Tyler could know exactly what behavior was expected. If he was unable to demonstrate a behavior adequately, it was modeled for him. More exacting expectations were required of

---

Name _____ Date _____

Rules of transition: (1) get materials, (2) sit in designated seat, (3) do tasks quickly and quietly without disturbance.

	1–2	2–3	3–4	4–5	5–6	6–7	7–Homeroom
M							
Tu							
W							
Th							
F							

TOTALS
(+) Followed rules _____
(−) Didn't follow rules _____

FIGURE 13.5   Card used to record student monitoring of transitions.

(continued)

Tyler as he progressed. He received 1 token for each successful transition during the first week. During the second week, he was required to make all transitions successfully before receiving the 7 tokens. However, after each successful transition, Tyler was praised immediately. During the first week of intervention, he was able to trade in 5 or more tokens for extra computer time at the rate of 5 minutes for each token.

As shown in the baseline and intervention graph (Figure 13.6), Tyler made more significant improvements (i.e., items he recalled) during the second week. He was able to reach criterion (the maximum number of successful transitions) during the second week, and he was able to maintain this performance during the maintenance phase. With verbal reinforcement, he was able to keep his performance at a high level. In this case, his academic work improved when he was better able to shift from one subject to another.

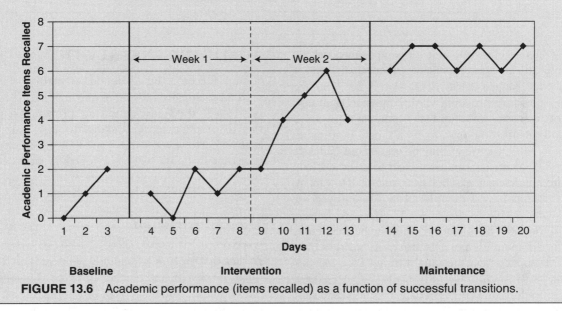

FIGURE 13.6   Academic performance (items recalled) as a function of successful transitions.

behavior and literally becoming their own "agent of change" (Porter, 2002). This represents a shift from external reinforcement by others to internal reinforcement, where students use self-talk to remind themselves when they have done a good job (Hanson, 1996). Self-monitoring has been used to manage many social and behavior problems, but it can also be used to self-monitor academic behavior (Rutherford, Quinn, & Mathur, 1996).

Self-monitoring can be used by students of all ages and disabilities (Agran et al., 2005; Hughes et al., 2002); it is appealing, relatively unobtrusive, inexpensive, and quick to implement (Carr & Punzo, 1993). Self-monitoring has been effective not only in increasing more appropriate behaviors but also in helping to improve on-task behavior, completion of homework,

and academic performance (Hallahan & Kauffman, 2003; Schunk, 1997; Smith, 2002). Self-monitoring is further effective in generalizing and maintaining skills over time as students can use this procedure at any time and in any place without help from a teacher or parent (Rutherford, Quinn, & Mathur, 2004).

To self-monitor, students will need to learn how to keep track of what they are doing and how they are thinking so that behaviors and thoughts can be adjusted to meet goals or complete tasks (Porter, 2002; Smith, 2002). The first step in teaching self-monitoring is to select and define a target behavior (Vaughn, Bos, & Schumm, 2000). Students must then establish learning and performance goals as well as identify consequences for either meeting or failing to meet these goals (Schunk, 1997). Students are also required to talk to themselves,

---

Definition of Peer Mediated Instruction

An alternative classroom arrangement in which students take an instructional role with classmates or other students. Many approaches have been developed in which students work in pairs (dyads) or small cooperative learning groups. To be most effective, students must be taught roles in the instructional episodes—to be systematic, elicit responses, and provide feedback. Research supports the use of these approaches as alternative practice activities; however, it does not condone the use of peers for providing instruction in "new" instructional content.

Source: Information from Hall, T. & Stegila, A. (2003). *Peer Mediated Instruction & Intervention*, Wakefield, MA: National Center on Assessing the General Curriculum, retrieved 6/11/08 from http://www.cast.org/publications/ncac/ncac_peermii.html.

---

focusing on a set of instructions for completing a task, or to periodically question themselves about their feelings or behaviors (Kamps & Kay, 2002; Porter, 2002; Smith, 2002). For example, students who are monitoring on-task behavior may ask "Am I on task?" when a timer cues them and record their answers on a sheet. As students learn to monitor, the timer may be phased out (Blick & Test, 1987). Students can also learn to ask questions about their performance or behavior, such as "How many math problems have I completed in 10 minutes?" or "How many problems are correct?" (Carr & Punzo, 1993). If the focus is on reading, the student might ask, "What is the main idea of this story?" (Guthrie et al., 1995). These steps can be taught either by a teacher (Schunk, 1997; Smith, 2002) or by peers (Gilberts, 2000). Such a procedure must be used daily by students to self-evaluate their successes (Vaughn, Bos, & Schumm, 2000). Of course, when the classroom environment is structured and supports the use of self-monitoring, it will be internalized as an automatic process.

Self-monitoring can best be maintained and generalized when combined with methods that allow students to evaluate themselves compared to prior performance and to reinforce themselves for success (Hallahan & Kauffman, 2003; Porter, 2002; Smith, 2002; Vaughn, Bos, & Schumm, 2000). Personal task reinforcements such as "I did a good job on this math work" or "I knew I could do it" or "It was hard but I completed it by staying with it" can be very useful. Again, the use of self-talk is important.*

---
*Much of this material was adapted from a series on highly effective practices by Catherine H. Kaser (2005). Permission granted by The Child Study Center at Old Dominion University.

ACADEMIC INSTRUCTION

The research on the academic instruction of students with EBD suggests teaching new material through direct (teacher-led) instruction and providing opportunities to practice learned skills through independent seatwork. However, Gunter and colleagues (2002) suggest that students be given worksheets one at a time rather than in a packet. Teachers must also carefully assign work that is doable yet challenging.

Direct Instruction

. . . .

Direct instruction is a method of instruction that is explicit, intensive, and teacher-directed. This method is based on a careful analysis of different content areas to determine the sequence of skills and concepts needed to master a wide variety of academic subjects.

. . . .

Direct instruction is an approach to instructional design and implementation that is based on 25 years of research development. Like precision teaching, direct instruction encounters resistance from educators because of its detailed scripting of the teacher's behavior. Nevertheless, direct instruction has been consistently associated with greater academic achievement, higher self-esteem, and enhanced problem-solving abilities in children than any other approach to teaching (Watkins, 1988).

. . . .

Precision teaching is a scientific system of strategies and their tactics for the monitoring of learning and for making data-based decisions about instruction.

. . . .

Precision Teaching

According to Lindsley (1990), the assumption of precision teaching is that learners respond in predictable ways to environmental variables; if learners act in undesirable ways, it is the responsibility of the teacher to alter those variables until they produce the desired result. By using daily charts such as the Student Behavior Chart or Standard Celeration Chart, teachers and students can make timely decisions about the effectiveness of the methods and materials used to assist them in achieving defined performance goals (Kubina & Morrison, 2000; Chapman, Ewing, & Mozzoni, 2005). Self-recording by students and sharing of results among teachers and students is another component of precision teaching that directly resulted from the methods used by behavior analysts (Kubina, Morrison, & Lee, 2002).

The failure of teachers to use strategies to minimize disruptive behavior may contribute to the high level of burnout experienced by teachers of students with EBD (Wehby et al., 2003). Although many teachers have been taught how to manage disruptive behavior, they have learned little about effective academic instruction. This may be one reason why teachers fail to use evidence-based practices in their classrooms. Another factor to be considered is that most students with EBD are often taught by teachers who are not certified in EBD (Wehby et al., 2003). This may be due in part to the constraints of IDEA, which requires that children with disabilities be educated in as normal an environment as possible with nondisabled classmates (Hallahan & Kauffman, 2003).

A study by Nelson (2001) indicated that teachers who were confident in their abilities to handle behavior problems and had a good relationship with their colleagues were under little job stress. However, this study involved mostly older, experienced teachers who did not typically educate students with EBD. Clearly, most general educators being certified today receive little training in special education, including EBD. With the increased number of students with special needs in the general education classroom, teachers may be forced to educate students with special needs early in their career. Future educators must become familiar with the research and effective teaching strategies for all types of disabilities. They also need to use a combination of academic instruction and classroom management strategies to provide a classroom that is conducive to learning. Future research needs to explore these two aspects together as strategies to reduce problem behaviors and to improve academic success.

REDUCING PROBLEM BEHAVIORS THROUGH ACADEMIC MANAGEMENT

Students who are confrontational or noncompliant frequently have poor academic skills, a low sense of self-efficacy as learners, and a very negative attitude toward school (Sprick, Borgmeier, & Nolet, 2002). Misbehavior often stems from, or is associated with, academic deficits. Educators who work with these behaviorally challenging learners, however, often make the mistake of overlooking simple academic strategies that have been shown to shape student behavior in powerful and positive ways (Penno, Frank, & Wacker, 2000). The following 10 research-based guidelines on academic management have been adapted from Wright (2004):

1. Do not assign work that is too easy or too difficult. It is surprising how often classroom behavior problems occur simply because students find the assigned work too difficult or too easy (Gettinger & Seibert, 2002). When assignments are too simple, students may become bored and distracted; when they are too hard, students are likely to feel frustrated and upset because they cannot complete the work. A significant discrepancy between the assignment and the student's abilities can foster misbehavior; teachers need to determine each student's academic skills and adjust assignments as needed to ensure that the student is appropriately challenged but not overwhelmed by the work.

2. Allow students to have frequent opportunities for choice in structuring their learning activities. Teachers who allow students a degree of choice typically have fewer behavior problems in their classrooms (Kern, Bambara, & Fogt, 2002). Offering choices provides students with a sense of autonomy and a voice in their learning. Remember that no teacher can possibly anticipate each student's idiosyncratic learning needs in every situation. If students are offered a choice in structuring their academic activities, however, they will frequently select those options that make their learning easier and more manageable. Students who

Some Examples of Academic Choices

An efficient way to promote choice in the classroom is for the teacher to create a master menu of options that allow students to select various learning situations. For example, during any independent assignment, students will always have a chance to (1) choose from at least two assignment options, (2) sit where they want in the classroom, and (3) select a peer-buddy to check their work. Student choice then becomes integrated seamlessly into the classroom routine. Another instructor may let the entire class vote on which of two lessons they would prefer to have presented that day. Choice can also be incorporated into individual assignments. In independent seatwork, for example, a student might choose which of several short assignments to do first, which books to read, or which research materials to use and in what response format (e.g., writing a short essay, preparing an oral report).

exercise academic choice are thus more likely to be active, motivated managers of their own learning and less likely to simply act out due to frustration or boredom.

3. Use high-interest or functional learning activities. Students are more motivated to learn when their instructional activities are linked to a topic of high interest (Kern et al., 2002). A teacher who discovers that her math group of seventh-graders loves NASCAR racing, for example, may be able to create engaging math problems based on car-racing statistics. Students may also be energized to participate in academic activities if they believe that these activities will give them functional real-life skills that they value (Miller, Gunter, Vern, Hammel, & Wiley, 2003). One instructor assigned to work with a special-education classroom of high school boys with serious behavior problems related that she had great difficulty managing the class until she realized that they all wanted to learn how to drive. She brought in copies of the state driver's education manual, which became the instructional text. The students' behavior improved because they were now motivated learners working toward the goal of learning how to drive.

4. Teach students at a brisk pace. A myth of remedial education is that special-needs students must be taught at a slower, less demanding pace than their general-education peers (Heward, 2003). Actually, a slow pace of instruction can cause significant behavior problems because students become bored and distracted. Teacher-led instruction should be dynamically delivered at a sufficiently brisk pace to

hold the student's attention. An important additional benefit of a brisk instructional pace is that students cover more academic material more quickly, accelerating their learning (Heward, 2003).

5. Structure lessons to foster more active student involvement. A powerful concept in behavior management is that it is very difficult for students to be actively engaged in academics and to misbehave at the same time. When teachers require that students participate in lessons rather than sit as passive listeners, they increase the odds that they will become caught up in the flow of the activity and not engage in misbehavior (Heward, 2003). There are many ways that students can become active learning participants. For example, a teacher may offer students several ways to respond to questions: (1) ask the class to give the answer in unison ("choral responding"); (2) pose a question, give the class "think time," and then draw a name from a hat to select a student to give the answer; or (3) direct students working independently on a practice problem to "think aloud" as they work through the steps of the problem. Students who have these types of opportunities to actively respond and receive teacher feedback demonstrate substantial gains in learning (Heward, 2003).

6. Integrate cooperative-learning opportunities with instruction. The traditional teacher lecture is frequently associated with high rates of student misbehavior. When misbehavior occurs in a large-group format, it can also have a major negative impact: one acting-out student who engages in a power-struggle with the teacher can interrupt learning for the entire class. However, when students are given

well-structured assignments and grouped into work-pairs of cooperative learning teams, behavior problems typically diminish (Beyda, Zentall, & Ferko, 2002). Furthermore, if a behavior problem should occur while cooperative groups are working together, the teacher is often able to approach and privately redirect the misbehaving student without disrupting learning in the other groups (Beyda, Zentall, & Ferko, 2002).

Even positive teacher practices can be more effective when used in cooperative-learning settings. When teachers engaged in a lecture format give extended feedback, coaching, and time to some students, other students can become disengaged and off-task. If students are working in pairs or small groups, though, teacher feedback may be given to one group or an individual and will not interrupt learning for other individuals or groups.

7. Give frequent teacher feedback and encouragement. Praise and other positive interactions between teacher and student serve an important instructional function; these exchanges regularly remind students about classroom behavioral and academic expectations and provide them with clear evidence that they are capable of achieving those expectations (Mayer, 2000).

Unfortunately, in most classrooms, educators tend to deliver many more reprimands than they do praise statements. This imbalance is understandable: after all, teachers are under pressure to devote most of their class time to delivering high-quality instruction, and they tend to interrupt that instruction only when forced to deal with disruptive behavior. A high rate of reprimands and low rate of praise, however, can result in several negative effects. If teachers do not routinely praise and encourage students who act appropriately, those positive student behaviors may whither away through lack of recognition. Students will probably find that a steady diet of reprimands is punishing, and they might eventually respond by withdrawing from participation or even avoiding the class altogether. A good goal for teachers should be to provide at least three to four positive interactions with students for each reprimand given (Sprick et al., 2002). Positive interactions might range from focused, specific praise to nonverbal exchanges such as a smile or "thumbs-up" from across the room, or even an encouraging note written on the student's

homework assignment. These positive interactions are brief and can often be delivered in the midst of instruction.

8. Provide correct models during independent work. In almost every classroom, students are expected to work independently on their assignments, but such independent seatwork can often be a prime trigger for serious student misbehavior (DuPaul & Stoner, 2002). One modest instructional adjustment that can significantly reduce problem behaviors is to supply students with several correctly completed models or work examples to use as a reference (Miller, Gunter, Vern, Hammel, & Wiley, 2003). For example, a math instructor teaching quadratic equations might provide four models in which all steps in solving the equation are shown. Students could refer to these models as needed when completing their own worksheets of similar algebra problems. Or an English/language arts teacher who asks students to write a letter to their U.S. senator might provide them with three "model" letters.

9. Be consistent in managing the academic setting. Picture this (not-uncommon) scenario: A teacher complains that her students routinely yell out answers without following the classroom rule of first raising their hands to be recognized. She invites an observer into the classroom to offer her some ideas for reducing the number of "blurt-outs." The observer quickly discovers that the teacher often ignores students who have raised their hands and instead accepts answers that are blurted out. Because the teacher is inconsistent in enforcing her classroom rules, she is actually contributing to student misbehavior.

As a group, students with challenging behaviors are more likely than their peers to become confused by inconsistent classroom attention. Teachers can minimize problem behaviors by teaching clear expectations for academic behaviors and then following through in enforcing those expectations consistently (Sprick et al., 2002). Classrooms run more smoothly when students are first taught routines for common learning activities such as participating in class discussion, turning in homework, breaking into cooperative learning groups, and handing out work materials. The teacher consistently enforces similar routines by praising students who follow them, reviewing those routines periodically, and, when appropriate, reteaching them.

10. Target interventions to coincide closely with point of performance. It is generally a good idea for teachers who work with a challenging group of students to target their behavioral and academic intervention strategies to coincide as closely as possible with that student's *point of performance*—the time that the student engages in the behavior that the teacher is attempting to influence (DuPaul & Stoner, 2002). Thus, a teacher is likely to be more successful in getting a student to take his colored pencils to afternoon art class if that teacher reminds the student (just as the class is lining up for art) than if she were to remind him at the start of the day. Also, student reward will have a greater impact if it is given near the time it was earned than if it is awarded after a two-week delay. Teacher interventions tend to gain in effectiveness as they are linked more closely in time to the students' points of performance that they are meant to influence. Skilled teachers employ many strategies to shape or manage challenging student behaviors. For instance, a teacher may give a "pre-correction" (reminder about appropriate behaviors) to a student who is about to leave the room to attend a school assembly, award a "good behavior" raffle-ticket to a student who displayed exemplary behavior in the hallway, or allow a student to collect a reward that she had earned for being on time to class for the whole week.

A good example of the use of effective strategies to educate and manage students with various disabilities is the model provided by the Morningside Learning Center.

THE MORNINGSIDE MODEL

The Morningside Model is an example of the application of scientific evidence in an educational setting that was established about 25 years ago initially as the Morningside Learning Center, and is today the Morningside Academy, a year-round school accredited by the state of Washington. With over 20 years of commitment to the ideals of educational accountability, there has been much empirical data to support the growth of this model (Johnson & Street, 2004).

While the Morningside Academy has many programs that are similar to any regular school, it is essentially a learning laboratory for designing instructional programs and classroom procedures using a precise focus on those skills that are essential for school success. Students typically gain from two to three grades in each academic skill per year, as measured by national standardized achievement tests (Snyder, 1992). The instructional materials represent a combination of Engleman's direct instruction programs in reading (Engleman & Brunner, 1995) and math (Engleman & Carnine, 1991). Direct instruction programs (Moran & Malott, 2004) are used in organizational and study skills and with thinking skills (Layng, Twyman, & Stikeleather, 2003).

The teacher's job during class sessions at Morningside Academy involves (1) alternating between teaching from various scripts, (2) troubleshooting with learners who need special fluency-building procedures, and (3) reinforcing interactions between peers as well as between student and teacher. If a teacher has never taught with others, there will be a need to adjust to the cooperative nature of the Morningside Model. The philosophy is that anything can be taught using the Morningside Model.

SUMMARY

The focus of this chapter is on the education of students with behavior disorders. Following a brief discussion of the relation between academic and behavioral problems, there is a general discussion of the No Child Left Behind Act of 2001. Current and future emphasis in educational practices will involve the use of scientifically based instruction and evidenced-based practice. Examples are given on how to implement such programs in the classroom. The nine categories of instructional strategies that are most likely to improve student achievement are presented, as are the three essential organizational needs for putting EBP in schools. Self-monitoring and opportunities to respond are discussed, and 10 research based guidelines on academic management are given. Lastly, the discussion focuses on the Morningside Model.

DISCUSSION QUESTIONS

1. Discuss the three basic findings in the study by Nelson, Brenner, Lane, and Smith (2004) on academic deficits.
2. What are the primary purpose and goals of NCLB?
3. List the six core elements of effective instruction of students with autism spectrum disorder as outlined by Iovannone and colleagues (2003).
4. How might practitioners put scientifically based research to work? Discuss the four steps that address this issue.
5. What is meta-analysis? Discuss its use.
6. Describe a normal distribution.
7. What is "effect size"? Explain its use.
8. List the nine categories of instructional strategies identified by Marzano, Pickering, and Pollock (2001) and explain each.
9. List two contextual influences in evidenced-based practices.
10. Explain the term "scaling-up."
11. What is a curriculum-based assessment?
12. How would you use self-monitoring to deal with staying on task?
13. Describe the two types of academic instruction.
14. What are the two things that teachers must combine to provide a classroom environment conducive to learning?
15. Briefly discuss 10 research-based ideas on academic management.
16. Describe the Morningside Model. Why is this an important instructional program?

PART V

Promising Directions for School-Wide Management

The presence of school-wide management can make a significant difference in the outcome of specific behavioral programs. The reality is that specific programs, which operate in the context of an overall positive behavioral framework, will be more successful. Variations in how school-wide programs are conceptualized and implemented are addressed first in Chapter 14. A school-wide program that is easy to implement is presented, and the concept of the wraparound school is discussed.

Schools have been more effective and manifest a number of benefits when operating in collaboration with a partner. Partnership programs are featured in Chapter 15, which describes their alliance with families and community. The federal guidelines for such alliances are also discussed. Involvement of siblings is often overlooked, but these resources clearly play a significant role in many school programs. The preparation of teachers with regard to partnerships is further addressed.

Chapter 16 focuses on the most promising direction for interventions with students who have behavior disorders. An important issue involves the focus on a model of prevention rather than a model of failure. This simply means that students who are having trouble need to be targeted before they fail. Recent developments using software for academic and behavioral interventions are explored, especially with regard to early childhood education. The training of teachers and related topics are emphasized—from dealing with teacher shortages and teacher burnout to the need for both general and special education teachers.

CHAPTER 14

Developing a School-Wide Behavioral Program

Overview

- Positive behavioral interventions and supports
- Discipline and development
- School-Wide Behavioral Programs
- Individual program support
- Resilience against violence
- Avoiding a negative behavioral orientation
- Improving the school and classroom environment
- Understanding the social needs of youth
- Teaching a social curriculum
- Current school discipline practices
- Applying discipline fairly
- Effectiveness of current discipline practices
- Steps in developing SW-PBS
- Primary prevention
- Secondary prevention
- Tertiary prevention
- Developmental considerations for SW-PBS
- History and development of the SW-PBS
- Schoolwide information system
- Wraparound schools

Case History

David is a 9-year-old third grader in a rural school. He is often off task and disrupts the class by refusing to stay at his desk during seatwork and talking disrespectfully to his teacher. He howls, makes clicking noises with his mouth, and talks out during instruction. David has been diagnosed with ADHD, but he is not on medication. The goal that has been set for David is for him to stay on-task and to work quietly. David is more disruptive when the teacher is in close proximity. The teacher's frequent redirections and reprimands have provided much attention. *What would you do?*

In the United States today, there are a growing number of students who exhibit disruptive behavior. These include the more serious issues of violence and gangs as well as significant behavior management issues in school. Disruptive behaviors have therefore become a primary concern for most educators (Martella, Nelson, and Marchand-Martella, 2003). Even if only a few students show inappropriate behavior, this can disrupt and interfere with learning for all students. One reason that such behavior problems can undermine the teacher's instruction is that these disruptive students have frequently been removed from the learning environment in the past (Brown & Beckett, 2007). Many of these students already have academic deficits, and when they are removed from the classroom for disciplinary reasons their academic deficits worsen. Increased frustration with learning tasks often results in additional behavior problems and consequently further exclusion. This self-perpetuating pattern may thus result in an escalating cycle of academic and social behavioral problems that brings about failure (Scott, Nelson, and Liaupsin, 2001). Academic problems may actually exacerbate behavior problems by increasing the student's time off-task and provide more opportunities to misbehave (Brown & Beckett, 2007; Scott, Nelson, & Liaupsin, 2001).

Disciplining students with chronic or serious behavior problems has been a long-standing challenge for educators. At the core of this challenge is the decision to choose between punitive and positive disciplinary procedures.

PUNITIVE DISCIPLINARY STRATEGIES: ZERO-TOLERANCE

Zero-tolerance policies exemplify punitive discipline that requires that students be expelled or suspended for serious misconduct or threats, especially when a student has possession of a weapon or drugs (Ghezzi, 2006). Although more common in recent years, zero tolerance has largely been shown to be ineffective at best and counterproductive at worst (Skiba, 2001). Research has indicated that expulsion, suspension, and other punitive consequences do not resolve dangerous and disruptive student behavior. The evidence suggests that these students may even become more dangerous as a result of such discipline. While no longer a dangerous threat in school, expelled students' problems often escalate and frequently endanger others outside of school. Some

expelled students may continue to carry grudges toward those still in school, and they are also more likely to associate with similar students and pose a real danger in the community. Expelled students are clearly not "safer" in school; they need to be involved in a structured treatment program that focuses on their aggressive behavior as well as their other problems. Zero-tolerance policies thus have many shortcomings (NASP, 2002):

■ They do not increase school safety.
■ They do not improve school climate or address the source of student alienation through expulsions and suspensions.
■ They are related to increased rates of school drop-out.
■ They may increase discriminating application of school discipline, negatively impacting minority students, with expulsions and suspensions.
■ They restrict access to a free and appropriate education, which may exacerbate the problems of students with various disabilities or academic problems and thus increase the probability of their dropping out. Dropouts further result in lost taxes and increased expenditures for welfare, mental-health care, and other social services.

POSITIVE DISCIPLINARY STRATEGIES

In contrast to zero-tolerance policies, positive disciplinary strategies focus instead on increasing desirable behaviors by improving the student environment instead of attempting to decrease undesirable behaviors through punishment. Positive reinforcement, modeling, and support from teachers and family are all examples of measures that may improve the student environment. This alternative to punitive discipline surely benefits all students.

The following information regarding students with disabilities has been provided by the Individuals with Disabilities Act (IDEA):

> The Individuals with Disabilities Education Act (IDEA) requires administrators to consider positive behavioral support (PBS) in all cases of students whose behavior impeded any student's learning. A report by Turnbull, Wilcox, et al. (2001) provides information to help educators understand how to legally handle students with behavioral (and other) disabilities. The article defines PBS and its role with

CENTRAL HIGH SCHOOL'S TEACHERS DISCOVER THE IMPORTANCE OF DATA.

IDEA, explains that PBS is a reputable presumption under IDEA, explains the definition of "appropriate education," and discusses state implementation of programming that will result in compliance with the law.

POSITIVE BEHAVIORAL INTERVENTIONS AND SUPPORTS IN SCHOOLS

Since 1966, schools have begun to emphasize school-wide positive behavior support in response to many requests to improve the purpose and structure of discipline systems. Currently, students in elementary and middle schools clearly require a preventive whole-school approach to deal with their problem behaviors (Sugai & Horner, 2002). Positive behavioral interventions and supports (PBIS) apply to positive behavioral

techniques to solve problem behaviors in the school setting—in the classroom as well as in hallways, cafeteria, playground, gym, etc. Although PBS and PBIS are used interchangeably in this discussion, the key attributes of PBS include proactivity, database decision making, and a problem-solving orientation (Horner, 2000; Sugai, Horner, Dunlap et al., 2000). PBS emphasizes a real-life focus in natural settings implemented by teachers, families, and perhaps other individuals using an array of assessment and support procedures (Turnbull & Turnbull, 1999).

Classrooms are often perceived as negative and unpleasant situations for students with academic and behavior problems. Consequently, these students are likely to show frustration and anger rather than perceiving the classroom positively as providing an opportunity to learn (Martella et al., 2003; Scott et al., 2001). It is therefore important for classrooms to decrease the probability of behavior problems that interfere with learning.

School discipline has typically focused primarily on reacting to undesirable behavior with some type of "punishment." However, research shows that the use of various punishment procedures without positive strategies is ineffective (Office of Special Education Programs [OSEP], 2005; Skiba and Peterson, 2000). For example, the use of suspensions and expulsions have been shown to be ineffective.

It was once thought that simply removing weapons from a school would reduce violent behavior (Sugai, Sprague, Horner, and Walker, 2000). However, this approach fails to consider the anxiety, threats, and other associated serious behavior problems that do not require a weapon (Scott et al., 2001).

The increase in the use of zero-tolerance policies for serious and less serious minimal offenses reflects the escalation of a punitive approach to behavior problems (Leone et al., 2003). However, those schools that continue to follow a zero-tolerance approach have been shown to be less safe than schools with fewer zero-tolerance policies (Leone et al., 2003; Skiba and Peterson, 2000).

Historically, there has been a general emphasis on punishment that has, however, slowly been replaced by School-Wide Positive Behavior Support (SW-PBS)—a proactive approach to discipline that uses both individual and systematic strategies based on positive behavioral interventions to improve both learning and social behavior while changing and preventing problem behaviors (Sugai, Horner, Dunlap et al., 2000; Turnbull et al., 2002). These proactive techniques can be used to manage undesirable behaviors and to improve students' active involvement in learning (Zuna and McDougall, 2004). Using empirically based (i.e., research-validated) practices, this approach is grounded in the science of human behavior and assumes that all behavior is learned through interactions and therefore can be unlearned or modified. The primary goal of SW-PBS is to remove the problem behaviors and to replace them with more desirable functional behavior. One must now look at the developmental aspects of discipline.

DISCIPLINE AND DEVELOPMENTAL PHASES

Children and their parents progress through social and emotional developmental phases in relation to each other. For school-aged children and their teachers, these phases become developmental tasks essential for optimal cognitive development. Discipline is necessary for accomplishing these tasks as well as ensuring the child's physical safety.

What the Federal Law (IDEA) Says About Discipline

Changes concerning the treatment of students who violate the code of conduct allows the school to change placement on a case-by-case basis. A manifestation determination may be conducted and educational services in alternative settings should be maintained.

As shown in Figure 14.1, however, discipline and punishment are not synonymous. Punishment may bring about more immediate suppression of the aggressive behavior, while discipline may require more time; punishment can be demeaning, while discipline can maintain respect; punishment may have no long-term effect, while discipline teaches skills that may be used in the future.

The aim of disciplining students within the school setting must be the development of character in the form of social conscience. In order for a society to successfully develop its children, they must understand that they share their society with others—that positive social interaction is essential.

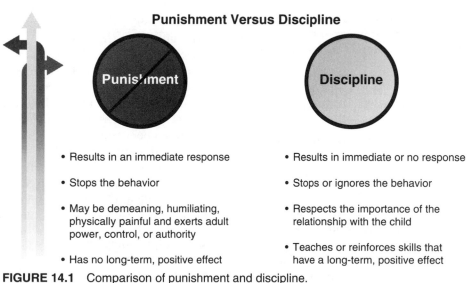

Punishment Versus Discipline

Punishment
- Results in an immediate response
- Stops the behavior
- May be demeaning, humiliating, physically painful and exerts adult power, control, or authority
- Has no long-term, positive effect

Discipline
- Results in immediate or no response
- Stops or ignores the behavior
- Respects the importance of the relationship with the child
- Teaches or reinforces skills that have a long-term, positive effect

FIGURE 14.1 Comparison of punishment and discipline.

Source: Information from The Ohio Department of Education, OCMS (1997; slide presentation). Reprinted by permission.

Adults too frequently resort to corporal punishment when discipline fails, thereby inhibiting a child's progress through normal developmental phases. Moreover, such punishment erodes the youngster's basic trust in others and stimulates anger and resentment toward authority figures.

By school age, children should have acquired a feeling of autonomy developed by teachers who delegate some control to students. Corporal punishment undermines this process and the teacher's ability to interpret a student's basic needs and to provide an environment of mutual trust conducive to learning. It slows or retards the development of a child's feeling of autonomy and produces shame and doubt. Teachers must separate themselves from their pupils and allow students to develop independently while they (the teachers) model optimal behavioral standards.

The development of a school-wide behavioral program can be beneficial to all students but especially to those students with a disability and particularly to those with a behavior disorder.

SCHOOL-WIDE BEHAVIORAL PROGRAMS

Positive behavioral support has strong conceptual and theoretical foundations in behavioral analysis and is used in school with different target students (Molina et al., 2005). These approaches may range from employing the *whole school* to focusing on *groups* or *individual students*. Positive behavioral support may be used in the following situations:

■ The whole school (all students, settings, and staff)
■ The classroom (instructional and behavior management)
■ A specific place (e.g., hallways, playgrounds, parking lots, cafeteria, gym)
■ Specialized interventions for the individual student (Sugai & Horner, 2002)

Positive behavioral interventions are clearly more effective when they are used on a whole-school *and* an individual-student basis. Adopting a school-wide approach allows students who have problem behaviors to learn skills they need to learn in order to reduce such behaviors and to reinforce positive behavior globally in the classroom and other school settings, and perhaps during after-school activities.

A school-wide disciplinary plan may foster a peaceful, caring student culture that is characteristic of a safe school. Positive school climates promote nurturance, inclusiveness, and a feeling of community (Walker, 1995). Students who are appreciated and recognized by at least one adult at school may be less likely to act-out against the school policy of nonviolence (Walker, 1995).

According to Walker, Colvin, and Ramsey (1995), a school-wide discipline plan should be designed to reach the following goals:

■ Teach students basic prosocial behaviors.
■ Reinforce these behaviors in clearly visible ways.
■ Consistently hold children accountable for their misbehavior. Various school personnel can not only encourage prosocial behaviors but also discourage misbehavior.

The actions of a principal can actually establish school norms of nonviolence, feelings of community, and caring relationships with students. By walking down the hall and visiting classrooms, the principal maintains a high profile, remains accessible to students, and reduces the likelihood of antisocial behavior (Bland & Read, 2000). The principal can also help students gain a sense of ownership of school programs and policies by sharing decision-making, instituting antiracism programs, speaking out against harassment, and making social services available to needy students (Natale, 1998). It is well to remember how students learn different behaviors.

Since students learn many violent behaviors through modeling and reinforcement, these same processes can be used to teach nonviolent behaviors (Committee for Children, 1989; Hausman, Pierce, & Briggs, 1996). Many middle and secondary schools have instituted peer conflict mediation programs that have reduced discipline referrals and improved school climate, while enhancing self-esteem, confidence, and student responsibility (Johnson & Johnson, 1996).

According to Sugai, Horner, Dunlap et al. (2000) there are five key features of positive behavioral support:

■ Clearly defining three to five universal behavioral expectations in simple, succinct, and positive ways.
■ Making expectations clear so that all students know exactly what is expected of them.
■ Implementing a comprehensive school-wide positive reinforcement system.

- Communicating the expectations on a school-wide basis (in other words, rewarding students by "catching them being good").
- Evaluating progress using a team of teachers to make data-based adaptations. An example of a research-based examination of SW-PBS is seen in the study that follows.

Turnbull, Turnbull, and Wilcox (2002) evaluate the school-wide positive referral system based on the five features of universal support. In this program, teachers and other school staff were encouraged to "catch" students demonstrating positive behaviors and to issue a positive referral ticket for that behavior. Students who engaged in the appropriate and desirable behavior were also asked to check off which one of the five universal expectations they had exhibited. Turnbull and colleagues (2002) found that the program was effective and resulted in an increase in appropriate behaviors in the school.

Nelson and colleagues (2002) evaluated another comprehensive school-wide program based on an effective behavioral support approach for preventing disruptive behaviors. The program consisted of five main elements: (1) a school-wide discipline program, (2) one-on-one tutoring and reading, (3) conflict resolution, (4) a video-based family management program, and (5) individualized, function-based, behavior intervention plans. Seven elementary schools in one district were studied for a period of 2 years. Comparisons with the districts' other 28 elementary schools suggested a strong positive effect on formal disciplinary actions and the school's academic performance. In addition to group programs, there are individual programs.

INDIVIDUAL PROGRAM SUPPORT

Individual program support: Student will benefit from a positive, supportive, and structured environment that offers programs to meet the needs of those students with disabilities.

At the heart of individual student support is a functional behavioral assessment (FBA) that identifies relationships between behaviors and the triggers that impede learning (Reid et al., 1999; Sugai, Sprague, Horner, & Walker, 2000). To reduce problem behavior, Lewis,

Powers, Kely, and Newcomer (2002) suggest that schools need to develop an array of positive-behavior supports that targets prevention, early intervention, and individualized student support systems for students with chronic problem behaviors.

RESILIENCE AGAINST VIOLENCE

Resilience against violence refers to the development of protective factors that allow both boys and girls to resist manifestations of violence despite exposure to risk factors that normally result in violent perpetration.

Some of the individual factors that increase resilience against violence include the following:

- *Caring relationships*: Research shows that developing relationships with caring adults protects "at-risk" youth against engaging in violence (McNeely, Nonnemaker, & Blum, 2002).
- *Sense of connection to family*: The 1994–1995 National Longitudinal Study of Adolescent Health found that young people's sense of connection to their parents and other family members was the most consistently protective factor across all the health outcomes. Teens with parents who were physically present in the home were less likely to engage in violent behavior (Williams, 1994).
- *Sense of connection to school*: Students who feel a part of their school and are treated fairly by teachers are generally more emotionally healthy and less inclined toward drug and alcohol abuse, suicidal thoughts or attempts, and involvement in violence (Catalano & Hawkins, 1996).
- *High expectations*: Students whose parents express high expectations for their performance in school are less likely to engage in violent behavior. Providing students with such messages helps to build their self-esteem and self-efficacy.

There are at least two factors within school and community settings that increase resilience:

- *Opportunities to participate and contribute*: Involving students in decisions about school policies and programs is a key factor in creating a school climate of inclusion, respect, and safety (U.S. Department of Education, 1998a). When students have opportunities to acquire skills and engage in social activities, their problem solving, communication, and analytical skills also improve. In addition, they demonstrate enhanced leadership and autonomous decision-making and are more likely to reach academic goals such as graduating from school.

■ *Participation in community networks*: Participation in community networks, neighborhood associations, and religious and school organizations helps students develop strong formal and informal ties with adults. It also increases their sense of connection and self-efficacy.

Resilience is defined as an individual's ability to adapt to change, involving stressful events, in healthy and flexible ways (Vandell & Su, 1999). Resilience has also been described in research studies as the characteristic of youth who, when exposed to multiple risk factors, successfully respond and learn from challenges to achieve successful outcomes (Goldstein, 2002; Hanlon et al., 2004).

Some researchers have pointed out that resilience may be less useful in the face of overwhelming risk, which almost invariably leads to poor outcomes (Vance et al., 2002). It has not been shown whether or not the presence of protective factors might weaken or lessen the severity of problems incurred by adolescents who are exposed to overwhelming risk. Like risk factors, protective factors (which foster resilience) may be strengthened through interaction with other protective factors. Individual protective factors include having a positive view of one's life circumstances and the ability to affect others as well as familiarity with stress-reducing strategies. Family protective factors include having a strong attachment to at least one family member who engages in proactive, healthy behavior (for example, someone who has high expectations for academic and social performance in and out of school or has shared values with family members).

Historically hyperactivity, limited attention span, restlessness, risk-taking, poor social skills, and certain beliefs and attitudes (for example, the necessity of retaliation) appear to favor the development of delinquent behavior. Students with disabilities such as emotional disturbance, attention-deficit disorders, specific learning problems, and conduct disorders are more likely to display antisocial behavior, suggesting that these conditions may be risk factors for aggressive and violent actions (Leone et al., 2000).

Negative conditions in the home (e.g., harsh and ineffective parental discipline, lack of parental involvement, family conflict, parental criminality, child abuse or neglect, and rejection) may also predict early onset and chronic patterns of antisocial behavior in youth (McEvoy & Welker, 2000). When such conditions are present, children may be literally trained to be aggressive during episodes of conflict with family members (Forgath & Patterson, 1998).

Reading skills serve as a protective factor among high-risk children in community samples (Werner and Smith, 1992). In a study by Vance et al. (2002), protective factors were the best predictors of behavioral outcomes, in contrast to the findings of studies of community-based samples, which have generally found risk factors to be more predictive of outcomes (Snowling, Bishop, and Stothard, 2000; Dekovic, 1999).

Some influences in the school and community also contribute to enduring patterns of aggressive and violent behavior. School factors include little school involvement, academic and social failure, lack of clarity and follow-through in rules and policies, poor or inconsistent administrative support, and few allowances for individual differences. In addition, disciplinary practices in many schools are inconsistent and inequitable (Skiba & Peterson, 2000). In spite of IDEA requirements, a disproportionate number of students with disabilities and students from diverse backgrounds are subjected to punitive consequences such as suspension or expulsion. Some communities lack features that help prevent antisocial lifestyles such as before and after school programs, recreational opportunities, and adult mentors. In addition, the absence of emotional or financial support with friends may lead to efforts to gain this support through antisocial behavior.

Prevention research has also shown that different risk and protective factors appear at different stages of a child's development (Bell, 1986). Some researchers have therefore cautioned practitioners to focus not just on protective interventions but also on risk reduction (Fraser, Richman, & Galinsky, 1999). Risk and resilience researchers have consistently noted the deleterious effects of an accumulation of four or more risk factors in the likelihood of developing a childhood psychiatric disorder (Kendler & Prescott, 2006; Rassool, 2006). Discussion now centers on further characteristics of resilience.

The length of time between the development of resilience and the development of cognitive and emotional skills lies in their both being acquired (i.e., learned) over time and within the context of supportive environments. From a developmental perspective, resilience is the capacity to successfully undertake the work of each successive developmental stage (Patterson & Blum, 1996). Chores and responsibilities at home are a key factor distinguishing those who function well from those who do not (Dunn, 2004). Rutter (1979) showed such experiences of "required helpfulness" assists in developing an internal locus of control that is a key to resilience in Western cultures. This philosophy by Rutter (1979) was also supported by Daniel and Wassell (2002). Rachman (1979) actually coined the term *required helpfulness* to capture the notion that those who contribute to the social good of a family or a community through successful completion of obligations should be recognized for their contributions. It is a concept Mitchell (1975) articulated when he spoke of the positive self-esteem value of youth participation in the community.

Patterson (1988) presented a transactional model for understanding risk and resilience within a social context. The "family adjustment and adaptation response" model suggested that an individual's reaction to stress is determined by a balance between demands (i.e., stresses and daily hassles) and capabilities (i.e., resources and coping behaviors).

In the school setting, both teachers and administrators can play an integral part in the development of resilience in youth exposed to multiple risks, providing positive and safe learning environments, setting high yet achievable academic and social expectations, and facilitating students' academic and social success. Also, youth who belong to a socially appropriate group sponsored and supported by the school are less likely to demonstrate aggression or violence (Catalano, Loeber, & McKinney, 1999).

Several longitudinal studies of resilience have indicated that some children exposed to high levels of risk nonetheless have positive life outcomes (Fergus & Zimmerman, 2005; Blum, 2005). Longitudinal studies conducted over the past 30 years have identified many factors in neighborhoods, families, schools, and peer groups as well as within the individual that predict problem behaviors (Hill et al., 2000; Bor, McGee, & Fagan, 2004). Exposure to an increasing number of risk factors was found to increase the likelihood of the child having problem behaviors, whereas exposure to an increasing number of protective factors was found to prevent problem behaviors in spite of the child's exposure to risks (Catalano et al., 2004). Thus, positive youth development programs seek to promote (1) resilience, (2) social competence, (3) emotional competence, (4) cognitive competence, (5) behavioral competence, (6) moral competence, and (7) recognition for positive behavior.

School violence-prevention experts need to recognize individual, family, and community assets and capacities that can help create resilience against violence. Violence-prevention strategies that build and support these capacities will help prevent school violence and foster healthy child and adolescent development while at the same time develop community strengths in the future.

Students are clearly shaped by the broader social context in which they live. Their individual behavior reflects not only their developmental level but also their experiences in families, neighborhoods, and schools (Garbarino, 1992). Practitioners who understand how these influences help to build resilience in young people are more likely to be able to successfully intervene to reduce and prevent school violence and improve the lives of young people.

Students, schools, and families can select from a range of activities that help to develop resilience. In doing so, leaders must ensure that selected activities are developmentally appropriate, culturally relevant, nonstigmatizing, and accessible to all youth (Moore, 2004). The following activities will help develop resilience:

- Peer support activities
- Structured after-school programs
- Service-learning

Service learning is an educational activity, program, or curriculum that seeks to promote students' learning through experiences associated with volunteerism or community service.

- Cross-age mentoring
- Work or training apprenticeships
- Art, music, dance, and other creative activities
- Sports and other recreational or outdoor experiences

AVOIDING A NEGATIVE BEHAVIORAL ORIENTATION

Policymakers at middle and secondary schools should follow two basic school program guidelines: (1) employ a positive approach to discipline and violence prevention, and (2) avoid negative behavioral orientation such as corporal punishment (a disciplinary procedure that should also be avoided at home).

Corporal Punishment

The use of corporal punishment in the home and school has been widely debated. Some believe it is a means of discipline while others label it as abuse. Not only does corporal punishment have no long-lasting positive effect on behavior, it also creates numerous side-effects, including emotional and physical problems.

Many parents and teachers are unsure of what is right or wrong concerning physical punishment. Too often the problem of discipline seems to be viewed only as how children can be controlled, while many parents and teachers today have been so intimidated by psychological publications and by legal action against child abuse that they are afraid to even appropriately assert themselves with their children. It is thus important for both parents and teachers to be aware of the findings about corporal punishment. For example, Curren (2000) reported that corporal punishment frequently escalates to child abuse.

Effective Discipline

Effective discipline includes both prevention and intervention programs and strategies that change student behavior, change school or classroom environments, and educate and support teachers and parents. The following strategies can help provide an atmosphere where learning can take place and where students learn to be self-disciplined:

■ Help students achieve academic success through identifying and ameliorating academic and behavioral deficiencies.
■ Use behavioral contracting where the student signs a contract to complete a specific task or engage in some appropriate behavior in order to obtain a desired consequence such as a reward.
■ Positively reinforce all appropriate behavior.

■ Use individual and group counseling.
■ Apply consequences that are meaningful to students and that have an instructional or thinking component. In short, it is important to develop strategies that not only teach specific appropriate behaviors but also encourage students to use their thinking processes to avoid the development of excessive dependency on others to do what they are told.

IMPROVING SCHOOL AND CLASSROOM ENVIRONMENTS

Improving the school and classroom environments will improve the effectiveness of behavior management, generally encouraging overall appropriate behavior and a positive behavioral focus. The following suggestions emphasize the importance of rules, personal responsibility, and communication and they will support and encourage appropriate behaviors in many contexts:

■ Encourage programs that emphasize early diagnosis and early intervention for staff and student problems.
■ Encourage programs that emphasize values, school pride, and personal responsibility as well as support the mental health needs of students.
■ Encourage development of fair, reasonable, and consistent rules.
■ Support strong parent–school and community–school communications and alliances.

UNDERSTANDING THE SOCIAL NEEDS OF YOUTH

Though it may not always be apparent, many children and adolescents are unaware of how to resolve social conflict (Optow, 1991) or to respond appropriately in benign social situations (Cunningham, 2000). Children who display noncompliant aggressive (even antisocial) behavior may believe that the most effective way to avoid physical abuse is to become physically abusive. Some learn to act-out to set limits, even if the consequence is harsh punishment (Flick, 1998b, 2000). Children with conduct disorders, perhaps as a function of their threatening home or harsh environment, may develop an antisocial mind-set: strike first and ask questions later (Dodge, 1993). Students who have a history of coercive family patterns may perceive a teacher's request for compliance as the initial phase of hassling where resistance needs to be quick and firm.

There are also links between antisocial behavior and academic underachievement (Beitchman & Young, 1997), which suggest that students with behavior problems often revert to disruptive or off-task behavior to escape from academic demands as the difficulty of the material increases. These students may avoid work that may cause them to look "dumb." Media violence has been associated with increased negative and aggressive interactions for both children and adolescents (Barenthin & Van Puymbroech, 2006; Anderson et al., 2003). It will therefore be important not only to limit the child's time

spent with media materials such as videos and comics but more importantly to monitor and control what the child is exposed to—for example, to make all violent videos, movies, games, and comics off-limits at all times.

Alternatives to Discipline and Punishment

Although punitive approaches might result in an immediate suppression of inappropriate behaviors, such procedures will not eliminate them. Some of the behavioral and emotional consequences of each approach are compared in Figure 14.2. Overall, the use of positive

Punitive Approaches	Positive Approaches
1. Rapidly stops behavior	1. Slowly stops behavior
2. Provides immediate relief for teacher	2. May provide no immediate relief to the teacher
3. Teaches the student and peers what not to do	3. Teaches the student and peers how to behave
4. Decreases positive self-statements (self-concept)	4. Increases positive self-statements (self-concept)
5. Decreases positive attitudes toward school and schoolwork	5. Increases positive attitudes toward school and schoolwork
6. Causes withdrawal (nontask, tardy, truancy, dropping out)	6. Promotes enhanced participation
7. Causes aggression (against property and others)	7. Decreases likelihood of aggression
8. Teaches students to respond in a punitive manner	8. Teaches students to recognize the positive
Results in suppression of undesirable behavior, not elimination	Results in alternative, positive behavior to replace maladaptive behavior

FIGURE 14.2   A comparison of punitive and positive approaches.

Source: Adapted with permission from Placer County SELPA (http://www.placercoe.k12.ca.us/documents405cdoc101.pdf).

approaches will result in more appropriate and adaptive behavior. While punitive approaches may harm the student–teacher relationship, positive approaches may enhance the relationship (Mayer, 1995).

TEACHING A SOCIAL CURRICULUM

Schools and teachers should make their expectations known to students through a social curriculum—school-wide instruction on social guidelines that may help address widespread misconceptions among youth about the nature of conflict and problem solving. The guidelines should include (1) verbal explanations (Skiba & Peterson, 2006), (2) written class and school rules, and (3) feedback with consequences (Alderman, 2004). In poorly managed classrooms, inconsistencies may confuse students about the social guidelines. For example, despite a rule to "raise your hand before speaking," some teachers selectively ignore the rule in order to encourage spontaneous discussion and then to enforce it *only* when the noise and conflict get out of hand. Such teachers thus fail to recognize and consistently reinforce appropriate behavior in as many situations as possible. Clearly followed rules foster the perception that *all* rules will be followed and promoted.

CURRENT SCHOOL DISCIPLINE PRACTICES

High school aggression and violence have become some of the most significant problems facing school administration public officials in the United States (Haas, 2000). Despite high levels of aggressive violent behavior in high schools, many school districts continue to rely on expensive, short-term, and poorly conceptualized policies and programs to adjust the problem of school violence.

Punitive procedures such as using metal detectors for guns and knives, in-school suspension, and zero-tolerance policies may temporarily reduce problem behaviors in the school, but they do not remove them. Zero-tolerance policies are supported by the Individuals with Disabilities Education Act (IDEA) in instances of (1) drug possession or use, and (2) carrying or possessing weapons (Wright & Wright, 2000).

Incidents of school violence and student misbehavior have received a lot of media attention. Local, state, and national policymakers have proposed, encouraged, and implemented a variety of preventive efforts, including zero-tolerance policies, metal detectors, and video monitoring. However, such strategies reflect narrow definitions of the term "school violence" and "school safety." It is therefore important to broaden these definitions to include other events that may have an individual relationship with school violence. For example, research shows that behaviors characterized as violent and unsafe by administrators, teachers, and students often are the outcome of a predictable chain of events that will sometimes begin with academic failure. For this reason, efforts to prevent school violence should include the promotion of effective academic instruction (Scott, Nelson, & Liaupsin, 2001).

Confronted by increasing incidents of violent behavior in schools, educators are being asked to make schools safer. One area of need resides in developing more specific directions for the use of existing discipline information to improve school-wide behavior support. Sugai, Sprague, and colleagues (2000) describe how office discipline referrals might be used as an information source to provide an indication of school-wide discipline and to improve the precision with which schools manage, monitor, and modify their universal interventions and their targeted interventions for students who exhibit problem behaviors.

Over the past few years, there has been growing public support for policies at all levels of government to increasingly address social problems through the police, courts, and prison system. As school safety became a top educational priority, zero-tolerance policies were broadened to include a range of behavioral infractions from possessing drugs or weapons to verbally threatening other students. A sense of perspective seems lost, as school systems across the country clamor for metal detectors, armed guards, see-through knapsacks, and in some cases, armed teachers. Some school systems are also investing in software that "profiles" students who might exhibit antisocial or criminal behavior. McConaughy (2005) has stated that profiling is one way that has been attempted to weed out violent students, but there are problems with such efforts.

American schools are increasingly marked by the foreboding presence of armed security guards patrolling the halls and cafeterias and by locked doors, video surveillance cameras, electronic badges, police dogs, and routine drug searches. Such an atmosphere conveys a deep distrust, if not hostility, toward young people.

Based on Colorado zero-tolerance law, the number of students expelled from public schools has skyrocketed since 1993, when 437 came before the law, to nearly 2,000 in the 1996–1997 school year. As the criminalization of young people finds its way into the classroom, it becomes easier to punish students rather than to listen to them or deal with their behavior. Columnist Ellen Goodman (2000) pointed out that zero tolerance has become a code word for "a quick and dirty way of kicking kids out of school."

Instead of investing in early childhood programs, repairing deteriorating school buildings, implementing antiviolence programs, or hiring more qualified teachers, schools now spend millions of dollars to upgrade security. In fact, many states now spend more on prisons than on university construction. Some young people are quickly led to believe that schools have more in common with military boot camps and prisons than they do with other institutions in American society.

Effective behavioral support procedures should be implemented by all school staff to provide a unified school-wide approach. Critical to the success of any program, however, is administrative support. While few procedures involving school policies outline specific administrative tasks, the typical approach adopted by many administrators requires training, monitoring, and possibly rewording goals. The administrator's role should be threefold:

- Provide leadership and communicate to all staff the importance of establishing a positive school-wide system and antiviolence program.
- Determine what resources are needed to provide staff with appropriate and comprehensive training along with time for planning.
- Continually monitor the overall plan and make sure that all staff members are participating.

Applying Discipline Fairly

In many school settings, the word *discipline* has been used almost synonymously with *zero tolerance*: Any misbehavior, however slight, is punished—sending a clear message to troublemakers. The infamous zero-tolerance approach has probably caused more problems than it has solved (Shellady & Sealander, 2003). In numerous controversial cases, students have been suspended or placed in alternative schools for pranks, with little consideration given to what may be a *real school threat*. The media have recorded some notable overreactions:

- In Colorado, a 6-year-old boy was suspended for half a day for giving candy to another child. A school official pointed out that bringing candy to school was as disruptive as bringing a gun.
- In Cape Central High School (Cape Girardeau, Missouri), 253 students who drove their cars to school were suspended. The assistant principal explained, "We have a strict policy against any student who brings a weapon that can cause harm, injury, or disruption." He continued to point out, "an automobile is the most dangerous legal weapon one can own and it's time we put a stop to this deadly menace."
- A sixth grader brought a knife to school (in Ocala, Florida) to cut her chicken in the lunchroom. Although she did ask the teacher if this was all right, she was subsequently arrested, taken from school in a police car, and then suspended.
- *USA Today* reported that two Illinois 7-year-olds were suspended for having nail clippers with "knife-like attachments" (Cauchon, 1999).

The most common form of school discipline under zero-tolerance policies is "suspension" (Skiba & Knesting, 2002). The general and sometimes flagrant use of suspension and expulsion has increased substantially since zero tolerance has been in effect in our schools (Brooks, Schiraldi, & Ziedenberg, 2000). The general result has been that neither suspension nor expulsion have been effective in managing behavior problems.

Nondiscrimination Procedure

In terms of school disciplinary practices, a student's right to not be discriminated against is not always upheld. As a result, many minority students are targeted for mild consequences and sometimes suspension. Minorities, especially blacks, have a long history of unequal opportunity and oppression; these inequities continue to be played out in educational settings (Skiba et al., 2002). The *New York Times* reported on several studies illustrating that black students in public schools across the United States are far more likely than white students to be suspended or expelled and far less likely to be in gifted or advanced-placement classes. For instance, blacks in San Francisco make up 52 percent of all suspended students, far in excess of their 16 percent representation in the general population.

A disproportionate number of young adolescent black males lose instructional time in the classroom as a result of being suspended for fighting at school. While many referrals for behavior problems lead only to mild consequences (Figure 14.3), the most common referrals lead to suspension (Figure 14.4), as noted by Skiba (2003).

Much of the literature addressing black culture suggests a correlation between socioeconomic status, households headed by single black females, and violent behavior of young black males (Kunjufu, 1990).

Mason (1996) studied the results of an anger management program taught primarily from the African American perspective by a black adult male. The sample population was limited to 51 seventh- and eighth-grade black males. Mason's findings suggested two significant group conclusions: (1) young adolescent black males get suspended and lose too much instructional (school) time because of aggressive behavior, and (2) young adolescent black males, especially those in

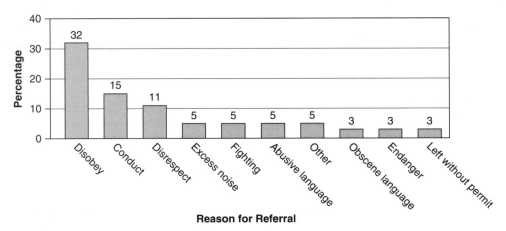

FIGURE 14.3 The most common referrals leading to mild consequences.
Source: Information from Skiba (2003). Reprinted by permission.

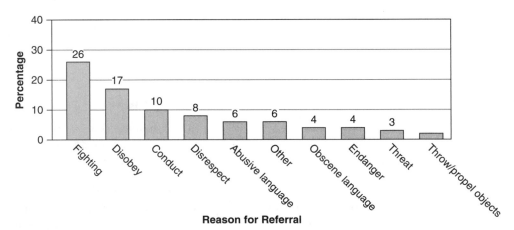

FIGURE 14.4 The most common referrals leading to suspension.
Source: Information from Skiba (2003). Reprinted by permission.

poor, female-dominated single-family homes, can benefit from anger management training.

For more than 25 years, black students have been suspended at rates of two to three times that of other students; similar data have been reported for office referrals, corporal punishment, and school expulsion (Skiba et al., 2002). Such differences cannot be accounted for merely on the basis of lower socioeconomic status (SES); no other evidence indicates that black students show higher rates of misbehavior. It has also been noted that black students have been punished for less severe rule violations than white students (Shaw & Braden, 1990) and punished more severely for similar offenses (McFadden, March, Price, & Hwang, 1992).

It is, therefore, difficult to argue that suspensions and expulsions reflect nondiscriminatory practice and instead seem to be more consistent with evidence of racial discrimination (Herr, Cramer, & Niles, 2004; Skiba, 2003). These findings are also combined with information that suggests racial disproportionality in suspension is greatly increased in schools that use suspension more frequently (Massachusetts Advocacy Center, 1986). The findings are reported in Figures 14.3 and 14.4. This data reflects clearly that blacks are disproportionate with regard to both the most common referrals that lead to mild consequences (Figure 14.3) as well as data that indicate that the most common referrals lead to suspension (Figure 14.4).

Special-Education Students

The discipline of special-education students has also created controversy; critics suggest that those provisions for special-education students create a dual system that limits the discipline options of school administrators. A review of the literature focusing on special-education students reveals little or no evidence that suspension contributes at all to reducing disruption or violence, and it reveals some evidence that expulsion procedures also target certain populations, including special-education students, disproportionately (Skiba et al., 2002). Despite a dramatic increase in the use of zero-tolerance procedures and policies, there is little evidence that school safety and appropriate student behavior have improved. A preventive early-response discipline approach increases the range of effective options for addressing violence and disruption across

both general and special-education students (Skiba & Peterson, 2000).

EFFECTIVENESS OF CURRENT DISCIPLINE PRACTICES

As Skiba and Peterson (2000) have noted, the term *discipline* comes from the Latin word *disciplina* or *discipere*, which means, "to teach." The question arises, how well do suspension, expulsion, and other supposedly preventive alternatives actually teach appropriate behavior in schools? The answer appears to be that disciplinary exclusion is associated with a myriad of negative outcomes for both students and the school climate.

Improved Student Behavior

A large number of students who are suspended from school appear to be repeat offenders (Bowditch, 1993; Massachusetts Advocacy Center, 1986), suggesting that such students are not "getting the message" that disciplinary removal allegedly teaches. In some obvious cases suspension may actually function as a reinforcer rather than a punishment (Tobin, Sugai, & Colvin, 2000). (See Chapter 8 regarding the underlying reasons for escape or avoidance behavior functions.)

For at-risk students with emotional and/or behavioral disorders, suspension and expulsion seem to increase the rate of disruption and eventually the delinquency and dropout rates (Ekstrom, Goertz, Pollack, & Rock, 1986). Some schools actually seem to use suspension to "push out" certain students, suspending them repeatedly as a means of "cleaning house" of troublemakers who are disrespectful, challenge school authority, and exhibit more aggressive behaviors (Bowditch, 1993).

Alternatives to Disciplinary Removal

In most cases, schools and school districts suspend and expel students simply because they do not know what else to do. However, numerous preventive alternatives are known to be effective in improving school discipline and reducing school disruption and violence (Elliott, Hatot, Sirovatka, & Potter, 2001; Gagnon & Leone, 2001; Mihalic et al., 2001; Thornton et al., 2000). The effective strategies and programs that have been researched represent the emergence of a new perspective in school discipline and in violence prevention. In contrast to largely ineffective suspension and expulsion, new strategies such as school-wide positive behavioral support programs, antiviolence programs, and various social skills programs have produced solid evidence of success in improving student behavior and school climate.

Litigation Issues

Educators are sometimes sued over issues that are commonly encountered in dealings with students with behavior problems. These disputes involve problems associated with corporal punishment, suspensions and expulsions, educational malpractice, search and seizure, and defamation of character. To avoid lawsuits, schools need to consider discontinuing disciplinary procedures such as corporal punishment, suspension, and expulsions while emphasizing educational procedures that are effective in targeting students with academic deficiencies or developmental lags. (Remember that such academic problems can precipitate behavior problems.)

Corporal Punishment Cases of assault and battery or charges of child abuse sometimes arise in instances of corporal punishment. Although many states still allow corporal punishment in schools, teachers should be aware that parents might strongly object to the use of such discipline. Although the state agency that handles child abuse and other allegations may clear the teacher or administrator who used punishment of legal wrongdoing, his or her name will remain on file in the agency's records. As a result, an educator's life can be severely disrupted by such a lawsuit.

In those cases in which corporal punishment appears to be unreasonable or excessive, the court may rule in favor of the student. The key words are "what is unreasonable and excessive?" Of course, the best policy is to ban the use of corporal punishment such as spanking in school.

Suspension and Expulsion Public-school educators who discipline using suspension or expulsion may also be subject to tort liabilities (Redding & Shalf, 2001). Such litigation usually deals with the right of students to due process prior to being excluded from school (Avant & Davis, 1984; Vacca & Hudgins, 1992). Students' rights to an education can be removed only after due process standards are met (see Avant & Davis, 1984). Students must understand the charges against them and have the opportunity to explain their behavior. In most cases, litigation involves an informal hearing whose extent depends on the severity of the punishment—the longer the suspension, the more formal the hearing.

Educational Malpractice Educational malpractice is a relatively new tort that has not had much success for plaintiffs. Based on the assumption of negligence, it holds educators liable for failure to provide adequate instruction, which may result in failure to learn how to read, get into college, or even get a job. Although the general climate of litigation for such claims has been negative, educational malpractice appears to be an evolving area of law that deserves some monitoring, especially in light of the No Child Left Behind Act of 2001. Clearly, many cases of disordered behavior can involve educational or academic deficiencies that must be addressed with greater intensity.

Search and Seizure With the advent of zero-tolerance programs and the many cases of violent acting-out behavior, educators frequently raise concerns over searching students and their belongings (Russo & Stefkovich, 1998). Such searches are often backed by lawmakers who view these searches as necessary to protect *all* of the students in school. The potential liability applies primarily to public schools and is associated with the Fourth Amendment, which provides that persons shall be free of unreasonable search and seizures by the state (in this case, by public school officials). Schools must post notices that lockers and other storage areas are school property and, as such, can be searched for drugs or dangerous weapons.

Although laws may vary from state to state, students generally may be searched under the following provisions: (1) the student has violated a school policy, (2) the search will provide evidence leading to disclosure of drugs or a dangerous weapon, (3) the search is based on the school's underlying need to maintain order, discipline, safety, supervision, and education for the student body, and (4) the search is not conducted for the sole purpose of obtaining evidence for criminal prosecution (Vacca & Hudgins, 1982). The two essential elements regarding the legal basis of the search are (1) the reason for the search, and (2) the way the search is conducted.

As a general rule, courts uphold searches in which a school official requires a student to remove personal effects from his clothing; however, courts are unlikely to uphold a strip search. When school officials personally go through a student's clothes, purses, school bag, etc. they face potential assault and battery charges; students must remove belongings on their own.

Defamation of Character   Educators may be held liable for the comments they write in a student's permanent record, a student's file that should contain only grades, attendance information, and standardized test scores. Statements about behavior in the student's file must be worded very carefully, emphasizing observable and factual information. However, students may receive any number of positive comments about appropriate behavior, as would be the case if a positive behavioral orientation is supported. For example, the educator may write, "Dylan has been in four fights this week." Since any other student, 18 or older, may have personal access to a student's entire file, defamatory comments made towards a teacher or another school might result in a lawsuit against the student's school.

A DESCRIPTION OF SCHOOL-WIDE BEHAVIORAL PROGRAMS

School-Wide Positive Behavior Support (SW-PBS) employs a three-tier model that involves *primary* (school-wide), *secondary* (classroom), and *tertiary* (individual) levels (Martella et al., 2003; Sugai, Horner, et al., 2000; Sugai, Sprague, et al., 2000). Figure 14.5 illustrates the three tiers of this model. These levels of intervention have two variables: (1) the number of students involved, and (2) the intensity of support (Turnbull, Edmonson, et al., 2002). Gresham (2004) has noted the importance of matching the intensity of the behavioral intervention with the severity of the problem behavior. The three-tier approach supports this combination by having a universal or primary level (the least intense) along with two other levels (secondary and tertiary) to provide additional interventions as needed. The three-tier positive behavioral support system is recommended (Lewis and Sugai, 1999) to create an environment that is conducive to both academic and social success.

Instead of using a patchwork of individual behavior management plans, a continuum of positive behavior support for all students is used in the classroom as well as in other areas of the school such as hallways, restrooms, lunchroom, gym, and playground.

A Systems Approach

A systems approach thus supports the adoption of evidence-based practices and procedures. The SW-PBS program stresses the formation of systems that not only support the implementation of evidence-based practices but also conform to school reforms. This process is basically the same as the SW-PBS and utilizes an interaction of four elements. According to Feinstein (2003), an interactive approach corrects and improves the four key elements in SW-PBS:

1. *Outcomes*—academic and behavioral targets that are endorsed by students, families, and educators.

2. *Practices*—interventions and strategies that are evidence-based.

3. *Data*—information that is used to identify the status, need for change, and effectiveness of interventions.

4. *Systems*—supports that are needed to enable the accurate and durable implementation of PBS practices.

The four elements are shown in Figure 14.6.

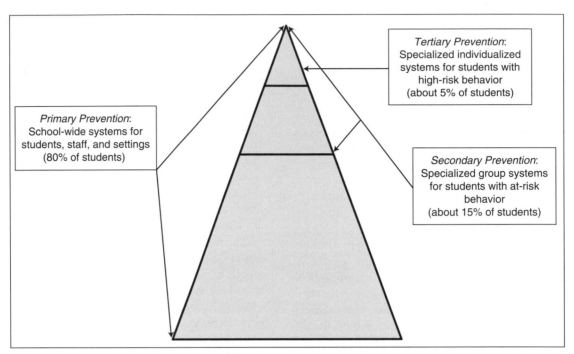

FIGURE 14.5 The three-tier model of School-Wide Positive Behavior Support.

Source: www.ode.state.or.us/teachlearn/conferencematerials/sped/sustaining_pbs.pdf.

Steps in Developing a SW-PBS

It is important to initially state that a SW-PBS system is a team approach that involves teachers, staff, and administrators. The team may take the following basic steps in setting up the system.

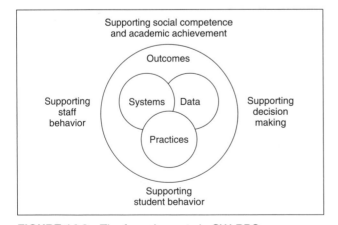

FIGURE 14.6 The four elements in SW-PBS.

Source: Luisella & Diament (2002) and www.ode.state.or.us/teachlearn/conferencematerials/sped/sustaining_pbs.pdf.

- Select three to five expectations and positively state them. An example might be to be *respectful*, be *responsible*, and be *safe*. Each one of these must be clearly explained in terms of rules that are clearly stated and communicated in order to help reduce behavior problems (Mayer, 1995).
- Review behavioral expectations regularly with students. Many educators falsely assume that students are aware of what is appropriate school behavior (Martella et al., 2003). It is likewise important to inform students about do's (how they are expected to behave) rather than don'ts (what they should not do) (Lewis, 1999; Flick, 1998b).
- Encourage and reinforce prosocial behavior. Some schools use a paper certificate, coupons, or tokens. The essential element is not the tangible reward but rather the verbal exchange between the teacher (staff) and the student, an important social acknowledgment (Lewis and Sugai, 1999).
- Have a clear understanding among the staff and administrators about which behaviors will be managed by teachers in the classroom and which ones by an administrator outside the classroom.

■ Address the consequences for rule infractions consistently without removing students from their academic environment. Establish clear and predictable procedures for minor as well as serious infractions of school rules.

■ Routinely collect, organize, and analyze data and the results from staff surveys in order to make decisions about where support is most needed (Sprague, Sugai, & Walker, 1998).

PRIMARY PREVENTION (INTERVENTION)

In all cases, *prevention* and *intervention* may be used interchangeably, as both are goals in any systems used in schools.

Primary prevention (intervention) involves system-wide efforts to prevent new instances of a behavior problem and/or academic problem while increasing as many appropriate behaviors as possible—a process

similar to vaccinating children against measles or chicken pox in order to prevent the outbreak of these diseases. Positive behavior support consists of rules, routines, and physical arrangements. For example, to prevent injuries from students running in the hallway, schools may (1) teach the rule "walk in the hallway," (2) have a staff member stationed in the hallway during transitions to supervise the movement of students, and (3) make sure that an adult is with any group when they are in the hallway. Teaching behavioral expectations and rewarding students for following the rules is a more proactive positive approach than waiting for the misbehavior to occur and then responding to it in a reactive fashion.

These primary or universal interventions are effective for those students who are without serious problem behavior, estimated at 80 percent to 90 percent of the school population (Office of Special Education Programs [OSEP], 2005; Sugai, Horner et al., 2000; Sugai, Sprague et al., 2000). Gresham (2004) notes that universal (primary) interventions are implemented in the same way for every student, daily or weekly. These interventions may include school-wide bully prevention programs, academic materials, social skills, and other areas according to need (Gresham, 2004; Martella & Nelson, 2003).

Implementation of Primary Prevention (Intervention)

When implementing primary prevention, there must be agreement on the main behavior problem to target, its nature, and how to go about changing it. When a wide majority of the school's staff (80 percent) agree that a certain student's behavior is a problem—for example, office discipline referrals from the classroom and the lunchroom have increased 60 percent since the last quarter—the next step is to conduct further assessments and consistently use a set of strategies to address the issue. Figure 14.7 illustrates how problem behavior may be processed. It is important that the staff agree on what the problems are and commit to work as a team on the strategies to address them.

Problem behaviors may be classified as either major or minor. Some examples of each are noted in Table 14.1.

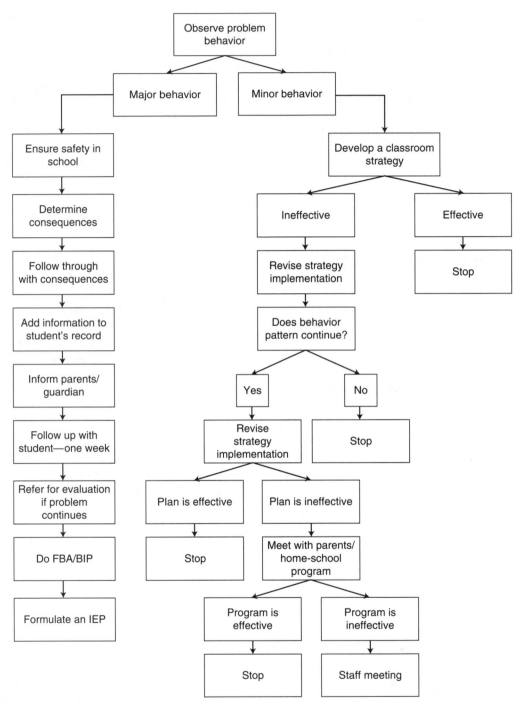

FIGURE 14.7 Dealing with problem behavior.

TABLE 14.1   Categories of Behavior

Minor Problem Behavior	Major Problem Behavior
Inappropriate language	Abusive language
Physical contact	Fighting (aggression)
Defiance/disrespect	Open defiance
Misuse of property	Vandalism
Disruptive behavior	Bullying/harassment

Office Discipline Referrals

Primary prevention works for over 80 percent of all students based on the number of office discipline referrals (ODR). However, in those cases where primary prevention does not reduce the number of office discipline referrals, students may need a more intense intervention. For example, a student (or group of students) with four or more office referrals per month may meet the criterion for moving to secondary prevention measures. However, note that the number of office referrals might be greater without primary prevention. An example of primary prevention through an application of SW-PBS at a middle school is described in the box below.

SECONDARY PREVENTION (INTERVENTION)

Secondary prevention (intervention) targets students who are at-risk for problem behavior and poor academic skills who are not responding to the primary prevention program. Such a group consists of about 5 to 15 percent of the school population (OSEP, 2005; Sugai, Horner, et al., 2000; Sugai, Sprague et al., 2000).

School-Wide Positive Behavior Support (SW-PBS)

Following a workshop on SW-PBS, the school's teachers developed three simple rules on behavioral expectations for their students:

- Be respectful of self, others, and property.
- Be responsible and prepared at all times.
- Be ready to follow directions and procedures.

These rules were printed on brightly colored posters and placed in strategic parts of the school (e.g., hallway, restroom, lunchroom, gym) where they were clearly visible.

The teachers then needed to explain to all other teachers as well as students about things like student attire and behavior. Pictures were made by teachers showing both appropriate and inappropriate clothing choices and other behavior. Students making the right choices got a small card, which could be later traded in for a special treat. When teachers caught students doing the appropriate thing (e.g., picking up trash or helping another student), their names were also recorded and once per month a name was drawn and announced over the intercom (an additional reinforcement). Students named were invited to join the assistant principal for a special lunch of pizza, soda, and dessert. Thus, only one name was announced but several students went to lunch. It was not only the rewards but also the attention these students received that was desirable. Students could also give a card to a teacher for doing something positive and special. Teachers' names could also be submitted to a drawing each month. The winning teacher would be surprised toward the end of the day when the assistant principal would bring a certificate saying that he or she was the winner and that the assistant principal would take over the class so the teacher could leave early. The teacher would also receive verbal praise for good work

Office discipline referrals were reduced from 45 percent to about 8 percent using this system. It was also estimated that the system saved about 145 hours or almost 21 days of contact time by the teachers. These data also correlated with higher achievement scores as teachers had more instructional time and more positive interactions with students.

Source: Information from Hieneman, Dunlap, and Kincaid (2005). Reprinted by permission.

Secondary prevention (intervention) is designed for use where there are more students who need behavior support than can be addressed by other programs and who are at-risk for chronic behavior problems without a need for high-intensity interventions. The purpose of this secondary level is to reduce current cases of problem behavior and academic failure by using specialized interventions that provide more support for groups of about 10 or more students. Common secondary prevention (intervention) practices include behavior contracts, conflict mediation, precorrection, self-management techniques along with remedial academic programs (Gresham, 2004; Martella and Nelson, 2003). Secondary prevention (intervention) thus addresses student needs for more support than is available in primary prevention (intervention) but less support than is available for students who need individualized tertiary interventions. While primary (universal) and secondary level interventions (preventions) successfully target about 93 to 99 percent of the students in a school, about 1 to 7 percent still need more intense interventions (Martella and Nelson, 2003).

TERTIARY PREVENTION (INTERVENTION)

Tertiary prevention (intervention) was originally designed to focus on the needs of students who showed specific and resistant patterns of problem behavior that were perhaps dangerous and highly disruptive and that impeded learning or resulted in social and/or educational exclusion. Most effective when school-wide (primary) and secondary classroom systems are in place, the tertiary level is the most individualized and intense of programs designed for students who display chronic academic and behavioral difficulties that clearly impede learning, are dangerous and disruptive, and may require that the student be placed in social or educational exclusion. According to Gresham (2004), even though these students are only 1 to 7 percent of the school population, they may account for 40 to 50 percent of the behavioral disruptions. The goal of tertiary prevention is to identify and reduce the frequency as well as the intensity of such students' behavior disruptions and also to improve adaptive skills and opportunities for an enhanced quality of life.

Tertiary prevention (intervention) involves conducting a functional behavioral assessment (FBA) and creating a behavior support plan for the identified student (Martella et al., 2003). The *behavior support plan (BSP)* and the *behavior intervention plan (BIP)* are essentially the same thing. BIP is the more common term (as it is used by IDEA). A BSP may be developed for groups or individuals while under IDEA; a BIP is individualized. Such a BSP would include a wide range of options, including (1) instruction on how to use new replacement skills for problem behaviors, (2) rearrangement of antecedents to prevent problem behavior and to encourage stronger behavior, and (3) development of procedures for monitoring, evaluating, and assessing the plan as needed. In some cases this plan may include emergency procedures to ensure student safety and to promote rapid de-escalation of severe behavior episodes. This is required in those cases where the student's behavior is dangerous and where there is a need for a change in school placement.

Tertiary intervention (prevention) focuses on the individual compared to the other primary and secondary interventions. IDEA requires that a functional behavioral assessment (FBA) be conducted and a BIP be developed when disciplinary measures result in the student's removal from the classroom for 10 cumulative days and for every change in placement. Support teams for tertiary interventions include the student's family, teachers, administrators, and other direct service providers such as counselors and psychologists. It is also important to have a team member who not only has expertise in applied behavior analysis but also is familiar with the design of interventions. A well-structured classroom management system can provide a good foundation for effective individual support.

Implementation of Tertiary Interventions (Preventions)

After the completion of the functional behavioral assessment and the behavioral intervention plan, the team must follow five general steps:

1. *Identify the goals of the intervention based on available information.* The support team may list the specific concerns and goals: (a) What are the problematic (observable) behaviors? (b) How frequent are these behaviors occurring? (c) What behavioral goals are to be achieved through the intervention?

2. *Gather the relevant information.* Information is obtained from (a) a review of school records,

(b) interviews with those who know the student, and (c) direct observation of behavioral patterns looking at antecedents, consequences, and the setting events or the context of behavior.

3. *Develop summary statements.* Information in these statements will assist the team in describing the relationships between the student's problem behaviors and their environments: (a) When, where, and with whom is the problem behavior most or least likely to occur? (b) What follows the problem behavior and what does the student get or avoid? (3) What other things (for example, time of day or day of the week) affect the student's problem behavior?

4. *Utilize the behavioral intervention plan.* Based on the available information that will be used to address the student's behavior problem in the environment in which it occurs, the BIP may either help to develop the IEP or to revise it. The BIP will include the following: (a) Adjustments to the environment will help reduce the probability of the behavior problem occurring or reoccurring. (b) The teaching of replacement skills will develop the general competencies of the student. (Remember that the desirable replacement skill must serve the same function as the undesirable problem behavior. For example, if attention is gained by the maladaptive behavior, then the alternate replacement behavior should also be instrumental in obtaining a similar degree of attention.) (c) Consequences must be selected that function to promote positive desirable behaviors and deter problem behaviors. (d) A crisis management plan may be formulated in case it is needed (when the problem behavior involved may be dangerous to self and others).

5. *Implement and monitor outcomes.* The BIP should be implemented with consistency in mind and should be effective in achieving its desired goals. The team decides what training and resources are needed, assigns responsibility for the plan, and evaluates the outcomes with data collection. It also determines whether adjustments in the plan are needed.

Effectiveness of the Behavioral Intervention Plan

Hopefully the BIP results in measurable changes in behavior and improvement with regard to quality of life goals—from increased participation and improved social relationships to greater independence and positive changes in self-sufficiency. There must be objective means to evaluate these outcomes and to determine which adjustments may be warranted when there is little progress within a reasonable time period (Ewell, 2001).

Crisis Management

If a severe episode or behavioral outburst occurs, it is important for schools to have a plan to provide a rapid response to ensure the safety of all as well as procedures that will result in a rapid de-escalation of the problem behavior. There not only should be specific crisis management procedures that are planned in advance but also training needs to be given beforehand so that the appropriate staff are prepared to deal with an episode of explosive aggressive behavior.

Schools that implement SW-PBS are making a conceptual shift from a reactive and aversive approach of managing behavior (through punishment) to one that is preventive and proactive in nature. Although it is clear that every child in school needs positive behavior support (Horner and Sugai, 2004), it is important to remember that schools must use procedures that have been empirically validated together with systems that have demonstrated effectiveness, efficiency, and relevance. SW-PBS allows schools to promote and facilitate both academic and behavioral success for all of its students.

DEVELOPMENTAL CONSIDERATIONS FOR IMPLEMENTING SW-PBS

Most serious behavior problems result from a myriad of complex interacting risk factors that are associated with individuals, families, schools, communities, and society (Gregg, 1996; Walker, Colvin, & Ramsey, 1995). Treatment must therefore be multimodal and must take place in varied settings such as home and school (Kazdin, 1997). Such serious behavior problems also develop along an age-related trajectory that may be established early (by third grade), reinforced during late elementary and early middle school, and stabilized and resistant to change by high school, as shown in Table 14.2. This developmental continuum addresses the purpose and efficacy of school-based interventions (Walker, Colvin, & Ramsey, 1995). Note that *prevention* is most appropriate up to third

Case Study

SW-PBS Individual

Lacie is a 6-year-old first grader who shows an escalating pattern of noncompliance, aggressive behavior toward peers and teachers, and tantrums. Lacie's elementary school has already implemented an SW-PBS for her three years ago. There was a set of universal expectations and social skill lessons to teach the expectations, along with clear routines and documented evidence of a general decrease in behavioral problems. The school has since then begun to implement some secondary, small group interventions for targeted social skill groups.

For Lacie, there have been teacher interviews, behavioral incidence data, and classroom observations. Based on this information, it is hypothesized that Lacie exhibits these problem behaviors to obtain teacher and peer attention. The tantrums serve to escape full disciplinary action (she has been sent to a time-out room near the principal's office). There are two components to the behavioral intervention plan for Lacie: (1) A self-management chart has been constructed to provide Lacie with a visual representation of her compliance with school-wide expectations; teachers and other staff also provide a high rate of specific verbal praise (attention) when they observe Lacie engaging in a behavior related to school-wide expectations. (2) Lacie is to report to the assistant principal's office when she has acquired a predetermined number of points on the self-management card. These visits provide additional attention and recognition under conditions of positive, rather than punitive, circumstances. While being escorted to the office, she is given clear and consistent instructions regarding her behavior; appropriate, expected behavior during this time receives considerable attention. In the office Lacie is to sit down and review what she is expected to do when asked to leave the classroom and what will happen in the office.

Initially, Lacie averaged three to five visits to the office per week along with daily reports of various problem behavior. At this time, Lacie has not had a single office visit in over 3 months, and all referral inquiries for additional services have been withdrawn except for the ongoing support for her family, which consists of progress reports and behavior management information.

Source: Information from Lewis (2005). Reprinted by permission of the author.

TABLE 14.2 Developmental Continuum of Services and Expectations for Serious Behavior Problems

Grade	Phase of Serious Behavior Problem	Services and Supports
Preschool	Prevention	Social skills
K	Prevention	Academic instruction
1	Prevention	Family support
2	Prevention	Early screening and identification
3	Prevention, remediation	
4	Remediation	Social skills
5	Remediation	Academic instruction
6	Remediation, amelioration	Family support
7	Amelioration	Self-control, academic skills
8	Amelioration, accommodation	Prevocational skills, family support
9	Accommodation	Survival skills
10	Accommodation	Vocational skills
11	Accommodation	Transition to work
12	Accommodation	Coping skills

Source: Walker, Colvin, and Ramsey (1995). Reprinted by permission.

grade, while *remediation* targets the late elementary grades, *amelioration* occurs in middle school, and *accommodation* in high school and beyond.

In order to interrupt the developmental course of students with serious behavior problems, Walker and colleagues (1995) suggest the following:

■ Identify those children who show signs of serious behavior problems such as aggression as early as possible through observation.
■ Use primary, secondary, and tertiary interventions to prevent the development of these behaviors.
■ Discontinue the use of expulsion, suspension, and other exclusion procedures as a means to deal with serious problem behavior.
■ Develop a variety of alternative placements such as hospitalization to not only deal with serious behavior problems but also keep these students in school when possible.

It is important to emphasize that early screening and identification of those students who are at-risk is essential. Successful outcomes in any prevention program will depend on the use of school-wide implementation as well as a primary focus on desired student behavior. The phrase "catch them being good" is relevant here. As Walker and colleagues (1995) assert, "one of the most critical mistakes made in classroom management is to take appropriate student behavior for granted" (p. 174).

HISTORY AND DEVELOPMENT OF SW-PBS

There are four basic models for using SW-PBS in schools. The following are models of SW-PBS using the three-tier approach:

The PREPARE Model

Project PREPARE (Proactive, Responsive, Empirical, and Proactive Alternatives in Regular Education) was proposed by Colvin, Kameenui, and Sugai (1993) as a school-wide behavior management program that had an empirically derived model of staff development focusing on the prevention of behavior problems. The PREPARE model grew out of the inadequacies of the traditional behavior management approaches of the

past that suffered from two major problems: a failure to consider staff development and issues and a restrictive (i.e., reactive) approach to discipline. The PREPARE model developed three primary objectives: (1) developing and evaluating the components of a pre-service and in-service training model based on an empirically derived model of staff development (Wilson & Berne, 1999); (2) applying empirically tested instructional principles to the understanding, management, and maintenance of social behavior problems in school; and (3) applying effective staff development and teacher change strategies. The PREPARE model focused on a proactive (positive) instructional approach to managing problem behaviors that viewed all school discipline as an instrument for student success. There was also a shift toward the use of more positive, preventive, and problem-solving approaches in managing problem behavior. The principal and general team leadership showed active involvement and support, reflecting a strong commitment to change. In a field test of initial development and evaluation of PREPARE, two middle schools were studied. While the control school (i.e., the school without SW-PBS) showed a 12 percent increase in office referrals for discipline, the target or experimental school showed a 50 percent decrease in such referrals. Some of the more common problem behaviors for office referrals such as harassment, defiance, disruption, and fighting noticeably decreased in the target school, but slightly increased in the control school with regard to various misbehaviors and detentions.

Notwithstanding the success of project PREPARE, Lewis and Sugai (1999) and Sugai, Horner, Dunlap et al. (2000) went on to develop the effective behavior support (EBS) system, an approach to proactive school-wide management designed to enhance the school's ability to adopt and consistently use effective behavioral strategies for the whole school.

The BEST Model

The Building Effective Schools Together (BEST) model provides a standardized staff-development program aimed at improving school and classroom discipline and associated outcomes such as reduction of violence and alcohol, tobacco, and other drug use (Sprague, Sugai, Horner, & Walker, 1999). This model is based on the effective behavior support (EBS) model (Sprague, Sugai, & Walker, 1998; Sprague, Walker,

Golly, White, Meyers, & Shannon, 2001), developed at the University of Oregon and the National Center on Positive Behavioral Interventions and Supports.

The mission of the BEST program is to facilitate the academic achievement and healthy social development of children and youth in a safe environment that is conducive to learning. This program includes intervention techniques based on more than 30 years of rigorous research regarding school discipline in a range of fields—from education and public health to psychology and criminology. Program components address whole-school, common area, classroom, and individual student interventions and are intended to be used in combination with other evidence-based prevention programs. Representative school staff team members develop and implement positive school rules, rule teaching, positive reinforcement systems, data-based decision making at the school level, effective classroom management methods, and curriculum adaptation to prevent problem behavior. Functional behavioral assessment and positive behavioral intervention are generally employed. Teams are also encouraged to integrate BEST principles with other prevention programs for maximum effectiveness.

Other researchers have replicated BEST and similar models that have been documented in a series of studies by researchers at the University of Oregon (Metzler, Biglan, Rusby, & Sprague, 2001; Sprague, Bernstein et al., 2002). Studies have shown reductions in office discipline referrals of up to 50 percent with continued improvement over a 3-year period in schools that sustain the intervention (Irvin et al., 2004). In addition, school staff report greater satisfaction with their work, compared to staff from schools that did not implement BEST. Comparison schools show increases or no change in office referrals, along with a general frustration with the school discipline program.

Studies are underway now to relate the quality of implementation to changes in student and staff behavior and to document changes in student attitudes and self-reported problem behavior. In studies employing the components included in the BEST program, reductions have been documented in antisocial behavior (Sprague, Bernstein et al., 2002), vandalism (Mayer, 1995), aggression (Grossman et al., 1997), later delinquency (Kellam, Mayer, Rebok, & Hawkins, 1998), and alcohol, tobacco, and other drug use in older students (Biglan et al., 2003). Positive changes in protective factors such as academic achievement (Kellam et al., 1998) and school engagement (O'Donnell et al., 1995) have also been documented using a positive school discipline program such as BEST in concert with other prevention interventions.

The PAR Model

The Prevent, Act, and Resolve (PAR) model is another school-wide behavior management program that is designed to meet the unique needs of a school. Functioning on a process-based operational plan, the model includes collaborative teams of teachers, school administrators, and related staff working together to arrive at a consensus on plans and strategies to (1) *prevent* the occurrence of problematic behavior, (2) *act*, or respond to, instances of rule compliance and noncompliance in a consistent way, and (3) *resolve* many of the issues that underlie or cause the problematic behavior. Essentially, these collaborative teams design their own unified plan of action based on data and researched procedures that have been documented to work. PAR training provides the school's staff with a framework and process for setting expectations and consequences as well as recognizing and rewarding positive behaviors throughout the school. The final result is a written discipline plan (manual) tailored to the particular school staff and students involved and a team consensus on the following plan components: (1) a mission statement, (2) a list of rules and expectations, (3) a list of consequences for rule violations, (4) an outline of crisis procedures, (5) procedures for family involvement, (6) ideas for adopting instruction as needed, and (7) an implementation section that details the "how's" of putting the plan into action.

PAR results have proved to be promising. In one middle school, fights decreased 75 percent over a 1-year period; in two other middle schools, both discipline referrals (out of classrooms) for disruptiveness and suspensions decreased approximately 50 percent over a 2-year period. Rosenberg (1998) explains that teachers are relaxed because they know the whole school agrees with the course of action. It enhances communication. Woodrow Rhoades, assistant principal at Hammond Middle School in Laurel, Maryland, admits that he and his colleagues were often overwhelmed by their undisciplined middle-school students. Many teachers had extensive experience handling the academic problems, but they were unprepared for behavior challenges. To illustrate the significant influence of the program on his school, Rhoades offers the example of a seventh-grade student with ADHD who had been described as "struggling." Before adopting the PAR philosophies, Rhoades said the child's teachers may have looked at ways to react to his disruptive behavior. "Now, we're sitting around wondering what we can do to help this kid make it," Rhoades said. "We're brainstorming for ways to turn this around." In the past, the teachers, administrators, and parents may have been inclined to assign blame for kids who cause problems. "That just doesn't happen anymore," Rhoades said. "The kids are happy, the teachers are happy, the parents are happy, and our test scores are going up...We are a real success story."

The ACHIEVE Model

The ACHIEVE model is an innovative school reform and school effectiveness program developed for use in preschool, elementary, and middle school settings by Dr. Howard Knoff, the director of Project ACHIEVE. It is designed to help schools, communities, and families develop, strengthen, and solidify students' resilience, protective factors, and self-management skills. Working to improve school and staff effectiveness, this model places particular emphasis on increasing student performance in the areas of (1) social skills and social-emotional development, (2) conflict resolution and self-management, (3) achievement and academic programs, and (4) positive school climate and safe school practices. Project ACHIEVE implements school-wide positive behavioral and academic prevention programs that focus on the needs of all students. It also develops and implements strategic intervention programs for at-risk and underachieving students, and it coordinates comprehensive and multifaceted "wrap-around" programs for students with intense needs.

Implemented in a series of steps that generally occur over a three-year period, the program uses professional development, in-service, and technical assistance to train the school staff. There are seven components to this model:

1. *Strategic planning and organizational analysis and development:* Analyzes the school's operations and recommends specific program objectives and action plans; it also coordinates meaningful evaluation procedures.

2. *Referral question consultation (RQC) problem-solving process:* Uses a systematic functional, problem-solving process to explain why students' problems are occurring and to link assessment to interventions that help students progress.

3. *Effective classroom and school processes/staff development:* Focuses on developing and reinforcing teachers, classroom behaviors, and school processes that maximize a student's academic engagement and learning.

4. *Instructional consultation and curriculum-based assessment and intervention:* Involves the functional assessment of referred students' learning problems. It evaluates their response to and success with the curriculum, and coordinates the instruction and interventions needed to teach them to master necessary academic skills.

5. *Social skills, behavioral consultation, and behavioral interventions:* Facilitates implementation of effective interventions that address students' curricular and behavioral problems, including "special situation" analyses, crisis prevention and intervention procedures as well as team development.

6. *Parent training, tutoring, and support:* Develops ongoing home–school collaborations, including the assessment, coordination, and use of community resources.

7. *Research, data management, and accountability:* Reinforces the collection of formative and summative outcome data (including consumer satisfaction and time- and cost-effectiveness data) to validate various aspects of a school-wide improvement process.

The "Stop and Think Social Skills Program" is Project ACHIEVE's curriculum for teaching students appropriate behavior and self-management skills (Knoff, 2001). It includes a social skills book and support materials along with a Referral Question Consultation (RQC) workbook. Using these materials, Project ACHIEVE is best installed in this sequence:

■ Year 1: Activities involve social skills training; RQC problem solving training; and providing teachers with release time for planning, meetings, and technical assistance.

■ Year 2: Activities include social skills/RQC training and booster sessions; behavioral observation and instructional environment assessment training;

curriculum-based assessment and measurement (CBA/CBM) training; and release time for planning, meetings, and technical assistance.

■ Year 3: Implementation requires booster sessions in all prior components; parent involvement planning; training and facilitation; grade-level intervention planning and implementation; and release time for planning, meetings, and technical assistance. After the third year, one day a month is devoted to release time for teachers to plan and implement the activities in their action plans.

The results for Project ACHIEVE are promising. Data suggest a 75 percent decrease in student office referrals in special education, a 28 percent decline in total disciplinary referrals, and a drop in school suspensions from 9 percent to 3 percent.

SCHOOL-WIDE INFORMATION SYSTEM (SWIS) PROGRAM

The School-Wide Information System (SWIS) is an online information system used by teachers, administrators, and other essential staff to improve the behavior support in elementary school through high school (May et al., 2000). The purpose of SWIS is to provide school personnel with accurate, timely, and practical information for making decisions about discipline systems. School personnel collect ongoing information about discipline events in their school and enter this information through protected, Web-based software. (There is a fee of $250 per school to subscribe to SWIS.)

The SWIS system for gathering problem-behavior information is flexible, allowing different schools to tailor the information they wish to enter. There is, however, a recommended list of problem-behavior categories as well as critical criteria requiring that the problem-behavior categories used within a school be mutually *exclusive* (a problem behavior cannot be placed in more than one category) and *exhaustive* (all problem behaviors must have a category, even if the category is "Other").

Schools that use SWIS typically start by self-assessing whether the way they collect information is *consistent* and *efficient*. They consider their current categories and ensure that effective procedures are retained. Often schools choose to have one clear set of "major" problem behaviors that are individually monitored and another

set of "minor" or "warning" problem behaviors that are monitored as a group.

SWIS provides information that allows school personnel to make more informed, immediate, and effective decisions in the design of behavioral interventions and support. This includes details about (1) the number of discipline events reported, (2) the kinds of problem behaviors occurring, (3) which students are receiving discipline referrals, (4) the locations of discipline problems, and (5) the times of day when problem behaviors are most likely.

School personnel are thus able to make decisions about (1) the design and management of school-wide behavior support systems, (2) targeted interventions for problem areas such as hallways and the cafeteria, and (3) individual student behavior support systems. When school teams have access to timely and accurate discipline information, they (1) identify problems early, (2) engage in more effective problem solving, and (3) are accurate and accountable in data gathering. When SWIS information is used by administrators, faculty, and staff to guide the design and improvement of behavior support, the result is an improved social culture.

THE WRAPAROUND PROCESS

The wraparound process builds constructive relationships and support networks among students with emotional and behavioral disorders, their families, teachers, and others (Eber, 2001). Careful and systematic application of the wraparound process can improve the likelihood that the appropriate supports and interventions are adopted, implemented, and sustained (Burns et al., 2000). PBIS is a systems approach for setting up a continuum of proactive, positive discipline procedures for all students and staff in varied school settings (Sugai, Sprague et al., 2000). Based on a three-tiered prevention model, PBIS provides a research-based approach for promoting pro-social behavior of (1) students without chronic behavior problems (primary prevention), (2) students at risk for problem behavior (secondary prevention), and (3) students with intensive behavioral needs (tertiary prevention). Elements of the wraparound process are evident within this model, especially at the secondary and tertiary levels; the comprehensive wraparound process is used to implement tertiary interventions for students with serious behavioral problems.

Case Study

The Wraparound Process

Lamar is a 9-year-old third grader who is having trouble with lying and stealing behaviors and being disrespectful to both adults and peers. He is often disruptive in class and is showing a decline in his grades. Lamar is a loner who does not participate in activities either at school or in his neighborhood. School officials placed Lamar in a group intervention program where he received increased monitoring and reinforcement for three school-wide expectations. The school has begun a case study evaluation for special education. Two members of the team (a social worker and the coach) met with Lamar's mother to engage her in the wraparound process while getting a social history. They learned that Lamar has a younger brother who is 5 years old and that his mother has severe visual impairment. Lamar's mother expressed concern about Lamar's isolation and was fearful of him playing outside because she might not be able to see him if he wandered away from their house.

Following the home visit, a wraparound planning meeting was held at school with Lamar and his mother. They discussed Lamar's strengths, which included his playing piano and guitar, his sense of humor with peers, his penchant for art, and the fact that he was helpful at home (mostly with hands-on attention). Lamar had no peer contacts outside of school. At school, his lying primarily involved exaggerated stories about his life, and he stole small things like pencils, sticky notes, and school supplies. His mother thought that much of Lamar's behavior was due to his feelings of helplessness about his life circumstances.

To build on his strengths, the school team suggested an after-school gym program to help with his sense of belonging and his confidence. His teacher also agreed to provide increased prompts and instructions about manners and appropriate language. After a visual exam, Lamar was prescribed eyeglasses, which increased his academic success, confidence, and behavior. His verbalizations with both adults and peers improved with prompts and reinforcers. When disrespectful behavior again increased, the team discovered that Lamar had overheard his mother crying on the phone about her increasing blindness. She did not discuss her deteriorating condition with him.

When Lamar was evaluated, an FBA revealed that he had a learning disability and that he would act out to avoid academic work. When it was time for him to transition to the fourth grade, the wrap team planned to meet with persons who could continue to provide prompts and reinforcements that he needed. They also helped Lamar's mother connect with an agency that would help her to become more independent in the community.

Source: Information from Hersen (2005). Reprinted by permission of Sage Publications.

Background and Need

Students with EBD have not fared well in public schools. They are more likely to drop out, to fail academically, and to be arrested, poor, or unemployed, and to become teen parents (Carson, Sitlington, & Frank, 1995; Kauffman, 2001; U.S. Department of Education, 1998). Most likely to be educated in restrictive or exclusionary placements (U.S. Department of Education, 1998, Publication #NCBS98013), such students have in general a poor prognosis. However, this prognosis can be improved with early intervention such as establishing an intervention program when the child is still young.

Defining and Describing Wraparound

The wraparound process has emerged from the concept known as a system of care, a community-based approach to providing comprehensive, integrated services through multiple professionals and agencies and in collaboration with families (Park & Turnbull, 2003; Eber & Nelson, 1997).

Wraparound is not a service or a set of services; it is instead a planning process that builds a consensus within a team of professionals, family, and supportive providers to improve the effectiveness, efficiency, and relevance of supports and services for children and their families. The wraparound process brings teachers, families, and community representatives together to unconditionally commit to a way of conducting problem solving and planning that gives equal importance and support to the child and family, teachers, and others.

Wraparound in Schools

The wraparound process can be integrated into school-based planning for students with special needs regardless of the type of special education label or multiagency involvement (Eber & Nelson, 1997). School systems are also applying the wraparound process directly through special education for students, especially EBD students, with the most intensive and complex needs (Eber, 2001; Eber & Nelson, 1997). Effective wraparound planning requires skilled facilitation of the planning process within the child–family team. The wraparound process is applied in school to increase the family/child voice in the design of school-based interventions and to achieve better outcomes across settings (Eber, 2001). In addition, from a policy and legal perspective, schools are being called upon to provide these interventions as part of the related services that must be provided by schools if it is determined that these are needed if a student is to receive an appropriate program (Maag & Katsiyannis, 1996).

Wraparound, Special Education, and IEP

The wraparound process is consistent with the values and mandates of the Education for All Handicapped Children Act of 1975, as well as its reauthorized version, the Individuals with Disabilities Education Act of 2004 (Skiba & Peterson, 2000; Smith, 2000). Wraparound can also be used to guide the development of effective IEPs that reflect the family's voice and include outcome-based supports, services, and interventions (Eber & Nelson, 1997). School-based wraparound can create access to more family and community supports that can enhance the effectiveness of academic and behavioral interventions for students with EBD. While wraparound is consistent with the intent of the IEP process, differences in implementation have occurred as the IEP process has evolved with a mandate focus (required attention) over the past 30 years. Application of the wraparound process requires professional and family members to think differently about each other and about the needs of a student with EBD.

School Features that Support Wraparound

The wraparound process organizes and supports programming for students with EBD and for those who are at-risk for significant problem behaviors along with their families. Prevention and early intervention for EBD are now recognized as critical needs in schools (Sprague & Walker, 2000; Walker et al., 1998). More educators are now recognizing the increased need for more system-wide approaches that will produce the pro-social behaviors required for safer schools (Council for Exceptional Children, 1999; Sugai & Horner, 2002).

Wraparound Process Features within SW-PBS

While dynamic and individualized, the wraparound process has defined features and processes. The wraparound process can be described as the following series of steps that are conducted by a team:

1. *Engage in initial conversations:* By engaging family members, information can be obtained on strengths, needs, behavioral data, and family concerns that can be used to design interventions that directly address outcomes across home, school, and other environments.

2. *Focus on strengths:* Different perspectives of the student's strengths are addressed across multiple life domains. All strengths should be specifically stated (e.g., "he likes to help others" rather than "nice kid").

3. *Develop a mission statement:* This should guide the team's actions to ensure that activities are connected to the mission (e.g., "the student will live at home and succeed at school").

4. *Identify needs across domains:* The team summarizes the needs of the student (e.g. "what does this student need to be more like a student who is doing OK in school?").

5. *Prioritize needs:* The team leader gets a consensus as to which specific needs will be strategized at the current meeting and which ones will be addressed in future meetings.

6. *Develop actions:* The team develops specific strategies for meeting needs and outcomes.

7. *Assign tasks/solicit commitments:* The person or persons responsible for implementing given actions should take ownership of the intervention design.

8. *Document the plan:* Each meeting should begin with a review and progress rating of actions defined at the previous meeting.

Decision Making on Academic and Behavioral Issues

The reduction of school violence and improved academic performance are complementary goals of the wraparound process: when one area is effectively targeted, the other improves as well. It, therefore, benefits the educator to address both areas in order to maximize the child's performance. Effective schools will have the following goals:

1. *Focus on the student's behavior.* An effective antiviolence program may actually increase a teacher's available time by reducing behavioral disruptions that will take time to deal with identifying students who need additional resources and are thus allowing the student to function in class more efficiently.

2. *Provide academic help early.* Schools that address student problems before they escalate may have a better chance of improving their students' skills and keeping them more invested in school. This may help to decrease dropout, gang membership, and delinquency rates.

3. *Establish a clear definition of "violence."* This should include verbal and physical acts that, intentionally or unintentionally, cause harm or embarrassment.

4. *Assess the current level of school-related violence.* Schools cannot effectively plan for antiviolence programs without a clear understanding of the magnitude of their current problem. Effective schools will track various indicators of school behavior, including attendance and tardiness problems, discipline referrals, and suspensions.

5. *Be informed about innovative programs and services.* Communications about new programs and services are paramount.

6. *Select school programs by need.* Monitor these programs over time to ascertain whether they are actually delivering expected improvement.*

7. *Establish a common set of behavioral standards between students and staff.* Phrase rules in positive terms (for example, "Speak in a normal tone using appropriate language" rather than "Don't yell or use profanity"). Rules should be posted, reviewed often, and shared with parents.

8. *Provide immediate and consistent consequences for misbehavior.* Emphasize appropriate behavior with praise (a positive approach) and provide mild consequences for misbehavior.

---

*Schools may obtain a School Needs Assessment Questionnaire by contacting Dr. Grad Flick at Seacoast Educational Consultants (drgflick@yahoo.com).

SUMMARY

This chapter focuses on the use of positive disciplinary techniques. Students with academic and behavior problems generally perceive classrooms as negative and unpleasant. Despite considerable evidence that they are inneffective, negative disciplinary techniques, including corporal punishment, are still used. Positive disciplinary techniques involve a proactive, not a reactive, approach. Such schools emphasize prevention and early intervention as well as individual student support. Violent behavior is a function of both risk and protective factors that foster resilience. There are several things that increase resilience against violent behavior, and a number of activities may be suggested by teachers.

Teachers must avoid negative orientation and educate students using a social curriculum and social guidelines. There are numerous problems with zero-tolerance, an approach that adversely affects a greater number of minority students and shows no evidence that it reduces disruptive behavior or violence. In contrast, viable alternatives to disciplinary removal—including SW-PBS, anti-violence programs, and social skill instruction—have shown positive improvements. An interactive approach corrects and improves the four key elements in a SW-PBS system (that is [1] outcomes, [2] systems, [3] data, and [4] practices). A team of teachers, staff, and administrators implement the six steps of SW-PBS.

There may be primary, secondary, and tertiary prevention approaches. There must be an objective way of measuring behavior changes and determining the effectiveness of the plan. There are also developmental considerations as there are differences in the services and supports for students at various grade levels. A number of variations of the three-tier approach in providing SW-PBS to schools are discussed. These include the PREPARE, BEST, PAR and ACHIEVE models. An on-line program for implementing SW-PBS is explored. The chapter concludes with a discussion of the wraparound process for building constructive relationships and support networks among students with EBD and families.

DISCUSSION QUESTIONS

1. What are some of the negative effects of zero-tolerance policies? In contrast, what are the advantages of positive disciplinary policies?
2. What are the key attributes of positive behavioral support (PBS)?
3. Discuss how classrooms are perceived by those students with academic and/or behavioral problems.
4. Is discipline and corporal punishment the same? Explain your answer.
5. Corporal punishment erodes the student's basic trust in others. Explain this statement.
6. What criteria determine the effectiveness of positive behavioral interventions?
7. What are the five key features of universal behavioral support according to Sugai, Horner, Dunlap, and colleagues (2000)? How did Turnbull and colleagues (2002) evaluate this school-wide referral system?
8. What are some general factors that favor the development of delinquent behavior?
9. Which negative conditions at home might predict early onset and chronic antisocial behavior problems?
10. Which factors at school contribute to patterns of aggressive and violent behavior?
11. According to Rutter (1979), what is "required helpfulness" and what does it assist in developing? This is a key element in what?
12. How can schools and administrators help develop resiliency?
13. What is the importance of risk and protective factors in developing problem behaviors?
14. Discuss some of the individual factors that increase resilience against violence.
15. List some of the activities that help develop resilience.
16. Effective discipline includes prevention and intervention programs. What strategies can provide an atmosphere for learning and self-discipline?
17. Explain the term "media violence." What can be done about it?
18. What should administrators do with regard to violence prevention?
19. What is the most common form of school discipline? What problems do minority students encounter with regard to discipline?
20. To avoid lawsuits, schools need to consider discontinuing disciplinary procedures. What must schools emphasize?
21. What is "educational malpractice"?
22. In the majority of cases, students may be "searched" for what reasons?
23. Explain how "defamation of character" applies to educators.
24. What are the basic steps in setting up a school-wide positive behavior support system?
25. Explain primary, secondary, and tertiary prevention approaches to behavior problems.
26. Describe the developmental continuum of services and expectations for serious behavior problems according to Bullis and Walker (1995).
27. Discuss one example of a school-wide behavior management model program.
28. What is a wraparound process? Describe the eight steps involved.

CHAPTER 15

Partnerships

No one is more important than parents in sending the signal that reading and education matter and that school work is not a form of drudgery but a ticket to a better life. . . . By giving their word to read to their children, to assist on homework, to engage the process of learning, parents can set an example for their children that is powerful and positive.

GRAY DAVIS, GOVERNOR OF CALIFORNIA, STATE OF THE STATE ADDRESS, JANUARY 7, 1999

Overview

- A program of partnership
- Parent involvement with school
- Family involvement in children's learning
- Levels of parent involvement
- Relationship-focused early intervention
- Sibling involvement
- Sibling areas of concern
- Sibshops
- School–family–community partnerships
- Impact of teacher training

If schools are to improve the effectiveness and generalization of schoolwide interventions, they must encourage families and community members to participate. Such involvement can have a positive impact on those skills that students learn within the context of the school setting. As Frey, Hirschstein, and Guzzo (2000) have noted, the generalization of prosocial skills is the ultimate goal of any prevention program. It is therefore necessary to influence behavior at school as well as at home. Training parents to manage behavior problems at home can help to improve behavior in school (Metzler et al., 1998). In order to establish universal behavior support, it is important to create a positive school and home partnership that is based on collaboration and communication (Gomez & Ang, 2007).

HISTORICAL EMPHASIS ON FAMILIES

Throughout history, the roles that families and community have played in education have changed. For example, during the 1600s laws were passed requiring families to be responsible for the religious education of their children (Barbour, 1990). During the twentieth century, home–school partnerships developed, especially with regard to academics. Family involvement in education has been valuable socially, while also improving academic achievement, reducing truancy, and increasing the rate of graduation (Tools for Schools, 1998). Although the importance of home–school collaboration is well documented, the research evaluation of these programs and the effectiveness of schools implementing them have not been published.

Results of surveys showed that schools were most effective in providing information on policies and academic achievement, and in contacting parents regarding volunteering. However, schools were noted to be deficient in giving to families knowledge of child development, parenting, and information about available community resources. Some examples of school reports are noted by Dingerson (2001); report cards, progress notes, and telephone communications too often focus on the curriculum, and little information is made available regarding a child's behavioral problems. The information conveyed to parents is typically negative and critical, offering no solutions. Receiving such communication often strikes fear in parents along with a sense of defensiveness and rarely promotes a desire to visit the school; most visits that do occur often become confrontational.

The significance and benefits of family involvement in academics is well established (Bauch & Goldring, 1995). There have been documented improvements in academic performance, attendance, a reduction in dropouts, along with increased graduation rates and post–high school goals (Chen & Chandler, 2001). With such an important emphasis on family involvement, the federal and state government have noted several initial cases associated with home–school collaboration. For example, schools receiving Chapter 1* funding must implement and improve programs associated with home–school collaboration (Kessler-Sklar & Baker, 2000). According to the Goals 2000: Educate America Act of March 1994, every school must "promote partnerships that will increase family involvement for the social, emotional, and academic growth of children" by the year 2000 (Barbour, 1990; McDermott, 2002). The Educational Partnership Act of 1988 also supported parent–school collaboration. Epstein (1995) identified the six types of parental involvement summarized in Table 15.1.

Type 1 includes helping parents understand what children are capable of doing at different developmental ages, and what parents can expect (Chandler & Vaden-Kiernan, 1996). Type 2 refers to the design of effective communications between home and school regarding a child's progress. These would include not only report cards but a parent conference that includes clear information about school policies (Epstein, 1995). Type 3 suggests that parents must be provided opportunities to volunteer in their child's school. Schools were noted to do well (Chen & Chandler, 2001) communicating opportunities to participate with parents via telephone calls, newsletters, classroom information, and mailings (Epstein, 1995). Because some parents still felt that donated time was not used well, Epstein (1995) suggested

---

*Chapter 1 of the Elementary and Secondary Education Act of 1965 grants funds for classroom services (primarily salaries and benefits for teachers/teacher assistants as well as supplies and equipment used in the classroom), support services (like curriculum development, teacher training, activities to increase student involvement, salaries and benefits for counselors and truant officers), and administration (salaries and benefits for Chapter 11 coordinators and administrative staff, and supplies and equipment for support of the program).

TABLE 15.1   Epstein's Six Types of Involvement in Successful School–Family–Community Partnerships

Type 1	**Parenting:** Assist families with parenting and child-rearing skills, understanding child and adolescent development, and setting home conditions that support children as students at each age and grade level. Assist schools in understanding families.
Type 2	**Communicating:** Communicate with families about school programs and student progress through effective school-to-home and home-to-school communications.
Type 3	**Volunteering:** Improve recruitment, training, work, and schedules to involve families as volunteers and audiences at the school or in other locations to support students and school programs.
Type 4	**Learning at Home:** Involve families with their children in learning activities at home, including homework and other curriculum-related activities and decisions.
Type 5	**Decision Making:** Include families as participants in school decisions, governance, and advocacy through PTA/PTO, school councils, committees, action teams, and other parent organizations.
Type 6	**Collaborating with Community:** Coordinate resources and services for students, families, and the school with businesses, agencies and other groups, and provide services to the community.

Source: Information from Epstein and colleagues (2002). Reprinted by permission.

that parents could donate time through tutoring programs, reading clubs, and other focused activities to enhance student learning. Type 4 emphasizes that parents should have information regarding how to assist their child with homework, and other academic goals specific to the child's grade level. Type 5 stresses the importance of including parents in decision-making through PTA, school councils, and other networks. While over 97 percent of schools reported that they included parents in decision making, only 75 percent of parents felt they were included and only 64 percent felt they had a real say in school policies (Chen & Chandler, 2001). Type 6 emphasizes not only home–school collaboration but also collaboration with the community. This includes giving the family needed information about community resources (e.g., health service, recreational activities, and social supports) so that parents can utilize these when their child's needs exceed the school resources (Chen & Chandler, 2001).

It is well known that those students who are successful in school are most always supported by their family. The question about how to develop this partnership requires some creative ways of thinking about family and community involvement (Epstein & Jansorn, 2004). Many parents are not involved but would be if there were some guidelines to improve basic academic performance, improve attendance, and meet other goals. Although parents have many time constraints, they want to know what they can do to help their children. One way to start improving the parent–school

partnership is by assessing parent practices. According to Epstein (1994), the following questions can help evaluate how well the school is reaching out to parents:

- Which partnership practices are currently working well at each grade level?
- Which partnership practices should be improved or added in each grade?
- How do you want your school's family involvement practices to look three years from now?
- Which current practices should change now and which should continue?
- Which families is the school reaching and which are hard to reach?
- What can be better done to communicate with the hard-to-reach families?
- What costs are associated with the improvements you want?
- How will you evaluate the results of your efforts?
- What opportunities will make it possible for teachers, parents, and students to share information on successful practices in order to strengthen their own efforts?

A PROGRAM OF PARTNERSHIPS

The new direction is to devise a program of school, family, and community partnerships linked to a school improvement plan (Epstein & Jansorn, 2004). This approach, developed in the National Network of Partnership

Schools at Johns Hopkins University, has noted that students learn and develop at home, at school, and in the community (Epstein, 2001); they are influenced by families, teachers, principals, and others in the community.

Partnership programs require teamwork that is best accomplished by forming an *action team for partnerships (ATP)*, which includes teachers, parents, the principal, and community leaders. Reporting to the school about action plans, committees, activities, progress, and results, this action team is also influential in improving family and community involvement.

Developing an Action Plan

The action plan developed by the ATP focuses on four major school improvement goals, two of which are academic, a third nonacademic (e.g., improving attendance, behavior, and respect), and a fourth designed to assist educators in creating a welcoming climate for partnering students, families, and educators.

Comprehensive partnership programs must include activities for the six types of parent involvement shown in Table 15.1 (Epstein & Sheldon, 2006). Included are: workshops, newsletters, parent–teacher conferences, volunteer functions, and a homework plan to involve all families. Each one of the school's programs is customized to meet specific goals that serve the families at an identified school in each community.

Principals may enhance the quality of their school's partnership programs by taking some of the following actions (Epstein et al., 2002):

■ Announce that your school is a partnership school whose entire staff aims to help all students succeed.
■ Give frequent feedback to let all students know the importance of families to students and the school.
■ Use funds for planned partnership activities of school, family, and community.
■ Discuss the ATP's mission in the first faculty meeting, emphasizing teamwork and support.
■ Recognize teachers for their contributions to partnership activities and help them communicate better with parents.
■ Publicize scheduled involvement activities throughout the year, encouraging a welcoming school climate.
■ Periodically report on ATP plans and accomplishments to school, parent, media, and community groups.

■ Locate resources that can enrich the curriculum.
■ Publicly thank ATP members for their time and contributions.
■ Work with administrators from other schools to coordinate professional development and to share ideas and challenges while improving school, family, and community partnerships.

When schools have good partnership programs, even hard-to-reach families get involved in their child's education (Epstein & Jansorn, 2004). For example, when schools welcome and train volunteers, more parents volunteer. Schools that have well-developed partnership programs encourage families to be involved, which results in students becoming more positive with improvement in learning. Research studies have found improvements in students' attendance, homework completion, and grades (Epstein, 2001; Epstein et al., 2002; Henderson & Mapp, 2002; Sheldon, 2003; VanVoorhis, 2003).

Given the effectiveness of good partnership programs, educators must work together to plan and establish a welcoming school environment. The No Child Left Behind Act of 2001 requires schools to have well-planned programs of family and community involvement to support student achievement and to communicate with families. Most schools can reach out to more families and limit their involvement to student achievement. At the National Network of Partnership Schools at Johns Hopkins University, educators, parents, and researchers are working together to continually improve programs. The result is an interplay in which research improves practice and practice improves research (Epstein & Jansorn, 2004). Principals hold the key to the success of these programs; it is through their leadership and support that teachers, parents, and community members are encouraged to work closely together for the benefit of the school and its students (Sanders, 2001; Sanders & Harvey, 2002; Hale & Moorman, 2003).

Types of Parents

The students at all schools have parents who display a broad range of involvement. There are parents who are committed to their children but do not participate, there are those who participate but are not necessarily supportive, and those who neither support nor participate in their child's education. Schools might thus do better to separate the dimensions of *support* and

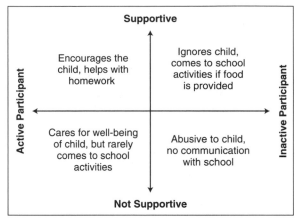

FIGURE 15.1   Four types of parents.
Source: http://www.mc3edsupport.org/community/
knowledgebases.php?c=297+node=119. Reprinted by permission.

participation in classifying the four basic types of parents. Figure 15.1 illustrates this concept.

At one end of the spectrum are parents who are both supportive and willing to participate (upper-left quadrant). They are likely to attend workshops and conferences, respond to notes and telephone calls, and get involved in decision-making roles through advisory committees and planning teams. Because this is not a comfortable role for many parents, it should not necessarily be considered the ultimate goal of parent involvement.

Some parents simply are not "joiners," even though they may care deeply about their child's education (lower-left quadrant). For them, several kinds of approaches hold promise. Newsletters with suggestions for home activities have proved to be successful, as have school-based activities where there is "safety in numbers" (for example, "make-and-take" workshops) and meeting parents on their own turf through home visits.

Perhaps a rarer parent—and the most difficult type to identify—is the one who pays lip service to education by attending events but is not supportive at home (upper-right quadrant). This type of parent may attend a parent-teacher conference only to go home and ignore or mistreat the child.

Parents who are unsupportive and do not participate (lower-right quadrant) are obviously the most difficult to reach but perhaps the most important group on which to focus efforts to improve communication. It is essential to determine the basis for their lack of involvement. In many cases, the reasons stem from the fact that the parents' own problems take precedence over their child's

education. If the situation involves an abusive environment, the only kind of solution possible may be to refer the parent to an outside agency. Parent liaisons or parent advocates who provide one-on-one assistance have successfully addressed the needs of these parents.

As expected, lack of parent participation is a prevalent problem among schools today. Perhaps more disturbing is the number of parents who are perceived as unsupportive and how this affects their children. Such parents may be at risk themselves. They may be drug addicts, alcoholics, or child abusers, or they may simply have bad memories of their own school experiences that result in the denigration of the value of education.

Gaining parents' support—for their children and for education—is a prerequisite for improving family involvement. Perhaps the best way to elicit the support of parents is by improving communication. Studies have shown that initial efforts to build support through improved communication with parents ultimately results in greater involvement. However, this improvement cannot always be measured by attendance at workshops or parenting classes.

The box on the following page describes an example of a parent involvement program at a school in Philadelphia.

PARENTAL INVOLVEMENT WITH SCHOOL

Parental involvement with school might encompass several different forms of participation in educational as well as other activities in the school (Gbadamosi & Lin, 2003). Participation might involve attending school functions, parent–teacher conferences, helping with homework, providing the appropriate environment for homework, modeling desired behavior such as reading, or some form of tutoring. Involving families in education may result in better attendance, more homework completed, improved attitudes toward school, better behavior, improved graduation rates, and post–high school involvement (Davis, 2000; Railsback, 2004).

Parents and Student Achievement

Parent involvement is positively related to the child's academic achievement, and the most effective parent involvement involves working on learning activities in the home (Rasinski, 1994). This and other forms of active involvement are more beneficial than passive ones

(text continued on page 326)

Restructuring an Inner-City School to Support Family Involvement

Ferguson Elementary School, an inner-city school in North Philadelphia, Pennsylvania, gets parents involved in their children's education by offering them a variety of opportunities through which they can improve their parenting and teaching skills and participate in school decision-making. When the Philadelphia public schools moved to site-based management in 1990, a group of Ferguson teachers formed a Parent Involvement Committee to assess community needs and explore strategies for involving parents in their children's education. With input from parents, the committee developed a parent involvement program coordinated by a Title I program support teacher and a full-time school–community coordinator. A parent center established with the help of Temple University serves as the headquarters for parent involvement activities, which include a Parent Network for fostering home–school communication, workshops on parenting and supporting learning at home, support groups for parents and grandparents, and adult education classes. Program success is measured by the growing number of students reading at or above grade level, a reduction in the number of referrals for discipline problems, and gains in student attendance.

Context

Ferguson Elementary School has implemented a school-wide program serving 750 low-income students in pre-kindergarten through grade 5. The school population is about 75 percent African American and 25 percent Latino. All students are eligible for free or reduced-price lunches, and 98 percent come from families with incomes below the federal poverty line. Most children attending Ferguson live in public housing projects, subsidized housing, or row houses in the immediate neighborhood. To create a more personalized atmosphere for students in this large school, Ferguson began the 1996–1997 school year by organizing students into four K–5 learning communities.

The principal and staff at Ferguson Elementary School made several changes to encourage parent involvement, many of which addressed the lack of time for staff and families to communicate with one another, a lack of information and training about the best ways to support family involvement, and the need to restructure the school to make it a more inviting place.

Overcoming Time and Resource Constraints

Finding Time for Working Parents

Finding the time for parents and teachers to communicate with one another challenges most attempts to bring the two groups together. Ferguson's Title I program support teacher also serves as the parent involvement program coordinator, and in this capacity she supervises volunteers, facilitates the parent support groups, and arranges parent workshops and classes. One change she has implemented addresses parents' time constraints. In the past, most parent involvement activities at Ferguson took place during the school day, while many parents were at work. In response to parents' requests, the school now offers more workshops and parent classes on weekends and in the evenings, and it also provides child care services during the parent sessions.

To reach out to parents, Ferguson teachers take the time to meet parents in the schoolyard each morning before the school day begins. Teachers also use a daily 45-minute planning period to meet with or to call parents. The principal encourages teachers to contact parents when their children are performing well, rather than just when they are performing poorly. Teachers are also encouraged to go out into the community and visit parents at home to welcome them into the school during three community outreach days each year. Usually, the principal, the parent involvement coordinator, the school–community coordinator, four parents, four students, and four or five teachers participate in these outreach events.

Finding Time for Teachers

Ferguson's school–community coordinator serves as a critical link between school and home, relieving some of the administrative burden placed on teachers. The coordinator's primary responsibility is to make home visits to families whom teachers have targeted for special attention. Teachers can request a visit for any reason, but most respond to changes in a student's behavior, attendance, or academic progress. In addition to making five or six home visits a day, the school–community coordinator also helps teachers arrange parent–teacher conferences.

Providing Information and Training to Parents and School Staff

Ferguson parents can participate in a variety of activities that provide them with the information and training they need to build an effective home–school partnership. These activities include the Parent Network, an outreach strategy that helps ensure ongoing home–school communication. Through the network, a core group of 10 parents contacts other parents in the school to share information on upcoming school activities and events. In addition to distributing informational fliers and monthly newsletters, the network makes two telephone calls to all parents in the school before any school activity that they are asked to attend. On at least three weekends each year, the Parent Network, teachers, the school–community coordinator, and students also conduct door-to-door family outreach to invite parents to the school.

Training Parents to Support Student Learning

Ferguson offers a variety of workshops and training opportunities for parents to learn more about how to help their children with schoolwork at home. Last year, the school offered Saturday morning workshops to help parents become active partners in teaching their children the school curriculum. Workshop topics included strategies to motivate the beginning reader, techniques to increase reading comprehension, and hands-on math activities. Between 100 and 150 parents attended the two workshops held at the end of the 1995–1996 school year.

Ferguson also hosts an annual Parents Make a Difference conference, a 2-day event that invites parents into their children's classrooms to observe and learn new techniques for helping their children succeed in school. While eating a box lunch provided by the school, parents hear talks given by guest speakers from the community, such as the authors of children's books. During the conference, parents also participate in workshops conducted by the guest speakers on such topics as how to read to your child in ways to increase their enjoyment and interest in reading. More than 300 parents participated in last year's conference.

A parent support group meets weekly in the parent room during the school day. The group sponsors workshops on parenting skills about six times a year. Workshop topics have included controlling anger, practicing assertive discipline, and preventing child abuse. The school psychologist, the school nurse, the parent involvement coordinator, and community resource people conduct the workshops. A grandparents' support group that meets three times a year was also formed; workshops focus on issues of specific concern to grandparents who are raising their grandchildren, including procedures for gaining child custody.

The school supports many parent-training opportunities. Three training sessions for parents and community members in the Community Assistants program are provided; this program provides stipends to parents and other community members to work for 10 weeks as classroom aides. The Parent Network receives training from the Title I teacher every month on school policies and activities, information they then share with other parents. Ferguson also helps parents increase their own skills by offering workshops during the school day on topics such as accessing community resources or writing a resume; these workshops, which are usually taught by the parent involvement coordinator, are held at least five times a year and are attended by 50 to 60 parents.

Training for Staff and Parents Working Together

During the 1995–1996 school year, all first-grade teachers received training from Temple University to improve parent involvement. First-grade teachers, Temple trainers, and parents first met to discuss how the school should and could involve parents. All first-grade teachers then met with Temple trainers to discuss priorities,

(continued)

chief among them being how to get parents to support learning at home and reinforce what students learn at school. Two of the first-grade teachers, along with Temple staff, then offered parents a series of five 2-hour workshops on how to help children with reading and math at home. Parents learned, for example, how to use a list of common words to help children make sentences, learn grammar, and sharpen their reading skills; they also learned how to use a "number line" manipulative to help children practice adding and subtracting. Each year, parents who have completed this training help train the parents of new first-grade students.

Restructuring Schools to Support Family Involvement

To support family involvement, Ferguson has reshaped its school program in several ways. It has created a more personalized and inviting environment by implementing both "schools within a school" and a parent center. They established a Parent Involvement Committee (PIC) in 1990 when a group of teachers involved in the school's move to site-based management wanted to assess community needs and explore strategies for involving parents in their children's education. Parent volunteering now includes parents in the classroom to support student achievement.

> *We want the same things for the children. By making the parents feel more comfortable, we're able to get their support in helping their children to achieve.*
> *Principal, Ferguson Elementary School*

Since the 1996–1997 school year, the school has been restructured into four kindergarten through grade 5 learning communities, each of which occupies its own space and benefits from the support of a parent support teacher or community leader. Each community leader is responsible for supporting the curriculum, instruction, and discipline within a learning community. In addition, Ferguson's parent center, which is located in an empty classroom on the second floor of the school, welcomes parents each school day. The center offers parents resources such as information on parenting skills, listings of job opportunities, and information about available programs for parents at the local library and at nearby community centers. An average of six or seven parents visit the parent center each day. The center is staffed in the mornings by a paid parent who operates a lending library of educational materials, such as "big book" story books and accompanying audio tapes and activity guides that parents can use with their children at home. Temple University provides training and support for the parent who staffs the center.

Giving Structure to Parent Decision Making Through the PIC

Parents at Ferguson play an active role in school decision making. Six parents (one for each grade level) sit on the school leadership team that is charged with making decisions on everything from funding to curriculum. In addition, all parents at the school are invited to participate in the PIC, which meets at least twice a month. The PIC determines all parent involvement activities for the coming month, based on parent needs and input from sources such as the Parent Network. Five teachers and two paraprofessionals that serve on the committee are usually joined by three or four parents.

Parent Volunteering to Support Student Achievement

Ferguson strongly encourages parents to get involved in their children's classrooms. Through the school's Community Assistants program, stipends and training are available for parents and other community members who commit to serve as classroom aides every morning for 10 weeks. Community assistant duties include working with small groups of students, tutoring students one-on-one, preparing bulletin boards, and assisting teachers with telephone calls and making copies. The parent involvement coordinator trains the assistants to do their jobs. There are three 10-week cycles of community assistants per year, with 10 assistants serving during each cycle. Most community assistants continue to serve after they have fulfilled their commitment. About 50 parents volunteer as classroom aides each week.

> *Every parent has something they can offer. They just need to hear someone say "we need you."*
> *Teacher, Ferguson Elementary School*

To encourage parent involvement, Ferguson offers both parents and teachers incentives for parent participation in school activities. Parents often receive school supplies or prizes such as T-shirts for their participation in workshops, and teachers are given pizza parties, popcorn parties, and banners outside their classrooms in recognition of high parent turnout at workshops.

Tapping External Supports for School–Family Partnerships

In addition to its Title I funding, community members such as Temple University support Ferguson's parent involvement program on several levels:

- *In-kind donations:* Temple provides furniture and other resources and equipment for the parent center, along with a stipend for the parent who staffs the center.
- *Training for teachers and the parent center staff.* Temple provides customized professional development for Ferguson teachers, and it places a number of its student teachers at the school. The university also provides stipends for teachers of the continuing education courses, which are described below, and for babysitters who watch over the children of parents while they take these classes and other workshops offered at the parent center.
- *Offering an adult evening school at Ferguson.* During the 1995–1996 school year, Temple offered classes in computer literacy and self-esteem at no cost to parents. During the 1996–1997 school year, computer literacy, English as a second language, and Spanish were offered. This program continues today, with courses taught by teachers, parents, and other individuals recruited from the community who receive a stipend from Temple. Adult evening school classes meet for 2 hours per week for 10 weeks. In the previous year, 24 parents were enrolled in the computer class, and 10 were enrolled in the self-esteem class.
- *Donations of food and other supplies.* The Philadelphia Gas Works utility company supports the parent involvement program at Ferguson through donations of food and supplies that parent center staff can distribute to families in need.

Evidence of Success

Ferguson measures program success by monitoring student achievement, student disciplinary referrals, and parent involvement in activities and workshops. Ferguson's parent involvement program appears to have had positive effects on students. The number of first-grade students reading at or above grade level has increased from 5 percent in June 1993 to 37 percent in June 1996. Student discipline has also improved, with the number of disciplinary referrals dropping steadily over the past few years, from 586 in 1993 to 267 in 1996. Average daily attendance is also up to about 90 percent, compared with about 80 percent when the parent involvement program began. Although it is impossible to attribute these improvements solely to the parent involvement program at Ferguson, school officials believe that helping parents become more involved has played a significant role in bringing these changes about.

> *I have a better and clearer understanding of what my children need to do in school because of my involvement, and I'm better able to help them.*
>
> *Parent, Ferguson Elementary School*

Parent involvement in school activities has also increased. The 1995–1996 fall Open House drew 350 parents, compared with fewer than 30 parents in 1989. Roughly 50 parents volunteer as classroom aides each week. Between 100 and 150 parents participated in the Saturday workshops offered during the spring of 1996, and more than 300 parents participated in last year's Parents Make a Difference conference. In addition, 25 parents received certificates of continuing education from Temple University last year, and one former community assistant is now earning her teaching credentials at La Salle University. Another former assistant has been hired as the school–community coordinator at another school in Philadelphia, and four are currently working at Ferguson as full-time classroom aides.

Source: http://www.ed.gov/pubs/famInvolve/ferguson.html. Reprinted by permission of the Philadelphia Board of Education.

such as signing notes from school. As Eccles and Howard (1996) and Ibanez and colleagues (2004) have pointed out, the school needs to help minority and low SES families. Schools can improve the relations between parents and the school, which can support increased student achievement and parent involvement (LaBahm, 1995). Also, the earlier the parent's involvement, the more powerful are its effects (Ewen & Neas, 2005). When parents are provided basic training in involvement, there is greater student achievement (Fan & Chen, 2001); however, when the training requires too much time and effort, parents may drop out of training. It is, therefore, important for this basic training to be simple and not require a great deal of time (Hoover-Dempsey, Bassler, & Brissie, 1987; Eccles & Howard, 1996).

Parents and Student Attitude and Behavior

Active parental involvement affects student attitude and behavior positively and improves relationships with school personnel—who also benefit, because students of involved parents tend to present fewer classroom problems (Hoover-Dempsey & Sander, 1995). Of course, when parents realize their involvement makes such a difference, then they, too, are gratified (Jeynes, 2005). For various reasons, many minority and/or low-income parents may be less involved with their child's education (Desimone, 1999); however, offered adequate training and encouragement, even parents having limited participation can have a noticeable positive impact on their children (Carter, 2002). For such parents, the concepts of "parents as partners" should be strongly emphasized (Berger, 2003). And obviously, parent involvement with students in special populations—those experiencing achievement problems and/or behavioral difficulties—benefit when parents are intimately involved in their children's learning.

Parents and School Rules

There is no evidence of any school program where parent participation in school decision making was directly linked to improved student achievement. However, this does not mean that parents should not be involved in some aspects of decision making. Perhaps when parents learn more about the school's structure and instructional programs and administrators learn that parents want to be involved, then the school administrators may feel more comfortable with parental input and involvement regarding school rules and general decision-making activities regarding the operation of the school.

Family Involvement in Children's Learning

Davis (1991) described family involvement as a shifting perspective that mirrors the changing nature of families and communities. He identified several important changes in recent times. A comparison of the old versus the new perspective is presented in Table 15.2.

Family involvement can be classified in several ways. According to the six types of parent involvement identified by Epstein (1995), various activities and other ways to encourage family involvement in child care, after-school activities, and other programs can be identified. This breakdown indicates not only how family members can show their involvement but also how programs can encourage that involvement. Table 15.3 presents information on the type of involvement, how

TABLE 15.2 Comparison of Old and New Perspectives

Old Perspective	New Perspective
Focused on parents	Focuses on families
Included families only	Includes families and community agencies
Worked in school settings	Works in home and neighborhood settings
Recruited eager families	Recruits hard-to-reach families
Based agendas on teacher and administrator priorities	Bases agendas on family priorities
Viewed urban families as deficient	Views all families as containing inherent strengths

Source: Information from Davis (1991). Reprinted by permission.

TABLE 15.3 Types of Involvement for Families and School Programs

Type of Involvement	How Family Members Show Involvement	How Programs Can Encourage Involvement
Volunteering Helping in the program or with program-related activities	• Serve as a chaperone on field trips • Work as a telephone-tree caller • Participate in a parent safety patrol • Teach a skill	• Recruit and organize volunteers • Identify available talents, times, and locations of volunteers • Match volunteers with appropriate opportunities • Offer training for volunteers • Recognize volunteer efforts
Parenting Establishing home environments that support children's learning and development	• Establish age appropriate rules and guidelines for children • Talk with children about their interests, activities, and friends • Explain their hopes and goals for their children to be children	• Offer clear parent-education information—via documents, workshops, discussion groups, videotapes, or classes—that shows respect for diversity of cultures, beliefs, values, needs, and goals
Communicating Engaging in two-way communications about children's progress and the program's activities and policies	• Read a progress report • Attend a parent conference • Read a program newsletter • Send a note to a staff member or call about the child's progress or problems	• Design effective program-to-home and home-to-program methods of communication • Provide clear information on program policies and activities that is appropriate for diverse literacy levels • Provide translations for written materials or interpreters for oral communications if needed • Send child's work home for the family to review
Supporting Learning at Home Helping children learn outside the classroom	• Discuss class work with children • Discuss homework assignments with children • Help children establish a homework routine • Visit the library with children • Help children rehearse for plays or concerts	• Sponsor family fun nights that focus on math, language, or other skills • Provide information and ideas about how families can help children with homework and other skill-building activities • Provide a lending library for educational books and games
Decision Making Participating in program decisions	• Join a friends of the program organization • Serve on an advisory committee, council, or board	• Reach out to families of all racial, ethnic, and socioeconomic groups • Offer leadership training
Collaborating with the Community Integrating school, community, and family resources to enhance programs, build partnerships, and support children's development	• Help children link to community resources, such as art, music, and theater • Encourage children to participate in community service, such as helping senior citizens, recycling, and peer tutoring	• Give parents a list of community resources and services that support learning • Develop partnerships, coalitions, or collaborations with other community resources and services

Source: Mulroy and Bothell (2003). Reprinted by permission.

family members can show involvement, and how schools or programs can encourage that involvement.

LEVELS OF PARENT INVOLVEMENT

Parent involvement may occur at several different levels, regardless of the age of the child (Hoover-Dempsey & Sandler, 1995). The sections that follow focus on parent involvement by phase or level of involvement.

Level 1: Assessment

The first step in Level 1, the assessment phase, is for parents to request for and consent to an evaluation. Following this, eligibility is considered for special educational classifications. For each level, the application of laws (based on the Individuals with Disabilities Education Act of 1997 and 2004) are discussed. Should the parent disagree with the findings, the conflict may be resolved informally or through mediation and due process.

During the assessment interview, parents will provide information on family background as well as subjective data on the identified child's problems. The information obtained during the interview will be used in conjunction with various test instruments, inventories, and rating scales administered to the parent, which will provide essential, objective information. Together the subjective and objective findings are used for educational diagnostic and placement purposes.

Level 2: Intervention

The Individualized Family Service Plan (IFSP) documents and guides the early intervention process for children with disabilities and their families. The IFSP allows for the implementation of early intervention (according to IDEA, Part C) and contains information about the services necessary to facilitate, in spite of disability, a given child's mental development. The IFSP enhances the family's capacity to facilitate the child's development by getting family members and service providers to work as a team to plan, implement, and evaluate services tailored to the family's unique concerns, priorities, and resources. The box below describes additional details about the IFSP.

Parents certainly should be involved in the IEP meeting to provide information and to discuss potential intervention, services, and placement that will best serve their child. Parents also may be involved in later discussions regarding recommendations made by the IEP team.

Level 3: Transition/Follow-Up

Transitions involve a basic continuity of care when the child moves from one program to another. Successful transitions must occur from early intervention programs to preschool or school-age programs. Family involvement—especially parent involvement—is essential (Morningstar, Turnbull, & Turnbull, 1995). Follow-up meetings, changes in the IEP, and any new condition or behaviors will also require parental participation (Bailey et al., 1998). The Hoover-Dempsey and Sandler model depicts parental involvement as levels of involvement. The model is described as follows.

The Hoover-Dempsey and Sandler Model of Parental Involvement Figure 15.2 illustrates the five levels of involvement in the Hoover-Dempsey and Sandler (HDS) model of parental involvement.

Understanding the Individualized Family Service Plan

An IFSP is a written plan that describes the specific early intervention services that are needed for a child under age 3 who has a delay in one or more of five key developmental areas. The IFSP also lists who will provide the services and where they will be provided. It also says how often, for how long, and how much of a service must be provided to the child (for example, direct physical therapy, two 30-minute sessions per week). The county and the early intervention provider *must* make arrangements for children to have all of the early intervention services that are listed in the IFSP.

Source: Information from www.elc.pa.org/pubs/downloads/english/dis-ei-under-3ifsp-11-02.pdf

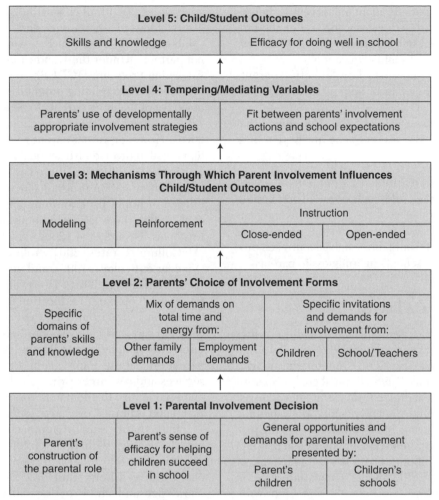

FIGURE 15.2   The Hoover-Dempsey and Sandler model.
Source: Permission granted through Copyright Clearance Center.

According to Lanthier, Wright-Cunningham, and Edmonds (2003), the HDS model of parental involvement is a five-level model with three research-based factors that influence parental involvement: (1) parental role construction, (2) parental self-efficacy, and (3) school invitingness. Level 1 of this model is illustrated in Figure 15.3.

In the HDS model, parental involvement relates to achievement in essentially a *three-level process*:

■ *Role construction* signifies how parents construct their roles as parents with regard to their child's

Level 1 of HDS

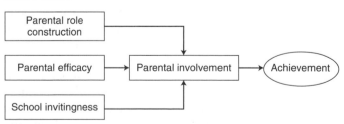

FIGURE 15.3   Level one of the Hoover-Dempsey and Sandler model.
Source: Information from www.goodschools.gwu.edu. Reprinted by permission obtained through Copyright Clearance Center.

education. Some parents adopt a passive role, believing that their child's education falls under the umbrella of the school system; others view themselves as an active part of their child's education.

■ *Parental efficacy* measures how effective parents view themselves in terms of helping their child succeed in school.

■ *School invitingness* reflects the frequency that schools actually invite parents to be involved in their child's school.

These three factors predict parental involvement and consequently, the child's achievement. By far, the most consistent predictor of parental involvement is school invitingness. Schools interested in fostering parental involvement would thus establish outreach programs to improve the school's invitingness to parents.

PARENT EDUCATION

Parent education typically refers to systematic activities to assist parents in acquiring knowledge and skills that allow them to mediate or extend the intervention with their child (Smith et al., 1998). Typical goals of parent education include teaching parents strategies to assist their children in attaining developmental skills, helping parents manage children's behavior, and enhancing parents' skills in engaging their younger children in play and social interaction (Mahoney et al., 1999). In fact, one of the most important developments in early intervention during the past 30 years has been the shift to provide services in collaboration with parents and families. This emphasis is reflected in family-centered approaches to care, direct family support, and the implementation of early intervention based on Individualized Family Service Plans (Mahoney et al., 1999).

Little discussion on parent education can be found in early intervention literature over the past few years. However, many of those who work in early intervention believe that parent education has become a major part of their job (Filer & Mahoney, 1996). Most publications put primary emphasis on a child-directed intervention (McBride & Peterson, 1997). Some question whether early intervention specialists have the knowledge and skills to offer to parents as their emphasis has been on working with children.

Historically, parents were viewed as peripheral to the child's education or at times even obstacles or adversaries (Turnbull & Turnbull, 1990). Professional efforts focused on parents and children separately (Mahoney et al., 1999); parents were viewed as clients, not partners. Under the Handicapped Children's Early Education Program (HCEEP),* it was "mandatory that projects develop training programs for parents with the objective of teaching parents to be effective in working with and teaching their own child" (Chen & Harsch, 2004). However, initial parent roles in early intervention entailed diverse instructional responsibilities.

In the past 20 years, there has been much criticism of parent education programs focusing on placing the burden of home programming on parents (DeBoard et al., 2006), the relationship between parent and professionals (Groark et al., 2002), the blaming of parents (McCollum & Yates, 2001), role conflict for parents (Vincent & Beckett, 1993), and potential cultural bias (Lynch & Hanson, 2004). However, there has been little research on parent education to deal with some of these issues. It is ironic that the emergence of family-centered care and family support (core features of early intervention) may have contributed to the decline of parent education. Family support emphasizes family services and resources primarily designed to help the family cope with the demands associated with caring for their child (Dunst, Trivette, & Jordy, 1997).

In the family support approach, parents' effectiveness in dealing with their children's developmental needs is affected primarily by socioeconomic and psychological well-being and only secondarily by their knowledge and child-rearing skills (Reynolds, 2000; Temple, Reynolds, & Miedel, 2000). In contrast, parent education emphasizes the importance of parents' child-rearing knowledge and specific skills for enhancing their child's development (Mahoney & Wheeden, 1997).

Needing a renewed focus on parent education (Mahoney et al., 1999), there is a need to focus on both educational achievement as well as on behavioral problems, as noted in the long-term effects of an early intervention program for behavior disorders (Reynolds et al., 2001). This means that there needs to be an emphasis on education achievement as well as on behavioral problems when addressing behavior disorders.

---

* The Handicapped Children's Early Education Program (HCEEP) is a discretionary grant program offering federal funds to public or private agencies that plan to develop new strategies for serving young handicapped children.

RELATIONSHIP-FOCUSED EARLY INTERVENTION

The term *relationship-focused early intervention* refers to the fostering of growth-producing parent–professional and parent–child relationships (Mahoney & Perales, 2005). According to Kelly and Barnard (1999), parent education is embedded in the relationship-focused approach. This approach is not new; in the 1980s researchers and program planners were emphasizing the important relationship between parent–child interaction intervention and child development (Mahoney & Powell, 1988).

An integral part of early intervention, parent education should be implemented as an important component of relationship-focused early intervention. Research has demonstrated the importance of the early parent–child relationship in influencing child growth and development. Recent research has pointed to the efficacy of making relationship-focused intervention the goal of early intervention efforts. To make the paradigm shift to relationship-focused intervention, program planners and service providers must understand the theoretical basis for the role of the parent–child relationship in early development and know how to design and implement appropriate and timely intervention activities that support and enhance the parent–child relationship as the foundation for early child development. Furthermore, service providers need training in effective adult teaching strategies to deliver relationship-focused early intervention. These same providers also need interpersonal communication skills to effectively use applicable teaching strategies to enhance parent–provider and parent–child relationships. Continued efficacy research, ongoing evaluation of training, and mentoring efforts along with the development of improved measurement strategies should guide efforts to deliver relationship-focused early intervention. Kelly and Barnard (1999) believe that a paradigm shift is occurring. There is evidence of renewed and reformed attention on the relationship-focused early intervention model, in which the educational process within a developmental context is related to the ongoing parent–child relationship (Kelly & Bernard, 1999; Mahoney et al., 1999).

SIBLING INVOLVEMENT

It is not unusual for siblings to be involved when there is a brother or sister who is the focus of treatment for some type of disability (Harry, 2002). When treatment programs are established outside of the school setting, it is not uncommon for the whole family to be involved in treatment. Siblings may participate in family therapy, and they are also involved when the identified student has had deficits in social skills and has conflicts with the sibling at home. According to Flick (1998b), both the identified student and sibling may be involved in developing more appropriate cooperation and/or play skills.

Clearly, when one child in a family has a disability, *all* family members are affected (Seligman & Darling, 1989). Parents certainly may struggle with their own emotions, which may first include denial but later, with continuing and unabating frustration, stress, and anger. There is at any point in time mixed emotions. Often, the child who is unimpaired may experience rejection, depression, and anger; there may be a sense of isolation (with loss of attention/support). At times, parents may have exceedingly high expectations for the typically developing child and even expect that child to compensate for the sibling who has a disability. Despite the many conflicts with their brothers or sisters, unimpaired children may frequently defend their impaired siblings from such things as name-calling or attacks by others.

SIBLING'S AREAS OF CONCERNS

In typically developing siblings there are often occasions for arguments and fights as well as rewarding emotional experiences. Conflicts, competition, and love span a wide range of emotional reactions between pairs of typically developing siblings. However, children who have siblings with special needs might also experience ambivalent feelings about their brothers and sisters. Clinical experience and the research literature show that there are numerous recurring themes that arise in children whose siblings have special needs (Meyer & Vadasy, 1994).

Overidentification

Overidentification occurs when a sibling wonders whether he or she shares—or will share—a sibling's problem or disability (Meyer & Vadasy, 1994). In some cases, many siblings might worry about acquiring their sibling's special needs (Sourkes, 1990).

> I'm really worried if I don't get an A in history, I won't get in the honor society. My parents have so many problems with my sister, I'd really like to

make them happy with my schoolwork. Do you think they will be disappointed if I don't get in the honor society?°

Overidentification is more likely to occur when the child with special needs is younger (Meyer & Vadasy, 1994). While parents may know that another child in the family cannot "catch" their sibling's disability, it may not be obvious to a child.

Embarrassment

Embarrassment may be caused by the unwanted attention the child and family receive when a sibling has behavior problems. Sometimes such embarrassment may actually be more common when the sibling's problems are mild or invisible.

> This will sound weird, but I wish my brother had Down syndrome. Some of the kids at our Sibshop group talk about how cool their sibs are even if they have Down's. My brother has ADHD and is a pain all the time! It is hard to find anything positive to say about him.

Being asked about their sibling's problem may also bring about embarrassment. Because there are many stages when children are more sensitive to their sibling's embarrassing problem behavior, parents will need to recognize this fact and also acknowledge the sibling's feelings of embarrassment. Handling such problems in a competent manner not only improves communication with the embarrassed sibling but also provides critical information needed to cope with the sibling's feelings. In most cases, embarrassment is temporary and siblings are able to reframe difficult situations in a more positive light.

Guilt

Guilt may result when children feel that they may have caused their sibling's disability, or they might experience survivor's guilt, guilt over their own abilities, guilt over sibling conflicts, and even guilt over caregiving.

> I blamed myself for my sister's problems. I always feel guilty around her. She's adopted and I know inside that it wasn't my fault but I feel so hurt and confused. I blame myself.

° The excerpts in this section have been adapted from Meyer and Vadasy (1994).

Children can feel responsible for their sibling's disability and feel that they are now somehow being punished for something they said, did, or thought at the time of diagnosis. Such siblings need reassurance that this was not the case. Siblings who express a form of survivor's guilt may wonder why this happened to their sibling and not to them. Some children have even expressed a desire to trade places with their disabled sibling (Koch-Hatten, 1986), and they may even experience guilt over their own typically normal developing abilities. Some siblings may also experience guilt over the usual sibling conflicts that normally occur during early development. Because of their "advantages," siblings are often told to compromise and may feel guilt if they tease or argue with their disabled siblings. Parents who put pressure on children to repress their feelings may see them later act-out their anger in a cryptic way. As siblings grow older, some may experience guilt over moving away from home and leaving their parents to care for their sibling with special needs.

Shame

Painful feelings of shame, guilt, and embarrassment are sometimes related to the stigma of having a sibling with a disability, although this has changed somewhat today as the stigma of various disabilities are not what they were in the past. Stigma may also be found in families with two children—one disabled and one who is not. Specifically, there is the stigma of shame for many siblings of disabled children.

> For a long time, I was embarrassed about my brother. I recall a constant conflict—you don't want to say anything because you don't want your parents to know you're ashamed.

Isolation

A sibling's disability can result in the typically developing sibling to experience various feelings of loss and isolation. These feelings are often exacerbated when there are only two children in the family. This isolation may take one of several forms.

First, there may be isolation from parental attention. When parents spend more time with one sibling because of a disability, the other sibling can feel neglected and isolated. Parents might become overwhelmed by a child's special needs and may be too exhausted or simply unable to recognize the sibling's need for attention (Campbell et al., 1996). Typically developing siblings who view their parents' hassles with the sibling with special needs may become reluctant to seek out parents about their own problems. During such trying times, the sibling may find a relative or friend in whom he or she can communicate and discuss their problems.

> The only way I could get them [parents] to pay attention to me was to get mad. That would get their attention.

Second, there is often isolation from information about their sibling with a disability. Later in life, some siblings have stated that their parents wished to protect them from the stress of the disability. In any case, there is a unique loneliness when parents fail to communicate about the sibling's disability.

Third, there is also isolation from peers. While many parents have the advantage of support groups, unaffected siblings do not have the support of peers that is so often essential in helping the sibling of a child with special needs. Despite a tremendous need for such sibling-oriented programs, there are few available. For this reason, the sibshops model was developed by Donald J. Meyer, director of the Sibling Support Project at the University of Washington (Meyer & Vadasy, 1994).

Resentment

Resentment is often expressed by siblings of children with special needs and frequently goes unnoticed by parents. Siblings may resent the attention, amount of care, time given, perceived unequal treatment, and expectations to do more chores than their disabled sibling. Loss of parental attention may stem from the perception that the sibling with special needs receives a greater share of the family's emotional and/or financial resources.

Unequal treatment and excessive demands may be associated with perceptions of the affected sibling being indulged, overprotected, or even permitted to engage in behaviors that are unacceptable to other family members. Siblings frequently complain that rules about behavior, chores, bedtime routines, etc., may not apply to the child with special needs.

> I'm confused. My sister has many behavior problems. I love my little sister and I'd like to play with her, but I'm afraid of her because she sometimes hurts me. She bites me and punches me. My mom says I shouldn't hit her back and I should play with her. What should I do?

There is also resentment regarding failure to plan for the future. In some families, there is the assumption that the unaffected sibling will become the guardian or may engage in long-term supervision of their disabled sibling. When parents fail to involve siblings in planning for the future, there may be resentment, especially in those cases where one child's disability is severe and where the prognosis for improvement is poor. When planning for the future is lacking, those siblings who become guardians may have a general lack of preparation along with feelings of resentment over their added responsibilities.

Increased Responsibilities

Early research on siblings of children with special needs typically focused on the caregiving demands assumed by siblings, especially sisters (Farber, 1960). Older sisters were more adversely affected because they were often pressured into a surrogate parent role with their sibling who had special needs (Cleveland & Miller, 1977). Not only were older sisters more likely to be at risk for educational failure (Tarcic & Hughes, 2004) and stress (Opperman & Alant, 2003), but they were most likely to enter "helping" professions as an adult (National Dissemination Center for Children with Disabilities [NICHCY], 1994). One study did show that preschool sisters of children with disabilities were likely to have more responsibility for child care and household chores than brothers in similar situations (Labato, Barbour, Hall, & Miller, 1987). Stoneman and colleagues (1991) found that younger siblings of children with special needs babysat, monitored, and helped care for their older siblings compared to their typically developing classmates. Stoneman and colleagues (1988) found that for siblings of children with special needs there was an increase in observed sibling conflict and a decrease in positive sibling interaction associated with child care responsibilities, which was not found with the comparison group. Similar findings were noted by Hodapp, Glidden, and Kaiser (2005).

> As an older sister, I knew I was very important to Terry. I was the one who took her to the rest room. I was the only one who could fix her hair, take her to a store, and stop her tantrums.

Researchers discovered that increased responsibilities involving helping with dressing and feeding were greater when the sibling with special needs had fewer adaptive skills (Stoneman et al., 1988, 1991). Many siblings who care for their brother or sister with special needs often take pride in the added responsibility and realize the importance of their work. Some general guidelines have been suggested by Stoneman and colleagues (1988) to help parents assign chores:

- The type of chores assigned are important to consider. Parents may even wish to offer the helping (normal) sibling a choice in their household responsibilities.
- The number of demands placed on the helping sibling should also be considered. Comparing the sibling's duties with peers may provide guidelines regarding whether a chore is excessive or whether the chore prevents the sibling from participating in some important outside activity.
- Which family member assumes the caregiving responsibilities should also be considered. Parents need to make sure that chores are divided equally and fairly among siblings of both sexes.

Pressure to Achieve

As noted by some early authors, parents often placed pressure on the typically developing sibling as if to compensate for the "failure" of the other child with a disability.

> I have an older brother and sister with special needs. My parents and teachers expect me to do everything right. They call me "the lucky normal one." I know my parents have lots of problems, so I want to make them happy, but sometimes I feel so much pressure! Do other kids feel this way?

Grossman (1972) found that this pressure to achieve was especially evident when the child with the disability was a son. It has also been noted that many siblings will place pressure on themselves as well. There can be many reasons for this self-pressure. One sibling mentioned that being successful in academics was one way to demonstrate that it was her sister who had the disability, not she. While many children who have siblings with special needs do well academically or otherwise, it is only those who exhibit a compulsive need to achieve perfection that may be of concern.

SIBSHOPS PROGRAM

Sibshops° is a program (Meyer & Vadasy, 1994) designed for brothers and sisters of children with special needs. The program offers siblings, ages 5 to 15 years, monthly meetings combining informal discussion with interactive educational activities in a fun-filled environment that is just for siblings. These "workshops" are led by a team of specially trained volunteers and health care providers. The Sibshop program has five basic goals:

- *Goal 1*: Sibshops will provide brothers and sisters of children with special needs an opportunity to meet other siblings in a relaxed recreational setting. This format has several benefits. First, it can reduce the sibling's sense of isolation. Second, the atmosphere can promote informal sharing and may develop friendship that continues outside of the program. Third, the recreational aspect makes sibshops enjoyable and not just another thing that they have to do because of their sibling.
- *Goal 2*: Sibshops will provide brothers and sisters with opportunities to discuss common joys and concerns with other siblings of children with special needs. Participants may share stories, experiences, and laughs with peers who understand the ups and downs of life with a disabled sibling. Siblings learn that they are not alone with their experiences and their frequent ambivalent feelings.
- *Goal 3*: Sibshops will provide siblings with an opportunity to learn how others handle situations commonly experienced by siblings of children with special needs. Such siblings often have unique experiences—ranging from defending a sibling from name calling or answering questions about the sibling from friends or strangers to dealing with lack of attention or exceedingly high expectations from parents. At Sibshops discussions about such common concerns, interests, and behavior problems may decrease the sibling's sense of feeling alone, and help the sibling learn how other peers cope with similar problems. From a broad range of solutions, siblings may choose the one that may be best suited for their situation.
- *Goal 4*: Sibshops will provide siblings with an opportunity to learn more about the implications of their sibling's special needs. Siblings need information to

---

°Sibshops are best described as opportunities for brothers and sisters of children with special health and development needs to obtain peer support and education within a recreational context.

answer questions about their sibling's special needs so that they can provide answers to questions posed by friends, classmates, and strangers.

■ *Goal 5*: Sibshops will provide parents and other professionals with opportunities to learn more about the concerns and opportunities frequently experienced by the siblings of children with special needs. Some activities also help parents to better understand "life as a sibling." Parents may learn from older siblings (adolescents and adults) what it was they appreciated in their own parents' treatment of children in the family and what they wished their parents had done differently.

A study by D'Arcy and colleagues (2005) evaluated the effectiveness of Sibshops from three disability agencies in Cork, Ireland. Both qualitative and quantitative data were obtained using semistructured interviews and the Piers-Harris Children's Self-Concept Scale with siblings, together with parent feedback. Results from the Piers-Harris showed that there was no significant increase in sibling self-esteem following attendance at the Sibshops. However, the interviews revealed that the majority of siblings enjoyed and benefited from the Sibshops. Parents also reported satisfaction with the Sibshops and believed that their children had benefited as well.

SCHOOL–FAMILY–COMMUNITY PARTNERSHIPS

Epstein (1995) has noted that the school, family, and community are extremely important because they "directly affect children's learning and development" (p. 702). She has encouraged schools to work with family and the community as partners who share responsibility for all students in both academic and behavioral areas. Such collaboration will ultimately benefit all students and especially those with behavioral problems. Community members share interests as well as responsibilities for students and work together to develop better programs and better opportunities for students.

Considering this shared responsibility, federal legislation concerning family and community involvement has stressed further development of school relationships with the family and with the community. Such collaboration allows families and community members a wide range of options to participate in school activities and to have input in the school's decision-making process with roles and responsibilities in school improvement. A good example of such collaboration is shown in Table 15.4.

TABLE 15.4   Examples of Collaboration Among Families, Communities, and Schools

Examples of stakeholder/community-wide collaborations	• Family–school–business partnerships; school-based community centers; corporate-school partnerships that include the community.
Business objectives/outcomes	• Improve the quality of K–12 education. • Enhance brand recognition and loyalty. • Be a good corporate citizen. • Send the message that school performance has meaning beyond the classroom by promoting the use of student records in hiring practices.
School objectives/outcomes	• Reduce incidents of school violence. • Raise academic and skill standards. • Attend to social and emotional needs of students. • Increase attendance and reduce truancy.

Eli Lilly and Company has started science camps which benefit working parents and their children during summer vacation. The first camp, which is on-site at Lilly in Indianapolis, Indiana, serves 350 children of employees. Lilly found the space, including the buildings and the pool, the **YMCA** came in and ran the camp, and Lilly scientists developed a science curriculum for campers. The science camp has been replicated at two additional sites. However, instead of limiting the science camps to Lilly employees, it is open to all children in the community. This is one example of a partnership that has tremendous benefits to all—Lilly employees and their families, Lilly customers, other area employers as well as families and children in the community.

Source: Information from http://www.ed.gov/pubs/strategicpartner/case.html.

Preparation of Teachers and Family Involvement

Teachers may be prepared to work with students, but they are not always prepared to effectively work with parents (Rasinski, Blachowicz, & Lems, 2006). Both regular and special education teachers must be sensitive to the feelings and needs of parents who have children with various disabilities.

One of the missing elements in teacher education programs is working with families (Hiatt-Michael, 2001). Until recently, most state teacher certifications did not require that teacher education programs include courses on family involvement issues. Gray (2001) reported a significant increase in the late 1990s of the number of states that required some credentialing statement regarding a teacher's knowledge and skills relating to family and community involvement.

A survey by Hiatt-Michael (2001) indicated that of 147 universities with a teacher education program (and 96 responding), only 7 had noted that parent involvement issues were not included in any course. Twenty-two offered a course on parent involvement, but it was not required for K–12 teacher education students. Such courses were developed for special education or for early childhood teachers or perhaps offered as an elective. It is significant that 93 percent of the universities reported that parent involvement issues were incorporated into existing teacher education courses (e.g., special education, reading methods, instructional methods, and early childhood education, in that order).

The most popular topic was reported to be the parent conference, the most pervasive home–school communication outside of the report card. Other topics (in rank order sequence) included parent concerns, parent newsletters, and working with the community (Hiatt-Michael, 2001). These findings are similar to those reported by Epstein (2001). Other forms of home–school partnerships, such as homework, parent workshops, class newsletters, and general planning programs, were also suggested by the research. Homework is one area that has almost ubiquitous support (Walker et al., 2004).

Research on parental involvement in children's homework was reviewed by Hoover-Dempsey and colleagues (2001). In general, parents choose to become involved in their child's homework because they believe they should be involved. Several authors have stressed the importance of teacher invitations in motivating parent involvement (Epstein & Van Voorhis, 2001; Kohl, Lengua, & McMahon, 2002; Simon, 2004). Teachers as well as parent leaders may be involved in after-school activities and are in a good position to bridge the gap with regard to communication between home and school on those issues concerning the student's learning and homework (Casden, Morrison, Albanese, & Mocias, 2001). It is important to know what parents do when they involve themselves in their child's homework. Table 15.5 presents some recommendations.

THE IMPACT OF TEACHER TRAINING

Clearly, teacher education courses that deal with family involvement make a difference in classroom practices. A study by Katz and Bauch (1999) using graduates from teacher education programs at Peabody College at Vanderbilt University reported that these new teachers felt prepared and used a diverse array of family involvement practices associated with the training they received.

Kirschenbaum (2001) and Hiatt-Michael (2001) summarize several of the promising practices for teachers regarding family involvement included in their university instruction. One of the most critical skills was the acquisition of skills needed to promote positive home–school communication. A primary recommendation was that university instructors should use case studies and role-playing to help future teachers become familiar with a positive parent conference. Various other suggestions included observation of trained teachers in classroom and their participation, as well as course and classroom activities that involve a family case study, a home visit, researching home–school literacy programs, preparing a class newsletter, and attending a school advisory council to name a few. If teachers fail to receive such training in their teacher education programs prior to entering the classroom, there may be limited opportunities to acquire such training later in the school setting.

The National Network of Partnership Schools based at Johns Hopkins University coordinates a network of schools, districts, and state agencies that use the

TABLE 15.5   What Do Parents Do When They Involve Themselves in Their Children's Homework?

1. Interact with the student's school or teacher about homework.
   • Communicate with the teacher about student's performance, progress, homework.
   • Meet school requests and suggestions related to homework (e.g., sign completed tasks, offer requested help, participate in homework intervention program).

2. Establish physical and psychological structures for the child's homework performance.
   • Specify regular times for homework, and establish structures for time use.
   • Articulate and enforce expectations, rules, and standards for homework behavior.
   • Help student structure time, space, and materials for homework.
   • Structure homework within the flow of family life; ensure parental "availability on demand."

3. Provide general oversight of the homework process.
   • Monitor, supervise, oversee the homework process.
   • Attend to signs of student success or difficulty related to task or motivation.

4. Respond to the student's homework performance.
   • Reinforce and reward student's homework efforts, completion, correctness.
   • Recognize and offer emotional support for student performance, ability, effort.
   • Review, check, correct homework.

5. Engage in homework processes and tasks with the student.
   • Assist, help, tutor, "work with" student, or "do" homework with student.
   • Teach student in direct, structured, convergent ways (e.g., learn facts, derive answers, drill, practice, memorize).
   • Teach student using indirect, more informal methods (e.g., respond to questions, follow student lead).

6. Engage in meta-strategies designed to create a fit between the task and student knowledge, skills, and abilities.
   • Break learning tasks into discrete, manageable parts.
   • Observe, understand, "teach to" student's developmental level.

7. Engage in interactive processes supporting student's understanding of homework.
   • Model or demonstrate appropriate learning processes and strategies.
   • Discuss problem-solving strategies.
   • Help student understand concepts, check for understanding.

8. Engage in meta-strategies helping the student learn processes conducive to achievement.
   • Support student's self-regulation skills, strategies, personal responsibility for homework processes and outcomes.
   • Help student organize personal thinking about assignments.
   • Encourage student to self-monitor, focus attention.
   • Teach and encourage the student to regulate emotional responses to homework.

Source: Information from Hoover-Dempsey and colleagues (2001). Reprinted by permission.

Epstein model of the six types of parent involvement (Epstein, 2001). They promote staff development, and create site action plans and assessment at each site. The Institute for Responsive Education at Boston University has researched and promoted family involvement issues for almost 40 years. This international group has helped develop partnerships across the nation and on every continent.

At the federal level, the Partnership for Family Involvement in Education within the U.S. Department of Education coordinates a wide range of activities and organizes staff development sessions, collects information on promising practices, and disseminates informative brochures. Parents are encouraged to join this partnership, a suggestion discussed in detail by Couchenour and Chrisman (2003).

SUMMARY

This chapter begins by outlining Epstein's (1995) six types of parental involvement. As part of the involvement, schools also need to develop programs such as an action team for partnerships (ATP). Parents can basically classify their involvement on two separate dimensions of support and participation. Based on federal legislation from Goals 2000 and the Educate America Act of 1994, the national education goals that relate to school partnerships are described. It is important to note that parental involvement can affect both achievement and behavior. Such involvement may occur at several levels: assessment, intervention, and transition/follow-up services. Notwithstanding, there is a clear need for a renewed focus on parent education, which is embedded in the relationship-focused approach. Although children who have a sibling with a disability have been neglected in the past, they may exhibit many concerns that need to be addressed. The Sibshop program has been designed with such nonimpaired siblings in mind. Clearly, parents need to be involved with their children as well as the community in which they live. Appropriate teacher training can make a difference in parent involvement along with positive classroom practices that improve behavior and achievement.

DISCUSSION QUESTIONS

1. Besides social factors, what does family involvement improve?
2. Who should be included on the action team for partnerships (ATP)?
3. Discuss the four types of parents who vary on the dimensions of support and participation.
4. Responsive teaching strategies are founded on the principle of "active learning." What does this mean?
5. How has family involvement in children's learning changed in recent times?
6. Based on federal legislation from Goals 2000 (Educate America Act of 1994), describe the three goals that relate to school partnerships.
7. Describe the three levels or phases of parent involvement, according to Hoover-Dempsey and Sandler (1995).
8. To what does the term *relationship-focused early intervention* refer?
9. The unimpaired sibling of a child with a disability may experience several feelings. Please describe.
10. What are some of the recurrent themes that are experienced by siblings of children with a disability? List and explain each.
11. Briefly explain the five goals of the Sibshop program.

CHAPTER 16

Future Directions
with EBD Students

Overview

- Early intervention
- Comprehensive behavior programs
- Extensive support network
- School-wide assessment
- Individual assessment
- Teacher education and student diversity
- General and special education teachers needed
- Teacher preparedness
- Future directions on the wraparound process
- The future of partnership programs
- Prevention of behavior disorders
- Family support and integrated services
- Researched interventions for behavior problems

Case History

Often there is more than one student in a classroom with similar problems. Seth is a 10-year-old third grader who has both behavioral and learning problems. Most of his time is spent in the special ed classroom, but he does spend some time in a general classroom. Seth can do addition, but has deficiencies with subtraction. Carlos is a 9-year-old third grader who has been diagnosed with EBD and ADHD, and he takes 15 mg of Ritalin. He is in the resource room for math and reading and engages in nonacademic activities in another special ed room with other students who have EBD. Carlos has severe deficiencies in multiplication and subtraction. Both boys are often off-task and when given difficult tasks look around and draw cartoons. Seth also shows aggression (e.g., tearing his paper, kicking the desk, throwing objects) along with other disruptive behaviors including talking, making noise, playing with objects, making faces and being out of his seat. *What would you do?*

There are three universal themes that are an integral part of successful intervention programs for children with EBD: (1) early identification and intervention, (2) comprehensive behavioral programs, and (3) an extensive support network.

EARLY IDENTIFICATION AND INTERVENTION

Early identification and intervention are essential to the success of at-risk children with behavior problems (Conroy et al., 2004; Nelson et al., 2005; Sinclair et al., 2005). Such programs are *proactive* thus avoiding placement in more restrictive alternative settings (Conroy, Hendrickson, & Hester, 2004; Nelson, Benner, & Gonzalez, 2004).

Conroy and colleagues (2004) highlight two model programs for elementary students with chronic behavior problems: (1) the Incredible Years, and (2) the First Step to Success. The Incredible Years is based on the needs of children aged 3–12 years who have conduct disorders. In this program, parents are able to improve their use of positive behavioral interventions (Webster-Stratton, Reid, & Hammond, 2001). The First Step to Success is for kindergarten-age children who are at-risk for developing EBD. This program teaches academic strategies and social skills to foster school success. Golly, Stiller, and Walker (1998) found that such children showed academic gains and learned adaptive skills as well as reduced their behavior problems and aggressive acting out. Another early intervention program, Promoting Alternative Thinking Strategies (PATHS), emphasizes emotional awareness and social competency via modeling and direct instruction. According to Kam, Greenberg, and Kusche (2004), this program decreases externalizing behaviors and depression in young children. The goal, in all cases, is to improve educational achievement and behavior for those children with serious evidence of emotional and behavior disorders. One approach is the use of comprehensive behavioral programs.

COMPREHENSIVE BEHAVIORAL PROGRAMS

Comprehensive behavioral programs focus on levels of academic engagement and modeling appropriate behavior to students with EBD (Kerr & Nelson, 2002).

Students with EBD may show coexisting academic problems, especially in reading (Barton-Arwood, Wehby, & Falk, 2005; Nelson et al., 2004). Many students with such problems may attempt to escape or avoid pressures in the classroom (Rosenberg, Wilson, Maheady, & Sindelar, 2004). Curriculum modifications may therefore reduce behavior problems by keeping these students actively engaged in the lesson (Lambert, Cartledge, Heward, & Lo, 2006; Sutherland, Alder, & Gunter, 2003). Clearly, academic skills are directly associated with the social adjustment of EBD students (Benner, Beaudoin, Kinder, & Mooney, 2005; Lambert, Cartledge, Heward, & Lo, 2006; Lane, Wehby, & Barton-Arword, 2005).

EXTENSIVE SUPPORT NETWORK

The collaboration of school and other community service agencies enhances the opportunities for students with EBD to successfully generalize their behaviors by extending services beyond schools and into the neighborhood communities (Armstrong, Dedrick, & Greenbaum, 2003; Rosenberg et al., 2004).

A personal mentor or significant tutor may also be a key element to a more positive life change (Todis et al., 2001). Since students with EBD often lack social supports, social networks can provide a wraparound system of care for children with EBD and their families (Armstrong et al., 2003). The complex issues of students with EBD requires support from a variety of agencies including schools, mental health centers, and child welfare and juvenile justice systems, all designed to improve the outcomes of students with EBD. It is well to review information previously discussed. Such information will be important in educational reform and in the development of more positive behavior programs in schools.

School-Wide Behavioral Programs

Students with EBD can most readily be identified without screening tools or in-service training (Liaupsin, Jolivette, & Scott, 2004). Early identification and intervention can prevent problem behaviors from escalating to more chronic and difficult-to-manage behaviors (McCurdy, Mannella, & Eldridge, 2003).

School-wide behavioral programs can create a positive highly structured environment compared to discipline referral programs that are often based on control through punitive consequences (Gresham, 2004; Rutherford, Quinn, & Mathur, 2004). Such a punishment-oriented approach with zero-tolerance policies has been reactive and generally ineffective with EBD students, excluding them from learning opportunities and exacerbating their academic skill deficits (Kerr & Nelson, 2002; Liaupsin et al., 2004). Schools can counter the effects of community and family risk factors by establishing a stable and rich environment where academic and social skills are taught and relationships with both peers and adults can be developed (Liaupsin et al., 2004; McCurdy et al., 2003).

Emphasis on Positive Behavioral Programs

Most school-wide programs use a three-tier approach that involves primary, secondary, and tertiary prevention (Gresham, 2004; Rosenberg et al., 2004). Primary interventions affect all students. They enhance the school climate, employ school-wide discipline, and focus on conflict and peer mediation groups (McCurdy et al., 2003; Rosenberg et al., 2004). Secondary interventions focus on students who do not respond to the primary intervention procedures (Gresham, 2004). These interventions utilize social skills instruction, behavioral contracting, and self-management (Gresham, 2004; Rosenberg et al., 2004). Tertiary interventions address the needs of students who exhibit frequent and intense problem behaviors; many EBD students can be included in this group, which requires more individualized and intense behavioral programs (Gresham, 2004; Rosenberg et al., 2004).

Schools must assess problem behavior of students in order that programs can be designed to deal with the problem behavior.

ASSESSMENT

There are two basic assessment procedures: (1) school-wide assessment, and (2) individual assessment.

School-Wide Assessment

School-wide programs are based on assessment of need and utilization of a positive approach to behavior change (McCurdy et al., 2003; Rosenberg et al., 2004). Examination of records and a needs assessment can identify where behavior problems exist. Students with EBD often have difficulty in school especially during transitions. The use of behavioral programs can help define clear behavioral expectations, the practice of routines during transitions along with the provision of highly structured environments in and out of the classroom (Gresham, 2004; McCurdy et al., 2003).

Individual Assessment

Replacement positive behaviors can be learned when individual assessment is based on interventions that focus on the context where problem behaviors occur, the antecedents and consequences (Gresham, 2004; Smith & Sugai, 2000). This process of functional behavioral assessment (FBA) consists of principles and practices used to understand the pattern of the behavior problem and to isolate those changes that may lead to improved rates of appropriate behaviors (Lewis, Lewis-Palmer, Newcomer, & Stichter, 2004). The assessment-based behavior interventions are thus built on information learned during FBA (Kern et al., 2006). While short-term interventions such as punishment can temporarily suppress behavior problems, the ultimate goal is to find a long-term resolution (Kern et al., 2006; Reid & Nelson, 2002).

Both teachers and parents should remember three key points;

- That it is most important to focus on appropriate behavior and to minimize attention to inappropriate behavior.
- That punishment will never tell the child *what to do*, only *what not to do*.
- That children need feedback on what they do—especially on their appropriate behavior.

CONCLUDING THOUGHTS

The concluding thoughts presented here focus on the future training of teachers, additional characteristics of behavior disorders, and future plans on how to prevent or reduce the frequency of behavior disorders in the classroom.

Teacher Education and Student Diversity

It is indeed difficult to influence long-held beliefs and attitudes about teacher education and student diversity during one education course (McDiarmid, 1990). However, a comprehensive program on diversity issues spread over several semesters (and courses) might allow for the development of greater cultural sensitivity and knowledge that will be beneficial for any teacher that inherits a culturally diverse classroom (McDiarmid & Price, 1993; Pohan, 1996). Clearly, student populations will continue to diversify (Peterson, 2004; National Center for Education Statistics [NCES], 2004; Willie, Alves, & Edwards, 2003), while the population of preservice teachers may become more homogeneous (Garmon, 2005; NCES, 2004).

An important goal for teacher education programs is to identify teachers who can display thoughtfulness and reflection; these are the best candidates to be open and receptive to new learning (Banks, 2001). There must also be a commitment to support sensitivity to cultural diversity in the classroom (Irvine, 2003). Teacher preparation programs must influence teacher beliefs about diversity, and teacher educators must ensure the continued development of knowledge and constructive beliefs with ongoing teacher support that will ultimately lead to the success of students with behavior disorders (Causey, Thomas, & Armento, 2000).

Teacher Attrition   Former teachers and teachers who transferred to another school at the end of the 1999–2000 school year complained of a lack of planning

time, too heavy a workload, too low a salary, and problematic student behavior among their top five sources of dissatisfaction with the school they left. Table 16.1 presents the numbers and percentages of teachers who did not teach at the same school during the 1987–2000 school years by turnover category (Ingersoll, 2001).

Teacher Burnout   A study by Singh and Billingsley (1996) indicated that the highest burnout area in special education may be working with students who have behavior disorders. Higher stress in classes with behavior disordered students was supported by Cegelka and Doorlag's (1995) report on attrition in special education teachers. They noted that severe behavior disorders and managing behavior problems was one of the four skill areas in which teachers rated themselves as least well prepared.

In many rural schools, teachers with new licenses have been hired to teach students with emotional and behavioral disorders at what is considered an entry-level position (Fore, Martin, & Bender, 2002). Although teachers burn out or leave teaching for varied reasons, the amount of training they receive is believed to be a primary contributor to their success or failure (Emmer & Stough, 2001; Billingsley, 2004). Consequently, there is a need to identify the effective methods of preparing

TABLE 16.1   Public and Private K–12 Teachers Who Made Transitions During the 1987–2000 School Years, by Turnover Categories

Turnover Categories	1987–1988		1990–1991		1993–1994		1999–2000	
	Number	Percent	Number	Percent	Number	Percent	Number	Percent
Total turnover at the end of the year	391,000	14	383,000	13	418,000	14	546,000	16
Transfers at the end of the year	218,000	8	209,000	7	205,000	7	269,000	8
Left school	173,000	6	174,000	6	213,000	7	278,000	8
Retired	35,000	1	46,000	2	48,000	2	66,000	2
Took other job	64,000	2	56,000	2	90,000	3	126,000	4
Went back to school	11,000	#	13,000	#	8,000	#	12,000	#
Left for family reasons	48,000	2	33,000	1	35,000	1	47,000	1
Other	14,000	1	25,000	1	30,000	1	26,000	1

Note: All numbers are estimates with confidence intervals varying from ±2,000 to ±34,000. Denominator used to calculate the percentage is the total number of teachers in the workforce during the Teacher Follow-up Survey year. Detail may not sum to totals because of rounding to zero.

Source: U.S. Department of Education, National Center for Education Statistics, Teacher Follow-up Survey (TFS), "Current Teacher Questionnaire" and "Former Teacher Questionnaire," 1988–89, 1991–92, 1994–95, and 2000–01. (Originally published on p. 13 of the complete report from which this article is excerpted.)

special education teachers (along with regular education teachers) to work with students with EBD.

The goal is to provide effective preparation to potential teachers in order to enhance their knowledge and skills and to develop the problem-solving skills that are needed to deal with problem behaviors. However, technologies such as case-based instruction, telecommunications, multimedia, and other electronic and computer support tools provide teacher educators with promising approaches to teach new techniques and for preservice teachers to learn new ways. For example, Fitzgerald and Semrau (1993–1997; 1998–2000) have developed, evaluated, and disseminated Teacher Problem Solving Skills (TPSS) through the Virtual Resources Center in Behavioral Disorders (VRCBD). This series of 10 interactive multimedia case studies focuses on students with emotional and behavioral disorders.

Initial research with TPSS shows that students (and teachers) are enthusiastic about their learning experiences and report the self-pacing, multiple learning options, and interactive participation as motivating and more realistic compared with traditional instruction (Fitzgerald & Semrau, 1998–2000; Semrau & Fitzgerald, 1995). However, Fitzgerald and colleagues (2003) note that further research is needed to document outcomes and transfer as well as process. In this case, the outcomes are the end point or how well the student performs. Transfer refers to the application of knowledge obtaining to other situations. The process refers to the mechanism of learning or how the information is acquired.

The Need for General and Special Education Teachers   A study by Nelson (2001) looked at the stress level of teachers whose students have EBD. Although this study involved mostly older and more experienced teachers, most teachers of EBD students are actually young and inexperienced. It is important that most future educators receive only minimal training on special education topics related to emotional and behavior disorders; sometimes only one class covers teaching students with special needs. However, with the increase in mainstreaming students with special needs in the general education setting, general education teachers will be forced to educate students with special needs, and they will therefore need to explore research and effective teaching strategies for students with all types of disabilities, not just EBD. Even if educators

can handle and minimize disruptive behavior by EBD students, this does not mean that these students will be successful. Teachers will need a combination of academic instruction skills as well as classroom management strategies to establish a classroom that is conducive to learning.

Teacher Preparedness   Teachers' perceptions of preparedness are also important. A survey in 1998 (NCES, 1999) revealed that teachers felt prepared for some of the most compelling classroom demands such as class discipline, but few felt they were well prepared to address students who lacked proficiency in English or who came from diverse cultural backgrounds. Of course, this survey may *not* have been representative of all teachers, and it was also clouded by the fact that newer teachers were far more likely to be mentored than the more experienced teachers, but the younger teachers felt less prepared to manage classrooms. According to the U.S. Department of Education (NCES, 1997), the content areas that teachers deemed most important in the survey were as follows:

- Maintain order and discipline in the classroom.
- Implement new methods of teaching such as cooperative learning.
- Implement state or district curriculum and performance standards.
- Use student performance assessment techniques.
- Address the needs of students with disabilities.
- Integrate educational technology into the grade or subject taught.
- Address the needs of students with limited English proficiency or from diverse cultural backgrounds.

More recent variations in the preparation of teachers has been discussed by Darling-Hammond, Chung, and Frelow (2002).

Future Directions on the Wraparound Process

Although it seems clear that more research is needed to conclude that the wraparound process and positive behavioral interventions supports (PBIS) have scientific support and can be used to solve problems (Franz, Miles, & Brown, 2003), current program data at various levels suggest that the wraparound process is promising, and there are some guidelines for effective implementation, training, and evaluation (Burns et al., 2000; Eber, 2003)

A systems framework for the PBIS approach supports the adoption and continued use of research-validated practices for all students, but especially for those with problematic behavior (Lewis & Sugai, 1999; Sugai & Horner, 1999). More research is also needed to support the effectiveness and efficiency of PBIS in providing proactive behavioral support to all school students. It is easy to support the integration of wraparound and PBIS as many of their components are similar. In addition, wraparound and PBIS are most effective when they are both used.

Future research must address the following:

- The practices used to educate students with emotional and behavior disorders are supported by research and are most likely to have a positive effect (Walker, Colvin, & Ramsey, 1995). However, it is not clear why schools do not adapt and use them.
- While a systems approach is clearly required to provide continued adaptation and use of effective components, the precise nature of the features that compromise the effective and efficient systems have not been scientifically validated.
- Although a proactive instructional approach is preferred, it is not clear why schools continue to maintain overreliance on negative solutions such as exclusion, suspension, and corporal punishment to deal with problematic behavior (Shores & Wehby, 1999). Factors must be isolated that prompt educators to use ineffective practices to determine why it is difficult to focus on prevention (Kauffman, 1999; Scott & Nelson, 1999) and how effective interventions can be substituted (Holas, 2002).
- Attempts must be made to understand why collaborative systems of care, which may have been initiated through mental health systems, have been reluctant to include schools (Eber, 2003; Eber, Nelson, & Miles, 1997).

The Future of Partnership Programs

Given the effectiveness of some of the excellent programs of school, family, and community partnerships, educators cannot let parents alone determine how they can be involved in their children's education (Deslandes et al., 1997). It has thus become important for educators, parents, and the community to work together planning and implementing complete programs, creating a school environment that is welcoming and that will help students succeed. The No Child Left Behind Act requires that schools offer well-planned programs of family and community involvement to provide support for student achievement and to communicate clearly with parents.

Most schools are attempting to involve families in their child's education by linking their involvement to student achievement. Research-based programs of partnership should be used. In fact, there is an emphasis on improvement of partnership programs. Involvement of families clearly results in increased levels of achievement and consequently greater student success. School principals appear to be a key factor in the success of these new partnership programs. It is only with their leadership and support that schools can work closely with teachers, parents, and community members to benefit schools and their students.

Prevention of Behavior Disorders

Kamps and Tankersley (1996) have identified some recurrent themes in the area of prevention: (1) early intervention and family-focused prevention services, including assistance in parenting skills and accessing community-based services, (2) school-based prevention programs, including effective teaching practices, peer mediation, social skills intervention, self-management, and classroom management, and (3) within-setting and across-setting collaboration. Clearly, it is important to have good communications in general among teachers, parents, and children.

Family Support and Integrated Services

Some children fail in the early grades for reasons that have nothing to do with their cognitive capabilities. Conflicts between parents and schools in values and expectations can undermine school success. Also, there are children who do not attend school regularly, who need eyeglasses or hearing aids, or who lack adequate nutrition. Family support and integrated service programs can solve many of these problems. Two national programs based largely on improving school–home collaboration and services for children are Comer's School Development Program (Comer, 1988) and Zigler's Schools of the 21st Century (Zigler, Finn-Stevenson, & Linkins, 1992).

Some excellent self-help resources are also available for parents (Clark, 1996; Flick, 1996; Flick, 1998b; Batshaw, 2001). Effective parenting is based on an understanding of the current developmental level and needs of children. Behavior is considered to be a problem, according to Batshaw (2001), when it occurs too often or too seldom or is inappropriate to the child's developmental level or for the situation at hand. As most authors suggest, it is most important to learn ways to encourage appropriate behavior in a child and to adapt a proactive rather than a reactive management style. There are now home-based treatment programs for specific disorders, such as ADHD (Flick, 1998b) and autism (Pomeranz, 1999).

Researched Interventions for Behavior Problems

Clearly, there are many approaches schools can use to prevent challenging behavior and to address it when it does occur. It is important to understand the following characteristics that are typical of the best systems (NICHCY, 1999):

■ Assessment of the student's behavior must be linked with interventions that follow the student through whatever placements the student has.

■ Multiple interventions are necessary for improving the behavior of most students. Any positive effect of a single strategy, especially when the intervention is short-term, is likely to be temporary. Just as behavior problems and risk factors come in packages, so too should interventions.

■ To produce lasting effects, interventions must address not only the behavior that led to disciplinary action but a constellation of related behaviors and contributing factors.

■ Interventions must be sustained and include specific plans for promoting maintenance over time and generalization across settings. Focusing on the student's behavior while placed in any short-term setting, such as an interim alternative educational setting, is not

sufficient. Interventions need to follow students to their next placement (and elsewhere). Generalization is a must.

■ A combination of proactive, corrective, and instructive classroom management strategies are needed. Interventions should target specific prosocial and antisocial behaviors as well as the "thinking skills" that mediate such behaviors. Such a combination provides an atmosphere of warmth, care, support, and essential structure.

■ Interventions must be developmentally appropriate, and they should address strengths and weaknesses of individual students and their environment.

■ Parent education and family therapy are critical components of effective programs for antisocial children and youth.

■ Interventions are most effective when provided early in life. Devoting resources to prevention reduces the later need for more expensive treatment.

■ Interventions should be guided by schoolwide and districtwide policies that emphasize positive interventions over punitive ones.

■ Interventions should be fair, consistent, culturally and racially nondiscriminatory, and sensitive to cultural diversity.

■ Interventions should be evaluated as to their short-term and long-term effectiveness in improving student behavior. Both the process and outcome of each intervention should be evaluated.

■ Teachers and support staff need to be well trained with respect to assessment and intervention. Staff working with students who have behavior problems will require ongoing staff development and continued support.

■ Effective behavioral interventions require collaborative efforts from the school, home, and community agencies. Helping children and youth is a shared responsibility.

SUMMARY

This chapter identified three important themes: (1) early intervention, (2) comprehensive behavioral programs, and (3) extensive support when looking at the future directions with EBD students. Both school and individual assessments can be of assistance. Teacher education is essential; if teacher training is delayed,

behavior change becomes quite difficult. Teachers will be faced with greater diversity in the school population. With more EBD students being educated in regular classrooms, more diverse training will be needed by regular education teachers. Clearly it is difficult to work with students who present behavior problems.

However, teachers are not alone. Greater attempts need to be made to include families and community agencies in the education of children with behavior problems. The chapter concludes with a summary of general research interventions that will help educators to work more effectively with students who have behavior and academic problems.

DISCUSSION QUESTIONS

1. Name two model programs for elementary students with chronic behavior problems.
2. Which skills are directly associated with social adjustment of EBD students?
3. What does the wraparound model provide for students with EBD and their families?
4. What do school-wide behavioral programs create? Why is this better?
5. Describe school-wide assessment.
6. How is individual assessment important?
7. Why is diversity an important issue?
8. What are some of the sources of dissatisfaction with school that causes teacher attrition?
9. What was the cause of highest burnout for teachers in special education according to Singh and Billingsley (1996)?
10. Why are rural schools affected most by students with EBD?
11. What is TPSS and why is it important?
12. Why would teachers in regular education need preparation to deal with EBD?
13. Elaborate on three research questions that schools need to address in the future.
14. How should schools attempt to involve families in the education of their children?
15. According to Kamps and Tankersley (1996), what are three recurrent themes in the area of prevention of behavior disorders?
16. What are the two national programs that address improvement in school–home collaboration and services for children?
17. What are some of the researched interventions for behavior problems?

APPENDIX A

ANSWERS TO PROBLEM CASES

Chapter 1   Lena's worksheets consisted of visual cues to compensate for her reading deficits. She was given more examples of how to complete a task, with some words highlighted. Her tasks were also shortened. Lena's disruptive behavior dropped significantly, and she was on-task for longer periods; her accuracy (i.e., items completed) also improved.

Chapter 2   For setting events, Shawn was provided with a classmate who modeled being calm and explained what was expected. Regarding antecedent strategies, Shawn was allowed to continue with a preferred activity if appropriately requested; easy/preferred tasks were mixed with more difficult ones and activities were made more appealing. Teachers encouraged Shawn to ask for help or a break. Consequent strategies involved providing assistance or a break when he asked appropriately. Staff members who became upset could ask for a replacement staff. The outcome was that the average number of aggressive incidents and disruption dropped from 21 to 2 per day. Participation increased. The aide now states that Shawn is no longer a behavior problem.

Chapter 3   Allen could earn coupons for spending time with a classmate of his (Allen's) choosing with the nonoccurrence of disruptive behavior. Time varied from 1 minute to 10 minutes with the classmate, but Allen could receive coupons only when he was on-task and not disruptive. Coupons were simply placed on his desk. When Allen was elsewhere, his classmates were told that they could earn coupons (for a snack or extra computer time) by not interacting with Allen or just remaining quiet. The amount of time on-task without disruptions was measured. Allen was able to reduce his inappropriate behaviors, and he eventually eliminated them. Average time on-task increased significantly. Allen continued his appropriate behavior even when he was required to show 10 minutes of on-task behavior without a disturbance to earn a coupon. Positive attention was used to maintain this behavior.

Chapter 4   Aston was first provided with a computer that enabled him to avoid his handwriting difficulties. He was encouraged to take time to think before brainstorming with a classmate. His teacher limited this activity to 2 minutes. Aston's percentage of time on-task improved significantly. He was given continued positive attention for improvements.

Chapter 5   The primary task for the teacher was to eliminate the consequences that maintain the problem behavior. Lauren was asked to return things stolen, but she received little or no attention from adults. She was not required to apologize, nor was she sent to the principal's office. If Lauren tried to discuss her stealing behavior, she was redirected to the classroom tasks. Her stealing incidents decreased to a minimum over a few weeks.

Chapter 6   The main target for Madison was to stay on-task. She was first taught an alternative behavior—asking for "help." She was then taught to ask for "attention" by saying "Am I doing good work?" The teacher used this appropriate attention-seeking behavior not more than three times per session. Madison decreased problem behaviors and increased time on-task when baseline was compared to outcome measures.

Chapter 7 Chris's desired behavior was to improve his time on-task during reading. In his case, the teacher assigned a peer tutor. The peer prompted Chris to find his book, get in his seat and conjointly read together. The peer was also taught to praise Chris when he was on-task. Chris' percentage of time on-task increased. When this arrangement was stopped, time on-task decreased; it increased again when it was reinstated.

Chapter 9 The desired behavior for Jordan was to go to school and stay there all day. A contract was developed and all parties agreed to follow it. The school would agree to provide extra computer time when he stayed all day. His parents would also provide time with friends (monitored and limited) and permission to watch 1 hour of TV for each day of attendance. Jordan showed significant improvement over initial baseline. However, when his parents requested that he not only attend school but also complete all of his homework, his improvement dropped to zero. Parents, however, agreed to the original contract and Jordan's behavior again increased. After 2 weeks, his parents could renegotiate.

Chapter 10 The desired target behavior for Tyler was being on-task during reading. Peer attention often maintained his problem behavior. Tyler was assigned a peer tutor. The peer was to help Tyler select his book and find his seat, and then the two would read together. This peer also provided some verbal praise (as the teacher had instructed) when Tyler was on-task. After the introduction of peer tutoring, Tyler improved significantly with on-task behavior. When tutoring was temporarily stopped, on-task behavior decreased. After a second implementation of peer tutoring, on-task behavior increased again.

Chapter 11 The desired behavior for Justin was for him to stay on-task and to complete his academic assignments. The intervention here involved modification of his curriculum. He was first given much positive behavioral support for appropriate behaviors and taught to self-monitor on-task behavior. He was to respond to a beep (on a tape recorder with head phones) given first every minute and then every 5 minutes. He was to mark whether he was on-task or off-task for each beep. An aide marked a sheet to see how accurate and honest he was. After the task, the data that Justin and the aide collected were compared. The lengths of his tasks were also shortened, and he was given more interesting problem solving tasks (instead of worksheets) in math. Also, handwriting was avoided in his English/spelling class; he was either assessed orally or he would use the computer. Change from baseline to outcome reflected significant improvement. Although tantrums were not monitored, they decreased as his on-task behavior improved.

Chapter 12 For Dylan, desirable behaviors consisted of staying on-task, following directions, being nondisruptive and showing either positive social interactions or no negative ones. There were four components in Dylan's program: (1) he was to complete independent work away from other students (e.g., in another class); (2) his group work was scheduled with those who would ignore his inappropriate behaviors and give praise for his positive ones; (3) he was taught to ask for a 1 or 2 minute break whenever he wished; and (4) all disruptive behavior was ignored by his teachers. Compared to baseline, Dylan's outcome measures showed significant improvement; his disruptive behavior was essentially eliminated. Requested breaks occurred several times per week, but they declined after 3 weeks. Dylan stopped asking for breaks. He was able to remain in the general education class.

Chapter 13 Crystal's expected desired behavior was to be able to trace words on four worksheets about the food groups without evidence of disruption or aggression. Her assignment was to choose food names to be traced and to use her completed worksheets as a grocery list in a mock shopping trip to a grocery store. All four food groups were shown with corresponding pictures, each on a different shelf. Crystal selected the four pictures of food groups and posted them under the correct label (at her seat). Child–teacher interaction time increased, while Crystal's disruptive behavior decreased. Her on-task time correspondingly increased.

Chapter 14 David's intervention had several components: (1) the teacher stopped reprimanding him for off-task behavior, (2) the teacher paid more attention to him when his behavior was appropriate (e.g., she responded immediately when he raised his hand), and (3) instead of reprimanding David for being out of his seat, she praised another student who behaved appropriately (but she did not compare the two). If David responded appropriately, he was then praised with a comment specific to what he did. If he did not respond, the teacher would comment in the form of a question ("What should you be doing at this time, David?") If he responded, she would give specific praise ("David, you know what to do and you did it. I'm proud of you"). With intervention, David's problem behavior often dropped to zero. Teacher attention was needed to maintain this behavior.

Chapter 16 Very often there is more than one student who needs to be managed in the classroom. The desired behavior for both Seth and Carlos is to stay on-task, especially during math, where the goal is for each of them to receive skill instruction until there is 85 percent accuracy in task performance. It is important to reduce the aversive characteristics of the task for each child. Before this intervention, Seth was off-task 40 percent of the time and Carlos was off-task 30 percent of the time. With appropriate instruction, both students' inappropriate behavior decreased significantly with continued praise; with no escape behavior permitted (i.e., being sent out of the room), both students progressed.

Remember that there may be more than one solution to behavior problems.

The answers above represent but one approach to such difficult to manage behavior. Perhaps there are other approaches that would be effective: monitoring the effects would therefore be most beneficial. In short, if the approach works continue to use it.

TABLE A.1 A.D.D. Warehouse Medication Chart to Treat Attention-Deficit/Hyperactivity Disorder

Drug	Form	Dosing	Common Side Effects	Duration of Effects	Pros	Precautions
Methylphenidate (MPH)						
Ritalin Methylin Metadate Generic MPH	Short-acting tablet 5 mg 10 mg 20 mg	Starting dose for children is 5 mg twice daily, 3–4 hours apart. Add third dose about 4 hours after second. Adjust timing based on duration of action. Increase by 5–10 mg increments. Daily dosage above 60 mg not recommended. Estimated dose range 0.3–0.6 mg/kg/dose	Insomnia, decreased appetite, weight loss, headache, irritability, stomachache, and rebound agitation or exaggeration of premedication symptoms as it is wearing off.	About 3–4 hours. Most helpful when need rapid onset and short duration.	Works quickly (within 30–60 minutes). Effective in over 70% of patients.	Use cautiously in patients with marked anxiety or motor tics or with a family history of Tourette's syndrome, or history of substance abuse. Don't use if patient has glaucoma or is on an MAOI.
Focalin (with isolated dextroisomer)	Short-acting tablet 2.5 mg 5 mg 10 mg	Start with half the dose recommended for normal short acting methylphenidate above. Dose may be adjusted in 2.5 to 5 mg increments to a maximum of 20 mg/day (10 mg twice daily).	As above; there is suggestion that Focalin (dextroisomer) may be less prone to causing sleep or appetite disturbance.	About 3–4 hours. Most helpful when need rapid onset and short duration. Only formulation with isolated dextroisomer.	Works quickly (within 30–60 minutes). Possibly better for use for evening needs when day's long-acting dose is wearing off.	As above; expensive compared to other short-acting preparations.

(*continued*)

Drug	Form	Dosing	Common Side Effects	Duration of Effects	Pros	Precautions
Ritalin-SR Methylin-ER Metadate-ER	Mid-acting tablet 20 mg Mid-acting tablet 10 mg 20mg	Start with 20 mg daily; may combine with short acting for quicker onset and/or coverage after this wears off.	Insomnia, decreased appetite, weight loss, headache, irritability, stomachache.	Onset delayed for 60–90 minutes; duration supposed to be 6–8 hours, but can be quite individual and unreliable.	Wears off more gradually than short acting, so there is less risk of rebound; lower abuse risk.	As above. *Note:* If crushed or cut, full dose may be released at once, giving twice the intended dose in first 4 hours, none in the second 4 hours.
Ritalin-LA (50% immediate release beads and 50% delayed release beads)	Mid-acting capsule 20 mg 30 mg 40 mg	Starting dose is 10–20 mg once daily; may be adjusted weekly in 10 mg increments to maximum of 60 mg taken once daily; may add short-acting dose in AM or 8 hours later in PM if needed.	Insomnia, decreased appetite, weight loss, headache, irritability, stomachache, and rebound potential.	Onset in 30–60 minutes. Duration about 8 hours.	May swallow whole or sprinkle ALL contents on a spoonful of applesauce. Starts quickly, avoids midday gap unless patient metabolizes medicine very rapidly.	Same cautions as for immediate release.
Metadate-CD (30% immediate release and 70% delayed release beads)	Mid-acting capsule 10 mg 20 mg 30 mg					If beads are chewed, may release full dose at once, giving entire contents in first 4 hours.
Concerta (22% immediate release and 78% gradual release)	Long-acting tablet 18 mg 27 mg 36 mg 54 mg	Starting dose is 18 mg or 36 mg once daily. Option to increase to 72 mg daily.	Insomnia, decreased appetite, weight loss, headache, irritability, stomachache.	Onset in 30–60 minutes; duration about 10–14 hours.	Works quickly (within 30–60 minutes); given only once a day; longest duration of MPH forms. Doesn't risk mid-day gap or rebound since medication is released gradually throughout the day; wears off more gradually than short acting, so less rebound; lower abuse risk.	Same cautions as for immediate release. Do not cut or crush.

Drug	Form	Dosing	Common Side Effects	Duration of Effects	Pros	Precautions
Dextroamphetamine						
Dextrostat	Short-acting tablet 5 mg 10 mg	For ages 3–5 years; starting dose is 2.5 mg of tablet; increase by 2.5 mg at weekly intervals, increasing first dose or adding/increasing a noon dose, until effective; for 6 years and over, start with 5 mg once or twice daily; may increase total daily dose by 5 mg/week until reach optimal level; tablet is given on awakening; over 6 years, one or two additional doses may be given at 4–6 hour intervals; usually no more than 40 mg/day needed.	Insomnia, decreased appetite, weight loss, headache, irritability, stomachache. Rebound agitation or exaggeration of premedication symptoms as it is wearing off; may also elicit psychotic symptoms.	Onset in 30–60 minutes; duration about 4–5 hours.	Approved for children under 6; good safety record. Somewhat longer action than short-acting methylphenidate.	Use cautiously in patients with marked anxiety or motor tics or with a family history of Tourette's syndrome, or history of substance abuse. Don't use if patient has glaucoma or is on MAOI; high abuse potential, particularly in tablet form.
Dexedrine (2004 Physician's Desk Reference [PDR] does not list short-acting Dexedrine tablets	Short-acting tablet 5 mg					
Dexedrine-Spansule	Long-acting capsule 5 mg 10 mg 15 mg	In children 6 and older who can swallow whole capsule, morning dose of capsule equal to sum of morning and noon short acting. Increase total daily dose by 5 mg/week until reach optimal dose to maximum of 40 mg/day.	Same as above.	Onset in 30–60 minutes. Duration about 5–10 hours.	May avoid need for noon dose; rapid onset; good safety record.	As above; less likely to be abused intranasal or IV than short acting; must use whole capsule.
Dextroamphetamine sulfate-ER	5 mg 10 mg 15 mg					

(*continued*)

Drug	Form	Dosing	Common Side Effects	Duration of Effects	Pros	Precautions
Mixed Amphetamine						
Adderall	Short-acting tablet 5 mg 7.5 mg 10 mg 12.5 mg 15 mg 20 mg 30 mg	Starting dose is 5 or 10 mg each morning (age 6 and older); may be adjusted in 5–10 mg increments, up to 30 mg/day.	Same as above.	Onset in 30–60 minutes; duration about 4–5 hours.	Wears off more gradually than dextroamphetamine alone, so rebound is less likely and more mild.	Same as for Dexedrine tablets.
Adderall-XR (50% immediate release beads and 50% delayed release beads)	Long-acting capsule 5 mg 10 mg 15 mg 20 mg 25 mg 30 mg	Starting dose is 5 or 10 mg each morning (age 6 and older); may be adjusted in 5–10 mg increments, up to 30 mg/day.	Same as above.	Onset in 60–90 minutes (possibly sooner); duration 10–12 hours.	May swallow whole or sprinkle ALL contents on a spoonful of applesauce; may last longer than most other sustained release stimulants; rebound less likely than with long-acting dextroamphetamine.	Same as for Dexedrine Spansules except that it has documented efficacy when sprinkled on applesauce.
Atomoxetine						
Strattera	Long-acting capsule 10 mg 18 mg 25 mg 40 mg 60 mg	Starting dose is 0.5 mg/kg; the targeted clinical dose is approximately 1.2 mg/kg; increase at weekly intervals; medication must be used each day; usually started in the morning, but may be changed to evening; it may be divided into a morning and an evening dose, particularly if higher doses needed.	In children: decreased appetite, GI upset (can be reduced if medication taken with food), sedation (can be reduced by dosing in evening), light-headedness. In adults: insomnia, sexual side effects, increased blood pressure.	Starts working within a few days to 1 week, but full effect may not be evident for a month or more; duration all day (24/7) so long as taken daily as directed.	Avoids problems of rebound and gaps in coverage; does not cause a "high," and thus does not lead to abuse; because it is not a controlled drug, it may be used with history of substance abuse.	Use cautiously in patients with hypertension, tachycardia, or cardiovascular or cerebrovascular disease because it can increase blood pressure and heart rate; has some drug interactions; while extensively tested, there is a short duration of population use.

Drug	Form	Dosing	Common Side Effects	Duration of Effects	Pros	Precautions
Buproprion						
Wellbutrin-IR	Short-acting tablet IR-75 mg 100 mg	Starting dose is 37.5 mg increasing gradually (wait at least 3 days) to maximum of 2–3 doses, no more than 150 mg/dose.	Irritability, decreased appetite, and insomnia.	About 4–6 hours.	Helpful for ADHD patients with comorbid depression or anxiety; may help after school until home.	Not indicated in patients with a seizure disorder or with a current or previous diagnosis of bulimia or anorexia; may worsen tics; may cause mood deterioration at the time it wears off.
Wellbutrin-SR	Long-acting tablet SR-100 mg 150 mg 200 mg	Starting dose is 100 mg/day, increasing gradually to a maximum of 2 doses; no more than 200 mg/dose.	Same as Wellbutrin-IR	About 10–14 hours.	Same for Wellbutrin-IR; lower seizure risk than immediate release form; avoids noon dose.	Same as Wellbutrin-IR. If a second dose is not given, may get mood deterioration at around 10–14 hours.
Wellbutrin-XL	Long-acting. tablet 150 mg 300 mg	Starting dose is 150 mg /day, increasing gradually to a maximum of 2 doses; no more than 300 mg/day.	Same as Wellbutrin-IR	About 24+ hours.	Same for Wellbutrin-IR; single daily dose; smooth 24 hour coverage; lower seizure risk than immediate release form.	Same as Wellbutrin-IR.
Alpha-2 Agonists						
Catapres (clonidine)	Tablet 0.1 mg 0.2 mg 0.3 mg	Starting dose is 0.025–0.05 mg/day in evening; increase by similar dose every 7 days, adding to morning, midday, possibly afternoon, and again evening doses in sequence; total dose of 0.1–0.3 mg/day divided into 3–4 doses; do not skip days.	Sleepiness, hypotension, headache, dizziness, stomachache, nausea, dry mouth, depression, nightmares.	Onset in 30–60 minutes; duration about 3–6 hours.	Helpful for ADHD patients with comorbid tic disorder or insomnia; good for severe impulsivity, hyperactivity, and/or aggression; stimulates appetite; especially helpful in younger children (under 6) with ADHD symptoms asociated with prenatal insult or disorders such as Fragile X syndrome.	Sudden discontinuation could result in rebound hypertension; minimize daytime tiredness by starting with evening dose and increasing slowly; avoid brand and generic formulations with red dye, which may cause hyperarousal in sensitive children.
Clonidine	Tablet 0.1 mg 0.2 mg 0.3 mg					

(*continued*)

Drug	Form	Dosing	Common Side Effects	Duration of Effects	Pros	Precautions
Catapres Patch	TTS-1 TTS-2 TTS-3	Corresponds to doses of 0.1 mg, 0.2 mg, and 0.3 mg/patch; if using 0.1 mg tablets, try TTS-2 (but will likely need TTS-3).	Same as Catapres tablet, but with skin patch there may be localized skin reactions.	Duration 4–5 days, so avoids the vacillations in drug effect seen in tablets.	Same as above.	Same as above; may get rebound hypertension and return of symptoms if a patch has accidentally come off or becomes loose; an immature student may get excessive dose from chewing on the patch.
Tenex (guanfacine)	1 mg 2 mg 3 mg	Starting dose is 0.5 mg/day in evening and increase by similar dose every 7 days as indicated; given in divided doses 2–4 times per day; daily dose range 0.5–4 mg/day; do not skip days	Compared to clonidine, lower chances/ severity of side effects, especially fatigue and depression; also less frequency of headache, stomachache, nausea, dry mouth; unlike clonidine, minimal problem of rebound hypertension if doses are missed.	Duration about 6–12 hours.	Can provide for 24/7 modulation of impulsivity, hyperactivity, aggression and sensory hypersensitivity; this covers most out-of-school problems, so stimulant use can be limited to school and homework hours; improves appetite; less sedating than clonidine.	Avoid formulations with red dye as above; hypotension is the primary dose-limiting problem; as with clonidine, important to check blood pressures with dose increases and if symptoms such as lightheadedness suggest hypotension.
Guanfacine tablets	1 mg 2 mg 3 mg					

This chart was updated 4/19/04.

Treatment of ADHD usually includes medical management, behavior modification. counseling, and school or work accommodations. The medications charted here include (1) the stimulants, (2) the nonstimulant Strattera (atomoxetine) with effects similar to stimulants, (3) the antidepressant Wellbutrin (bupropion), and (4) two antihypertensives—Catapres (clonidine) and Tenex (guanfacine). Stimulants include all formulations of methyphenidate (Ritalin, Focalin, Metadate, and Methylin) and all forms of amphetamines (Dexedrine, Dextrostat, and Adderall).

Note: Individuals respond in unique ways to medication depending upon their physical make-up, severity of symptoms, associated conditions, and other factors. Careful monitoring should be done by a physician in collaboration with the teacher, therapist, parents, spouse, and patient. Medications to treat ADHD and related conditions should only be prescribed by a physician. Information presented here is not intended to replace the advice of a physician.

Source: Thanks go to Dorothy Johnson, M.D., for her invaluable assistance in preparing this chart. Permission granted by Harvey Parker, PhD, of the ADD Warehouse.

TABLE A.2

Medications for Conduct Disorders and Oppositional Defiance Disorder
From Clinically Researched Double-Blind Studies

Medication (Trade Name)	Treatment Target
Clonidine (Catapres)	Effective in reducing symptoms of overarousal, aggression, and defiance, especially when ODD/CD is comorbid with ADHD.
Haloperidal (Haldol)	Reduces severe aggression.
Tazodone (Dergrel)	Reduces impulsivity, temper tantrums, and overt aggression, especially when ODD/CD is comorbid with ADHD.
Venlataxine (Effexor)	Improves ADHD, aggression, and mood disturbances, especially when ODD/CD is comorbid with ADHD.

Helpful Medications

Medication (Trade Name)	Treatment Target
Buspirone (Buspar)	Reduces irritability, defiance, anger, and aggression.
Carbamazeprine (Tegretol)	Reduces impulsivity and aggression.
Guanfacine (Tenex)	Reduces overarousal and aggression.
Risperidone (Risperdal)	Reduces impulsivity, aggression, overarousal, and defiance.

Medications for Tics and Tourette's Syndrome
From Clinically Researched Double-Blind Studies

Medication (Trade Name)	Treatment Target
Clonidine (Catapres)	Reduces tics along with impulsivity, inattention, overactivity, and disruptive behavior.
Fluoxetine (Prozac)	Reduces OCD symptoms.
Guanfacine (Tenex)	Reduces vocal/motor tics, symptoms of ADHD, and disruptive behavior.
Haloperidal (Haldol)	Reduces motor and vocal tics.
Primozide (Orap)	Reduces motor and vocal tics.
Risperidone (Risperdal)	Reduces motor and vocal tics.

Primary Medications for Depression
From Clinically Researched Double-Blind Studies

Medication (Trade Name)	Treatment Target
Clomipramine (Anafranil)	Reduces depression.
Fluoxetine (Prozac)	Reduces depression.
Fluvoxamine (Luvox)	Reduces severity of depression.
Nefazodone (Serzone)	Reduces severity of depression symptoms.
Paroxetine (Paxil)	Reduces severity of depression symptoms.
Sertraline (Zoloft)	Reduces severity of depression symptoms.

(*continued*)

Medications for Bipolar Disorder
From Clinically Researched Double-Blind Studies

Medication (Trade Name)	Treatment Target
Lithium (Eskalith, Lithane, Lithobid, Lithonate)	Reduces manic and rapid cycling symptoms.
Carbamazepine (Tegretol)	Reduces manic symptoms.
Clozapene (Clozaril)	Reduces bipolar symptoms.
Risperidene (Risperdal)	Reduces manic symptoms.
Valproic acid (Depakote)	Reduces manic symptoms.

Medications for Behavioral Disturbances of Autism and Asperger Syndrome

Medication (Trade Name)	Treatment Target
Risperidone (Risperdal)	Reduces aggression and behavioral problems.
Olonzapine (Zyprexa)	Reduces aggression and disruptive behavior.
Haloperidal (Haldol)	Most useful for symptoms of autism.
Thioridazine (Mellaril)	Useful for decreasing aggression and agitation.
Naltrexone (Revia)	Reduces self-injurious and aggressive behavior.
Clonidine (Catapres)	Reduces stereotypic body movements, self-stimulation, hyperactivity, hypervigilance, sedation, and fatigue as side effects.
Valproic acid (Depakote, Depakene)	Reduces rage.
Carbamazepine (Tegretol)	Reduces rage.
Propranolol (Inderal)	Reduces rage.
Clomipramine (Anafranil)	Improves repetitive behavior, OCD symptoms, and aggression.
Fluoxetine (Prozac)	Improves repetitive behavior, OCD symptoms, and aggression.
Fluvoxamine (Luvox)	Improves repetitive behavior, OCD symptoms, and aggression.
Sertraline (Zoloft)	Improves repetitive behavior, OCD symptoms, and aggression.
Olanzapine (Zyprexa)	Reduces aggressiveness and distractive behavior.

Medications for Psychotic Disorders
From Clinically Researched Double-Blind Studies

Medication (Trade Name)	Treatment Target
Clozapine (Clozaril)	Good alternative to conventional neuroleptics.
Haloperidol (Haldol)	Reduces schizophrenic symptoms.
Loxapine (Daxlin, Loxitane)	Reduces schizophrenic symptoms.
Thioridazine (Mellavil)	Reduces schizophrenic symptoms.
Thiothixene (Navane)	Reduces schizophrenic symptoms.
Other Helpful Medications	
Olanzapine (Zyprexa)	Somewhat effective in reducing schizophrenic symptoms.
Risperidone (Risperdal)	Effective in reducing schizophrenic symptoms.

Source: Information from Phelps, Brown, and Power (2002).

TABLE A.3   Key to Psychological Test Procedures

WISC–III	Wechsler Intelligence Scale for Children–III
WASI	Wechsler Abbreviated Scale of Intelligence
WPPSI-R	Wechsler Preschool and Primary Scale of Intelligence–Revised
WRAT-3	Wide Range Achievement Test–3
PPVT-III	Peabody Picture Vocabulary Test–III
LDDI	Learning Disabilities Diagnostic Inventory
Beery VMI	Beery Developmental Test
SSRS	Social Skills Rating System
RCDS	Reynolds Child Depression Scale
RADS	Reynolds Adolescent Depression Scale
RCMAS	Revised Children's Manifest Anxiety Scale
CAFAS	Child and Adolescent Functional Assessment Scale
CBCL	Child Behavior Checklist
TRF	Teacher's Report Form (Achenback)
K-SADS	Kiddie–Schizophrenia and Affective Disorders Scales
CRS	Conners Rating Scales
BASC-2	Behavior Assessment System for Children–2nd edition
ADDES	ADD Evaluation Scales
DBDRS	Disruptive Behavior Disorders Rating Scale
PHCSCS	Piers-Harris Children's Self-Concept Scale
WRAML	Wide Range Assessment of Memory and Learning
WJ-R(Ach)	Woodcock-Johnson Psychoeducational Battery–Revised
TOPS–R	Test of Problem Solving–Revised
TOKEN	Token Test for Children
DSI	Dyslexia Screening Inventory
BRIEF	Behavior Rating Inventory of Executive Functions
TGMD-2	Test of Gross Motor Development–2
TAP	Test of Auditory Processing
GADS	Gilliam Asperger Disorder Scale
CARS	Childhood Autism Rating Scale
ABI	Adaptive Behavior Inventory
CDS	Conduct Disorder Scale
PKBS-2	Preschool and Kindergarten Behavior Scales–2
THS	Test of Handwriting Skills
ABS-S2	Adaptive Behavior Scales–School 2
Vineland	Vineland Adaptive Behavior Scales–Classroom Edition
NEPSY	A Developmental Neuropsychological Assessment
SCAN-C	Test for Auditory Processing Disorders in Children–Revised
ADD-H	ADD-H Comprehensive Teacher (Parent) Rating Scale
ACPT	Auditory Continuous Performance Test
Conners CPT-II	Conners' Continuous Performance Test–II
Conners K-CPT	Conners' Kiddie Continuous Performance Test
TOVA	Test of Variables of Attention
TOVA-A	Test of Variables of Attention–Auditory
IVA	Integrated Visual and Auditory Continuous Performance Test
CMDQ	Conners' March Developmental Questionnaire
WISC–IV	Wechsler Intelligence Scale for Children—4th edition
KBIT–2	Kaufman Brief Intelligence Test—2nd edition
Stanford-Binet	Stanford-Binet Intelligence Scale
WRAT–4	Wide Range Achievement Test—4th edition
WIAT–II	Wechsler Individual Achievement Test—2nd edition
PIAT–R	Peabody Individual Achievement Test–Revised
PPVT–IV	Peabody Picture Vocabulary Test–4th edition
TOLD–I–2	Test of Language Development—Intermediate 2nd edition
Bender Gestalt	Bender Gestalt Test

APPENDIX B

FUNCTIONAL BEHAVIORAL ASSESSMENT COMPONENT 1: DEFINE THE PROBLEM

Student _____   Date _____

Describe the problem behavior in observable terms. Be as specific as possible. Indicate how serious each problem is (destructive, disruptive, or distracting). Decide which behavior(s) you will begin to gather information on first in order to design a behavioral intervention plan.

Description of Problem Behavior   **Level of Seriousness**

1. _____

_____

_____

_____

_____

_____

_____

2. _____

_____

_____

_____

_____

_____

_____

3. _____

_____

_____

_____

_____

_____

_____

Description of Problem Behavior   **Level of Seriousness**

4. _____

_____

_____

_____

_____

_____

_____

FUNCTIONAL BEHAVIORAL ASSESSMENT COMPONENT 2: IDENTIFY EVENTS, TIMES, AND SITUATIONS

Student _____ Date _____

Target behavior _____

Answer these questions in measurable terms using specific data gathered from all the assessment tools used by the evaluation team. Patterns of behavior may emerge as you answer the questions. Be as specific as possible. General data and information will not assist the IEP team in developing an effective behavioral intervention plan.

Who is present...

when the behavior tends to occur?

_____

_____

_____

_____

when the behavior does not occur?

_____

_____

_____

_____

What is going on...

when the behavior tends to occur?

_____

_____

_____

_____

when the behavior does not occur?

_____

_____

_____

_____

When does the behavior...

tend to occur?

_____

_____

_____

_____

almost never occur?

_____

_____

_____

_____

Where does the behavior...

tend to occur?

_____

_____

_____

_____

almost never occur?

_____

_____

_____

_____

How often does the behavior occur...

per hour? _____   per day? _____   per week? _____

How long does the behavior occur...

per episode? _____

FUNCTIONAL BEHAVIORAL ASSESSMENT COMPONENT 3: GATHER INFORMATION

Student _____ Date _____

Consider the following factors and record any relevant information that has or may have an impact on the student's behavior. Information can be gathered from interviews or reviews of a student's record.

1. Medical, physical, and social concerns (such as medications, illnesses, disfigurements, allergies, lack of friends, inappropriate sexual contacts).

_____

_____

_____

_____

_____

2. Eating, diet, and sleep routines.

3. Substance abuse history (types, frequency of use, when and where use occurs, legal problems related to abuse, recent increase or decrease in use).

4. Stressful events and family history (family, information, siblings, difficult transitions, emotional losses, etc.).

FUNCTIONAL BEHAVIORAL ASSESSMENT COMPONENT 4:
IDENTIFY CONSEQUENCES MAINTAINING THE BEHAVIOR

Student _____ Date _____

Target behavior _____

Answer these key questions regarding what happens after the behavior occurs. Be specific using data collected about consequences. Responses that are too general do not assist in the development of an effective behavioral intervention plan.

What are the reactions...

of other people in the environment?

_____

_____

_____

_____

of the student toward the other people?

_____

_____

_____

_____

When the behavior occurs, what do...

teachers do?

_____

_____

_____

_____

peers do?

_____

_____

_____

_____

parents do?

_____

_____

_____

_____

What consequence methods have been used...

in the past at school and how did they work?

_____

_____

_____

_____

at home and how did they work?

_____

_____

_____

_____

What seems to improve the behavior. . .

in a short period of time?

_____

_____

_____

_____

if all else fails?

_____

_____

_____

_____

FUNCTIONAL BEHAVIORAL ASSESSMENT COMPONENT 5: DEVELOP A THEORY

Student _____ Date _____

Target behavior _____

Use the assessment information collected about the behavior and decide what purpose or function it has for the student. The following checklist may be helpful in developing a theory. Write a theory statement at the bottom.

Determining the Purpose of a Problem Behavior

N = Never   S = Sometimes   O = Other

1. The purpose of the behavior may be **attention** if . . .
   _____ It occurs when you are not paying attention to the student (e.g., you are talking to someone else in the room, talking on the phone, too busy to have a chat).
   _____ It occurs when you stop paying attention to the student.

2. The purpose of the behavior may be to **get/obtain something** if . . .
   _____ It occurs when you take away a favorite activity, food, toy, free time, etc.
   _____ It stops soon after you give the student what he or she seems to want or has recently requested.
   _____ It occurs when the student can't have what he or she desires.

3. The purpose of the behavior may be **escape/avoidance** if . . .
   _____ It occurs when you ask the student to do something (e.g., getting ready to change activities, write assignments, speak in front of peers, read in class) that he or she doesn't seem to like or want to do.
   _____ It stops after you stop "making demands."

4. The purpose of the behavior may be **play** if . . .
   _____ It occurs over and over again in a cyclical manner with friends or peers.
   _____ It occurs when no one else is around or the student seems to enjoy performing the behavior (e.g., smiles, laughs).
   _____ The student seems to be in his or her "own world" and can't do other things at the same time.

5. The purpose of the behavior may be **self-stimulation** if . . .
   _____ It tends to be performed over and over again, in a rhythmic or cyclical manner.
   _____ It tends to happen when there is either a lot going on or very little (e.g., noise, movement, people, activity).
   _____ The student can still do other things at the same time as performing the behavior.

6. The purpose of the behavior may be **control/power** if . . .
   _____ The student tends to be bossy.
   _____ The student wants to show others he or she can't be pushed around.
   _____ The student refuses to comply and seems to want to disrupt the established order.

7. The purpose of the behavior may be to get **justice** or **revenge** if . . .
   _____ The student appears to be getting back at another student.
   _____ The student appears to be defending another student for some real or imagined action.

8. The purpose of the behavior seems related to **acceptance** and/or **affiliation** with a group if . . .
   _____ The student's behavior is related to attempts to impress members of a peer group.
   _____ The student talks excessively about being a member of some group.

9. The purpose of the behavior appears to be an **expression** of **self** if . . .

_____ The student's behavior seems to show his or her independence.

_____ The student's behavior is associated with talk of acting alone.

_____ The student appears to take delight in what he or she can do alone.

The main purpose or function of the behavior is . . .

_____

_____

_____

_____

Source: Information from Durand and Crimmins (1988).

FUNCTIONAL BEHAVIORAL ASSESSMENT SUMMARY

Student _____

Date of birth _____ Age _____ Grade _____

1. **Behavior:** What is the inappropriate or unacceptable behavior to be targeted for intervention? Be specific; give examples.

   _____

   _____

   _____

   _____

2. **Events, Times, and Situations:** What specific events trigger the behavior? Include who, what, when, where, and how often information is obtained from interviews, observations, assessments, or record reviews.

   _____

   _____

   _____

   _____

3. **Relevant Information:** What circumstances make the behavior more likely to occur (medical concerns, diet and sleep routines, substance abuse, family history, emotional losses or social concerns, etc.)?

   _____

   _____

   _____

   _____

4. **Consequences:** What responses or reactions occur after the behavior that appear to maintain the behavior?

   _____

   _____

   _____

   _____

5. **Consequences:** What responses or reactions occur that appear to diminish/discourage the behavior?

   _____

   _____

   _____

   _____

6. **Function of the Behavior:** To gain/obtain or escape/avoid something are the most common reasons. (Consider reasons related to attention, acceptance or affiliation, power and control, self-stimulation, self-expression, justice or revenge, a means of communication, etc.).

_____

_____

_____

_____

7. **Hypothesis Statement:** For example, "On mornings when Marty misses breakfast (*condition*) and rides the bus for an hour (*condition*), he becomes angry (*internal event*) when his peers tease him (*precipitating event*). He starts to hit (*behavior*) students who are teasing him and says abusive words (*behavior*), and then they stop to tell an adult about his behavior (*consequence*). Escaping the teasing appears to be the purpose of the behavior."

_____

_____

_____

_____

8. **Prediction:** What statements will answer the question, "What might happen if . . . ?" Brainstorm possible solutions to prevent the behavior, teach new skills, or use positive or negative responses. Here are some examples:

If Marty eats breakfast, he will not react to the teasing by hitting other students.
If Marty is taught a way to respond to teasing and control his anger, hitting will not occur.
If Marty receives positive rewards for days he does not hit others, the hitting will stop.

_____

_____

_____

_____

_____

_____

_____

9. Select one or more of the predictions to test the hypotheses. Develop a behavioral intervention plan. Provide ongoing support to the person(s) implementing the plan. Use the data collected during implementation of the plan in the functional behavioral assessment over time.

Source: Information from the Idaho Special Education Manual (2007). Reprinted by permission of the Special Education Department, Idaho State Department of Education.

Positive Strategies
Setting Events Checklist

Student ________________		**Date** ________	
Behavior ________	**Location** ________	**Time** ________	

Instructions: Check the appropriate column for events according to their time frame. For long-standing influences, note only those that contribute to the current incident or behavior.	**Time frame in relation to problem behavior**			
Setting Events (by type)	Same Day	Day Before	Within Week	Long-Standing
Physical				
Meal time changed or meal missed				
Sleep pattern (including duration) atypical or insufficient				
Medications changed or missed				
Medication side effects				
Appeared or complained of illness				
Appeared or complained of pain or discomfort				
Allergy symptoms				
Seizure				
Chronic health condition				
Other (specify):				
Learning and Self-Regulation				
Specific disability (specify):				
Learning difficulties (specify):				
Low frustration tolerance/impulsive				
Short attention span				
Poor organizational or planning skills				
Anger management problems				
Atypical sensory needs				
Other (specify):				
Social-Emotional				
Anxious				
Irritable or agitated				
Depressed, sad, or blue				
Experienced disappointment (specify):				
Refused a desired object or activity				
Disciplined or reprimanded, especially if atypical				
Fought, argued, or had other negative interaction(s)				
Difficulty with peer(s) (specify):				
Chronic/acute stress in home or community (specify):				
Otter (specify):				
Environment and Routines				
Routine was altered; change in activity, order, pacing				
Routine was disrupted				
Change in caregiver or teacher				
Absence of preferred caregiver or teacher				
Was "made" to do something				
Change in school placement (specify):				
Changes in living environment (specify):				
Other (specify):				

Source: Westchester Institute for Human Development/UCE, revised 2004. Adapted from Gardner, Cole, Davidson, and Karan (1986). Reprinted by permission.

FUNCTIONAL BEHAVIORAL ASSESSMENT INTERVIEW FORM

Focus student _____ Date of Birth _____ Sex: M _____ F _____

Interviewer _____ Date _____

Student answering the interview questions _____

Describing the Problem Behaviors

1. Describe each problem behavior that is of concern. Include information about what it looks like, how often it occurs (per day, week, month), how long the behavior lasts, and how damaging or destructive the behaviors are when they occur.

   a. _____

   b. _____

   c. _____

   d. _____

   e. _____

   f. _____

Describing the Student's Social Behaviors

2. Describe positive social behaviors you have observed the student perform. Include information about what it looks like, how often it occurs (per day, week, month), and when you are most likely to see the behavior.

   a. _____

   b. _____

   c. _____

   d. _____

   e. _____

   f. _____

3. Which of the behaviors described above are likely to occur together in some way? Do you see positive behaviors occurring before problem behaviors occur? Do all of the behaviors occur about the same time? If you see behaviors occurring in a sequence from least to more problematic, describe the order in which they occur.

   _____

   _____

Describing Setting Events

4. Describe any setting events that you think are associated with a higher likelihood of problem behaviors.

   _____

   _____

Physiological Setting Events

5. Is the student taking any medications that may have an effect on behavior?

_____

_____

6. Does the student have medical or physical problems that may affect behavior (e.g., gastrointestinal problems, allergies, ear or sinus infections, seizures, headaches)?

_____

_____

_____

7. Does the student have normal sleeping patterns or does he or she have any problems getting enough rest at night?

_____

_____

_____

8. Are there any dietary or eating problems that might have an impact on the problem behavior?

_____

_____

_____

Environmental and Social Setting Events

9. Make a list of the activities where the student is successful and does not engage in problem behavior. Include the times when these activities occur. List problematic activities.

Successful Activities	Problematic Activities
_____	_____
_____	_____
_____	_____
_____	_____
_____	_____

10. Are the activities on the daily schedule predictable for the student? Does the student know what to expect after one activity ends and the next begins? Is it clear to the student who they will be spending time with and for how long?

_____

_____

_____

11. Does the student get a chance to make choices about what he or she will be doing each day? Does the student choose what to wear in the morning, the activities that he or she will be experiencing, and when he or she will be able to engage in fun and reinforcing events?

_____

_____

_____

12. Are there usually a lot of people around at home, school, or work (including staff, classmates, family members, or roommates)? How does the student respond to crowded or noisy settings?

_____

_____

_____

13. What kinds of support does the student receive at home, school, work, and other settings? Do you believe there may be issues related to the number of staff, level of family support, staff or family training needs, or certain types of social interactions that may be related to the student's problem behaviors?

_____

_____

_____

14. Define specific immediate antecedent events that predict when the behaviors are likely and not likely to occur.

Settings Most and Least Likely to Trigger Problem Behavior

Most Likely   **Least Likely**

_____   _____

_____   _____

_____   _____

_____   _____

_____   _____

_____   _____

Times Most and Least Likely to Trigger Problem Behavior

Most Likely   **Least Likely**

_____   _____

_____   _____

_____   _____

_____   _____

_____   _____

_____   _____

People Most and Least Likely to Trigger Problem Behavior

Most Likely

_____

_____

_____

_____

_____

Least Likely

_____

_____

_____

_____

_____

Activities Most and Least Likely to Trigger Problem Behavior

Most Likely

_____

_____

_____

_____

_____

Least Likely

_____

_____

_____

_____

_____

15. Describe something that you could do or say that almost always results in problem behavior. This may include a certain tone of voice (authoritarian, aloof, overly concerned, etc.), particular words or phrases ("no, that's not right, do it again").

_____

_____

16. Briefly describe what the student would do in the following situations.

    The person is asked to complete a difficult task.

_____

_____

    A highly preferred activity naturally ends or is interrupted.

_____

_____

    There is a sudden and unexpected change in the student's daily schedule.

_____

_____

A preferred item or activity is visible but the student needs assistance to obtain it.

_____

_____

The student is left alone (e.g., for 15 minutes).

_____

_____

The student is in the room with other people but no one is interacting with him or her.

_____

_____

Identifying the Consequences or Outcomes of Problem Behaviors

17. Think of each of the behaviors you listed previously, and identify a specific routine (getting up in the morning, going to the store, etc.). Describe what happens right after the behavior. Does the student obtain something? Does the student escape or avoid something?

Problem Behavior	Routine	What Does the Student Obtain?	What Does the Student Escape or Avoid?

Positive Behavior	Routine	What Does the Student Obtain?	What Does the Student Escape or Avoid?

18. Consider how much effort it takes to engage in each of the problem and positive behaviors. Think about (a) How much physical effort it takes to engage in each behavior, (b) How often a behavior occurs before it is reinforced, and (c) How long the student has to wait to get the reinforcer.

Problem Behaviors	Low Effort				High Effort
_____	1	2	3	4	5
_____	1	2	3	4	5
_____	1	2	3	4	5
_____	1	2	3	4	5
_____	1	2	3	4	5
Positive Behaviors					
_____	1	2	3	4	5
_____	1	2	3	4	5
_____	1	2	3	4	5
_____	1	2	3	4	5
_____	1	2	3	4	5

19. What *functional alternative* behaviors does the student already know how to do? Which socially appropriate behaviors or skills listed previously generate the same outcomes or reinforcers produced by the problem behavior?

_____

_____

20. How does the student communicate with other individuals? Describe the most common strategies the student uses and what communication strategies are available. The student may communicate through the use of speech, signs and gestures, communication boards, and electronic devices. Are there any problems with assistive communication systems that are currently used?

_____

_____

_____

21. Describe the student's receptive communication skills and ability to understand others. Can the student follow spoken requests or instructions that are simply stated? Give examples of simple and more complicated (if applicable) requests or instructions that can be followed.

_____

_____

22. Does the student seem to understand and respond to requests or instructions that are signed or gestural? Give several examples of signed or gestural instructions that can be followed.

_____

_____

23. Can the student imitate actions if shown how to do something? Give several examples of the types of actions that can be imitated.

_____

_____

24. How does the student typically communicate *yes or no* when given a choice or being told to do something?

_____

_____

25. Describe things that you should do and that should be avoided when working with and supporting this student. Describe what you do to improve the likelihood that activities or other things will go well when you are with this student.

_____

_____

26. Describe the things you do to avoid interfering with or disrupting an event or activity when you are with this student.

_____

_____

_____

27. Describe the things that the student likes and finds reinforcing.

Favorite foods: _____

_____

_____

Toys, games, or items: _____

_____

_____

In-home activities: _____

_____

_____

Community activities: _____

_____

_____

Other events, people, or activities: _____

_____

_____

28. Describe what you know about the history of problem behaviors identified previously or other problem behaviors that no longer are present. Include information about any interventions that have been tried in the past and how effective those interventions were at the time.

Past Problem Behaviors	Interventions	Effectiveness
a.		
b.		
c.		
d.		
e.		
f.		
g.		
h.		
i.		
j.		

29. Write down hypothesis statements for each major trigger and/or consequence.

Setting Event		Immediate Antecedent (Trigger)		Problem Behavior		Consequence Maintaining Behavior
	—		—		—	
	—		—		—	
	—		—		—	
	—		—		—	
	—		—		—	

Source: Information from O'Neill and colleagues (1997). Reprinted by permission.

FUNCTIONAL ASSESSMENT CHECKLIST FOR TEACHERS AND STAFF (FACTS–PART B)

Step 1 Student/Grade _____ Date _____

Step 2 Interviewer _____ Respondent(s) _____

Routine/Activities/Context: Which routine (only one) from the FACTS–Part A is assessed?

Step 3

Routine/Activities/Context	Problem Behavior(s)

Provide more details about the problem behavior(s):

Step 4

What does the problem behavior(s) look like?

How often does the problem behavior(s) occur?

How long does the problem behavior(s) last when it does occur?

Step 5

What is the intensity/level of danger of the problem behavior(s)?

What are the events that predict when the problem behavior(s) will occur? (Predictors)

Related Issues (Setting Events)		Environmental Features	
___ Illness	Other:_____	___ Reprimand/correction	___ Structured activity
___ Drug use	_____	___ Physical demands	___ Unstructured time
___ Negative social	_____	___ Socially isolated	___ Tasks too boring
___ Conflict at home	_____	___ With peers	___ Activity too long
___ Academic failure	_____	___ Other: _____	___ Tasks too difficult

Step 6

Step 7

Step 8

What consequences appear most likely to maintain the problem behavior(s)?

Things Obtained		Things Avoided or Escaped From	
____ Adult attention	Other: _____	___ Hard tasks	Other: _____
____ Peer attention	_____	___ Reprimands	_____
____ Preferred activity	_____	___ Peer negatives	_____
____ Money/things	_____	___ Physical effort	_____
		___ Adult attention	_____

Summary of Behavior

Identify the summary that will be used to build a plan of behavior support.

Setting Events and Predictors	Problem Behavior(s)	Maintaining Consequence(s)

How confident are you that the Summary of Behavior is accurate? Use scale below to estimate (1) or (2).

(1) **Strategies for Preventing Problem Behavior** Estimate = ( )			(2) **Consequences for Problem Behavior** Estimate = ( )		
Not very confident					Very Confident
1	2	3	4	5	6

What current efforts have been used to control the problem behavior?

Strategies for Preventing Problem Behavior		Strategies for Responding to Problem Behavior	
____ Schedule change	Other: _____	____ Reprimand	Other: _____
____ Seating change	_____	____ Office referral	_____
____ Curriculum change	_____	____ Detention	_____

Source: Information from March and colleagues (2000). Reprinted by permission of the University of Oregon, Educational and Community Supports.

PROBLEM BEHAVIOR QUESTIONNAIRE

Respondent Information

Student _____ DOB _____ Grade _____ Sex: M   F   IEP: Y   N

Teacher _____ School _____

Telephone _____ Date _____

STUDENT BEHAVIOR: Please briefly describe the problem behavior(s).

DIRECTIONS: Keeping in mind a typical episode of the problem behavior, circle the frequency at which each of the following statements are true.

		Never	10%	25%	50%	75%	90%	Always
					PERCENT OF THE TIME			
1.	Does the problem behavior occur and persist when you make a request to perform a task?	0	1	2	3	4	5	6
2.	When the problem behavior occurs, do you redirect the student to get back to task or follow rules?	0	1	2	3	4	5	6
3.	During a conflict with peers, if the student engages in the problem behavior do peers leave the student alone?	0	1	2	3	4	5	6
4.	When the problem behavior occurs, do peers verbally respond or laugh at the student?	0	1	2	3	4	5	6
5.	Is the problem behavior more likely to occur following a conflict outside the classroom (e.g., bus write up)?	0	1	2	3	4	5	6
6.	Does the problem behavior occur to get your attention when you are working with other students?	0	1	2	3	4	5	6
7.	Does the problem behavior occur in the presence of specific peers?	0	1	2	3	4	5	6
8.	Is the problem behavior more likely to continue to occur throughout the day following an earlier episode?	0	1	2	3	4	5	6
9.	Does the problem behavior occur during specific academic activities?	0	1	2	3	4	5	6
10.	Does the problem behavior stop when peers stop interacting with the student?	0	1	2	3	4	5	6
11.	Does the behavior stop when peers are attending to other students?	0	1	2	3	4	5	6
12.	If the student engages in the problem behavior, do you provide one-on-one instruction to get student back on-task?	0	1	2	3	4	5	6
13.	Will the student stop doing the problem behavior if you stop making requests or end an academic activity?	0	1	2	3	4	5	6
14.	If the student engages in the problem behavior, do peers stop interacting with the student?	0	1	2	3	4	5	6
15.	Is the problem behavior more likely to occur following unscheduled events or disruptions in classroom routines?	0	1	2	3	4	5	6

Source: Information from Lewis, Scott, and Sugai (1997). Reprinted by permission.

PROBLEM BEHAVIOR QUESTIONNAIRE PROFILE

Student _____ Grade _____

School _____ Date _____

DIRECTIONS: Circle the score given for each question from the scale below the corresponding question number (in bold) (i.e., item # on Problem Behavior Questionnaire).

PEERS						ADULTS						SETTING EVENTS			
Escape			Attention			Escape			Attention						
3	**10**	**14**	**4**	**7**	**11**	**1**	**9**	**13**	**2**	**6**	**12**	**5**	**8**	**15**	Item #
6	6	6	6	6	6	6	6	6	6	6	6	6	6	6	
5	5	5	5	5	5	5	5	5	5	5	5	5	5	5	
4	4	4	4	4	4	4	4	4	4	4	4	4	4	4	
3	3	3	3	3	3	3	3	3	3	3	3	3	3	3	
2	2	2	2	2	2	2	2	2	2	2	2	2	2	2	
1	1	1	1	1	1	1	1	1	1	1	1	1	1	1	
0	0	0	0	0	0	0	0	0	0	0	0	0	0	0	

ANALYSIS OF POSSIBLE FUNCTION(S) OF STUDENT BEHAVIOR

Source: Information from Lewis, Scott, and Sugai (1994). Reprinted by permission.

ABC Observation Form

Student _____ Grade _____ School _____

Date _____ Observer _____

Behavior of Concern _____

	Date _____ Time _____	Date _____ Time _____	Date _____ Time _____
CONTEXT OR CIRCUMSTANCES			
ANTECEDENT (what happens just prior)			
BEHAVIOR			
CONSEQUENCE (what happens, right after)			
COMMENTS OR OTHER OBSERVATIONS			

Source: Information from New Mexico Public Education Department, *Technical Assistance Manual: Addressing Student Behavior.* Reprinted by permission.

SCATTERPLOT

Student _____ Grade _____ School _____

Date(s) _____ Observer _____

Behavior of Concern _____

_____ Additional Relevant Information _____

_____

Code Used (if any) _____

Setting or Class	Times or Intervals	Day/Date	Day/Date	Day/Date	Day/Date	Day/Date	Total Times Observed

Observation Notes

Provide specific circumstances under which the behavior occurred, particular antecedents that triggered the behavior, times/conditions during which the behavior does not occur, patterns observed, etc.

_____

_____

_____

_____

_____

Source: New Mexico Public Education Department, *Technical Assistance Manual: Addressing Student Behavior.* Reprinted by permission.

DATA TRIANGLE CHART

Student _____ Grade _____ Dates _____

Behavior of Concern _____

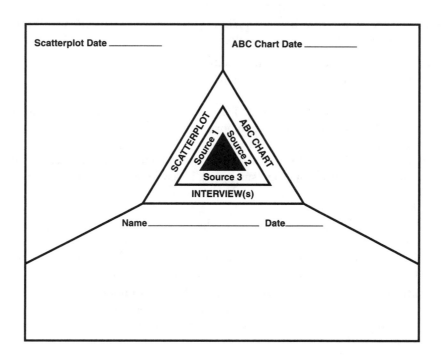

• **Precipitating Events** (conditions/circumstances under which target behavior occurs): _____

_____

• **Functions that Maintain the Behavior** (what student gets, controls, or avoids as a consequence of the action):

_____

• **Deficit(s)** (skill or performance): _____

_____

Interpretation Summary: _____

_____

_____

Source: New Mexico Public Education Department, *Technical Assistance Manual: Addressing Student Behavior.* Reprinted by permission.

FUNCTIONAL BEHAVIORAL ASSESSMENT CHECKLIST

Date _____

Student _____

Team Members _____

The following steps need to be addressed when completing a functional assessment. Use this outline as a guide for completing the functional assessment during team meetings.

1. **Collect functional behavioral assessment information.**
   - ❑ Gather a team of individuals who know the student well, and include people who will be implementing the future positive behavior support plan.
   - ❑ Schedule a person-centered planning meeting if the student's behavior is moderate to severe. This step may not be necessary when problem behaviors are minor.
   - ❑ Summarize the person-centered planning information.
   - ❑ Check to see when the student's last physical exam was conducted. If setting events such as sleeping problems, allergies, and other medical issues are suspected, it may be necessary to schedule an appointment with a physician.
   - ❑ Review the student's records.
   - ❑ Interview the student and the individuals who know the student well.
   - ❑ Define the key problem behaviors.
   - ❑ Collect initial direct observation data including when and where problem behaviors are occurring.
   - ❑ Identify in what settings and situations problem behavior *does not* occur.

2. **Identify the hypothesis or hypotheses maintaining problem behavior.**
   - ❑ Set up a team meeting to begin developing the hypothesis or hypotheses.
   - ❑ Include within the hypothesis statement setting events, antecedents, and consequences associated with problem behavior in specific routines.
   - ❑ Determine the level of confidence that team members have in the hypothesis established for each routine.

3. **Confirm that the hypothesis or hypotheses are correct.**
   - ❑ Create a plan for collecting direct observation data with the team.
   - ❑ Include data measuring behavior for baseline purposes so that the team can evaluate the impact of future interventions on current frequency and intensity.
   - ❑ Collect data confirming the hypothesis statement (including setting events, antecedents, and consequences in specific routines).
   - ❑ Determine whether initial hypotheses are correct based upon the data collected.

4. **Create a written summary of functional assessment findings.**
   - ❑ The functional assessment may be combined with the positive behavior support plan in situations where problem behavior is not complex.
   - ❑ A more detailed functional assessment report may be needed in situations where moderate to severe problem behavior is present.
   - ❑ Include in the summary:
     - ❑ problem behavior being assessed,
     - ❑ functional assessment methods that were used,
     - ❑ hypothesis statement, and
     - ❑ evidence confirming the hypotheses (include direct observation data or summarized results).

A SAMPLE FUNCTIONAL BEHAVIORAL ASSESSMENT SUMMARY REPORT WITH A BEHAVIOR INTERVENTION PLAN

Student <u>Marcus</u>   Date <u>December 3, 2010</u>

Eligibility <u>Emotionally impaired/OHI</u>   School _____

Parent _____   Grade <u>6th</u>

Teacher _____   Support Staff _____

Administrator _____

Marcus is currently in General Education for all of his classes, but he receives Resource Room support for math. He accumulated an excess of 10 suspension days during the first 2 months of the school year for aggressive and insubordinate behaviors. Marcus sees a therapist occasionally through community mental health.

Target Problem Behaviors

Disruptive: walks around class, blurts out answers, throws materials
Off-task: slow starting, refuses to work (especially anything that involves writing)
Defiant: argues with adults, threatening comments/behavior

Marcus exhibits a pattern beginning with off-task behaviors (avoidance) leading to disruptive attention-seeking behaviors, which result in teacher intervention in the form of redirections, corrections, and/or warnings. At times, he will continue the behaviors after multiple warnings, may escalate to defiance, inappropriate, and/or threatening comments made to adults or peers. These escalated behaviors usually result in office referrals and suspensions.

Functional Behavior Assessment Summary

FBA interviews were conducted with teachers, support staff, parent, and Marcus. His file was reviewed. Scatterplot and ABC data have been taken since November 12, 2010. (*Methods*)

Marcus appears to perform disruptive behaviors because he is reinforced by attention from other students and by negative attention from his teachers. His difficulty with organizational skills causes him to avoid tasks that appear too difficult for him. He does not ask for help from his general education teachers on his own. Off-task behaviors are frequently associated with difficulties with attention and concentration. Sometimes Marcus may act aggressively when he feels others are gossiping or talking about him. (*Antecedents and Consequences*)

The FBA revealed that Marcus has a number of strengths. He is very outgoing and is often seen as a leader by his peers because of his social nature. Marcus is also very artistic and athletic. He is known for his ability to work well with small children. (*Strengths*)

Intervention Plan

Objectives

- Increase Marcus's ability to stay on task, complete work, and hand it in for credit.
- Increase Marcus's positive attention-seeking behaviors from peers and adults.
- Increase Marcus's ability to use coping skills with peers and adults.
- Reduce Marcus's incidents of defiant, disruptive, and aggressive behaviors in school.

Preventive Strategies

Organization and Monitoring

- The Resource Room teacher or paraprofessional will meet with Marcus every morning for 10 minutes to monitor and teach him how to organize his folders and materials. They will highlight completed homework so that he does not forget to hand it in. They will also help Marcus work on time management skills.
- At the end of the day, Marcus's homeroom teacher will remind him to put his books and materials in his backpack so that he can complete his homework that evening.
- Incomplete classroom assignments will be sent home daily and completed as homework.
- A weekly progress report will be sent home by Marcus's teachers, signed by his mother, and returned.

Teaching and Reinforcing Replacement Behaviors

Classroom Assignments

- Encourage Marcus to ask questions and to request help when needed.
- Occasionally ask Marcus questions and to repeat directions to assess his level of understanding of the assignment/material.
- Help him get started.
- If he has trouble staying on task,
    Remind him of his reward activities.
    Ask him if he would like to work at a desk in a quiet area.
- Marcus may choose to have 10 minutes to draw, read, do a puzzle, socialize, or just take a break after finishing an assignment.

Positive Attention

- At least once or twice per hour Marcus will receive positive attention from his teachers and other adults for desirable behaviors such as on-task behaviors and cooperation.
- Marcus will help tutor students in a lower elementary class on a weekly basis.

Teaching Coping Skills

- The school social worker will assist Marcus's general education teachers in showing the entire class various social and conflict management skills. Topics will include anger styles, responding to taunting or someone else's anger, and effective communication strategies. Sessions will occur for 20 minutes once a week.
- Marcus's teachers will reinforce the skills taught in these sessions with all students every day.
- Marcus will continue to meet with his outside therapist.

Increase Rule-Following/Reduce Reinforcement for Problem Behaviors

- Marcus will be taught behavioral expectations, rules, and consequences both individually and with his class. Schedule a time to review these expectations with Marcus and his mother together in a positive manner.
- For mild incidents of noncompliance, disruptive, and disrespectful behaviors, give Marcus one warning.
    Keep verbal directives calm, firm, and matter-of-fact.
    State the expected behavior in positive terms after telling him the inappropriate behavior. If possible, speak to him privately.
- If Marcus persists with the problem behavior, implement an exclusion time-out in the time-out area identified outside of the classroom.
    Time-out will last 15 minutes and will be supervised by a classroom paraprofessional. A timer or watch will be used to make sure that the time-out is carried out properly.
- For more severe incidents, the administration may implement in-school suspension. If necessary, the behavior intervention team will meet with Marcus's mother to develop a home intervention.

HOME INTERVENTION

Marcus's mother has indicated that she will carefully monitor her son's homework, review expectations, and implement consequences to reinforce the objectives of his plan.

Program Review Schedule

Review meetings will be held monthly, or as needed.

Source: Information from *Guidelines for Conducting Functional Behavior Assessment and Developing Behavior Intervention Plans* (2003). Reprinted by permission of the Wayne County Regional Educational Service Agency.

APPENDIX C

I.D.E.A.—FUNCTIONAL BEHAVIOR ANALYSIS

School District Name
Special Education Department
1234 Main Street
Anytown, AA 12345

FBA Date: 01/31/2001
Review Date: 01/31/2003

Student Information

Student:	John Doe	Grade:	05
Student ID:	12345	Home School:	Jefferson Elementary
Gender:	Male	Receiving School:	Richman Elementary
Ethnicity:	White		
Date of Birth:	6/1/90		
Chronological Age:	10-8		
Primary Language:	English	Date Determined: 12/12/00	
Determine by:	School Records	❑ Interpreter needed for student	

Parent/Guardian Information

Parent/Guardian:	Jack and Jane Doe	Relationship:	parents
Home Address:	123 Candy Cane Lane	Home Phone:	(123)555–7800
	Apt#12	Work Phone:	(234)555–8901
	Anytown, CA 12345-1234		
Primary Home			
Language:	English	Date Determined:	5/1/00
Determined by:	Parent report	❑ Interpreter needed for parent	

❑ Procedural Safeguards were given to the parent

❑ Information was given to John and his parents regarding John's rights upon reaching the age of majority

Team Members

The following individuals were consulted in the development or this Functional Behavior Assessment
Team member signature indicates attendance at the meeting.

NAME	TITLE	SIGNATURE
Ben Ewing	Psychologist	
Jack Doe	Parent	
Sandra Duran	Teacher	
Jack Terrio	Principal	

Student Name: John Doe   Student ID: 12345   Date: 1/31/01

Reason For Referral

John was referred for Functional Behavior Assessment by Sandra Duran, his teacher, on 02/02/2002. He is currently receiving special education in the area of Emotionally Disturbance with placement, services, and supplementary aids and services identified in the IEP created on 12/31/2000. A Behavior Intervention Plan is not currently in place and the need for one will be evaluated in this functional assessment.

Behaviors of concern at this time include being off-task, talking out, poor social skills, picking on others, fighting, bossiness, and physical aggression. John demonstrates behavior problems that are self-injurious and likely to result in significant property damage. These serious behaviors are pervasive and maladaptive for which the instruction/behavioral approaches specified in his IEP are found to be ineffective.

The negative ramifications of these behaviors are disruption, interference with learning, violation of the rights of others, and a danger to others.

Educationally Relevant Background Information

John presently resides with his parents. A total of three children live in the home.

John's activity level is typical of others his age. His friends tend to be the same age. John's ability to get along with his peers is rated as typical for his age.

John's general health is good. He does not have a history of prior or current medications that might impact his academic performance or behavior. His health history shows no conditions likely to affect academic performance.

John has a prior court history. Specifically, he has been adjudicated a delinquent child. John is currently under the supervision of probation with probation officer Jason Beskind.

John attended a preschool program. He was five years old when he entered kindergarten. John's educational career appears to be relatively stable. He has not changed schools frequently during any one year. John has a satisfactory attendance history.

Summary of Assessment

Review of Previous Assessments

The information available for review included his last comprehensive evaluation conducted 12/31/2001, and one other prior evaluation, 12/12/1998. Additional information available for review included probation officer input, special education teacher input, general education teacher input, report cards, and observation.

The Team does not suspect that an unidentified educational disability is affecting John's behavior.

Direct/Indirect Assessments

John's behavior was assessed using standardized assessment, observation, and teacher report.

John was indirectly assessed using the BASC Teacher on 12/12/2001 by Sandra Ewing and the BASC Parent on 12/13/2001 by Jack Doe.

John was directly assessed by reinforcement survey on 12/14/2001 by Ben Ewing, student interview on 12/14/2001 by Ben Ewing, classroom observation on 12/13/2001 by Chris Guttierrez, and classroom observation on 12/13/2001 by Ben Ewing.

Observation of Reading

John was observed by Ben Ewing, psychologist, in Reading class. John was calm and acted in a manner typical for children his age during the observation.

John showed good effort in the classroom. His concentration span was inconsistent. John was able to restart tasks without cues from others.

John related adequately to others. His maturity level seemed typical for his age. He complied when limits were set. He followed rules with cues. His approach to tasks appeared to be disorganized.

John was observed for 30 minutes using a 30 second interval recording system. Every 30 seconds, John was observed for 3 seconds and appropriate behavior and inappropriate behavior were recorded. During the observation period, John was off-task 52% of the intervals. He attempted to engage other students during 21% of the intervals. He was on-task the remaining intervals or 17% of the intervals observed.

Student Name: John Doe   Student ID: 12345   Date: 1/31/01

Observation of Math

John was observed by Chris Guttierrez in Math class. John's activity level during the observation was unremarkable.

Functional Analysis Assessment

Target Behavior: FIGHTING

Definition: John instigates and promotes fights with other students.

Functional Analysis: The fighting behavior occurs 1 time per week. The intensity of the behavior results in danger to others, creates arguments with peers, and interruption to teaching. Each incident lasts 10 minutes and the problem has existed for 6 months.

The fighting behavior generally occurs in the classroom setting during activities involving partner tasks and individual work. The fighting behavior tends to occur in the morning.

Prior to demonstrating the fighting behavior, John appears to be in an extreme emotional state. The fighting behavior occurs most often when the teacher is ignoring John's attempts to obtain attention. The fighting behavior occurs during or immediately after John is provoked by his peers.

Immediately or as a result of the fighting behavior, the teacher issues a warning to John, implements a time-out procedure, refers John for In-School Suspension, suspends John, and implements contract contingencies. In response to the fighting behavior, his peers communicate their disapproval to him, retaliate against him, and provoke John.

Based on the behavioral analysis, the team hypothesizes that John's fighting behavior appears be a function of a need to control his peers.

The team consensus is that John does not demonstrate an appropriate alternative behavior because he has the skills for the appropriate behavior, but the fighting behavior is being reinforced.

Behavior Reduction Interventions/Strategies:

Replacement Behaviors and Goals

Goal #1—John will demonstrate a positive replacement behavior to fighting by identifying the meaning of a verbal message.

Conditions:	When social situation requires	
Mastery Level:	100%	
Evaluation Frequency:	Continuously	
	Method 1	**Method 2**
Evaluation Method:	Teacher observation	Parent observation
Number of Trials:	4 out of 5 trials	4 out of 5 trials
Person Responsible for:		
• *Implementing Goal:*	Sandra Duran	
• *Coordinating Changes:*	Ben Ewing	
• *Team Communication:*	Ben Ewing	
• *Monitoring Progress:*	Jack Terrio	

Goal #2—John will demonstrate a positive replacement behavior to fighting by improving ability to make friends.

Conditions:	When situation dictates
Mastery Level:	100%
Evaluation Frequency:	Per 5 days

Student Name: John Doe   Student ID: 12345   Date: 1/31/01

Replacement Behaviors and Goals (Continued)

	Method 1	Method 2
Evaluation Method:	Teacher observation	Parent observation
Number of Trials:	1 out of 2 trials	1 out of 2 trials

Person Responsible for:
- *Implementing Goal:*   Sandra Ewing and Jack Doe
- *Coordinating Changes:*   Ben Ewing
- *Team Communication:*   Ben Ewing
- *Monitoring Progress:*   Jack Terrio

Further explanation of the intervention plan goes here.

Manifestation Determination

Target Behavior: FIGHTING

Analysis: The team is considering the appropriateness of the following proposed disciplinary action: 4-day suspension

John has been removed from the school for 3 days due to disciplinary action this school year. The proposed disciplinary action will result in John being removed from school for a total of 7 days this school year. The IEP team determined that this does not constitute a change of placement. The IEP team and other qualified personnel (as appropriate) determined that in relationship to the proposed disciplinary action, the IEP and placement were not appropriate and the team should reconvene to develop an appropriate IEP and placement and clarify the special education services. John's disability impairs his ability to understand the impact and consequences of the fighting behavior.

Progress and Success

Reporting: Progress will be reported to the team members 2 time(s) per quarter. The team will meet to discuss progress and the appropriateness of this behavior plan no later than 01/31/2003

Target Behavior: FIGHTING

Success Criteria: The behavior Intervention plan will be considered successful when the frequency of the fighting behavior decreases by 100 percent from the present level of 1 times per week or when the behavior no longer results in danger to others, creates arguments with peers, or interruption to teaching. Progress towards the specific goals in the behavior intervention plan will be reported separately.

Emergency Procedures

The purpose of this Behavior Intervention Plan is to reduce the inappropriate target behavior and teach more adaptive behaviors. However, if John demonstrates a behavior (whether previously identified or not) that is assaultive and/or self-injurious and results in significant property damage, is potentially criminal, or is otherwise considered a serious behavior problem, then the regular school or district procedures for serious behavior will be implemented, his parent(s) will be contacted immediately by phone, and the school or district security will be contacted and operate within their policies and procedures. If the emergency procedures are implemented, John will not be allowed to reenter the school without a meeting with the parent(s) or guardian at the school or district office.

Source: The Architext Behavior Planner. Copyright © 2002 NCS Pearson. Published and distributed exclusively by NCS Pearson, Minneapolis, MN 55440. Reprinted by permission of NCS Pearson.

Positive Behavioral Intervention Plan
Planning Form

IEP teams can use this form to guide them through the process of developing the Positive Behavioral Intervention Plan.

Student _____ Age _____ Sex _____

Teacher(s) _____ Grade _____

Case Manager _____ Date _____

Reason for intervention plan:

Participants (specify names):

( ) student _____   ( ) special education administrator _____
( ) family member _____   ( ) general education administrator _____
( ) special educator _____   ( ) school psychologist _____
( ) general educator _____   ( ) other agency personnel _____
( ) peer(s) _____
( ) others (specify) _____
_____

Fact Finding

1. **General learning environment:** Describe the student's classroom structure (i.e., schedule, grouping, content area). Include any special programs or services.

2. **Problem behavior:** Define the problem behavior(s) in observable, measurable, and countable terms (i.e., topography, event, duration, seriousness, and/or intensity). Include examples of the behavior.

3. **Setting events:** Describe important things that are happening in the student's life that may be affecting the behavior(s) of concern.

4. **Review existing data:** Summarize previously collected information (records review, interviews, observations, and test results) relevant to the behavior(s). Attach additional sheets if necessary.

Possible Explanations

5. **Identify likely antecedents:** Precipitating events to the behavior(s).

6. **Identify likely consequences:** Occurrences immediately following the behavior(s).

7. **Identify and describe any academic or environmental context(s) in which the problem behavior(s) does *not* occur.**

Validation

8. **Functional assessment:** Do you already have enough information on the possible function(s) of the behavior to plan an effective intervention?
   a. If yes, go to Step 9; if no, then what additional data collection is necessary?
   - ( )   Review of IEP goals and objectives
   - ( )   Review of medical records
   - ( )   Review of previous intervention plans
   - ( )   Review of incident reports
   - ( )   ABC (across time and situations)
   - ( )   Motivational analysis
   - ( )   Ecological analysis
   - ( )   Curricular analysis
   - ( )   Scatterplot

( ) Parent questionnaire/interview
( ) Student questionnaire/interview
( ) Teacher questionnaire/interview (specify who) _____
( ) Other (explain) _____

b. Summarize data. Attach additional sheets if necessary.

Planning

9. **Formulate hypothesis statement:** Using the table below, determine why the student engages in problem behavior(s), whether the behavior(s) serves a single function or multiple functions, and what to do about the behavior(s).

	Internal	External
Obtain Something		
Avoid Something		

10. **Current level of performance:** Describe problem behavior(s) in a way the team will recognize; include onset and conclusion of behavior(s).

11. **Describe replacement behavior(s) that are likely to serve the same function as the behavior(s) identified in Step 9.**

12. **Measurement procedures for problem behavior(s) and replacement behavior(s):**

a. Describe how (e.g., permanent products, event recording, scatterplot, when and where student behavior(s) will be measured.

b. Summarize data by specifying which problem behavior(s) and replacement behavior(s) will be targets for the intervention

13. **Behavioral intervention plan:**

a. Specify goals and objectives (conditions, criteria for acceptable performance) for teaching the replacement behavior(s).

b. Specify instructional strategies that will be used to teach the replacement behavior(s).

c. Specify strategies that will be used to decrease problem behavior(s) and increase replacement behavior(s).

d. Identify any changes in the physical environment needed to prevent problem behavior(s) and to promote desired (replacement) behavior(s), if necessary.

e. Specify extent to which intervention plan will be implemented in various settings; specify settings and persons responsible for implementation of the plan.

14. **Evaluation plan and schedule:** Describe the plan and timetable to evaluate effectiveness of the intervention plan.

a. Describe how, when, where, and how often the problem behavior(s) will be measured.

b. Specify persons and settings involved.

c. Specify a plan for crisis/emergency intervention, if necessary.

d. Determine a schedule to review/modify the intervention plan, as needed. Include dates and criteria for changing/teaching the plan.

15. **Describe the plan and timetable to monitor the degree to which the plan is being implemented.**

Source: Reprinted by permission from CECP/AIR. Obtained online at cecp.air/fba/problembehavior3/appendix.htm.

NEW HAMPSHIRE CENTER FOR EFFECTIVE BEHAVIORAL INTERVENTIONS AND SUPPORTS

BEHAVIOR SUPPORT PLAN FEEDBACK FORM

School _____ Team _____ Date _____

Overview

Section 1: Brief summary and background information	

Comments	✓
1. The background section was complete with all important information included.	
2. The background section was only partially complete and some important information is missing.	
3. The background section was missing all or most of the important information.	
4. Written expression was consistent with program standards.	
5. There were problems with written expression.	

Section 2: Summary of problem behavior and context	
Hypothesis statement with function included	
Behavior pathway	

Comments	✓
6. The problem behavior or class of behaviors were defined in observable and measurable terms; data about frequency, duration, and intensity of behavior is included; the settings where the behavior is most likely and least likely to occur are delineated; early indicators of the problem behavior were included; a hypothesis statement about the likely function(s) of the behavior was included and was reasonable, based on the evidence.	
7. The problem behavior or class of behaviors were not defined in observable and measurable terms.	
8. Data about frequency, duration, and intensity of behavior was missing or incomplete.	
9. The setting(s) where the behavior was most likely to occur is not delineated.	
10. The setting(s) where the behavior was least likely to occur is not delineated.	
11. Early indicators of the problem behavior were missing or incorrect.	
12. A hypothesis statement about the likely function(s) of the behavior was missing or incorrect based on the evidence.	

	✓
13. The behavior pathway was complete, accurate, and consistent with the narrative report.	
14. The behavior pathway was mostly complete and accurate, but there were errors or inconsistencies with the narrative report.	
15. The behavior pathway had major errors or was missing.	
16. Written expression was consistent with program standards.	
17. There was a problem with written expression.	

Section 3: The replacement/ prosocial behavior	

Comments	✓
1. The expected replacement behavior or prosocial alternatives to the misbehavior were described clearly in observable and measurable terms and related to the function of the behavior.	
2. The expected replacement behavior or prosocial alternatives to the misbehavior were described clearly in observable and measurable terms, but not related to the function of the behavior.	
3. The expected replacement behavior or prosocial alternatives to the misbehavior were not described clearly in observable and measurable terms or they are missing.	
4. Written expression was consistent with program standards.	
5. There were problems with written expression.	

Section 4: Intervening prior to the problem behavior	
Context manipulation or environmental rearrangements	
Teaching or behavioral rehearsal	
Reinforcement strategies	
Connection to the function of the behavior	

Comments:	✓
6. The context manipulation or environmental rearrangements strategies were clearly delineated and likely to prevent the problem behavior from occurring in the first place.	
7. The context manipulation or environmental rearrangements strategies were missing, unclear, or unlikely to prevent the problem behavior from occurring in the first place.	

8. The strategies for teaching the prosocial alternative or related skills were correctly identified, detailed, and related to the function of the behavior.	
9. The strategies for teaching the prosocial alternative or related skills were missing, not detailed enough, or incorrectly identified.	
10. The strategies for teaching the prosocial alternative or related skills were not connected to the function of the behavior.	
11. The reinforcement plan was specific, connected to the prosocial behavior, and likely to be influential.	
12. The reinforcement plan was specific and connected to the prosocial behavior but unlikely to be influential.	
13. The reinforcement plan was not specific enough to determine whether it was likely to be influential.	
14. The reinforcement plan was not connected to the prosocial behavior.	
15. The behavior plan was directly related to the function of behavior.	
16. The behavior plan was not directly related to the function of behavior.	
17. Written expression was consistent with program standards.	
18. There were problems with written expression.	

Section 5: Intervening after the problem behavior	

Comments	✓
19. There were clear and detailed consequences, interventions, or relational strategies delineated to address the problem behavior when it occurs. The strategies were likely to decrease the problem behavior from recurring in the context of the entire plan.	
20. Clear and detailed consequences, interventions, or relational strategies delineated to address the problem behavior when it occurs were missing or incomplete.	
21. There were clear and detailed consequences, interventions, or relational strategies delineated to address the problem behavior when it occurs. However, the strategies were unlikely to decrease the problem behavior from recurring in the context of the entire plan.	
22. Written expression was consistent with program standards.	
23. There were problems with written expression.	

Section 6: Monitoring plan, notification, and follow-up	

Comments	✓
24. The plan to monitor and inform other members of the team and family was complete. It included the case manager, a detailed description of how it would be shared with others, and a method for evaluating success or failure.	
25. The plan to monitor and inform other members of the team and family was only partially complete. It did not include the case manager.	
26. The plan to monitor and inform other members of the team and family was only partially complete. It did not include a detailed description of how it would be shared with others.	
27. The plan to monitor and inform other members of the team and family was only partially complete. It did not include a method for evaluating success or failure.	
28. The plan to monitor and inform other members of the team and family was missing.	
29. Written expression was consistent with program standards	
30. There were problems with written expression.	

Section 7: Goals and objectives	
The annual goal(s)	
The behavioral objectives	

Comments	✓
31. The expected replacement behavior or prosocial alternatives have been translated into annual goals for the IEP or IFSP. They include a grade, age or skill level standard, and the date of completion.	
32. The expected replacement behavior or prosocial alternatives have not been translated accurately into annual goals for the IEP or IFSP that are observable and measurable. They are missing a grade, age or skill level standard and/or the date of completion.	
33. There was a sequence of 3–5 behavioral objectives matched to each annual goal. They all include conditions under which learning occurs, observable and measurable behavior, and criteria for success.	
34. There was not a sequence of 3–5 behavioral objectives matched to each annual goal.	
35. The objectives have problems with the conditions under which learning occurs.	
36. The objectives have problems with observable and measurable behavior.	
37. The objectives have problems with criteria for success.	
38. Written expression was consistent with program standards.	
39. There were problems with written expression.	

Overall Comments:

Source: Reprinted by permission of Howard S. Muscott, New Hampshire Center for Positive Behavioral Interventions and Supports.

SAMPLE CRISIS/EMERGENCY PLAN

Student _____   Date _____

School _____   Grade _____

Reason for crisis/emergency plan: _____

_____

_____

Persons responsible for developing the plan (indicate position): _____

_____

_____

Parental Approval

Indicate level of parent/guardian participation and approval of the plan: _____

_____

Parent/guardian signature: _____

_____

1. Give a full description of the behavior that poses a risk of physical injury to the student or to others, damage to physical property and/or serious disturbance of the teaching/learning process and for which a crisis/emergency plan is required, including both the frequency of occurrence and magnitude of behavior.

2. Give a full description of previous interventions (including those in the student's IEP or existing behavioral intervention plan) that have been applied and have not been successful, including length of implementation.

3. Give a full description of the strategies or procedures included in the plan, the times, places, and situations under which the plan may be introduced, person(s) responsible for its implementation, and any potential risks associated with the plan.

4. Give a full description of how, when, and where measurement procedures that will be used to evaluate the effectiveness of the plan, the criteria against which the plan will be judged, and the timetable for its evaluation.

5. Give the timetable for review of the plan.

6. Give a full description of the behavior that will be strengthened and/or taught to the student to replace the behavior of concern, including steps to provide frequency opportunities for the student to engage in and be reinforced for the desired behavior.

7. Give a full description of the plan for withdrawing the crisis/emergency plan and the less restrictive and intrusive intervention that will replace it, including the timetable for withdrawal of the crisis/emergency plan.

8. Give a full description of the steps that will be taken to eliminate future occurrences of the behavior, including changes in the social/physical environment, teaching of replacement behavior, or both.

9. Indicate the person(s) responsible for notifying the parent/guardian when the crisis/emergency plan has been introduced and the way in which that notification will be documented.

10. Indicate the person(s) responsible for the written report of the outcome of the crisis/emergency plan.

Source: Retrieved from cecp.air.org/fba/problembehavior3/appendixd1.htm. Reprinted by permission from CECP/AIR.

RECONSIDERING THE BEHAVIORAL INTERVENTION PLAN

Student _____ Date _____

Age _____ Grade _____

Teacher _____ School _____

At this point, evaluate the implementation and effectiveness of the plan.

1. Has everyone been able to follow the plan that was written . . .

   For preventing:

   For teaching:

   For responding:

   For crisis management:

2. Do you feel that the theory about the purpose of the behavior was correct?

   _____

   _____

   _____

3. What positive changes have you seen? _____

   _____

   _____

   _____

   _____

4. What areas of the plan need to be continued? _____

   _____

   _____

   _____

5. What areas of the plan need to be changed? _____

   _____

   _____

   _____

Source: Idaho Special Education Manual (2007). Reprinted by permission of the Special Education Department, Idaho State Department of Education. Retrieved from www.sed.idaho.gov/specialeducation/docs/manual/manual%20appendices/chapter12.pdf.

MANIFESTION OF HANDICAPPNG CONDITION DECISION

Student _____ Date of Meeting _____

School Year _____ Purpose for Meeting (please check) _____ Behavior _____ Attendance

Number of Absences _____ (Of this total, please specify: Excused _____ Unexcused _____ Due to suspension _____)

If behavior offense, explain incident(s):

_____

_____

_____

1. Was the offense or record of excessive absences a manifestation of the student's handicapping condition? (*Indicate Yes/No below.*)

    _____ Does the student understand the difference between right and wrong?

    _____ Does the student understand the school rules?

    _____ Does the student understand the consequences of his/her behavior? (*Consider impulsivity vs. premeditation.*)

    _____ Is the student able to control his/her behavior in such a way that we can expect him/her to be able to follow the school rules with little or no difficulty on a day to day basis?

    _____ Has any significant event(s) occurred in the student's life recently, such as divorce or death of a family member? If so, explain: _____

2. Is the student's current educational placement appropriate? (*Indicate Yes/No below.*)

    _____ Does the student's IEP meet his/her needs?

    _____ Has the student's IEP been fully implemented to address his/her needs?

    _____ Is the most recent evaluation current, complete, and relevant to the specific behavior and/or attendance problem?

> **DECISION: This student's [ ] attendance record   [ ] behavior**
> **[ ] IS   [ ] IS NOT a manifestation of his/her handicapping condition.**

Recommendations: (*Check all that apply.*)

_____ Develop behavior plan to deal with absenteeism and/or offense.

_____ Implement interventions. (*List options.*) _____

_____ Other. (*Specify recommendations.*) _____

_____ Do further evaluation. (*List options.*) _____

_____ If parent is not present at IEP meeting, make contact by telephone or in writing.

_____ Refer to at-risk coordinator for excessive absences. (*Attach a copy of this form.*)

IEP Team Members Present:

Name	Position	Name	Position

Name	Position	Name	Position

Source: Reprinted by permission of the Sevier County Board of Education, Sevier, TN.

MANIFESTATION DETERMINATION REVIEW

(Applicable to all students receiving special education)

Student _____   Date of Birth _____

I.D. _____   School _____

Date of Meeting _____

Required Committee Membership: Parent, administrator, special education teacher, appraisal person, regular teacher, and student, if appropriate.

1. To determine whether the behavior was/was not a manifestation of the disability(ies), the Committee needs to consider all relevant information in terms of the behavior subject to disciplinary action. Please check data sources that are available.

   Yes _____   No _____   School Resource Officer (SRO) Incident Report

   Yes _____   No _____   Office referrals

   Yes _____   No _____   Evaluation and diagnostic results

   Yes _____   No _____   Diagnostic results/relevant information provided by the parent(s)

   Yes _____   No _____   Observations of the student

   Yes _____   No _____   Student's IEP and placement

   Yes _____   No _____   Documentation of behavior intervention plan strategies/level and/or point system

   Yes _____   No _____   Progress reports

2. In relation to the behavior subject to disciplinary action, the Committee considered the following:

   Program is appropriate as evidenced by:

   Yes _____   No _____   IEP is appropriate.

   Yes _____   No _____   Placement is appropriate.

3. Continuum of services has been considered and documented for this student. (Continuum of services: regular education with modifications, supplementary aids and services, itinerant support, resource, self-contained, self-contained separate campus–Parkway, Alternate Learning Center [ALC]).

   Yes _____   No _____   Supplementary aids and services provided are consistent with the IEP and placement.

   Yes _____   No _____   Special education services are consistent with the IEP and placement.

   Yes _____   No _____   Behavior intervention strategies are consistent with the IEP and placement.

   Yes _____   No _____   The student's disability did not impair the ability of the student to understand the impact and consequences of the behavior subject to disciplinary action.

   Yes _____   No _____   The student's disability did not impair the ability of the student to control the behavior

IEP Supplement for Manifestation Determination Review Reward

Guideline to determination:

Manifestation: If the answer to any of the statements in Section B is *No*, the disability is linked to the behavior. Make appropriate changes to the student's program. Consider where the student is on the continuum of services and look at available options.

No Manifestation: If the answer to all of the statements in Section B is *Yes*, the disability is not linked to the behavior. Student may be disciplined as regular education student.

Manifestation Determination Decision

The behavior subject to disciplinary action is a manifestation of the student's disabilities. (*List all of the student's disabilities.*)

Yes _____   No _____   Primary disability _____

Yes _____   No _____   Secondary disability _____

Yes _____   No _____   Tertiary disability _____

Source: Reprinted by permission of the Sevier County Board of Education, Sevier, TN. Retrieved from www.sic.sevier.org/forms.htm.

MANIFESTATION DETERMINATION

Name _____ School _____

Student # _____ Date of Birth _____ Grade _____

Date of MD
Meeting _____ 　Date of
Incident _____ 　Date of Decision
to Suspend $\geq$ 10 Days _____

Behavior prompting suspension _____

I. Appropriateness of Program

A. **Current Classification** _____

B. **Prereferral** (Was behavior previously noted as area of concern?) _____ Yes _____ No _____ N/A

　If yes, date of prereferral _____ Concerns noted _____

　Source(s) of information _____

C. **Referral** (Was behavior leading to suspension noted as a concern of the referral?) _____ Yes _____ No

　If yes, date of referral _____ Concerns noted _____

　Source(s) of information _____

D. **Evaluation** Date of last ESE evaluation _____ _____ N/A

　1. Does existing evaluation address current areas of educational concern? _____ Yes _____ No

　2. Additional evaluation needed in the following area(s):

　　_____ Complete evaluation 　_____ Intellectual development 　_____ Academic achievement

　　_____ Communication 　_____ FBA/BIP 　_____ Adaptive/social/behavioral

　　_____ Other _____

E. **Individual Educational Plan (IEP)** Date of last IEP _____ Is IEP in compliance? _____ Yes _____ No _____ N/A

　1. Have services consistent with the IEP been provided? _____ Yes _____ No _____ N/A

　　If no, explain: _____

　　_____

　2. Are behavioral goals included on the IEP? _____ Yes _____ No _____ N/A

　　If yes, do they address the behavior subject to disciplinary action? _____ Yes _____ No _____ N/A

　　Sources of information _____

F. **Ancedotal Records** Is there a record of behavior subject to disciplinary action? _____ Yes _____ No _____ N/A

　Sources of information _____

G. **School Performance** Statement regarding student's present school performance (grades, attendance) _____

　_____

　Source(s) of information _____

H. **Placement** Is an Informed Consent for Placement in evidence? _____ Yes _____ No _____ N/A

Source(s) of information _____

I. **Summary Statement** After a review of the above information, this team his concluded the following:

The student **was** _____ **was not** _____ properly evaluated.

The student's parent(s) **were** _____ **were not** _____ included in the IEP process.

The IEP and placement **are** _____ **are not** _____ reasonably calculated to confer educational benefit.

II. Ability to Understand Impact and Consequences

A. Has the student received information regarding the school's code of conduct? _____ Yes _____ No

Source(s) of information _____

B. Has the student previously demonstrated the ability to follow school rules? _____ Yes _____ No

Source(s) of information _____

C. Has the student expressed that this or similar conduct is wrong? _____ Yes _____ No

Source(s) of information _____

D. Has the student expressed an understanding of the consequences of this or similar behavior? _____ Yes _____ No

Source(s) of information _____

E. **Statement of ability to understand impact of behavior** After review of the above relevant information, it is the finding of the IEP Team _____

III. Ability to Control Behavior

A. What is the nature and severity of the disability (eligibility, criteria, behavioral characteristics, DSM-IV)?

_____

B. Is this an isolated instance of this behavior or is it recurrent? _____

_____

C. Was behavior affected by psychological/social event(s) unrelated to disability (e.g., illness, death, family conflict, substance abuse)? _____

_____

D. Was behavior premeditated or impulsive? _____

_____

E. Is there pertinent medical information (diagnosis, medications)? _____

_____

F. In the opinion of the team, would similarly situated students without disabilities in a like circumstance react in a different manner? _____

_____

G. **Statement of ability to control behavior** After careful review of the above relevant information, it is the finding of the IEP Team that at the time of the offense, as a result of the disability, the student was _____ **unable** _____ **able** to conform to the code of conduct of the school.

IV. Manifestation Determination

In order to make a determination that the behavior was not a manifestation, the team must find that (1) the program was appropriate, (2) the student had the capacity to understand the impact of the conduct, and (3) the student was able to conform to the code of conduct.

> **Based upon the information considered, it is the consensus of the IEP Team that the conduct was _____ was not _____ a manifestation of the student's disability.**

Record of Participation

°LEA Rep. _____   District Rep. _____

°°Parent _____   Guidance Counselor _____

°ESE Teacher _____   Behavior Specialist _____

°Regular Ed. Teacher _____   Administrator _____

Student _____   Other _____

°Required to attend.   °°Notified/given opportunity to participate.

Source: Retrieved from www.sic.sevier.org/manifestationdetermination.doc. Reprinted by permission of the Sevier County Board of Education, Sevier, TN.

INDIVIDUALIZED EDUCATION PROGRAM (IEP)

Name __Danny__   Date of Birth __age 10__   Grade Level __4__   ☐ Male   ☐ Female

Student Identification Number _____

Child/Student Address _____

Parent/Guardian _____

Parent Address _____   Home Phone _____   Work Phone _____

Effective IEP Dates from _____ to _____   Meeting Date _____   ☐ Initial IEP   ☐ Periodic Review

District of Residence _____   District of Service _____

Step 1   Discuss future planning.
(Family and student preferences and interests)

Danny's Mom and Dad support his interest in farm operation and machinery. He spends time assisting on his uncle's farm and he is able to handle many tasks on his own. Danny and his family are frustrated about his difficulty in learning to read though his Dad reported that he too had similar problems in school. They would like him to be independent enough in reading to do his daily functional tasks and also to fit in with his peers. Mom and Dad recognize that Danny's attention has improved since he started medication last year but they would like to work toward getting him off the medication.

Step 2   Discuss present levels of performance.
(What do we know about this child, and how does that relate in the context of content standards, or for preschool children, in the context of appropriate activities and how the disability affects the student's involvement in the general curriculum.)

Danny has a strong interest in building replicas of buildings and machinery. He can reproduce parts of farm machinery and can explain how they work. Danny has a learning disability in the areas of basic reading skills and written expression and he has ADHD. His ability to participate and make progress in the general curriculum is limited because he is not able to read grade-level material, demonstrate knowledge in writing at grade level expectations or independently manage his assignments. Math is an academic strength for him, but he is missing some grade level skills due to missed instruction practice related to attention and organizational factors (ADHD). Danny can follow the general education content and sequence in mathematics with accommodations for reading (directions, written problems, tests read aloud) and assistance with managing assignments. (Final 2003 grading period, he turned in 60% of his assignments, many incomplete).

Danny's performance in Language Arts is significantly below grade level. He does not demonstrate mastery of the K–3 benchmarks related to word recognition, but his spoken vocabulary and listening comprehension skills are age-appropriate. Danny uses initial and final consonants sounds to help decode words, but he does not use vowel sounds or rules. On 5/12/03, he identified by sight 20/200 Dolch words. Danny uses picture and context clues independently but due to limited word recognition, he is not fluent in reading or comprehending primer level materials.

Danny's writing attempts are 1–2 words. He uses a word box and can locate some words by initial and final consonant. He can dictate a short story or set of directions and can edit his dictated sentences for capitalization of initial letter and end punctuation. With accommodations for reading and writing skills and support for organization and attention, Danny can access science and social studies content and can demonstrate what he has learned.

410

INDIVIDUALIZED EDUCATION PROGRAM (IEP)

Annual Goals and Short-Term Objectives

Step 3: Identify needs that require specially designed instruction

Danny needs to build organizational skills to stay on-task and complete assignments.

Step 4: Identify measurable annual goals

Goal # 1   Content area addressed: Study Skills

Given a motivational contract daily check-in, and an assignment management system, Danny will complete at least 3/4 assignments in general education classes.

Benchmarks or short-term objectives

1a.   Given a ticket system with an on-task check sheet completed daily by Danny with general education teacher's signature, Danny will achieve 3/4 on-task ratings in a target week by the end of the 2nd grading period

1b.   Given an assignment folder and daily check-in and support for directions/written material to be read aloud to him, Danny will complete and turn in 75% of general education assignments.

Statement of Student Progress

(Include how the child's progress towards annual goals will be measured and how the parents will be informed of the extent to which the child's progress is sufficient to enable him/her to achieve the goals by the end of the year)

Danny's special education and general education teachers will jointly document progress toward short-term objectives and report in writing to parents each 9 week grading period.

Step 5: Identify services

Service: Consultation and Specially Designed Instruction   **Initiation date:** 9/02/03   **Expected duration:** 1 school year **Frequency:** (how often) 60 min. daily *(Identify all services needed for the child to attain the annual goal and progress in the general curriculum. Services may include specially designed instruction, related services, supplementary aids, or, on behalf of the child, a statement of program modifications, testing accommodations or supports for school personnel)*

Danny will spend 30 minutes daily in the Resource Room for support with general education classes including daily check of assignment folder and assignment/test assistance. The special education teacher will spend 30 minutes daily providing assistance in/or making accommodations for general education classes. The special education teacher will prepare and monitor the contract. (Read aloud, change format for responses)

Step 6: Determine least restrictive environment

Determine where services will be provided

(Include an explanation of the extent, if any, to which the child will not participate with nondisabled peers.)

Special education resource room – 0% with nondisabled peers.
General education classes –100% with nondisabled peers. Danny will participate in general education with nondisabled peers 5 1/2 of 7 hours daily.

411

INDIVIDUALIZED EDUCATION PROGRAM (IEP)

Annual Goals and Short-Term Objectives

Step 3: Identify needs that require specially designed instruction

Danny needs to build skills in using graphic systems and visual displays, computer word processing, dictation and his own writing to help him record and recall information and to demonstrate knowledge.

Step 4: Identify measurable annual goals

Goal # 2   Content area addressed: Writing (Standards: Processes, Conventions and Communication, Oral and Visual)
Danny will use writing, dictation and graphic systems and visual displays (prepared in advance and pre-taught) to record information presented in general-education classes and to demonstrate knowledge.

Benchmarks or short-term objectives

2a.   Given a set of graphic/visual displays prepared for him with pre-taught reading or writing components, Danny will fill in key words from a word bank to take notes or study with 75% accuracy.
2b.   Given a project in which Danny needs to convey information, he will utilize writing, computer word processing, dictation and graphic and visual displays and will achieve on a project rubric at 75% or above.

Statement of Student Progress
(Include how the child's progress towards annual goals will be measured and how the parents will be informed of the extent to which the child's progress is sufficient to enable him/her to achieve the goals by the end of the year)
Danny's special education and general education science/social studies teachers will jointly document progress on short-term objectives and provide a written summary to parents each 9 week grading period.

Step 5: Identify services

Service: Consultation and Specially Designed Instruction   **Initiation date:** 9/02/03   **Expected duration:** 1 school year   **Frequency:** (how often) 60 min. daily *(Identify all services needed for the child to attain the annual goal and progress in the general curriculum. Services may include specially designed instruction, related services, supplementary aids, or, on behalf of the child, a statement of program modifications, testing accommodations, or supports for school personnel)*
Danny will spend 30 minutes daily in the special education resource room for support with general education classes. Danny will have directions, assignments and tests read aloud in a small group with additional time for completion. For writing, he will use a word box, Franklin device and computer word processing. Danny's special education teacher will spend 30 minutes daily providing assistance in/or accommodations for general education classes.

Step 6: Determine least restrictive environment

Determine where services will be provided
(Include an explanation of the extent, if any, to which the child will not participate with nondisabled children in the regular classroom)

412

Annual Goals and Short-Term Objectives

Step 3: Identify needs that require specially designed instruction

Danny needs to demonstrate 4th grade-level comprehension skills when listening to grade-level materials read aloud, using non-text materials or reading at his own level.

Step 4: Identify measurable annual goals

Goal # 3   Content area addressed: Reading (standards: concepts of Print, Comprehension…and Informational… Text)

Danny will demonstrate targeted 4th grade comprehension skills when listening to general education class materials read aloud, when using non-text materials, or reading at his own level.

Benchmarks or short-term objectives

3a.   Given study assistance and materials, Danny will make predictions and inferences and draw conclusions to demonstrate comprehension of non-fiction materials he reads at his level with 70% accuracy on comprehension questions.

3b.   Given different sources of non-text materials such as maps, charts, pictures and diagrams, Danny will locate and explain important details of non-fiction topics assessed on a rubric with 75% performance level on 3 projects.

3c.   Given grade level concepts presented orally in general education classes, Danny will respond with an average of 70% accuracy to comprehension checks following the oral presentations.

Statement of Student Progress

(Include how the child's progress towards annual goals will be measured and how the parents will be informed of the extent to which the child's progress is sufficient to enable him/her to achieve the goals by the end of the year)

Danny's special education and general education science/social studies teachers will jointly document progress toward short-term objectives and report in writing to parents each 9 week grading period.

Step 5: Identify services

Service: Consultation and Specially Designed Instruction   **Initiation date:** 9/02/03   **Expected duration:** 1 school year   **Frequency:** (how often) 120 min. daily

(Identify all services needed for the child to attain the annual goal and progress in the general curriculum. Services may include specially designed instruction, related services, supplementary aids, or, on behalf of the child, a statement of program modifications, testing accommodations, or supports for school personnel)

This goal will be addressed both in specially designed small group instruction and in consultation providing support for general education classes. The special education teacher will read aloud text, assignments or tests or provide audio tapes and will prepare specially designed study and assignment materials. She will also provide assistance with Danny's use of computer word processing or act as a scribe as appropriate.

Step 6: Determine least restrictive environment

Determine where services will be provided

(Include an explanation of the extent, if any, to which the child will not participate with nondisabled children in the regular classroom)

INDIVIDUALIZED EDUCATION PROGRAM (IEP)

Annual Goals and Short-Term Objectives

Step 3: Identify needs that require specially designed instruction

Danny needs to recognize and decode printed words to read fluently and accurately.

Step 4: Identify measurable annual goals

Goal # 4   Content area addressed: Reading (Standards: Phonemic Awareness, Word Recognition and Fluency, and Acquisition of vocabulary (K-3 Band))

Given multi-sensory instruction, Danny will recognize and decode printed words to read first grade level vocabulary-controlled books accurately.

Benchmarks or short-term objectives

4a.   Given reading materials controlled for vocabulary and rules taught, Danny will decode by using letter-sound matches and common word families and patterns with 75% accuracy.

4b.   Given multi-sensory practice and memory aids, Danny will recognize by sight 75/200 Dolch words.

Statement of Student Progress

(Include how the child's progress towards annual goals will be measured and how the parents will be informed of the extent to which the child's progress is sufficient to enable him/her to achieve the goals by the end of the year)

Danny's special education teacher will document progress on short-term objectives and report in writing to parents each 9 week grading period.

Step 5: Identify services

Service: Specially Designed Instruction.   **Initiation date:** 9/02/03   **Expected duration:** 1 school year   **Frequency:** (how often) 60 min. daily

(Identify all services needed for the child to attain the annual goal and progress in the general curriculum. Services may include specially designed instruction, related services, supplementary aids, or, on behalf of the child, a statement of program modifications, testing accommodations, or supports for school personnel)

Danny will have 60 min. daily of individual and small group language arts instruction. Specially designed materials and strategies will be used.

Step 6: Determine least restrictive environment

Determine where services will be provided

(Include an explanation of the extent, if any, to which the child will not participate with nondisabled children in the regular classroom)

414

INDIVIDUALIZED EDUCATION PROGRAM (IEP)

Special Factors

Based on discussions of the information provided regarding relevant special factors and other considerations as noted below, the following is applicable and incorporated into the IEP.

	Incorporated into IEP (Check box)
Behavior: In the case of a student whose behavior impedes his or her learning or that of others.	☐
Limited English proficiency (LEP)	☐
Children/students with visual impairments (See IEP page _____)	☐
Communication	☐
Deaf or hard of hearing	☐
Assistive technology services and devices	☐

Other Considerations

Physical education—Danny will participate fully in general education for PE	☐
Extended school year services	☐
Beginning at age 14...transition service needs which focus on the student's courses of study [See IEP page _____]	☐
Transition services statement, no later than age 16 [See IEP page _____]	☐
Testing and assessment programs, including proficiency tests [See IEP page _____]	☐
Transfer of rights beginning at least one year before the student reaches the age of majority under state law (Ohio law is age 18)	☐

Relevant Information/Suggestions (e.g., medical information, other information):
  Danny takes medication for ADHD   (Physician: Dr. Rose–Medical Plaza)
  Check most recent Physician's Report
  for schedule and dosage.

INDIVIDUALIZED EDUCATION PROGRAM (IEP)

Statewide and Districtwide Testing

Student Name ___Danny___ **Student Grade** (when scheduled to take this test): __4__ **Student ID:** _____

School Year: ___2003–2004___ **IEP Meeting Date:** _____

STATEWIDE TESTING

Areas of Assessment	Grade Level of Test to Be Administered	Will Take Test without IEP Accommodations	Will Take Test with IEP Accommodations	Will Participate in Alternate Assessment
Reading	4		X	
Writing	4		X	
Math	4		X	
Science	4		X	
Citizenship	4		X	
Technology				
ITAC				

DISTRICTWIDE TESTING

	Grade Level of Test to Be Administered	Will Take Test without Accommodations	Will Take Test will Accommodations	Will Participate in Alternate Assessment

Excused from the consequences associated with not passing the test (Graduation Test) in the following area(s) of assessment: _____

Met participation requirements ☐ Yes ☐ No   Date _____
(Graduation Tests)

Area of Assessment	List Accommodations to Assessment	Area of Assessment	List Accommodations
Reading	Directions and questions read aloud, small group, additional time	Other (Specify)	
Writing	Computer, scribe, small group, additional time	Other (Specify)	
Math	Directions, word problems read aloud, small group, additional time	Other (Specify)	
Science	Read aloud, small group, additional time	Other (Specify)	
Citizenship	Read aloud, small group, additional time	Other (Specify)	

INDIVIDUALIZED EDUCATION PROGRAM (IEP)

Name ___Danny___   **IEP summary for effective dates** _____   **Date of next IEP review** _____

IEP Meeting Participants' Signatures

_____ Parent	_____ Child/Student's Special Education Teacher/Provider
_____ Child/Student's Regular Education Teacher	_____ Child/Student
_____ District Representative	
_____ Other Titles	_____ Other Titles
_____ Other Titles	_____ Other Titles

Summary of special education services: 90 minutes daily resource room (60 minutes language arts instruction, 30 minutes language arts instruction, 30 minutes general education support) 30 minutes consultation in/for general education classes.

Consent

☐ I give consent to initiate special education and related services specified in this IEP.*

☐ I give consent to initiate special education and related services specified in this IEP except for _____ **

☐ I do not give consent for special education services at this time.**

☐ I give consent for a change of placement.

Parent Signature _____ Date _____

*This IEP serves as prior written notice if there is agreement.

**If there is not agreement, the district must provide prior written notice to the parents.

Reevaluation (State and federal rules and regulations mandate that every child/student with a disability be reevaluated at least every three years.)

Your child's last MFE was _____

The next MFE shall occur by _____

You will be invited to participate in this meeting as part of the team. Parent permission is required for reevaluation if additional assessment is to be conducted.

Parent Notice of Procedural Safeguards

☐ I have received a copy of the parent notice of procedural safeguards; or

☐ I have a current copy of the parent notice of procedural safeguards.

☐ I waive my right to notification of special education and related services by certified mail.

Parent Signature _____   Date: _____

Note: *The student receives notice of procedural safeguards at least one year prior to his/her 18th birthday.*

Student Signature _____   Date: _____

Reason for Placement in Separate Facility (if applicable)

Having considered the continuum of services and the needs of the student, this IEP team has decided that placement in a separate facility is appropriate because:

Source: Retrieved from http://www.ode.state.oh.us/gd/templates/pages/ODE/ODEgooglesearch.aspx?page=221&query=pr07. Form dated 2007. Data/information on sample form is not part of the form. Reprinted by permission of the Ohio Department of Education.

417

APPENDIX D

SCHOOL ACCOMMODATIONS AND MODIFICATIONS

Some students need special accommodations or modifications to their educational program to be successful in school. An *accommodation* allows a student to complete the same assignment or test as other students, but with a variation in time, format, setting, and/or presentation. This adjustment to an assignment or a test-taking situation does not change the meaning of the student's score. Examples of accommodations include a student who is blind taking a Braille version of a test or a student taking a test alone in a quiet room.

A *modification* is an adjustment to an assignment or a testing situation that changes the standard for a particular student. Examples of possible modifications include a student completing work on *part* of a standard or a student completing an alternate assignment that is more easily achievable than the standard assignment.

Needed modifications and accommodations should be written into a student's Individualized Education Program (IEP) or Section 504 Plan. They should be chosen to fit the student's learning style. It's important to include the student when discussing accommodations and modifications. Ask the student what would be helpful.

Here are some ideas for changes in textbooks and curriculum, the classroom environment, instruction and assignments, and behavior expectations. When reviewing these suggestions, keep in mind that any accommodations or modifications you choose must be based on the individual student's needs.

Textbooks and Curriculum

Books
❑ Provide alternative books with similar concepts, but at an easier reading level.
❑ Provide audiotapes of textbooks and have the student follow the text while listening.
❑ Provide summaries of chapters.
❑ Provide interesting reading material at or slightly above the student's comfortable reading level.
❑ Use peer readers.
❑ Use marker to highlight important textbook sections.
❑ Use word-for-word sentence fill-ins.
❑ Provide two sets of textbooks, one for home and one for school.
❑ Use index cards to record major themes.
❑ Provide the student with a list of discussion questions before reading the material.
❑ Give page numbers to help the student find answers.

Curriculum
❑ Shorten assignments to focus on mastery of key concepts.
❑ Shorten spelling tests to focus on mastering the most functional words.

❑ Substitute alternatives for written assignments (clay models, posters, panoramas, collections, etc.).
❑ Change the percentage required for a passing grade on a test or assignment.
❑ Specify and list exactly what the student will need to learn to pass. Review this frequently.
❑ Modify expectations based on student needs (e.g., "When you have read this chapter, you should be able to list three reasons for the Civil War").
❑ Give alternatives to long written reports (e.g., write several short reports, preview new audiovisual materials and write a short review, give an oral report on an assigned topic).

Classroom Environment

❑ Develop individualized rules for the student.
❑ Evaluate the classroom structure against the student's needs (flexible structure, firm limits, etc.).
❑ Keep workspaces clear of unrelated materials.
❑ Keep the classroom quiet during intense learning times.
❑ Reduce visual distractions in the classroom (mobiles, etc.).
❑ Provide a computer for written work.
❑ Seat the student close to the teacher or a positive role model.
❑ Use a study carrel. (Provide extras so that the student is not singled out.)
❑ Seat the student away from windows or doorways.
❑ Provide an unobstructed view of the chalkboard, teacher, movie screen, etc.
❑ Keep extra supplies of classroom materials (pencils, books) on hand.
❑ Use alternatives to crossword puzzles or word finds.
❑ Maintain adequate space between desks.

Instruction and Assignments

Directions
❑ Use both oral and printed directions.
❑ Give directions in small steps and in as few words as possible.
❑ Number and sequence the steps in a task.
❑ Have student repeat the directions for a task.
❑ Provide visual aids.
❑ Show a model of the end product of directions (e.g., a completed math problem or finished quiz).
❑ Stand near the student when giving directions or presenting a lesson.

Time/transitions
❑ Alert student several minutes before a transition from one activity to another is planned; give several reminders.
❑ Provide additional time to complete a task.
❑ Allow extra time to turn in homework without penalty.
❑ Provide assistance when moving about the building.

Handwriting
❑ Use worksheets that require minimal writing.
❑ Do not return handwritten work to be recopied by the student. Do not grade handwriting on written work.
❑ Use fill-in questions with space for a brief response rather than a short essay.
❑ Provide a "designated notetaker" or photocopy of other student or teacher notes. (Do not require a peer notetaker or a student with no friends to arrange with another student for notes.)
❑ Provide a print outline with videotapes and filmstrips.
❑ Provide a print copy of any assignments or directions written on the blackboard.
❑ Omit assignments that require copying, or let the student use a tape recorder to dictate answers.

Grading
❑ Provide a partial grade based on individual progress or effort.
❑ Use daily or frequent grading averaged into a grade for the quarter.
❑ Weight daily work higher than tests for a student who performs poorly on tests.
❑ Mark the correct answers rather than the incorrect ones.
❑ Permit a student to rework missed problems for a better grade.
❑ Average grades out when assignments are reworked, or grade on corrected work.
❑ Use a pass-fail or an alternative grading system when the student is assessed on his or her own growth.
❑ Permit the student to retake a test until it is passed.
❑ If a portion of the grade is based on class participation, modify participation expectations.

Tests
❑ Go over directions orally.
❑ Teach the student how to take tests (e.g., how to review, to plan time for each section).
❑ Provide a vocabulary list with definitions.
❑ Permit as much time as needed to finish tests.
❑ Allow tests to be taken in a room with few distractions (e.g., the library).
❑ Have test materials read to the student, and allow oral responses.
❑ Divide tests into small sections of similar questions or problems.
❑ Use recognition tests (true-false, multiple choice, or matching) instead of essays.
❑ Allow the student to complete an independent project as an alternative test.
❑ Give progress reports instead of grades.
❑ Grade spelling separately from content.
❑ Provide typed test materials, not tests written in cursive.
❑ Allow take-home or open-book tests.
❑ Provide possible answers for fill-in-the-blank sections.
❑ Provide the first letter of the missing word.

Math
❑ Allow the student to use a calculator without penalty.
❑ Group similar problems together (e.g., all addition in one section).
❑ Provide fewer problems on a worksheet (e.g., 4 to 6 problems on a page, rather than 20 or 30).
❑ Require fewer problems to attain passing grades.
❑ Use enlarged graph paper to write problems to help the student keep numbers in columns.
❑ Provide a table of math facts for reference.
❑ Tape a number line to the student's desk.
❑ Read and explain story problems, or break problems into smaller steps.
❑ Use pictures or graphics.

Other
❑ Use Post-it notes to mark assignments in textbooks.
❑ Check progress and provide feedback often in the first few minutes of each assignment.
❑ Place a ruler under sentences being read for better tracking.
❑ Introduce an overview of long-term assignments so the student knows what is expected and when it is due.
❑ Break long-term assignments into small, sequential steps, with daily monitoring and frequent grading.
❑ Have the student practice presenting in a small group before presenting to the class.
❑ Hand out worksheets one at a time.
❑ Sequence work, with the easiest part first.

❑ Use blackline copies, not dittos.
❑ Provide study guides and study questions that directly relate to tests.
❑ Reinforce student for recording assignments and due dates in a notebook.
❑ Draw arrows on worksheets, chalkboard, or overheads to show how ideas are related, or use other graphic organizers such as flow charts.

Behavior
❑ Arrange a "check-in" time to organize the day.
❑ Pair the student with a student who is a good behavior model for class projects.
❑ Modify school rules that may discriminate against the student.
❑ Use nonverbal cues to remind the student of rule violations.
❑ Amend consequences for rule violations (e.g., reward a forgetful student for remembering to bring pencils to class, rather than punishing the failure to remember).
❑ Minimize the use of punishment; provide positive as well as negative consequences.
❑ Develop an individualized behavior intervention plan that is positive and consistent with the student's ability and skills.
❑ Increase the frequency and immediacy of reinforcement.
❑ Arrange for the student to leave the classroom voluntarily and go to a designated "safe place" when under high stress.
❑ Develop a system or a code word to let the student know when behavior is not appropriate.
❑ Ignore behaviors that are not seriously disruptive.
❑ Develop interventions for behaviors that are annoying but not deliberate (e.g., provide a small piece of foam rubber for the desk of a student who continually taps a pencil on the desktop).
❑ Be aware of behavior changes that relate to medication or the length of the school day; modify expectations.

Source: Information from Families and Advocates Partnership for Education (FAPE) from the PACER Center. Retrieved from www.fape.org/pubs/FAPE-27.pdf. Reprinted by permission.

INTERVENTION STRATEGIES—SECTION 504 ACCOMMODATION CHECKLIST

If you have a child who does not qualify for special education under IDEA but has a mental or physical impairment which substantially limits one or more major life activities, including learning, that child may qualify for special help in a regular classroom setting under Section 504 of the Rehabilitation Act of 1973.

The following is a list of accommodations that may help your child succeed in the classroom. The list can be used as a reference for parents and school personnel.*

Physical Arrangement of Room
- ❑ Seat student near the teacher.
- ❑ Seat student near a positive role model.
- ❑ Stand near the student when giving directions or presenting lessons.
- ❑ Avoid distractions (air conditioner, high traffic area, etc.)
- ❑ Increase distance between desks.

Lesson Presentation
- ❑ Pair students to check work.
- ❑ Write key points on the board.
- ❑ Provide peer tutoring.
- ❑ Provide visual aids, large print, films.
- ❑ Provide peer notetaker.
- ❑ Make sure directions are understood.
- ❑ Include a variety of activities during each lesson.
- ❑ Repeat directions to the student after they have been given to the class, then have student repeat and explain directions to teacher.
- ❑ Provide a written outline.
- ❑ Allow student to tape-record lessons.
- ❑ Have student review key points orally.
- ❑ Teach through multisensory modes, visual, auditory, kinesthetics, olfactory.
- ❑ Use computer-assisted instruction.
- ❑ Accompany oral directions with written directions for student to refer to blackboard or paper.
- ❑ Provide a model to help students, then post the model and refer to it often.
- ❑ Provide cross-age peer tutoring to assist the student in finding the main idea. Use underlining, highlighting, cue cards, etc., to break longer presentations into shorter segments.

Test Taking
- ❑ Allow open book exams.
- ❑ Give exams orally.
- ❑ Give take-home exams.
- ❑ Use more objective items (fewer essay responses).
- ❑ Allow student to give test answers on tape recorder.
- ❑ Give frequent short quizzes, not long exams.
- ❑ Allow extra time for exam.
- ❑ Read test item to student.
- ❑ Avoid placing student under pressure of time or competition.

Organization
- ❑ Provide peer assistance with organizational skills.
- ❑ Assign volunteer homework buddy.
- ❑ Allow student to have an extra set of books at home.
- ❑ Send daily/weekly progress reports home.
- ❑ Develop a reward system for in-school work and homework completion.
- ❑ Provide student with a homework assignment notebook.

Assignments/Worksheets
- ❑ Give extra time to complete tasks.
- ❑ Simplify complex directions.
- ❑ Hand worksheets out one at a time.
- ❑ Reduce the reading level of the assignments.
- ❑ Require fewer correct responses to achieve grade (quality vs. quantity).
- ❑ Allow student to tape record assignments/homework.
- ❑ Provide a structured routine in written form.
- ❑ Provide study skills training/learning strategies.
- ❑ Give frequent short quizzes and avoid long tests.
- ❑ Shorten assignments; break work into smaller segments
- ❑ Allow typewritten or computer printed assignments prepared by the student or dictated by the student and recorded by someone else if needed.

*Adapted from http://www.come-over.to/FAS/IDEA504.htm.

❑ Use self-monitoring devices.
❑ Reduce homework assignments.
❑ Do not grade handwriting.
❑ Do not allow student to use cursive or manuscript writing.
❑ Do not mark reversals and transpositions of letters and numbers as wrong; these should be pointed out for corrections.
❑ Do not require lengthy outside reading assignments.
❑ Monitor students involved in self-paced assignments (daily, weekly, biweekly).
❑ Arrange for homework assignments to reach home with clear, concise directions.
❑ Recognize and give credit for student's oral participation in class.

Behaviors

❑ Use timers to facilitate task completion.
❑ Structure transitional and unstructured times (recess, hallways, lunchroom, locker room, library, assembly, field trips, etc.).

❑ Praise specific behaviors.
❑ Use self-monitoring strategies.
❑ Give extra privileges and rewards.
❑ Keep classroom rules simple and clear.
❑ Make "prudent use" of negative consequences.
❑ Allow for short breaks between assignments.
❑ Cue student to stay on task (nonverbal signal).
❑ Mark student's correct answers, not mistakes.
❑ Implement a classroom behavior management system.
❑ Allow student time out of seat to run errands, etc.
❑ Ignore inappropriate behaviors not drastically outside classroom limits.
❑ Allow legitimate movement.
❑ Contract with the student.
❑ Increase the immediacy of rewards.
❑ Implement time-out procedures.

TEACHER POINT SYSTEM (AGES 6–8)

Name _____ Age _____

Behavior	Points	M	T	W	Th	F	Total
Follows instructions	4/class						
Completes work	4/class						
Obeys class rules	4/class						
Gets along with peers	4/class						
Completes homework	4/class						
Works on-task	4/class						
Bonus Points	2/class						
Total Points							
Total Cum. Points							
Points Used							
Net Points							
Privilege	**Points Used**	**M**	**T**	**W**	**Th**	**F**	**Totals**
First in line							
Class helper							
Store item (F)							
Homework pass (F)							
Popcorn party for class (F)							
Totals							
	Based on 4 classes						____ Pts leftover
Rules	• Follow instructions (start work after instructions). • Obey class rule (raise hand to answer). • Get along with peers (work/play cooperatively/share).						

Note: (F) = Friday.

Source: Information from Flick (1998). Reprinted by permission.

TEACHER POINT SYSTEM (AGES 9–12)

Name _____   Age _____

Behavior	Points	M	T	W	Th	F	Total
Follows instructions	5/class						
On-task	5/class						
Completes work	10/class						
Obeys class rules	5/class						
Works/plays cooperatively	10/class						
Completes homework	20/class						
Bonus Points	2/class						
Total Points							
Total Cum. Points							
Points Used							
Net Points (savings)							
Privilege	**Points Used**	M	T	W	Th	F	**Totals**
Store items (F)							
Homework pass (F)							
Extra computer time							
Free time							
Totals							
Rules	• Follow instructions (start work after instructions). • Obey class rule (raise hand to answer/keep hands and feet to self). • Work/play cooperatively (cooperate, share, and help).						

Note: (F) = Friday.

Source: Information from Flick (1998). Reprinted by permission.

GENERAL BEHAVIOR CONTRACT

I, _____ , agree to _____
        (Student's Name)

_____
        (Perform some task expected by parent/teacher)

This is to be completed by _____.*
              (date)

In return, I would like _____
                 (Some wished-for reward)

I therefore agree to the contract specified above.

_____   _____
Parent's/Teacher's Signature   *Student's Signature*

*If no deadline is set for completion of the contract, put NA (Not Applicable).

Source: Information from Flick (1998). Reprinted by permission.

DAILY BEHAVIOR CONTRACT

Date _____

My goal for today will be to _____

_____

_____

When this goal is achieved, I will get _____

_____

Should I fail to achieve this goal today, I will accept the following consequence:

_____

_____

_____   _____
Student's Signature   *Teacher's Signature*

Source: Information from Flick (1998). Reprinted by permission.

COMPLEX BEHAVIOR CONTRACT

I, _____ , agree to do the following:
                 (*Student's Name*)

1. Complete written assignments with 80% accuracy or better before lunch time.
2. Remain quiet and keep my hands to myself when going out to recess or lunch.
3. Play cooperatively (i.e., no fights) at recess.
4. Write the assignment for homework for each period.

Each day that I do the above things, I may choose one of the following:

1. Use the class computer for 20 minutes for work or play at the end of the day.
2. Choose the next available class job (e.g., errand) the next day.
3. Receive 20 minutes of free time at the end of the day.

If I complete 1 week of the above daily list, I will earn one of the following:

1. Have a friend sleep over.
2. Rent a selected movie.
3. Be excused from one weekend chore (e.g., folding clothes).

I agree to fulfill this contract.

_____   _____
      Student's Signature   *Teacher's Signature*

_____   _____
       Parent's Signature   *Date Completed*

This contract is in effect as of _____ . It will expire on _____ .
                               Date   *Date*

At the end of this contract, a new contract may be written.

Source: Information from Flick (1998). Reprinted by permission.

GRAPHIC DEPICTION OF RULES

_____

Name:	Response Cost Card					
Date:	M	T	W	Th	F	Total
Rule Above	Points Lost					
Name:	Response Cost Card					
Date:	M	T	W	Th	F	Total
 quiets down						
Rule Above	Points Lost					
Name:	Response Cost Card					
Date:	M	T	W	Th	F	Total
 raises hand						
Rule Above	Points Lost					

Name:	Response Cost Card					
Date:	M	T	W	Th	F	Total
pays attention						
Rule Above	Points Lost					

Name:	Response Cost Card					
Date:	M	T	W	Th	F	Total
waits turn						
Rule Above	Points Lost					

Name:	Response Cost Card					
Date:	M	T	W	Th	F	Total
works hard						
Rule Above	Points Lost					

Name:	Response Cost Card					
Date:	M	T	W	Th	F	Total

is positive | | | | | | |
Rule Above	Points Lost					
Name:	Response Cost Card					
Date:	M	T	W	Th	F	Total

uses manners | | | | | | |
Rule Above	Points Lost					
Name:	Response Cost Card					
Date:	M	T	W	Th	F	Total

knows how to ignore | | | | | | |
| Rule Above | Points Lost | | | | | |

RECORDING SHEET FOR SOCIAL SKILLS

Social Skills	M	T	W	Th	F	Totals
Listening						
Following rules						
Sharing						
Working/playing cooperatively						
Problem solving						
Controlling anger						
Totals						

BEHAVIOR CHECK CARD

Behavior	M	T	W	Th	F
Working cooperatively					
Playing cooperatively					
Cumulative totals					
Date	Point total goal this week				

Source: Information from Flick (1998). Reprinted by permission.

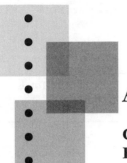

APPENDIX E

CHILDREN'S CLASSROOM REINFORCEMENT SURVEY FOR TEACHERS

Student _____ Age _____ Date of Rating _____

Rating _____ Grade Level _____

Survey Guidelines

The survey should be filled out in the presence of the student. Ask each question in the relevant sections, recording their response. If they refuse to answer, rely on your own judgement or on that of the parent(s).

In order to determine the most desired reinforcer in each category, employ the data received from the student's responses. Use the section marked "teacher notations" to record that information.

The suggested reinforcers listed are just that—suggestions. You and the student determine what is the best reinforcer in your situation. You will find that the lists will be particularly helpful when they have difficulty giving an answer, "I don't know."

The reinforcer decided upon should be one you are comfortable with the student receiving, and one you feel the student is really motivated to work for.

Try and determine social reinforcers or reinforcing school activities that will motivate the child before going on to material or home administered reinforcers. This survey is designed to help you go only so far as is necessary to find a functional reinforcer; use only that part of the survey that you need to find a reinforcer that your student will work for.

1. If you did a good job, who would you like to know? _____

   _____

2. The classmates you enjoy being with most are: _____

   _____

3. My favorite adult at school is: _____

4. A person at school I would do almost anything for is: _____

5. If I did better at school, I wish my teacher would: _____

   _____

6. The friend or person I would most like to spend more time with at school is: _____
   What would you most like to do together? _____

Teacher's Notations

What social reinforcers do you and your child feel he will most want to earn?

_____

_____

People to send positive notes of progress to: 1. _____

2. _____

3. _____

(in order of preference)

People to spend more time with and the activity:

1. _____

2. _____

3. _____

School Activity Reinforcers What the student does or would wish to do at school with additional free time (e.g., art projects, recess, monitor jobs).

1. If I had a chance at school, I sure would like to: _____

_____

2. Something I really want to do at school is: _____

_____

3. I feel terrific at school when I'm doing: _____

_____

4. My favorite school subject is: _____

_____

5. Use the following list only if the student is having difficulty thinking of activities they would like to work toward. Which of the following would you most like to work toward?

_____ Select topic for group to discuss	_____ Use radio with earphones
_____ Read to a friend	_____ Be first in line
_____ Read with a friend	_____ Assist teacher with teaching
_____ Tutor a slower classmate	_____ Help custodian
_____ Have free time in the library	_____ Run errands
_____ Be in a class play	_____ Read a story
_____ Have five minutes to discuss something with the teacher	_____ Select game/object for recess
_____ Care for class pets/flowers, etc.	_____ Work puzzle (free time)
_____ Earn time for the entire class to do a favorite activity	_____ Choose seat for specified time
_____ Dusting, erasing, cleaning, arranging chairs, etc.	_____ Choose group activity

Which two would be your favorites?

1. _____

2. _____

Teacher's Notations

Which activities would the child most want to earn (in order of preference)?

1. _____
2. _____
3. _____
4. _____

DO NOT GO BEYOND THIS IF ACTIVITY REINFORCERS PROVE ADEQUATE TO MOTIVATE THE TEACHER'S STUDENT

Material Reinforcers

The things the child does not own or have ready access to which would most likely be something he or she would work toward. Remember, be realistic and include the parent's financial support whenever possible.

1. What is your favorite food? _____
2. If I had my choice of any of the following foods, I would pick:

_____ Ice cream	_____ Peanuts	_____ Marshmallows
_____ Soft drinks	_____ Animal crackers	_____ Apples
_____ Cookies	_____ Jaw breakers	_____ Gum
_____ Candy bars	_____ Lemon drops	_____ Crackers
_____ Potato chips	_____ Raisins	_____ Life savers
_____ M & M's	_____ Cake	_____ Candy kisses
_____ Candy canes	_____ Popsicles	_____ Popcorn
_____ Milk	_____ Fruit	_____ Candy corn
_____ Sugar-coated cereals	_____ Crackerjacks	

Check all of those named. (Use only if having difficulty in picking his/her favorite or favorite is not realistic.)

Teacher's Notations

Do I have parents' financial support? _____ Yes _____ No

Limits? _____

With these limits in mind, his/her favorite foods would be:

1. _____
2. _____
3. _____
4. _____
5. _____

Which three would be the student's favorites?

1. _____
2. _____
3. _____

Teacher's Notations

With the financial limits in mind, which material reinforcers would the student most want to work for? (in order)

1. _____
2. _____
3. _____
4. _____

IF YOU FEEL THIS REINFORCER WOULD BE SUFFICIENT TO MOTIVATE YOUR CHILD, STOP HERE AND DESIGN A PROGRAM AROUND THE CHOSEN REINFORCER. IF NOT, GO ON TO THE NEXT SECTION.

Home Interventions

Home reinforcers should only be used with the complete cooperation of the parents. Use the relevant questions from the previous questions, if applicable.

My two favorite TV shows are: 1. _____
2. _____

The thing I like to do most with my mother is: _____

_____

The thing I like to do most with my father is: _____

_____

When I have money at home, I like to: _____

_____

I spend most of my time at home: _____

_____

Something I would like to do more of at home, but presently cannot is: _____

_____

When I have money, I like to: _____

_____

If I had a dollar, I'd: _____

_____

What is the best reward I could give you? _____

_____

What is your favorite toy or game? _____

_____

If I could pick any of the following items to have, I'd pick:

(Use only if having difficulty in isolating rewarding contingencies.)

_____ Balls	_____ Banks	_____ Boats
_____ Puzzles	_____ Rings	_____ Blocks
_____ Combs	_____ Flowers	_____ Comics
_____ Storybooks	_____ Miniature cars	_____ Jump ropes
_____ Chalk	_____ Marbles	_____ Balloons
_____ Clay	_____ Toy jewelry	_____ Medals
_____ Address books	_____ Cups	_____ Fans
_____ Flashlight	_____ Silly putty	_____ Stamps
_____ "Good deed" charts	_____ Whistles	_____ Bookmarkers
_____ Make-up kits	_____ Bean bags	_____ Toys
_____ Pencils with names	_____ Jumping beans	_____ Book covers
_____ Cartoons	_____ Crayons	_____ Paints
_____ Stuffed animals	_____ Coloring books	_____ Straw hats
_____ Pick-up sticks		

Which three of the above would you most want to earn?

1. _____
2. _____
3. _____

Some place I would like to go, but have not been able to as much as I would like is: _____

_____

The person at home or in your neighborhood who you would most like to spend more time with is: _____

_____

What would you like to do with that person? _____

_____

Teacher's Notations

Possible suggestions for home contingencies in order of practicality:

1. _____
2. _____
3. _____
4. _____

Additional Comments

Is there anything at all that was not already mentioned that you would be willing to work for or earn? _____

_____

Is there anyone you would want to be like when you are _____ years old? (Suggest an age five years older than student.)

_____

Teacher's Notations

Additional comments: _____

_____

_____

_____

_____

_____

_____

Source: Special Education Department K–6, Minneapolis Public Schools. Retrieved from www.pc.mplsk12.mn.us/ site1/97711090-59b5-4f98-964e-932ab29cf5bc/uploads/classroom_reinforcement_survey_for_teacher.pdf.

STUDENT REINFORCEMENT SURVEY

This survey can be used if you are attempting to discover activity reinforcers for students.

Activity Reinforcers

1. List what activity you would like to do at school if you had a chance.

   _____

   _____

2. Something that we should do at school is

   _____

   _____

3. I feel great at school when I am doing

   _____

   _____

4. My favorite class at school is

   _____

   _____

5. My favorite activity that we do in class is

   _____

   _____

6. After my work is done and when there is more time, I would like to

   _____

   _____

   _____

7. When I have time to choose something to do quietly, I like to

   _____

   _____

8. Circle three activities that you might like to do at school:

Reading with a friend	Being outside with friends	Working on a project
Having free time in the library	Listening to CDs with headphones	Drawing, painting, or using clay
Being in a class discussion	Being first to leave class	Talking with friends
Doing chores for a teacher	Running errands	Playing a game with friends
Talking with a teacher	Reading something I choose	Playing a class game
Eating lunch with an adult	Eating lunch in a classroom	Walking to a nearby restaurant

STUDENT REINFORCEMENT SURVEY #2

If you discovered that a student prefers adult attention, this survey could help to identify the adults that a child wishes to spend more time with or that would motivate a child.

Survey of Reinforcers

1. If I did well on an assignment, I would like for someone to tell this adult at my school:

   _____

2. My favorite adult in the school is _____

   because _____

   _____

3. A person at school who I would do almost anything for is _____

   _____

   _____

4. If I did better at school, I wish teachers would _____

   _____

   _____

5. The adult that I would like to spend more time with at school is _____

   _____

6. The member of my family I would most want to be proud of my progress at school is

   _____

Source: Reprinted by permission of the Wake County Public School System. Retrieved from www.wcpss.net/positive-behavior/day_two06-07/index.html.

IMPULSIVITY SCALE

Measure of Behavioral Inhibition

Name _____ Age _____ Sex _____

Grade _____ Date of Birth _____ Date assessed _____

School _____ Ratings by Parent _____ Teacher _____

Other (write in) _____

Name of Medication _____ Dose _____

Name of Medication _____ Dose _____

Dear Rater: The following scale was designed to measure various forms of impulsivity or behavioral inhibition. There are three subscales: (1) behavioral, (2) cognitive, and (3) emotional impulsivity. Please rate each item on each of the following scales: (0) Not characteristic of this person (None), (1) Somewhat characteristic (Mild), (2) Fairly Typical (Moderate), (3) Very characteristic (Extreme), (4) Extremely characteristic (Profound). Thus, on this scale of 0 to 4, the teen is rated on how prominent he/she exhibits each item. Circle the most descriptive rating number (#) for each item on the scale.

Behavioral Impulsivity	Severity Rating				
This Youngster or Teen	None	Mild	Mod.	Extreme	Profound
1. Blurts out embarrassing comments.	0	1	2	3	4
2. Interrupts conversations.	0	1	2	3	4
3. Acts before thinking about consequences.	0	1	2	3	4
4. Wears clothing inappropriate for the situation.	0	1	2	3	4
5. Asks questions about something that has already been covered.	0	1	2	3	4
6. Shows poor judgment.	0	1	2	3	4
7. Acts in a rush manner.	0	1	2	3	4
8. Shows a prominent startle response—jumps at loud sounds or sudden actions.	0	1	2	3	4
9. Generally does things quickly.	0	1	2	3	4
10. Takes chances—engages in risky behavior.	0	1	2	3	4
11. Acts on whatever pops into his/her mind.	0	1	2	3	4
12. Cannot wait for things—has to have them now.	0	1	2	3	4
13. Looks for immediate pleasure.	0	1	2	3	4
14. Fails to appreciate the future consequences of his/her actions.	0	1	2	3	4

Behavioral Impulsivity	Severity Rating				
This Youngster or Teen	None	Mild	Mod.	Extreme	Profound
15. Does not follow rules in games or class.	0	1	2	3	4
16. Makes rash decisions and "pays the price" later.	0	1	2	3	4
17. Does not stay in assigned area for specified time.	0	1	2	3	4
18. Moves from one subject or task to another without completion.	0	1	2	3	4
Cognitive Impulsivity	**Severity Rating**				
This Youngster or Teen	None	Mild	Mod.	Extreme	Profound
1. Rushes through work.	0	1	2	3	4
2. Does work hurriedly.	0	1	2	3	4
3. Makes careless mistakes.	0	1	2	3	4
4. Has trouble shifting from one activity to another.	0	1	2	3	4
5. Does work sloppily.	0	1	2	3	4
6. Misses important details in assignments.	0	1	2	3	4
7. Shows handwriting that is hard to read.	0	1	2	3	4
8. Misinterprets math problems.	0	1	2	3	4
9. Misinterprets what is read too quickly.	0	1	2	3	4
10. Handwriting/drawings are sloppy.	0	1	2	3	4
11. Exhibits a rapid cognitive tempo (i.e., seems to think "too fast").	0	1	2	3	4
12. Thinks faster than he/she can talk.	0	1	2	3	4
13. Overlooks critical details.	0	1	2	3	4
14. Thinks faster than he/she can write.	0	1	2	3	4
15. Appears unable to slow down.	0	1	2	3	4
16. Does not wait for directions to start.	0	1	2	3	4
17. Shifts from one activity to another.	0	1	2	3	4
18. Reads and rereads material without understanding.	0	1	2	3	4
Emotional Impulsivity	**Severity Rating**				
This Youngster or Teen	None	Mild	Mod.	Extreme	Profound
1. Seems to overreact in emotional situations.	0	1	2	3	4
2. Has trouble controlling temper.	0	1	2	3	4

Emotional Impulsivity	Severity Rating				
This Youngster or Teen	None	Mild	Mod.	Extreme	Profound
3. Gets caught fighting.	0	1	2	3	4
4. Is quick to cry.	0	1	2	3	4
5. Seems too sensitive.	0	1	2	3	4
6. Seems to wear emotions "on the sleeve."	0	1	2	3	4
7. Is quick to anger.	0	1	2	3	4
8. Has a low level of frustration tolerance.	0	1	2	3	4
9. Responds in a way that is out of proportion to whatever happened.	0	1	2	3	4
10. Goes too far when expressing self.	0	1	2	3	4
11. Is quick to express anger to self or others.	0	1	2	3	4
12. Is easily frustrated and becomes tense and agitated.	0	1	2	3	4
13. Is moody and emotionally volatile.	0	1	2	3	4
14. Has hurt others or self before realizing what has happened.	0	1	2	3	4
15. Easily becomes physically aggressive with others.	0	1	2	3	4
16. Makes rude comments.	0	1	2	3	4
17. Is easily angered, annoyed, or upset.	0	1	2	3	4
18. Is loud, boisterous, or arrogant.	0	1	2	3	4

Comments: Please write any general comments about this youngster's impulsive behavior (if any) or his/her ability to inhibit/control such behavior.

SURVEY OF TEACHER BEHAVIORAL PRACTICES

Teacher's name _____ Student's name _____

Teacher's school _____ Phone _____

Date _____ Student's age _____ Student's date of birth _____ Sex _____ Grade _____ School _____

Dear Teacher:

The following is a survey of behavioral practices that focuses on your knowledge of behavior modification techniques. The purpose of this survey is to determine your strengths and weaknesses in the use of behavioral techniques with children. While it is not exhaustive, it does cover a wide range of behaviors and applications. Respond to each statement by circling the "T" if you believe the statement is true and the "F" if you believe the statement is false. Your answers will generate a profile reflecting your knowledge of behavioral principles. The use of this information may increase the efficiency of your behavioral training skills.

1.   T   F   Rewarding a behavior will cause it to become stronger and occur more frequently.

2.   T   F   When you praise a child, it is important to be very specific about what he/she did.

3.   T   F   When a child is assigned additional tasks immediately after rapidly completing regularly assigned tasks, it may be difficult to get the child to complete future tasks.

4.   T   F   When a child gets what he/she wants after whining, whining will occur more often and may become more difficult to deal with.

5.   T   F   Punishment of inappropriate behavior is more effective when more appropriate behavior is rewarded as well.

6.   T   F   Almost all punishment is bad for children.

7.   T   F   Children know basic rules and expectations without discussing these matters with their teachers.

8.   T   F   Communications are better when you have eye contact with the child.

9.   T   F   When you communicate clearly and have good eye contact, you can be sure that a child understands your message and knows what to do.

10.   T   F   "Put your math classwork in your math folder" is an example of a clear, concise, and specific command.

11.   T   F   Rules that are posted and reviewed with a child are not likely to be followed.

12.   T   F   A child who understands commands and messages but does just the opposite is noncompliant and may have a behavior disorder.

13.   T   F   Ignoring students when they speak sarcastically and praising them for appropriate speech is a good example of reinforcing alternative, good behavior.

14.   T   F   When students are given a treat before doing a task, they will surely be motivated to carry out the task.

15.   T   F   Parents and teachers will sometimes need to model an appropriate behavior for a child so that the child knows exactly what is expected.

16.   T   F   When good behaviors are rewarded and opposite, bad behaviors are either ignored or punished, a balanced behavioral program is established; such a balanced behavioral program is more powerful than either procedure used alone.

17.   T   F   Once a decision is made to actively ignore an inappropriate behavior such as whining, it is OK to attend to it only when this behavior becomes truly obnoxious.

18.   T   F   Scolding, nagging, and reprimands can be an effective way to manage bad behavior exhibited by a child.

19.   T   F   A threat to punish a child may be just as effective as the actual punishment.

20.   T   F   An example of a behavior penalty or response cost procedure would be for a child to lose a privilege because of some bad behavior.

21. T F Compared to physical punishment (such as spanking), time-out and behavior penalty are rarely effective for a child.

22. T F A bad behavior may persist because the rewards of that behavior (e.g., attention, or power and control over a victim) may outweigh the punishment received for the behavior.

23. T F Bad behavior may continue when it (the "bad behavior") is modeled. (For example, spanking a child for hitting another child simply models the very behavior one is trying to extinguish or remove.)

24. T F When a teacher simply says, "No," or, "Stop that," each time a certain inappropriate behavior occurs, these behaviors may actually be reinforced as though the child were receiving a candy reward each time.

25. T F At times a student may play quietly and cooperatively with a classmate. Although the teacher might be tempted to say something, more often nothing is said for fear that a fight might erupt, the teacher thinking, "I'd better not disturb them now—they're playing so nicely."

26. T F Behavior penalty or loss of privileges has often been so effective that a teacher may wish to use it more often, adding one penalty on top of another each time a student exhibits a minor bad behavior. Although the child may seem increasingly depressed or angry, the teacher may feel comfortable with this approach.

27. T F If after each time-out a student receives a hug from the teacher to communicate that the child is still loved, this child's behavior will improve more rapidly.

28. T F Time-out may generally be effective with most children from ages 2 to 12; it may not be effective with teenagers, but much depends on the age and maturity level of the student.

29. T F The following would be an acceptable and advisable procedure in managing behavior: after each time-out, students should be asked to say that they are sorry for what they have done and make a solemn commitment to never again exhibit the behavior that got them in trouble.

30. T F Before time-out is used, it is best to review the procedure with the child and actually role-play the sequence of steps from the time the bad behavior is shown until the child comes out of time-out.

31. T F Lecturing a child who is yelling and screaming is an effective way of managing such inappropriate behavior.

32. T F The so-called "acting out" behaviors such as hitting, sassing, and spitting are the ones that respond best to time-out.

33. T F Putting a child in time-out just before bedtime is an effective way to deal with resistance to going to bed.

34. T F When students misbehave in class, it is clearly a punishment when they are sent to the principal's office and they have to talk with the principal, help sort papers, and sit in a swivel chair while looking out the window.

35. T F Time-outs as well as other punishments are given frequently to one student in a classroom. When trouble erupts, the teacher often assumes that the identified child is the source of the problem (from previous episodes) and sends that child to time-out even though a classmate was the culprit and now seems to be giggling. Resentments over such experiences are common and are likely to dissipate and be forgotten by the child who is punished.

36. T F A boy who screams when put in time-out in one room is now allowed to serve his time-out in another room. He has to promise not to play with his toys, look out the window, or go to sleep. If this boy remains quiet in time-out, his behavior will most probably improve.

37. T F A timer is not really necessary to use time-out effectively.

38. T F It is just as effective to tell a child, "When you can behave you can come out of time-out" as it is to use a timer.

39. T F Children who tell their teacher that "time-out won't work—forget it" should be believed; some other technique needs to be used.

40. T F Scolding or giving lectures to a child who is in time-out will make the time-out more effective.

41. T F Time-out is really not effective when the child becomes angry or annoyed when leaving time-out.

42. T F A child who stomps off in anger after time-out clearly needs to be punished again.

43. T F When time-out does not appear to be working, it is a good idea to double the amount of time in time-out.

44. T F If inappropriate behavior gets worse when time-out or behavior penalty is first used, this is an immediate sign that the procedure will not work with this child.

45. T F When teachers implement new procedures to deal with some inappropriate behaviors, many children will "test" the teacher to see if they "really mean what they say."

46. T F Students will often show improved behavior when tokens or points are given for appropriate behavior because they enjoy the immediate attention given and it is a signal for the ultimate reward that they will eventually get within a short time.

47. T F One of the problems with punishment is that it never lets students know what appropriate behavior is expected; it only tells them which behaviors are not desired.

48. T F In writing teacher–child contracts, the teacher must be clear and explicit about what is expected and what consequence(s) will follow when the child complies; contracts must be written down and signed by both teacher and child, along with a witness.

49. T F When two classmates or siblings are caught fighting, it is best to send both to time-out rather than try to discover who started the fight.

50. T F When two classmates or siblings fight over a toy, the simplest solution may be to put the toy in time-out for a short period of time.

51. T F When teachers use a point reward system, there is no need to verbally praise students for any good behavior.

52. T F The one situation where it is appropriate to "slap" a child who is misbehaving is while riding in a car, since this misbehavior may result in a serious accident.

53. T F It is not possible to use time-out in public places because it would be an embarrassment and waste of time for the teacher.

54. T F Behavior penalty can be used with one or more children who misbehave in public places.

55. T F It is helpful to review what behaviors are expected of children when visiting or going out in public places.

56. T F It is useful to employ some signal with students so that they may be given the opportunity to change their behavior in a positive direction and thereby receive reward and recognition for making the change without being told.

57. T F Whenever a child spontaneously shows a more appropriate behavior (e.g., inhibiting his/her normal tendency to blurt out answers or to hit another student when teased), this change should be enthusiastically reinforced by a teacher.

58. T F Some teachers believe that children need not be rewarded for their good behavior.

59. T F Children who show aggression may often receive more attention for their inappropriate behavior. The more such behavior is shown, the more attention is received, the stronger the behavior becomes, and the more likely it will occur.

60. T F Grounding can work fairly well with older children and teens as long as the grounding period is not excessive (e.g., a few days) and they have an opportunity to work off some of their "time" through good behavior.

61. T F Positive practice is just another form of punishment where the child learns very little appropriate behavior.

62. T F Restitution should be used along with positive practices when a child has been especially disrespectful.

63. T F The only real criterion for a token or point system is that it should be successful.

64. T F When setting up token or point systems, it is important to have many fines (for inappropriate behavior) and only have a few rewards for appropriate behavior.

65. T F Punishing a child for "laziness" and "having a bad attitude" will most likely be effective in changing these patterns.

66. T F It is sometimes easier to deal with the behavior of identified students when the teacher knows that their behavioral inconsistencies, impulsivity, forgetfulness, attentional problems, and distractibility all have a neurobiological basis.

67. T F When students are made to do distasteful or difficult tasks before easier tasks (where they feel more competent), completion of the more difficult task is thus strengthened by the second task through its association with completion of the second task.

68. T F It is sometimes difficult to think about and reinforce appropriate behaviors since so much attention is drawn to a child's inappropriate behaviors.

69. T F Children are expected to behave appropriately and should not receive any rewards, tangible (e.g., a treat) or social (e.g., praise), for doing what is expected.

70. T F Very often children will force teachers to use more restrictive and more punitive commands even though there is little success achieved using these commands.

71. T F Over a period of time teachers may develop a sense of "helplessness" when it seems like nothing seems to work in their attempts at disciplining a child.

72. T F Sometimes teachers must use a variety of rewards (i.e., reinforcers) since children may become bored or satiated on a certain reward; and while some things may be universally rewarding most times, some change in a specified reward may be needed to maintain each child's motivation.

73. T F Good, or appropriate, behavior should be rewarded.

74. T F Bad, or inappropriate, behavior should be punished or ignored.

75. T F It is important to reward a good behavior or punish a bad behavior as soon as possible after it appears.

76. T F Physical punishment for children is generally not effective in the long run.

77. T F The use of time-out for bad behavior will always work with any child.

78. T F Physical punishment will control hyperactivity.

79. T F A good example of "Grandma's Rule" is "When you eat your dinner, you can have your dessert."

80. T F A good application of "Grandma's Rule" is "When you do your daily chores, you can go out to play."

81. T F Differential reinforcement involves the selection of one behavior out of many that will receive attention and reward.

82. T F A typical behavior sequence involves an antecedent event (e.g., a command) followed by behavior (e.g., complies) with a specific consequence (e.g., a reward).

83. T F Inappropriate behavior may continue or get worse when a teacher simply attends to it by saying "stop that."

84. T F It is generally better for students to do more difficult homework last as easier work will probably put them in a "better mood" to complete the more difficult task.

85. T F When grounding teenagers it is best to use a short period and to allow them to get out early when showing some really appropriate behavior.

86. T F It is OK to use some high probability behavior to get compliance just to reinforce compliance.

87. T F While overcorrection is technically punishment, it focuses on the development of an appropriate behavior so it is typically viewed as a proactive or positive approach to behavior management.

88. T F Point systems are inappropriate for use with all teenagers.

89. T F The probability that a teenager will exhibit any specific behavior will not change even if you obtain compliance (i.e., a yes) on several preceding behaviors.

90. T F It is OK to allow teenagers some privilege listed in a point system even though they do not have enough points to get it because they are older and generally more responsible about completing agreements.

91. T F While spanking is inappropriate, it is OK to slap teenagers when they break a rule.

92. T F Teenagers may not comply with time-out, but they can be encouraged to view this procedure as "a time to calm down and chill out" when they are upset.

93. T F A behavior penalty should never be given to teenagers even if they exhibited some inappropriate behavior.

94. T F If you continue to tell teenagers everything that they need to do, they will have a difficult time developing a sense of responsibility and thinking for themselves.

95. T F Assertive communication should never be used with a teenager.

96. T F It is never OK to ignore an inappropriate behavior. All inappropriate behaviors should be punished, no matter what age the child.

97. T F Behavioral contracts should never be used with teenagers.

98. T F If teenagers are caught lying, it is best to question them until the truth comes out—then punish them by taking away all privileges.

99. T F It is difficult to deny privileges to teenagers since they like so few things.

100. T F If a teenager has a long history of reinforced inappropriate behavior, it may be more difficult to focus on the development of appropriate behavior for that student.

ANSWER KEY

Survey of Teacher Behavioral Practices

1	T	26	F	51	F	76	T
2	T	27	F	52	F	77	F
3	T	28	T	53	F	78	F
4	T	29	F	54	T	79	T
5	T	30	F	55	T	80	T
6	F	31	F	56	T	81	T
7	F	32	T	57	T	82	T
8	T	33	F	58	T	83	T
9	F	34	F	59	T	84	F
10	T	35	F	60	T	85	T
11	F	36	F	61	F	86	T
12	T	37	F	62	T	87	F
13	T	38	F	63	T	88	F
14	F	39	F	64	F	89	F
15	T	40	F	65	F	90	F
16	T	41	F	66	T	91	F
17	F	42	F	67	T	92	F
18	F	43	F	68	T	93	F
19	F	44	F	69	F	94	T
20	T	45	T	70	T	95	F
21	F	46	T	71	T	96	F
22	T	47	T	72	T	97	F
23	T	48	T	73	T	98	F
24	T	49	T	74	T	99	F
25	T	50	T	75	T	100	T
Totals							

Grand Total Correct _____

TEACHER HANDOUT ON BEHAVIORAL MANAGEMENT

We briefly review here the basic behavioral techniques that a teacher will need in dealing with students who have behavior disorders. These techniques are mostly good behavioral procedures that will work with any student, with or without a disability.

Problem behavior may certainly be influenced by many factors, but the main problems appear to center around learning. This means that many inappropriate behaviors are learned and reinforced through years of use. Since such behaviors are learned, they can be unlearned. In short, some of the inappropriate behaviors are reinforced and developed because they continue to work for the child. These behaviors either allow the child to *get something* or to *get out of something*. What most teachers want to do is (1) to get rid of the inappropriate (undesirable) behavior and (2) to replace it with more appropriate (desirable) behavior or (3) to simply develop more appropriate (desirable) behavior. Let's consider each component.

Removing Inappropriate Behavior

In many cases, the inappropriate behavior is just annoying or perhaps it causes the teacher to become angry. The first thought might be "I've got to punish this behavior to stop it." Physical punishment does result in suppression of a behavior, but it does not get rid of it. When a teacher uses physical punishment, several things happen:

1. The child stops the behavior but returns to it later.

2. The child initially learns to inhibit the behavior *only* in the presence of the punishing teacher.

3. The teacher often models the very behavior he or she wished to remove. This means that the teacher shows how to deal with a problem. If it is aggression toward a classmate, the message is "Don't do to your classmate what I'm doing to you." It sends a message to the child that the way you handle problems like this is to use physical punishment (i.e., to hit someone).

4. Physical punishment may also result in the child avoiding the punishing teacher or perhaps tuning out the teacher so that further socialization (and teaching) is limited.

5. Over time, the child may develop a lack of sensitivity to physical punishment or even consider it a "mark of toughness."

Thus, physical punishment becomes even less effective and may even backfire (i.e., when the child is bigger, he or she may retaliate). It is also important to note that physical punishment is often given long after the child exhibits the inappropriate behavior; the most effective rewards and punishment are given as soon as possible after the behavior (best given immediately after it). The bottom line is *do not use physical punishment in school*. Basically, it is totally ineffective in dealing with a chronic behavior problem. The philosophy that is suggested here is to use more positive forms of reinforcement and to focus on developing more desirable and appropriate behaviors.

Emphasis on Positive Reinforcement. The emphasis should be on positive reinforcement for all behavior management. However, there may be times when inappropriate behavior must be addressed with a punishment technique. There are two mild techniques that can be easily used in the school situation: (1) ignoring and (2) withdrawal of a privilege. Whether one or the other is used will often depend on the seriousness of the misbehavior. Ignoring can be used for less serious misbehavior; withdrawal of a privilege is used with more serious misbehavior.

Ignoring. When a behavior is annoying or mildly disruptive, the first procedure to use is ignoring. The teacher will know quickly if this behavior is under attentional control for it will get worse when ignored. Paying attention to the behavior by saying "stop" or "no" or giving a lecture about how inappropriate the behavior is, will only serve to make it worse. When a teacher decides to ignore a behavior, it must be consistently ignored for as long as it continues. To pay attention to a behavior after it was initially ignored will do two things: (1) it will reinforce the behavior at a higher level of intensity and (2) it will cause the child to be persistent. Thus, the unacceptable behavior will become worse, and it will persist for a longer period of time. Essentially, the child does not know when the teacher will attend to it; frustration-tolerance is therefore "built-in." Teachers must be able to predict how strong the initial behavior is and how long it will last. A child who receives no attention for a behavior is experiencing extinction of that behavior.

Many students will often "test" teachers to see if they mean what they say or if they will pay attention to the inappropriate behavior. Of course, when this happens, the child will be more likely to show that behavior again. In fact, each time the behavior receives attention it becomes stronger and more likely to occur.

Therefore, when a teacher ignores a child's behavior, the behavior is influenced and is less likely to occur. There are many behaviors that will respond to ignoring: yelling, temper outbursts, swearing, and demanding behaviors are just a few. This would be especially true for those behaviors that are elicited and maintained by attention. A teacher will know if attention plays a part in a behavior if it gets worse when attention is withdrawn. For example, if a child says, "Get me that book!" to the teacher and the teacher does not respond, the child might repeat the statement louder. The teacher might then let the child know that he or she must ask appropriately for the book while continuing to ignore the inappropriate behavior. When the child changes the behavior and asks appropriately for the book, the teacher must reinforce this change saying, "Now, that's a lot better way of asking—which book would you like?"

Teachers must be prepared for two things: (1) that the inappropriate behavior will get worse before it gets better, and (2) that they must not assume that the child *knows* the appropriate behavior. You can say to a student, "How do you ask for something that you want?" If the child answers correctly, reinforce that verbalization by saying, "That's right—now use it." If the child does not know, then, model the correct verbal behavior. When the child imitates it, say, "Good, that's it—you said it just the way I showed you."

Withdrawal of a Privilege.　When there is a generally positive reinforcing environment, this procedure works quite well. However, if a teacher is more accustomed to focusing on problem behavior, then this procedure may not be as effective. In short, it will be important to focus on positive, appropriate behaviors. This teaches the child what to do instead of what not to do. Many children simply do not know what to do. They lack the skills needed to deal with different situations. *Teach them what they need to know.*

In some cases, it will be important to take something away from the child so that the behavior is deemed unacceptable and the message is to stop their behavior. These are generally more serious misbehaviors such as violent acting out behavior that can hurt either the child or someone else. Remember that too many rules may just be overwhelming and may prompt a student to test out what teachers will do. Rules should be few in number and must be periodically reviewed. It may not be essential to query the child in question, but asking another (good) student may serve to not only remind the student but also review the rule.

Behavior is governed by consequences. While a behavior may be triggered by some situation or event, it is the consequence that determines what will happen to the behavior. If it is a positive consequence, the behavior will continue. If it is a negative consequence, the behavior may be weakened or suppressed. It may not happen the first time, and suppression may require several occasions to fully extinguish the behavior. If the privilege that is withdrawn is important and if it is something the child likes, the withdrawal will be effective; if it is not something the child likes, the withdrawal may fail. So, if a child hates to miss computer time, its withdrawal may be effective. If a child hates math and he is not allowed to do it, the withdrawal may actually be reinforcing. Taking math away will result in no real consequence. It is important to use only those things that are not involved in the child's social development or to use a relaxation strategy. Thus, the child should not be deprived of recess or lunch or anything else that is given to all students. Computer time may be a special reward that is available to only a select few students. Each child is different, and each situation is different. The teacher must evaluate the consequence that is proposed to be withdrawn to see if it is effective. A consequence that is effective will indicate that it is a good one to use with a particular child. Remember that the same privilege will not work for every child.

Predictable Sequence.　In many cases a teacher will know that a particular sequence of behavior will escalate to disrespect and perhaps aggressive acting out behavior. For example, let's assume that a child needs to develop behaviors that support his ability to think and prepare for class. In short, he will be responsible for coming to class prepared and ready to work. This might mean bringing a pencil or pen to complete his work. Another child might need to work on disrespectful behavior toward authority. If the first child fails to bring a pencil, the second might offer him one. This would obviate his need to come to class prepared to work.

The second child might become upset if the first is not allowed to take the pencil that he offers. He might think that the teacher is being unfair to him for not allowing him to offer the pencil. He may therefore get upset and argumentative with the teacher. This scenario could be avoided by (1) informing the class that help is not to be offered to the student, (2) reminding the student by asking questions the day before, "Now, John, what will you need to bring to class tomorrow in order to be prepared?" (3) commenting on occasions when the second student does not offer assistance when this was possible. The issue is not whether the second student does or does not offer assistance; the issue concerns the first boy's need to come prepared for class. In fact, this would be a prerequest for all students in class. The second student should not receive attention for his improper behavior. It would be far better for the teacher to avoid the escalation by giving no comment to the second boy. If the first boy does not have what is needed to do the class work, there should be an accepted procedure for getting it. An example might be for the teacher to say, "When you don't have what you need for class, raise your hand and I will assist you." This would then apply to all students.

Development of Appropriate Behavior

In general, it is important to think that the best behavior techniques are the more *positive* ones. These will be emphasized in this brief summary of behavior management procedures. There are many other techniques that are available for use and the interested teacher may consult one of the reference resources listed in this book.

A Word About Time-Out. Time-out is a very controversial procedure for students and teachers alike. It is best not used in a formal manner in the classroom. However, students can be taught how to use it for themselves and identify it as a chill-out procedure. For example, you might say to a student, "You can put *yourself* in a time-out. Whenever you are upset or angry, you can go to a specific place where there is a comfortable chair—sit down and calm down. After you get control of yourself, you can then go back to where you were." Make available to students some place in the classroom (e.g., a beanbag chair) where they can go to the back of the room when upset. Perhaps, a place can also be identified on the school ground (e.g., a bench) where students

can go to calm down. This self-imposed, self-control technique can be used by any student. The teacher might say, "I noticed that you were real upset about what happened, and I liked the way you handled it by giving yourself a 'chill-out.' You must feel a lot better, and you look much calmer, too. I'm really proud of you for recognizing what you needed and for doing it."

Grandma's Rule. Grandma's Rule is a motivational procedure that can be used to get students to do something that they haven't been doing by reminding them about what grandma said: "When you eat your dinner, then you can have your dessert." This can be put in a *when-then format*. For example, "*When* you finish your homework, *then* you can watch TV," or "*When* you do your chores, *then* you can go out and play." This simple procedure is the basis for almost all behavior management.

There are a few conditions to consider:

1. What you want the child to do must be developmentally appropriate and reasonable. If you ask a child to clean the whole classroom, this might be unreasonable. If you ask for something that students have difficulty doing (e.g., math work), they might still resist. If you then ask the question, "Well, what is it that's so difficult about this task?" you must find out if there is some reason for the difficulty. For example, many children who have ADHD may have trouble remaining still, paying attention, or showing self-control. All of these problems may be associated with differences in the nervous system (i.e., it's physiological).

2. The payoff must be reasonable. For example, few children would clean their classroom for a penny. The payoff must be appropriate to the task expected. Perhaps it will even be appropriate to talk to the child and to come up with reasonable tasks and expected rewards.

3. If the task is one that the child has not done, it may be necessary to model the behavior first so the child can imitate it. Remember, too, that you can be lenient with the child's behavior at first, and then expect more as the child shows that behavior more often (i.e., gets better at doing it). Cleaning one's desk is a good example. It is unlikely that a child will be able to do this very well the first time. *Accept improvement*. Be sure to review what is

meant by *clean your desk*. The teacher might know, but the child may not. List those things that must be done to get the desk clean and be specific (e.g., books placed in desk neatly, all papers sorted in appropriate folders, trash thrown out, etc.).

Communication.   Communication is the *input* into the system, so it is important to be clear about what a child should expect and what rules to follow. Rules should be few in number (maximum five), simple, clearly stated and posted (i.e., make signs). They also need to be reviewed periodically.

It is also best not to have to give many directives (i.e., to tell the child what to do) unless the behavior is a new one that is in development. It is best to ask questions. For example, instead of telling the older child what to do at math time say, "What are you supposed to do at this time?" If the child answers correctly (i.e., knows what to do) say, "That's right—do it." If the child does not answer correctly, say what needs to be done and ask again, "Now, what is it you have to do?" This gives you a chance to give verbal praise when the child gets it right. After assignments are given, query the child about what needs to be done: "Now what was the assignment I gave you to do?" If the child answers correctly, say, "Good, you were listening very well and you get the assignment. Now go ahead and do it."

When giving specific instruction, it is best to do so when you are directly in front of the child and while you have eye contact. This allows you to reinforce students for "looking at you." If they have trouble with this, you might gently (i.e., no force) hold a younger child's head so that he or she will look at you. You can then ask, "Now what did I just ask you to do?" Again if the child's answer is correct, reinforce with verbal praise: if not correct, repeat the instruction and ask again. Each time the child gets it right, he or she deserves verbal praise. Say, "That's right—do it!" If the child hesitates, count to three. Say (very emphatically), "I'll give you to the count of three to do it!" If the child does what you ask *before three* say, "Very good, I'm glad you decided to do that." Count slowly, 1-2-3, one per second. If the behavior is a new one under development, model that behavior and give the child a chance to imitate it, reinforcing any positive correct response. Abide by the following basic rules of behavior management:

1. Be *generous* (especially with verbal praise).
2. Be *watchful* (for any good behavior or any improvement).
3. Be *reasonable* (with expectation/rules and consequences).
4. Be *clear* (stating rules/expectations and communications clearly).
5. Be *specific* (especially with verbal praise).
6. Be *consistent* (over time and across teachers).
7. Be *patient* (behavior change is a slow process).
8. Be *strong* (remember bad behavior gets worse before it gets better).
9. Be *persistent* (behaviors are slow to change—stay with what works).
10. Be *smart* (use the positive approach wisely).

Verbal Praise.   Verbal praise is reinforcing, but it is important to know how to give it. First, be *very specific* and describe exactly what you like about the child's behavior. For example, "I really like the way you asked that question." Second, it is important to give praise immediately after the child shows the appropriate behavior. It is not very effective when you say, "You know that was very good the way you talked to me yesterday." That's not very specific and it is too late to be effective. Third, it is important whenever you are trying to develop a behavior that is weak to be consistent about giving verbal praise each time you see the behavior. Once the behavior is developed, you can taper off reinforcement (i.e., give less verbal praise).

There are three occasions to give praise. The first is when the child shows any appropriate behavior. Sometimes, many of these behaviors are taken for granted and not noticed. A child with a behavior disorder needs as much verbal praise as possible. Focus on any good behavior. Make a list so that you will be familiar with all of the child's good behavior. No matter how much inappropriate behavior is shown, the child will always show some appropriate behavior as well.

A second occasion for verbal praise is when the child shows an improvement in behavior. Again, this could be academic or social behavior—anything from handwriting and throwing a ball to language, grades, sitting still. The list would be very long. When you see such improvement, note it by saying, "You know your handwriting has improved a great deal. Keep up the good work," or "I've noticed that you're dressing a lot better. You're looking good and I'm proud of you!"

A third occasion for the use of verbal praise is when you are trying to establish a new behavior. This means you are trying to teach the child something that is an appropriate behavior that may be a replacement for an undesirable behavior. Verbal praise should then be immediate and consistent (i.e., every time you see the behavior). For example, you may wish to teach the child appropriate social behaviors such as saying *please* and *thank you*. First, model this behavior and when the child imitates you say, "That's right—you got it." It is important to vary the reinforcement from time to time so you do not say the same thing each time. For example, "I like to hear you say please" or "You said please—that's very good" or "Saying please is a very grown up thing to do." You may want to practice ways of giving praise by first writing them down and then practicing them in front of a mirror or using a tape recorder to hear how they sound. Remember though that praise should be honest and automatic—which means it

should not sound like it was practiced. It is also important to use language that you feel comfortable with and to avoid just saying "That was good." Remember that you must describe what you liked about the behavior. "Good" by itself does not say anything about what you liked about a child's behavior.

Perhaps the most important thing about behavior management is consistency. This means to be consistent with: (1) those behaviors you reinforce, (2) those expectations you have, (3) doing these things in the same way over time, and (4) doing these things the same way for each teacher. It is detrimental for only one teacher to use these "postive techniques." In fact, any difference may be confusing and might interfere with learning. Teachers should not allow one child to play one teacher against another.

Resources

Books

Artesani, J. (2001). *Understanding the Purpose of Challenging Behavior: A Guide to Conducting Functional Assessments*. Upper Saddle River, NJ: Prentice Hall.

Baker, J. (2003). *The Social Skills Practice Book*. Arlington, TX: Future Horizons.

Bigler, E., Clark, E., & Farmer, J. (Eds.). (1997). *Childhood Traumatic Brain Injury: Diagnosis, Assessment & Intervention*. Austin, TX: Pro-Ed.

Brickson, M. T. (1998). *Behavior Disorders of Children & Adolescents: Assessment, Etiology and Intervention* (3rd ed.). Upper Saddle River, NJ: Prentice Hall.

Chandler, L. K. & Dahlquist, C. M. (2002). *Functional Assessment: Strategies to Prevent and Remediate Challenging Behavior in School Settings*. Upper Saddle River, NJ: Merrill/Pearson Education.

DuPaul, G. J. & Stoner, G. (2004). *ADHD in the Schools*. New York, NY: Guilford Press.

Idol, L., Nevin, A., & Paolucci-Whitcomb, P. (1999). *Models of Curriculum-Based Assessment: A Blueprint for Learning*. Austin, TX: Pro-Ed.

Kellner, M. H. (2001). *In Control: A Skill Building Program for Teaching Young Adolescents to Manage Anger*. Champaign, IL: Research Press.

McIntyre, T. (2003). *The Behavior Survival Guide for Kids*. Minneapolis, MN: Free Spirit.

Meyer, D., & Vadasy, P. (1996). *Living with a Brother or Sister with Special Needs* (2nd ed.). Baltimore, MD: Paul H. Brooks.

Nelson, R., Roberts, M. L., & Smith, D. J. (2000). *Conducting Functional Behavioral Assessments: A Practical Guide*. Longmont, CO: Sopris West.

Pierangelo, R. & Giuliana, J. D. (2007). *The Educator's Diagnostic Manual of Disabilities and Disorders*. San Francisco, CA: Jossey-Bass.

Pierangelo, R. & Jacoby, R. (1996). *Parent's Complete Special Education Guide: Tips, Techniques & Materials for Helping Your Child Succeed in School and Life*. New York: The Center for Applied Research in Education.

Rhode, G., Jenson, W. R., & Reavis, H. K. (1992). *The Tough Kid Book: Practical Classroom Management Strategies*. Longmont, CO: Sopris West.

Rosenberg, M. S., Wilson, R., Maheady, C., & Sindelar, P. T. (2004). *Educating Students with Behavior Disorders*. Boston, MA: Allen & Bacon.

Reif, S. R. (2005). *How to Reach and Teach Children with ADD/ADHD*. San Francisco, CA: Jossey-Bass.

Sugai, G. & Horner, R. H. (2000). *Functional Behavioral Assessments*. Mahwah, NJ: Lawrence Erlbaum Associates.

Zager, D. B. (Ed.). (1999). *Autism: Identification, Education & Treatment* (2nd ed.). Mahwah, NJ: Lawrence Erlbaum Associates.

Videos

Attwood, T. (1998). *Asperger Syndrome: A Guide for Parents & Professionals*. Arlington, TX: Future Horizons.

Goldstein, S. & Goldstein, M. (1990). *Educating Inattentive Children*. Salt Lake City, UT: Neurology Learning & Behavior Center.

Reif, S. (1993). *Inclusive Instruction & Collaborative Practices*. New York, NY: National Professional Resources.

Robin, A. L. & Weiss, S. K. (1997). *Managing Oppositional Youth: Effective, Practical Strategies for Managing the Behavior of Hard to Manage Kids & Teens*. Plantation, FL: Specialty Press.

Videos Specifically for Educators

Behavior Intervention Strategies—An in-depth look at practical strategies that can help regular and special classroom teachers change the behavior of their students. (Available from the National Training Network.)

Functional Assessment and Behavioral Intervention Plans: Part 1—A two-hour video workshop on functional behavioral assessment (FBA). Covers definitions and origins of FBA as well as how to conduct the FBA and the criteria used to determine when one is needed. (Available from the Training and Technical Assistance Center.)

Positive Approaches to Solving Behavior Challenges—An 8-module training video package designed to teach a person-centered model for solving behavior challenges with nonadversive strategies. (Available from the Institute on Applied Behavior Analysis.)

Self-Management Training Program: Teaching Individuals with Developmental Disabilities to Manage Their Disruptive Behavior (with training manual)—Teaches about the education of those with developmental disabilities, and appropriate and needed behavioral skills in daily life. (Available from Research Press.)

Suicide Prevention: The Classroom Teacher's Role—Focuses on factors that contribute to adolescent suicide, special warning signals that a teacher should be sensitive to, and procedures for student referral. (Available from the Bureau for At-Risk Youth.)

Time for School—Presents social skills in the context of school. It features elementary school-age children demonstrating appropriate social skills in the classroom, library, on the playground, and in the hallway.

Writing Social Stories with Carol Gray (booklet included)—A DVD workshop complete with workbook. (Available from The Gray Center.)

Catalogues

ADD Warehouse
300 NW 70th Ave.
Suite 102
Plantation, FL 33317
Phone: 954-792-8944
Orders: 1-800-233-9273

Childswork/Childsplay
135 Dupont St.
PO Box 760
Plainview, NY 11803-0760
Phone: 1-800-962-1141
Web: www.childswork.com

Sunburst Media
PO Box 9120
Plainview, NY 11803-9020
Phone: 1-800-461-1934
Web: www.sunburst-media.com

Games

Catch Them Being Good: Professional Version (Ages 3–8) 2–4 players°

Conflict Resolution Game (Ages 6–12) 2–6 players °°°°
Look Before You Leap (Ages 5–12) 2–4 players°°
Mountaineering (Cooperation) (Ages 7+) 2–6 players °°°
No More Bullies (Ages 5–12) 2–4 players°°
Overheating (Ages 6–9) 2–4 players°°
Stop, Relax & Think (Ages 6–12) 2–4 players°°
Talking, Feeling & Doing Game (Ages 4–15) 2–6 players°
The Classroom Behavior Game (Ages 5–12) 2–4 players°
The Impulse Control Game (Ages 7–13) 2–6 players °°°°
You & Me: A Game of Social Skills (Ages 6–10) 2–6 players°

° Available from The ADD Warehouse
°° Available from Childswork/Childsplay
°°° Available from Cooperative Games
°°°° Available from Self Help Warehouse

Internet Resources

Addressing Student Problem Behavior: Part 1 (1998)—http://www.air.org/cecp/fba/problembehavior/main.htm
Addressing Student Problem Behavior: Part 2 (1998)—http://www.air.org/cecp/fba/problembehavior2/main2.htm
Addressing Student Problem Behavior: Part 3 (1999)—http://www.air.org/cecp/fba/problembehavior3/main3.htm
Behavior Advisor—www.behavioradvisor.com
Comprehensive Collection of Resources for Educators—www.pbis.org
Discipline Help—www.disciplinehelp.com
Early Warning, Timely Response: A Guide to Safe Schools (2000)—http://www.air.org/cecp/guide/default.htm
Education World®—www.educationworld.com
Effective Procedures for Early Intervention—www.challengingbehavior.org
IDEA Partnership—www.ideapartnership.org
Incorporating PBS into the IEP—www.beachcenter.org
Lesson Plan for Teachers, Special Educators, etc.—www.youthchg.com
NICHCY Publications—http://www.nichey.org/pubs1.htm
One ADD Place—http://www.oneaddplace.com
Peer Mediated Instruction & Intervention—http://www.cast.org/publications/ncac_peermii.html
Resources for Students with Behavioral/Discipline Problems—http://www.taalliance.org/research/discipline.htm

Teacher Education Videos & DVDs—www.business-marketing.com
Teacher Posters: Interventions for Students with Behavior Disorders—www.youthchg.com
Teaching Strategies for Social & Emotional Development—http://csetel.uiuc.edu
The Best of Attainment—www.attainmentcompany.com
The Future of Children—http://www.futureofchildren.org
The Teacher's Guide to the U.S. Dept. of Education (2000)—http://www.ed.gov/pubs/teachersguide/index.html
Self Realization Publications: Adolescent & Juvenile Issues—www.srpublications.com
Special Education Resources & Information—www.educationworld.com
Students with Emotional Disturbance (1994)—http://www.air.org/cecp/resources/20th/intro.htm
Violence Prevention: What Middle School Teachers and Students Should Know—www.researchpress.com

Newsletters

CCBD: Newsletter
Council for Children with Behavioral Disorders
1110 N. Globe Rd., Suite 300
Arlington, VA 22201-5704
Web: http://www.ccbd.net
ITN (Innovative Teaching Newsletter)—http://surfaquarium.com/newsletter/specialized.htm
Mental Health Information (Disruptive Behavior Disorders)—http://www.athealth.com/practitioner/newsletter/fpn_subscribe.html
My ADHD
ADD Warehouse
Web: www.myADHD.com
The Social Stories Quarterly—http://www.thegraycenter.org/store

Organizations/Associations

American Academy of Special Education Professionals
Phone: 800-424-0371
Web: http://aasep.org
America Counseling Association
Phone: 800-347-6647
Web: www.counseling.org
American Federation of Teachers
Phone: 202-879-4400

Web: www.aft.org
E-mail: online@aft.org
American Psychological Association (APH)
Phone: 202-336-5500, 800-374-2721
Web: www.apa.org
Beach Center on Disability
Phone: 785-864-7600
Web: www.beachcenter.org
Cambridge Center for Behavioral Studies
Phone: 978-369-2227
Web: www.behavior.org
Center for Effective Collaboration and Practice
Phone: 888-457-1551
Web: http://cecp.air.org
Children and Adults with Attention Deficit Disorder (CHADD)
Phone: 800-233-4050
Web: www.chadd.org
CYKE (A Media Co-Dedicated to Improving the Emotional and Physical Health of Children)
Web: http://www.cyke.com
International Dyslexia Association
Phone: 800-222-3123
Web: www.interdys.org
Learning Disabilities Association (LDA)
Phone: 412-341-1515
Web: www.ldanatl.org
Leslie Packer, PhD, Site
Web: www.schoolbehavior.com/index.htm
National Association of School Psychologists (NASP)
Phone: 301-657-0270
Web: www.nasponline.org/index2.html
E-mail: nasp@naspweb.org
National Association of Special Education Teachers (NASET)
Phone: 800-754-4421
Web: http://www.naset.org
National Association on Mental Illness (NAMI)
Phone: 703-524-7600
Web: www.nami.org
National Education Association
Phone: 202-833-4000
Web: www.nea.org
National Information Center for Children and Youth with Disabilities (NICHCY)
Phone: 800-695-0285
Web: www.nichcy.org
National Mental Health Information Center (SAMHSA)
Phone: 800-789-2647
Web: http://mentalhealth.samhsa.gov

Orton Dyslexia Society
Phone: 800-222-3123
Web: www.selu.edu/academics/education/tbc/orton.htm

School Social Worker Association of America
Phone: 847-289-4642
Web: www.sswaa.org
E-mail: sswa@aol.com

School Violence Prevention Initiative
Phone: 800-789-2647
Web: www.mentalhealth.samhsa.gov/schoolviolence

Society for Developmental and Behavioral Pediatrics
Phone: 703-556-4222
Web: http://www.sdbp.org

The American Academy of Child and Adolescent Psychiatry
Phone: 202-966-7300
Web: http://www.aacap.org

The Center for Evidence-Based Practice: Young Children and Challenging Behavior
Phone: 813-974-2200
Web: http://challengingbehavior.fmhi.usf.edu

The Council for Children with Behavioral Disorders (CCBD)
Phone: 913-239-0550
Web: www.ccbd.net

The Council for Exceptional Children
Phone: 800-328-0272
Web: www.cec.sped.org

The PACER Center
Phone: 952-838-9000
Web: http://www.pacer.org

The Technical Assistance Center on Positive Behavior Interventions and Supports
Web: www.pbis.org/english

Publishers

Academic Therapy Publications
Phone: 800-422-7249
Web: www.academictherapy.com

Corwin Press
Phone: 800-818-7243
Web: www.corwinpress.com

Free Spirit Publishing
Phone: 800-735-7323
Web: www.freespirit.com

Guilford Press
Phone: 800-365-7006
Web: www.guilford.com

John Wiley & Sons
Phone: 877-762-2974
Web: www.wiley.com

Jossey-Bass
Phone: 415-433-1740
Web: www.josseybass.com

Magination Press
Phone: 800-374-2721
Web: www.maginationpress.com

Paul H. Brooks
Phone: 800-638-3775
Web: www.brookespublishing.com

Prentice Hall/Pearson Education
Phone: 201-236-7000
Web: www.pearsonhighered.com

Pro-Ed
Phone: 800-897-3200, 512-451-3246
Web: www.proedinc.com

Research Press
Phone: 217-352-3273
Web: www.researchpress.com

Sage Publications
Phone: 800-818-7243
Web: www.sagepub.com

Scholastic, Inc.
Phone: 800-SCHOLASTIC
Web: www.scholastic.com/index.asp

Sopris West
Phone: 800-547-6747
Web: sopriswest.com

Teachers College Press
Phone: 800-575-6566
Web: www.teacherscollegepress.com

Woodbine House
Phone: 800-843-7323
Web: www.woodbinehouse.com/

Behavioral Journals

Behavior Analysts Today
Web: www.behavior-analyst-online.org

Behavioral Interventions
Phone: 800-825-7550
Web: www3.interscience.wiley.com/cqi-bin/jhome/24375

Behavior Modification
Phone: 800-818-7243
Web: www.sagepub.com/journal.aspx?pid=152

Child Development
Phone: 800-232-4636
Web: www.srcd.org/cd.html

Developmental Psychology
Phone: 800-374-2721
Web: www.apa.org/journals/dev/description.html

Journal of Education for Students Placed at Risk (JESPAR)
Phone: 502-852-0616
Web: www.csos.jhu.edu/jespar/past.htm

Journal of Applied Behavior Analysis
Phone: 785-841-4425
Web: http://seab.envmed.rochester.edu/jaba

Journal of Behavioral Education
Phone: 212-460-1500
Web: www.kluweronline.com/issn/1053-0819

Journal of Positive Behavioral Interventions
Phone: 212-352-1404
Web: http://jpbi.sagepub.com

Journal of School Psychology
Phone: 402-472-5923
Web: www.elsevier.com/locate/jschpsyc

Glossary

Behavior Terms—www.coedu.usf.edu/abaglossary/main.asp

Behavioral Health Terms—www.uihealthcare.com/depts/uibehavioralhealth/patiented/glossary/html

Behavioral Intervention Terms—www.usu.edu/teachall/text/behavior/BEHAVglos.htm

More Behavior Terms—www.thecol.org/guide/glossary.html

Terms Used in Behavior Research—www.psychology.uiowa.edu/faculty/wasserman/glossary/index%20set.html

Treatment Description—www.aacap.org/publications/factsfam/continum.htm

References

Abikoff, H., Jensen, P., Arnold, L., Hoza, B., Hechtman, L., Pollack, S., et al. (2002). Observed classroom behavior of children with ADHD: Relationship to gender and co-morbidity. *Journal of Abnormal Child Psychology, 30,* 349–359.

Ackenbach, T. M. (1999). Empirically based assessment and epidemiology across the lifespan. In A. M. Koot, A. M. Crijnen, & R. R. Ferdinand (Eds.), *Child psychiatric epidemiology: Accomplishment and future directions* (pp. 1–31). Assen, Netherlands: Van Gorcum.

Acosta, M. T., Arcos-Burgos, M., & Muenke, M. (2004). Attention deficit hyperactivity disorder (ADHD): Complex phenotype; simple genotype? *Genetics in Medicine, 6,* 1–15.

Agran, M., Sinclair, T., Alper, M., Cavin, M., Wehmeyer, M., & Hughes, C. (2005). Using self-monitoring to increase following-direction skills of students with moderate to severe disabilities in general education. *Education and Training in Developmental Disabilities, 40,* 3–13.

Ahearn, W. H., Clark, K. M., Gardenier, N. C., Chung, B., & Dube, W. V. (2003). Persistence of stereotypic behavior: Examining the effects of external reinforcers. *Journal of Applied Behavior Analysis, 36,* 439–448.

Ahmad, S. A., & Warriner, E. M. (2001). Review of the NEPSY: A developmental neuropsychological assessment. *Clinical Neuropsychologist, 15,* 240–249.

Alberto, P. A., & Troutman, H. C. (1999). *Applied behavior analysis for teachers.* Upper Saddle River, NJ: Merrill/Pearson Education.

Alderman, M. K. (2004). *Maturation for achievement: Possibilities for teaching and learning.* Mahwah, NJ: Lawrence Erlbaum.

Alexander, S., McKenzie, J., & Geissinger, H. (2002). *An evaluation of information technology projects for university learning (executive summary).* Australian Government Committee for University Teaching and Staff Development.

Allen, K. E., & Cowdery, G. E. (2004). *The exceptional child: Inclusion in early childhood education* (5th ed.). Albany, NY: Thompson/Delmar Publishers.

Allen, R. (2002). Big schools: The way we are. *Educational Leadership, 59,* 36–42.

Althoff, R. R., Faraone, S. V., Rettew, D. C., Morley, C. P., & Hudziak, J. J. (2005). Family, twin, adoption and molecular genetics studies of juvenile bipolar disorder. *Bipolar Disorders, 7,* 598–609.

American Academy of Neurology. (1949). Retrieved 10/1/09 at http://www.physorg.com/partners/american-academy-of-neurology/.

American Institutes for Research (AIR). (2002). *Evidence of effects on student achievement.* Unpublished manuscript. U.S. Department of Education: Washington, D.C.

American Psychiatric Association. (1994). *Diagnostic and statistical manual of mental disorders* (4th ed.). Washington, DC: Author.

America Psychological Association. (1993). *Violence and youth: Psychology's response.* Washington, DC: Author.

Anderson, C. A., Berkowitz, L., Donnerstein, E., Huesmann, L. R., Johnson, J. D., Linz, D., et al. (2003). The influence of media on youth. *Psychological Science in the Public Interest, 4,* 81–110.

Anderson, C. W., Ryan D. W., & Shaprio, B. J. (1989). *International association for the evaluation of educational achievement: International studies in educational achievement* (Vol. 4). Oxford: Pergamon Press.

Anderson, V. (2006). Advances in postacute rehabilitation after childhood-acquired brain injury: A focus on cognitive, behavioral and social domain. *American Journal of Physical Medicine and Rehabilitation, 85,* 767–778.

Anderson, V. A., Anderson P., Northam, B., Jacobs, R., & Catroppa, C. (2001). Development of executive functions through late childhood and adolescence in an Australian sample. *Developmental Neuropsychology, 20,* 385–406.

Anderson, V. A., Morse, S. A., Catroppa, C., Haritou, F., & Rosenfeld, J. V. (2004). Thirty month outcome from early childhood head injury: A prospective analysis of neurobehavioral recovery. *Brain, 127,* 2608–2620.

Armstrong, K. H., Dedrick, R. F., & Greenbaum, P. E. (2003). Factors associated with community adjustment of young adults with serious emotional disturbance: A longitudinal analysis. *Journal of Emotional and Behavioral Disorders, 11,* 66–90.

Arroyos-Jurado, E., Paulsen, J. S., Ehly, S., & Max, J. E. (2006). Traumatic brain injury in children and adolescents: Academic and intellectual outcomes following injury. *Exceptionality, 14,* 125–140.

Asperger, H. (1991). *Autistic psychopathology in childhood.* In U. Frith (Ed.), (1991), *Autism and asperger syndrome* (pp. 37–92). Cambridge, England: Cambridge University Press.

Attwood, T. (2006). *The complete guide to Asperger's syndrome.* London: Jessica Kingley.

Audette, B., & Algozzine, B. (1997). Re-inventing government? Let's re-invent special education. *Journal of Learning Disabilities, 30,* 378–383.

August, G. J., Braswell, L., & Thuras, P. (1998). Diagnostic stability of ADHD in a community sample of school-aged children screened for disruptive behavior (attention-deficit hyperactivity disorder). *Journal of Abnormal Child Psychology, 26,* 345–360.

Austin, J. L. (2004). Preparing tomorrow's behavior-analytic researchers: A review of research methods in applied behavior analysis by John Bailey and Mary Burch. *Journal of Applied Behavior Analysis, 37,* 243–248.

Autti-Ramo, R. (2000). Twelve-year follow-up of children exposed to alcohol in utero. *Developmental Medicine and Child Neurology, 42,* 406–411.

Avant, G. R., & Davis, H. J. (1984). *The U.S. Constitution in school: The rights of the student.* Document Reproduction Service No. (ERIC 244899).

Ayers, B. J., & Hedeen, D. L. (1996). Been there, done that, didn't work: Alternative solutions for behavior problems. *Educational Leadership, 53,* 48–50.

Aylward, G. P. (1994). *Practitioner's Guide to Developmental and Psychological Testing.* New York: Plenum.

Bailey, D. B., McWilliam, R. A., Darkes, L. A., Hebbeler, K., Simeonsson, R. J., Spiker, D., et al. (1998). Family outcomes in early intervention: A framework for program evaluation and efficacy research. *Exceptional Children, 64,* 313–328.

Bandura, A. (1969). *Principles of behavior modification.* New York: Holt, Rinehart & Winston.

Bandura, A. (1986). *Social foundations of thought and action: A social cognitive theory.* Upper Saddle River, NJ: Prentice Hall.

Banks, J. A. (2001). Citizenship education and diversity. *Journal of Teacher Education, 52,* 5–16.

Barbour, I. (1990). *Religion in an age of science.* San Francisco: Harper.

Barenthin, J., & Van Puymbroech, M. (2006). *The joystick generation: Video games have measureable social effects on adolescents.* National Park Association. Retrieved from http://www.nrpa.org/content/default.aspx?documentId=4626.

Barkley, R. A. (1981). *Hyperactive children: A handbook for diagnosis and treatment.* New York: Guilford Press.

Barkley, R. A. (1990). *Attention deficit/hyperactivity disorder: A handbook for diagnosis and treatment.* New York: Guilford Press.

Barkley, R. A. (1997). Behavioral inhibition, sustained attention, and executive functions: Constructing a unifying theory of ADHD. *Psychological Bulletin, 124,* 65–94.

Barkley, R. A. (1998). *Attention deficit hyperactivity disorder: A handbook for diagnosis and treatment.* New York: Guilford Press.

Barkley, R. A. (2000). Commentary on the multimodal treatment study of children with ADHD. *Journal of Abnormal Child Psychology, 28,* 595–599.

Barkley, R. A. (2002). Major life activity and health outcomes associated with attention-deficit-hyperactivity disorder. *Journal of Clinical Psychiatry, 63,* 10–15.

Barkley, R. A., Edwards, G., & Robins, A. R. (1999). *Defiant teens: A clinician's manual for family training.* New York: Guilford Press.

Barkley, R. A., Fischer, M., Edelbrock, C. S., & Smallish, L. (1990). The adolescent outcome of hyperactive children diagnosed by research criteria: I. An 8-year prospective follow-up study. *Journal of the American Academy of Child and Adolescent Psychiatry, 29,* 545–547.

Barkley, R. A., & Murphy, K. R. (2006). *Attention deficit hyperactivity disorder: A clinical workbook* (3rd ed.). New York: Guilford Press.

Barkley, R. A., Murphy, K. R., & Kwasnik, D. (1996). Motor vehicle driving competencies and risks in teens and young adults with attention deficit hyperactivity disorder. *Pediatrics, 98,* 1089–1095.

Baron, I. S., Fennell, E. B., & Voeller, K. K. (1995). *Cardiovascular disease. Pediatric neuropsychology in the medical setting* (pp. 343–369). New York: Oxford University Press.

Baron-Cohen, S. (1990). Autism: A specific cognitive disorder of "mind-blindness." *International Review of Psychiatry, 2,* 81–90.

Barton-Arwood, S., Wehby, J. A., & Falk, K. B. (2005). Reading instruction for elementary-age students with emotional and behavioral disorders: Academic and behavioral outcomes. *Exceptional Children, 72,* 7–27.

Bates, E., & Roe, K. (2001). *Language development in children with unilateral brain injury.* In C. Nelson, & M. Luciana (Eds.). *Handbook of developmental cognitive neuroscience* (pp. 281–307). Cambridge, MA: MIT Press.

Batshaw, M. L. (2001). *When your child has a disability.* Baltimore, MD: Paul Brooks.

Bauch, P., & Goldring, E. (1995). Parent involvement and school responsiveness: Facilitating the home–school connection in schools of choice. *Educational Evaluation and Policy Analysis, 17,* 1–22.

Bauman, L. J., & Friedman, S. B. (1998). Corporal punishment. *Pediatric Clinics of North America, 45,* 403–414.

Beghetto, R. (2003). *Scientifically based research.* Eugene, OR: ERIC Clearinghouse on Educational Management.

Begley, S. (1998). Homework doesn't help. *Newsweek, 131*(13), 50–52.

Beitchman, J. H., & Young, H. A. (1997). Learning disorders with a special emphasis on reading disorders: A review of the past 10 years. *Journal of the American Academy of Child and Adolescent Psychiatry, 36,* 1020–1032.

Bell, R. Q. (1986). Age specific manifestations in changing psychosocial risk. In D. Farran & J. D. McKinney (Eds.), *The concept of risk in intellectual and psychosocial development* (pp. 283–310). New York: Academic Press.

Bellah, E. (2002). *President's commission on excellence in special education. New report.* Retrieved from http://www.tsbui.edu/outreach./seehear/fall02president.htm.

Benner, G. J., Beaudoin, K., Kinder, D., & Mooney, P. (2005). The relationship between beginning reading skills and social adjustment of a general sample of elementary aged children. *Education and Treatment of Children, 28,* 280–284.

Berger, E. H. (2003). *Parents as partners in education: Families and schools working together* (7th ed.). Upper Saddle River, NJ: Merrill/Pearson Education.

Berkowitz, M. J., & Martens, B. K. (2001). Assessing teachers' and students' preferences for school-based reinforcers: Agreement across methods and different effort requirements. *Journal of Developmental and Physical Disabilities, 12,* 373–387.

Berkson, G., & Tupa, M. (2000). Early development of stereotyped and self-injurious behaviors. *Journal of Early Intervention, 23,* 1–19.

Berner, M. L., Fee, V. E., & Turner, H. D. (2001). A multi-component social skills training program for pre-adolescent girls with few friends. *Child and Family Behavior Therapy, 23,* 1–18.

Bettenhausen, S. (1998). Make proactive modifications to your classroom. *Intervention in School and Clinic, 33,* 182–183.

Beyda, S. D., Zentall, S. S., & Ferko, D. J. K. (2002). The relationship between teacher practices and the task-appropriate and social behavior of students with behavioral disorders. *Behavioral Disorders, 27,* 236–255.

Biederman, J., Faraone, S., Keenan, K., Knee, D., & Tsuang, M. T. (1990). Family-genetic and psychosocial risk factors in DSM-III: Attention-deficit-disorder. *Journal of the American Academy of Child and Adolescent Psychiatry, 29,* 526–533.

Biederman, J., Faraone, S., Mick, E., & Moore, P. (1996). Child behavior check list findings further support co-morbidity between ADHD and major depression in a referred sample. *Journal of the American Academy of Child and Adolescent Psychiatry, 35,* 734–742.

Biederman, J., Mick, E., & Faraone, S. V. (1998). Normalized functioning in youths with persistent attention deficit/hyperactivity disorder. *Journal of Pediatrics, 133,* 544–551.

Biederman, J., Rosenbam, T., Boldus-Murphy, E., Faraone, S., Chaloff, T., Hirschfeld, D., et al. (1993). A three-year follow-up of children with and without behavioral inhibition. *Journal of the American Academy of Child and Adolescent Psychology, 32*, 814–821.

Biederman, J., Wilens, T., Mick, E., Milberger, S., Spencer, F. O., & Faraone, S. V. (1995). Psychoactive substance use disorders in adults with attention deficit disorder (ADHD): Effects of ADHD and psychiatric co-morbidity. *American Journal of Psychiatry, 152*, 1652–1658.

Biglan, A., Margaret, C., Wang, M. C., & Walberg, H. J. (2003). *Preventing youth problems*. New York: Kluwer Academic/ Plenum Publications.

Bigler, E. D., Clark, E., & Farmer, J. E. (Eds.). (1997). *Childhood traumatic brain injury: Diagnosis, assessment and intervention*. Austin, TX: Pro-Ed.

Billingsley, B. (2004). Promoting teacher quality and retention in special education. *Journal of Learning Disabilities, 37*, 370–376.

Bird, H. R., Canino, G., Davis, M., Ramirez, R., Chavez, L., Duarte, C., et al. (2005). Brief Impairment Scale (BIS): A multidimensional scale of functional impairment for children and adolescents. *Journal of the American Academy of Child and Adolescent Psychiatry, 44*, 699–707.

Birmaher, B., Ryan, N. D., Williamson, D. E., Brent, D. A., Kaufman, J., Dahl, R. E., et al. (1996a). Childhood and adolescent depression: A review of the past 10 years. Part I. *Journal of the American Academy of Child and Adolescent Psychiatry, 35*, 1427–1439.

Birmaher, B., Ryan, N. D., Williamson, D. E., Brent, D. A., & Kaufman, J. (1996b). Childhood and adolescent depression: A review of the past 10 years. Part II. *Journal of the American Academy of Child and Adolescent Psychiatry, 35*, 1575–1583.

Black, S. (1997). Doing our homework on homework. *The Education Digest, 62*, 36–39.

Black, P., & William, D. (1998). Assessment and classroom learning. *Assessment in Education, 5*, 7–74.

Blackerby, J., & Wopner, M. (1996). Longitudinal postschool outcomes of youth with disabilities. Findings from the national longitudinal transition study. *Exceptional Children, 62*, 399–414.

Bland, N., & Read, T. (2000). *Policing antisocial behavior*. London: Home Office Policing and Reducing Crime Unit.

Blick, D. W., & Test, D. W. (1987). Effects of self-recording on high-school students' on

task behavior. *Learning Disability Quarterly, 10*, 203–213.

Blum, R. W. (2005). *Protective factors in the lives of youths: The evidence base*. Retrieved from World Bank HDNCY Youth Development Lecture Series at www.worldbank.org/childrenandyouth.

Bodilly, S. (1998). *Lessons from new American schools' scale-up phase: Prospects for bringing designs to multiple schools*. Santa Monica, CA: The Rand Corporation.

Bohnert, A. M., Crnic, K. A., & Lim, K. G. (2003). Emotional competence and aggressive behavior in school-age children. *Journal of Abnormal Child Psychology, 37*, 79–91.

Bondy, A., & Frost, L. (2001). The picture exchange communication system. *Behavior Modification, 25*, 725–744.

Bor, W., McGee, T. R., & Fagan, A. A. (2004). Early risk factors for adolescent antisocial behavior: An Australian longitudinal study. *Australian and New Zealand Journal of Psychiatry, 38*, 365–372.

Boss, S. (2000). Big lessons on a small scale. Retrieved 10/5/09 at http://www.nwrd.org/ mwedu/winter_00/1.html.

Bowditch, C. (1993). Getting rid of trouble makers: High school disciplining procedures and the production of dropouts. *Social Problems, 40*, 493–507.

Bowen, J. M., Jenson, W. R., & Clark, E. (2004). *School-based interventions for students with behavior problems*. New York: Kluwer Academic/Plenum Publications.

Bowlby, J. (1951). *Maternal care and mental health*. Geneva, Switzerland: World Health Organization.

Bowley, D. M., Khavandi, A., Boffard, K. D. et al. (2002). Rule out TBI? Serum markers for traumatic brain injury. *Annals of Emergency Medicine, 39*, 342–343.

Boyd, R., & Richardson, P. (1985). *Culture and the evolutionary process*. Chicago: University of Chicago Press.

Boyle, G. J., & Haines, S. (2002). Severe traumatic brain injury: Some effects on family caregivers. *Psychological Reports, 90*, 415–425.

Brenner, V., & Fox, R. A. (1998). Parental discipline and behavior problems in young children. *Journal of General Psychology, 159*, 251–256.

Bronnell, M. (2002). Musically adapted social stories to modify behaviors in students with autism: four case studies. *Journal of Music Therapy, 39*(2), 117–144.

Brooks, K., Schiraldi, V., & Ziedenberg, J. (2000). *Schoolhouse hype: Two years later*. Washington, DC: Justice Policy Center/ Children's Law Center.

Brooks, R., & Goldstein, S. (2002). Can do kids. Retrieved 12/23/09 online at http:// www.cdl.org/resource-Library/articles/can-do_kids.php.

Brophy, J. (1996). Working with shy or withdrawn students. *Eric Digest*. Retrieved 10/1/09 at http://www.ericdigests.org/1997-3/shy.html.

Brown, D. S. (2000). *Learning a living: A guide to planning your career and finding a job for people with learning disabilities: Attention-deficit disorder and dyslexia*. Bethesda, MD: Woodbine House.

Brown, L. A., & Beckett, K. S. (2007). Parent involvement in an alternative school for students at risk of educational failure. *Education and Urban Society, 39*, 498–523.

Brown, W. E., & Payne, T. (1988). Policies/ practices in public school discipline. *Academic Therapy, 23*, 297–301.

Buehler, A. (2004). *Initial perceptions of labels to initial perceptions of common humanity: A paradigm shift in the disability field. The psychology of humiliation*. Retrieved from Teachers College, Columbia University at www.humiliationstudies.org/documents/ buehlerlabels.pdf.

Bullis, M., & Walker, H. M. (1995). *Characteristics and causal factors of troubled youth*. In C. M. Nelson, B. I. Wolford, & R. B. Rutherford (Eds.) *Comprehensive and collaborative systems that work for troubled youth: A national agenda*, pp. 15–28. Richmond, KY: National Coalition for Juvenile Justice Services.

Burd, L., Kerbeshian, J., Wikenheiser, M., et al. (1986). A prevalence study of Gilles de La Tourette syndrome in North Dakota school-age children. *Journal of the American Academy of Child and Adolescent Psychiatry, 25*, 552–553.

Burden, P. R. (2003). *Classroom management: Creating a successful learning community* (2nd ed.). New York: Wiley.

Burns, B. J., Schoenwald, S. K., Burchard, J. D., Faw, L., & Santos, A. B. (2000). Comprehensive community-based interventions for youth with severe emotional disorders. Multisystemic therapy and the wraparound process. *Journal of Child and Family Studies, 9*, 283–314.

Buschbacker, P. W., & Fox, L. (2003). Understanding and intervening with the challenging behavior of young children with autism spectrum disorder. *Language, Speech, and Hearing Services in Schools, 34,* 217–227.

Bush, S. P., & Kahn, M. D. (1982). *The sibling bond.* New York: Basic Books.

Bushman, B. T., & Anderson, C. A. (2001). Media violence and the American public: Scientific facts versus media misinformation. *American Psychologist, 56,* 477–489.

Button, T., Thapar, A., & McGuffin, P. (2005). Relationship between antisocial behavior, attention deficit hyperactivity disorder, and maternal prenatal smoking. *British Journal of Psychiatry, 187,* 155–160.

Campbell, M., Armenteros, J. L., Malone, R. P., Adams, P. B., Eisenberg, Z. W., & Overall, J. E. (1997). Neuroleptic-related dyskinesias in autistic children: A prospective, longitudinal study. *Journal of the American Academy of Child and Adolescent Psychiatry, 36,* 835–843.

Campbell, M., Schopler, E., Cueva, J. E., & Hallin, A. (1996). Treatment of autistic disorder. *Journal of the American Academy of Child and Adolescent Psychiatry, 35,* 134–143.

Cangelosi, J. S. (2000). *Classroom management strategies: Gaining and maintaining student's cooperation* (4th ed.). New York: Wiley.

Carlson, G. A., & Meyer, S. E. (2000). Bipolar disorder in youth. *Current Psychiatry Report, 2,* 90–94.

Carpenter, S. L., & McKee-Higgins, B. (1996). Behavior management in inclusive classrooms. *Remedial and Special Education, 17,* 195–203.

Carr, E. G. (1994). Emerging themes in the functional analysis of problem behavior. *Journal of Applied Behavior Analysis, 27,* 393–399.

Carr, E. G. (1977). The motivation of self-injurious behavior: A review of some hypothesis. *Psychological Bulletin, 84,* 800–815.

Carr, E. G., Horner, R. H., Turnbull, A. P., Marquis, J. G., Mogito-McLaughlin, D., McAtee, M. L., et al. (1999). *Positive behavior support for people with developmental disabilities: A research synthesis.* Washington, DC: American Association of Mental Retardation.

Carr, S. C., & Punzo, R. P. (1993). The effects of self-monitoring of academic accuracy and productivity on the performance of students with behavioral disorders. *Behavior Disorders, 18,* 241–250.

Carson, R., Sitlington, P., & Frank, A. (1995). Young adulthood for individuals with behavioral disorders: What does it hold? *Behavioral Disorders, 20,* 127–135.

Carter, M. (2002). Communicative spontaneity in individuals with high support needs: An exploratory consideration of causation. *International Journal of Disability, Development, and Education, 49,* 225–242.

Carter, M. (2003). Communicative spontaneity of children with high support needs who use augmentative and alternative communication systems II: Antecedents and effectiveness of communication. *Argumentative and Alternative Communication, 19,* 155–169.

Casden, M., Morrison, G., Albanese, A. L., & Mocias, S. (2001). When homework is not home work: After school programs for homework assistance. *Educational Psychologist, 36,* 211–221.

Castellanos, F. X., Giedd, J. N., Marsh, W. L., Hamburger, S. D., Vaituzis, A. C., Dickstein, D. P., et al. (1996). Quantitative brain magnetic resonance imaging in attention-deficit-hyperactivity disorder. *Archives of General Psychiatry, 53,* 607–616.

Catalano, R. F., Berglund, M. C., Ryan, J. A., Lonezak, H. S., & Hawkins, J. D. (2004). Positive youth development in the United States: Research findings on evaluations of positive youth development programs. *Annals of the American Academy of Political and Social Science, 591,* 98–124.

Catalano, R. F., & Hawkins, J. D. (1996). The social development model: A theory of antisocial behavior. In J. D. Hawkins (Ed.), *Delinquency and crime: Current theories* (pp. 149–177). New York: Cambridge University Press.

Catalano, R. F., Loeber, R., & McKinney, K. C. (1999, October). School and community interventions to prevent serious and violent offending. *Juvenile Justice Bulletin,* 1–12.

Catroppa, C., Anderson, V. A., Morse, S. A., Haritou, F., & Rosenfeld, J. V. (2007). Children's attention skills 5 years post TBI. *Journal of Pediatric Psychology, 321,* 354–369.

Cauchon, D. (1999, April 13). Zero tolerance policies lack flexibility. *USA Today,* 1–5.

Causey, V. E., Thomas, C. D., & Armento, B. J. (2000). Cultural diversity is basically a foreign term to me: The challenges of diversity for preservice teacher education. *Teaching and Teacher Education, 16,* 33–45.

Cegelka, P., & Doorlag, D. (1995). *Personnel preparation: Relationship to job satisfaction*

(Draft Report, Working Paper #7). Paper presented at the National Dissemination Forum on Issues Relating to Special Education Teacher Satisfaction, Retention and Attrition, Washington, DC.

Center for Mental Health in Schools at UCLA. (1999). Retrieved from http://smhp.psych.ucla.edu/.

Center for Research on the Education of Students Placed at Risk. (1998). *Tools for schools.* Johns Hopkins University. Retrieved from http://www.ed.go/pubs/toolsforschools/2way.html.

Chamberlain, P., & Patterson, G. R. (1995). Discipline and child compliance. In M. H. Bornstrain (Ed.), *Handbook of parenting. Vol. 4: Applied and practical parenting* (pp. 205–223). Mahwah, NJ: Lawrence Erlbaum.

Chance, P. (1999). *Learning and behavior* (4th ed.). Pacific Grove, CA: Brooks/Cole.

Chandler, K., & Vaden-Kiernan, N. (1996). *Parents' report of school practices to involve families.* Washington, DC: U.S. Department of Education. National Center for Education Statistics.

Chandler, L. K., & Dahlquist, M. (2002). *Functional assessment: Strategies to prevent and remediate challenging behavior in school settings.* Upper Saddle River, NJ: Merrill/Pearson Education.

Chandler, L. K., Dahlquist, C. M., Repp, A. C., & Feltz, C. (1999). The effects of team-based functional assessment on the behavior of students in classroom settings. *Exceptional Children, 66,* 101–122.

Chandler, L. K., & VanLaarhoven, T. (2004). *Functional behavioral assessment.* Paper written for the Illinois Autism Project, Springfield, IL.

Chang, K., Steiner, H., Deiner, K., Adelman, N., & Kettier, T. (2003). Biological offspring: A window into bipolar disorder evolution. *Biological Psychiatry, 53,* 945–951.

Chang, K. D., Blasey, C., Ketter, T. A., & Steiner, H. (2001). Family environment of children and adolescents with bipolar parents. *Bipolar Disorders, 3,* 73–78.

Chapman, S. S., Ewing, C. B., & Mozzoni, M. P. (2005). Precise teaching and fluency training across cognitive, physical, and academic tasks in children with traumatic brain injury: A multiple baseline study. *Behavioral Interventions, 20,* 37–49.

Charney, D. S., Nestler, E. I., & Bunney, B. S. (Eds.). (2004). *Neurobiology of mental illness* (2nd ed.). New York: Oxford University Press.

Checkley, K. (2003). When homework works. *Classroom Leadership, 7*(1). Retrieved from Association for Supervision and Curriculum Development, www.ascd.org/affiliates/articles/cf200309_checkley.html.

Chen, J. Q., & Harsch, P. (2004). *Effective partnering for school change: Improving early childhood education in urban classrooms.* New York: Teachers College Press.

Chen, X., & Chandler, K. (2001). *Effects by public K–8 schools to involve parents in children's education: Do schools and parent reports agree?* (NCES2001-076). Washington, DC: U.S. Department of Education. National Center for Education Statistics. Retrieved from http://mces.ed.gov/pubresearch/mdx.asp.

Chesapeake Institute. (1994). *National agenda for achieving better results for children and youth with serious emotional disturbance.* Washington, DC: Department of Education, Office of Special Education and Rehabilitative Services, Office of Special Education Programs.

Chowdbury, U. (2004). *Tics and Tourette syndrome: A handbook for parents and professors.* New York: Jessica Kingsley.

Cicchetti, D., & Carlson, V. (Eds.). (1989). *Child maltreatment: Theory and research on the causes and consequences of child abuse and neglect.* New York: Cambridge University Press.

Cicchetti, D., & Cohen, D. (Eds.). (2006). *Developmental psychopathology: Theory and method* (2nd ed. Vol. 1). New York: Wiley.

Cicchetti, D., & Rogosch, F. A. (2002). A developmental psychopathology perspective on adolescence. *Journal of Consulting and Clinical Psychology, 70,* 6–20.

Cicchetti, D., & Toth, S. L. (1998). The development of depression in children and adolescents. *American Psychologist, 53,* 221–241.

Cicchetti, D., & Toth, S. L. (2006). A developmental psychopathology perspective on preventive interventions with high-risk children and families. In A. Renninger & I. Sigel (Eds.), *Handbook of child psychology* (6th ed.). New York: Wiley.

Cicchetti, D., & Walker, E. F. (Eds.). (2003). *Neurodevelopmental mechanisms in psychopathology.* New York: Cambridge University Press

Clark, L. (1996). *SOS! Help for parents: A practical guide for handling common everyday behavior problems* (2nd ed.). Bowling Green, KY: Parents Press.

Clarke, S., Dunlap, G., & Stichter, J. P. (2001). A descriptive analysis of intervention research in emotional and behavioral disorders from 1980 through 1999. *Behavior Modification, 6,* 355–374.

Cleveland, D. W., & Miller, N. (1977). Attitudes and life commitments of older siblings of mentally retarded adults: An exploratory study. *Mental Retardation, 15,* 38–41.

Cloninger, L. R., Van Eudewegh, P., Goate, A., Edenberg, H. J., Blangero, J., Hesselbrock, V., et al. (1998). Anxiety proneness linked to epistatic loci in genome scan of human personality traits. *American Journal of Medical Genetics, 81,* 313–317.

Cogan, B. (1996). Diagnosis and treatment of bipolar disorder in children and adolescents. *Psychiatric Times, 13,* 1–2.

Cohen, J. A., et al. (2002). Childhood traumatic grief: Concepts and controversies. *Trauma, Violence and Abuse, 3,* 307–327.

Cohen, N. J., Vallance, D. D., Barwick, M., Im, N., Menna, R., Horodezky, N. B., et al., (2000). The interface between ADHD and language impairment: An examination of language achievement and cognitive processing. *Journal of Child Psychology and Psychiatry, 41,* 353–362.

Cole, J. D., & Miller-Johnson, S. (2001). Peer factors and interventions. In R. Loeber, & D. P. Farrington (Eds.), *Serious and violent juvenile offenders: Risk factors and successful interventions* (pp. 191–209). Thousand Oaks, CA: Sage.

Coleman, M., & Vaughn, S. (2000). Reading interventions for students with emotional/behavioral disorders. *Behavioral Disorders, 25,* 93–105.

Coleman, M. C., & Webber, J. (2002). *Emotional and behavioral disorders: Theory and practice.* Boston: Allyn and Bacon.

Colvin, G. (2005). *Understanding and managing severe problem behavior.* Powerpoint presentation, University of Oregon/Behavior Associates.

Colvin, G., Kameenui, E., & Sugai, G. (1993). Reconceptualizing behavior management and school-wide discipline in general education. *Education and Treatment of Children, 16,* 361–381.

Colvin, G., Sugai, G., Good, R. H., & Lee, Y. Y. (1997). Using active supervision and precorrection to improve transition behaviors in elementary school. *School Psychology Quarterly, 12,* 344–363.

Colvin, G., Sugai, G., & Patching, B. (1993). Precorrection: An instructional approach for managing predictable problem behaviors. *Interventions in School and Clinic, 28,* 143–150.

Comer, J. P. (1998). Educating poor minority children. *Scientific American, 259,* 42–48.

Comings, D. E. (1990). *Tourette syndrome and human behavior.* Duarte, CA: Hope Press.

Comings, D. E. (2001). Clinical and molecular genetics of ADHD and Tourette syndrome: Two related polygenic disorders. *Annals of the New York Academy of Science, 931,* 50–83.

Comings, D. E., Wu, S. J., Chiu, C., Muhleman, D., & Suerd, J. (1996). Studies of the e-harvey-ras gene in psychiatric disorders. *Psychiatry Research, 63,* 25–32.

Committee for Children. (1989), *Second step: A violence-prevention curriculum, grades 1–3* (2nd ed., Teacher's Guide). Seattle, WA: Author.

Condon, K. A., & Tobin, T. J. (2001). Using electronic and other new ways to help students improve their behavior. *Teaching Exceptional Children, 34,* 44–51.

Conduct Disorder-Biological Factors: http://family.jrank.org/pages/303/Conduct-Disorder-Biological-Factors.html.

Cone, J. D. (1978). The behavior assessment grid (BAG): A conceptual framework and a taxonomy. *Behavior Therapy, 9,* 882–888.

Cone, J. D. (1988). Psychometric considerations and the multiple models of behavioral assessment. In A. S. Bellack & M. Hersen (Eds.), *Behavioral assessment: A practical handbook* (3rd ed.), pp. 42–66. Boston: Allyn and Bacon.

Conroy, M. A., & Brown, W. H. (2004). Early identification, prevention, and early intervention with young children at risk for emotional or behavioral disorders: Issues, trends, and a call for action. *Behavioral Disorders, 29,* 224–236.

Conroy, M. A., Hendrickson, J. M., & Hester, P. P. (2004). Early identification and prevention of emotional and behavioral disorders. In R. B. Rutherford, M. M. Quinn, & S. R. Mathur (Eds.), *Handbook of research in emotional and behavioral disorders* (pp. 199–215). New York: Guilford Press.

Cook, B. G., Landrum, T. J., Tankersley, M., & Kauffman, J. M. (2003). Bringing research to bear on practice: Effecting evidence-based instruction for students with emotional or behavioral disorders. *Education and Treatment of Children, 26,* 345–361.

Cook, M. N. (2003, October). Social skills training in schools. *Counseling and Human Development.* FindArticles.com. Retrieved on 10/24/09 at http:// findarticles.com/p/articles/ mi_qa9939434/is_200310/ai_n9322569/.

Cooke, B. G., Young, L. T., Mohri, L., Blake, P., & Joffe, R. T. (1999). Family of origin characteristics in bipolar disorder: A controlled study. *Canadian Journal of Psychiatry, 44,* 379–381.

Cooke, S. F., & Bliss, T. U. P. (2006). Plasticity in the human central nervous system. *Brain, 129,* 1659–1673.

Cooper, C. S., Peterson, N. L., & Meier, J. A. (1987). Variables associated with disrupted placement in a select sample of abused and neglected children. *Child Abuse and Neglect, 11,* 75–86.

Cooper, H. (1989). *Homework.* White Plains, NY: Longman.

Cooper, H. M., Lindsay, J. J., Nye, B. A., & Greathouse, S. (1998). Relationships among attitudes about homework assigned and completed and student achievement. *Journal of Educational Psychology, 90,* 70–83.

Copeland, S. R., Sutherland, K. S., & Wehby, J. H. (2000). Effect of varying rates of behavior on the on-task behavior of students with BBD. *Journal of Emotional and Behavior Disorders, 8(1),* 2–8.

Copeland, S., Sutherland, K. S., & Wehby, J. H. (2001). Catch them while you can: Monitoring and increasing the use of effective praise. *Beyond Behavior, 11,* 46–49.

Cornish, K., Kogan, C., Turk, J., Manly, T., Janes, N., Mills, A., et al. (2005). The emerging Fragile X premutation phenotype: Evidence from the domain of social cognition. *Brain and Cognition, 57,* 53–60.

Corrigan, P., River, P., Lundin, R., et al. (2001). Three strategies for changing attributions about severe mental illness. *Schizophrenia Bulletin, 27,* 187–195.

Costello, E. J. (1989). Child psychiatric disorders and their correlates: A primary care pediatric sample. *Journal of the American Academy of Child and Adolescent Psychiatry, 28,* 851–855.

Couchenour, D., & Christman, K. (2003). *Families, schools, and communities: Together for young children* (2nd ed.). Independence, KY: Delmar Learning.

Council for Exceptional Children. (1999). *IDEA 1997: Let's make it work. Preliminary analysis: The law and regulations, revised.* Reston, VA: Author.

Cox, N., Reich, T., Rice, J., Elston, R., Schober, J., & Keats, B. (1989). Segregation and linkage analysis of bipolar and major depressive illnesses in multigenerational pedigrees. *Journal of Psychiatric Research, 23,* 109–123.

Crain, W. (2000). *Theories of development* (4th ed). Upper Saddle River, NJ: Prentice Hall.

Crandell, L. E., Patrick, M. P. H., & Hobson, R. P. (2003). "Still-face" interactions between mothers with borderline personality disorder and their 2-month-old infants. *British Journal of Psychiatry, 183,* 239–247.

Crawford, D. C., Acuna, J. M., & Sherman, S. L. (2001). FMR1 and the Fragile-X syndrome: Human genome epidemiology review. *Genetic Medicine, 3,* 359–371.

Crone, D. A., & Horner, R. H. (2003). *Building positive behavior support systems in schools: Functional behavioral assessment.* New York: Guilford Press.

Crone, D. A., & Horner, R. H. (2000). Contextual, conceptual and empirical foundations of functional behavioral assessments in schools. *Exceptionality, 8,* 161–172.

Croonenberghs, J., Deboutte, D., & Maes, M. (2002). Pathophysiology of autism: Current opinions. *Acta Neuropsychiatrica, 14,* 93–102.

Cruse, H., Winiarek, M., Marshburn, J., Clark, O., & Djulbegovic, B. (2002). Quality and methods of developing practice guidelines. *Bio-Medical Central Health Services Research, 2,* 1186–1472.

Cunningham, J. A. (2000). *Curriculum terms* (Web Institute for Teachers, University of Chicago). Retrieved from http://cuip .uchicago.edu/wit2000/curriculum/home roommodules/curriculumterms/extra.htm# develop.

Curran, L. (2000, November). *The national human rights register Australian Children's Rights News, 27,* 1–32.

Curry, S. A., & Hatlen, P. H. (1988). Meeting the unique educational need of visually impaired pupils through appropriate placement. *Journal of Visual Impairment and Blindness, 82,* 417–424.

Daly, E. J. III, & Murdoch, A. (2000). Direct observation in the assessment of academic skills problems. In E. S. Shapiro &

T. R. Kratochwill (Eds.), *Behavioral assessment in schools: Theory, research, and clinical foundations* (2nd ed., pp. 46–77). New York: Guilford Press.

Daniel, B., & Wassell, S. (2002). *Adolescence: Assessing and promoting resilience in vulnerable children, III.* London: Jessica Kingsley.

D'Arcy, F., Flynn, J., McCarthy, Y., O'Connor, C., & Tierney, E. (2005). Sibshops. *Journal of Intellectual Disabilities, 9,* 43–57.

Darling-Hammond, L., Chung, R., & Frelow, F. (2002). Variation in teacher preparation. *Journal of Teacher Education, 53,* 286–302.

Davis, D. (1991). Schools reaching out: Family, school and community partnerships for student success. *Phi Delta Kappan, 72(5),* 376–382.

Davis, D. (2000). *Supporting parent, family and community involvement in your school.* Portland, OR: Northwest Regional Educational Laboratory.

Davis, G., Governor. (1999). *Family school partnerships: Overview of the issues.* State of the State Address, (California), January 7, 1999.

Dawson, G., & Fernald, M. (1987). Perspective-taking ability and its relationship to the social behavior of autistic children. *Journal of Autism and Developmental Disorders, 17,* 487–498.

DeBoard, K., Bower, D., Goddard, H. W., Wilkins, J. K., Kobbe, A., Meyers-Walls, J. A., Mulroy, M., & Ozretich, R. (2006). A professional guide for parenting educators: The national extension parenting educators' framework. *Journal of Extension, 44(3).* Retrieved from http://www.joe.org/ joe/2006june/a8.shtml.

Deitz, T. L. (2000). Disciplining children: Characteristics associated with the use of corporal punishment. *Child Abuse and Neglect, 24,* 1529–1542.

Dekovic, M. (1999). Risk and protective factors in the development of problem behavior during adolescence. *Journal of Youth and Adolescence, 28,* 667–685.

DelBello, M. P., & Geller, B. (2001). Review of studies of child and adolescent offspring of bipolar parents. *Bipolar Disorders, 3,* 325–334.

Dempsey, I., & Foreman, P. (2001). A review of educational approaches for individuals with autism. *International Journal of Disability Development and Education, 48,* 103–116.

Deno, S. L., Foegen, A., Robinson, S., & Espin, C. (1996). Commentary: Facing the realities of inclusion for students with mild disabilities. *Journal of Special Education, 30,* 345–357.

Desimone, L. (1999). Linking parent involvement with student achievement: Do race and income matter? *Journal of Educational Research, 93,* 11–30.

Deslandes, R., Royer, E., Turcotte, D., & Bertrand, R. (1997). School achievement at the secondary level: Influence of parenting style and parent involvement in schooling. *McGill Journal of Education, 32,* 191–207.

Dew-Hughes, D. (2004). *Educating children with Fragile-X syndrome.* New York: Falmer Press.

Diamond, A. (1990). Rate of maturation of the hippocampus and the developmental progression of children's performance on the delayed non-matching to sample and visual paired comparison tasks. *Annals of the New York Academy of Science, 608,* 394–426.

Dilling, H. (2000). Classification. In M. G. Gelder, J. J. Lopez-Ibor, & N. C. Andreasen (Eds.), *New Oxford textbook of psychiatry* (pp. 109–133). Oxford, England: Oxford University Press.

Dingerson, L. (2001). Working with indicators on your school report card. Retrieved from Center for Community Change at http://www.communitychange.org.

Dishion, T. J., & Patterson, S. G. (1996). *Preventive parenting with love, encouragement, and limits: The pre-school years.* Eugene, OR: Castalia.

Dixon, M. R., & Cummings, A. (2001). Self-control in children with autism: Response allocation during delays to reinforcement. *Journal of Applied Behavior Analysis, 34,* 491–495.

Dodge, K. (1993). Social cognitive mechanisms in the development of conduct disorder and depression. In J. W. Santrock (Ed.), *Adolescence* (p. 7). Boston: McGraw-Hill.

Domino, M. L., & Domino, G. (2006). *Psychological testing: An introduction.* Cambridge, England: Cambridge University Press.

Dowd, T., & Tierney, J. (2005). *Teaching social skills to youth* (2nd ed.). Boys Town, New England: Boys Town Press.

Doyle, J. (2005). Children's mental health services, EMQ children and family services. Paper presented at the Women in Government Conference. Campbell, CA.

Drabick, D. A. G., Strassberg, Z., & Kees, M. R. (2001). Measuring qualitative aspects of preschool boys' noncompliance: The response style questionnaire. *Journal of Abnormal Child Psychology, 29,* 129–139.

Drew, C., & Hardman, M. (2004). *Mental retardation: A lifespan approach to people with disabilities* (8th ed.). Upper Saddle River, NJ: Merrill/Pearson Education.

Dube, W. V., McIlvane, W. J., Mazzitelli, K., & McNamara, B. (2003). Reinforcer rate effects and behavioral momentum in individuals with developmental disabilities. *American Journal of Mental Retardation, 108,* 134–143.

Duffy, M. L., & Forgan, J. (2005). *Mentoring new special education teachers.* Thousand Oaks, CA: Corwin Press.

Dunn, L. (2004). Validation of the CHORES: A measure of school-age children's participation in household tasks. *Scandinavian Journal of Occupational Therapy, 11,* 179–190.

Dunn, N. (1999). *The Sensory Profile Manual.* The Psychological Corporation, San Antonio.

Dunst, C. J., Trivette, C., & Jordy, W. (1997). Influences of social support on children with disabilities and their families. In M. Guralnick (Ed.), *The effectiveness of early intervention* (pp. 499–522). Baltimore, MD: Brookes.

DuPaul, G. J., & Stoner, G. (1994). *ADHD in the schools: Assessment and intervention strategies.* New York: Guilford Press.

DuPaul, G. J., & Stoner, G. (2002). Interventions for attention problems. In M. Shinn, H. M. Walker, & G. Stoner (Eds.), *Interventions for academic and behavioral problems II: Preventive and remedial approaches* (pp. 913–938). Bethesda, MD: NASSP.

DuPaul, G., & Stoner, G. (2003). *ADHD in the schools: Assessment and intervention strategies.* New York: Guilford Press.

DuPaul, G. J. (1991). Parent and teacher ratings of ADHD symptoms: Psychometric properties in a community-based sample. *Journal of Clinical Child Psychology, 20,* 245–253.

Durand, V. M., & Crimmins, D. B. (1988). Identifying the variables maintaining self-injurious behavior. *Journal of Autism and Developmental Disorders, 18,* 99–117.

Durrant, J. E. (1999). Evaluating the success of Sweden's corporal punishment ban. *Child Abuse and Neglect, 23,* 435–448.

Easton, V. J., & McColl, J. H. (1997). *Statistics glossary.* Retrieved on 10/24/09 from http://www.stats.gla.ac.uk/steps/glossary/confidence_intervals.html.

Eber, L. (2001). *School-based wrap around and its connection to positive behavior interventions and supports: A component of safe/effective schools for all students.* Paper presented at the annual meeting of the National Association of School Psychologists, Washington, DC.

Eber, L. (2003). *The art and science of wraparound: Completing the continuum of school wide behavioral support.* Bloomington: Forum on Education at Indiana University.

Eber, L., & Nelson, C. M. (1997). Integrating services for students with emotional and behavioral needs through school-based wraparound planning. *American Journal of Orthopsychiatry, 67,* 385–395.

Eber, L., Nelson, C. M., & Miles, P. (1997). School-based wraparound for students with emotional and behavioral challenges. *Exceptional Children, 63,* 539–555.

Eccles, J. S., & Howard, R. D. (1996). Family involvement in childrens' and adolescents' schooling. In A. Bootz & J. F. Dunn (Eds.), *Family-school links* (pp. 3–34). Mahwah, NJ: Lawrence Erlbaum.

Eddy, J. M. (2003). *Conduct disorders: The latest assessment and treatment strategies.* Kansas City, MO: Compact Clinicals.

Edgar, R., Levine, P., & Maddox, M. (1986). *Statewide follow-up studies of secondary special education in transition* (Working paper of the Networking and Evaluation Teams). Seattle, WA: University of Washington.

Education for All Handicapped Children Act (1975). From Public Law 94-142 (5,6). Retrieved from http://asclepius.com/angel/special.html.

Ehlers, S., & Gillberg, C. (1993). The epidemiology of Asperger syndrome: A total population study. *Journal of Child Psychology and Psychiatry, 34,* 1327–1356.

Ehrensaft, M. K., Cohen, P., Brown, J., Smailes, E., Chen, H., & Johnson, J. C. (2003). Intergenerational transmission of partner violence: A 20-year prospective study. *Journal of Consulting and Clinical Psychology, 71,* 741–753.

Ekstrom, R. B., Goertz, M. E., Pollack, J. M., & Rock, D. A. (1986). Who drops out of high school and why? Findings from a national study. *Teachers College Record, 87,* 357–373.

Elgar, F. J., Knight, J., Worrall, G. J., & Sherman, G. (2003). Attachment characteristics and behavioral problems in rural and urban juvenile delinquents. *Child Psychiatry and Human Development, 34,* 25–47.

Elliott, D., Hatot, N. J., Sirovatka, P., & Potter, B. B. (2001). *Youth violence: A report of the surgeon general.* Washington, DC: U.S. Office of the Surgeon General.

Emmer, E. T., & Stough, L. M. (2001). Classroom management: A critical part of educational psychology with implications for teacher education. *Educational Psychologist, 36,* 103–112.

Emmons, P. G., & Anderson, L. M. (2005). *Understanding sensory dysfunction in learning, development and sensory dysfunction in autism spectrum disorders, ADHD, learning disabilities and bipolar disorder.* London: Jessica Kingsley.

Engel, G. L. (1977). The need for a new medical model. *Science, 196,* 129–138.

Engleman, S., Becker, W., Carnine, D., & Gresten, R. (1988). The direct instruction follow-through model: Designs and outcomes. *Education and Treatment of Students, 11,* 303–317.

Engleman, S., & Brunner, E. (1995). *Reading Mastery.* Worthington, OH: McGraw Hill.

Engleman, S., & Carnine, D. (1991). *Theory of instruction: Principles and applications* (rev. ed.). Eugene, OR: ADI Press.

Epstein, H. (1986). Stages in human brain development. *Brain Research, 395,* 114–119.

Epstein, H. T., & Epstein, E. B. (1978). The relationship between brain weight and head circumference from birth to age 18 years. *American Journal of Physical Anthropology, 48,* 471–473.

Epstein, J. L. (1995). School/family/community partnerships: Caring for the children we share. *Phi Delta Kappan, 76,* 703.

Epstein, J. L. (2001). *School, family and community partnerships: Preparing educators and improving schools.* Boulder, CO: Westview Press.

Epstein, J. L., & Jansorn, N. R. (2004). Developing successful partnership programs: Principal leadership makes a difference. *Principal, 8,* 10–15.

Epstein, J. L., Sanders, M. G., Simon, B. S., Salinas, K. C., Jansorn, N. R., & VanVoorhis, F. L. (2002). *School, family and community partnerships: Your handbook for action* (2nd ed.). Thousand Oaks: Corwin Press.

Epstein, J. L., & Sheldon, S. B. (2006). Moving forward: Ideas for research on school, family and community partnerships. In C. F. Conrad & R. Serlin (Eds.), *SAGE handbook for research in education: Engaging ideas and enriching inquiry* (pp. 117–137). Thousand Oaks, CA: Sage.

Epstein, J. L., & Van Voorhis, F. L. (2001). More than minutes: Teachers' roles in designing homework. *Educational Psychologist, 36,* 181–193.

Epstein, M. H., Polloway, E. A., Foley, R. M., & Patton, J. R. (1990). Comparison of performance on academic probes by students with mild retardation, learning disabilities and behavior disorders. *Special Services in the Schools, 6,* 121–134.

Erchul, W. P., & Martens, B. K. (2002). *School consultation: Conceptual and empirical bases of practice* (2nd ed.). New York: Kluwer Academic/Plenum Publications.

Erikson, E. H. (1968). *Identity, youth and crisis.* New York: Norton.

Euggenheim, M. A. (2004). Familial Tourette syndrome. *Annals of Neurology, 5,* 104.

Evans, A. C. (2006). The NIH MRI study of normal brain development. *Neuroimage, 30,* 184–202.

Evans, E. D., & Richardson, R. C. (1995). Corporal punishment: What teachers should know. *Teaching Exceptional Children, 27,* 33–36.

Ewell, P. T. (2001). *Accreditation and student outcomes: A proposed point of departure.* Washington, DC: Council on Higher Education Accreditation (CHEA).

Ewen, D., & Neas, K. B. (2005). *Preparing for success: How Head Start helps children with disabilities and their families.* Washington, DC: Center for Law and Social Policy.

Ewing-Cobbs, L., Barnes, M. A., & Fletcher, J. M. (2003). Early brain injury in children: Development and recognition of cognitive function. *Developmental Neuropsychology, 24,* 669–704.

Ewing-Cobbs, L., Kramer, L., Prasad, M., Canales, D. N., Louis, P. T., Fletcher, J. M., et al. (1998). Neuroimaging, physical, and developmental findings after inflicted and noninflicted traumatic brain injury in young children. *Pediatrics, 102,* 300–307.

Exkorn, K. S. (2005). *The autism source book.* New York: HarperCollins.

F-Foldi, R. (2004). Importance of neuropsychological assessment in diagnostics of learning disabilities and behavioral disorders. *Hungarian Psychological Review, 59,* 19–40.

Fahey, J. C. (2006). Developmental changes in attention performance and their relationship to behavior and school problems. Retrieved from http://idea.library.drexel .edu/dspace/handle/860/872.

Fan, X. T., & Chen, M. (2001). Parental involvement and students' academic achievement: A meta-analysis. *Educational Psychology Review, 130,* 1–22.

Faraone, S. V., Biederman, J., Wozniak, J., Mundy, E., Mennin, D., & O'Donnell, D. (1997). Is comorbidity with ADHD a marker for juvenile-onset mania? *Journal of the American Academy of Child and Adolescent Psychiatry, 36,* 1046–1055.

Farber, B. (1960). Family organization and crisis: Maintenance of integration in families with a severely mentally retarded child. *Monographs of the Society for Research in Child Development, 25,* (1, Serial #75), 1–523.

Farrell, E. F. (2004). Asperger's confounds colleges. *Chronicle of Higher Education. 51*(7), A35.

Farmer, R. F., & Nelson-Gray, R. O. (2005). *Personality guided behavior therapy.* Washington, DC: American Psychological Association.

Fee, V. E., Holloway, K. S., & Seay, H. A. (2003). Multicomponent treatment package to increase anger control in teacher referred boys. *Child and Family Behavior Therapy, 25,* 1–18.

Feinstein, S. (2003). School wide positive behavior supports. *Journal of Correctional Education, 54,* 163–174.

Feldman, R. A., Caplinger, T. E., & Wodarski, J. S. (1983). *The St. Louis conundrum: The effective treatment of antisocial youths.* Upper Saddle River, NJ: Prentice Hall.

Fergus, S., & Zimmerman, M. A. (2005). Adolescence resilience: A framework for understanding healthy development in face of risk. *Annual Review of Public Health, 26,* 399–419.

Ferrer, M., Fugate, A., & Rivera, I. (2007). *Working with school-age children, part 1: Preventing misbehavior.* Gainesville: University of Florida IFAS Extension.

Feuer, M. J., Towne, L., & Shavelson, R. J. (2002). Scientific culture and educational research. *Educational Research, 31*(8), 4–14.

Filcheck, H. A., Greco, L. A., & Herchell, A. D. (2002). Who's testing whom? Ten suggestions for managing the disruptive behavior of young children during testing. *Intervention in School and Clinic, 37,* 140–148.

Filer, J., & Mahoney, G. (1996). Collaboration between families and early intervention service providers. *Infants and Young Children, 9,* 22–30.

Fisher, S. E., Francks, C., McCracken, J. T. et al. (2002). A genome-wide scan for loci involved in attention-deficit/hyperactivity disorder. *American Journal Human Genetics, 70,* 1183–1196.

Fitzgerald, G., Hollingsead, C., Koury, K., & Miller, K. (2003). *Implementation of case-based instruction in multiple contexts: Process, outcomes, and transfer of knowledge and skills* (Project #H327A030072). Washington, DC: U.S. Department of Education.

Fitzgerald, G., & Semrau, L. (1993–1997). *An interactive video disc program to enhance teacher problem-solving skills for behavior disorders* (Project #H029K36210). Washington, DC: U.S. Department of Education.

Fitzgerald, G., & Semrau, L. (1998–2000). *Virtual resource center in behavior disorders* (Project #H029K70089). Washington, DC: U.S. Department of Education.

Flick, G. L. (1996). *Power parenting for children with ADD/ADHD: A practical parents' guide for managing difficult behaviors.* San Francisco, CA: Jossey-Bass.

Flick, G. L. (1998a). 24 ways to manage ADHD in the classroom without medication. *Researching Today's Youth, 2,* 37–40.

Flick, G. L. (1998b). *ADD/ADHD behavior change resource kit.* San Francisco: Jossey-Bass.

Flick, G. L. (1999). *Managing difficult behavior in the classroom: A pocket guide for teachers.* Biloxi, MS: Seacoast Publications.

Flick, G. L. (2000). *How to reach and teach teenagers with ADHD: A step-by-step guide to overcoming difficult behaviors at school and at home.* San Francisco: Jossey-Bass.

Flick, G. L. (2001). *Homework skills improvement kit: A training program to help children with ADD/ADHD.* Biloxi, MS: Seacoast Publications.

Flick, G. L. (2002). Controversies in ADHD: Fundamental questions being answered slowly, but scientifically. *Advance for Nurse Practitioners, 10,* 34–36.

Foglianni, C., Chaumoitre, K., Chapon F. et al. (2005). Assessment of certical maturation with prenatal MRI. Part I: Normal certical maturation. *European Radiology, 15,* 1671–1685.

Fombonne, E. (1999). The epidemiology of autism: A review. *Psychological Medicine, 29,* 769–786.

Fore, III, C., Martin, C., & Bender, W. N. (2002). Teacher burnout in special education: The causes and recommended solutions. *High School Journal, 86,* 36–44.

Forehand, R., & Wierson, M. (1993). The role of developmental factors in planning interventions for children: Disruptive behavior as an example. *Behavior Therapy, 24,* 117–141.

Forehand, R. L., & McMahon, R. J. (1981). *Helping the noncompliant child: A clinician's guide to parenting.* New York: Guilford Press.

Forgath, M. S., & Patterson, G. R. (1998). Behavioral family therapy. In F. M. Dattelo (Ed.), *Case studies in couple and family therapy: Systematic and cognitive perspectives* (pp. 85–107). New York: Guilford Press.

Forsterling, F. & Binser, M. J. (2002). Depression, school performance, and the verdicality of perceived grades and causal attributions. *Personality and Social Psychology Bulletin, 28,* 1441–1449.

Fowle, C. (1973). The effect of a severely mentally retarded child on his family. *American Journal of Mental Deficiency, 73,* 468–473.

Fox, C. L., & Boulton, M. T. (2005). The social skills problems of victims of bullying: Self, peer, and teacher perceptions. *British Journal of Educational Psychology, 75,* 313–328.

Fox, J. J., & Gable, R. A. (2004). Functional behavioral assessment. In R. B. Rutherford, M. M. Quinn, & S. R. Mathur (Eds.). *Handbook of research in emotional and behavioral disorders* (pp. 143–162). New York: Guilford Press.

Fox, J. J., & McEvoy, M. A. (1993). Assessing and enhancing generalization and social validity of social skills interventions with children and adolescents. *Behavior Modification, 17,* 339–366.

Frankel, F., & Feinberg, D. (2002). Social problems associated with ADHD vs. ODD in children referred for friendship problems. *Child Psychiatry and Human Development, 33,* 125–146.

Franz, J., Miles, P., & Brown, N. (2003). *Taming the wrap around gremlins.* Retrieved on 10/29/2009 from www.paperboat.com/calliope/greml.html.

Fraser, M., Richman, J., & Galinsky, M. (1999). Risk, protection and resilience: Toward a conceptual framework for social work practice. *Social Work Research, 23,* 131–143.

Frasure-Smith, N., Lesperance, F., Gravel, G., Masson, A., Janeau, M., Talajic, M., et al. (2000). Social support, depression, and mortality during the first year after myocardial infarction. *Circulation, 101,* 1919–1924.

Freedman, R., Coon, H., Myles-Worsley, M., et al. (1997). Linkage of a neurophysiological deficit in schizophrenia to a chromosome 15 locus. *Proceeding of the National Academy of Sciences USA, 94,* 587–592.

Freeman, R., Eber, L., Anderson, C., Irvin, L., Horner, R., Bounds, M., et al. (2006). Building inclusive school cultures using school-wide positive behavior support: Designing effective individual support systems for students with significant disabilities. *Research and Practice for Persons with Severe Disabilities, 31,* 4–17.

Freud, S. (1949). *An outline of psychoanalysis.* New York: Norton.

Frey, K. S., Hirschstein, M. K., & Guzzo, B. H. (2000). Second step: Preventing aggression by promoting social competence. *Journal of Emotional and Behavioral Disorders, 6,* 66–80.

Friedman, M. J. (2004). Acknowledging the psychiatric cost of war. *New England Journal of Medicine, 351,* 75–77.

Fuchs, L. S. (2004). The past, present, and future of curriculum-based measurement research. *School Psychology Review, 33,* 188–192.

Gaddes, W. A. & Edgell, D. (1994). *Learning disabilities and brain function: A neuropsychological approach* (3rd ed.). New York: Springer-Verlag.

Garbarino, J. (1992). *Children and families in the social environment.* Piscataway, NJ: Transaction Publishers.

Garber, J., & Hillsman, R. (1992) Cognition, stress, and depression in children and adolescents. *Child and Adolescent Psychiatric Clinics of North America, 1,* 129–167.

Gardner, W. I., Cole, C. L., Davidson, D. P., & Karan, O. C. (1986). Reducing aggression in individuals with developmental disabilities: An expanded stimulus control, assessment, and intervention models. *Education and Training of the Mentally Retarded, 21,* 3–10.

Garland, A. E., Hough, R. L., McCabe, K. N., Yeh, M., Wood, P. A., & Aarons, G. A.

(2001). Prevalence of psychiatric disorders in youth across five sectors of care. *Journal of the American Academy of Child and Adolescent Psychiatry, 40,* 409–448.

Garmon, M. A. (2005). Six key factors for changing preservice teachers' attitudes/beliefs about diversity. *Educational Studies: A Journal of the American Education Studies Association, 38,* 275–286.

Garrison, C. Z., Waller, J. L., Cuffee, S. P., McKeown, R. E., Addy, C. L., & Jackson, K. L. (1997). Incidence of major depressive disorder and dysthymia in young adolescents. *Journal of the American Academy of Child and Adolescent Psychiatry, 36,* 438–465.

Gbadamosi, T., & Lin, H. L. (2003). Parent's interests, current involvement and level of parental involvement in school activities. ERIC #ED482552.

Geffner, D. (2006). Language and auditory processing problems in ADHD. *ADHD Report, 14,* 1–6.

Geller, B., Cooper, T. B., Sun, K., et al. (1998). Double-blind and placebo controlled study of lithium for adolescent bipolar disorders with secondary substance dependency. *Journal of the American Academy of Child and Adolescent Psychiatry, 37,* 171–178

Geller, B., & Luby, J. (1997). Child and adolescent bipolar disorder: A review of the past 10 years. *Journal of the American Academy of Child and Adolescent Psychiatry, 36,* 1168–1176.

Geller, B., Sun, K., Zimmerman, B., Luby, J., Frazier, J., & Williams, M. (1995). Complex and rapid cycling in bipolar children and adolescents: A preliminary study. *Journal of Affective Disorders, 34,* 259–268.

Geller, B., Zimmerman, B., Williams, M., et al. (2000). Diagnostic characteristics of 93 cases of a prepubertal and early adolescent bipolar disorder phenotype by gender, puberty and comorbid attention deficit hyperactivity disorder. *Journal of Child and Adolescent Psychopharmacology, 10,* 157–164.

Gershoff, E. T. (2002). Parental corporal punishment and associated child behaviors and experiences: A meta-analytic and theoretical review. *Psychological Bulletin, 128,* 539–579.

Gettinger, M., & Seibert, J. K. (2002). Best practices in increasing academic learning time. In A. Thomas (Ed.), *Best practices in school psychology IV* (4th ed., Vol. 4,

pp. 773–787). Bethesda, MD: National Association of School Psychologists.

Ghaemi, S. N. (2003). *Mood disorders: A practical guide.* Hagerstown, MD: Williams and Wilkins.

Ghezzi, P. (2006, March 20). Zero tolerance for zero tolerance. *Atlanta Constitution,* March 20, 2006.

Giedd, J. N. (2001). Bipolar disorder and ADHD in children and adolescents. *Journal of Attention Disorders, 5,* 56.

Gilberts, G. H. (2000). *The effects of peer delivered self-monitoring strategies on the participation of students with disabilities in general education classrooms.* Paper presented at Capitalization on leadership in rural special education: Making a difference for children and families. Alexandria, VA.

Gillberg, C. (1993). Autism and related behaviors. *Journal of Intellectual Disability Research, 37,* 343–372.

Gillberg, C., & Billstedt, E. (2000). Autism and Asperger syndrome: Co-existence with other clinical disorders. *Acta Psychiatrica Scandinavica, 102,* 321–330.

Gillot, A., Furniss, F., & Walter, A. (2001). Anxiety in high-functioning children with autism. *Autism, 5,* 277–286.

Glasser, W. (1992). *The quality school.* New York: HarperCollins.

Goldenthal, P. (2000). *Beyond sibling rivalry: How to help your child become cooperative, caring, and compassionate.* New York: Holt.

Goldfried, M. R., & Kent, R. N. (1972). Traditional versus behavioral personality assessment: A comparison of methodological and theoretical assumptions. *Psychological Bulletin, 77,* 409–420.

Goldstein, A. P. (1988). *The prepare curriculum: Teaching pro-social competencies.* Chicago: Research Press.

Goldstein, H. (2002). Communication intervention for children with autism: A review of treatment efficacy. *Journal of Autism and Developmental Disorders, 32,* 373–396.

Goldstein, H., Arkell, C., Ashcroft, S. C., Hurley, O. L., & Lilly, S. M. (1975). Schools. In N. Hobbs (Ed.). *Issues in the classification of children* (pp. 4–61). San Francisco: Jossey-Bass.

Golly, A., Stiller, B., & Walker, H. M. (1998). Replication and social validation of an early intervention program. *Journal of Emotional and Behavioral Disorders, 6,* 243–250.

Gomez, B. J., & Ang, P. M. (2007). Promoting positive youth development in schools. *Theory into Practice, 46,* 97–104.

Good, T. L., & Brophy, J. (2008). *Looking in classrooms* (10th ed.). Boston: Allyn and Bacon/Pearson Education.

Goodman, E. (2000, January 4). Zero tolerance means zero chance for troubled kids. *Centre Daily Times,* p. 8.

Gootman, M. (2001). *The caring teacher's guide to discipline: Helping young students learn self-control, responsibility, and respect.* San Francisco: Corwin Press.

Grant, B. F., et al. (2002). Childhood traumatic grief: Concepts and controversies. *Trauma, Violence, and Abuse, 3,* 307–327.

Gray, C. (1994). *The new social story book.* Arlington, TX: Future Horizons.

Gray, C. (2002). *Social Stories 10.0.* Arlington, TX: Future Horizons.

Gray, C., & Garland, J. (1993). Social stories: Improving responses of students with autism with accurate social information. *Focus on Autism, 8,* 1–13.

Gray, S. (2001). *A compilation of state mandates for home school partnership education in pre-service teacher training programs.* Unpublished paper, Pepperdine University, Culver City, CA.

Green, C. W., Reid, D. H., White, L. K., Halford, R. C., Brittain, D. P., & Gardner, S. M. (1988). Identifying reinforcers for persons with profound handicaps: Staff opinion versus systematic assessment of preferences. *Journal of Applied Behavior Analysis, 21,* 31–43.

Greenbaum, P., Dedrick, R., Friedman, R., Kutash, K., Brown, E., Lardierh, S., et al. (1996). National Adolescent and Child Treatment Study (NACTS). Outcomes for children with serious emotional and behavioral disturbance. *Journal of Emotional and Behavioral Disorders, 4,* 130–146.

Gregg, S. (1996). *Preventing antisocial behavior in disabled and at-risk students* (AEL Policy Briefs). Charleston, WV: Appalachia Educational Laboratory.

Gresham, F. M. (1998). Designs for evaluating behavior change: Conceptual principles of simple case methodology. In T. S. Watson & F. M. Gresham (Eds.), *Handbook of child behavior therapy* (pp. 23–40). New York: Plenum Press.

Gresham, F. M. (2004). Current status and future directions of school-based behavioral interventions. *School Psychology Review, 33,* 326–343.

Gresham, F. M., & Elliott, S. N. (1984). Assessment and classification of children's social skills: A review of methods and issues. *School Psychology Review*, *13*, 292–301.

Gresham, F. M., & Gansle, K. A. (1992). Misguided assumptions of DSM III-R: Implications for school psychological practice. *School Psychology Quarterly*, *72*, 79–95.

Gresham, F. M., & Lopez, M. F. (1996). Social validation: A unifying concept for school-based consultation research and practice. *School Psychology Quarterly*, *11*, 204–227.

Groark, C. J., Mehaffie, K. E., McCall, R. B., Greenbey, M. T., & the University Children's Policy Collaborative. (2002). *From science to policy: Research on issues, programs and policies in early care and education* (pp. 87–98). Pittsburgh, PA: University Children's Policy Collaborative Executive Summary in Early Care and Education: Pennsylvania, Governor's Task Forum on Early Childhood Care and Education.

Grossman, D. C., Neckerman, H. J., Koepsell, L., Liu, P., Asher, K. N., Beland, K., Frey, K., et al. (1997). Effectiveness of a violence prevention curriculum among children in elementary school. *Journal of the American Medical Association*, *277*, 1605–1611.

Grossman, F. K. (1972). *Brothers and sisters of retarded children: An exploratory study*. New York: Syracuse University Press.

Guidry, J., & Kent, T. A. (1999). New genetic hypothesis of schizophrenia. *Medical Hypothesis*, *52*, 69–75.

Gunter, P. L., Coutinho, M. J., & Cade, T. (2002). Classroom factors linked with academic gains among students with emotional and behavioral problems. *Preventing School Failure*, *46*, 126–132.

Guskey, T. R. (2002). Does it make a difference? Evaluating professional development. *Educational Leadership*, *59*, 45–51.

Guthrie, J. T., Schafer, W., Wang, Y. Y., & Afflerbach, P. (1995). Relationships of instruction to the amount of reading: An exploration of social, cognitive, and instructional connections. *Reading Research Quarterly*, *30*, 8–25.

Haas, S. M. (2000). *High school aggression: A social learning analysis*. Unpublished doctoral dissertation, University of Cincinnati.

Hagiwara, T., & Myles, B. (1999). A multimedia social story intervention: Teaching skills to children with autism. *Focus on Autism and Other Developmental Disabilities*, *14*, 82–95.

Hale, E., & Moorman, H. (2003). *Preparing school leaders*. Washington, DC, and

Edwardsville, IL: Institute for Educational Leadership and the Illinois Education Research Council.

Halgin, R. P., & Whitbourne, S. K. (2006). *Abnormal psychology with Mindmap II*. CD-ROM and Power Web. New York: McGraw-Hill.

Hall, T., & Steglia, A. (2003). *Peer Mediated Instruction and Intervention*. Wakefield, MA. National Center on Assessing the General Curriculum retrieved on 6/11/09 from http://www.cataloguepublication/NCAE/NCAC_peer.

Hallahan, D. P., & Kauffman, J. M. (2003). *Exceptional learners: Introduction to special education* (9th ed.). Boston: Allyn and Bacon.

Hamre, B. K., & Pianta, R. C. (2001). Early teacher-child relationships and the trajectory of children's school outcomes through eighth grade. *Child Development*, *72*, 625–638.

Hanlon, T. E., Bateman, R. W., Simon, B. D. O'Grady, K. E., & Carswell, S. B. (2004). Antecedents and correlates of deviant activity in urban youth manifesting behavioral problems. *Journal of Primary Prevention*, *24*, 285–309.

Hansen, C., Weiss, D., & Last, C. G. (1999). ADHD boys in young adulthood: Psychosocial adjustment. *Journal of the American Academy of Child and Adolescent Psychiatry*, *38*, 165–170.

Hanson, M. (1996). Self-management through self-monitoring. In K. Jones & T. Charlton (Eds.), *Overcoming learning and behavior difficulties* (pp. 173–191). London: Routledge, Partnership with Pupils.

Harman, P., Egelson, P., Hood, A., & O'Donnell, D. (2004). Observing life in small-class size classrooms. *International Journal of Educational Policy Research and Practice*, *4*, 111–122.

Harris, K., et al. (1986). *The ICD survey of disabled Americans: Bringing disabled Americans into the mainstream*. New York: Author.

Harry, B. (2002). Trends and issues in serving culturally diverse families of children with disabilities. *Journal of Special Education*, *36*, 131–138.

Hasazi, S., Gordon, L., & Roe, C. (1985). Factors associated with the employment status of handicapped youth exiting high school from 1979–1983. *Exceptional Children*, *51*, 455–469.

Hausman, A., Pierce, G., & Briggs, L. (1996). Evolution of comprehensive violence

prevention education: Effects on student behavior. *Journal of Adolescent Health*, *19*, 104–110.

Hawley, C. A., Ward, A. B., Magnay, A. R., & Long, J. (2004). Outcomes following childhood head injury: A population study. *Journal of Neurosurgery and Psychiatry*, *15*, 737–742.

Henderson, H. T., & Mapp, K. L. (2002). *A new wave of evidence: The impact of school, family and community connections on student achievement*. Austin, TX: Southwest Educational Laboratory.

Herndon, R. W., & Iacono, W. G. (2005). Psychiatric disorders in the children of antisocial parents. *Psychological Medicine*, *35*, 1815–1824.

Herr, E. L., Cramer, S. A., & Niles, S. G. (2004). *Career guidance and counseling through the lifespan* (6th ed.). Upper Saddle River, NJ: Pearson Education.

Hersen, M. (2005). *Encyclopedia of Behavior Modification and Cognitive Behavior Therapy*. New York: Sage.

Hessel, D., Dyer-Friedman, J., Glaser, B., Wisbeck, J., Barajas, R. G., Taylor, A., & Reiss, A. L. (2001). The influence of environmental and genetic factors in behavior problems and autistic symptoms in boys and girls with Fragile-X syndrome. *Pediatrics*, *108*, E88.

Heward, W. L. (2003). Ten faulty notions about teaching and learning that hinder the effectiveness of special education. *Journal of Special Education*, *36*, 186–205.

Hewett, F. M. (1967). Educational engineering with emotionally disturbed children. *Exceptional Children*, *33*, 450–457.

Hiatt-Michael, D. (Ed.). (2001). *Promising practices for family involvement in school*. Greenwich, CT: Information Age Publishing.

Hieneman, M., Dunlap, G., & Kincaid, D. (2005). Positive support strategies for students with behavioral disorders in general education settings. *Psychology in the Schools*, *42*, 779–794.

Hill, K. G., White, H. R., Chung, I., Hawkins, J. D., & Catalano, R. F. (2000). Early adult outcomes of adolescent binge drinking: Person- and variable-centered analyses of binge drinking trajectories. *Alcoholism: Clinical and Experimental Research*, *24*, 892–901.

Hill, S. Y., Locke, J., Lowers, L., & Connolly, J. (1999). Psychopathology and achievement in children at high risk for developing alcoholism. *Journal of the American Academy of Child and Adolescent Psychiatry*, 38, 883–891.

Hobbs, N. (1975). *The futures of children: Categories, labels, and their consequences.* (ERIC Document Reproduction Service No. BD115069).

Hodapp, R. M., Glidden, L. M., & Kaiser, A. P. (2005). Siblings of persons with disabilities: Toward a research agenda. *Mental Retardation*, 43, 334–338.

Hojnoski, R. L., Morrison, R., Brown, M., & Matthews, W. J. (2006). Performance-based assessment in schools. *Journal of Psychoeducational Assessment*, 24, 145–159.

Holas, E. (2002). Symbolism and social phenomena: Toward the integration of past and current theoretical approaches. *European Journal of Social Theory*, 5, 351–366.

Holcutt, A. (1996). Effectiveness of special education: Is placement the critical factor? *Special Education for Students with Disabilities*, 6, 77–102.

Holmes, S. E., Slaughter, J. R., & Kashani, T. (2001). Risk factors in childhood that lead to the development of conduct disorder and antisocial personality disorder. *Child Psychiatry and Human Development*, 31, 183–193.

Hong, S., & Jun, W. (2004). *A Fundamental Web-Board System Toward the Adaptive Mobile School Web Site.* Heidelberg, Germany: Springer Berlin.

Hoover-Dempsey, K. V., Bassler, O. C., & Brissie, J. (1987). Parent involvement: Contributions of teacher efficacy, school socioeconomic status and other school characteristics. *American Educational Research Journal*, 24, pp. 417–435.

Hoover-Dempsey, K. V., Battiato, A. C., Walker, J. M. T., Reed, R. P., DeJong, J. M., & Jones, K. P. (2001). Parental involvement in homework. *Educational Psychologist*, 36, 195–209.

Hoover-Dempsey, K. V., & Sander, H. M. (1995). Parental involvement in children's education: Why does it make a difference? *Teachers College Record*, 97, 310–331.

Hoover-Dempsey, K. V., & Sandler, H. M. (1997). Why do parents become involved in their children's education? *Review of Educational Research*, 67, 3–42.

Horner, R., & Carr, E. G. (1997). Behavior support for students with severe disabilities: Functional assessment and comprehensive intervention. *Journal of Special Education*, 37, 84–104.

Horner, R., Carr, E. G., Strain, P. S., Todd, A. W., & Reed, H. K. (2002). Problem behavior interventions for young children with autism: A research synthesis. *Journal of Autism and Developmental Disorders*, 32, 426–446.

Horner, R., & Sugai, G. (2004). *School-wide positive behavior support, implementers' blueprint and self-assessment.* Eugene, OR: University of Oregon, OSEP Center on Positive Behavior Support.

Horner, R. J. (2000). Positive behavior supports. *Focus on Autism and Other Developmental Disabilities*, 15, 97–105.

Horner, R. H., Sugai, G., Todd, A. W., & Lewis-Palmer, T. (2000). Elements of behavior support plans: A technical brief. *Exceptionality*, 8, 205–216.

Horner, R. H., Todd, A. W., Lewis-Palmer, T., Irvin, L. K., Sugai, G., & Boland, J. B. (2004). The school-wide evaluation tool (set): A research instrument for assessing school-wide positive behavior support. *Journal of Positive Behavior Interventions*, 6, 3–12.

Horner, R. H., Vaughn, B. J., Day, H. M., & Ard, W. R. (1996). The relationship between setting events and problem behavior: Expanding our understanding of behavior support. In L. K. Koegel & A. G. Dunlap (Eds.), *Positive behavioral support including people with difficult behavior in the community* (pp. 381–402). Baltimore: Brookes.

Howard, K. I., Krause, M. S., & Orlinsky, D. E. (1986). The attrition dilemma: Toward a new strategy for psychotherapy research. *Journal of Consulting and Clinical Psychology*, 54, 106–110.

Hruz, T. (2002, July). The growth of special education in Wisconsin. Thiensville, WI: *Wisconsin Policy Research Institute Report*, 15(5), 80 pages.

Huebner, K. M. (1989). *The education of students with disabilities: Where do we stand?* Unpublished Congressional testimony. New York: American Foundation for the Blind.

Hughes, C., Copeland, S. R., Agran, M., Wehmeyer, M. C., Rodi, M. S., & Presley, J. A. (2002). Using self-monitoring to improve performance in general education high school classes. *Education and Training in Mental Retardation and Developmental Disabilities*, 37, 262–271.

Hultman, C. M., Sparen, P., Cnattingius, S. (2002). Perinatal risk factors for infantile autism. *Epidemiology*, 13, 417–423.

Hunt, P. (1996). *International companion encyclopedia of children's literature.* London: Routledge.

Hunter, S. J., & Donders, J. (Eds). (2007). *Pediatric neuropsychological intervention.* Cambridge, England: Cambridge University Press.

Hyman, S. (2000). Goals for research on bipolar disorder: The view from NIMH. *Biological Psychiatry*, 48, 436–441.

Ibanez, G. E., Kuperminc, G. P., Jurkovic, G., & Perilla, J. (2004). Cultural attributes and agitations linked to achievement motivation among Latino adolescents. *Youth and Adolescence*, 33, 559–568.

Idaho State Department of Education (2007). *Idaho Special Education Manual.* Retrieved 3/20/09 at http://www.ste.idaho.gov/specialeducationmanual.asp.

Imlay, J. (2004). Effective behavior interventions and strategies in United States of America (USA) classrooms. Doctoral of Philosophy, curriculum and Instruction: Special Education, University of Toledo.

Ingersoll, B. D., & Goldstein, S. (1995). *Attention deficit disorder and learning disabilities: Realities, myths and controversial treatment.* New York: Doubleday.

Ingersoll, B. D., & Goldstein, S. (1995). *Lonely, sad and angry: A parent's guide to depression in children and adolescents.* New York: Bantam Doubleday Dell.

Ingersoll, R. (2001). Teacher turnover and teacher shortages: An organizational analysis. *American Educational Research Journal*, 38, 499–534.

Ingram, S., Hechtman, L., & Morgenstern, G. (1999). Outcome issues in AD/HD: Adolescent and adult long-term outcome. *Mental Retardation and Developmental Disabilities Research Reviews*, 5, 243–250.

Iovannone, R., Dunlap, D., Hunter, H., & Kincaid, D. (2003). Effective educational practices for students with autism spectrum disorders. *Focus on Autism and Other Developmental Disabilities*, 18, 150–165.

Irvin, L. K., Tobin, T. J., Sprague, J. T., Sugai, G., & Vincent, C. G. (2004). Validity of office discipline referral measures as indices of school-wide behavioral status and effects of school-wide behavioral interventions. *Journal of Positive Behavioral Interventions*, 6, 131–147.

Irvine, J. J. (2003). *Educating teachers for diversity: Seeing with a cultural eye.* New York: Teachers College Press.

Iwata, B. A., Smith, R. G., & Michael, J. (2000). Current research on the influence of establishing operations on behavior in applied settings. *Journal of Applied Behavior Analysis, 33,* 411–418

Jablensky, A. V., & Kalaydieva, L. V. (2003). Genetic epidemiology of schizophrenia: Phenotypes, risk factors, and reproductive behavior. *American Journal of Psychiatry, 160,* 425–429.

Jackson, L., & Panyon, M. (2002). *Positive behavioral support in the classroom: Principles and practices.* Baltimore: Brookes.

Jacobson, E. (1938). *Progressive relaxation.* Chicago: University of Chicago Press.

Jacobson, S. W., Jacobson, J. L., Sokal, R. J., Chiodo, L. M., & Corobana, R. (2004). Maternal age, alcohol abuse history, and quality of parenting as moderators of the effects of prenatal alcohol exposure on 7.5-year intellectual function. *Alcoholism: Clinical and Experimental Research, 28,* 1732–1745.

Janus, M. (2002). 20 ways to build resilience. *Intervention in School and Clinic, 38,* 117–121.

Jayanthi, M., & Sawyer, V. (1995). Recommendations for homework communication problems: From parents, classroom teachers and special education teachers. *Remedial and Special Education, 16,* 212–227.

Jenkins, E., & Bell, C. (1997). Exposure and response to community violence among children and adolescents. In J. Osofsky (Ed.), *Children in a violent society* (pp. 19–31). New York: Guilford Press.

Jenkins, J. R., & Heinen, A. (1989). Students' preferences for service delivery: Pull-out, in-class, or integrated models. *Exceptional Children, 55,* 516–523.

Jensen, P. S. (1998). Developmental psychopathology courts developmental neurobiology: Current Issues and future challenges. *Seminars in Clinical Neuropsychiatry, 3,* 333–337.

Jensen, P. S., Bhatara, V. S., ViTiello, B., Hoagwood, K., Feil, M., & Burke, L. B. (1999). Psychoactive medication prescribing practices for U.S. children: Gaps between research and clinical practice. *Journal of the American Academy of Child and Adolescent Psychiatry, 38,* 557–565.

Jeynes, W. H. (2005). A meta-analysis of the relation of parental involvement to urban elementary school student academic achievement. *Urban Education, 40,* 237–269.

Jick, H., Beach, K. J., & Kaye, J. A. (2006). Incidence of autism over time. *Epidemiology, 17,* 120–121.

Jimerson, L. (2006). The Hobbit Effect: Why Small Works in Public Schools. Retrieved on 10/5/09 at http://www.smallschoolsproject.org/PDFS/RSCT_hobbit-effect.pdf.

Jimerson, S. R., & Brock, S. E. (2004). Threat assessment, school crisis preparation, and school crisis response. In M. J. Furlong, M. P. Bates, D. C. Smith, & P. M. Kingery (Eds.), *Appraisal and prediction of school violence: Context, issues and methods.* Hauppauge, NY: Nova.

Johnson, D. W., & Johnson, R. T. (1996). Conflict resolution and peer mediation programs in elementary and secondary schools: A review of the research. *Review of Educational Research, 66,* 459–506.

Johnson, K., & Street, E. M. (2004). The morningside model of generative instruction: An integration on research-based practices. In D. J. Moran & R. Malott (Eds.), *Empirically supported educational methods* (pp. 247–265). St. Louis, MO: Elsevier Science/Academic Press.

Johnson, K. R., & Layng, T. V. J. (1992). Breaking the structural barrier: Literacy and numeracy with fluency, *American Psychologist, 47,* 1475–1490.

Johnston, C., & Ohan, J. L. (1999). Externalizing disorders. In W. K. Silverman & T. H. Ollendick (Eds.), *Developmental issues in the clinical treatment of children* (pp. 279–294). Boston: Allyn and Bacon.

Joint Committee on Teacher Planning for Students with Disabilities (1995). *Planning for academic diversity in America's classrooms: Windows on reality, research, change and practice*: Lawrence, KS: Author.

Jolivette, K., Stichter, J. P., Nelson, C. M., Terrance, M., & Liaupsim, C. J. (2000). *Improving post-school outcomes for students with emotional and behavioral disorders.* Arlington, VA: ERIC Clearinghouse on Disabilities and Gifted Education. #E597.

Jonas, M. (2002). Twenty ways to build resilience. *Intervention in School and Clinic, 38,* 117–121.

Jones, K. M., & Lungaro, C. J. (2000). Teacher acceptability of functional assessment-derived treatments. *Journal of Educational and Psychological Consultation, 11,* 323–332.

Jones, V. F., & Jones, L. S. (2001). *Comprehensive classroom management: Creating communities of support and solving problems* (6th ed.). Boston: Allyn and Bacon.

Joyce, B., Weil, M., & Calhoun, E. (2003). *Models of teaching* (7th ed) Boston: Allyn and Bacon.

Justen III, J., & Howerton, D. (1993). Clarifying behavior management terminology. *Intervention in School and Clinic, 29,* 36–40.

Kadesjo, B., & Gillberg, C. (2000). Tourette's disorder: Epidemiology and comorbidity in primary school children. *Journal of the American Academy of Child and Adolescent Psychiatry, 39,* 548–555.

Kagan, J. (1994). *Galen's prophecy.* New York: Basic Books.

Kagan, J. (1995). On attachment. *Harvard Review of Psychiatry, 3,* 104–106.

Kagan, J., Kearsley, R. B., & Zelazo, P. R. (1978). *Infancy: Its place in human development.* Cambridge, MA: Harvard University Press.

Kagan, J., Snidman, N., & Arcus, D. (1998). Childhood derivatives of high and low reactivity in infancy. *Child Development, 69,* 1483–1493.

Kaiser, A. P., Hancock, T. B., & Nietfeld, J. P. (2000). The effects of parent-implemented enhanced mileau teaching on the social communication of children who have autism. *Journal of Early Education and Development, 11,* 423–446.

Kalb, L. M., & Loeber, R. (2003). Child disobedience and noncompliance: A review. *Pediatrics, 111,* 641–652.

Kam, C. M., Greenberg, M. T., & Kusche, C. A. (2004). Sustained effects of the PATHS curriculum on the social and psychological adjustment of children in special education. *Journal of Emotional and Behavioral Disorders, 12,* 66–78.

Kamps, D., & Tankersley, M. (1996). Prevention of behavioral and conduct disorders: Trends and research issues. *Behavioral Disorders, 22,* 41–48.

Kamps, D. M., & Kay, P. (2002). Preventing problems through social skills instruction. In B. Algozzine & P. Kay (Eds.), *Preventing problem behaviors: A handbook of successful prevention strategies* (pp. 57–84). Thousand Oaks, CA: Corwin Press.

Kaplan, H. I., & Sadock, B. J. (1998). *Kaplan and Sadock's synopsis of psychiatry; Behavioral science/clinical psychiatry* (8th ed.). Baltimore: Williams and Wilkins.

Karp, N. (1996). Individualized wraparound services for children with emotional, behavior, and mental disorders. In G. H. Singer, L. E. Powers, & A. L. Olson (Eds.), *Redefining family support* (pp. 291–310). Baltimore: Brookes.

Kaser, C. (2006). Highly Effective Practices. Retrieved on 11/18/09 from http://www.googlesyndicatedsearch.com/u/odu?q=catherine&Kaser.

Katsiyannis, A., & Maag, J. (2001). Manifestation determination as a golden fleece. *Exceptional Children, 68*, 85–96.

Katz, L., & Bauch, J. P. (1999). The Peabody family involvement initiative: Preparing pre-service teachers for family/school collaboration. *School Community Journal, 9*, 49–69.

Kau, A. S., Reider, E. E., Payne, L., Meyer, W. A., & Freund, L. (2000). Early behavior signs of psychiatric phenotypes in Fragile-X syndrome. *American Journal of Mental Retardation, 105*, 286–299.

Kauffman, J. M. (1999). How we prevent the prevention of emotional and behavioral disorders. *Exceptional Children, 65*, 448–468.

Kauffman, J. M. (2001). *Characteristics of emotional and behavioral disorder of children* (7th ed.). Upper Saddle River, NJ: Merrill/Pearson Education.

Kauffman, J. M., Bantz, J., & McCullough, J. (2002). Separate and better: A special public school class for students with emotional and behavioral disorders. *Exceptionality, 10*, 149–170.

Kauffman, J. M., & Hallahan, D. P. (Eds.). (1995). *The illusion of full inclusion: A comprehensive critique of a current special education bandwagon*. Austin, TX: Pro-Ed.

Kazdin, A. E. (1997). Practitioner review: Psychosocial treatments for conduct disorder in children. *Journal of Child Psychology and Psychiatry, 32*, 161–178.

Kazdin, A. E. (1982). *Simple case research design*. New York: Oxford University Press.

Kazdin, A. E. (2001). *Behavior modification in applied setting*. Belmont, CA: Wadsworth Thompson Learning.

Kazdin, A. E. (2001). Treatment of conduct disorders. In J. Hill & B. Maughan (Eds.), *Conduct disorders in childhood and adolescence* (pp. 408–448). Cambridge, England: Cambridge University Press.

Kazdin, A. E., & Bootzin, R. R. (1972). The Token economy: An evaluation review. *Journal of Applied Behavior Analysis, 5*, 343–372.

Kee, M., Hill, S. M., & West, M. D. (1999). School-based behavior management of cursing, hitting, and spitting in a girl with profound retardation. *Education and Treatment of Children, 22*, 171–178.

Keenan, H. T., Hooper, S. R., Wetherington, et al. (2007). Neurodevelopmental outcomes following traumatic brain injury. *Pediatrics, 119*, 616–623.

Kellam, S. G., Mayer, L. S., Rebok, G. W., & Hawkins, W. E. (1998). Effects of improving achievement on aggressive behavior and of improving aggressive behavior on achievement through two preventive interventions: An investigation of causal paths. In B. P. Dohrenwend et al. (Eds.), *Adversity, stress and psychopathology* (pp. 486–505). New York: Oxford University Press.

Kelly, J. F., & Barnard, K. E. (1999). Parent education within a relationship-focused model. *Topics in Early Childhood Special Education, 19*, 151–157.

Kemich, C. A. (2004). Traumatic brain injury: Patient and family fact sheet. *Neurologist, 10*, 291–292.

Kendall, P. C., & Braswell, L. (1993). *Cognitive-behavioral therapy for impulsive children* (2nd ed.). New York: Guilford Press.

Kendler, K. S., & Prescott, C. A. (2006). *Genes, environment and psychopathology: Understanding the causes of psychiatric and substance use disorders*. New York: Guilford Press.

Kenny, T. J., Holden, W., & Santilli, L. (1991). The meaning of measures: Pitfalls in behavioral and developmental research. *Journal of Development and Behavioral Pediatrics, 12*, 355–360.

Kern, L., Bambara, L., & Fogt, J. (2002). Classwide curricular modification to improve the behavior of students with emotional or behavioral disorders. *Behavioral Disorders, 27*, 317–326.

Kern, L., & Clemens, N. A. (2006). Antecedent strategies to promote appropriate classroom behavior. *Psychology in the Schools, 44*, 65–75.

Kern, L., & Dunlap, G. (1999). Assessment-based interventions for children with emotional and behavioral disorders. In A. C. Repp & R. A. Horner (Eds.), *Functional analysis of problem behavior: From effective assessment to effective support* (pp. 197–218). Belmont, CA: Wadsworth.

Kern, L., Gallagher, P., Starosta, K., Hickman, W., & George, M. (2006). Longitudinal outcomes of functional behavioral assessment-based intervention. *Journal of Positive Behavior Interventions, 8*, 67–78.

Kern, L., Mantegna, M. E., Vorndran, C. M., Ballin, D., & Hilt, A. (2001). Choice of task sequence to increase engagement and reduce problem behaviors. *Journal of Positive Behavior Interventions, 3*, 3–10.

Kern, L., & Vorndran, C. M. (2000). Functional assessment and intervention for transition difficulties. *Journal of the Association for Persons with Severe Handicaps, 25*, 212–216.

Kerr, M. M., & Nelson, C. M. (1998). *Strategies for managing behavior problems in the classroom* (3rd ed.). Upper Saddle River, NJ: Merrill/Pearson Education.

Kerr, M. M., & Nelson, C. M. (2002). *Strategies for addressing behavior problems in the classroom* (4th ed.). Upper Saddle River, NJ: Merrill/Pearson Education.

Kerr, M. M., & Nelson, C. M. (2006). *Strategies for addressing behavior problems in the classroom* (5th ed.). Upper Saddle River, NJ: Merrill/Pearson Education.

Kesler, S. R., Adams, H. F., Blasey, C. M., & Bigler, E. D. (2003). Premorbid intellectual functioning education and brain size in traumatic brain injury: An investigation of the cognitive reserve. *Applied Neuropsychology, 10*, 153–162.

Kessler-Sklar, S. L., & Baker, A. J. L. (2000). School district parent involvement policies and programs. *Elementary School Journal, 101*, 101–118.

Keyes, G. K. (1994). Motivating reluctant students: The time on computer program. *Teaching Exceptional Children, 27*, 20–23.

Kim, E. Y., & Miklowitz, D. J. (2002). Childhood mania, attention deficit hyperactivity disorder and conduct disorder: A critical review of diagnostic dilemmas. *Bipolar Disorders, 4*, 215–225.

Kirschenbaum, H. (2001). Educating professionals for school, family, and community partnerships. In D. B. Hiatt-Michael (Ed.), *Promising practices for family involvement in schools* (pp. 185–206). Greenwich, CT: Information Age Publishing.

Knoff, H. M. (2001). *The stop and think social skills program (preschool–grade 1, grades 2/3, grades 4/5, middle school (6–8)*. Longmont, CO: Sopris West.

Koch-Hatten, A. (1986). Siblings' experience of pediatric cancer: Interviews with children. *Health and Social Work*, 107–117.

Koeb, B., Gibb, R. & Gorny, G. (2000). Cortical plasticity and the development of behavior after early frontal cortical injury. *Developmental Neuropsychology, 18,* 423–444.

Koegel, L. K., Koegel, R. L., & Dunlap, G. (Eds.) (1996). *Positive behavioral support: Including people with difficult behavior in the community.* Baltimore: Brookes.

Kohl, G. W., Lengua, L. J., & McMahon, R. J. (2002). Parent involvement in school: Conceptualizing multiple dimensions and their relations with family and demographic risk factors. *Journal of School Psychology, 38,* 501–523.

Kohn, A. (2006). *The homework myth.* Cambridge, MA: DeCapo Lifelong Books.

Konrad, K., Gauggel, S., Manz, A., & Scholl, M. (2000). Inhibitory control in children with traumatic brain injury (TBI) and children with attention deficit/hyperactivity disorder (ADHD). *Brain Injury, 14,* 859–875.

Korkman, M. (1999). Applying Luria's diagnostic principles in the neuropsychological assessment of children. *Neuropsychology Review, 9,* 89–105.

Korkman, M., Kemp, S. L., & Kirk, U. (2001). Effects of age on neurocognitive measures of children ages 5 to 12: A cross-sectional study on 800 children from the United States. *Developmental Neuropsychology, 20,* 331–354.

Korkman, M., & Peltomoa, K. (1991). A pattern of test findings predicting attention problems at school. *Journal of Abnormal Child Psychology, 19,* 451–467.

Korvatska, E., Van de Water, J., Anders, T. F., & Gershwin, M. E. (2002). Genetic and immunologic considerations in autism. *Neurobiological Diseases, 9,* 107–125.

Kostelnik, M. J., Whiren, H. P., Soderman, A. K., Stein, L. C., & Gregory, K. (2002). *Guiding children's social development: Theory to practice.* Clifton Park, NY: Delmar.

Kovacs, M., Devlin, B., Pollock, M., Richards, C., & Mukerji, P. (1997). A controlled family history study of childhood-onset depressive disorder. *Archives of General Psychiatry, 54,* 613–623.

Kovacs, M., Goldston, D., Obrasky, D. S., & Bonar, L. K. (1997). Psychiatric disorders in youth with IDDM: Rates and risk factors. *Diabetes Care, 20,* 36–44.

Koyanagi, C. (1994). Is there a national policy for children and youth with serious emotional disturbance? *Policy Studies Journal, 22,* 669–680.

Krain, A. L., Kendall, P. C., & Power, T. J. (2005). The role of treatment acceptability in the initiation of treatment for ADHD. *Journal of Attention Disorders, 9,* 425–434.

Kratochwill, T. R., Sladeczek, I. E., & Plunge, M. (1995). Re-evolution of behavior consultation. *Journal of Educational and Psychological Consultation, 6,* 145–157.

Kriedler, W. J. (1997). *Conflict resolution in the middle school.* Cambridge, MA: Educators for Social Responsibility.

Kubina, R. M., & Morrison, R. S. (2000). Fluency in education. *Behavior and Social Issues, 10,* 83–99.

Kubina, R. M., Morrison, R. S., & Lee, D. L. (2002). Benefits of adding precision teaching to behavior interventions for students with autism. *Behavioral Interventions, 17,* 233–246.

Kunjufu, J. (1990). *Countering the conspiracy to destroy Black boys* (Vol. 3). Chicago: African American Images.

Kuo, A. Y., Reiss, A. L., Freund, L. S., & Huffman, L. C. (2002). Family environment and cognitive abilities in girls with Fragile-X syndrome. *Journal of Intellectual Disability Research, 46,* 328–339.

Kupferman, F. (2006). *Special education handbook bureau of Jewish education of San Francisco.* San Francisco, CA; Peninsula, Marin, and Sonoma Counties.

Kurita, H. (2001). Current status of autism studies. *Sushin Shinkerigaku Zasshi, 103,* 64–75.

Kurlan, R., Como, P. G., Miller, B., Palumbo, D., Deeley, C., Andressen, E. M., et al. (2002). The behavioral spectrum of tic disorders: A community-based study. *Neurology, 59,* 414–420.

Kushner, H. I. (2000). *A cursing brain? The histories of Tourette syndrome.* Boston: Harvard University Press.

Kyler, S. J., Bumbarger, B. K., & Greenberg, M. T. (2005). Technical Assistance Facts Sheet: Evidence-based programs. University Park: Penn State University, Prevention Research Center for the Promotion of Human Development.

Labato, D., Barbour, L., Hall, L. J., & Miller, C. T. (1987). Psychosocial characteristics of preschool siblings of handicapped and non-handicapped children. *Journal of Abnormal Psychology, 15,* 329–338.

LaBahn, J. (1995). *Education and parental involvement in schools: Problems, solutions,* and effects. Educational Psychology Interactive. Valdosta, GA: Valdosta State University. Retrieved from http://chiron.valdosta.edu/whutt/files/parinvol.html.

Lahey, B. B., Mofitt, T. E., & Caspi, A. (Eds.). (2003). *The causes of conduct disorder and juvenile deliquency.* New York: Guilford Press.

Lahey, B. B., Waldman, I. D., & McBurnett, K. (1999). Annotation: The development of antisocial behavior, an integrative causal model. *Journal of Child Psychology and Psychiatry, 40,* 669–682.

Lalli, J. S., & Casey, S. D. (1996). Treatment of multiply-controlled problem behavior. *Journal of Applied Behavior Analysis, 29,* 391–395.

Lambert, M. C., Cartledge, G., Heward, W. L., & Lo, Y. Y. (2006). Effects of response cards on disruptive behavior and academic responding during math lessons by fourth-grade urban students. *Journal of Positive Behavior Interventions, 8,* 85–102.

Lamphear, B. P., Hernring, R., Khoury, J., Yolton, K., Baghurst, P., Bellinger, D. C., et al. (2005). Low level environmental lead exposure and children's intellectual function: An international pooled analysis. *Environmental Health Perspectives, 113,* 894–899.

Landry, S. H., Swank, P., Stuebing, K., Prasad, M., & Ewing-Cobbs, L. (2004). Social competence in young children with inflicted traumatic brain injury. *Developmental Neuropsychology, 26,* 707–733.

Lane, K., Gresham, F., MacCilan, D., & Bocian, K. (2001). Early detection of students with antisocial behavior and hyperactivity problems. *Education and Treatment of Children, 24,* 294–308.

Lane, K. L., & Wehby, J. (2002). Addressing antisocial behavior in the schools: A call for action. *Academic Exchange Quarterly, 6,* 4–9.

Lane, K. L., Wehby, J., & Barton-Arwood, S. M. (2005). Students with and at risk for emotional and behavioral disorders: Meeting their social and academic needs. *Preventing School Failure, 49,* 6–11.

Lanthier, R. P., Wright-Cunningham, K., & Edmonds, E. A. (2003). *Factors influencing levels of parent involvement: Findings from research.* Washington, DC: National Clearinghouse for Comprehensive School Reform.

Lau, A. S., & Weisz, J. R. (2003). Reported maltreatment among clinic-referred children: Implications for preventing problems, treatment attrition, and long-term outcomes. *Journal of the American Academy of Child and Adolescent Psychiatry, 42,* 1327–1334.

Laucht, M., Esser, G., Baving, L., Gerhold, M., Hoesch, R., Ihle, W., et al. (2000). Behavioral sequence of perinatal insults and early family adversity at 8 years of age. *Journal of the American Academy of Child and Adolescent Psychiatry, 39,* 1229–1237.

Layng, T. V. J., Twyman, J. S., & Stikeleather, G. (2003). Headsprout early reading: Reliably teaching children to read. *Behavioral Technology Today, 3,* 7–20.

Lechman, J. R., Peterson, B. S., Pauls, D. C., & Cohen, D. J. (1997). Tic disorders. *Psychiatric Clinics of North America, 20,* 839–861.

Lee, D. L. & Laspe, A. K. (2004). Using high-probability request sequences to increase journal writing. *Journal of Behavioral Evaluation, 12,* 261–273.

Leonard, H. C., Rapoport, J. L., & Swedo, S. E. (1997). Obsessive-compulsive disorder. In J. M. Weiner (Ed.), *Textbook of child and adolescent psychiatry* (2nd ed., pp. 481–490). Washington, DC: American Academy of Child and Adolescent Psychiatry, American Psychiatric Press.

Leone, P. E., Christle, C. A., Nelson, C. M., Skiba, R., Frey, A., & Jolivette, K. (2003). School failure and disability: Promoting positive outcomes, decreasing vulnerability for involvement with the juvenile delinquency system. National Center on Education, Disability, and Juvenile Justice web site. Retrieved from http://www.edjj.org/Publications/List/Leone_et_al_2003.pdf.

Leone, P. E., Mayer, M. J., Malmgren, K., & Misel, S. M. (2000). School violence and disruption: Rhetoric, reality, and reasonable balance. *Focus on Exceptional Children, 33,* 1–20.

Lerner, J. (1997). *Learning disabilities: Theories, diagnosis, and teaching strategies* (7th ed.). Boston: Houghton Mifflin.

Lewinsohn, P. M., Clarke, G. N., Seely, J. R., & Rhode, F. (1994). Major depression in community adolescents: Age at onset, episode deviation and time to reoccurrence. *Journal of the American Academy of Child and Adolescent Psychiatry, 33,* 809–818.

Lewinsohn, P. M., Klein, D. N., & Seeley, J. R. (1995). Bipolar disorders in a community sample of older adolescents: Prevalence,

phenomenology, comorbidity and course. *Journal of the American Academy of Child and Adolescent Psychiatry, 34,* 454–463.

Lewis, J. J., & Newcomer, L. L. (2005). Reducing problem behavior through school-wide systems of positive behavior support. In P. Clough, P. Garner, J. T. Pardeek, & F. Yen (Eds.), *Handbook of emotional and behavioral difficulties* (pp. 261–272). Thousand Oaks, CA: Sage.

Lewis, R. (1999). Teacher support for inclusive forms of classroom management. *International Journal of Inclusive Education, 3,* 269–285.

Lewis, S. P., & Waschbusch, D. A. (2007). Alternative approaches for conceptualizing children's attributional styles and their associations with depressive symptoms. *Depression and Anxiety, 24,* B37–B46.

Lewis, T. J. (2005). Implementing school-wide positive behavior supports. *Impact, 18,* 26–27.

Lewis, T. J., Lewis-Palmer, T., Newcomer, L., & Stichter, J. (2004). Applied behavior analysis and the education and treatment of students with emotional and behavioral disorders. In R. B. Rutherford Jr., & M. M. Mathur (Eds.), *Handbook of research in emotional and behavioral disorders* (pp. 523–545). New York: Guilford Press.

Lewis, T. J. and Newcomer, L. L. (2005). Reducing problem behavior through school-wide systems of positive behavior support. In P. Clough, P. Garner, J. T. Pardeck, and F. Yuen (Eds.). (2005). *Handbook of Emotional Behavioral Difficulties.* Thousand Oaks, CA: Sage Publications.

Lewis, T. J., Scott, T. M., & Danko, C. D. (1994). The problem behavior questionnaire: A teacher-based instrument to develop functional hypotheses of problem behavior in general education classroom. *Diagnostique, 19,* 103–115.

Lewis, T. J., Powers, L. J., Kely, M. J., & Newcomer, L. L. (2002). Reducing problem behaviors on the playground: An investigation of the application of schoolwide positive behavior supports. *Psychology in the Schools, 39,* 181–190.

Lewis, T. J., & Sugai, G. (1999). Effective behavior support: A systems approach to proactive school wide management. *Focus on Exceptional Children, 31,* 1–24.

Liaupsin, C. J., Jolivette, K., & Scott, T. M. (2004). School-wide systems of behavior support. Maximizing student success in schools. In R. Rutherford Jr., M. Quinn, &

S. Mathur (Eds.), *Handbook of research in emotional and behavioral disorders* (pp. 487–501). New York: Guilford Press.

Liberty, K. A., & Billingsley, F. F. (1988). Strategies to improve generalization. In N. G. Haring (Ed.), *Generalization for students with severe handicaps* (pp. 1–33). Seattle: University of Washington Press.

Lieber, C. S. (2000). Alcohol: Its metabolism and interaction with nutrients. *Annual Review of Nutrition, 20,* 395–430.

Limond, J., & Leeke, R. (2005). Practitioner review: Cognitive rehabilitation for children with acquired injury. *Journal of Clinical Child Psychology and Psychiatry, 46,* 339–352.

Lindsley, O. R. (1990). Precision teaching: By children for teachers. *Teaching Exceptional Children, 22,* 10–15.

Linnet, K. M., Wisborg, K., Obel, C., Secher, N. J., Thomsen, P. A., Agerbo, E., et al. (2005). Smoking during pregnancy and the risk for hyperkinetic disorder in offspring. *Pediatrics, 116,* 462–467.

Lipkin, W. I., & Hornig, M. (2004). Psychotropic viruses: A review. *Current Opinions in Microbiology, 7,* 420–425.

Lipsey, M. W., & Wilson, D. B. (2001). *Practical meta-analysis.* Thousand Oaks, CA: Sage.

Lipsky, D. K., & Gartner, A. (1998). Taking inclusion into the future. *Educational Leadership 56,* 78–81.

Loeber, R., & Farrington, D. P. (Eds.). (1998). *Serious and violent juvenile offenders: Risk factors and successful interventions.* Thousand Oaks, CA: Sage.

Lombardo, L. (1997). Behavior intervention: Place the emphasis on the positive. *Counterpoint, Vol. 18,* Alexandria, VA: National Association of State Directors of Special Education.

Lonigan, C. J., Elbert, J. C., & Johnson, S. B. (1998). Empirically supported psychosocial interventions for children: An overview. *Journal of Clinical and Child Psychology, 27,* 138–145.

Lovitt, T. C. (1995). *Tactics for teaching* (2nd ed.). Upper Saddle River, NJ: Prentice Hall.

Lubs, H. A. (1969). A marker X chromosome. *American Journal of Human Genetics, 21,* 231–244.

Lucyshyn, J. M., Horner, R. H., Dunlap, G., Albin, R. W., & Ben, K. R. (2002). Positive behavior support with families.

In J. M. Lucyshyn, G. Dunlop, & R. W. Albin (Eds.), *Families and positive behavior support: Addressing problem behavior in family contexts* (pp. 3–34). Baltimore: Brookes.

Luis, C. A., & Mittenburg, W. (2002). Mood and anxiety disorders following pediatric traumatic brain injury: A prospective study. *Journal of Clinical and Experimental Neuropsychology, 24,* 270–279.

Luiselli, J. K., & Diament, C. (Eds.). (2002). *Behavior psychology in the schools: Innovations in evaluation, support and consultation.* Binghamton, NY: Haworth Press.

Luman, J., Oosterlaan, J., & Sergeant, J. A. (2005). The impact of reinforcement contingencies on AD/HD: A review on theoretical appraisal. *Clinical Psychology Review, 25,* 183–213.

Lynch, E. W., & Hanson, M. J. (2004). *Developing cross-cultural competence: A guide for working with children and their families* (3rd ed.). Baltimore: Brookes.

Lyon, D., & Morgan-Judge, T. (2000). Childhood depressive disorders. *Journal of School Nursing, 16,* 26–31.

Maag, J. W. (1989). Assessment in social skills training: Methodological and conceptual issues for research and practice. *Remedial and Special Education, 10,* 6–17.

Maag, J. W. (2001). Rewarded by punishment: Reflections on the disuse of positive reinforcement in the schools. *Exceptional Children, 67,* 173–186.

Maag, J. W., & Katsiyannis, A. (1996). Counseling as a related service for students with emotional or behavioral disorders: Issues and recommendations. *Behavioral Disorders, 21,* 293–305.

MacAulay, D. J. (1990). Classroom environment: A literature review. *Educational Psychology, 10,* 239–253.

Macciomei, N. R., & Ruben, D. H. (1999). *Behavioral management in the public schools: An urban approach.* Westport, CT: Praeger.

Mace, F. C., & Belfiore, P. (1990). Behavior momentum in the treatment of escape-motivated stereotypy. *Journal of Applied Behavior Analysis, 23,* 507–514.

Maestrini, E., Paul, A., Monaco, A., & Bailey, A. (2000). Identifying autism susceptibility genes. *Neuron, 28,* 19–24.

Mahoney, A., Donnelly, W. O., Lewis, T., & Maynard, C. (2000). Mother and father self-reports of corporal punishment and severe physical aggression toward

clinic-referred youth. *Journal of Clinical Child Psychology, 29,* 266–281.

Mahoney, G., Kaiser, A., Girolametta, L., McDonald, T., Robinson, C., Safford, P., & Spiker, D. (1999). Parent education in early intervention: A call for renewed focus. *Topics in Early Childhood Special Education, 19,* 131–140.

Mahoney, G., & Perales, F. (2005). Relationship-focused early intervention with children with pervasive developmental disorders and other disabilities: A comparative study. *Journal of Developmental and Behavioral Pediatrics, 26,* 77–85.

Mahoney, G., & Powell, A. (1988). Modifying parent-child interaction: Enhancing the development of handicapped children. *Journal of Special Education, 22,* 82–96.

Mahoney, G., & Wheeden, C. (1997). Parent-child interaction—the foundation for family centered early intervention practice: A response to Baird and Peterson. *Topics in Early Childhood Special Education, 17,* 165–187.

Maier, S. E., & West, J. R. (2001). Drinking patterns and alcohol-related birth defects. *Alcohol Research and Health, 25,* 168–174.

Main, M., & Solomon, J. (1990). Procedure for identifying infants as disorganized/disoriented during the Ainsworth strange situation. In M. Greenberg, D. Cicchetti, & E. M. Cummings (Eds). *Attachment during preschool years* (pp. 121–160). Chicago: University of Chicago Press.

Malmgren, K., Edgar, E., & Neel, R. S. (1998). Postschool status of youth with behavioral disorders. *Behavior Disorders, 23,* 257–263.

Maras, P., & Kutnick, P. (1998). *Developing a typology of EBD.* Unpublished paper for the EBD subgroup of the National Advisory Group on Special Educational Needs, Department of Education and Employment.

March, R., Horner, R. A., Lewis-Palmer, T., Brown, D., Crone, D., Todd, A. W., et al. (2000). *Functional assessment checklist for teachers and staff (FACTS).* Eugene, OR: University of Oregon, Department of Educational and Community Supports.

March, R. E., & Horner, R. H. (2002). Feasibility and contributions of functional behavioral assessment in schools. *Journal of Emotional and Behavioral Disorders, 10,* 158–170.

Marcus, B. A., Vollmer, T. R., Swanson, V., Roane, H. R., & Ringdahl, J. E. (2001).

An experimental analysis of aggression. *Behavior Modification. 25,* 189–213.

Margolis, H., & McCabe, P. P. (1997). Homework challenges for students with reading and writing problems: Suggestions for effective practice. *Journal of Educational and Psychological Consultation, 8,* 41–74.

Marsh, E. J., & Barkley, R. A. (2006). *Treatment of childhood disorders.* New York: Guilford Press.

Martella, R. C., & Nelson, J. R. (2003). Managing classroom behavior. *Journal of Direct Instruction, 3,* 139–165.

Martella, R. C., Nelson, J. R., & Marchand-Martella, N. E. (2003). *Managing disruptive behaviors in the schools: A school-wide, classroom and individualized social learning approach.* Boston: Allyn and Bacon.

Martin, E. P., & Dear, C. (2000). *A grandfather's love letter to his grandson with autism.* Arlington, TX: Future Horizons.

Marx, A., Fuhrer, U., & Hartig, T. (1999). Effect of classroom seating arrangements on children's question asking. *Learning Environments Research, 2,* 249–263.

Marzano, R. J. (2003). *What works in schools: Translating research into action.* Alexandria, VA: Association for Supervision and Curriculum Development.

Marzano, R. J., Pickering, D. J., & Pollock, J. E. (2001). *Classroom assessment that works.* Alexandria, VA: Association for Supervision and Curriculum Development.

Mash, E. J., & Hunsley, J. (2005). Evidence-based assessment of child and adolescent disorders: Issues and challenges. *Journal of Clinical Child and Adolescent Psychology, 34,* 362–379.

Mash, E. J., & Wolfe, D. A. (1999). *Abnormal Child Psychology.* New York: Brooks/Cole.

Mason, J. A. (1996). The effect of anger management on young adolescent African-American males and fighting at school. (Doctoral dissertation, University of North Carolina, 1996). *Dissertation Abstracts International 57,* 11-A, 4640.

Massachusetts Advocacy Center. (1986). *The way out: Student exclusion practices in Boston middle schools.* Boston: Author.

Mather, N., & Goldstein, S. (2001). *Learning disabilities and challenging behaviors: A guide to intervention and classroom management.* Baltimore: Brookes.

Matthews, T. J. (2001). Smoking during pregnancy during the 1990s. *National Vital Statistics Report, 49,* 1–14.

Mattison, R. E., Hooper, S. R., & Glassberg, L. A. (2002). Three-year course of learning disorders in special education students classified as behavior disorder. *Journal of the American Academy of Child and Adolescent Psychiatry, 41*, 1454–1461.

Max, J. B., Levin, H. S., Schachar, R. J., et al. (2006). Predictors of personality change due to traumatic brain injury in children and adolescents six to twenty-four months after injury. *Journal of Neuropsychiatry and Clinical Neuroscience, 18*, 21–32.

May, P. A., & Gossage, J. P. (2001). Estimating the prevalence of fetal alcohol syndrome: A summary. *Alcohol Research and Health, 25*, 159–167.

May, S., Ard III, W., Todd, A. W., Horner, R. H., Glasgow, A., Sugai, G., et al. (2000). *School-wide information system.* Eugene, OR: Educational and Community Supports, University of Oregon.

Mayer, G. R. (1995). Preventing antisocial behavior in the schools. *Journal of Applied Behavior Analysis, 28(4)*, 462–492.

Mayer, G. R. (2000). *Classroom management: A California resource guide.* Los Angeles, CA: Los Angeles County Office of Education and California Department of Education.

Mayer, W., Niveleau, A., Walter, J., Fundele, R., & Haaf, T. (2000). Demethylation of the zygotic paternal genome. *Nature, 403*, 501–502.

McAfee, J. K., Schwilk, C., & Mitruski, M. (2006). Public policy on physical restraint of children with disabilities in public schools. *Education and Treatment of Children, 29*, 711–728.

McBride, S., & Peterson, C. (1997). Home-based early intervention with families of children with disabilities: Who is doing what? *Topics in Early Childhood Education, 17*, 209–234.

McCain, A. P., & Kelley, M. L. (1994). Improving classroom performance in underachieving pre-adolescents: The additive effects of response cost to a school-home note system. *Child and Family Behavior Therapy, 16*, 27–41.

McCartan, L. M. (2007). Inevitable or unnecessary? Explaining the utility of genetic explanation for development behavior. *Journal of Criminal Justice, 35*, 219–233.

McCauley, R. J., & Swisher, L. (1984). Use and misuse of norm-referenced tests in clinical assessment. *Journal of Speech and Hearing Disorders, 49*, 328–348.

McClure, I., & Conteur, A. L. (2007). Evidence-based approaches to autism spectrum disorders. *Child: Care, Health and Development, 33(5)*, 509–512.

McCollum, J. A., & Yates, T. J. (2001). *Cross-cultural perspectives on approaches to parent-infant interaction intervention, technical report.* Champaign, IL: CLAS Early Childhood Research Institute.

McConaughy, S. H. (2005). Direct observational assessment during test sessions and child clinical interviews. *School Psychology Review, 34*, 489–506.

McCrory, P. R. (2003). Brain injury and heading in soccer. *BMJ (British Medical Journal), 327*, 327–352.

McCurdy, B. L., Mannella, M. C., & Eldridge, N. (2003). Positive behavior support in urban schools: Can we predict the escalation of antisocial behavior? *Journal of Positive Behavior Interventions, 5*, 158–171.

McDermott, D. (2002). Theoretical background: Perspectives informing parenting education. *Prepare tomorrow's parents.* Retrieved on 3/28/09 from www.parenting-project.org/background.htm.

McDiarmid, G. W. (1990). Challenging prospective teachers' beliefs during early field experience: a quixotic undertaking? *Journal of Teacher Education, 41*, 12–20.

McDiarmid, G. W., & Price, J. (1993). Preparing teachers for diversity: A study of student teachers in a multicultural program. In M. J. O'Haire & J. Price (Eds.), *Diversity and teaching: Teacher education yearbook 1* (pp. 31–59). New York, NY: Harcourt Brace Jovanovich.

McEvoy, A., & Welker, R. (2000). Antisocial behavior, academic failure and school climate: A critical view. *Journal of Emotional and Behavioral Disorders, 8*, 130–140.

McEvoy, M. A., & Reichle, J. (2000). Further considerations of the role of the environment on stereotypic and self-injurious behavior. *Journal of Early Intervention, 23*, 22–23.

McFadden, A. C., March, G. E., Price, B. J., & Hwang, Y. (1992). A study of race and gender bias in the punishment of handicapped school children. *Urban Review, 24*, 239–251.

McGee, R., Williams, S., & Feehan, M. (1992). Attention deficit disorder and age of onset of problem behaviors. *Journal of Abnormal Child Psychology, 20*, 487–502.

McGraw, M. B. (1946). Maturation of behavior. In L. Carmichael (Ed.) *Manual of child psychology* (pp. 332–369). New York: Wiley.

McIntosh, K., Herman, K., Sanford, A., McGraw, K., & Florence, K. (2004). Teaching transitions: Techniques for promoting success between lessons. *Teaching Exceptional Children, 37*, 32–38.

McKenna, K., Gordon, C. T., Lenane, M., et al. (1994). Looking for childhood-onset schizophrenia: The first 71 cases screened. *Journal of the American Academy of Child and Adolescent Psychiatry, 33*, 636–644.

McMahon, R. J., & Forehand, R. I. (2003). *Helping the noncompliant child: Family-based treatment for oppositional behavior* (2nd ed.). New York: Guilford Press.

McNeely, C., Nonnemaker, J., & Blum, R. (2002). Promoting school connectedness: Evidence from the national longitudinal study of adolescent health. *Journal of School Health, 72*, 138–146.

McNeill, S. L., Watson, T. S., Henington, C., & Meeks, C. (2002). The effects of training parents in functional behavior assessment on problem identification, problem analysis and intervention design. *Behavior Modification, 26*, 499–515.

McVey, M. D. (2001). Teacher praise: Maximizing the motivational impact: Teaching strategies. *Journal of Early Education and Family Review, 8*, 29–34.

Meltzer, H. (2000). Genetics and etiology of schizophrenia and bipolar disorder. *Biological Psychiatry, 47*, 171–173.

Mercer, L. D., & Mercer A. R. (1998). *Teaching students with learning problems.* Upper Saddle River, NJ: Merrill/Pearson Education.

Mercer, N. (1995). *The guided construction of knowledge: Talk amongst teachers and learners.* Clevedon, UK: Multilingual Matters.

Metzler, C., Biglan, A., Rusby, J., & Sprague, J. (2001). Evaluation of a comprehensive behavior management program to improve school-wide positive behavior support. *Education and Treatment of Children, 24*, 448–479.

Metzler, C. W., Taylor, T. K., Gunn, B., Fowler, R. C., Biglan, A., & Ary, D. (1998). A comprehensive approach to the prevention of behavior problems: Integrating family and community-based approaches to strengthen behavior management programs in school. *Effective School Practices, 17*, 1–24.

Meyer, D. J., & Vadasy, P. F. (1994). *Sibshops: Workshops for siblings of children with special needs.* Baltimore: Brookes.

Meyer, G. J., Finn, S. E., Eyde, L. D., Kay, G. G., Moreland, K. L., Dier, R. R., et al. (2001). Psychological testing and psychological assessment: A review of evidence and issues. *American Psychologist, 56,* 128–165.

Michaelsen, L. K. (1998). Three keys to using learning groups effectively. *Essay on Teaching Excellence, 9,* Valdosta, GA: POD Network.

Michel, S. (2001). *What do you really think? Assessing student and faculty perspectives of a web-based tutorial to library research* (pp. 317–332). Chicago, IL: College and Research Libraries.

Mick, E., Biederman, J., Faraone, S. U., Sayer, J., & Klinman, S. (2002). Case control study of attention-deficit hyperactivity disorder and maternal smoking, alcohol use, and drug use during pregnancy. *Journal of the American Academy of Child and Adolescent Psychiatry, 41,* 378–385.

Mick, E., Biederman, J., Jetton, J., & Faraone, S. V. (2000). Sleep disturbances associated with attention-deficit hyperactivity disorder: The impact of psychiatric comorbidity and pharmacotherapy. *Journal of Child and Adolescent Psychopharmacology, 10,* 223–231.

Mid-Continent Research for Education and Learning. (2002). Scientifically based research emerges as national issue. *Changing Schools.* Retrieved from http://www.mcrel.org/PDF/ChangingSchools/5022NLCSSummer2002.pdf.

Mihalic, S., Irwin, K., Elliott, D. S., Fagan, H., & Hansen, D. (2001). OJJDP Juvenile Justice Bulletin. Washington, DC. U.S. Department of Justice, Office of Justice Programs, Office of Juvenile and Justice Delinquency Prevention: 2001 Blueprints for Violence Prevention.

Miller, J. A., Tansey, M., & Hughes, T. L. (1998). Functional behavioral assessment: The link between problem behavior and effective intervention in schools. *Current Issues in Education, 1*(5). Retrieved from http://cie.asu.edu/volume1/number5/.

Miller, K. A., Gunter, P. L., Vern, M. J., Hummel, J., & Wiley, L. P. (2003). Effects of curricular and materials modifications on academic performances and task engagement of three students with emotional or behavioral disorders. *Behavioral Disorders, 28,* 130–149.

Miller, P. J., Hengst, J. A., & Wang, S. (2003). Ethnographic methods: Applications from developmental cultural psychology. In P. M. Camic, J. E. Rhodes, & L. Yardley (Eds.), *Qualitative research in psychology: Expanding perspectives in methodology and design* (pp. 219–242). Washington, DC: American Psychological Association.

Milofsky, C. D. (1974). Why special education isn't special. *Harvard Educational Review, 44,* 437–458.

Mitchell, R. (1975). The incidence and nature of child abuse. *Developmental Medicine and Child Neurology, 17,* 641–644.

Mithaug, D., Horinchi, C., & Fanning, P. (1985). A report on the Colorado statewide follow-up survey of special education students. *Exceptional Children, 51,* 397–404.

Mohr, W. K. (2001). Bipolar disorders in children. *Journal of Psychosocial Nursing Mental Health, 39,* 12–23.

Molina, B. S. G., Smith, B. H., & Pelham Jr., W. E. (2005). Development of a school-wide behavior program in a public middle school: An illustration of the deployment-focused intervention development, stage 1. *Journal of Attention Disorders, 9,* 333–342.

Mooney, P., Ryan, J. B., Whing, B. M., Reid, R., & Epstein, M. H. (2005). A review of self-management interventions targeting academic outcomes for students with emotional and behavioral disorders. *Journal of Behavioral Education, 14,* 203–221.

Moore, A. D. (2004). *The relationship between the use of developmentally appropriate practice and the inclusion of product-producing art activities in infant programs.* Master's thesis, East Tennessee State University.

Moran, D. T., & Malott, R. W. (Eds.) (2004). *Evidence-based educational methods.* New York: Academic Press.

Morgan, D. P., & Jenson, W. R. (1988). *Teaching behaviorally disordered students: Preferred practices.* Columbus, OH: Merrill.

Morningstar, M. E., Turnbull, A. P., & Turnbull, H. R. (1995). What 10 students with disabilities tell us about the importance of family involvement in the transition from school to adult life? *Exceptional Children, 62,* 249–260.

Moss, P. A. (1994). Can there be validity without reliability? *Educational Researcher, 23,* 5–12.

Mowrey, L. (2008). Contributions to manuscript, "Understanding and managing emotional and behavioral disorders in the classroom."

Mrug, S., Hoza, B., & Gerdes, A. C. (2001). Children with attention deficit/hyperactivity disorder: Peer relationships and peer-oriented interventions. In D. Nangle & C. A. Erdley (Eds.). *The role of friendship in psychological adjustment* (pp. 51–77). San Francisco: Jossey-Bass.

Msall, M. E., & Tremont, M. R. (1999). Measuring functional status in children with genetic impairments. *American Journal of Medical Genetics, 89,* 62–74.

Mueller, M. M., Moore, J. W., & Sterling-Turner, H. E. (2005). Towards developing a classroom-based functional analysis condition to assess escape-to-attention as a viable maintaining problem behavior. *School Psychology Review, 34,* 425–431.

Mueller, M. M., Sterling-Turner, H. E., & Scattone, D. (2001). Functional assessment of hand flapping in a general education classroom. *Journal of Applied Behavior Analysis, 34,* 233–236.

Mulroy, M. T., & Bothell, J. (2003). *The CYFAR supporting family involvement in children's learning best practices for nonformal educational settings training model.* Storrs, CT: University of Connecticut Cooperative Extension System, College of Agriculture and Natural Resources.

Mundy, P., & Neal, R. (2001). Neural plasticity, joint attention and a transactional social-orienting model of autism. *International Review of Mental Retardation, 23,* 139–168.

Muscott, H. S. (1997). Behavioral characteristics of elementary and secondary students with emotional/behavioral disabilities in four different cascade placements. *Education and Treatment of Children, 20,* 336–356.

Natale, J. (1998). Education in black and white: How kids learn racism and how schools can help them unlearn it. *American School Board Journal, 185,* 18–23.

Nathan, A. (1998). *Surviving homework.* Minneapolis, MN: Millbrook Press.

National Association of School Psychologists (NASP) and Anderson, G. E., Whipple, A. D., & Jimerson, S. R. (2002). *Grade retention: Achievement and mental health outcomes.* Santa Barbara, CA: NASP.

National Association of School Psychologists (NASP). (1994). *The role of the school psychologist in assessment.* Washington, DC: Author.

National Association of School Psychologists. (2002). *Fair and effective discipline for all students: Best practice strategies for educators.*

Retrieved 11/18/09 at http://www.nasponline. org/communications/spawareness/effdiscpts .pdf.

National Association of State Boards of Education (NASBE). 1992.

National Center for Education Statistics (NCES). (1997). *State indicators in education 1997.* Washington, DC: U.S. Department of Education.

National Center for Education Statistics (NCES). (1999). *Teacher Quality in the United States: Data on Preparation and Qualifications.* Washington, DC: U.S. Department of Education.

National Center for Educational Statistics (NCES). (2003). Washington, DC: U.S. Department of Education.

National Center for Education Statistics (NCES). (2004). *The condition of education 2004.* Washington, DC: U.S. Department of Education.

NICHCY (1994). Children with disabilities: Understanding sibling issues. *NICHCY News Digest #N.11,* 1988 (updated 1994).

National Institute of Mental Health (NIMH). (1998). *Genetics and mental disorders: Report of the national institute of mental health's genetics workgroup* (NIH Publication No 98-4268). Rockville, MD: Author.

National Institute of Mental Health (NIMH). (2000). *Depression in children and adolescents: A fact sheet for physicians.* Bethesda, MD: Department of Health and Human Services.

National Institute on Alcohol Abuse and Alcoholism. (1991). *Fetal alcohol syndrome* (No. 13PH297 July, 1991). Bethesda, MD: National Institute on Alcohol Abuse and Alchoholism (NIAA).

National Longitudinal Transition Study. (2006). U.S. Department of Labor. National Longitudinal Surveys. Available from http://www.bls.gov/nis/.

National Reading Panel. (2000). *Teaching children to read: An evidence-based assessment of the scientific research literature on reading and its implications for reading instruction: Reports of the subgroups.* Washington, DC: National Institutes of Child Health and Development.

National Research Council. (2001). Commission on behavioral and social sciences and education. Retrieved from http://www7. nationalacademics.org/cnstat.

Needleman, H. C., Schell, A., Bellinger, D., Leviton, A., & Allred, E. N. (1990). The long-term effects of exposure to low doses of lead in childhood. An 11-year follow-up report. *New England Journal of Medicine, 322,* 83–88.

Neef, N. A., Bicard, D. F., Endo, S., Coury, D. L. & Aman, M. G. (2005). Evaluation of pharmacological treatment of impulsivity in children with attention deficit hyperactivity disorder. *Journal of Applied Behavior Analysis, 38,* 135–146.

Neihart, M. (2000). Gifted children with Asperger's syndrome. *Gifted Child Quarterly, 44,* 222–230.

Neill, J. (2004). How to choose tools, instruments, and questionnaires for intervention, research, and evaluation. Retrieved on 10/1/09 from http://wilderdon.com/tools/ ToolsHowChoose.html.

Nelson, R. J. (2001). Sources of occupational stress for teachers of students with emotional and behavioral disorders. *Journal of Emotional and Behavioral Disorders, 9,* 123–131.

Nelson, J. R., Martella, R. M., & Marchand-Martella, N. (2002). Maximizing student learning: The effects of a school based program for preventing problem behavior. *Journal of Emotional and Behavioral Disorders, 10,* 136–148.

Nelson, J. R., Benner, G. J., & Gonzales, J. (2005). An investigation of the effects of a prereading intervention on the early literacy skills of children at risk of emotional disturbance and reading problems. *Journal of Emotional and Behavioral Disorders, 13,* 3–12.

Nelson, T. R., Benner, G. J., Lane, K., & Smith, B. W. (2004). Academic achievement of K–12 students with emotional and behavioral disorders. *Exceptional Children, 71,* 59–73.

Neves-Pereira, M., Mundo, E., Muglia, P., King, N., Macciardi, F., & Kennedy, J. L. (2002). The brain-derived neurotropic factor gene confers susceptibility to bipolar disorder: Evidence from a family-based association study. *American Journal of Human Genetics, 71,* 651–655.

Nevin, J. A., Mandell, C., & Atak, T. R. (1983). The analysis of behavioral momentum. *Journal of the Experimental Analysis of Behavior, 39,* 49–59.

Newcomer, L. L., & Lewis, T. J. (2004). Functional behavioral assessment: An investigation of assessment reliability and effectiveness of function-based intervention. *Journal of Emotional and Behavioral Disorders, 12,* 168–181.

Nicholls, J. G., McKenzie, M., & Shufro, J. (1994). Schoolwork, homework, life's work: The experience of students with and without learning disabilities. *Journal of Learning Disabilities, 27,* 562–569.

NICHCY-National Dissemination Center for Children with Disabilities. (1994). *Children with disabilities: Understanding sibling issues.* LD Online web. Retrieved from http://www.ldonline.org/article/6054.

NICHCY-National Committee to Prevent Child Abuse. (1995). *Current trends in child abuse reporting and fatalities: The results of the 1994 annual 50 state survey.* Chicago: Author.

NICHCY-National Dissemination Center for Children with Disabilities. (2003). *Visual impairments.* Fact Sheet #13. Retrieved from http://www.nichcy.org/pubs/factshe/ fs13txt.htm.

NICHCY-National Dissemination Center for Children with Disabilities. (2006). *Traumatic brain injury* Fact Sheet #18. Retrieved from www.nichy.org.

NICHCY-National Dissemination Center for Children with Disabilities. (2003). *Interventions for chronic behavior problems.* Retrieved on 3/8/09 from www.nichcy. org/products/pages/default.aspx?ProductD= 7581.

NICHCY-National Information Center for Children and Youth with Disabilities. (1999). Interventions for chronic behavior problems. Research brief. U. S. Department of Education, Office of Educational Research and Improvement, Educational Resource Information Center, Washington, DC.

Nicpon, M. F., Wodrich, D. L., & Kurpius, S. R. (2004). Utilization behavior in boys with ADHD: A test of Barkley's theory. *Developmental Neuropsychology, 26,* 735–751.

Nielson, S., Olive, M., Donovan, A., & McEvoy, M. (1999). Challenging behaviors in your classroom? In S. Sandall and M. Ostrosky (Eds.), *Young exceptional children: Practical ideas for addressing challenging behaviors* (pp. 5–16). Longmont, CO: Sopris West.

Nigg, J. T., Blaskey, L. G., Huang-Pollock, C. L., & Rappley, M. D. (2002). Neuropsychological executive functions in DSM IV ADHD subtypes. *Journal of the American Academy of Child and Adolescent Psychology, 41,* 59–66.

Nixon, R. D. V. (2001). Changes in hyperactivity and temperament in behaviorally disturbed pre-schoolers after parent-child interaction therapy (PCRT). *Behavior Change, 18,* 168–176.

No Child Left Behind Act of 2001, Pub I, No. 107-110, 115 Stat. 425 (2002).

Noell, G. H., & Gresham, F. M. (1993). Functional outcome analysis: Do the benefits of consultation and pre-referral intervention justify the cost? *School Psychology Quarterly, 8,* 200–227.

Nordquist, V. M., & McEvoy, M. A. (1983). Punishment as a factor in early childhood imitation. *Analysis and Intervention in Developmental Disabilities, 3,* 339–357.

Norris, D. (2007). *ADHD and other behavior problems.* Retrieved on 3/6/09 from http://ezinearticles.com/?ADHD-and-other-behavior-problems&id=804603.

O'Connor, R. E., Harty, K. R., & Fulmer, D. (2005). Ties of intervention in kindergarten through third grade. *Journal of Learning Disabilities, 38,* 532–538.

O'Donnell, J., Hawkins, J., Catalano, R., Abbott, R., & Day, L. (1995). Preventing school failure, drug use, and delinquency among low-income children: Long-term intervention in elementary schools. *American Journal of Orthopsychiatry, 65,* 87–100.

O'Neill, J. (2004). How to choose tools, instruments, and questionnaires for intervention research and evaluation. Retrieved on 3/5/09 from http://wilderdom.com/tools/ToolsHowChoose.html.

O'Neill, R. E., Horner, R. H., Sprague, J. R., Albin, R. W., Storey, R., & Newton, J. S. (1997). *Functional assessment and program development for problem behavior: A product handbook.* Pacific Grove, CA: Brooks/Cole.

O'Riordan, M., & Passetti, F. (2006). Discrimination in autism within different sensory modalities. *Journal of Autism and Developmental Discordance, 36,* 665–675.

O'Shaughnessy, T., Lane, K., Gresham, F., & Beebe-Frankenberger, M. (2003). Children placed at risk for learning and behavioral difficulties: Implementing a school-wide system of early identification and prevention. *Remedial and Special Education, 24,* 27–35.

Office of Special Education Programs (OSEP) (1993). http://www.eg.gov/pubs/biemial/315.html.

Office of Special Education Programs (OSEP) (2005). Technical Assistance Center of Positive Behavioral Interventions and Supports (2004). Retrieved from http://www.pbis.org.

Olds, D., Robinson, J., Song, N., Little, C., & Hill, P. (1999). *Reducing risks for mental disorders during the first five years of life: A review of preventive interventions.* Rockville, MD: Center for Mental Health Statistics.

Ollendick, T. H., Grills, A. E., & King, N. J. (2001). Applying developmental theory to the assessment and treatment of childhood disorders: Does it make a difference? *Clinical Psychology and Psychotherapy, 8,* 304–314.

Ollendick, T. H., King, N. J., & Muris, P. (2004). Phobias in children and adolescents: A review. In M. H. Akishal, J. J. Lopez, & A. Okasha (Eds.), pp. 245–279. W. Sussex, England: John Wiley and Sons.

Ollendick, T. H., & Vasey, M. W. (1999). Developmental theory and the practice of clinical child psychology. *Journal of Clinical Child Psychology, 28,* 457–464.

Olsen, J. L., & Platt, J. M. (2000). *Teaching children and adolescents with special needs* (3rd ed.). Upper Saddle River, NJ: Merrill/Pearson Education.

Opperman, S., & Alant, E. (2003). The coping responses of the adolescent siblings of children with severe disabilities. *Disability and Rehabilitation, 25,* 441–454.

Optow, S. V. (1991). Adolescent peer conflicts: Implications for students and for schools. *Education and Urban Society, 23,* 416–441.

Ornoy, A. (2003). The impact of intrauterine exposure versus postnatal environment in neurodevelopmental toxicity: Long-term neurobehavioral studies in children at risk for developmental disorders. *Toxicology Letters, 140–141,* 171–181.

Osher, D., & Hanley, T. V. (2001). Implementing the SED national agenda: Promising programs and policies for children with emotional and behavioral disorders. *Education and Treatment of Children, 24,* 374–403.

Otten, K. L., & Tuttle, J. L. (2004). *Structured behavioral skills: A practitioner's model program for students with severe EBD.* Paper presented at the Council for Exceptional Children International Convention and Expo, New Orleans, LA.

Paclawskyj, T. R., Matson, J. L., Rush, K. S., Smalls, Y., & Vollmer, T. R. (2000). Questions about behavioral function (QABF): A behavioral checklist for functional assessment of aberrant behavior. *Research in Developmental Disabilities, 21,* 223–229.

Paclawskyj, T. R., Matson, J. L., Rush, K. S., Smalls, Y., & Vollmer, T. R. (2001). Assessment of the convergent validity of the questions about behavioral function scale with analogue functional analysis and the motivation assessment scale. *Journal of Intellectual Disability Research, 45,* 484–494.

Padeliadu, S., & Zigmond, N. (1996). Perspective of students with learning disabilities about special education placement. *Learning Disabilities Research and Practice, 1,* 15–23.

Paine, S. C., Radicchi, J., Rosellini, C. C., Deutchman, L., & Darch, C. B. (1983). *Structuring your classroom for academic success.* Champaign, IL: Research Press.

Papolos, D. M., & Papolos, J. (2002). *The bipolar child: The definitive and reassuring guide to childhood's most misunderstood disorder.* New York: Broadway Books.

Park, J., & Turnbull, A. P. (2003). Service integration in early intervention: Determining interpersonal and structural factors for its success. *Infants and Young Children, 16,* 48–58.

Park, J., Turnbull, A. P., & Turnbull, H. R. (2002). Impacts of poverty on quality of life in families of children with disabilities. *Exceptional Children, 68,* 151–170.

Parker, H. C. (1992). *Listen, look, and think: A self-regulation program for children.* Plantation, FL: Specialty Press.

Parker, L. B. (2005). Tic-related school problems: Report on functioning, accommodations, and interventions. *Behavior Modification, 29,* 876–899.

Parmar, R., & Cawley, J. (1991). Challenging the routines and passivity that characterize authentic instruction for children with mild handicaps. *Remedial and Special Education, 12,* 23–32.

Patterson, G. R. (1982). *Coercive family process.* Eugene, OR: Castalia.

Patterson, G. R. (1996). Some characteristics of a developmental theory for early-onset delinquency. In M. F. Lenzenweger and J. J. Haugaard (Eds.), *Frontiers in developmental psychology* (pp. 81–124). New York: Oxford University Press.

Patterson, G. R., DeBaryshe, B. D., & Ramsey, E. (1989). A developmental perspective on antisocial behavior. *American Psychologist, 44,* 329–335.

Patterson, G. R., & Guillon, M. E. (1968). *Living with children: New methods for parents and teachers.* Champaign, IL: Research Press.

Patterson, J. (1988). Families experiencing stress: The family adjustment and adaptation response model, family systems medicine. *Family Systems Medicine, 6*, 200–237.

Patterson, J., & Blum, R. W. (1996). Risk and resilience among children and youth with disabilities. *Archives of Pediatrics and Adolescent Medicine, 150*, 692–698.

Paulson, R. H. (1997). Patient information: Depression up to date. Retrieved 1/6/09 from http://patients.uptodate.com/topic.asp?file=menti_h/2952.

Paus, T. (2005). Mapping brain maturation and cognitive development during adolescence. *Trends in Cognitive Sciences, 9*, 60–68.

Peden, A. R., Rayens, M. K., Hall, L. A., & Grant, E. (2004). Negative thinking and the mental health of low-income single mothers. *Journal of Nursing Scholarship, 36*, 337–344.

Pennington, B. (2004). The development of psychopathology: Nature and nurture. *Journals of Developmental and Behavioral Pediatrics, 25*, 214–215.

Penno, D. A., Frank, A. R., & Wacker, D. P. (2000). Instructional accommodations for adolescent students with severe emotional or behavioral disorders. *Behavioral Disorders, 25*, 325–343.

Penza, K. M., Heim, C., & Nemeroff, C. B. (2003). Neurobiological effects of childhood abuse: Implications for the pathophysiology of depression and anxiety. *Archives of Women and Mental Health, 6*, 15–22.

Petermann, F., & Petermann, U. (1997). *Training with aggressive children*. Weinheim, Germany: Beltz.

Peterson, B. (2004). *Cultural intelligence: A guide to working with people from other cultures*. Yarmouth, ME: Nicholas Brealy (Intellectual Press).

Peterson, B. C. (1995). Neuroimaging in child and adolescent neuropsychiatric disorders. *Journal of the American Academy of Child and Adolescent Psychiatry, 34*, 1560–1576.

Peterson, K. M. H., & Shinn, M. R. (2002). Severe discrepancy models: Which best explains school identification practices for learning disabilities? *School Psychology Review, 31*, 459–476.

Phelps, L., Brown, R. T., & Power, T. J. (2002). *Pediatric Psychopharmacology: Combining Medical and Psychosocial Interventions*. Washington, DC: APA Books.

Phillips, D. R., Schwean, V. L., & Saklofske, D. H. (1997). Treatment effects of a school-based cognitive-behavioral program for aggressive children. *Canadian Journal of School Psychology, 13*, 60–67.

Piaget, J. (1951). *Psychology and intelligence*. London: Routledge and Kegan Paul.

Piazza, C. C., Fisher, W. W., Hagopian, L. P., Bowman, L. G., & Toole, L. (1996). Using a choice assessment to predict reinforcer effectiveness. *Journal of Applied Behavior Analysis, 29*, 1–9.

Pierce, W. D., & Epling, W. F. (1995). *Behavior analysis and learning*. Upper Saddle River, NJ: Prentice Hall.

Pierre, C. B., Nolan, E. E., Gadow, K. D., Sverd, J., & Sprafkin, J. (1999). Comparisons of internalizing and externalizing symptoms in children with attention-deficit-hyperactivity disorder with and without comorbid tic disorder. *Journal of Developmental and Behavioral Pediatrics, 20*, 170–176.

Pilowsky, D. J., Wickramaratne, P., Nomura, Y., Weissman, M. M., et al. (2006). Family discord, parental depression, and psychopathology in offspring: 20-year follow up. *Journal of the American Academy of Child and Adolescent Psychiatry, 45*, 452–460.

Pine, D. S. (1997). Childhood anxiety disorders. *Current Opinion in Pediatrics, 9*, 329–338.

Pine, D. S. (2006). Understanding developmental psychopathology: Two steps forward; one step back? *Journal of Child Psychology and Psychiatry*. Oxford, England: Blackwell Publishing.

Pinneau, S. R. (1955). The infantile disorder of hospitalism and anaclitic depression. *Psychological Bulletin, 52*, 429–452.

Piven, J., & O'Leary, D. (1997). Neuroimaging in autism. In B. S. Peterson & M. Lewis (Eds.), *Child and adolescent psychiatric clinics of North America: Neuroimaging* (Vol. 6, pp. 305–324). Philadelphia: Saunders.

Placer County SELPA. *Strategies and procedures that support positive behaviors*. http://www.placercoe.k12.ca.us/documents 405cd101.pdf. Retrieved 7/24/08. http://www.placeroe.k12.ca.us/Studentsand Parents/Documents/SELPA/Behavior Intervention Handbook.pdf. Retrieved 1/14/2010.

Plaud, J. J., & Gaither, G. A. (1996). Human behavioral momentum: Implications for applied behavior analysis and therapy. *Journal of Behavior Therapy and Experimental Psychiatry, 27*, 139–148.

Pliszka, S. R. (1992). Comorbidity of attention-deficit hyperactivity disorder and overanxious disorder. *Journal of the American Academy of Child and Adolescent Psychiatry, 28*, 882–887.

Plomin, R. (1996). Beyond nature vs. nurture. In L. L. Hall (Ed.), *Genetics and mental illness: Evolving issues for research and society* (pp. 29–50). New York: Plenum Press.

Pohan, L. A. (1996). Pre-service teachers' beliefs about diversity: Uncovering factors leading to multicultural responsiveness. *Equity and Excellence in Education, 29*, 62–69.

Polloway, E. A., Foley, R., & Epstein, M. H. (1992). A comparison of the homework problems of students with learning disabilities and non-handicapped students. *Learning Disabilities: Research and Practice, 7*, 203–209.

Pomeranz, K. (1999). Home-based behavioral treatment. *Journal of Autism and Developmental Disorders, 29*, 425.

Pond, W. G., Boleman, S. L., Flarotto, M. L., Ho, H., Kabe, D. A., Mersmann, H. J., et al. (2000). Perinatal ontogeny of brain growth in the domestic pig. *Proceedings of the Society for Experimental Biological Medicine, 223*, 102–108.

Porrata, J. L. (1998). Eliminating temper tantrums in a four-year-old by parent eliciting incompatible behavior. *Perceptual and Motor Skills, 86*, 42.

Porter, L. (2002). Cognitive skills. In C. Porter (Ed.), *Educating young children with special needs* (pp. 191–209). Crows Nest, Australia: Allen and Unwin.

Powell, S. W., & Barber-Foss, K. D. (1999). Traumatic brain injury in high school athletes. *Journal of the American Medical Association, 282*, 958–963.

Prasad, M. R., Ewing-Cobbs, L., Swank, P. R., & Kramer, L. (2002). Predictors of outcome following traumatic brain injury in childhood and adolescence. *Pediatric Neurosurgery, 36*, 64–74.

Prins, P. J. M., & Van Manen, T. G. (2005). Aggressive and antisocial behavior in youth. In A. Freeman, S. H. Felgoire, C. M. Nezu, A. M. Nezu, & M. A. Reinecke (Eds.), *Encyclopedia of cognitive behavior theory*. New York: Springer.

Pruslow, T. (2000). *A comparison of the costs and educational outcomes of three models of service delivery for special needs students.* Paper presented at the annual meeting of the American Educational Research Association, New Orleans, LA.

Purcell, A. E., Jeon, O. K., & Pevsner, J. (2001). The abnormal regulation of gene expression in autistic brain tissue. *Journal of Autism and Developmental Disorders, 31,* 545–549.

Purvis, K., & Tannock, R. (1997). Language abilities in children with attention deficit hyperactivity disorder, reading disabilities, and normal controls. *Journal of Abnormal Child Psychology, 25,* 133–145.

Quay, H., & Hogan, A. (Eds.). (1999). *Handbook of disruptive behavior disorders.* New York: Plenum Press.

Qi, C. H., & Kaiser, F. P. (2003). Behavioral problems of preschool children from low-income families: Review of the literature. *Topics in Early Childhood Special Education, 23,* 188–216.

Quinn, M. M., Osher, D., Warger, C. L., Hanley, T. V., Bader, B. D., & Hoffman, C. C. (2000). *Teaching and working with children who have emotional and behavioral challenges.* Longmont, CO: Sopris West.

Rachmen, S. (1979). The concept of required helpfulness. *Behavior Research Therapy, 17,* 1–6.

Railsback, J. (2004). *Increasing student attendance: Strategies from research and practice.* Portland, OR: Northwest Regional Educational Laboratory.

Raine, A., Brennan, P., & Mednick, S. A. (1997). Interaction between both complications and early maternal rejection in predisposing individuals to adult violence: Specificity to serious early-onset violence. *American Journal of Psychiatry, 154,* 1263–1271.

Raine, A., Reynolds, C., Veneabler, P. H., Mednick, S. A., & Farrington, D. F. (1998). Fearlessness, stimulation-seeking, and large body size at age 3 years as early predispositions to childhood aggression at age 11 years. *Archives of General Psychiatry, 55,* 743–751.

Rasinski, T., Blachowicz, C., & Lems, K. (2006). *Fluency instruction: Researched-based best practices.* New York: Guilford Press.

Rasinski, T. V. (1994). Fast start: A parental involvement reading program for primary grade students. Paper presented at the annual meeting of the College Reading Association, New Orleans, LA.

Rassool, G. H. (2006). Current issues and forthcoming events. *Journal of Advanced Nursing, 54,* 132–134.

Redding, R. E., & Shalf, S. M. (2001). The legal context of school violence: The effectiveness of federal, state, and local law enforcement efforts to reduce gun violence in schools. *Law and Policy, 23,* 297–343.

Reed, H., Thomas, E., Sprague, J. R., & Horner, R. H. (1997). The student guided functional assessment interview: An analysis of student and teacher agreement. *Journal of Behavioral Education, 7,* 33–49.

Reid, J., Eddy, S. M., Fetrow, R., & Stoolmiller, M. (1999). Descriptions and immediate impacts of a preventive intervention for conduct problems. *American Journal of Community Psychology, 27,* 483–517.

Reid, M. J., Walter, A. L., & O'Leary, S. G. (1999). Treatment of young children's bedtime refusal and nightmares wakings: A comparison of standard and graduated ignoring procedures. *Journal of Abnormal Child Psychology, 27,* 5–16.

Reid, R., & Lienemann, T. O. (2006). Self-regulated strategy development for written expression with students with attention deficit/hyperactivity disorder. *Exceptional Children, 73,* 53–68.

Reid, R., & Nelson, J. R. (2002). The utility, acceptability, and practicality of functional behavior assessment for students with high-incidence problem behaviors. *Remedial and Special Education, 23,* 15–23.

Reimers, C., & Brunger, B. A. (1999). *ADHD in the young child: Driven to redirection.* Plantation, FL: Specialty Press.

Reinke, W., & Hernan, K. (2002). A research agenda for school violence prevention. *American Psychologist, 57,* 790–797.

Reinke, W. M., Lewis-Pamer, T., & Martin, E. (2007). The effect of visual performance feedback on teacher use of behavior-specific praise. *Behavior Modification, 31,* 247–263.

Remschmidt, H. E., Schulz, E., Martin, M., Warnke, A., & Trott, G. E. (1994). Childhood-onset schizophrenia: History of the concept and recent strides. *Schizophrenia Bulletin, 20,* 727–745.

Reschly, D. (1996). Identification and assessment of students with disabilities. *The future of children: Special education for students with disabilities* (pp. 40–53). Princeton, NJ: Princeton University.

Reschly, D. J., Tilly III, W. D., & Grimes, T. P. (Eds.). (1999). Special education in transition: Functional assessment and noncategorized programming. Longmont, CO: Sopris West.

Reynolds, A. (2000). *Success in early intervention: The Chicago child-parent centers.* Lincoln: University of Nebraska Press.

Reynolds, A. J., Temple, J. A., Robertson, D. L., Dylan, L., & Mann, E. A. (2001). Long-term effects of an early childhood intervention on educational achievement and juvenile arrest: A 15-year follow-up of low-income children in public schools. *Journal of the American Medical Association, 285,* 2339–2346.

Rhode, G., Jenson, W. R., & Reavis, H. K. (1996). *The tough kid book: Practical classroom management strategies.* Longmont, CO: Sopris West.

Rice, J. K. (1999). The impact of class size on instructional strategies and the use of time in high school mathematics and science courses. *Education Evaluation and Policy Analysis, 21,* 215–229.

Riffel, C. L. (2005). Positive interventions and effective strategies. Retrieved on 3/6/09 at www.pbsga.org.

Riley-Tillman, T. C., Chafouleas, S. M., Eckert, T. L., & Kelleher, C. (2005). Bridging the gap between research and practice: A framework for building research agendas in school psychology. *Psychology in the Schools, 42,* 459–473.

Rivara, J., Jaffe, K., Polissar, N., Fay, G., Liao, S., & Martin, K. (1996). Predictors of family functioning and change 3 years after traumatic brain injury in children. *Archives of Physical Medicine and Rehabilitation, 77,* 554–564.

Roach, V., Ascroft, T., Stranp, A., & Kysilko, D. (Eds.). (1995). *Winning ways: Creating inclusive schools, classrooms and communities.* Alexandria, VA: National Association of State Boards of Education.

Roberts, J. M. (2004). A review of the research to identify the most effective models of best practice in the management of children with autism spectrum disorders. Sydney, Australia: Center for Developmental Disability Studies. Retrieved from www.dadhc.nsw.gov.au.

Roberts, N., Parker, K. C. H., Woogh, C., Cripps, L. F., & Arthur, P. (2000). Bipolar disorder in ADHD children grown up (letter to the editor). *Journal of American Academy of Child and Adolescent Psychiatry, 39,* 678–679.

Robertson, M. M. (2000). Tourette Syndrome, associated conditions, and the conplexities of treatment (PDF). *Brain, 123(3)*, 425–462.

Robin, A. L. (1998). *ADHD in adolescents: Diagnosis and treatment.* New York: Guilford Press.

Roderique, T. W., Polloway, E. A., Cumblad, C., Epstein, M. H., & Bursuck, W. D. (1994). Homework: A survey of policies in the United States. *Journal of Learning Disabilities, 27,* 481–487.

Rogers, M. F., & Myles, B. S. (2001). Using social stories and comic strip conversations to interpret social situations for an adolescent with Asperger syndrome. *Interventions in School and Clinic, 36,* 310–313.

Rogers, S. S., Wehner, E. A., & Hagerman, R. (2001). The behavioral phenotype in Fragile X symptoms of autism in very young children with Fragile X syndrome: Ideopathic autism and other developmental disorders. *Journal of Developmental and Behavioral Pediatrics. 22,* 409–417.

Rolland, J. S., & Walsh, F. (2005). Systematic training for health care professionals: The Chicago Center for Family Health approach. *Family Process, 44,* 283–301.

Rose, D. J., & Church, R. J. (1998). Learning to teach: The acquisition and maintenance of teaching skills. *Journal of Behavioral Education, 8,* 5–35.

Rosenberg, M. (1998, January 20). Grant will broaden PAR program. *Johns Hopkins Gazette, 27*(18).

Rosenberg, M. S. (1989). The effect of daily homework assignments on the acquisition of basic skills by students with learning disabilities. *Journal of Learning Disabilities, 22,* 314–323.

Rosenberg, M. S., Wilson, R. J., Maheady, L., & Sindelar, P. T. (2004). *Educating students with behavior disorders* (3rd ed.). Boston: Allyn and Bacon.

Rosenshine, B. (1995). Advances in research on instruction. *Journal of Educational Research, 88,* 262–268.

Rosenshine, B., & Stevens, R. (1986). Teaching functions. In M. C. Witrock (Ed.), *Handbook of research on teaching* (3rd ed., pp. 376–391). New York: Macmillan.

Rothstein, L. F. (2000). *Special education law* (3rd ed.). New York: Addison Wesley Longman.

Rourke, B. (2005). Neuropsychology of learning disabilities: Past and future. *Learning Disabilities Quarterly, 28,* 111–114.

Rowe, R., Maughan, B., Pickler, A., Costello, E., & Angold, A. (2002). The relationship between DSM-IV oppositional defiant disorder and conduct disorder: Findings from the Great Smoky Mountains study. *Journal of Child Psychology and Psychiatry and Allied Disciplines, 43,* 365–373.

Ruef, M., Higgens, C., Glaeser, B., & Patnode, M. (1998). Positive behavioral support: Strategies for teachers. *Intervention in School and Clinic, 34,* 21–31.

Russo, C., & Stefkovich, J. (1998). Search and seizure in the schools. *NASSP Bulletin, 82,* 26–33.

Rutherford, R. B., Quinn, M. M., & Mathur, S. R. (Eds.). (2004). *Handbook of research in emotional and behavior disorders.* New York: Guilford Press.

Rutter, M. (1978). Diagnosis and definition. In M. Rutter & E. Schopler (Eds.), *Autism: A reappraisal of concepts and treatments* (pp. 1–25). New York: Plenum.

Rutter, M. (1979). Protective factors in children's response to stress and disadvantage. In M. Kent & J. Roif (Eds.), *Primary prevention in psychopathology. Vol. 3: Social competence in children* (pp. 49–74). Hanover, NH: University Press of New England.

Rutter, M. (1995). Clinical implications of attachment concepts: Retrospect and prospect. *Journal of Child Psychology and Psychiatry, 36,* 549–571.

Rutter, M. (2005). Incidence of autism spectrum disorders: Changes over time and their meaning. *Acta Pediatrica, 94,* 2–15.

Rutter, M., & Lockyer, L. (1967). A five to fifteen year follow-up of infantile psychosis: I. Description of sample. *British Journal of Psychiatry, 113,* 1109–1183.

Rutter, M., & Sroufe, L. A. (2000). Developmental psychopathology: Concepts and challenges. *Developmental Psychopathology, 12,* 265–296.

Sachs, G. S., Printz, D. J., Kahn, D. A., et al. (2000). The expert consensus guidelines series: Medication treatment of bipolar disorder. *Postgraduate Medical Specialties,* (April) 1–104.

Safer, D. J., Zito, J. M., & Fine, E. M. (1996). Increased methylphenidate usage for attention deficit disorder in the 1990s. *Pediatrics, 98,* 1084–1088.

Safran, S., Safran, J., & Ellis, K. (2003). Interventions ABCs for children with Asperger syndrome. *Topics in Language Disorder, 23,* 154–165.

Sailor, W., Freeman, R., Britten, J., McCart, A., Smith, C., & Scott, T. M. (1999–2000). Using information technology to prepare personnel to implement functional behavioral assessment and positive behavioral support. *Exceptionality, 8,* 217–229.

Sainato, D. M. (1990). Classroom transitions: Organizing environments to promote independent performance in preschool children with disabilities. *Education and Treatment of Children, 13,* 288–297.

Salmon, H. (2006). Educating students with emotional or behavioral disorders. *Law and Disorder, 1,* 49–53.

Salzinger, S., Feldman, R. S., Wg-Mak, D. S., Mojica, E., & Stockhammer, T. (2001). The effect of physical abuse on children's social and affective states: A model of cognitive and behavioral processes explaining the association. *Development and Psychopathology, 13,* 805–825.

Sameroff, A. J. (1995). General symptoms theories and developmental psychopathology. *Developmental Psychopathology, 1,* 659–695.

Sampson, R. J., & Laub, J. H. (1993). *Crime in the making: Pathways and turning points through life.* Cambridge, MA: Harvard University Press.

Sanders, M. G. (2001). The role of "community" in comprehensive school, family and community partnership programs. *School Community Journal, 102,* 19–34.

Sanders, M. G., & Harvey, A. (2002). Beyond the school walls: A case study of principal leadership for school-community collaboration. *Teachers College Record, 104,* 1345–1368.

Sanders, M. R. (1999). Triple p-positive parenting program: Towards an empirically validated multilevel parenting and family support strategy for the prevention of behavioral and emotional problems in children. *Clinical Child and Family Psychology Review, 2,* 71–90.

Sasso, G. M., Conroy, M. A., Stichter, J. P., & Fox, J. J. (2001). Slowing down the bandwagon: The misapplication of functional assessment for students with emotional and behavioral disorders. *Behavioral Disorders, 26,* 282–296.

Savage, T. V. (1999). *Teaching self-control through management and discipline.* Boston: Allyn and Bacon.

Scattione, D., Wilezynski, S. M., Edwards, R. P., & Rabian, B. (2002). Decreasing disruptive behaviors of children with autism using social stories. *Journal of Autism and Developmental Disorders, 32*, 535–543.

Schloss, P. J., & Smith, M. A. (1987). Guidelines for the ethical use of manual restraint in public school settings for behaviorally disordered students. *Behavior Disorders, 12*, 207–213.

Schmidt-Neven, R., Anderson, V., & Godber, T. (2002). *Attention-deficit/hyperactivity disorder: A disease of our time.* Sydney, Australia: Allen and Unwin.

School to Work Opportunities Act. (1994). Public Law 103-239. 103rd U.S. Congress.

Schuler, A. L. (2001). Autistic syndrome. *Autism, 5*, 331–340.

Schultz, R. T. (2005). Developmental deficits in social perception in autism: The role of the amygdala and fusiform face area. *International Journal of Developmental Neuroscience, 23*, 125–141.

Schunk, D. H. (1997). *Self-monitoring as a motivator during instruction with elementary school students.* Paper presented at the annual meeting of the America Educational Research Association, Chicago.

Schutte, R. C., & Hopkins, B. L. (1970). The effects of teacher attention on following instructions in a kindergarten class. *Journal of Applied Behavior Analysis, 3*, 117–122.

Scott, T. M., & Nelson, C. M. (1998). Confusion and failure in facilitating generalized social responding in the school setting: Sometimes 2 and 2–5. *Behavioral Disorders, 23*, 264–275.

Scott, T. M., & Nelson, C. M. (1999a). Using functional behavioral assessment: Implications for training and staff development. *Behavioral Disorders, 24*, 249–252.

Scott, T. M., & Nelson, C. M. (1999b). Using functional behavioral assessment to develop effective intervention plans: Practical classroom applications. *Journal of Positive Behavioral Interventions, 1*, 242–251.

Scott, T. M., Nelson, C. M., & Liaupsin, C. J. (2001). Effective instruction: The forgotten component in preventing school violence. *Education and Treatment of Children, 24*, 309–322.

Segal, Z. V., & Shaw, B. F. (1988). Cognitive assessment: Issues and methods. In K. S. Dobson (Ed.), *Handbook of cognitive-behavioral therapies* (pp. 39–84). New York: Guilford Press.

Seligman, M., & Darling, R. B. (1989). *Ordinary families, special children.* New York: Guilford Press.

Semrau, L., & Fitzgerald, G. (1995). Interactive case studies in behavior disorders: Looking at children from multiple perspectives. *Education and Treatment of Children, 18*, 348–359.

Semrud-Clikeman, M. (2001). *Traumatic brain injury in children and adolescents: Assessment and intervention.* New York: Guilford Press.

Serra, M., Loth, F. L., VanGeret, P. L., Hurkens, E., & Minderaa, R. B. (2002). Theory of mind in children with a lesser variant of autism: A longitudinal study. *Journal of Child Psychology and Psychiatry, 43*, 885–900.

Severson, H., & Walker, H. (2002). Proactive approaches for identifying children at risk for sociobehavioral problems. In K. Lane, F. M. Gresham, & T. E. O'Shaughnessy (Eds.), *Intervention for children with or at risk for emotional and behavioral disorders* (pp. 33–53). Boston: Allyn and Bacon.

Shapiro, E. S., & Cole, L. L. (1994). *Behavior change in the classroom: Self-management interventions.* New York: Guilford Press.

Shapiro, E. S., & Eckert, T. L. (1993). Curriculum-based assessment among school psychologists: Knowledge, use and attitudes. *Journal of School Psychology, 31*, 375–384.

Shapiro, E. S., & Heick, P. F. (2004). School psychologist assessment practices in the evolution of students referred for social/behavioral/emotional problems. *Psychology in the Schools, 44*, 551–561.

Shapiro, E. S., & Kratochwill, T. R. (Eds.). (2000). *Conducting school-based assessments of child and adolescent behavior.* New York: Guilford Press.

Shavelson, R. J., & Towne, L. (Eds.) (2002). *Scientific research in education.* Washington, DC: National Academy Press.

Shaw, D., Owens, E., Giovannelli, J., & Winslow, E. (2001). Infant and toddler pathways leading to early externalizing disorder. *Journal of the American Academy of Child and Adolescent Psychiatry, 40*, 36–43.

Shaw, S. R., & Braden, J. P. (1990). Race and gender bias in the administration of corporal punishment. *School Psychology Review, 19*, 378–383.

Shaywitz, S. E., Cohen, D. J., & Shaywitz, B. A. (1980). Behavior and learning difficulties in children of normal intelligence born to alcoholic mothers. *Journal of Pediatrics, 96*, 978–982.

Shechtman, Z., & Pastor, R. (2005). Cognitive-behavioral and humanistic group treatment for children with learning disabilities: A comparison of outcomes and process. *Journal of Counseling Psychology, 52*, 322–336.

Sheldon, S. B. (2003). Linking school-family-community partnerships in urban elementary schools to student achievement on state tests. *Urban Review, 35*, 149–165.

Sheldon, S. B. (2005). Testing a structural equation model of partnership program implementation and parent involvement. *Elementary School Journal, 106*, 171–187.

Shellady, S. M., Sealander, K. A. (2003). Rethinking school-wide discipline. *Principal Leadership, 142*, 29–34.

Shinn, M. R., Stoner, G., & Walker, H. M. (Eds.). (2002). *Interventions for academic and behavior problems: Preventive and remedial approaches.* Silver Springs, MD: National Association of School Psychologists.

Shore, B. A., & Iwata, B. A. (1999). Assessment and treatment of behavior disorders maintained by nonsocial (automatic) reinforcement. In A. C. Repp & R. H. Horner (Eds.), *Functional analysis of problem behavior: From effective assessment to effective support* (pp. 117–146). Belmont, CA: Wadsworth.

Shore, K. (1998). *Special kids problem solver.* Paramus, NJ: Prentice Hall.

Shores, R., & Wehby, J. (1999). Analyzing the classroom social behavior of students with EBD. *Journal of Behavior Disorders, 7*, 194–199.

Simon, B. S. (2004). High school outreach and family involvement. *Social Psychology of Education, 7*, 185–209.

Sinclair, I., Wilson, K., & Gibbs, I. (2005). *Faster placements: Why they succeed and why they fail.* London: Jessica Kingsley.

Singer, A. S. (1997). Neurobiology of Tourette's syndrome. *Neurologic Clinic, 15*, 357–379.

Singh, K., & Billingsley, B. S. (1996). Intent to stay in teaching: Teachers of students with emotional disorders versus other special educators. *Remedial and Special Education, 17*, 37–47.

Skiba, R. (2003). *Children left behind: The disproportionate impact of school discipline on students of color.* Paper presented at a meeting of the Open Society Institute Forum, Baltimore.

Skiba, R., Michael, R., Nardo, A., & Peterson, R. (2002). The color of discipline: Sources of racial and gender disproportionality in school punishment. *Urban Review, 34,* 317–342.

Skiba, R., & Peterson, R. (2006). *The dark side of zero tolerance: Can punishment lead to safe schools?* Retrieved on 5/6/09 from http://pdkinel.org/kappan/rski9901.htm.

Skiba, R. J. (2001). Zero tolerance: Solution or problem? Key note presentation to the Ohio State Chiefs of Police Association 8th Annual Reducing School Violence Conference.

Skiba, R. J., & Knesting, K. (2002). Zero tolerance, zero evidence: An analysis of school disciplinary practice. In R. J. Skiba & G. G. Nunn (Eds.), *New directions for youth development (#92). Zero tolerance: Can suspension and expulsion keep schools safe?* (pp. 17–43). San Francisco: Jossey-Bass.

Skiba, R. J., & Peterson, R. L. (2000). School discipline at a crossroads: From zero tolerance to early response. *Exceptional Children, 66,* 335–347.

Skibam, R. (2001). *Zero tolerance, zero evidence: An analysis of school disciplinary practice.* Bloomington, IN: Indiana Education Policy Center, Indiana University.

Skinner, B. F. (1938). *The behavior of organisms.* New York: Appleton-Century Crofts.

Skinner, B. F. (1953). *Science and human behavior.* New York: Free Press.

Skinner, B. F. (1971). *Beyond freedom and dignity.* New York: Knopf.

Skinner, B. F. (1974). *About behaviorism.* New York: Knopf.

Slavin, R. E. (2003). A reader's guide to scientifically based research. *Educational Leadership, 60,* 12–16.

Slee, P. T. (1996). Family climate and behavior in families with conduct disordered children. *Child Psychiatry and Human Development, 26,* 255–265.

Smalley, S. L., Asarnov, R. F., & Spence, M. A. (1988). Autism and genetics. *Archives of General Psychiatry, 45,* 953–961.

Smart, J. L. (1991). Critical periods in brain development. *CIBA Foundation Symposium, 156,* 109–124.

Smith, B. W., & Sugai, G. (2000). A self-management functional assessment-based behavior support plan for a middle school student with EBD. *Journal of Positive Behavior Interventions, 2,* 131–152.

Smith, C. R. (2000). Behavioral and discipline provisions of IDEA '97: Implicit competencies yet to be confirmed. *Exceptional Children, 66,* 403–412.

Smith, M. C., Van Loon, P. C., DeFrates-Densch, N., & Schrader, T. O. (1998). Content changes in parent education books for parents of adolescents. *Family and Consumer Sciences Research Journal, 27,* 194–213.

Smith, R. G., & Iwata, B. A. (1997). Antecedent influences on behavior disorders. *Journal of Applied Behavior Analysis, 30,* 343–376.

Smith, S. W. (2002). *Applying cognitive-behavioral techniques to social skills instruction.* Arlington, VA: ERIC Clearinghouse on Disabilities and Gifted Education.

Smith, T. B. C., Polloway, E., Patton, J. R., & Dowdy, C. A. (2004). *Teaching students with special needs in inclusive settings* (4th ed.). Boston: Allyn and Bacon.

Snowling, M. L., Bishop, D. V. M., & Stothard, S. E. (2000). Is pre-school language impairment a risk factor for dyslexia in adolescence? *Journal of Child Psychology and Psychiatry, 41,* 587–600.

Snyder, G. (1992). Morningside academy: A learning guarantee. *Performance Management Magazine, 10,* 29–35.

Solomon, D., & Sparadeo, F. (1992). Effects of substance use on persons with traumatic brain injury. *Neurorehabilitation, 29,* 16–26.

Sourkes, B. (1990). Siblings count two. *Candlelighters Childhood Cancer Foundation Youth Newsletter, 12,* 2–6.

Spencer, T. J., Biederman, J., Wozniak, J., & Faraone, T. E. (2001). Passing pediatric bipolar disorder from its associated comorbidity with the disruptive behavior disorders. *Biological Psychiatry, 49,* 1062–1070.

Spencer, V. G., Scruggs, T. E., & Mastropieri, M. A. (2003). Content-area learning in middle school social studies classrooms and students with emotional or behavior disorders: A comparison of strategies. *Behavioral Disorders, 28,* 77–93.

Spitz, R. A. (1945). Hospitalism: An inquiry into the genesis of psychiatric conditions in early childhood. *Psychoanalytic Studies of Childhood,* 53–74.

Spoth, R. L., Redmond, C., & Shin, C. (2000). Reducing adolescents' aggressive and hostile behaviors. *Archives of Pediatric and Adolescent Medicine, 154,* 1248–1257.

Sprague, J. (2002). Getting effective school discipline practices to scale: B.E.S.T. practices staff development. *NASP Communique, 30,* 28–32.

Sprague, J., Bernstein, L., Munkres, A., Golly, A., & March, R. (1999). BEST practices: *Building effective schools together.* Eugene, OR: University of Oregon, Institute on Violence and Destructive Behavior.

Sprague, J., Sugai, G., Horner, R. H., & Walker, H. (1999). Using office discipline referral data to evaluate school-wide discipline and violence prevention. *Interventions OSSC Bulletin, 42(3).*

Sprague, J., Sugai, G., & Walker, H. M. (1998). Antisocial behavior in schools. In T. S. Watson & F. M. Gresham (Eds.), *Handbook of child behavior therapy* (pp. 451–474). New York: Plenum Press

Sprague, J., & Walker, H. (2000). Early identification for youth with antisocial and violent behavior. *Exceptional Children, 66,* 367–379.

Sprick, R. S., Borgmeier, C., & Nolet, V. (2002). Prevention and management of behavior problems in secondary schools. In M. Shinn, H. M. Walker, & G. Stoner (Eds.), *Interventions for academic and behavioral problems II: Preventive and remedial approaches* (pp. 373–401) Bethesda, MD: National Association of School Psychologists.

Sprick, R. S., Garrison, M., & Howard, L. (1998). *CHAMPs: A proactive and positive approach to classroom management.* Eugene, OR: Pacific Northwest Publishing.

Stainback, S., & Stainback, W. (1996). *Inclusion: A guide for educators.* Baltimore: Brookes.

Stanovich, P. J., & Stanovich, K. E. (2003). *Using research and reason in education.* Portsmouth, NH: RMC Research Corporation.

Steele, H. (Ed.). (2004). Editorial: New perspectives on attachment through the life cycle. *Attachment and Human Development, 6,* 1–2.

Steiner, L. (2000). A review of the research literature on scaling up in education. Retrieved on 6/4/09 from http://ncrel.org/csri/resources/scaling/review.htm.

Steinhausen, H. C., Von Gontard, A., Spohr, H. C., Hauffa, B. P., Eiholzer, U., Backer, M., et al. (2002). Behavior phenotypes in four mental retardation syndromes: Fetal alcohol syndrome, Prader-Willi syndrome, Fragile X, and Tuberosis Sclerosis, *111,* 381–387.

Steinhausen, H. C., Willms, J., & Spohr, H. L. (1993). Long-term psychopathological and cognitive outcomes of children with fetal alcohol syndrome. *Journal of American Academy of Child and Adolescent Psychiatry, 32,* 990–994.

Stewart, S. C., & Evans, W. H. (1997). Setting the stage for success: Assessing the instructional environment. *Preventing School Failure, 41,* 53–56.

Stokes, T. (2002). Terror and violence perpetrated by children. In C. E. Stout (Ed.), *The psychology of terrorism. Vol. 4: Programs and practices in response and prevention* (pp. 77–90). Westport, CT: Praeger.

Stokes, T., & Baer, D. M. (1977). An implicit technology of generalization. *Journal of Applied Behavior Analysis, 10,* 349–367.

Stokes, T., Mowrey, D., Dean, K. B., & Hoffman, S. J. (1997). Nurturance: Traps of aggression, depression and regression affecting childhood illness. In D. M. Baer & E. M. Pinkston (Eds.), *Environment and behavior* (pp. 147–154). Boulder, CO: Westview Press.

Stoneman, Z., Brody, G. H., Davis, C. H., & Crapps, J. M. (1988). Childcare responsibilities, peer relations, and siblings conflict: Older siblings of mentally retarded children. *American Journal of Mental Retardation, 93,* 174–183.

Stoneman, Z., Brody, G. H., Davis, C. H., Crapps, J. M. & Malone, D. M. (1991). Ascribed role relations between children with mental retardation and their younger siblings. *American Journal of Mental Retardation, 95,* 537–550.

Straus, M. A., & Donnelly, D. A. (2001). *Beating the devil out of them: Corporal punishment in American families and its effect on children.* New Brunswick, NJ: Transaction.

Straus, M. A., Sugarman, D. B., & Giles-Sims, T. (1997). Spanking by parents and subsequent antisocial behavior of children. *Archives of Pediatrics and Adolescent Medicine, 151,* 761–767.

Strauss, B., Sherman, E. M. S., & Spreen, O. (2006). *A compendium of neuropsychological tests: Administration, norms, and commentary.* Oxford, England: Oxford University Press.

Streissguth, A. P. (1997). *Fetal alcohol syndrome: A guide for families and communities.* Baltimore: Brookes.

Streissguth, A. P., et al. (2004). Risk factors for adverse life outcomes in fetal alcohol syndrome and fetal alcohol effects. *Journal of Developmental Pediatrics, 25,* 228–238.

Streissguth, A. P., Aase, J. M., Clarren, S. K., Randels, S. R., LaDine, R. A., & Smith, D. F. (1991). Fetal alcohol syndrome in adolescents and adults. *Journal of the American Medical Association, 265,* 191–196.

Strother, D. B. (1984). Another look at time on task. *Phi Delta Kappan, 65,* 714–717.

Sturm, W. (2007). Neuropsychological assessment. *Journal of Neurology, 254,* 1432–1459.

Suen, H. R. (1990). *Principles of test theories.* Hillsdale, NJ: Lawrence Erlbaum.

Sugai, G., & Horner, R. H. (1999). Discipline and behavioral support: Preferred processes and practices. *Effective School Practices, 17,* 10–22.

Sugai, G., & Horner, R. (2002). The evolution of discipline practice: School-wide positive behavior supports. *Child and Family Therapy, 24,* 23–50.

Sugai, G., Horner, R. H., Dunlap, G., Hieneman, M., Lewis, T. J., Nelson, C. M., et al. (2000). Applying positive behavioral support and functional behavioral assessment in schools. *Journal of Positive Behavioral Interventions and Support, 2,* 131–143.

Sugai, G., Lewis-Palmer, T., & Hogan-Burke, S. (2000). Overview of the functional behavioral assessment process. *Exceptionality, 8,* 149–160.

Sugai, G., Sprague, J. R., Horner, R. H., & Walker, H. M. (2000). Preventing school violence: The use of office discipline referrals to assess and monitor school-wide discipline interventions. *Journal of Emotional and Behavioral Disorders, 8,* 94–101.

Sullivan, P. M., & Knutson, J. F. (2000). Maltreatment and disabilities: A population-based epidemiological study. *Child Abuse and Neglect, 24,* 1257–1273.

Sutherland, K. S. (2000). Promoting positive interactions between teachers and students with emotional/behavioral disorders. *Preventing School Failure, 44,* 110–115.

Sutherland, K. S., Alder, N., & Gunter, P. L. (2003). The effect of varying rates of opportunities to respond to academic requests on the classroom behavior of students with EBD. *Journal of Emotional and Behavioral Disorders, 11,* 239–298.

Sutherland, K. S., & Wehby, J. H. (2001). The effects of self-evaluation on teaching behavior in classrooms for students with emotional and behavioral disorders. *Journal of Special Education, 35,* 161–171.

Sutherland, K. S., Wehby, J. H., & Yoder, P. J. (2002). Examination of the relationship between teacher praise and opportunities for students with EBD to respond to academic requests. *Journal of Emotional and Behavioral Disorders, 10,* 5–13.

Tabor, M. B. W. (1996, April 6). Homework is keeping grade-schoolers busy. *New York Times.* p. 64.

Tarcic, E. K., & Hughes, R. S. (2004). Caregiving influenced by gender and spirituality. *Journal of Religion, Disability and Health, 7,* 41–53.

Taylor, H. G. (2004). Research on outcomes of pediatric traumatic brain injury: Current advances and future directions. *Developmental Neuropsychology, 25,* 199–225.

Teeter, P. A., & Semrud-Clikeman, M. (1997). *Child neuropsychological assessment and intervention.* Boston: Allyn and Bacon.

Temple, A. J., Reynolds, A. J., & Miedel, W. T. (2000). Can early intervention prevent high school dropout? Evidence from the Chicago child-parent centers. *Urban Education, 35,* 31–56.

Thapar, A., & McGuffin, P. (1994). A twin study of depressive symptoms in childhood. *British Journal of Psychiatry, 165,* 259–265.

Thiemann, K. S., & Goldstein, H. (2001). Social stories, written text cues, and video feedback: Effect on social communication of children with autism. *Journal of Applied Behavior Analysis, 34,* 425–446.

Thornton, T. N., Craft, C. A., Dahlberg, L. L., Lynch, B. S., & Baer, K. (2000). *Best practices of youth violence prevention: A sourcebook for community action.* Atlanta: Centers for Disease Control and Prevention, National Center for Injury Prevention and Control.

Thurlow, M., Ysseldyke, J., & Anderson, A. (1995). *High school graduation requirements: What's happening for students with disabilities?* (Synthesis Report 20). Minneapolis: University of Minnesota, Institute on Community Interpretation, National Center on Educational Outcomes.

Thweatt, K. S., & McCroskey, J. C. (1996). Teacher non-immediacy and misbehavior: Unintentional negative communication. *Communication Research Reports, 13,* 198–204.

Tiano, J. D., Fortson, B. L., McNeil, C. B., & Humphreys, L. A. (2005). Managing classroom behavior of head start children using response cost and token economy procedures. *Journal of Early and Intensive Behavior Intervention, 2,* 28–39.

Tieghi, C. (1997). A behaviorally-based teacher-driven meeting system. Survival dissertation submitted to University of Kansas.

Till, C., Westall, C., Rovet, J. F., & Koren, G. (2001). Prenatal exposure to organic solvents and color vision impairment. *Teratology*, *64*, 134–141.

Tillman, L. C. (2005). Monitoring new teachers: Implications for membership practice in urban school. *Educational Administration Quarterly*, *41*, 609–629.

Tobin, T., Sugai, G., & Colvin, G. (2000). Using discipline referrals to make decisions. *NASSP Bulletin*, *84*, 106–117.

Tobin, T. J. (2000). Function-based support at school: Summaries of research examples. Retrieved on 6/3/09 from http://www.uoregon.edu/~tobin/enufhtml.htm.

Todd, R., Geller, B., Neuman, R., Fox, L. W., & Hickok, J. (1996). Increased prevalence of alcoholism in relatives of depressed and bipolar children. *Journal of the American Academy of Child and Adolescent Psychiatry*, *35*, 716–724.

Todis, B., Bullis, M., Waintrup, M., Schultz, R., & D'Ambrosio, R. (2001). Overcoming the odds: Qualitative examination of resilience among formerly incarcerated adolescents. *Exceptional Children*, *68*, 119–139.

Toga, H. W., Thompson, P. M., Sowell, E. S., et al. (2006). Mapping brain maturation. *Trends in Neuroscience*, *29*, 148–159.

Tolan, P., Gorman-Smith, D., & Henry, D. (2001). New study to focus on efficacy of "whole school" prevention approaches. *Emotional and Behavioral Disorders in Youth*, *2*, 5–7.

Tomblin, J., Xuyang, Z., Buckwalter, P. & Catts, H. (2000). The association of reading disability, behavioral disorders, and language impairment among second grade children. *Journal of Child Psychology and Psychiatry and Allied Disciplines*, *41*, 473–482.

Tompkins, J. R., & Tompkins-McGill, P. L. (1993). *Surviving in schools in the 1990s: Strategic management of school environments*. Lanham, MD: University Press of America.

Tools for Schools. (1998). Conflict Resolution. *Tools for Schools, Vol 2(3)*, December.

Torrey, E. F. (1994). *Schizophrenia and manic depressive disorder: The biological roots of mental illness as revealed by the landmark study of identical twins*. New York, Basic Books.

Torrey, E. (1997). Seasonality of births in schizophrenia and bipolar disorder: A review of the literature. *Schizophrenia Research*, *28*, 1–38.

Torrey, E. F. (1997). *Out of the shadows: Confronting America's mental illness crisis*. New York: Wiley.

Toth, S. L., & Cicchetti, P. (1996). Patterns of relatedness expressive symptomatology, and perceived competence in maltreated children. *Journal of Consulting and Clinical Psychology*, *64*, 32–41.

Touchette, P. E., MacDonald, R. F., & Langer, S. N. (1985). A scatter plot for identifying stimulus control of problem behavior. *Journal of Applied Behavior Analysis*, *18*, 343–351.

Turnbull, A., Edmonson, H., Griggs, P., Wickham, D., Sailor, W., Freeman, R., et al. (2002). A blueprint for school-wide positive behavior support: Implementation of three components. *Exceptional Children*, *68*, 377–402.

Turnbull, A. P., & Turnbull, H. R. (1999). Comprehensive life style support for adults with challenging behavior: From rhetoric to reality. *Education and Training in Mental Retardation and Developmental Disabilities*, *34*, 373–394.

Turnbull, A. P., & Turnbull, H. R. (1990). A tale about of lifestyle changes: Comments on "Toward a technology of non aversive behavioral support." *Journal of the Association for Persons with Severe Handicaps*, *15*, 142–144.

Turnbull, H. R., Turnbull, A. P., & Wilcox, B. L. (2002). Family interests and positive behavior support: Opportunities under the individuals with disabilities education act. In J. M. Lucyshyn, G. Dunlap, & R. W. Albin (Eds.), *Families and positive behavior support: Addressing problem behavior in family contexts* (pp. 57–72). Baltimore: Brookes.

Turnbull, H. R., Wilcox, B. L., Stowe, M. J., & Turnbull, A. P. (2001). BAD requirements for use of PBS: Guidelines for responsible agencies. *Journal of Positive Behavior Support. 3(1)*, 11–18.

University of Rochester Medical Center. (2006, February 7). Children with asthma more likely to have behavior difficulties. *Science Daily*.

U. S. Department of Education. (1998a) *Annual report on school safety*. Washington, DC: Department of Justice.

U. S. Department of Education. (1998b). *Twenty-third annual report to Congress on the implementation of the Individuals with Disabilities Education Act*. Washington, DC: Author.

U. S. Department of Education. (1999). *Educational excellence for all children*. Act of 1999. Fact sheet available from http://www.ed/gov/offices/OSSE/ESBA/factsheet.html. Retrieved 10/3/09.

U. S. Department of Justice, Office of Juvenile Justice and Delinquency Prevention. (2000, March). *Want to resolve a dispute? Try mediation (#15)*. Retrieved from http://www.mcjrs/gov/html/ojjdp/youthbulletin/200_03_1/contents.html.

Vacca, R. S., & Hudgins, H. C. Jr. (1982). *The legacy of the Burger court and the schools: 1969–1986*. (NOLPE1991).

Van Acker, R. (2002). *Establishing and monitoring a school and classroom climate that promotes desired behavior and academic achievement* (ERIC Document Reproduction Service No. ED 466862). CASE/CCBD Mini-Library Series on Safe, Drug Free, and Effective Schools.

Van Ijzendoorn, M. H., Juffer, F., & Duyvesteyn, M. G. (1995). Breaking the international cycle of insecure attachment: A review of the effects of attachment-based interventions on maternal sensitivity and infant security. *Journal of Child Psychology and Psychiatry*, *36*, 225–248.

Van Os, J., & Marcells, M. (1998, July). The ecogenetics of schizophrenia: A review. *Schizophrenia Research*, *32*, 127–135.

Van Voorhis, F. L. (2003). Interactive Homework in Middle School: Effects on family involvement and student's science achievement. *Journal of Educational Research*, *6*, 323–339.

Vance, E. J., Bowen, N. K., Fernandez, G., & Thompson, S. (2002). Risk and protective factors as predictors of outcome in adolescents with psychiatric disorder and aggression. *Journal of the American Academy of Child and Adolescent Psychiatry*, *41*, 36–43.

Vandell, D. L., & Su, H. (1999). Childcare and school-age children. *Young Children*, *54(6)*, 62–71.

Vanderploeg, R. D. (1999). *Clinician's guide to neuropsychological assessment*. Hillsdale, NJ: Lawrence Erlbaum.

Varlas, L. (2002). Getting acquainted with the essential nine. *Curriculum Update* (Winter 2002), 1–4. Retrieved from http://www.ascd.org/members/curr_update/2002winter/carlas.html.

Vaughn, S., & Bos, C. (1987). Knowledge and perception of the resource room: The students' perspective. *Journal of Learning Disabilities, 26*, 545–555.

Vaughn, S., Bos, C. S., & Schumm, J. S. (2000). *Teaching exceptional, diverse, and at-risk students in the general education classroom* (2nd ed.). Boston: Allyn and Bacon.

Villa, R., & Thousand, J. S. (2003). Making inclusive education work. *Educational Leadership 61,* 19–23.

Vincent, L. J., & Beckett, J. A. (1993). Family participation: DEC recommended practices. In *DEC recommended practices: Indicators of quality in programs for infants and young children with special needs and their families.* Pittsburg, PA: Council for Exceptional Children.

Vollmer, T. R., Borrero, J. C., Lalli, J. S., & Daniel, D. (1999). Identifying possible contingencies during descriptive analysis of severe behavior disorders. *Journal of Applied Behavior Analysis, 32,* 451–466.

Wagner, M. (1995). Outcomes for youths with serious emotional disturbance in secondary school and early adulthood. *Future of Children: Critical Issues for Children and Youths, 5,* 90–112.

Wakschlag, U. S., Pickett, K. E., Kasza, K. B., & Loeber, R. (2006). Is prenatal smoking associated with a developmental pattern of conduct problems in young boys? *Journal of the American Academy of Child and Adolescent Psychiatry, 45,* 461–467.

Walker, H., Colvin, G., & Ramsey, E. (1995). *Antisocial behavior in the classroom: Strategies and best practices.* Pacific Grove, CA: Brooks/Cole.

Walker, H. M. (1995). *The acting-out child: Coping with classroom disruption* (2nd ed.). Longmont, CO: Sopris West.

Walker, H. M., Kavanaugh, K., Stiller, B., Golly, A., Severson, H. H., & Fell, E. G. (1998). First step to success: An early intervention approach for preventing school antisocial behavior. *Journal of Emotional and Behavioral Disorders, 6,* 66–80.

Walker, H. M., & Severson, H. (2002). Developmental prevention of at risk outcomes for vulnerable antisocial children and youth. In K. C. Lane, F. M. Gresham, & T. E. O'Schoughnessy (Eds.), *Interventions for children with or at risk for emotional and behavioral disorders* (pp. 177–194). Boston: Allyn and Bacon.

Walker, H. M., & Walker, J. E. (1991). *Coping with non-compliance in the classroom: A positive approach for teachers.* Austin, TX: Pro-Ed.

Walker, J. E., & Shea, T. M. (1991). *Behavior management: A practical approach for educators* (5th ed.). Upper Saddle River, NJ: Merrill/Pearson Education.

Walker, J. E., & Shea, T. M. (1999). *Behavior management: A practical approach for educators* (7th ed.). Upper Saddle River, NJ: Merrill/Pearson Education.

Walker, J. M. T., Hoover-Dempsey, K. V., Whetsel, D. R., & Green, C. L. (2004). *Parental involvement in homework: A review of current research and its implications for teachers, after school program staff and parent leaders.* Cambridge, MA: Harvard Graduate School of Education, Harvard Family Research Project.

Wallace, M. D., Doney, J. K., Mintz-Resudek, C. M., & Targox, R. S. F. (2004). Training educators to implement functional analysis. *Journal of Applied Behavior Analysis, 37,* 89–92.

Warger, C. (1999). *Positive behavior support and functional assessment.* Arlington, VA: Council for Exceptional Children. (ERIC Document Reproduction Service No. E580).

Warschausky, S., Kewman, D., & Day, J. (1999). Empirically supported psychological and behavioral therapies in pediatric rehabilitation of TBI: Neurobehavioral issues in pediatric head trauma. *Journal of Head Trauma Rehabilitation, 14,* 373–383.

Waschbusch, D. A., & Willoughby, M. T. (2007). Attention-deficit/hyperactivity disorder and callous-unemotional traits as moderators of conduct problems when examining impairment and aggression in elementary school children. *Aggressive Behavior, 33,* 1–15.

Wasley, P. A. (2002). Small classes, small schools: The time is now. *Educational Leadership, 59(5),* 6–10.

Waterman, G. S., & Ryan, N. D. (1993). Pharmacological treatment of depression and anxiety in children and adolescents. *School Psychology Review, 22,* 228–242.

Watkins, C. L. (1988). Project follow through: A story of the identification and neglect of effective instruction. *Youth Policy, 10,* 7–11.

Watkins, M. W., & Pacheco, M. (2000). Interobserver agreement in behavioral research: Importance and calculation. *Journal of Behavioral Education, 10,* 205–212.

Watling, R., Deitz, J., & White, O. (2001). Comparison of sensory profile scores of young children with and without autism spectrum disorders. *American Journal of Occupational Therapy, 55,* 416–423.

Webb, L. D., & Myrick, R. D. (2003). Group counseling intervention for children with attention-deficit-hyperactivity disorder. *Professional School Counseling, 7,* 108–115.

Webster-Stratton, C. (1996). Early intervention with videotape modeling: Programs for families with children with oppositional defiant disorder or conduct disorder. In E. D. Hibbs, & P. S. Jensen (Eds.), *Psychosocial treatments for child and adolescent disorders empirically based strategies for clinical practice* (pp. 435–474). Washington, DC: American Psychological Association.

Webster-Stratton, C. (1996). Videotape modeling intervention programs from families of young children with oppositional defiant disorder or conduct disorder. In B. D. Hill & P. S. Jensen (Eds.), *Psychosocial treatment research of child and adolescent disorders: Empirically based strategies for clinical practice.* Washington, DC: APA.

Webster-Stratton, C., & Dahl, R. W. (1995). Conduct disorder. In M. Hersen & R. T. Ammerman (Eds.), *Advanced abnormal child psychology* (pp. 333–352) Hillsdale, NJ: Lawrence Erlbaum.

Webster-Stratton, C., & Reid, M. J. (2004). Strengthening social and emotional competence in young children—The foundation for early school readiness and success. *Infants and Young Children, 17,* 96–113.

Webster-Stratton, C., Reid, M. J., & Hammond, M. (2001). Preventing conduct problems, promoting social competence: A parent and teacher training partnership in Head Start. *Journal of Clinical Child Psychology, 30,* 283–302.

Wechsler, D. (1991). *Wechsler Intelligence Scale for Children* (3rd ed.). San Antonio, TX: Psychological Corporation.

Wehby, J. H., Lane, K. L., & Falk, J. B. (2003). Academic instruction for students with emotional and behavioral disorders. *Journal of Emotional and Behavioral Disorders, 11,* 194–197.

Wehman, P. (2002). A new era: Revitalizing Special Education for children and their families. *Focus on Autism and Other Developmental Disabilities, 17(4),* 194–197.

Weinstein, C., Tomlinson-Clarke, S., & Curren, M. (2004). Toward a conception of cultural responsive classroom management. *Journal of Teacher Education, 55,* 25–38.

Weiss, G., & Hechtman, L. T. (1993). *Hyperactive children grown up*. New York: Guilford Press.

Weiss, H., Caspe, M., & Lopez, M. E. (2006). *Family involvement in early childhood education*. Cambridge, MA: Harvard Graduate School of Education. Harvard Family Research Project.

Weiss, N. J., & Harris, S. L. (2001). *Reaching out, joining in: Teaching skills to young children with autism*. Bethesda, MD: Woodbine House.

Weissman, M. M., Warner, V., Wickramaratne, P., Moreau, D., & Olfson, M. (1997). Offspring of depressed parents: Ten years later. *Archives of General Psychiatry, 54,* 932–940.

Weissman, M. M., Wickramaratne, P., Nomura, Y., Warner, V., Pilowsky, D., & Verdeli, H. (2006). *American Journal of Psychiatry, 163,* 1001–1008.

Weisz, J. R., Weiss, B., Han, S. S., Granger, D. A., & Morton, T. (1995). Effect of psychotherapy with children and adolescents revisited: A meta-analysis of treatment outcome studies. *Psychological Bulletin, 117,* 450–468.

Weller, E., Weller, R. A., & Dogin, J. W. (1998). A rose is a rose is a rose. *Journal of Affective Disorders, 51,* 189–193.

Weller, E. B., Weller, R. A., & Fristad, M. A. (1995). Bipolar disorder in children: Misdiagnosis, under diagnosis and future directions, *Journal of the American Academy of Child and Adolescent Psychiatry, 34,* 709–714.

Werner, E. E., & Smith, R. S. (1992). *Overcoming the odds: High-risk children from birth to adulthood*. Ithaca, NY: Cornell University Press.

Werner, E. E., & Smith, R. S. (2001). *Journeys from childhood to midlife: Risk, resilience and recovery*. Ithaca, NY: Cornell University Press.

Wetherington, C. E., & Hooper, S. R. (2006). Preschool traumatic brain injury: A review for the early childhood special educator. *Exceptionality, 14,* 155–170.

What Works Clearinghouse (WWC). (2002). *Evidence report topics*. Retrieved from http://w-w-c.org/61.html.

Wheldhall, K., & Lam, Y. Y. (1987). Rows versus tables II. The effects of two classroom seating arrangements on classroom disruption rate, on-task behavior and teacher behavior in three special school classes. *Educational Psychology, 7,* 303–312.

Whitaker, A. H., Van Rossem, R., Feldman, T. F., Schonfeld, R. S., Pinto-Martin, J. H., Tore, C., et al. (1997). Psychiatric outcomes in low-birth-weight children at age 6 years: Relation to neonatal cranial ultrasound abnormalities. *Archives of General Psychiatry, 54,* 847–856.

Whitehurst, G. J. (2002). Evidence-based education (slide presentation). Retrieved on 6/10/09 from http://www.ed.gov/nclb/methods/whatworks/eb/evidencebased.pdf.

Wickramaratne, P. J., & Weissman, M. M. (1998). Onset of psychopathology in offspring by developmental phase and parental depression. *Journal of American Academy of Child and Adolescent Psychiatry, 37,* 933–942.

Wielkiewicz, R. M. (1986). *Behavior management in the schools: Principles and procedures*. New York: Pergamon.

Wildenauer, D. B., Schwab, S. G., Maier, W., Detera-Wadleigh, S. D. (1999). Do schizophrenia and affective disorder share susceptibility genes? *Schizophrenia Research, 30,* 107–111.

Wilens, T. E., & Biederman, J. (2006). Alcohol, drugs and attention-deficit/hyperactivity disorder: A model for the study of addictions in youth. *Journal of Psychopharmacology, 20,* 580.

Will, M. (1986). Clarifying the standards. Placement in a least restrictive environment. *OSERS News in Print*, Washington, DC. *1*(2).

Williams, J. H. (1994). Understanding substance use, delinquency involvement, and juvenile justice system involvement among African-American and European-American adolescents. Unpublished doctoral dissertation, University of Washington, Seattle.

Williams, K. (1995). Understanding the student with Asperger syndrome. *Focus on Autistic Behavior, 10*(2). Austin, TX: Pro-Ed. Retrieved from http://www.udel.edu/bkirby/asperger/.

Williamson, D. E., et al. (2004). First episode of depression in children at low and high familial risk for depression. *Journal of the American Academy of Child and Adolescent Psychiatry, 43,* 291–297.

Willie, C. V., Alves, M. J., & Edwards, R. (2003). *Student diversity, choice, and school improvement*. Westport, CT: Bergin and Gorvey.

Wilson, S. M., & Berne, J. (1999). Teacher learning and the acquisition of professional knowledge: An examination of research on contemporary professional development. *Review of Research in Education, 24,* 173–209.

Wing, L., & Potter, D. (2002). The epidemiology of autistic spectrum disorders: Is the prevalence rising? *Mental Retardation and Developmental Disabilities Research Reviews, 8,* 151–161.

Witt, J. C., & Eliott, S. N. (1982). The response cost lottery: A time efficient and effective classroom intervention. *Journal of School Psychology, 20,* 155–161.

Wohlstetter, P., Malloy, C. L., Hentschke, G. C., & Smith, T. (2004). Improving service delivery in education through collaboration: An exploratory study of the role of cross-sectional alliances in the development and support of charter schools. *Social Science Quarterly, 85,* 1078–1096.

Wolery, M., Bailey, D. D., & Sugai, G. M. (1988). *Effective teaching: Principles and procedures of applied behavior analysis with exceptional students*. Boston: Allyn and Bacon.

Wolf, M. M. (1978). Social validity: The case for subjective measurement or how applied behavior analysis is finding its heart. *Journal of Applied Behavior Analysis, 11,* 203–214.

Wolfgang, C. H. (1996). *The three faces of discipline for the elementary school teacher: Empowering the teacher and students*. Boston: Allyn and Bacon.

Wolfgang, C. H., & Glickman, C. D. (1986). *Solving discipline problems: Strategies for classroom teachers*. Boston: Allyn and Bacon.

Wolpe, J. (1958). *Psychotherapy by reciprocal inhibition*. Stanford, CA: Stanford University Press.

Wolraich, M. L., Wibbelsman, C. J., Brown, T. E., et al. (2005). Attention deficit/hyperactivity disorder among adolescents: A review of the diagnosis, treatment, and clinical implications. *Pediatrics, 115,* 1734–1746.

Wood, F. H. (1990). Issues in the education of behaviorally disordered students. In M. Wang, M. Reynolds, & A. Walberg (Eds.), *Special education research and practice: Synthesis of findings* (pp. 110–118). Toronto, Ontario: Pergamon Press.

Woodruff, T., Axelrad, D., Kyle, A., Nweke, G., & Miller, G. (2003). *America's children and the environment: Measures of contaminants, body burdens and illnesses*. Washington, DC: U.S. Environmental Protection Agency.

Wozniak, J., Biederman, J., Kiely, K., Ablon, J. S., Faraone, S. V., Mundy, E., & Mennin, D. (1995). Mania-like symptoms supportive of childhood onset bipolar disorder in clinically referred children. *Journal of the American Academy of Child and Adolescent Psychiatry, 34,* 867–876.

Wozniak, J., Crawford, M. H., Biedermann, T., Faraone, S. V., Spencer, T. J., Taylor, A., & Blier, H. K. (1999). Antecedents and complications of trauma in boys with ADHD: Findings from a longitudinal study. *Journal of the American Academy of Child and Adolescent Psychotherapy, 38,* 48–55.

Wright, J. (2004). Reducing problem behaviors through good academic management: 10 strategies. Retrieved on 11/18/09 from http://www.interventioncentral.org/htmdocs/interventions/behavior/edtchng.php.

Wright, W. D., & Wright, P. D. (2000). *Wrights law: Special education law.* Hartfield, VA: Harbor House Press.

Yeargin-Allsopp, M., Rice, C., Karapurka, T., Doernberg, N., Boyle, C., & Murphy, C. (2003). Prevalance of autism in a US metropolitan area. *Journal of the American Medical Association, 289,* 49–55.

Yesseldyke, J., & Christenson, S. (2002). *Functional assessment of academic behavior: Creating successful academic environments.* Longmont, CO: Sopris West.

Yesseldyke, J. E., Algozzine, B., & Rickey, L. (1982). Judgment under uncertainty: How many children are handicapped? *Exceptional Children, 48,* 531–534.

Yudofsky, S. C., Hales, R. E., & Stuart, C. (Eds.). (2002). *Neuropsychiatry and clinical neurosciences* (4th ed). Washington, DC: American Psychiatric Publishing.

Zarcone, J. R., Iwata, B. A., Mazaleski, J. L., & Smith, R. G. (1994). Momentum and extinction effects on self-injurious escape behavior and noncompliance. *Journal of Applied Behavior Analysis, 27,* 649–658.

Zigler, E. F., Finn-Stevenson, M., & Linkins, K. W. (1992). Meeting the needs of children and families with schools of the 21st century. *Yale Law and Policy Review, 10,* 69–81.

Zilbovicius, M., Garreau, B., Samson, Y., Remy, P., Bartholemy, C., Syrota, A., et al. (1995). Delayed maturation of the frontal cortex in childhood autism. *American Journal of Psychiatry, 152,* 248–252.

Zilz, W. (2006). Manifestation determination: Rulings of the courts. *Education and the Law, 18,* 193–206.

Zirpoli, T. (2007). *Behavior management: Applications for teachers* (5th ed.). Upper Saddle River, NJ: Merrill/Pearson Education.

Zirpoli, T. J., & Mellow, K. J. (1993). *Behavior management: Application for teachers.* Upper Saddle River, NJ: Merrill/Pearson Education.

Zohar, A. H., Apter, A., King, R. A., et al. (1999). Epidemiological studies. In J. F. Leckman & D. J. Cohen (Eds.), *Tourette's syndrome—tics, obsessions, compulsions: Developmental psychopathology and clinical care* (pp. 177–192). San Francisco: Wiley.

Zuna, N., & McDougall, D. (2004). Using positive behavioral support to manage avoidance of academic tasks. *Teaching Exceptional Children, 37,* 18–24.

Zwaigenbaum, L. (2001). Autistic spectrum disorders in preschool children. *Canadian Family Physician, 47,* 2037–2042.

Name Index

Abikoff, H., 261, 262
Achenbach, T. M., 11
Acosta, M. T., 21
Agran, M., 240, 277
Ahearn, W. H., 200
Ahmad, S. A., 95
Alant, E., 333
Albanese, A. L., 336
Alberto, P. A., 205
Alder, N., 340
Alderman, M. K., 296
Alexander, S., 170
Algozzine, B., 13, 42
Allen, K. E., 227
Allen, R., 170
Althoff, R. R., 63
Alves, M. J., 342
Anderson, A., 38
Anderson, C. A., 224, 295
Anderson, L. M., 108
Anderson, V., 50, 66
Anderson, V. A., 65, 261
Ang, P. M., 318
Arcos-Burgos, M., 21
Armento, B. J., 342
Armstrong, K. H., 340
Arroyos-Jurado, E., 66
Atak, T. R., 200
Attwood, T., 76
Audette, B., 42
August, G. J., 51
Austin, J. L., 135
Autti-Ramo, R., 69
Avant, G. R., 300
Ayers, B. J., 173

Bailey, A., 73
Bailey, D. D., 222
Baker, A. J. L., 318
Bambara, L., 279
Bandura, A., 10, 36
Bantz, J., 26
Barber-Foss, K. D., 65
Barbour, I., 318
Barbour, L., 333
Barenthin, J., 295
Barkley, R. A., 29, 32, 33, 52, 58, 61, 86, 93, 95
Barnard, K. E., 331
Barnes, M. A., 65
Baron, I. S., 95
Baron-Cohen, S., 75

Bartoon-Arword, S. M., 340
Bassler, O. C., 326
Batshaw, M. L., 345
Bauch, P., 318
Baucsh, J. P., 336
Bauman, L. J., 183
Beach, K. J., 73
Beaudoin, K., 340
Beckett, J. A., 330
Beckett, K. S., 287
Beebe-Frankenberger, M., 261
Beghetto, R., 262
Begley, S., 182
Beitchman, J. H., 295
Belfiore, P., 200
Bell, C., 22
Bell, R. Q., 292
Bellah, E., 42
Bender, W. N., 342
Benner, G. J., 261, 340
Berger, E. H., 326
Berkley, R. A., 28
Berkowitz, M. J., 176
Berkson, G., 108
Berner, M. L., 174
Bernstein, L., 310
Bettenhausen, S., 169
Beyda, S. D., 281
Biederman, J., 22, 52, 55, 62, 86
Biglan, A., 310
Bigler, E. D., 31
Billingsley, B., 342
Billingsley, F. F., 204, 342
Billstedt, E., 75
Binser, M. J., 61
Bird, H. R., 100
Birmaher, B., 22, 23, 61, 62
Bishop, D. V. M., 292
Blachowicz, C., 336
Black, S., 181, 182
Bland, N., 290
Blasey, C., 32
Blick, D. W., 278
Blum, R., 291
Bocian, K., 262
Bohnert, A. M., 224
Bor, W., 293
Bos, C., 43, 275, 277, 278
Boulton, M. T., 230
Bowditch, C., 299, 300
Bowen, J. M., 189
Bowlby, J., 25

Bowley, D. M., 65
Boyd, R., 248
Boyle, G. J., 66
Braden, J. P., 299
Braswell, L., 51, 218
Brennan, P., 24
Brenner, V., 183
Brissie, J., 326
Brock, S. E., 224
Brooks, K., 297
Brophy, J., 174, 275
Brown, L. A., 287
Brown, N., 343
Brown, W. E., 187
Brunger, B. A., 227
Bunney, B. S., 31
Burden, P. R., 172, 173
Burns, B. J., 312, 343
Buschbacker, P. W., 121
Bushman, B. T., 224

Cade, T., 275
Calhoun, E., 174
Campbell, M., 79, 333
Cangelosi, J. S., 172, 173
Caplinger, T. E., 24
Carlson, G. A., 52
Carnine, D., 282
Carr, E. G., 109, 121, 123
Carr, S. C., 277, 278
Carson, R., 313
Carter, M., 204
Cartledge, G., 340
Casden, M., 336
Casey, S. D., 227
Caspe, M., 248
Castellanos, F. X., 29
Catalano, R. F., 291, 293
Catroppa, C., 66
Cauchon, D., 297
Causey, V. E., 342
Cawley, J., 172
Cegelka, P., 342
Chance, P., 208
Chandler, K., 318, 319
Chandler, L. K., 103, 106, 107, 110, 116, 121, 134
Chang, K. D., 32, 63
Chapman, S. S., 279
Charney, D. S., 31
Checkley, K., 181
Chen, J. Q., 330

491

Subject Index

Note: Page numbers followed by "f" or "t" refer to figures or tables respectively.